MUHAMMAD
AT MEDINA

MUHAMMAD AT MEDINA

BY

W. MONTGOMERY WATT

OXFORD
AT THE CLARENDON PRESS
1956

Oxford University Press, Amen House, London E.C.4
GLASGOW NEW YORK TORONTO MELBOURNE WELLINGTON
BOMBAY CALCUTTA MADRAS KARACHI CAPE TOWN IBADAN
Geoffrey Cumberlege, Publisher to the University

PRINTED IN GREAT BRITAIN

PREFACE

THE present volume is a sequel to *Muhammad at Mecca*, and the two together are intended to constitute a history of the life of Muḥammad and of the origins of the Islamic community. The plan of the book should be clear from the table of contents. I have endeavoured to write so as to be easily understood by the historian who has no knowledge of Arabic, but I have probably often fallen short of this aim. In particular, in discussions of a pioneering character, such as those in the fourth and fifth chapters, I have necessarily written at greater length than the intrinsic importance of the topic warranted, and thereby upset the balance of the various parts. In such cases all I can do is to advise the non-specialist to 'skip' judiciously.

In a subject like that of this book where there is a vast mass both of source material and of scholarly discussions, it is difficult not to overlook points here and there. I trust, however, that nothing of importance has been omitted. The exhaustive treatment of a subject is a noble ideal to have before one's eyes, but in scholarship as in economics the law of diminishing returns is operative. A point is reached at which further heavy labour leads to a negligible improvement in the product. While few readers are likely to be as fully aware as I am of the places where further study is possible, I have decided that, for the moment at least, I have said my say about Muḥammad, and, if I try to say more, am as likely to mar as to better the impression I have tried to convey.

It is appropriate at this point to draw attention to two gaps of which I have become aware in the course of my work, and which the normal type of European or American orientalist is incapable of filling. One is the production of a map of Arabia as it was in Muḥammad's time. For this the information to be gathered from the old Arab geographers has to be transferred to a series of large-scale modern maps of the country; and that can hardly be done without access to all the localities. An excellent beginning has been made by one Muslim scholar,[1] and it is to be hoped that others will continue the work.

The other serious gap is that the study of life in pre-Islamic

[1] Cf. p. 153 below.

Arabia has not kept pace with the development of social anthropology. I have done what I could to fill in this gap in so far as pre-Islamic conditions are necessary as a background for an understanding of Muḥammad's social reforms. From my colleague, Dr. Kenneth L. Little, head of the Department of Social Anthropology in the University of Edinburgh, I received valuable help, and I am much indebted to him for enabling me to correct some elementary mistakes. My fumbling attempts, however, have convinced me that the adequate study of pre-Islamic life demands someone who is primarily a social anthropologist, but who is at the same time able to deal directly with the Arabic source material. The non-anthropologist inevitably overlooks the significance of many details in the material.

The transliteration of Arabic names is the same as in *Muhammad at Mecca* with one small exception. Where two letters indicate a single Arabic sound (e.g. sh, dh), many writers place a ligature under the letters (as s̲h̲, d̲h̲). It is rare, however, to find these combinations of letters indicating *two* Arabic sounds. Consequently it seems reasonable to use these pairs of letters without ligature for the single sound, and to find some other way of marking the cases where they represent two sounds. For this I suggest the apostrophe. This could not be confused with *hamzah* by the Arabist, and it would indicate to the non-Arabist that the letters did not coalesce. This apostrophe is only absolutely necessary in cases where neither letter has a dot (of which there are none in this book), but I have used it where there was a dot or dots, and even in a word like 'Ash'hal'. I hope this innovation may commend itself to fellow orientalists.

With regard to the form of Arabic names also I have tried to avoid puzzling the non-specialist. A brief explanation here may be of value, however. An Arab's name has several parts. Thus Muḥammad could be called Abū Qāsim Muḥammad b. ʿAbdallāh al-Hāshimī al-Qurashī, that is, the father of Qāsim, Muḥammad, son of ʿAbdallāh, of (the clan of) Hāshim, of (the tribe of) Quraysh. Any part of this name that is sufficiently distinctive may be used by itself. With a few exceptions (such as Ibn Ubayy for ʿAbdallāh b. Ubayy) I have kept to one form for each man. The last part of the name is often a *nisbah* or relative adjective, formed by adding 'ī', and usually indicating at this period the tribe or clan to which a man belonged.

Both Christian and Muslim dates have generally been given, the Muslim months being indicated by Roman numerals since the names would convey little to most readers. Muslim dating is convenient when dealing with the sources, but the Christian dating is essential in order to understand the relation of Muḥammad's career to Byzantine and Persian history.

The Qur'anic quotations are normally from Richard Bell's *Translation*, by kind permission of the publishers, Messrs. T. & T. Clark. For help of various kinds my thanks are due to the Reverend E. F. F. Bishop and Glasgow University Library, to Professor J. Robson, to Professor G. H. Bousquet, to Mr. J. R. Walsh and to Dr. Pierre Cachia. For the compilation of the index and other secretarial assistance I am greatly indebted to Miss Elizabeth Whitelaw.

W. M. W.

Edinburgh
July 1955

CONTENTS

BIBLIOGRAPHICAL ABBREVIATIONS

Aghānī = Abū 'l-Faraj al-Isfahānī, *Kitāb al-Aghānī* (20 vols.), Būlāq (1868)/1285.

Bell, *Translation* = Richard Bell, *The Qur'ān, translated with a critical rearrangement of the surahs* (2 vols.), Edinburgh, 1937–9. (See also under Q.)

al-Bukhārī = al-Bukhārī, *Al-Jāmi' aṣ-Ṣaḥīḥ*. The reference is by the name (and number) of the *Kitāb* and the number of the *Bāb*.

Buhl, *Muhammad* = Frants Buhl, *Das Leben Muhammeds* (German tr. by H. H. Schaeder), Leipzig, 1930.

Caetani = Leone Caetani, *Annali dell' Islam*, Milan, 1905, &c.

EI (1) = *Encyclopaedia of Islam* (4 vols. and supplement), Leiden, 1913, &c.

EI (2) = *Encyclopaedia of Islam* (second edition), Leiden, 1954, &c.

EI (S) = *The Shorter Encyclopaedia of Islam*, Leiden, 1953.

IH = Ibn Hishām, *Kitāb Sīrat Rasūl Allāh* (*Das Leben Muhammeds nach . . . Ibn Ishāk bearbeitet von . . . Ibn Hischām*), ed. F. Wüstenfeld (2 vols.), Göttingen, 1859–60.

IS = Ibn Sa'd, *Ṭabaqāt* (Ibn Saad, *Biographien . . .*), ed. E. Sachau (9 vols.), Leiden, 1905, &c.

M/Mecca = W. Montgomery Watt, *Muhammad at Mecca*, Oxford, 1953.

Q = *Qur'ān* (with the official Egyptian numbering of the verses, followed by Flügel's where it differs); the translation is normally that of Richard Bell, but occasionally, for the sake of harmonizing with the context, this has been modified or replaced by some other rendering. In certain places an attempt has been made to indicate by letters Bell's provisional dating of passages, as follows:

A = very early.
B = early, early Meccan, early Qur'ān period.
C = Meccan.
D = late Meccan.
E = early Medinan.
E+ = Medinan.
F = connected with Badr.
G = connected with Uḥud.
H = up to al-Ḥudaybiyah.
I = after al-Ḥudaybiyah.
— = revised.

Ṭab. = aṭ-Ṭabarī, *Ta'rīkh ar-Rusul wa 'l-Mulūk* ('*Annales*'), ed. M. de Goeje (15 vols.), Leiden, 1879–1901. All references are to the page of the Prima Series; the third volume of this contains the life of

Muḥammad up to A.H. 8 (pp. 1073–1686); the rest is in the fourth volume.

Ṭab., *Tafsīr* = aṭ-Ṭabarī, *Jāmiʿ al-Bayān fī Tafsīr al-Qurʾān* (30 vols.), Cairo, (1903)/1321.

Usd = Ibn al-Athīr, *Usd al-Ghābah* (5 vols.), Cairo, (1869)/1286.

WK = al-Wāqidī, *Kitāb al-Maghāzī*, ed. von Kremer, Calcutta, 1856.

WW = al-Wāqidī, *Kitāb al-Maghāzī*, tr. J. Wellhausen (*Muhammed in Medina; das ist Vakidi's Kitab alMaghazi in verkürzter deutscher Wiedergabe*), Berlin, 1882.

Particulars of other works are given at the first occurrence, and this may be found in the Index under the author's name.

I

THE PROVOCATION OF QURAYSH

1. THE SITUATION AT THE HIJRAH

THE Medinan period of Muḥammad's career begins with his arrival at Qubā' in the oasis of Medina on or about 4 September 622 (12/iii/1). Life in Mecca had become intolerable or even impossible for him, owing to the opposition he had aroused, and he had come to an agreement with the leading men of Medina. The precise nature of this agreement will be discussed later. On the religious side it meant the acceptance of Muḥammad as prophet, and on the political side the acceptance of him as arbiter between the opposing factions in Medina. Many seem to have been sincere in their acceptance of his prophethood, but others probably looked only at the political side. Relying on this agreement, some seventy of Muḥammad's Meccan followers preceded him to Medina, where they were given lodging by his Medinan adherents. Thus on his arrival at Medina Muḥammad had a large religious following and a position in the community of some political importance, though his powers may not have been exactly defined. His Meccan and Medinan followers came to be known respectively as the Emigrants (*muhājirūn*, those making the *hijrah*) and the Anṣār or 'helpers'.[1]

After a few days at Qubā' Muḥammad rode towards the centre of the oasis, and selected a spot for his house, being lodged near by until it was built. This house and courtyard later became the mosque, which is at the centre of the modern town; but it is doubtful whether in Muḥammad's time the population was denser here than at other parts of the oasis. The earliest settlements were more to the south in the 'Āliyah or 'high lands'. Here then Muḥammad settled in the midst of his followers. During the first months at Medina he must have been busy directing and ordering the affairs of his community, religious and secular. His activity had many sides, but, except in the case of the external affairs—the 'expeditions'—there are few chronological data. It is therefore

[1] The name of Anṣār is probably derived from Q. 61. 14; cf. 3. 52/45; 8. 72/73; 9. 100/101, 117/118. Cf. also J. Horovitz, *Koranische Untersuchungen*, Berlin, 1926, 99 f., with further references.

convenient to deal first with external affairs, that is, relations with the pagan Meccans and with the nomadic tribes, and then to consider, in systematic rather than chronological order, the various internal aspects of the life of the Muslim community.

2. THE EARLIEST EXPEDITIONS

The first attempts to collect biographical material about Muḥammad were called *al-maghāzī*, that is, the 'expeditions' or 'campaigns'; and, although the Medinan period was not entirely filled with expeditions, these did play a large part in it, and it is natural to date an event roughly by its relation to some expedition. Of the seventy-four expeditions listed by al-Wāqidī seven are assigned to the first eighteen months after the Hijrah.[1] They are of slight importance, in that nothing seemed to happen, but they are excellent illustrations of Muḥammad's attitude towards the Meccans shortly after his departure from their city.

The chief point to notice is that the Muslims took the offensive. With one exception these seven expeditions were directed against Meccan caravans. The geographical situation lent itself to this. Caravans from Mecca to Syria had to pass between Medina and the coast. Even if they kept as close to the Red Sea as possible, they had to pass within about 80 miles of Medina, and, while at this distance from the enemy base, would be twice as far from their own base. The attackers thus required to deal only with the force accompanying the caravan, and would easily be home before any rescue party came near them. The idea in these expeditions, as in most of the fighting of the desert Arabs, was doubtless to catch the opponents at a disadvantage—by ambushing them, for instance. In these early expeditions the favourable opportunity apparently did not present itself; but its absence did not make the Muslims sufficiently desperate to risk a frontal attack. They merely withdrew.

In the first two or three expeditions the numbers involved are given as from 20 to 80. In those of the later part of 623 (ii–vi/2), however, when Muḥammad himself took part, they are said to have ranged up to 200. The caravans attacked were mostly large—one of 2,500 camels is mentioned—and figures of 200 to 300 are given for the men accompanying them. These numbers are perhaps

[1] Details will be found in Excursus B, pp. 339 ff. below; references given in this Excursus will frequently be omitted from the footnotes.

exaggerated, since there were only 70 men with the important caravan which was the occasion of the battle of Badr, but it was conceivably its weakness which made Quraysh come out in force.

If Muḥammad had with him as many as 200 men, or even 150, the Anṣār must have taken part. The sources tend to agree that the great expedition of Badr was the first on which Anṣār were present; but they are not quite unanimous. In the only passage where the authorities are named[1] suspicion is roused by the fact that the last names in the chain of authorities are already late and are the names of persons much involved in legal disputes; in addition all belong to B. Makhzūm of Quraysh. Since Muḥammad had well under a hundred Emigrants with him at Badr, where practically all were present, there is a strong presumption (unless the figures are completely wrong) that the Anṣār took part at least in the larger of the early expeditions.

Muḥammad had indeed some opportunities for getting men in addition to the original Emigrants. Further Meccans joined him, ʿAyyāsh b. Abī Rabīʿah (Makhzūm) and Hishām b. al-ʿĀṣ (Sahm) are said to have left Mecca in the course of A.H. 1, their departure perhaps being connected with the death of al-Walīd b. al-Mughīrah, the old chief of Makhzūm. Miqdād b. ʿAmr and ʿUtbah b. Ghazwān (confederates of B. Zuhrah and B. Nawfal respectively) changed sides during the expedition of ʿUbaydah. Further, some nomads may have been attracted to him for material reasons; this certainly happened in later years, but may not have occurred before Badr. These additional sources, however, could not bring the numbers up to 150. Apart from this argument about numbers, the action of Majdī b. ʿAmr of B. Juhaynah, during the expedition of Ḥamzah, in mediating between the Muslims and a superior force of Meccans, is probably due to the presence in the raiding party of Medinans, confederate with Juhaynah.[2]

Although there was no fighting on any of these seven expeditions, they were not without positive result for the Muslims. The mere fact that Muḥammad was able to go about with a comparatively large force, and appeared to have the intention of attacking the redoubtable Meccans, must have impressed the nomads. B. Juhaynah was presumably already friendly, since some at least were confederates of some of the Anṣār. In addition, pacts of mutual non-aggression were made with Banū Ḍamrah and B. Mudlij.

[1] WW, 33, last part of §1.

[2] IH, 419; WW, 33.

According to one account the terms were that neither party was to make raids on the other, to join in hostile concentrations against the other, or to help the other's enemies.[1]

In all this we may see a deliberate intention on Muḥammad's part to provoke the Meccans. In so far as the Anṣār joined in they must have been aware of the plan; indeed, their leaders were presumably aware of Muḥammad's policy before they invited him to Medina. It is difficult, however, to know how far ahead Muḥammad was looking at this moment. Was his aim primarily negative, to destroy the trade of Quraysh? Or did he look beyond this to a conquest of Mecca? There are no signs at this period that Muḥammad had any thoughts of securing the Meccan trade for Medina (though one of the later expeditions was partly commercial); he still was not sufficiently strong in Medina and did not have any manpower to spare. The one early expedition which was not against the Meccans, that against Kurz al-Fihrī, illustrates the dangers against which he had to be constantly on guard; it was an attempt to punish a freebooter of the neighbouring region for stealing some of the Medinan pasturing camels.

Though Quraysh suffered no losses they were probably seriously perturbed at the threat to their trade. Despite the fullest precautions on their part the chances were that one day the Muslims would find the opportunity they looked for, and that would mean serious loss to Quraysh. For the moment Quraysh did nothing, but their eagerness to fight the Muslims at Badr is a measure of their annoyance.

The Qur'ān does not refer explicitly to the early expeditions, but it gives some glimpses of the attitude of the Muslims to fighting. What appears to be the earliest passage implies that the Emigrants wanted to fight, since it speaks of God permitting them to do so; 'permission is granted to those who fight because they have suffered wrong, . . . who have been expelled from their dwellings without any cause (or justification) except that they say, "Our Lord is God"'.[2] Later the Muslims, presumably both Emigrants and Anṣār, receive by revelation a direct command to fight; 'fight in the way of God, and know that God is one who hears and knows'.[3] There was apparently, however, some disinclination to

[1] IS, ii/1. 3. 17–20; cf. p. 84 below and the translation on p. 354.

[2] 22. 39/40 E—.

[3] 2. 244/245 'early Medinan' (E), but perhaps after Badr; cf. 9. 123/124.

obey this command, for there are several references to the unwillingness of many to fight.[1] A fresh incentive is therefore given; the Muslims are told that God prefers fighters to those who sit still, that is, remain inactive at home; for the fighters there is a 'mighty hire', a reward in Paradise.[2] Clearly the Muslims regarded their political and military activities as taking place within a religious setting.

3. THE FIRST FIGHTING[3]

The standard account of the first fighting between the Muslim Emigrants and the pagan Quraysh, that during the expedition to Nakhlah, is the one in the version of Ibn Isḥāq, which was based on the report of 'Urwah and transmitted by az-Zuhrī and also Yazīd b. Rūmān. According to this account 'Abdallāh b. Jaḥsh, a confederate of B. 'Abd Shams, was sent out with a small party of from eight to twelve, all Emigrants. Muḥammad gave him a sealed letter of instructions which he was not to read till they were two days' journey from Medina. In due course they opened the letter, and found in it an order to proceed to Nakhlah on the road from aṭ-Ṭa'if to Mecca and there to ambush a Meccan caravan. They eventually met a Meccan caravan at Nakhlah and lulled the suspicions of the Meccans by making out that they were pilgrims. Having found a suitable opportunity they attacked. Of the four Meccans who appear to have been the sole attendants of the caravan, they killed one, 'Amr b. al-Ḥaḍramī, and captured two, while the fourth escaped. Although warning was thus given to the enemy, the party appears to have had no difficulty in bringing the caravan and their prisoners back to Medina. There, however, some misgivings were expressed on account of the Meccan having been killed in the sacred month of Rajab, when bloodshed was forbidden. Muḥammad at first kept the booty undistributed and did not accept the fifth they offered him. But eventually a revelation[4] justified their action. A Meccan deputation came to Medina to arrange for the ransom of the prisoners, and Muḥammad agreed to do this for 1,600 dirhams apiece after the safe return of two Muslims who had become separated from the rest of the party.

The first point to notice in this story is that Muḥammad took

[1] E.g. 2. 216/212 E; 4. 77/79 ? E; 2. 246/247.
[2] 4. 95/97 E—, 77/79 ? E; 3. 195/194.
[3] IH, 423–7; WW, 34–37.
[4] 2. 217/214.

elaborate precautions to ensure secrecy. Not merely did he give the leader of the expedition sealed instructions, whose content was presumably known only to himself, his scribe, and one or two trusted advisers; he also sent the party off by the Najd road, roughly in an easterly direction, although their ultimate goal was almost due south. Doubtless this was all done to prevent the Meccan espionage system from discovering what he was about. Perhaps some of the previous expeditions had failed through their intentions being communicated to the enemy. But in any case, as this expedition was to go to a spot much closer to Mecca than to Medina, it would have been dangerous for the participants had any news of their plan leaked out.

Further, the reason for the hesitation of the party when they read Muḥammad's orders was almost certainly the obvious danger of the enterprise and not any scruples about possibly dishonourable aspects of what they were asked to do. The Arab may be recklessly daring when his blood is up, but in cold blood he tries to avoid serious danger. That was doubtless why Muḥammad told ʿAbdallāh b. Jaḥsh to send back anyone who was not entirely willing to carry out the plan (if this part of the source material is to be accepted). In this connexion the case of Saʿd b. Abī Waqqāṣ and the companion who shared his camel, ʿUtbah b. Ghazwān, is of interest. That their camel had strayed and that in their search they became cut off from the main party was the story they told when they got back to Medina several days *after* the successful raiders. But, while it may be a fact that this was the story they told, it does not follow that the story is true. One version suggests that it is not.[1] The two had certainly wasted a lot of time, and it is curious that this should be in the territory of B. Sulaym, the tribe of ʿUtbah's birth. Another unfortunate incident at a later date also tended to mar Saʿd's reputation for courage. At the great battle of Qādisīyah in 635/14 which broke the power of the Persian empire Saʿd commanded the Muslims, but owing to illness had to direct his forces from a litter at the rear. It is probably to counteract the bad appearance of these two incidents that so much is made in the traditional material of the fact that Saʿd was the first to strike a blow for Islam.[2] Much more is made of this than of the fact that, in killing ʿAmr b. al-Ḥaḍramī at Nakhlah, Wāqid b. ʿAbdallāh was the first to kill a man for the cause of Islam.

[1] Ṭab. i. 1278. 19–1279. 1.

[2] IH, 166; IS, iii/1. 99 f.; &c.

Probably this difference is due to the fact that Wāqid died at the beginning of the caliphate of ʿUmar and left no descendants, whereas Saʿd lived for a further forty years or so and became one of the leading men in the state with a numerous progeny. Many of the notices of Saʿd's feat (which contain several discrepancies) are from himself or members of his family.

The essential part of Muḥammad's sealed orders to ʿAbdallāh b. Jaḥsh was to go to Nakhlah and ambush a caravan of Quraysh. The further clause (in some versions) about bringing back a report to Muḥammad is clearly a later addition intended to give the word *taraṣṣadū* the meaning 'keep a watch' instead of 'lay an ambush'; in this way all responsibility for blood shedding would be removed from Muḥammad. There can be no doubt, however, that Muḥammad sent out the raiders on an errand which he realized might involve deaths among both his own men and the enemy. It is not clear whether Muḥammad knew definitely that this particular caravan would be passing Nakhlah about this date, or whether he sent the men because of the general probability that there would be caravans then. He may have surmised that any caravans on the comparatively safe route from aṭ-Ṭā'if to Mecca would be lightly guarded in view of the efforts that had been expended on protecting the caravans to Syria which had to run the gauntlet of Medina. It seems most likely that Muḥammad acted on the general probability, but it is not impossible that he had specific information.

A more serious question is whether Muḥammad expected the caravan to be ambushed during the sacred month of Rajab. Al-Wāqidī places the incident at the end of Rajab and indicates that the Muslims, if they were to attack this caravan at all, had either to do so during the sacred month or else after it had entered the sacred territory of Mecca. If this account could be accepted, it might be the case that the caravan had upset Muḥammad's calculations by being a little before time. The suggestion that the attackers were uncertain whether the sacred month had or had not ended looks like an attempt to whitewash what is known to be black. It is very suspicious that, while some sources say the date was the end of Rajab, others make it the beginning. It seems that it was only known that the event was alleged to have taken place in Rajab, and that the rest is extenuating conjecture. If that is so, the incident may well have taken place about the middle of the month, and the orders given by Muḥammad may have contemplated an ambush during the sacred month.

If we suppose that Muḥammad intended the violation of the sacred month (although it is by no means proved that he did so), it does not mean that he was contemplating anything scandalous or dishonourable. The sacredness of the month of Rajab was bound up with the pagan religion which he was denouncing. Violation of the sacred month would be on a par with the destruction of idols. But, on this supposition, what are we to make of Muḥammad's hesitation before accepting a fifth of the booty? We cannot fairly regard him as abandoning his companions, nor as being afraid of Quraysh—although some of the Jews of Medina made puns on the names of slayer and slain which indicated that war was as good as declared. The easiest solution is to hold that after the event he discovered that there was a far stronger feeling on the question of violation than he had anticipated. Possibly many were afraid of the punishment to be meted out by offended deities, a punishment which might affect the whole community if they accepted the booty. Others certainly pointed to the contradiction between this breaking of Divine Law and Muḥammad's call to worship and serve God; 'Muḥammad imagines that he is keeping obedience to God, they said, but he is the first who has profaned the sacred month and he has killed our comrade during Rajab'.[1]

The question of the sacred months is a difficult one.[2] Muslim writers, following the Qur'ān, 9. 36, hold that four always had been regarded as sacred, namely, Rajab, Dhū 'l-Qa'dah, Dhū 'l-Ḥijjah, al-Muḥarram (vii, xi, xii, i, respectively). But elsewhere —2. 194/190; 2. 217/214; 5. 2; 5. 97/98—the Qur'ān speaks of 'the' sacred month. It has been suggested that different districts had different usages, and that the number four is an attempt at compromise. This may explain why the reaction in Medina to the incident at Nakhlah took Muḥammad by surprise. Perhaps also the Medinans clung more closely to the old beliefs than the Meccans, for the latter had had experience of a war in which sacred things were violated.

The revelation which ended Muḥammad's hesitation ran thus:[3]

They will ask thee about the sacred month, fighting therein; say:

[1] Ṭab. 1278, 3, from as-Suddī. For the 'fifth' cf. p. 255 below.
[2] Cf. M. Plessner, arts. 'al-Muḥarram' and 'Radjab' in EI (1).
[3] Q. 2. 217/214.

'Fighting therein is serious, but debarring [people] from the way of God, and unbelief in Him . . . is in God's sight more serious still'; persecution is more serious than killing. . . .

This admits that the violation of the sacred month was 'serious', but it reminds the Muslims that the offences of Quraysh against God were more serious; the intended inference is perhaps that punishment is more likely to fall on Quraysh. The word 'serious' (*kabīr*) might almost have the connotation of 'sin', but the verse is not a prohibition of fighting for the future (though some Muslim writers take it in this way and then say it is abrogated); it is rather a justification of what has been done in the past. It may be that for some years after the affair at Nakhlah Muḥammad tried to avoid giving offence by not sending out expeditions in Rajab. Al-Wāqidī indeed mentions two in that month, in the years 6 and 8 (627 and 629), but on neither apparently was any enemy blood shed though some Muslims were killed in 6.[1] Several expeditions undoubtedly took place in the other sacred months; and in the light of this and of other matters it is commonly stated by Muslim scholars that the prohibition of fighting in the sacred months was abrogated.[2]

Among the probabilities and uncertainties through which we have been wading there is a little firm ground. It is clear that people accused ʿAbdallāh and his party of having violated the month of Rajab, and also that Muḥammad was not in a position to demonstrate that the Muslims had *not* done so. It is tolerably certain that Muḥammad himself had few scruples about fighting in the sacred months, but that he had to respect the scruples of an important section of his followers and to guard against repercussions which might weaken his prophetic authority. And it must be insisted that, even if Muḥammad intended the raiding party to violate the sacred month, there was in Arab eyes nothing dishonourable or disgraceful about that, especially in view of his general attack on paganism. Finally, in addition to losing a life and a valuable caravan Quraysh would be thoroughly infuriated by the fact that these acts were perpetrated under their very noses, as it were.

[1] See Excursus B.

[2] Cf. WW, 29–31; Ṭab., *Tafsīr*, ii. 199 (on Q. 2. 217/214); Abū Jaʿfar an-Naḥḥās, *K. an-Nāsikh wa 'l-Mansūkh*, Cairo, 1938/1357, 32 f.

4. THE BATTLE OF BADR

(March 624 = ix/2)[1]

The booty from Nakhlah gave a fillip to the policy of raiding Meccan caravans, and for his next expedition Muḥammad was able to collect 300 men, at least a hundred more than on any previous occasion. The excess was doubtless mainly from the Anṣār, since it may be assumed that practically all the Emigrants took part in the earlier large raid. According to Ibn Sa'd's reckoning there were 238 of the Anṣār at the battle of Badr and only 86 Emigrants.[2] Muḥammad apparently heard in good time that a large caravan was setting out from Gaza to return to Mecca and realized that it was well worth plundering. Although only 70 men (or perhaps even fewer) accompanied it, the merchandise was later said to be worth 50,000 dīnārs. All the leading Meccan merchants and financiers had an interest in it; indeed, nearly everyone in Mecca was concerned for its safe return. Perhaps several smaller caravans—some of them having been the object of Muslim attentions on their way north—had joined together for greater safety.[3]

In charge of the caravan was Abū Sufyān b. Ḥarb, one of the most astute men in Mecca. He seems to have realized at an early stage that Muḥammad would try to attack his caravan and to have sent a timely request to the Meccans to dispatch a force to cover the caravan at the danger-point. (Some sources say that he sent his message only after hearing of Muḥammad's preparations, but considerations of timing make this impossible.)

The Meccans, led by Abū Jahl, responded to Abū Sufyān's message by sending a large force, said to be about 950. Nearly all the fighting men of Mecca went, after a neighbouring chief of the B. Kinānah had given his word that, even if Mecca were denuded of defenders, it would not be attacked by the section of Kinānah which had a blood-feud with Quraysh. The size of the force shows that Abū Jahl probably intended to overawe Muḥammad and his

[1] IH, 427–539; WW, 37–90; Ṭab. 1281–1359; Caetani, i. 472–518; M. Hamidullah, *The Battlefields of the Prophet Muhammad*, Woking, 1953/1373, 11–17 (reprinted, with continuous paging, from *The Islamic Review*, 1952, 1953). The strategy of this and other battles is discussed by Muḥammad 'Abd al-Fattāḥ Ibrāhīm in *Muḥammad al-Qā'id*, Cairo, 1945/1364.

[2] IS, iii/2, iii/1.

[3] IH, 421 f., 428; WW, 34, 39 f.; contrast Caetani, i. 463, n. 1.

followers and any potential followers, and so to scare them from meeting him in battle and from raiding caravans in the future. Some days out from Mecca Quraysh got word that the caravan had eluded Muḥammad and was safe. The only cause of war now was the blood of ʿAmr b. al-Ḥaḍramī, and ʿUtbah b. Rabīʿah of ʿAbd Shams was ready to pay blood-money to keep peace, but Abū Jahl skilfully shamed ʿUtbah into withdrawing his offer, and so forced Quraysh to advance; he was presumably hoping to get rid of Muḥammad once for all.

Such, at least, is the account of the Meccan proceedings given by several sources. Even if they are unduly hostile to Makhzūm and friendly to ʿAbd Shams, there is probably much truth in what they say. There was certainly no strong bond of unity among Quraysh; two clans, Zuhrah and ʿAdī, withdrew completely after it was decided, even though the caravan was safe, to advance to Badr. Doubtless they felt that Abū Jahl and his friends would stand to benefit most by the destruction of Muḥammad. Fear of a conflict would have little to do with the action of the Meccans, since the majority presumably believed that the Muslims would not venture to attack them.

The Muslims certainly did not expect a conflict when they set out. According to the oldest source, ʿUrwah's letter to ʿAbd al-Malik,[1] 'neither the Messenger of God nor his Companions heard of the expedition of Quraysh until the prophet came to Badr'. Had the Muslims known there was likely to be a battle they might have shrunk from taking part in the expedition. There is a curious story of how some of Muḥammad's party captured one of the Meccan water-carriers and questioned him; when he told them the truth about Abū Jahl's force, they thought he was lying and punished him, but when he told them lies about Abū Sufyān they believed him, and it was only when Muḥammad himself interviewed him that the real state of affairs was discovered. Whether in this way or some other way, Muḥammad appears to have had definite news of Quraysh before they had any exact information about him, and so to have had the tactical initiative. The phrase in the Qur'ān (8. 7) about God 'promising that one of the two parties (*sc.* the caravan or the relief force) should be yours' would seem to imply that Muḥammad knew about Abū Jahl sufficiently long before the battle for it to be uncertain with which party contact would be

[1] Ṭab. 1284 ff.; tr. by Caetani, i. 472 ff.

made. It is also said that the Anṣār were pledged to defend Muḥammad only within Medinan territory and that, before committing himself to a course leading to battle, Muḥammad conferred with them and asked if they would support him in these circumstances. It is conceivable that when the Muslims learnt about Quraysh they were so close to them that retreat would have involved loss of face; but it is more likely that Muḥammad saw an opportunity of attacking Quraysh with conditions in his favour, and managed to convince his followers of the soundness of such a course.

The date given for the battle is the 17th, 19th, or 21st of Ramaḍān (ix) in the year 2 (= 13, 15, or 17 March 624). On the night before it Muḥammad, aware that Abū Jahl was making for Badr, seized the water-supply there, blocked up all the wells except one round which he stationed his men—the one nearest to Mecca—and so forced his opponents, presumably now in need of water, to fight on ground and under conditions of his choosing. Quraysh was not ambushed, but it was apparently placed in a position in which it could not avoid fighting, though the conditions were unfavourable. If the sources can be trusted on points of detail, Quraysh on the evening before the battle learnt that Muḥammad was close to them, but not his precise whereabouts. Next morning his presence at the wells took them by surprise. Nevertheless there seems to have been a series of single combats between champions, the normal prelude to Arab set battles. There was also arrow-shooting on both sides, and latterly a general mêlée, which turned into the flight of Quraysh. In the course of the battle from forty-five to seventy of Quraysh were killed, including Abū Jahl himself and several other leaders. A similar number were taken prisoner. For the Muslims there was much booty, and to prevent the quest for loot from interfering with the pursuit of the enemy, Muḥammad had to announce that the booty, apart from the spoils from those killed and the ransoms of those taken prisoner, would be divided equally among those who took part in the battle.

One or two of the prisoners were treated with the harshness and ferocity which were probably not unusual among the Arabs of that age. The common attitude was that a man might do what he liked with his prisoner; the only point for him to consider was what was profitable or advisable for himself and his clan. At Badr in at least one instance a pagan was being led off by a Muslim captor when a group of Emigrants who particularly hated him noticed him, and at once set on him and killed him; the captor incidentally lost the potential ransom. Such excesses Muḥammad put a stop to. In general his policy was to hold prisoners to ransom, but those belonging to his own clan or in some other way specially related to the Muslims, and those not sufficiently influential or wealthy to be ransomed, he usually set free without ransom. He may already have begun to realize how important it was going to be for him to win the hearts of the Meccans. An exception to this lenient policy was ʿUqbah b. Abī Muʿayṭ, who was executed for his former hostility to Muḥammad, and in particular because he had composed verses about him. An-Naḍr b. al-Ḥārith, who had claimed that his stories about things Persian were as good as those of the Qur'ān, was likewise executed.[1]

A number of factors combined to bring about this notable victory for the Muslims. One was the lack of unity among Quraysh, which has been noticed above. By defections their number had been reduced far below the original 950, perhaps to 600 or 700; and of these many were not whole-hearted supporters of Abū Jahl's policy. They were also over-confident. Against such a foe the spirit of the Muslims would count for much. Their belief in a future life probably gave them greater courage in battle, and Muḥammad's confidence inspired them with confidence. His generalship also won for them a tactical advantage. These seem to be the main reasons for the Muslim victory. There are no grounds for holding that the fighting qualities of the Anṣār were superior to those of Quraysh. The list of pagans killed often mentions the name of the Muslim who killed a particular man, but too much reliance cannot be placed upon details; the large numbers killed by ʿAlī and Ḥamzah must be exaggerations. If, however, after allowing for exaggeration, we may accept the general impression made by the list and other relevant details, it is that the farmers of Medina were not markedly superior fighters to the merchants of Mecca. It has to be remembered that the pagans, or at least many of those killed, were considerably older than the majority of the Emigrants, and were probably suffering from thirst. Though the numbers of the Emigrants were only about one-third of those of the Anṣār, they appear to have taken their full share in the battle.

[1] IH, 458 ff.; WW, 78 ff.

5. THE SITUATION AFTER BADR

The loss of trained men was a disaster of the first magnitude for Mecca. Besides Abū Jahl (of Makhzūm) the following leaders were killed: ʿUqbah b. Abī Muʿayṭ, ʿUtbah b. Rabīʿah, and Shaybah b. Rabīʿah of the clan of ʿAbd Shams; al-Ḥārith b. ʿĀmir and Ṭuʿaymah b. ʿAdī of Nawfal; Zamʿah b. al-Aswad, Abū 'l-Bakhtarī, and Nawfal b. Khuwaylid of Asad; an-Naḍr b. al-Ḥārith of ʿAbd ad-Dār; Munabbih b. al-Ḥajjāj and his brother Nubayh of Sahm; and Umayyah b. Khalaf of Jumaḥ.[1] There can hardly have been left alive in Mecca a dozen men of similar ability and experience. Abū Sufyān, of course, was safe with the caravan and now became the most prominent man in the city. Suhayl b. ʿAmr was a prisoner, but was ransomed, and Ḥakīm b. Ḥizām and various others managed to escape from the battlefield. There were younger men, too, coming forward. Nevertheless the catastrophe was considerable.

With this went no little loss of prestige, even though there was no immediate change in the political situation. The Arabs of the Ḥijāz realized that this battle did not mean that Muslim Medina had replaced Mecca as chief power in the area. Further tests of Muḥammad's strength were required before everyone flocked to him from far and near. It was now clear, however, that Abū Jahl had been correct in rating very high the seriousness of the threat from Muḥammad, even if he had made errors of judgement in other points. Muḥammad had now, as it were, thrown down a gauntlet which the Meccans could not honourably refuse to pick up. He had effectively challenged them to a full-scale trial of strength.

Although neither party when they left home expected to fight, the outcome of the battle was no accident. The Meccan belief that Muḥammad would be so overawed that he would avoid them rested on a misappraisal of the relative strength and fighting quality of the two parties; and this in turn was doubtless due to over-confidence in their own powers and failure to realize how much these had been weakened by the malaise of the age—for example, by the reliance on money and other vices attacked in the Qur'ān. Muḥammad, on the other hand, though he might not have deliberately organized an expedition to seek an engagement

[1] IH, 507 ff.; WW, 81 ff.

with Quraysh, had shown himself disposed to attack them in circumstances favourable to the Muslims. When chance made it difficult for him to avoid fighting at Badr—or perhaps we should say, helped him to persuade the Anṣār to fight—he kept his head and made the fullest possible use of the opportunity. Thus, though the fighting was unpremeditated, the result fairly reflected the relative strength of the two sides within the limits of a small engagement. Of course, only a small part of the total available forces of Quraysh had been involved. It therefore remained to be seen whether Muḥammad could increase the manpower at his disposal sufficiently rapidly to be in a position to hold the larger army which Quraysh were sure to put in the field against him.

In Medina itself the victory considerably strengthened Muḥammad's position, which had perhaps been deteriorating during the previous few months when it looked as if he was unlikely to achieve anything. Usayd b. Ḥuḍayr, for example, one of the chief early converts, was not sufficiently enthusiastic in his support of Muḥammad to take part in the expedition, though he made his excuses as soon as Muḥammad returned victorious.[1] Muḥammad further used the flush of victory to eliminate some weaknesses. Two persons who had written poems against him—ʿAṣmāʾ bint Marwān of Umayyah b. Zayd and Abū ʿAfak of B. ʿAmr b. ʿAwf—were killed by persons belonging to their own or related clans, but nothing was said and no blood-feud followed.[2] About the same time the Jewish tribe of B. Qaynuqāʿ was attacked after a trivial dispute had led to the death of a Muslim, was besieged for a fortnight, and, when they surrendered, sent away from Medina. Thereby Muḥammad's chief rival, ʿAbdallāh b. Ubayy lost perhaps as many as 700 of his confederates.[3]

The most important result of the battle, however, was the deepening of the faith of Muḥammad himself and his closest Companions in his prophetic vocation. After years of hardship and a measure of persecution, after the weary months at Medina when nothing seemed to be going right, there came this astounding success. It was a vindication of the faith which had sustained them through disappointment. Very naturally they regarded it as miraculous, the work of God, as the Qur'ān asserted (8. 17): 'Ye did not kill them, but God killed them, and when thou didst

[1] WW, 38, 72; cf. p. 181 below.
[2] IH, 994–6; WW, 90–92.
[3] Cf. pp. 181 f., 209 f. below.

throw, it was not thou but God who threw. . . .'[1] Moreover, this disaster which had overtaken the pagans was the punishment which had been foretold in the Meccan revelations,[2] and thus Muḥammad's claim to prophethood was verified.

So much is certain. It is further probable that the word *furqān*, at least in some passages of the Qu'rān, is to be interpreted as Richard Bell suggested.[3] In 8. 41/42 'the day of the *furqān*, the day the two parties met' must be the day of Badr; and *furqān*, in virtue of its connexion with the Syriac word *pūrqāna*, 'salvation', must mean something like 'deliverance from the judgement'. This being so the *furqān* which was given to Moses[4] is doubtless his deliverance when he led his people out of Egypt, and Pharaoh and his hosts were overwhelmed. Similarly, Muḥammad's *furqān* will be the deliverance given at Badr when the Calamity came upon the Meccans. That was the 'sign' which confirmed his prophethood. Perhaps there is also a reference to the experience, analogous to the receiving of revelation, which Muḥammad apparently had during the heat of the battle, and as a result of which he became assured that the Muslims had invincible Divine assistance.[5]

[1] For the traditional story cf. p. 312 below.
[2] Q. 8. 30–35, &c.
[3] *The Origin of Islam in its Christian Environment*, London, 1926, 118 ff.
[4] Q. 2. 53/50; 21. 48/49.
[5] WW, 54; cf. Q. 8. 43/45 f.

II

THE FAILURE OF THE MECCAN RIPOST

1. MUḤAMMAD PREPARES FOR THE IMPENDING STRUGGLE[1]

AFTER his success at Badr Muḥammad must have realized that he was committed to 'total war' with the Meccans. Their prosperity depended to a great extent on their prestige, and in order to maintain their position they must in no uncertain fashion retrieve what they had lost at Badr, in addition to loosening Muḥammad's hold on their route to the north. From the Meccans, therefore, Muḥammad could expect nothing but an intensification of the struggle, so that he must clearly devote all his energies to strengthening himself and weakening his enemies.

The mere news of Badr and the sight of the booty had brought an accession of strength to Muḥammad. The people of Medina were much readier to join Muḥammad's expeditions; for that to Dhū Amarr in September 624 (iii/3) he was able to muster 450. The friendly tribes between Medina and the sea were presumably more ready to help Muḥammad openly; at least Quraysh did not venture to send any caravan to Syria by that route in the summer of 624. When Quraysh marched north for the battle of Uḥud men of Khuzā'ah passed information to Muḥammad. Pagan nomads in the neighbourhood of Medina were much readier to profess Islam; mention is made not merely of one or two individuals but also of the whole tribe of Muḥārib, who followed their chief, Du'thūr b. al-Ḥārith.[2]

The increased forces at his disposal were employed by Muḥammad to create a healthy respect for the new Medinan state among nomadic tribes friendly with Mecca. When Abū Sufyān raided Medina to show that Mecca was not 'down and out', Muḥammad gave a counter-display of his power by pursuing him with at least 200 men. The strong tribes of Sulaym and Ghaṭafān, which later helped Quraysh at the siege of Medina, were raided in the expedition of al-Kudr and a large number of camels driven off. A little later another raid with 300 men was made against Sulaym, and,

[1] General sources for §§ 1 and 2: IH, 539–55, 994–6; WW, 73–76, 90–101.
[2] IH, 544; WW, 99–101.

though no booty was captured, the expedition was doubtless not without effect.

In all Muḥammad's planning he was fully aware of the importance for him of what may be called the ideological aspect and of his pre-eminence there. It was always possible for him to win enemies over to his side by converting them; one at least of the pagans who came to arrange for the ransom of prisoners after Badr was so impressed by some of the things he saw in Medina that he became a Muslim, though previously he had been plotting to kill Muḥammad. Muḥammad's decision (contrary to the views of some of his supporters) that in general the prisoners from Badr were to be held to ransom is not simply a mark of leniency of disposition and of the great need for improving the financial position of the Muslims; it is perhaps also the beginning of the realization that, to achieve the distant aims he was beginning to see over the horizon, he required the administrative abilities of the Meccans, and that therefore his task must be not to destroy Quraysh but to win them for his cause.

Out of the same awareness of the importance of the ideological aspect sprang events like the assassinations of ʿAṣmāʾ bint Marwān and Abū ʿAfak who had made verses criticizing Muḥammad, and the expulsion from Medina of the Jewish tribe of Qaynuqāʿ. The assassination of Kaʿb b. al-Ashraf a little later was similar. Kaʿb was the son of an Arab from the distant tribe of Ṭayyi', but was reckoned as belonging to his Jewish mother's tribe of an-Naḍīr, in which he was one of the leading men. When he heard the news of Badr, he set out for Mecca, and by his verses helped to rouse the Meccans to grief and anger and the desire for revenge. Eventually he returned to Medina—apparently because the Muslim poet Ḥassān b. Thābit ridiculed the families whose guest he was. Muḥammad now made it known that he would welcome Kaʿb's removal, and five doughty Muslims laid a plot. Abū Nā'ilah, Kaʿb's foster-brother, won his confidence by complaining about the state of affairs in Medina as a result of Muḥammad's presence. The points mentioned are the general enmity of the Arabs, the difficulty of travelling, the payment of contributions (*ṣadaqah*), with the consequent impoverishment of their families and lack of food; these may be the points most keenly felt by Muḥammad's opponents at this period. Kaʿb agreed to give the men food and was to receive their arms as security. This gave the conspirators an excuse for meeting Ka'b privately by night with their arms. He was overpowered and killed, and his head carried off and flung at Muḥammad's feet.

Such measures made it clear that Muḥammad was not a man to be trifled with. For those who accepted him as leader there were material advantages; for those who opposed him there were serious disadvantages. Thus, apart from Muḥammad's preaching, men had many reasons for taking his side. Consequently, although the Meccans had 3,000 men in the field at the battle of Uḥud, the outcome of the battle is never said to be due to the fact that the Muslims were outnumbered; and, though this point could partly be explained away, it does perhaps give us some justification for thinking that Muḥammad may have had about 2,000 men that day.

2. MECCAN REACTIONS TO BADR

The news of Badr was received at Mecca at first with incredulity, then with a dismay which inhibited all effective action. Abū Sufyān took control of affairs and for a time forbade mourning for the dead; this was ostensibly to prevent the Muslims gloating over their plight and to avoid dissipating the energies of the Meccans when all their strength was required to prepare for revenge,[1] but perhaps really to avoid a complete collapse of morale. For a similar reason he announced that he had vowed to have nothing to do with oil or women till he had carried out a raid against Muḥammad. The pent-up feelings, however, at length swept away the prohibition, which had perhaps served its turn. Ka'b b. al-Ashraf in his poems encouraged the expression of grief among the Meccans in order subsequently to stir up their desire for revenge. This and the need for restoring their position was no doubt uppermost in their minds once they had recovered from the first shock of the disaster. Thus Ṣafwān b. Umayyah b. Khalaf of Jumaḥ, whose father had been killed at Badr, persuaded a member of his clan, 'Umayr b. Wahb by name, to try to assassinate Muḥammad while in Medina negotiating for his brother's ransom (though what actually happened was that 'Umayr became a Muslim). A more positive step was Abū Sufyān's proposal to devote to preparations for war all the profits of the caravan he had brought safely back; those concerned seem to have agreed.

Some ten weeks after Badr, Abū Sufyān, in fulfilment of his

[1] WW, 73 = WK, 114 f.

vow, led a party of 200 (or 400) men to raid Medina. His primary aims were doubtless to restore confidence among the Meccans and to show the world that the day of Quraysh was not yet over. With such a force—less numerous than the Muslims at Badr—he cannot have intended to inflict any serious damage on Muḥammad, unless he expected more than half the inhabitants of Medina to join him (which is unlikely). He must have had a firm grip on all information leaving Mecca for he apparently reached the outskirts of Medina without Muḥammad's knowledge. A friend, the chief of the Jewish tribe of the Naḍīr, gave him a meal and presumably information (if we may trust the account), but nothing more, and he decided to retreat immediately. To fulfil his oath two houses were burnt and some fields laid waste. On the way back the Meccans abandoned some excess provisions, mainly barley-meal (*sawīq*), and this was picked up by the Muslims. In consequence the expedition was known to the Muslims as 'the barley-meal raid'.[1]

In the existing state of affairs it was clearly wiser not to attempt to force the passage of a caravan to Syria through territory friendly to Muḥammad, but to concentrate on raising an army which could destroy his power. No caravans were therefore sent to Syria by the usual route which passed between Medina and the sea. A group of Quraysh, however, headed by Ṣafwān b. Umayyah (who was perhaps setting up as a rival to Abū Sufyān), decided to risk sending a caravan by a route well to the east of Medina, and found a reliable guide. Unfortunately for them, however, Muḥammad got wind of the plan, sent out Zayd b. Ḥārithah with 100 men, and captured merchandise worth 100,000 dirhams; the men in charge of it escaped, doubtless being, at this period between Badr and Uḥud, thoroughly terrified at the prospect of fighting with Muslims.[2]

Meanwhile a large force was being raised to go against Medina. Embassies were sent to various tribes, including Thaqīf of aṭ-Ṭā'if and the nomadic 'Abd Manāt (which was closely related to Quraysh and included Bakr). The Aḥābīsh who followed Quraysh were also summoned.[3] About 11 March 625 (25/ix/3) the Meccans set out with an army of 3,000 well-equipped men, of whom 700 had coats of mail; there were 3,000 camels and 200 horses. Abū Sufyān was in command, since to command in battle was one of the privileges

[1] IH, 543 f.; WW, 94.
[2] IH, 547 f.; WW, 100 f.
[3] WK, 199. 9, 201 foot; cf. al-Wāḥidī, *Asbāb an-Nuzūl*, Cairo (1897)/1315, 177; also p. 81 n. below.

of his clan, but others, notably Ṣafwān b. Umayyah, had an important share in the direction of the campaign. The army advanced by easy stages and reached the oasis of Medina on Thursday, 21 March (5/x). For their camp they selected a site on the far side of the oasis from Mecca near the hill of Uḥud. In this neighbourhood there were fields of corn, now in the ear, and they deliberately pastured their animals there in order to provoke the Medinans to come out to fight. Apart from this the peculiar Medinan strongholds or *aṭām*, at various points in the oasis, were able to hold out for far longer than the Meccans were capable of besieging them.

3. THE BATTLE OF UḤUD

(Saturday, 23 March 625 = 7/x/3)

There is a great mass of material in the early sources about the battle of Uḥud,[1] but much consists of accounts of trivial incidents redounding to the glory of individuals (and so preserved by their descendants or clansmen), or rebutting accusations against them. From this mass it is not possible to give a full or clear account of the battle. Nevertheless, if we accept the general soundness of the material, a rough outline does emerge. This runs somewhat as follows.

The Meccans advanced by Wādi 'l-'Aqīq and camped to the north of Medina near Uḥud on Thursday, 21 March. Almost at once a scout brought Muḥammad exact information about their strength, and some of the leading Anṣār kept guard at Muḥammad's door all night. Early on the Friday a council of war was held in Medina. Muḥammad, 'Abdallāh b. Ubayy, and some of the senior men were for remaining in the centre where the buildings were closer, and so forcing the enemy to undertake a combination of siege and house-to-house fighting; but younger men, together with one or two men of weight, argued that to allow the Meccan army to lay waste their fields as it was doing would make them seem cowards and ruin their reputation in the eyes of the nomadic tribes; so they must go out to the enemy. Eventually Muḥammad decided on this course, and, though some of the hotheads cooled down and said they were willing to accept Muḥammad's original plan, he (very properly) stuck to his decision with the remark that

[1] IH, 555–638; WW, 101–48; Ṭab. 1383–1427; discussed in detail by Caetani, i. 540–66. Cf. Hamidullah, *Battlefields of Muhammad*, 18–24. See also the map, p. 152 below.

once a prophet has put on armour he must not take it off until God has decided between him and his enemy. Later in the day the Medinan forces set out in the direction of the enemy camp. Muḥammad is said to have rejected the help of a Jewish contingent, confederates of ʿAbdallāh b. Ubayy, because they were not believers. Some distance short of the enemy they halted for the night, then very early next morning, using their superior knowledge of the terrain, they made their way unobserved to a position on the lower slopes of the hill of Uḥud, with the enemy roughly between them and the city. The left flank was protected by fifty archers under ʿAbdallāh b. Jubayr.

The departure of ʿAbdallāh b. Ubayy and his followers shortly before the battle is curious. The sources suggest that he was annoyed because Muḥammad did not adopt the plan he advocated on the previous day. But this is difficult to believe, since he seems to have gone with Muḥammad right to the site of the battle. It is conceivable that he retired, in agreement with Muḥammad, in order to defend the main settlement against a possible enemy attack.[1] In sources not friendly to him his motives could easily be blackened, especially when, after the battle, he made no secret of his joy at the discomfiture of his rival, Muḥammad. If he acted independently it may have been from the calculation that neutrality during the battle would strengthen his position with both parties afterwards; he is said to have acted in a similar way at the battle of Buʿāth between the Aws and the Khazraj.

The Meccans had to move forward to the attack across a wadi. The cavalry may have attacked first, but, if so, they were driven back by the Muslim archers. Then the Meccan standard-bearer moved forward, perhaps with a view to single combat, but soon a general mêlée developed round the standard. The clan of ʿAbd ad-Dār who had the privilege of bearing the standard fought with great gallantry against overwhelming odds. Nine members of the clan seem to have been killed defending the standard—a large number for a small clan. The standard did not fall into Muslim hands, but the Meccan forces withdrew before the Muslim onslaught, perhaps even fled. However, as victory seemed to be almost within the grasp of the Muslims, there was a sudden reversal of fortune. The cavalry on the Meccan right under Khālid b. al-Walīd, observing the Muslim ranks in some disorder and in

[1] Cf. WW, 138.

particular the archers advancing from their post, quickly overran the few remaining archers and attacked the Muslim flank and rear. A scene of great confusion followed, especially as the cry went up that Muḥammad had been killed. Muslims wounded other Muslims—in at least one case mortally. Muḥammad was not in fact killed, but for some time there was a fierce hand-to-hand struggle round him, in which he received two or three wounds on the face and leg, and inflicted a spear wound on one of the Meccans which caused the latter's death subsequently.[1] Eventually Muḥammad and the group round him managed to reach the slopes of Uḥud, and here the Muslims were rallied and given some sort of order. A section, however, had become separated from the main body and had made for the stronghold of the clan of Ḥārithah in the direction of the city; of these a number, perhaps nearly all, were killed.[2] The position on the hill—the Muslims were perhaps a little higher up now than before the battle—still had the advantages for defence which Muḥammad saw when he originally chose it, and the Meccans soon ceased to attack, though they remained on the field for some time longer. With a final taunt to the Muslims Abū Sufyān ordered withdrawal, and both the fighting men and the baggage train moved off. For a time it seemed possible that they might attack the town of Medina itself, but they left it alone and headed for Mecca.

Such then is the outline account of the battle into which the numerous incidents recorded by Ibn Isḥāq and al-Wāqidī are fitted. The unsatisfactory outcome of the battle is attributed to the disobedience of the majority of the archers. That this outline is in essentials the official Muslim account of the battle is confirmed by the Qur'ān (3. 152/145 ff.), although the archers are not specifically mentioned.

> God made good His promise to you when ye were sweeping them away by His permission, until when ye flinched and vied in withdrawing from the affair (or, disputed with one another about the affair), and disobeyed after He had shown you what ye love; then He turned you from them, that He might try you . . . when ye were making for the skyline without turning aside for anyone though the Messenger was calling to you from behind you. . . .

If this, then, was the official account, can it be accepted as reliable?

So far as the individual incidents go, it is obvious that sources

[1] IH, 575; WW, 119. [2] WW, 121 f.

friendly to a man (and these are the majority) will magnify his merits and try to hide any faults. For many it is claimed that they stood firm with Muḥammad and helped him to regain the hill. Those who fled to the stronghold of the clan of Ḥārithah are said to have turned back to fight, but one may wonder whether they were not simply killed as they fled. Usually the discreditable acts are anonymous; only the archers who stood firm are named. An exception to the rule of anonymity is the suggestion that it was Juʿāl b. Surāqah who first cried out that Muḥammad had been killed; but two of the other archers witnessed to his brave bearing, and the generally accepted view came to be that the cry had been raised by the Devil in Juʿāl's form! Some incidents are remembered chiefly for their legal interest, like the case of the man who had just become a Muslim and achieved martyrdom without once having performed the Worship.[1] The story of Quzmān, a non-Muslim Medinan who fought bravely on the Muslim side but eventually hastened his own death and went to Hell, is frequently referred to from the legal and theological standpoint.[2] The ascription of the attack on the Muslim rear to Khālid is perhaps due to the hostility of the sources to him, as the cavalry is elsewhere said to have been under Ṣafwān b. Umayyah.[3] The presence of such tendencies, however, in the accounts of the separate incidents does not greatly affect the general outline, and we must consider whether this outline is similarly open to criticism.

The first question to ask is whether the initial Muslim success was as extensive as some of the source material suggests, for the Muslims are said to have reached the Meccan camp and started plundering. This is distinctly doubtful, for the same source material also admits that they did not in fact secure any booty.[4] It seems probable, then, that, while the Meccan infantry was thrown back, perhaps in disorder, the Muslim advance was not nearly so extensive as is claimed. On the other hand, the Meccan retreat rather presupposes that the Muslims had been definitely superior when fighting on foot under equal conditions.

The next point is whether the plundering instincts of the archers were the main reason that the Muslim rear was exposed to the Meccan cavalry. The words 'what ye love' in the Qur'anic passage could certainly refer to booty. It seems not impossible, however,

[1] WW, 124.
[2] Ibid. 109; cf. al-Bukhārī, *Qadar*, 5 (iv. 253); &c.
[3] WW, 108; WK, 219.
[4] WW, 111; contrast 112.

that they were simply overrun by a well-led charge while still in position (as the sources admit happened to the remnant), but their own slackness when they saw the good fortune of their side may have contributed. It is curious that the man to whom the rumour of Muḥammad's death is attributed should have been one of ʿAbdallāh b. Jubayr's band of archers. Moreover, it is conceivable that this flank attack was not the sudden inspiration of a moment but part of the Meccan plan of battle. The Meccan foot were too undisciplined to carry out a planned withdrawal in the face of enemy pressure, but those who directed the battle may well have foreseen the likelihood of such a retreat and held the cavalry in readiness for just such an attack as they made. The fact that the Meccans had dug trenches somewhere might indicate a deliberate attempt to cause confusion in the Muslim ranks, but the references are too slight to permit a definite opinion.[1] In the light of this total picture it is impossible not to entertain the suspicion that the Meccan success was largely due to skilful generalship. Khālid b. al-Walīd is one of the great generals of all time, and presumably made his contribution at the council of war before the battle, but the supreme commander, Abū Sufyān, and the other leaders, were by no means devoid of military skill.

We may admit, then, that the official Muslim account has to be modified along these lines. From the standpoint of Muḥammad, however, there is a sense in which it is true. There had been a great upsurge of confidence in their military superiority among the believers after Badr. Qur'ān 8. 65/66 may be taken as an illustration of their general attitude:

> O thou prophet, stir up the believers to fight: 'If there be twenty of you who endure, they will overcome two hundred, and if there be a hundred of you they will overcome a thousand of those who have disbelieved. . . .'

Muḥammad doubtless realized that there was an element of exaggeration in this, as is shown by his hesitation about going out to meet the Meccans, but probably felt that it was necessary to speak thus in order to counter the long-standing reputation of Quraysh and strengthen the morale of the Muslims. This may be the implication of Qur'ān 3. 126/122 (though the primary reference is to the promise of angels):

> God only set that forth as good news for you, that your hearts thereby might be at peace.

[1] Ibid. 117, &c.

It is interesting that 8. 66/67, which must have been revealed some time after verse 65/66, reduces from a thousand to two hundred the number of pagans a hundred Muslims can overcome. Now after Uḥud Muḥammad had to explain how it was that the Muslims had not overcome Quraysh. He could not consistently say that it was due to the superior numbers of the enemy; and indeed that was not true since to begin with the Muslims had shown themselves capable of dealing with (presumably) larger numbers. It would have lowered Muslim morale to attribute it to the fact that the Meccans had a large force of cavalry while the Muslims had none. Such indications as are given in al-Wāqidī's casualty list suggest that most of the Muslims who fell were struck down by horsemen. But Muḥammad had been aware of the danger from the cavalry and had made allowance for it in his plans. As the matter appeared to Muḥammad, then, the unfortunate result of the battle was due neither to the Meccans' superior numbers nor to their cavalry (nor to their generalship, he would doubtless have added), but to the combination of indiscipline and love of plunder among the Muslims. As the Qur'ān put it, 'ye flinched . . . and disobeyed after He had shown you what ye love'. And this decline in the military qualities of the Muslims is no doubt connected with their increase in numbers. During the past year Muḥammad had been aware that he would need a far larger force than that at Badr, and he had not turned away men attracted to Islam by prospects of booty. Because of this there was serious indiscipline at Uḥud and lack of steadfastness not merely among the archers but in various other ways. This was therefore the point on which he had to concentrate as he prepared for the next round of the struggle. His rejection of the Jewish contingent which offered to fight for him is, if authentic, perhaps partly due to the awareness that morale was not as good as it ought to be, and that the Jews might set a bad example.

Finally, the common assumption that Uḥud was a great defeat for the Muslims and a great victory for the Meccans must be considered. For the Muslims Uḥud was certainly a setback. They had over seventy killed, including some old and trusted followers of Muḥammad, and his father's brother, Ḥamzah; and among the Arabs the loss of each individual tended to be felt. More serious, however, was the ideological aspect. Lower morale among the combatants was dealt with by the official account of the battle.

Muḥammad's earlier claim that Badr was a sign of God's favour raised theological difficulties, which his opponents in Medina and elsewhere were not slow to press. Did Uḥud not show that God favoured the Meccans, and that Muḥammad was no prophet?[1] The theological problems are referred to in various passages of the Qur'ān:

(Recall) when ye were making for the skyline without turning aside for anyone though the Messenger was calling to you from behind you; so He recompensed you with distress upon distress; in order that ye may not grieve for what ye have missed or for what has befallen you. . . . (3. 153/147.)

What befell you on the day when the two hosts met was by the permission of God, and in order that He might know the believers and in order that he might know the hypocrites. . . . (166/160.)

Let not those who have disbelieved think that such respite as We give them (*sc.* the Meccans) is for their good; We give them respite simply that they may increase in guilt, and for them is a punishment humiliating. God is not one to leave the believers in the situation in which ye are until He distinguishes the bad from the good (*sc.* till doomsday). (173/172 f.)

Western scholars have sometimes thought that the sources try to hide the full extent of the disaster at Uḥud. Scrutiny suggests, however, that the opposite is rather the case, and that the Muslims themselves paint Uḥud in gloomier colours than it merits. This might in part be a reflection of the animosity of the Anṣār (who were almost the sole sufferers, losing seventy men to the Emigrants' four) against Quraysh and especially the ancestors of the Umayyad dynasty. The passages from the Qur'ān, however, give grounds for another explanation in that they show that after Uḥud the average Muslim, who was more sharply aware of the loss of life than of the wider strategic context, was plunged into profound spiritual chaos, since some of his cherished beliefs had been shattered. His gloom was not lessened by certain events of the next few months, when nomads, doubtless responsive to Meccan propaganda, showed their contempt for Muḥammad by deliberately shedding Muslim blood.

If Uḥud was not an out-and-out defeat for the Muslims, still less was it a Meccan victory. The Meccan strategic aim was the destruction of the Muslim community and nothing less, and they

[1] WW, 145.

had fallen far short of this. For many of the Meccans the conscious motive was revenge for the blood shed at Badr; and, if we take the lower figure of about fifty for Meccan dead at Badr, then the Muslims killed at Badr and Uḥud together are slightly more than the Meccans killed in the two battles (though with the higher figure of seventy Meccans killed at Badr the total Muslim dead are slightly fewer). Quraysh as a whole then had had its revenge, even if some individuals were not yet satisfied, as subsequent events showed. But at best Quraysh had merely taken a life for a life, whereas they had boasted they would make the Muslims pay several times over. In more general terms the implication of Uḥud was that Muḥammad was almost able to hold his own against Quraysh, and that Quraysh were not capable of doing much more than holding their own against Muḥammad. What humiliation for the proud merchant princes of Mecca who recently had thought that they had all western Arabia under their control!

Why, then, since this was so, did Abū Sufyān withdraw from Medina without pressing home his advantage? He at least must have been aware of the strategic necessity of destroying Muḥammad's power, and he apparently knew before he left the battlefield that the claim of Ibn Qamīyah to have killed Muḥammad was false. ʿAmr b. al-ʿĀṣ (as reported by al-Wāqidī) sums up the position from the Meccan standpoint:

> When we renewed the attack against them, we smote a certain number of them, and they scattered in every direction, but later a party of them rallied. Quraysh then took counsel together and said, The victory is ours, let us depart. For we had heard that Ibn Ubayy had retired with a third of the force, and some of the Aws and the Khazraj had stayed away from the battle, and we were not sure that they would not attack us. Moreover we had a number of wounded, and all our horses had been wounded by the arrows. So they set off. We had not reached ar-Rawḥā' until a number of them came against us, and we continued on our way.[1]

In other words, the Meccans were not in a position to do anything further. They could not with any hope of success attack either Muḥammad or the strongholds constituting the main settlement of Medina. It is conceivable that they hoped to win over Ibn Ubayy by diplomacy, and so did not want to attack him; but this is not likely. At the same time they had been roughly handled by

[1] WK, 291; cf. WW, 138.

the Muslims; their infantry had been proved inferior, and the horses to which they owed their success were temporarily out of action. Their morale must now have been low, and their withdrawal tends to confirm the Muslim claim to have been victorious at first. To return home was clearly the wisest course.

Muḥammad and the Muslims returned to their homes late on the day of the battle, after burying the dead. Overnight Muḥammad had time to reflect on the position and realized, if he had not done so already, that he had suffered no irretrievable disaster and that much depended on his actions in the immediate future. On the following morning, therefore, he summoned those who had been with him at Uḥud to set out in pursuit of the retreating Meccans. It was the normal and expected thing for an Arab to do when he had been the victim of a raid. Muḥammad had presumably no intention of attacking the Meccans, any more than they can have thought seriously of attacking him. It was an act of defiance and at the same time a sufficient show of strength to deter the Meccans from returning to the attack. The latter had apparently spent the Saturday night at Ḥamrā' al-Asad, a few miles from Medina, and thither the Muslims proceeded on the Sunday, and camped for three or four days. Contact was not made with the enemy, though they were apparently still in the vicinity. To make his demonstration more impressive Muḥammad had his men work hard collecting wood by day and lighting fires by night. A friendly nomad of Khuzā'ah helped to lower the morale of Quraysh by exaggerating the number of the Muslims. Quraysh seem to have remained near by for a day or two—they must not appear to be running away from a renewal of the fighting—and Abū Sufyān tried to spread disquieting rumours among the Muslims. Muḥammad, however, did not flinch. The enemy made no attempt to bring him to battle, and eventually continued on their way to Mecca.

4. THE ROUSING OF THE NOMADS

(a) *The Meccans' last chance*

Long before they reached Mecca Abū Sufyān and the other leaders must have realized that their position was critical. They had made a great effort and had not succeeded. Unless they could do something much better they were faced with disaster. For the expedition of Uḥud they had collected all the available men from Quraysh and the surrounding tribes friendly to them. The only possibility of raising a more powerful army was to attract the active support of some of the great nomadic tribes to the east and north-east of Medina, using propaganda about Muḥammad's weakness, memories of the prestige of Quraysh, promises of booty, and even straight bribes. To this task Quraysh now devoted their energies, as we may surmise from the incidents that have been recorded and from the account of the army they brought together in the year 627/5.[1]

It was not only among tribes like Sulaym and Ghaṭafān that Quraysh tried to make an impression. The chief of B. Ḍamrah (a little north-west of Mecca) had been led to believe that Muḥammad was 'finished' after Uḥud, and was greatly surprised to see the strong Muslim force at Badr in April 626 (xi/4).[2] However, the tribes round Medina already friendly to Muḥammad seem to have stood firm, and numbers of individuals from more distant tribes were now attaching themselves to him.

By their exaggerations the Meccans probably did themselves more harm than good in the end, for the appearance of a strong force of Muslims soon showed up the lies. Muḥammad's policy in the two years following Uḥud was, as far as possible, to forestall hostile moves against Medina. As soon as he heard of a concentration of tribesmen threatening Medina—and he had a good information service—he sent out an expedition to break it up. Such was the raid to Qaṭan against B. Asad led by Abū Salamah with 150 men in June 625 (i/4). Exactly a year later Muḥammad himself led a similar raid to Dhāt ar-Riqāʿ against B. Anmār and Thaʿlabah with 400 (or 800) men. In these raids little seemed to be accomplished apart from the capture of a small quantity of booty; but their effect as demonstrations of Muslim strength was important, and they doubtless made it much more difficult for the Meccans to organize their great confederation.

Another measure employed by Muḥammad where opportunity was given to him was assassination. In the period between Uḥud and the siege of Medina there are two instances of this (according to the more probable dating). Sufyān b. Khālid b. Nubayh, chief of B. Liḥyān, a branch of Hudhayl, was killed by ʿAbdallāh b. Unays (a confederate of B. Salimah of the Khazraj belonging to

[1] IH, 638–68; WW, 149–90; Ṭab. 1431–65; contrast Caetani, i. 568–613.
[2] WW, 169.

B. Juhaynah).[1] Again, after the expulsion of B. an-Naḍīr from Medina and their settlement in Khaybar, one of their leaders, Abū Rāfiʿ Sallām b. Abī 'l-Ḥuqayq, who was engaged in anti-Muslim intrigues with B. Ghaṭafān and other tribes in the vicinity, was assassinated by a group of five Muslims from Medina, including the same ʿAbdallāh b. Unays.[2] To such envoys Muḥammad gave permission to say what they liked about himself and to pretend that they wanted to fight against him. Thus any would-be enemy had to be constantly on his guard against tricks of this sort, just as Muḥammad also had to be constantly on guard against the enemy's wiles and ruses. Two happenings which incidentally illustrate this point are worthy of separate consideration; they are rather different from the other 'expeditions' of the period after Uḥud.

(b) *Bi'r Maʿūnah*[3]

The disaster at the well of Maʿūnah has been given overmuch prominence by some Western biographers of Muḥammad. There was certainly considerable loss of life for the Muslims, and some encouragement for other enemies to take similar measures. But it did not raise theological difficulties as the battle of Uḥud had done; and in the total strategic picture of the period after Uḥud it is hardly noticeable, except as an instance of the difficulties with which Muḥammad had constantly to contend.

The story is that a leading man of the tribe of ʿĀmir b. Ṣaʿṣaʿah, Abū 'l-Barā' ʿĀmir b. Mālik, was invited by Muḥammad to become a Muslim and showed some readiness to do so provided there was sufficient support in his tribe. To obtain this he asked Muḥammad to send missionaries to the region where its pasture-grounds were, and undertook to act as their protector (*jār*). Muḥammad was dubious about the proposition but sent 40 (or 70) young men (but even 40 may be an exaggeration as the names of less than 20 are recorded). Another leader of B. ʿĀmir, ʿĀmir b. Ṭufayl, was apparently hostile to Muḥammad, had the envoy with Muḥammad's letter killed, and tried to get his tribe to attack the Muslim party; but the tribe insisted on observing the protection given by Abū 'l-Barā'.[4] ʿĀmir b. Ṭufayl, however, persuaded some neighbouring clans of B. Sulaym to attack, and the Muslims were killed, apart from two. One of these was seriously wounded and left on the

[1] IH, 981–3 (cf. 310, 501); WW, 224 f.; *Usd*, iii. 119 f. For the date cf. Caetani, i. 578–80. [2] IH, 981; WW, 170–2. [3] IH, 648–52; WW, 153–6.
[4] Cf. p. 97 below.

field for dead. The other, ʿAmr b. Umayyah al-Kinānī, was taken prisoner, but set free because of some relationship to his captors. On the way home he met two members of B. ʿĀmir and killed them. When ʿĀmir b. Ṭufayl asked Muḥammad for blood-money for these two members of his tribe, he was paid it, as the tribe was in alliance with the Muslims.

The puzzle in this account is that Muḥammad pays blood-money to ʿĀmir b. Ṭufayl for two men and does not make any counter-claim for nearly forty Muslims for whose death ʿĀmir b. Ṭufayl had just been responsible. It has been suggested that the Muslims had done something which caused them to forfeit the right to blood-money; but this is improbable. An explanation that does little violence to the existing texts is that, while ʿĀmir b. Ṭufayl had encouraged the Sulamī clans to massacre the Muslims and so was morally responsible, he was not their leader in any sense and so not technically responsible; it was probably also they who killed the letter-carrier.

This explanation of the blood-money can be made part of a consistent account of the whole affair. Abū ʾl-Barāʾ, who was the uncle of ʿĀmir b. Ṭufayl, had a strong following within the tribe which disapproved of ʿĀmir. His appeal to Muḥammad was at bottom an appeal for help against rivals within the tribe. Muḥammad, anxious to bring B. ʿĀmir to his own side, decided to interfere in the internal politics of the tribe, though he realized the riskiness of doing so. When ʿĀmir b. Ṭufayl discovered he was not strong enough to bring the tribe to disown Abū ʾl-Barāʾ's 'protection', he persuaded his neighbours of B. Sulaym to attack the Muslims, and doubtless gave them help by way of information.

It was, of course, shameful for B. ʿĀmir to allow men under its protection to be killed. The Muslim poet, Kaʿb. b. Mālik, is quite clear on the point: 'You left your protégés to Banū Sulaym, in abject weakness fearing their attack. . . .'[1] On the other hand, Ḥassān b. Thābit, who was friendly with the descendants of Abū ʾl-Barāʾ, blamed rather the treachery of ʿĀmir b. Ṭufayl: 'Death came upon him (one of the victims) through league with a tribe whose league-making was rendered ineffectual by treachery. . . .'[2] Muḥammad could not abandon his alliance with B. ʿĀmir without giving up many hopes, but nothing prevented him praying that God would punish ʿĀmir.[3] Perhaps Muḥammad's attempt to make

[1] IH, 652. 3. [2] Ibid. 651. 18. [3] WW, 155.

the Naḍīr, who were confederates of B. ʿĀmir, contribute a portion of the blood-money of the two ʿĀmirīs was in part a way of paying back ʿĀmir b. Ṭufayl.

(c) *Ar-Rajīʿ*[1]

The small expedition of seven men which met with disaster at ar-Rajīʿ (on the Najd road) raises several difficulties, but our information permits sufficient accuracy to make the event a useful illustration of the conditions in which Muḥammad and the Muslims lived.

One version, that of ʿUrwah, was that Muḥammad sent out the seven men to get information about Quraysh—presumably about their intrigues with the great nomadic tribes. The common version, however, is that B. Liḥyān wanted to avenge the assassination of their chief at Muḥammad's instigation, and bribed two clans of the tribe of Khuzaymah to say they wanted to become Muslims and ask Muḥammad to send instructors. At ar-Rajīʿ the would-be converts left the 7 Muslims alone and informed their enemies, who surrounded them, killed 4 who resisted and took the other 3 prisoners, after making fair promises to them. One of the 3 escaped from his bonds on the way to Mecca and died sword in hand, but the other 2 were sold in Mecca to relatives of men killed at Badr; after the sacred month was over they were taken outside the sacred area, summoned to recant from Islam and when they refused put to death not altogether painlessly.

The difficulty lies in the motive of B. Liḥyān, for a commonly expressed view is that the assassination of the chief did not take place till the year 627/5 or even later. Though some sources give the date as the 35th month after the Hijrah (June 625 = i/4), others say it was the 54th or 55th month (about January 627 = viii/5). In view of the alleged motive for the attack on the Muslims at ar-Rajīʿ in July 625 (ii/4), however, and in view of the fact that Muḥammad cursed B. Liḥyān along with those responsible for Biʾr Maʿūnah,[2] it is probable that the assassination took place in the 35th month before the affair of ar-Rajīʿ. The two explanations, moreover, may well be complementary. The seven may have been both spies for Muḥammad and instructors for Arab tribes. The incident is trivial, but it shows how the Arabs expected men to

[1] IH, 638–48; WW, 156–60; Caetani, i. 581–4.
[2] WW, 155; WK, 341.

take care of themselves and to be on their guard against duplicity. The treatment of prisoners suggests that feelings were now pretty high on both sides.

(d) *Growing Muslim strength*

The battle of Uḥud, it has been maintained, was not a great military disaster for the Muslims, though it caused them some theological heart-searchings. The expeditions to Ḥamrā' al-Asad and Qaṭan (March and June 625) were not unsuccessful. The misfortunes at Bi'r Maʿūnah and ar-Rajīʿ (about July 625) may have caused temporary gloom in Medina, but for the rest of the period up to the siege the tide seemed to be turning in favour of the Muslims.

The expulsion of the tribe of an-Naḍīr from Medina in August 625 (iii/4) will be considered more fully in connexion with the internal politics of Medina, but it has also some connexion with Bi'r Maʿūnah, and may further have been intended to cheer up the Muslims after the news of the two disasters had reached them. Certainly a few months later (April 626 = xi/4) Muḥammad was able to raise a force of 1,500 men and 10 horses to go to Badr.[1] This was by far the largest number of men he had so far collected. The story (which may or may not be true) is that before Abū Sufyān left the field at Uḥud he shouted to the Muslims, 'We would like to meet you at Badr next year!', and ʿUmar replied in Muḥammad's name, 'We will be there!' Each side tried to scare away the other by exaggerated accounts of its strength. Eventually the 1,500 Muslims spent the eight days of the market and fair at Badr, and did not come into contact with the 2,000 men and 50 horses which Abū Sufyān brought out to meet them. Presumably both sides wanted to avoid fighting and merely to make a demonstration of strength. The Muslims, however, seem to have had the better of their opponents in this matter, and the tribes of the coastal region were suitably impressed.[2] It is possible that the Muslims circulated the story of the rendezvous merely to discredit their opponents.

During the next few months Muḥammad acted with severity whenever he heard of men massing with hostile intentions against Medina. As already mentioned, Abū Rāfiʿ was assassinated (May 626). The tribes of Anmār and Thaʿlabah were raided at Dhāt ar-Riqāʿ (June 626). Another large force of 1,000 men broke up

[1] IH, 666–8; WW, 167–70. [2] WW, 169.

what was possibly an enemy concentration at Dūmat al-Jandal (August and September 626). This expedition receives scant notice in the sources, but in some ways it is the most significant so far. As Dūmah was some 500 miles from Medina there can have been no immediate threat to Muḥammad, but it may be, as Caetani suggests,[1] that communications with Syria were being interrupted and supplies to Medina stopped. It is tempting to suppose that Muḥammad was already envisaging something of the expansion which took place after his death. It may be, however, that his primary aim was to deter these northern tribes from joining the Meccan grand alliance against him; but what he now learnt about conditions in the north may have shown him the possibility of expansion in this direction. Certainly his rapid march with such a large force must have impressed all who heard of it. Despite Uḥud Muslim strength was clearly increasing.

The expedition to al-Muraysī'[2] against B. al-Muṣṭaliq, a branch of Khuzā'ah, is placed by al-Wāqidī in viii/5 (= January 627), though Ibn Isḥāq places it later after the siege of Medina. The chief of the tribe or clan was said to be arming the men for an attack on Medina (perhaps in concert with the expedition the Meccans were planning). Muḥammad attacked the small group unexpectedly with overwhelming force, and after only a brief resistance all were taken prisoner. The presence of Hypocrites in the Muslim force and the quarrels to which this led belong rather to the internal history of Medina. As al-Muraysī' is near the Red Sea coast, north-west of Mecca, the expedition is an indication of how Muḥammad's sway was encroaching on the sphere where Mecca recently had been supreme.

Thus in the period between Uḥud and the siege of Medina, while Muḥammad was unable to prevent the Meccans forming a confederation against him, he probably stopped many from joining it, and he certainly increased the forces at his own disposal. From the purely human point of view he could not regard the threatened attack without anxiety, yet he had also good grounds for hope.

5. THE SIEGE OF MEDINA

The siege of Medina,[3] known to Muslims as the expedition of the Khandaq or Trench, began on 31 March 627 (8/xi/5) and

[1] i. 597. [2] IH, 725–40; WW, 175–90; Caetani, i. 599–606.
[3] IH, 668–713; WW, 190–210; Ṭab. 1463–85; Q. 33. 9–27; Hamidullah, *Battlefields of Muhammad*, 25–30.

lasted about a fortnight.[1] It was the supreme effort of the Meccans to break Muḥammad's power. For it they had gathered a vast confederacy, including some of the nomadic tribes in no way subject to them. The Jews of an-Naḍīr, now in exile at Khaybar and eager to regain their lands at Medina, had much to do with the collecting of the confederacy; half the date harvest of Khaybar was promised to B. Ghaṭafān if they would join in the attack.[2]

The Meccan confederacy had 10,000 men in three (or perhaps two) armies. Quraysh and their closer allies constituted one army of 4,000 men; Ghaṭafān was the leading tribe in another, and Sulaym in a third; but the latter seem to have shared a camp site with the Ghaṭafān group.[3] Three branches of Ghaṭafān, Fazārah, Ashja', and Murrah, supplied respectively 1,000, 400, and 400 men, and Sulaym 700. That makes only 6,500, and the other tribe mentioned as participating, Asad, could not account for 3,500, but it is idle to speculate about the discrepancy. Quraysh themselves had 300 horses, and there was a like number in the army of Ghaṭafān.

To oppose this enormous force Muḥammad could count on about 3,000 men, that is, practically all the inhabitants of Medina with the exception of the Jewish tribe of Qurayẓah, who seem to have tried to remain neutral. There were some Medinans in league with the Meccans, but they were presumably, like Abū 'Āmir ar-Rāhib, exiled from Medina for the time being. There was a considerable degree of unity among the Muslims, but some of the Hypocrites were critical of Muḥammad's methods and sceptical of a successful result. The Qur'ān makes it clear that a number of them would have been only too glad to be out of the fighting and might even have gone over to the enemy had there been a favourable opportunity.[4]

As in the campaign of Uḥud the enemy approached Medina by Wādi' l-'Aqīq, and camped partly there and partly beside mount Uḥud. The latter arrangement may have been intended to prevent the Muslims obtaining the strong position there which had been so advantageous to them on the previous occasion. Such a precaution, however, was vain, for Muḥammad had adopted another form of defence, indeed, one hitherto unknown in Arabia. Wherever Medina lay open to cavalry attack he had dug a trench, the

[1] WW, 190.
[2] Ibid. 191.
[3] Ibid. 191 n.
[4] 33. 9–25, esp. 12–15.

Khandaq. The idea may have come from Persia, and the Persian convert Salmān is credited with an important share in the detailed planning. The work was set afoot as soon as it was known that the Meccans had started out—it would have been difficult to rouse enthusiasm for it earlier—and most of the Muslims worked hard at it for six days until it was completed. Muḥammad established his headquarters on mount Salʿ, and from this spot could presumably command a view of the whole northern front. Had the enemy crossed the trench, Salʿ would presumably have given the defenders some of the advantages they had at Uḥud.

On one occasion a small party of horsemen crossed, but they were too few to accomplish anything of importance, and in the end retired with the loss of two of their number. Apart from this the Meccans failed to cross the trench at all. They made several assaults by night, but the trench was guarded constantly. To effect a crossing the infantry also would have had to engage the Muslims at close quarters, and that they seem to have been unwilling to do, for they probably regarded the Muslims as more than a match for them in hand-to-hand fighting. The one hope of the Meccans under these circumstances would have been to make several attacks at once. They seem to have hoped to persuade B. Qurayẓah to attack the Muslims from the south, but nothing came of the negotiations. The Muslims were sufficiently well organized and sufficiently numerous to contain all assaults from the north. After a fortnight spent in this way the Meccans gave up hope of success, and the great confederacy split up into its separate contingents, and retired. Exceptionally cold weather and a storm of wind gave the *coup de grâce* to the morale of the besiegers. Six of the Anṣār are reported to have been killed and three of the Meccans.

On the military side the reason for the Meccan failure was the superior strategy of Muḥammad, and probably also his superior information service and secret agents. In particular his adoption of the trench was well suited to the circumstances. Meccan hopes of victory rested mainly on the superiority of their cavalry, for previous battles had shown that the Muslims were likely to overcome their opponents in an infantry mêlée unless heavily outnumbered. The trench effectively countered the menace from the cavalry and forced the Meccans to fight in conditions where they derived little advantage from their 600 horses.

The Meccans suffered from a further disadvantage. In the

campaign of Uḥud they had arrived at Medina about ten days earlier, before the grain was harvested; and the fields had provided fodder for the Meccan horses, while the sight of their devastation had provoked the Medinans to march out in defence despite the disadvantageous circumstances. In 627/5 the grain had been harvested a month before the Meccans arrived—probably earlier than usual because of Muḥammad's foresight—and they had great difficulty in obtaining fodder for their horses. Moreover, as there was no provocation, the Anṣār were content to remain behind the trench. This point seems to indicate slackness or lack of foresight on the part of the Meccan leaders.

Apart from these purely military considerations, the result was due to the relative unity of the Muslims and their discipline, in contrast to the lack of cohesion in the confederacy and the lack of confidence of the various groups in one another. Of this disunity Muḥammad's diplomacy took full advantage. The main group of nomads in the confederacy, Ghaṭafān, had only been persuaded to come by a bribe, and Muḥammad made tentative offers to them of a presumably higher bribe if they would withdraw. The report is that he offered them a third of the date-harvest of Medina, but that at first they demanded a half, and only after some time agreed to accept a third; when this came to the ears of some of the leading Medinans they protested that Medina had never before sunk to this depth of ignominy, and insisted that the negotiations should be broken off. Whatever the exact details may have been, Ghaṭafān had compromised themselves by discussing such matters with Muḥammad. The whole was a battle of wits in which the Muslims had the best of it; without cost to themselves they weakened the enemy and increased the dissension.

The same is true of the intrigues in which the tribe of Qurayẓah was involved. They seem to have had a treaty with Muḥammad, though it is not clear whether, in the event of an attack on Medina, they were to help him or merely to remain neutral. They are said to have supplied the Muslims with some implements for the digging of the trench. Later, however, Ḥuyayy b. Akhṭab of an-Naḍīr persuaded them that Muḥammad was certain to be overwhelmed and they changed their attitude. As they would be exposed to Muslim retaliation should the confederacy retire without destroying Muḥammad, they demanded hostages from Quraysh and Ghaṭafān. Negotiations over this were protracted. A secret agent of Muḥammad's, acting in accordance with hints from him, so increased the suspicion with which the different parties viewed one another that the negotiations came to nothing, and the threatened 'second front' was never opened. The importance of this diplomatic success can hardly be overestimated, for an attack from the south on the Muslim rear by Qurayẓah might have put an end to Muḥammad's career.

The break-up of the confederacy marked the utter failure of the Meccans to deal with Muḥammad. The outlook for them now was dismal. They had exerted their utmost strength to dislodge him from Medina, but he remained there, more influential than ever as a result of the fiasco of the confederacy. Their trade with Syria was gone, and much of their prestige lost. Even if Muḥammad did not attack them, they had no hope of retaining their wealth and position; but he might very well use armed force against them, and try to annihilate them as they had tried to annihilate him. It would be strange if some of the Meccans—a practical people—had not begun to wonder whether it would not be best to accept Muḥammad and his religion.

III

THE WINNING OF THE MECCANS

1. THE EXPEDITIONS OF THE YEAR AFTER THE SIEGE

THE great interest of the period from the end of the siege of Medina to the conclusion of the treaty of al-Ḥudaybiyah is that in it new trends become manifest in Muḥammad's policy. To speak of a reorientation would be to exaggerate, or rather to confess that one had failed to understand Muḥammad's policy so far. Hitherto he had had to concentrate on the struggle with Mecca, and it would be natural to suppose that he had had no thought beyond the defeat of the Meccans and the conquest of their city. Soon after the siege, however, it is clear that Muḥammad's aims are much vaster and more statesmanlike; and when one scrutinizes the early history there appear slight indications that these wider aims were present all along, or at least since the victory at Badr had shown that great changes were possible. The study of this period will therefore most profitably be directed to attempting to understand the underlying aims of Muḥammad's overt actions.

In such a study we necessarily use an analytic and discursive mode of thought. Muḥammad himself, however, almost certainly thought intuitively and not analytically. He was aware of all the factors we laboriously enumerate, but, without isolating these in his thinking, he was presumably able to decide on a course of action that was an adequate response to them. In particular the religious aspect of events was the dominant one for Muḥammad, even where he was most fully aware of political implications; and he would almost certainly have described his supreme aim at this period as the summoning of all the Arabs to Islam. The implied corollary, namely, the political unity of all the Arabs cannot have escaped Muḥammad, but it remained in the background.

To speak at this stage of *all* the Arabs may seem to be going too far ahead, since Islam had touched only a few tribes in the neighbourhood of Mecca and Medina. But Muḥammad had sufficient width of vision to look beyond immediate concerns, and it would be natural for him to take as his potential unit the Arabian peninsula, or rather the totality of tribal groups with some claim to the name Arab. On the other hand, the suggestion of some Muslim sources, though not the earliest, that he conceived of Islam as a universal religion and summoned the Byzantine and Persian emperors and other lesser potentates to accept it, is almost certainly false. Islam indeed from its beginnings was potentially a universal religion, and it is not fortuitous that with the expansion of the Islamic state it became in fact a universal religion. But it is barely credible that a wise statesman like Muḥammad should have made this precise appeal at this precise stage in his career; and examination shows that the reports of the embassies to the various sovereigns are full of inconsistencies.

The usual account[1] is that on one day shortly after his return to Medina from al-Ḥudaybiyah Muḥammad sent out six messengers with letters for the Najashī or Negus of Abyssinia, for the governor of Bostra (Buṣrā) to hand on to the Byzantine emperor, for the Persian emperor (perhaps sent by way of the Yemen), for the Muqawqis or ruler of Egypt, for al-Ḥārith b. Abī Shāmir, prince of Ghassān, and for Hawdhah b. ʿAlī, chief of Ḥanīfah. The messengers who carried the letters are named and the actual texts allegedly reproduced. The critical discussions of European scholars have shown that, while the story cannot be taken as it stands, there is a kernel of truth in it. According to the story Muḥammad's envoys were favourably received and given presents, apart from the one to the Persian emperor. But this is incredible if the message was a summons to become a Muslim and accept Muḥammad as religious leader; we cannot conceive of a Roman emperor or a Negus of Abyssinia responding to such a message. But, if we admit that the persons named actually carried some message from Muḥammad to their respective destinations (though probably at different dates) and were well received, it is not impossible that the contents of the letters have been somewhat altered in the course of transmission. This may be either because the details were not known to the messenger (who is the presumptive source of information), or because later developments made the message seem trivial and unworthy of a great prophet. On this hypothesis we might suppose that, while Muḥammad may have made some reference to his religious beliefs, the real point was

[1] IS, i/2, 15–18 (§§ 1–7); commented on by J. Wellhausen, *Skizzen und Vorarbeiten*, iv, Berlin, 1889, 97–102; Caetani, i. 728–39; Buhl, *Muhammed*, 294–8. Cf. Excursus D, p. 345 below.

political. Perhaps he proposed a neutrality pact. Perhaps he was merely anxious to prevent the Meccans getting foreign help and to counteract the effects of the biased accounts they gave of their relations with him. It would have been most inappropriate for Muḥammad at this period to summon these powerful rulers to accept Islam. But after the siege of Medina he was sufficiently important to have some rudimentary diplomatic contacts with them; and that is presumably the truth of the matter. This is in keeping with the view that Muḥammad was now interested in more than the defeat of Quraysh.

In the alliances made during this period Muḥammad does not seem to have insisted that those on whom the privilege of being his allies was conferred should be Muslims. The words of Ibn Saʿd suggest that the treaty with Ashjaʿ was concluded some time before they became Muslims; and Caetani has argued that the people of Dūmat al-Jandal did not cease to be Christians.[1] Other possible instances will be mentioned in the next chapter.

Of the various events placed by al-Wāqidī in the year between the siege and the expedition to al-Ḥudaybiyah, one section might be described as an aftermath of the failure of the Meccan confederacy at the siege.[2] There was first of all the punishment of the Jewish tribe of Qurayẓah for their intrigues with the Meccans; this will be considered more fully elsewhere. Then there was the raid on Muḥammad's private herd of camels by ʿUyaynah b. Ḥiṣn al-Fazārī, who was doubtless annoyed because Muḥammad had broken off negotiations with him over the withdrawal of Ghaṭafān. The raid was a small affair. Only 40 enemy horsemen were involved, and the booty was only 20 milking camels; 8 Muslims pursued on horseback, recovered half the camels, and killed 4 of the raiders for the loss of 1 of their own number. Muḥammad, however, seems to have been afraid of a large-scale attack, for he collected 500 (or 700) men before following up the 8 Muslim horsemen, and Saʿd b. ʿUbādah was left on guard in Medina with 300 men under arms. A poem by Ḥassān b. Thābit[3] suggests that ʿUyaynah hoped to lay Medina waste and obtain much booty; this is doubtless poetical exaggeration, but it is an indication of what was in the minds of the Muslims. Later in the year Zayd b. Ḥārithah had a mishap at the hands of B. Badr b.

[1] IS, i/2. 48 f. (§ 92); Caetani, i. 701; cf. p. 364 below.

[2] For detailed references see Excursus B.

[3] IH, 724.

Fazārah, a part of ʿUyaynah's tribe, but subsequently avenged it.

Several of the small expeditions of the period were directed, in part at least, against other members of the Meccan confederacy, especially Asad and Thaʿlabah (a part of Ghaṭafān). It appears, however, from various remarks in the sources, that rain, and therefore also fodder, was scarce this year, and in particular that Muḥārib, Thaʿlabah, and Anmār had left their usual pasture-grounds owing to lack of rain and had come nearer to Medina. It may therefore be that the Muslim raids were not so much a requital for what had gone before as a warning not to encroach on the lands of Medina. The same may be true of the expedition against B. Bakr b. Kilāb (a part of ʿĀmir b. Ṣaʿṣaʿah of Ḥawāzin), although these were, at least potentially, allies of the Meccans. A group of B. ʿUraynah (which lived among the same Kilāb) came to Medina (perhaps in distress through lack of food) and professed Islam; because they were suffering from fever they were allowed to go to the pasture-grounds of Muḥammad's private herd to enjoy the plentiful milk there. But when they recovered their strength, they killed one of the herdsmen and made off with fifteen camels; they were quickly captured and cruelly put to death. Similar to these incidents was the expedition led by Muḥammad himself to punish B. Liḥyān who had treacherously attacked a small Muslim party at ar-Rajīʿ in July 625 (ii/4).

The Jewish participants in the Meccan confederacy continued their intrigues. They offered bribes for military help to Arab tribes, including that of Saʿd (? Saʿd b. Bakr), and a Muslim expedition was sent against Saʿd which captured 500 camels and 2,000 sheep as a warning that it was dangerous to fraternize with the enemies of Islam. The Jews themselves were given a similar warning by the assassination of their leader, Usayr b. Rāzim.

A second group of events during the period under review aimed at developing closer relations with the tribes on the road to Syria. Attention has already been called to the great expedition to Dūmah in the latter half of 626 (iii–iv/5). Several events in the year after the siege point to an expansion of interest in this direction, but our information is tantalizingly meagre.

A series of incidents involves Diḥyah b. Khalīfah al-Kalbī and B. Judhām. Diḥyah was sent as envoy to Caesar, that is, presumably, to the nearest Byzantine governor. (This is probably the embassy which is commonly placed among the six.) On his way back Diḥyah was robbed of the Byzantine presents, which he was carrying to Muḥammad, by a few members of the tribe of Judhām. He reported the theft to Muḥammad, who sent out Zayd b. Ḥārithah to punish the offenders. Meantime, however, other members of Judhām were persuading the tribe to accept Islam; complaints were made to Muḥammad that Zayd's punitive measures were illegal, and 'Alī had to be sent to straighten out the matter. The details are obscure, but it is clear that at least a section of Judhām entered into alliance with Muḥammad about this time.

Following upon this Zayd set out on a trading journey to Syria in the course of which he was wounded and robbed by B. Badr b. Fazārah.[1] This is the first mention of a trading journey by any Muslim from Medina. But the next expedition, one of 700 men to Dūmat al-Jandal, was led by 'Abd ar-Raḥmān b. 'Awf, who had the reputation of being the shrewdest merchant and financier among the Muslims; at some time or other (probably after Muḥammad's death) he appears as the organizer of a caravan of 500 camels.[2] On the expedition in 627/6 the prince of Dūmat al-Jandal made a treaty of alliance with Muḥammad, and gave his daughter Tumāḍir in marriage to 'Abd ar-Raḥmān.

These scanty details are sufficient to show that Muḥammad's interest in the tribes on the route to Syria was not simply a matter of chance. These tribes were either Christian or had some acquaintance with Christianity, and because of this may have been more attracted to Islam than the pagans farther south, especially while the Persians were occupying Syria. But our sources do not justify the supposition that Muḥammad was interested in the northern tribes because they showed themselves interested in Islam. It is more likely that his interest was due to the importance of the Syrian trade in the Meccan economy. By his raids on Meccan caravans he had blocked the Meccan path to the north, and alliances with the northern tribes would serve to tighten the blockade, if Muḥammad so desired. The expeditions of Zayd and 'Abd ar-Raḥmān were probably designed to bring part of the Syrian trade to Medina. This trade was perhaps more important in the life of Medina than our sources indicate. As the population of the oasis grew through the attraction of Islam, imports of food would presumably be necessary.

[1] IS, ii/1. 65. 16; cf. 64. 16 f.; WW, 236, 238.
[2] IS, iii/1. 93. 17 ff.

Another point was doubtless present in Muḥammad's mind. He forbade fighting and raiding between Muslims, and consequently, if a large number of Arab tribes accepted Islam or even merely accepted Muḥammad's leadership, he would have to find an alternative outlet for their energies. Looking ahead, Muḥammad probably realized that it would be necessary to direct the predatory impulses of the Arabs outwards, towards the settled communities adjacent to Arabia, and he was probably conscious to some extent of the development of the route to Syria as a preparation for expansion.

Thirdly, in contrast to all this activity to the north and east of Medina, there was no attempt to attack Mecca directly. On the expedition against Banū Liḥyān Muḥammad seems to have made a feint against Mecca;[1] but it cannot have caused more than a temporary flurry. More serious was the attack by Zayd with 170 men on the caravan returning to Mecca from Syria by the 'Irāq road. The goods, including silver belonging to Ṣafwān b. Umayyah, were all captured, and a number of prisoners made. The lenient treatment of one of these, however, may be the expression of a new policy of leniency directed to winning over the Meccans. This man was Abū 'l-'Āṣ b. ar-Rabī', husband of Muḥammad's daughter Zaynab; he sought and publicly received her protection (*jiwār*), although this was perhaps contrary to the constitution. Muḥammad denied prior knowledge of Zaynab's declaration but asserted that he was ready to uphold it, and Abū 'l-'Āṣ consequently received back his property that was among the booty.

From a consideration of these events of 627/6, together with what happened subsequently, it seems clear that Muḥammad was not preparing for a direct assault on Mecca. His policy was instead to weaken Mecca by preventing the movement of caravans to and from Syria, while at the same time increasing the number of tribes in alliance with himself and consolidating the strength of this group. The conversion of Ashja', one of the weaker tribal bodies joining in the siege, showed that the Meccans and their confederates were not able to provide for their members as Muḥammad was. The peace of Islam, as administered by the iron hand of Muḥammad, would bring prosperity for the Arabs, but only if the means of subsistence were correspondingly increased. But the number of camels and sheep the desert could support could not

[1] IS, ii/1. 57. 16–18; contrast WW, 227 = IS, ii/1. 57. 6.

be greatly increased. Consequently the Islamic state was under the necessity of constantly expanding its sphere of influence. From now on Muḥammad seems to be more concerned with the positive building up of strength and prosperity than with the negative aim of defeating the Meccans. Soon it becomes apparent that the Meccans have an important part to play in the positive side of his policy.

2. THE EXPEDITION AND TREATY OF AL-ḤUDAYBIYAH

This series of events was brought to a close, which was indeed a consummation, by Muḥammad's expedition to al-Ḥudaybiyah; and an endeavour must now be made to elucidate this event. The outline of the story as given in the sources[1] is that as the result of a dream Muḥammad decided to go on pilgrimage (*'umrah*) to Mecca. He called on the Muslims (and perhaps others) to join him and to bring animals for sacrifice. Eventually he set out with from 1,400 to 1,600 men, among whom were nomads of Khuzā'ah, though other tribes who might have been expected to take part made excuses for abstaining. When the Meccans heard of this approaching force, they assumed that Muḥammad's intentions were hostile, and sent out 200 cavalry to bar the way. By taking an unusual route across difficult hilly country Muḥammad circumvented the Meccan cavalry and reached al-Ḥudaybiyah on the edge of the sacred territory of Mecca. At this point his camel refused to go farther, and he decided it was time to halt.

The Meccans threatened to fight if Muḥammad tried to perform the pilgrimage. Messengers came and went between them and the Muslims, and eventually a treaty was agreed on. This year the Muslims were to retire, but in the following year the Meccans were to evacuate their city for three days to enable the Muslims to carry out the various rites connected with the pilgrimage. At a moment when it looked as if the negotiations would break down, the Muslims made a pledge to Muḥammad known as the Pledge of Good Pleasure, or the Pledge under the Tree. On the conclusion of the treaty, Muḥammad killed his sacrificial animal and had his hair shaved, and the Muslims, apparently after some hesitation, followed his example. Then they set off home.

The dream mentioned by al-Wāqidī (though not by Ibn Hishām and Ibn Sa'd) may be accepted as fact in the light of the Qur'anic

[1] IH, 740–55; WW, 241–64; IS, ii/1. 69–76; Ṭab. 1528–51.

verse, 'Assuredly God hath given to His messenger a true and right vision';[1] but the account of the contents of the dream is probably influenced by later events. It was doubtless by a dream that the idea first came to Muḥammad of making the pilgrimage, and he was naturally puzzled when what he regarded as a Divine promise was not fulfilled. The idea, however, must also have commended itself to him for practical political reasons. He can hardly have hoped to conquer Mecca, for he must have known that the morale of the Meccans was still good, and his force was too small to overcome them in battle. His primary intention was no doubt simply what he said, to perform the pilgrimage; but this had certain political implications, and it was probably in these that he was chiefly interested. The performance of the pilgrimage would be a demonstration that Islam was not a foreign religion but essentially an Arabian one, and in particular that it had its centre and focus in Mecca. A demonstration of such a kind at such a time would impress upon the Meccans that Islam was not a threat to the religious importance of Mecca. It would also suggest that Muḥammad was prepared to be friendly—on his own terms, of course.

Unfortunately, however, Muḥammad's proposed action, if carried out, would make it appear that Quraysh were too weak to stop him. It was, of course, one of the sacred months in which there was supposed to be no bloodshed, but Muḥammad had not shown himself specially observant of sacred times, and was clearly relying, not solely on the sanctity of the season, but partly on the number of his followers. In the light of the failure of Quraysh in besieging Medina, the triumphant progress of Muḥammad through Mecca would look bad. It was therefore understandable that they should decide to oppose. The compromise eventually agreed on saved their face and their prestige, while Muḥammad obtained all that he really wanted.

The terms of the treaty are given as follows:

In Thy name, O God. This is the treaty which Muḥammad b. ʿAbdallāh made with Suhayl b. ʿAmr. They agreed to remove war from the people for ten years. During this time the people are to be in security and no one is to lay hands on another. Whoever of Quraysh comes to Muḥammad without permission of his protector (or guardian), Muḥammad is to send back to them; whoever of those with Muḥammad comes

[1] 48. 27.

to Quraysh is not to be sent back to him. Between us evil is to be abstained from,[1] and there is to be no raiding or spoliation. Whoever wants to enter into a covenant and alliance with Muḥammad is to do so; and whoever wants to enter into a covenant and alliance with Quraysh is to do so. . . . You are to withdraw from us this year and not enter Mecca against us; and when next year comes we shall go out in front of you and you shall enter it (Mecca) with your companions and remain in it three days; you shall have the arms of the rider, swords in scabbards; you shall not enter it bearing anything else.[2]

This is probably not an exact reproduction of the original text of the treaty, in view of the abrupt changes of person,[3] but it may be accepted as an adequate account of the provisions. It gives some satisfaction to both parties. The abandonment of hostilities for ten years expresses Muḥammad's peaceful intentions towards Mecca, and gives Quraysh a respite from the desperate struggle against his growing power. The postponement of the pilgrimage rites by the Muslims saved the face of Quraysh, but Muḥammad achieved his aim of demonstrating his intentions and attitudes by the permission to perform pilgrimage in the following year; indeed he had largely achieved it by the very conclusion of the treaty. The clause about returning persons under protection (chiefly minors and clients presumably) was a concession to the feelings of Quraysh which cost the Muslims little. The son of one of the Meccan negotiators is said to have come to Muḥammad while his father was still with him and to have been told he must remain in Mecca; but Muḥammad made the other two negotiators present guarantee his safety in view of his strained relations with his father. The fact that this clause was not reciprocal is perhaps mainly an expression of Muḥammad's belief in the superior attractiveness of Islam.

The remaining clause was apparently one on which Muḥammad set considerable store, for on his way to Mecca he is said to have told one of his messengers that he was ready to make peace with Quraysh if they would allow him a free hand with the nomadic tribes. The clause suggests that the two sides are being treated equally, and in a sense it is a recognition by Quraysh of Muḥammad's equality with themselves. In fact it is a concession by Quraysh,

[1] The meaning of this phrase is obscure; cf. E. W. Lane, *Arabic-English Lexicon*, London, 1863–93, *s.v.* *'aybah*.

[2] IH, 747 f.; cf. IS, ii/1. 70 f.; WW, 257.

[3] Cf. Caetani, i. 718, n. 2.

permitting tribes to abandon the Meccan alliance for that of Muḥammad; and Khuzāʿah speedily made the exchange.

This is part of Muḥammad's programme of consolidating his own strength and building a complex of tribes in alliance with himself. It should further be noticed that by agreeing to a pact of non-aggression for ten years Muḥammad had by implication given up the blockade of Mecca. Mecca could presumably now resume her trade with Syria, though her monopoly of this trade was gone. While flinging away this weapon, however, Muḥammad was strengthening himself in other ways, and, if need be, could meet Quraysh in battle at some future date with good hopes of success. Meantime he was reducing his pressure on Mecca and showing himself disposed to be friendly and ready to respect Meccan feelings in various ways. In other words, instead of vigorously prosecuting the struggle with Mecca, he was angling for the conversion of Quraysh to Islam. About what lay behind this aim we cannot be quite certain. Perhaps he was merely disgusted at the recent refusal of the nomads to join in his pilgrimage, and felt they were very unreliable, compared with his fellow tribesmen. But possibly he saw that in the new Islamic state their administrative and organizing ability would be in demand. Certainly from this time onward, whatever may have been the case previously, he was aiming at winning the Meccans for Islam and the Islamic state. (The believing men and women for whose sake Mecca was said to be spared[1] were doubtless people who did not yet believe but were potential believers; they can hardly have been people who already believed but concealed their faith. This is tantamount to saying that Muḥammad hoped to win many of the Meccans for Islam.)

The treaty was thus favourable to Muḥammad's long-term strategy, but for the moment left him to deal with the disappointment of his followers at the apparent failure of the expedition. In this crisis smouldering embers of dissatisfaction within Muḥammad were fanned into flame, and he acted vigorously. He had been disappointed when some of the allied nomads refused to join in the pilgrimage. They had seen no prospect of booty, and had suspected that the Muslims might not even return safely.[2] Besides making Muḥammad's demonstration less impressive, their action had shown slight interest in Islam as a religion and little loyalty to Muḥammad.

[1] Q. 48. 25. [2] Ibid. 12.

It is against this background that the Pledge of Good Pleasure (*bayʿat ar-riḍwān*) must be considered. The usual account is that Muḥammad eventually sent ʿUthmān b. ʿAffān to discuss matters with the Meccans; as a member of the clan of ʿAbd Shams he had powerful protection in Mecca. When he was long in returning and a rumour got about that he had been killed, Muḥammad called the Muslims to himself under a tree and made them pledge themselves to him. A few sources say that this was a pledge to fight to the death (*bāyaʿū ʿalā ʾl-mawt*), but most of them explicitly deny that and say it was a pledge not to flee. One account, however, says it was a pledge to do whatever Muḥammad had in mind.[1]

It is tempting to think that the last gives the essence of the pledge. What the situation demanded most of all was that the Muslims should accept Muḥammad's decision, even if it seemed to them unsatisfactory; and they did in fact agree to the renunciation of the plan of making the pilgrimage that year. ʿUmar is said to have protested; and the unwillingness of most of the Muslims to sacrifice the animals and shave their hair after the signing of the treaty may be due to a feeling that they had not duly performed the rites. Such a pledge to accept Muḥammad's decision would be an advance on his part towards the position of autocrat; but the refusal of many nomads to join the expedition may have made him regard some such strengthening of his position as necessary. It must have been about this time that he started in suitable cases to insist on acceptance of Islam and readiness to obey the Messenger of God as conditions for alliance with himself.

While general considerations point to this interpretation of the pledge, it has to be admitted that the evidence is slender. The Arabic name, *bayʿat ar-riḍwān*, could conceivably mean a pledge to do what seemed good to Muḥammad, but it is almost certainly derived from the Qur'ānic words: 'God was well-pleased (*raḍiya*) with the believers when they took the pledge to thee under the tree.'[2] On the other hand, the commonest version, namely, that it was a pledge not to flee, not a pledge to the death, is compatible with the interpretation just suggested. The insistence that it was not a pledge to the death is perhaps an indication that it was not solely connected with fighting. It is indeed curious that so much should be made of the distinction between 'not fleeing' and 'fighting to the death', for the latter seems to be involved in the former. It

[1] WW, 254. [2] Q. 48. 18.

is simplest, therefore, to suppose that the pledge was not an oath never under any circumstances to flee, but an oath not to make for safety unless with Muḥammad's permission. Though this was the aspect emphasized at the time, it may well be that the pledge was essentially one to accept his judgement in general. The period of tension when it looked as if the Meccans would decide to fight would be a convenient opportunity for demanding such a pledge.

Whatever the precise content of the pledge, Muḥammad was certainly well able to control the Muslims at al-Ḥudaybiyah, and, as the sources indicate, this made a great impression on some of the Meccan negotiators. It was natural, however, for an Arab to feel that virtue could not be allowed to go unrewarded; and before long—perhaps on the way back to Medina—Muḥammad had evolved the scheme of attacking the rich Jewish settlement of Khaybar, but allowing only those who took the pledge at al-Ḥudaybiyah to participate. There were weighty military reasons for the attack, but it would also, if successful, reward those who had been faithful to him. Some six months later he carried out the plan.

As he rode home to Medina, Muḥammad must have been well satisfied with the expedition. In making a treaty with the Meccans as an equal he had received public recognition of the position that was clearly his after the failure of the siege of Medina. More important was the fact that, by ending the state of war with Mecca, he had gained a larger measure of freedom for the work of extending the influence of the religious and political organization he had formed. He doubtless realized that some of the pagan Meccans had been impressed. Yet in stopping the blockade Muḥammad had made a great military and economic concession, and what he had gained in return was chiefly among the *imponderabilia*. The treaty of al-Ḥudaybiyah was only satisfactory for the Muslims in so far as one believed in Islam and its attractive power. Had Muḥammad not been able to maintain and strengthen his hold on the Muslims by the sway of the religious ideas of Islam over their imaginations, and had he not been able to attract fresh converts to Islam, the treaty of al-Ḥudaybiyah would not have worked in his favour. Material reasons certainly played a large part in the conversion of many Arabs to Islam. But any historian who is not biased in favour of materialism must also allow as factors of supreme importance Muḥammad's belief in the message of the Qur'ān, his belief in the future of Islam as a religious and political system, and his unflinching devotion to the task to which, as he believed, God had called him. These attitudes of Muḥammad underlay the policy he followed at al-Ḥudaybiyah.

This expedition and treaty mark a new initiative on the part of Muḥammad. His had been the activity which provoked Quraysh after his migration to Medina. Their ripost had failed. The obvious way for Muḥammad to follow up his advantage would have been to set about destroying the influence of Mecca. Instead of that, however, he tried something new.

3. AFTER AL-ḤUDAYBIYAH

In the period of nearly two years between the treaty of al-Ḥudaybiyah (March 628) and the capture or surrender of Mecca (January 630) some seventeen Muslim expeditions are recorded, though of some practically no details are given.[1] These expeditions, if that to Khaybar is neglected, may conveniently be regarded as falling into three groups.

Firstly, there are a number of expeditions against tribes which were ceasing to oppose Muḥammad but were not yet completely quiescent. Ghaṭafān, including Murrah and Thaʿlabah, attracted most attention. A small expedition to Fadak against Murrah led by Bashīr b. Saʿd was unfortunate, and most of the Muslim party were killed; but revenge was taken immediately by a larger expedition under Ghālib b. ʿAbdallāh. The same Bashīr successfully led a force of 300 men against Ghaṭafān two months later. Presumably only some sections of Ghaṭafān were involved, and not the whole; but ʿUyaynah the chief, to whom Muḥammad had made a gift from the spoils of Khaybar, was present and took to flight.[2] Another old enemy, Sulaym, was the object of an expedition under Ibn Abī 'l-ʿAwjā', himself a Sulamī. Though most of the fifty participants were killed, there is no mention of revenge being taken, so it is probable that this was an old quarrel within the tribe which was being prosecuted by one party in the name of Islam. Less than a year after this a large contingent of Sulaym joined Muḥammad for the expedition against Mecca. The expedition of Ghālib b. ʿAbdallāh al-Laythī against a branch of Layth called Mulawwiḥ is probably also a repayment of old scores. The expedition of Abū ʿUbaydah against some of the Juhaynah in

[1] General sources for the section: IH, 788–802; WW, 297–319; Ṭab. 1552–1618; Caetani, ii/1. 3–105.

[2] Cf. IS, iii/2, 84.

November 629 (viii/8) is puzzling, as most of Juhaynah were in alliance with the Muslims.

Secondly, there are a number of expeditions against parts of Hawāzin. These were perhaps of no great importance in themselves; but they are significant as an indication of the geographical expansion of Muḥammad's power and as a premonition of the events which culminated in the battle of Ḥunayn.

Thirdly, there are the expeditions to the north, which may be reckoned as three in number, namely, that under Ka'b al-Ghifārī to Dhāt Aṭlāḥ, that to Mu'tah, and that under 'Amr b. al-'Āṣ to Dhāt as-Salāsil. Some of the expeditions of the first group may also have been concerned with the road to Syria. Certainly Muḥammad was intensely interested in the route to the north. The expedition to Dūmat al-Jandal in the autumn of 626[1] marks an early stage in the growth of this interest. There were further expeditions towards the end of 627 and the beginning of 628. Now the expedition to Mu'tah in September 629 (v/8), led by Muḥammad's adopted son, Zayd b. Ḥārithah, shows the high importance attached to the northern road. Three thousand men took part in this expedition—nearly twice as many as at al-Ḥudaybiyah, and half as many again as at Khaybar. Muḥammad doubtless did not tell many of his followers the plans that were in his mind, and consequently our sources are exasperatingly silent on events connected with Muḥammad's 'northern' policy. We do not know, for example, on what errand Muḥammad had sent Ka'b al-Ghifārī and his party of fourteen over the border into Syria; we may be almost certain, however, that they were not mere raiders, but were carrying out part of some far-reaching plan. The massacre of this party by men of Quḍā'ah would be part of the reason for the two later expeditions, since there were some Quḍā'ah among the enemy at Mu'tah.[2]

The great expedition to Mu'tah is not merely part of the mysterious 'northern' policy, but is in itself mysterious. A messenger from Muḥammad to the prince of Bostra (Buṣrā) had been intercepted and put to death by Shuraḥbīl b. 'Amr of Ghassān, and Zayd was sent out with 3,000 men to exact a penalty. Muḥammad may have thought of taking part himself, in view of the importance and size of the expedition, for it was apparently only after the men were collected that Zayd was appointed supreme

[1] Cf. p. 35 above. [2] WW, 314.

commander; in the end, however, poor health (perhaps the result of an attempt to poison him at Khaybar) or pressure of affairs kept him at home. The expedition made its way north, and at Maʿān heard of a large Byzantine army ahead of them, including many Arab tribesmen. They decided, however, to proceed, and at Mu'tah the two forces met. Zayd and two other prominent Muslims were killed. The Muslims are said to have taken to flight, but to have been rallied by Thābit b. Aqram of the Anṣār and Khālid b. al-Walīd. After some further fighting (in which according to one source the enemy fled) Khālid decided to lead the force back to Medina. On reaching Medina the army is said to have been greeted with derision presumably because they had retired without taking due revenge for the fallen.

The story of Mu'tah has been greatly manipulated in transmission, and it is impossible to be certain of more than the barest outline of events. The chief source of confusion has been the desire to vilify Khālid. Thus the account of how Muḥammad appointed Jaʿfar b. Abī Ṭālib and ʿAbdallāh b. Rawāḥah to succeed Zayd if he fell is probably an invention to support the accusation that Khālid unjustifiably assumed supreme command. (Jaʿfar and ʿAbdallāh were perhaps second and third in command of the centre.) The story of how Thābit b. Aqram insisted on his taking command is primarily an attempt to counter this. Again, the emphasis on the hostile reception of the army on its homecoming is a denigration of Khālid's decision to return to Medina, though this was presumably the wisest thing to do in the circumstances. The exaggerated reports of the enemy numbers—100,000 men—may be part of the defence of Khālid's action. When allowance is made for this hostility to Khālid, and for the usual glorification of the part played by members of one's family, the following points seem to remain: (1) there was some sort of an encounter with an enemy force; (2) Zayd, Jaʿfar, and ʿAbdallāh were killed, but not many others; (3) the army returned to Medina under the command of Khālid without serious loss.

Beyond these points there is much uncertainty. It is unlikely that the encounter was with the whole of the opposing army. Al-Wāqidī says only 8 Muslims were killed, but Ibn Hishām adds 4 other names. This is an incredibly small casualty list, however, for a pitched battle between 3,000 men on one side and, say, 20,000 or 10,000 or even 3,000 on the other—unless, indeed, the Muslims completely routed the enemy. On the other hand, had there been more casualties they would have been mentioned to blacken Khālid, if for no other reason; but in fact the sources do not seem to try to conceal Muslim losses. It is possible, then, that the encounter was of the nature of a skirmish. It is difficult to conceive a skirmish in which the general and two staff officers were killed, but hardly anyone else; but, in view of Arab methods of fighting, it is not an absolute impossibility. In this encounter the Arabs may well have had the best of it; otherwise the losses would have been heavier. The decision to return would be dictated not by danger from the enemy or by cowardice, but by the length of absence from the base and perhaps also by Khālid's ignorance of the precise aims of the expedition. (The alleged instructions to Zayd given in the sources seem to belong to a later date.)[1] This is practically all that can be said.

While the expedition was doubtless successful in increasing respect for Muslim power, the death of the general may have had a contrary effect in some quarters. At least in the following month (October 629 = vi/8) an expedition was sent under ʿAmr b. al-ʿĀṣ, another recent convert, against the tribes of Balī and Quḍāʿah which (or part of which) had been on the Byzantine side at Mu'tah, and were reported to be preparing a further concentration of men against Medina. After reinforcements had come from Medina and a dispute about leadership had been settled, the threatening concentration was completely dispersed.

With his power over a wide area as secure as power could be in Arabian conditions, Muḥammad was now in a position to march on Mecca as soon as he found an occasion for interference.

4. MECCAN REACTIONS TO MUḤAMMAD'S SUCCESSES

Before we consider Muḥammad's triumphal entry into Mecca, it will be convenient to review the course of the internal politics of Mecca since the battle of Badr. The sources give us no more than a glimpse of what was happening even if we assume their general reliability. In later times a man's descendants would pass over in silence or minimize his opposition to Muḥammad, while the enemies of the man or of his descendants would exaggerate it, and thus there is a ground for doubting the sources on this topic over and above the normal grounds for doubting sources. The

[1] Ibid. 309. 22–33; cf. Caetani, ii/1. 82, n. 2.

items of information to be considered in this section, however, are too varied in their 'tendency' to be explicable as inventions to the honour or dishonour of the actors.

The political changes at this period illustrate the progressive disintegration of the clan system at Mecca. That system was still the basis of social security, but apart from that it was unimportant. Not merely were the old alliances shifting, but it becomes common to find members of the same clan on opposite sides. Politics tends to be a matter of individuals rather than of clans.

The political divisions at the time of Badr may be taken as reflected in men's approval or disapproval of the policy of Abū Jahl (Makhzūm). The latter apparently wanted to precipitate the battle, whereas, after the caravan was out of danger, Abū Sufyān tried to avoid a clash and considered that Abū Jahl rather 'fancied himself' as leader—he was presumably entitled to lead in war only during Abū Sufyān's absence, since 'Abd Shams was entitled to the *qiyādah* or leadership in war.[1] The following table summarizes the statements of al-Wāqidī[2] (an asterisk indicates those killed at Badr):

Clan	*Approved*	*Disapproved*
Makhzūm . .	*Abū Jahl 'Abdallāh b. Rabī'ah	. .
Jumaḥ . . .	'Umayr b. Wahb	*Umayyah b. Khalaf
Sahm . . .	. .	*Munabbih b. al-Ḥajjāj
'Abd ad-Dār . .	*an-Nadr b. al-Ḥārith	. .
'Āmir . . .	Suhayl b. 'Amr Ḥuwayṭib	. .
Nawfal . . .	*Ṭu'aymah b. 'Adī al-Ḥārith b. 'Āmir (?)	. .
'Abd Shams . .	*'Uqbah b. Abī Mu'ayṭ	Abū Sufyān *'Utbah b. Rabī'ah *Shaybah " "
Asad . . .	*Zam'ah b. al-Aswad	Ḥakīm b. Ḥizām
Zuhrah . . .	. .	al-Akhnas

From this it appears that some clans were divided in their attitude to Abū Jahl, and that 'Abd Shams was not united behind Abū Sufyān. It is noteworthy, too, that the clans of 'Āmir and Nawfal which did not belong to the old clan-group of the Aḥlāf[3] were now apparently whole-hearted supporters of Makhzūm. On the other hand, there are signs that the Aḥlāf ('Abd ad-Dār, Makhzūm,

[1] WW, 45. [2] Ibid. 41–43, 50–53. [3] *M/Mecca*, 5–7.

Jumaḥ, Sahm, ʿAdī) are breaking up; ʿAdī had already gone because of a quarrel with Sahm, and now Sahm appears to be going, while Jumaḥ is restive.

The death at Badr of so many of the leaders caused some shifting of the balance of power, while the catastrophic change in the fortunes of Mecca made men forget for a time the old rivalry between the groups associated with Makhzūm and ʿAbd Shams respectively. Al-Wāqidī's list of the women taken with them by the Meccans on the expedition of Uḥud appears to give an indication of the leading men and tribes.[1] These women, with two exceptions, were wives of chiefs of clans, and the fact that Abū Sufyān and Ṣafwān b. Umayyah took two each suggests that these were now the leaders of the rival factions. Abū Jahl's son ʿIkrimah was apparently not yet on a level with Ṣafwān. The men of Quraysh who took wives were:

ʿAbd Shams . .	Abū Sufyān (2).
Jumaḥ . . .	Ṣafwān (2).
Makhzūm . .	ʿIkrimah (1); al-Ḥarith b. Hishām (1).
ʿAbd ad-Dār .	Ṭalḥah b. Abī Ṭalḥah (1).
Sahm . . .	ʿAmr b. al-ʿĀṣ (1).
ʿĀmir . . .	Perhaps represented by Khunās bint Mālik who accompanied her son Abū ʿUzayr of ʿAbd ad-Dār.

The other five women were from tribes allied with Quraysh. Sufyān b. ʿUwayf of B. ʿAbd Manāt b. Kinānah had both wife and daughter-in-law, and so was almost on a level with Abū Sufyān and Ṣafwān. Ad-Dughaynah (or ad-Dughunnah) accompanied her two sons, perhaps chiefs of al-Ḥārith b. ʿAbd Manāt b. Kinānah, and so of the Aḥābīsh.[2] The remaining two I have not been able to identify; they may be from Thaqīf, unless one is from the clan of Nawfal of Quraysh. Ṣafwān's wives were from Thaqīf and Kinānah respectively.

Divided counsels made their appearance immediately after the battle of Uḥud. Ṣafwān's view of the situation was that the Meccans ought to be content with the success they had achieved and not endanger it, whereas ʿAmr b. al-ʿĀṣ and Abū Sufyān thought they

[1] WW, 102; cf. IH, 557.

[2] Cf. IH, 245, and note in 'Kritische Anmerkungen', p. 80; in IH, 852 (= WW, 364) a Sulamī is son of ad-Dughunnah.

ought to drive home their advantage by attacking Medina.[1] We might conjecture that Ṣafwān was afraid that, as Abū Sufyān was supreme commander, a successful campaign might redound too much to the latter's glory. It is also possible, however, that Abū Sufyān was more of a statesman. In opposing Ṣafwān's earlier suggestion of cutting down the palm-trees at Medina he may have been hoping to win over some of the Medinans (unless the report is simply later white-washing of the Umayyads).[2] He also pursued a milder course a few months later when the tribe of Liḥyān brought the Muslims captured at ar-Rajīʿ to Mecca. In its bitterness against the Muslims the 'Makhzūm group' to which Ṣafwān belonged bought these captives and put them to death to avenge their own losses at Muslim hands; the clans involved were Nawfal, Jumaḥ, Makhzūm, ʿĀmir, Zuhrah, and ʿAbd ad-Dār.[3] Abū Sufyān had nothing to do with this affair, though his son and other members of his clan had been killed at Badr; a confederate of the clan seems to have been involved, however.

The rivalry between Abū Sufyān and Ṣafwān b. Umayyah abated sufficiently to allow a united expedition to Badr in April 626 (xi/4) and the attempt to capture Medina in April 627 (xi/5), but the dissensions between the Meccan leaders led to delay on both occasions. Abū Sufyān had the supreme command in view of the hereditary privilege of his clan. ʿIkrimah, however, began to come into prominence at the siege of Medina, especially in negotiations with the Jews;[4] and by the time of Muḥammad's expedition to al-Ḥudaybiyah in March 628 (xi/6) we find the triumvirate of Ṣafwān b. Umayyah, Suhayl b. ʿAmr (ʿĀmir), and ʿIkrimah b. Abī Jahl constituting the core of the resistance to the Muslims. When Muḥammad suggested negotiations, however, the triumvirate was divided. ʿIkrimah was against any negotiations, and at one point maltreated Muḥammad's envoy, but he was opposed by Ṣafwān along with al-Ḥārith b. Hishām of Makhzūm.[5] ʿIkrimah was eventually won over, and when it came to the final negotiation of the treaty, this was entrusted to the third of the triumvirate, Suhayl, assisted by two of his fellow clansmen. In all this there is no mention of Abū Sufyān; and mere absence[6] is not enough to

[1] WW, 138, 146, 150. [2] Ibid. 103.

[3] IH, 638 ff., esp. 645; WW, 158–60; Saʿīd b. ʿAbdallāh b. ʿAbd Qays b. ʿAbd Wudd (ʿĀmir) is probably a brother of the ʿAmr b. ʿAbd (Wudd) b. ʿAbd Qays killed at the Khandaq. [4] WW, 201, 206. [5] Ibid. 250, 253.

[6] Cf. ibid. 323; but contrast IH, 745 and Ṭab. 1542 f.

explain this silence, though absence—if he were absent—would help. Perhaps he felt that there was little point in continuing the struggle; the old position of Mecca was irretrievably lost; one had to accept a decrease in dignity and prosperity and make the best of it. He certainly expected Muḥammad to be successful at Khaybar, as soon as he heard of the expedition.[1] Perhaps, too, he was growing weaker compared with the 'Makhzūm group'. His own clan was not giving him wholehearted support, for a member of it, al-Ḥakam b. Abī 'l-ʿĀṣ (father of the caliph Marwān), joined ʿIkrimah in opposing the negotiations at al-Ḥudaybiyah, although Abū Sufyān, whether present or absent, presumably supported the policy of negotiating.[2] Further, he may have known that Muḥammad was proposing to marry his daughter, Umm Ḥabībah, and, although she had been a Muslim for over a dozen years, this may have influenced him.[3]

After the first breath of relief at the signing of the treaty of al-Ḥudaybiyah, Mecca must have felt a doomed city. The older men and those with vested interests would want to carry on, but the younger men must have seen that there was no future for them in Mecca. Abū Jandal, a son of the Meccan plenipotentiary, Suhayl b. ʿAmr, is said to have made his way to the Muslim camp to profess Islam at the very time when his father was arranging the treaty; and in accordance with the terms of the treaty he was handed back to his father.[4] The most notable converts were ʿAmr b. al-ʿĀṣ, probably now chief of Sahm, and Khālid b. al-Walīd, a prominent member of Makhzūm, already noted for his military ability. These came to Medina in the summer of 629, and were almost immediately given a leading place in the Muslim community and put in command of expeditions. With them came a third Meccan, ʿUthmān b. Ṭalḥah (ʿAbd ad-Dār), but he was less prominent. There were doubtless others, however, not mentioned by Ibn Hishām and al-Wāqidī. Thus Abān b. Saʿīd (ʿAbd Shams), who had given protection (*jiwār*) to ʿUthmān b. ʿAffān when he entered Mecca as Muḥammad's envoy to arrange the treaty, is said to have been converted between the expeditions of al-Ḥudaybiyah and Khaybar;[5] and Jubayr b. al-Muṭʿim was perhaps converted before the fall of Mecca.[6] Presumably many, even if not all, of the 700

[1] WW, 289.
[2] Ibid. 250.
[3] Ṭab. 1571. 10; cf. Caetani, ii/1. 55, &c.
[4] WW, 256.
[5] *Usd*, i. 35 f.; cf. ad-Diyārbakrī, *Al-Khamīs*, (Cairo), (1884)/1302, ii. 46 f.
[6] *Usd*, i. 270.

Emigrants said to be at Ḥunayn were from Quraysh.[1] At least one woman went to Medina in the period in question, for her advent raised a problem about the interpretation of the treaty.[2] And two cousins of Muḥammad's, Abū Sufyān b. al-Ḥārith b. ʿAbd al-Muṭṭalib (Hāshim)[3] and ʿAbdallāh b. Abī Umayyah (Makhzūm), the son of ʿĀtikah bint ʿAbd al-Muṭṭalib, joined him while he was on his way to Mecca in January 630.

Al-ʿAbbās b. ʿAbd al-Muṭṭalib, Muḥammad's uncle, also went to meet him on his way to Mecca, along with Makhramah b. Nawfal (Zuhrah), but it is possible that he was converted earlier. As the eponymous ancestor of the ʿAbbāsid dynasty, al-ʿAbbās had to be 'white-washed' by ʿAbbāsid propagandists and historians, and an attempt was made to show that his long residence in Mecca was due to his acting as a secret agent for Muḥammad. This is hardly credible before Muḥammad's pilgrimage in March 629 (xi/7). Al-ʿAbbās was a banker and financier, doubtless in a small way, though he probably made something out of the *siqāyah* or right of providing water for the pilgrims. He had no importance in the affairs of Mecca, and life there cannot have been very comfortable for him. Muḥammad's marriage to Maymūnah was primarily an attempt to win al-ʿAbbās to Muḥammad's cause or to seal his allegiance to it. Maymūnah was sister of the wife of al-ʿAbbās and belonged to a family where matrilineal kinship was important; by marrying her Muḥammad was forging a strong link with al-ʿAbbās.[4] The fact that another member of the matrilineal family (and of the household of al-ʿAbbās), Ḥamzah's daughter ʿAmmārah or Umāmah was taken to Medina at the same time—was it for safety?—supports the view that al-ʿAbbās became a Muslim at this point and remained in Mecca to work for Muḥammad.

While some Meccans were thus abandoning the ship, the remainder were trying to make the most of the advantages they derived from the treaty. Things did not go smoothly, however, and events occurred which at the very least caused some friction. There was a clause in the treaty according to which Muḥammad was to send back anyone of Quraysh who went to Medina without permission of his protector. In the case of married women Muḥammad refused to apply this; perhaps it was because, as a matter of principle, he

[1] WW, 358; IH, 754 f.
[2] WW, 262 f.
[3] To be distinguished from the better-known Abū Sufyān, who is Abū Sufyān b. Ḥarb.
[4] Cf. p. 288 below.

insisted on treating women as independent persons.[1] In the affair of Abū Baṣīr, too, he connived at and possibly encouraged what looks like a breach of the treaty, though certainly by Arab standards, and perhaps even by those of the West, his conduct was formally correct; it was not officially questioned by the Meccans. This affair is worth describing in detail.[2]

Abū Baṣīr 'Utbah b. Usayd, by origin belonging to Thaqīf, but now a confederate of the clan of Zuhrah at Mecca, had been imprisoned for his Muslim sympathies, but managed to make his way to Medina to Muḥammad. On his heels, however, came a man of the clan of 'Āmir bearing a letter from the heads of Zuhrah demanding his extradition. Muḥammad acknowledged the justice of the request, and, when Abū Baṣīr protested, said that God would make a way out of his difficulties and would not allow him to be seduced from his religion. The 'Āmirī, his freedman and their prisoner had not gone many miles before Abū Baṣīr seized an opportunity. When they halted for lunch he won the confidence of the others by sharing his dates with them; they had only dry bread, for dates were a Medinan product. The 'Āmirī took off his sword to be more comfortable, and on Abū Baṣīr's praising it and asking if it were sharp unsheathed it and let him put his hand on the hilt. It was the work of a minute to kill the unwary captor. The freedman escaped to Muḥammad, but when Abū Baṣīr also appeared and Muḥammad gave the freedman the chance of escorting him back to Mecca, he not surprisingly declined. As Abū Baṣīr had been handed over to Quraysh, he was no longer technically a Muslim and Muḥammad had no responsibility technically for the bloodshed. To maintain his correct attitude Muḥammad refused the fifth of the booty offered to him.

Quraysh, however, would now be more than ever incensed at Abū Baṣīr and could require him from Muḥammad; so with some words of encouragement from Muḥammad he left Medina and went to a spot near the coast which commanded Quraysh's route to Syria. Here—again probably not without Muḥammad's encouragement—there gathered round him seventy would-be Muslims from Mecca, whom Muḥammad would have had to hand back had they gone to Medina. This band attacked small caravans belonging to Quraysh and killed any man that came into their power. In this way, without breaking the letter of the treaty, Muḥammad

[1] Cf. p. 283 below.

[2] IH, 751–3; WW, 261 f.

partly restored the boycott. As these men were not officially members of his community he had no responsibility for their actions. Quraysh, on the other hand, though free to use violence on the men so far as Muḥammad was concerned, were now too weak to do so at such a distance from Mecca. In the end they appealed to Muḥammad to take the men into his community, presumably agreeing to waive their rights under the treaty. Abū Baṣīr unfortunately died just as Muḥammad's letter to this effect reached him. This incident illustrates how the attraction of the religio-political system of Islam outweighed the apparent advantages Quraysh received from the treaty.

The affair which put an end to the peace with Muḥammad and led to his triumph over Mecca was the plot against his allies the Khuzāʿah.[1] The prime mover was Nawfal b. Muʿāwiyah of ad-Du'il, but most of the leading men of the 'Makhzūm group' supported him. Before the coming of Islam there had been a feud between B. Bakr b. ʿAbd Manāt (a part of Kinānah) and Khuzāʿah. It was quiescent for a time, but broke out afresh when Khuzāʿah killed a man of ad-Du'il (a section of Bakr) who had composed verses hostile to Muḥammad. After al-Ḥudaybiyah Khuzāʿah had openly pronounced themselves allies of Muḥammad and Bakr of Quraysh. Nawfal b. Muʿāwiyah secretly got a quantity of weapons from the leaders of Quraysh and plotted to take Khuzāʿah by surprise. Things went according to plan and Khuzāʿah, after some losses, fled to the houses of two fellow tribesmen in Mecca. The Meccan leaders had aided and abetted the plotters. Ṣafwān and two men of ʿĀmir were even said to have been present in disguise, but this is probably later calumny, though they were certainly privy to the plot. So also were Suhayl and ʿIkrimah. On the other hand two important members of Makhzūm knew about it but thought it unwise—al-Ḥārith b. Hishām and ʿAbdallāh b. Abī Rabīʿah. Abū Sufyān was evidently ignorant.

A man of Khuzāʿah reported at once to Muḥammad. Quraysh, after stopping the fighting and presumably sending the men of Bakr out of the city, realized that the situation was serious. If they were not to submit to Muḥammad, they had a choice between three courses: they might disown the section of Bakr involved, Nufāthah, and let Muḥammad do what he liked with them; they might pay blood-money; they might declare war on Muḥammad.

[1] IH, 802 ff.; WW, 319 ff.

Suhayl was for the first option, perhaps influenced by the fact that his mother was of Khuzāʿah, and also by an old feud between ʿĀmir and Bakr.[1] The other courses likewise found some support, but there was no agreement about which was best. To pay blood-money would mean a great loss of face, whereas a rupture of the treaty would lead to economic loss and there was little hope of defeating Muḥammad. In the end Abū Sufyān persuaded Quraysh to attempt a compromise, and he himself was sent to Medina to try to secure this. It was a sign of how the mighty Quraysh had fallen that they now had to go to Muḥammad and ask him humbly for a favour. The sources do not give a clear account of the compromise hoped for, but it seems to have been something analogous to the position of Abū Baṣīr—an attempt to use against Muḥammad the principles involved in that case. Quraysh, it seems, were to admit that a wrong had been done, but to maintain that they were not responsible for it, possibly because the wrong-doers were not included in the treaty or because they had acted on their own; they were to renew the treaty, however, from now on so as to include these people. Unfortunately Muḥammad was not prepared to play their game, and he was in a much stronger position than Quraysh had been with regard to Abū Baṣīr. After Abū Sufyān's mission Quraysh was left with the same three or rather four choices as before; but Abū Sufyān was now turning to the fourth—submission to Muḥammad.

The accounts of what happened while Abū Sufyān was in Medina are highly coloured. He is said to have gone first to his daughter Umm Ḥabībah, now Muḥammad's wife, but she refused to let him sit on her bed even, since he was an unbeliever and it was used by the prophet. Muḥammad himself refused to speak to him. He then went in turn to Abū Bakr, ʿUmar, Uthmān, and ʿAlī to ask assistance, but all he got was some advice from ʿAlī. Now, while Umm Ḥabībah's lack of filial respect is not inconceivable at this period, though unlikely if Muḥammad used his marriages to win over opponents, the excessive reverence for the person of the prophet must belong to a later date; and the naming of the first four caliphs in order is also suspicious. All we can be certain about is that Muḥammad refused Abū Sufyān's original proposal. After that, even if we reject the story of his visiting the four caliphs-to-be, it is possible that while still in Medina he made some

[1] WW, 43.

pronouncement of *jiwār* or giving of protection (as ʿAlī is said to have advised). It may be, however, that the pronouncement was made later. Whatever its date, Abū Sufyān was the first of the Meccan leaders to accept the inevitability of submission to Muḥammad, and his pronouncement of *jiwār*, whether of B. Nufāthah or of Quraysh in general, must be linked up with this change of attitude. He could not have hoped to protect men against Muḥammad. On the other hand, if he had made terms with Muḥammad, then Muḥammad would support his *jiwār*. For others to accept the *jiwār* of a man who had submitted to Muḥammad was tantamount to submitting to Muḥammad; but for the proud Meccans the bitter pill of submission was thereby sugared over. Abū Sufyān's part in the Muslim capture of Mecca is much more important than is commonly realized. It has probably been deliberately obscured by the sources to avoid making his role appear more glorious than that of al-ʿAbbās.

What Abū Sufyān did in the last critical days, however, when Muḥammad with a large army was nearing Mecca, could not be concealed. The 'Makhzūm group' under Ṣafwān, ʿIkrimah, and Suhayl were trying to organize some resistance. Abū Sufyān, on the other hand, went out to meet Muḥammad, accompanied by Ḥakīm b. Ḥizām (Asad) and Budayl b. Warqā', who, though belonging to Khuzāʿah, had a house in Mecca. This seems to indicate that those outside the 'Makhzūm group' had decided to capitulate. Muḥammad showed himself eager to avoid bloodshed, and acknowledged Abū Sufyān's *jiwār* by ordering that those who took refuge in Abū Sufyān's house or closed their own houses would be safe. In this way the resistance was greatly reduced. The ground had doubtless been carefully prepared by Abū Sufyān. The leaders only of the 'Makhzūm group' fought, along with one or two others, notably some tribesmen of Hudhayl. Most of the group took advantage of the amnesty gained by Abū Sufyān.

Abū Sufyān seems to have had a more statesmanlike grasp of realities than his Meccan opponents and, after the failure of the great confederacy at the siege of Medina, to have seen the hopelessness of continued resistance. He was probably reconciled to a decrease in dignity and importance and to a lower standard of living. His influence seems to have been on the side of moderation. Both before and after the siege we find him fostering unity among Quraysh and trying to prevent internal strife. It is not surprising that in the period after the siege we hear less of him than of his more vociferous opponents. The dignity and honour of their clans, their vested interests, and some sheer pigheadedness made these resist after resistance was hopeless. When the force of Muslim arms pushed them out of Mecca, they fled in various directions and went into hiding. Most were at length reconciled to Muḥammad and swallowed their pride, but perhaps most typical of their defiant spirit was Hubayrah b. Abī Wahb (Makhzūm) who remained in Najrān for the rest of his life.[1]

5. THE SUBMISSION OF MECCA[2]

The size and consequent importance of the expedition to Mu'tah is an indication that Muḥammad's strategic aim by 629/8 was the unification of the Arabs under himself and their expansion northward. The capture of Mecca was therefore not an end in itself. Nevertheless Mecca and the Meccans were important for Muḥammad. Mecca had long since been chosen as the geographical focus of Islam, and it was therefore necessary that the Muslims should have complete freedom of access to it. Could Mecca be brought under his sway, his prestige and power would be greatly increased; without Mecca his position was comparatively weak. Moreover, as the affairs of the Islamic community grew in volume, Muḥammad had need of the military and administrative abilities of the Meccans. Sooner or later he must try to get Mecca on his side.

In the year 628 at al-Ḥudaybiyah it had suited Muḥammad to make peace and end the blockade, for he was then able to devote greater energy to the work among the nomadic tribes. In the twenty-two months following the treaty, however, his strength grew rapidly; and when his allies of Khuzāʿah appealed for help he apparently felt that the moment had come for action. If he was still uncertain, Abū Sufyān's visit to Medina presumably made him realize that few in Mecca would now resist and that the 'diehard' leaders of the 'Makhzūm group' would have little support. He therefore set about collecting a force sufficient to overawe the Meccans and ensure that none but the most inveterate opponents resisted actively.

During the preparations for the expedition Muḥammad took precautions to secure a large measure of secrecy. Nothing was said

[1] Caetani, ii/1. 134.

[2] IH, 802–40; WW, 319–51.

in Medina about the goal of the expedition, a small party was sent towards Syria to put men on a false scent, and the roads to Mecca were sealed off. By a strange lapse (which he alleged to be due to anxiety about wife and children in Mecca) one of the veterans of Badr tried to give information to Quraysh, but his letter was intercepted. Muḥammad's messengers to the various allied tribes were successful, and on 1 January 630 (10/ix/8) he was able to set out with an army which, including those who joined *en route*, numbered about 10,000 men. This included contingents from the tribes: 1,000 men from Muzaynah, 1,000 (or 700) from Sulaym, 400 each from Aslam and Ghifār, and unspecified numbers from Juhaynah, Ashjaʿ, Khuzāʿah (*sc.* Kaʿb), Ḍamrah, Layth, and Saʿd b. Bakr; there were also small groups from Tamīm, Qays, and Asad.[1]

In due course the army encamped at Marr aẓ-Ẓahrān, two short stages from Mecca, but still on the road an army would take if making for aṭ-Ṭā'if or the country of Hawāzin. The Meccans were thus not quite certain of the destination of the army, and indeed had probably received little exact information about it. Ten thousand fires lit by Muḥammad's orders increased their dismay. To this camp Abū Sufyān came to make his submission; and from it he went back to Mecca with word of the general amnesty. The following night Muḥammad pitched camp nearer to Mecca at Dhū Tuwā; in the morning his forces, divided into four columns, advanced into Mecca from four directions. Only one column, that under Khālid, met with resistance, and that was soon overcome. After twenty-four men of Quraysh and four of Hudhayl had been killed, the rest fled. Two Muslims were killed when they mistook their way and ran into a body of the enemy. With such negligible bloodshed did Muḥammad achieve this great triumph.[2] The date was probably about 11 January 630 (20/ix/8).[3]

This event came to be known as the Fat'ḥ or Conquest *par excellence*.[4] The word *fat'ḥ* properly means 'opening', but it is also used in other ways, for example of God's bestowing gifts, especially rain, on men. The phrase *fataḥa bayna-hum*, literally 'he opened between them', means 'he judged between them',[5] and so the noun *fat'ḥ* comes to be 'used in the sense of something which will clear up a doubtful situation'.[6] In late Meccan and early Medinan

[1] IH, 810, 828; WW, 326, 332; cf. 358.
[2] IH, 810–18; WW, 330–5.
[3] IH, 840; WW, 355; cf. IH, 810 and WW, 330, but contrast WW, 350.
[4] Cf. Q. 57. 10.
[5] Lane, *s.v.*
[6] Bell, *Translation*, note on 110. 1.

days Muḥammad and his followers seem to have expected a *fat'ḥ*, a decision between themselves and the pagans, or perhaps 'a decisive clearing away of the clouds of opposition and distress which surrounded' them, and the Qur'ān has to meet the objection that the *fat'ḥ* was long in coming.[1] With the victory of Badr it was said to have come.[2] But the conception was a wide one and apparently could also apply to the signing of the treaty of al-Ḥudaybiyah.[3] Muḥammad's triumphal entry into Mecca, however, was the final and absolute decision between the Muslims and their chief opponents, the pagan Quraysh, and as such it came to be regarded as the supreme *fat'ḥ*, though the Qur'ānic basis for this use of the term is slender.[4] Since this event was also a victory and a conquest, the word was used by the next generation of Muslims to describe their overrunning of the Persian and Byzantine empires. The meaning of conquest, however, is derived from this conception of the conquest of Mecca as a judgement or clearing-up.

The pursuit of the fleeing pagans was not energetic seeing that Muḥammad had proclaimed a general amnesty. ʿAbdallāh b. Abī Rabīʿah (or Zuhayr b. Abī Umayyah) and al-Ḥārith b. Hishām, both of Makhzūm but critics of the attack on Khuzāʿah, fled to the house of a fellow clansman, Hubayrah b. Abī Wahb, whose wife was a daughter of Abū Ṭālib and so a cousin of Muḥammad's. Suhayl b. ʿAmr went to his own house and sent a son to ask for security. His friend Ḥuwayṭib was found and assured that all was well by the celebrated Abū Dharr, who apparently knew him. Ṣafwān b. Umayyah evidently judged it wise to flee to the Red Sea coast, but a member of his clan of Jumaḥ obtained an explicit guarantee of his security from Muḥammad and communicated this to him. Muḥammad's policy of forbidding all pillage meant that some of his poorer followers were now in want, and from some of the rich men of Mecca whom he had treated so magnanimously Muḥammad requested loans. Ṣafwān is said to have lent 50,000 dirhams, and ʿAbdallāh b. Abī Rabīʿah and Ḥuwayṭib 40,000 each; from this the men in need received 50 dirhams apiece.[5] These

[1] Q. 32. 28–30; Bell, op. cit., note on 32. 9/8.

[2] 8. 19, and probably 48. 1 originally.

[3] 48. 1; cf. Bell's interpretation, also remarks in E. M. Wherry, *A Comprehensive Commentary on the Qurān; comprising Sale's Translation and Preliminary Discourse with Additional Notes and Emendations*, Boston, 1882–6, *ad loc.*

[4] Cf. 57. 10 as commonly interpreted; but contrast Bell, *ad loc.*

[5] IH, 820, 825 f.; WW, 336, 343–8.

leaders were not forced to become Muslims; they and doubtless many others remained pagan at least till after al-Ji'rānah.

There was also a small number of persons specified by name as excluded from the general amnesty. Apparently only one of the active leaders of the resistance to Muḥammad was on this list, 'Ikrimah b. Abī Jahl, though it is not clear why he was given this prominence. His wife, however, after submitting to Muḥammad, begged pardon for him and obtained it, and had an adventurous journey to the Yemen to find him and bring him back. He did not receive a gift in the distribution of the spoil at al-Ji'rānah, but this may be because he had not yet returned to Mecca at that time.

The other proscribed persons were all guilty of specific faults. Ibn Abī Sarḥ ('Abdallāh b. Sa'd b. Abī Sarḥ) had been one of the Emigrants at Medina and had acted as Muḥammad's amanuensis. When Muḥammad dictated a phrase of the Qur'ān such as *samī' 'alīm*, 'Hearing, Knowing' (with reference to God), he had written, for example, *'alīm ḥakīm*, 'Knowing, Wise', and Muḥammad had not noticed the change; he had therefore doubted the reality of Muḥammad's inspiration, become an apostate, and gone to Mecca. Muḥammad pardoned him, after some hesitation, on the intercession of 'Uthmān. 'Abdallāh (b. Hilāl) b. al-Khaṭal, of one of the lesser clans of Quraysh, had been sent out from Medina by Muḥammad to collect *ṣadaqah* or legal alms; he became so annoyed with the deficiencies of his servant, also a Muslim, that he gave him a beating from which he died; he then made for Mecca, taking with him the money he had collected. Worse than this he composed verses satirizing Muḥammad, and these were sung in public by two singing-girls of his who were now also proscribed; he himself and one of the girls were executed, but the other was pardoned. Another singing-girl, Sārah, was also proscribed; according to Ibn Hishām she was eventually pardoned, but al-Wāqidī says she was executed, since, after being pardoned, she repeated the offence.[1]

Besides these spreaders of anti-Muslim propaganda, some perpetrators of acts of violence were put to death where they had contravened the basic principles of social security in the Islamic state or had attacked women of Muḥammad's family. Miqyas b. Ḍubābah (or Ṣubābah) al-Laythī had been a Muslim; when his brother was killed by mistake on the expedition to Muraysī' in January 627 (viii/5), he had accepted the blood-money paid by Muḥammad, and

[1] IH, 820; WW, 347.

the affair ought to have been settled; but when the opportunity came, he killed the man responsible and fled to Mecca; he was now executed. Al-Ḥuwayrith b. Nuqaydh of B. ʿAbd of Quraysh was executed for knocking down Muḥammad's daughters when al-ʿAbbās was taking them to Medina. Habbār b. al-Aswad, guilty of similar conduct which had caused Zaynab to have a miscarriage, managed later at Medina to appear before Muḥammad and, before the latter had time to order his punishment, to repeat the *shahādah* or profession of faith; this made him a Muslim, and he was pardoned. Hind, the wife of Abū Sufyān, perhaps proscribed because she instigated Waḥshī to kill Ḥamzah, also appeared before Muḥammad and made her submission, which was accepted. Thus in the end very few persons were put to death.

Muḥammad remained fifteen or twenty days in Mecca. The Kaʿbah and the private houses were cleansed of idols. Parties were sent to destroy Manāt at Mushallal (between Mecca and Medina), ʿUzzā at Nakhlah, and various others. A number of pressing administrative matters were dealt with, especially the defining of the boundaries of the sacred territory of Mecca. Most of the old offices or privileges of Quraysh were abolished, but ʿUthmān b. Ṭalḥah of ʿAbd ad-Dār retained the custody of the Kaʿbah and al-ʿAbbās the right of supplying water to pilgrims.

Foremost among the reasons for this success of Muḥammad's was the attractiveness of Islam and its relevance as a religious and social system to the religious and social needs of the Arabs. In *Muhammad in Mecca* an attempt was made to analyse the malaise of the times, and its root was traced to the transition from a nomadic to a settled economy. The Meccan leaders adhered to the old tribal standards and customs when it was to their advantage; but those who were not leaders were chiefly aware of the disadvantages. As hardships multiplied through the Muslim blockade, the private interests of the leaders would come more and more into conflict with one another, and unity became more and more difficult to preserve. Abū Sufyān probably saw more clearly than the others the need for unity among Quraysh, and as hopes of this faded he must also have been aware that by going over to Muḥammad before the last possible moment he would probably strengthen his position relatively to the 'Makhzūm group'.

Again, Muḥammad's own tact, diplomacy, and administrative skill contributed greatly. His marriages to Maymūnah and Umm

Ḥabībah would help to win over al-ʿAbbās and Abū Sufyān, and he probably gained advantages from the discord at Mecca of which we are not aware. Above all, however, his consummate skill in handling the confederacy he now ruled, and making all but an insignificant minority feel they were being fairly treated, heightened the contrast between the feeling of harmony, satisfaction and zest in the Islamic community and the malaise elsewhere; this must have been obvious to many and have attracted them to Muḥammad.

In all this one cannot but be impressed by Muḥammad's faith in his cause, his vision and his far-seeing wisdom. While his community was still small and devoting all its energies to avoiding being overwhelmed by its enemies, he had conceived a united Arabia directed outwards, in which the Meccans would play a new role—a role no less important than their old role of merchants. He had harried them and provoked them; then he had wooed them and frightened them in turn; and now practically all of them, even the greatest, had submitted to him. Against considerable odds, often with narrow margins, but nearly always with sureness of touch, he had moved towards his goal. If we were not convinced of the historicity of these things, few would credit that a despised Meccan prophet could re-enter his city as a triumphant conqueror.

6. THE BATTLE OF ḤUNAYN

During the time he spent in Mecca Muḥammad sent out at least three small expeditions to secure the submission of tribes in the surrounding district. These expeditions were presumably successful, but few details have been preserved except about the third, that of Khālid against B. Jadhīmah (of Kinānah). The standard account of this expedition, however, is hardly more than a circumstantial denigration of Khālid, and yields little solid historical fact. It is not surprising that there are few memories of these events, for much else was happening at the time. The Muslims, especially the Emigrants, had to adjust their feelings to the sudden change whereby their bitterest enemies had become allies. Muḥammad himself had taken over the responsibility for the administration of Mecca. Above all there was a serious military threat in that Hawāzin and Thaqīf were collecting an army twice the size of Muḥammad's only two or three days' march away.

For an understanding of the campaign of Ḥunayn it is important to realize that Hawāzin and Thaqīf were old enemies of Quraysh; during Muḥammad's lifetime there had been fierce fighting on several occasions. This had been connected with the trade rivalry between Mecca and aṭ-Ṭā'if (the city of B. Thaqīf). The trade of aṭ-Ṭā'if had come under the control of the Meccan merchants, who worked through one of the two political groups into which Thaqīf were divided, the Aḥlāf. The decline in the prestige of Quraysh must have upset the balance of power in aṭ-Ṭā'if and given the upper hand to the other group, B. Mālik, so that in January 630 the city as a whole joined Hawāzin against Quraysh. This helps to explain why B. Mālik fought stubbornly at Ḥunayn and lost nearly a hundred men, whereas the Aḥlāf fled almost at once and lost only two.[1] While many of Thaqīf obviously hoped to assert their independence of Quraysh, the precise expectations of Hawāzin are obscure. They are said to have started concentrating as soon as they heard of Muḥammad's preparations at Medina, and this may indicate that they regarded the expansion of Muḥammad's power as a threat to themselves, though, in view of his policy of uniting the Arabs, it is unlikely that he planned to attack them. The weakness of Mecca may have made them think they could bring it into subjection, but probably they only hoped to pay off old scores. A conflict between Muḥammad and the Meccans must have seemed inevitable, and the presumed exhaustion of both sides would give an advantageous opportunity for attacking one or both.

On the Meccan side there was realization of this danger. At no point in the sources is there any suggestion that the leaders of the Meccan resistance to Muḥammad sought help from Hawāzin and Thaqīf. Even when they fled none of them, so far as we know, went in this direction. Feeling between these tribes and Quraysh must have been strong. In this situation Muḥammad, on becoming conqueror of Mecca, at once became also its champion against the threatening enemy. It was self-preservation rather than hope of booty that made the pagan Quraysh go out with him to Ḥunayn. Ṣafwān b. Umayyah thought submission to Muḥammad preferable to subjection to Thaqīf or Hawāzin;[2] and he lent arms to Muḥammad as well as the money mentioned above. Altogether Muḥammad was able to add 2,000 men to his army, and judged himself strong

[1] WW, 362; for the tribal relations cf. p. 101 below.
[2] IH, 845; WW, 357, 363.

enough to march out and give battle to an enemy reputed to have a force of 20,000.

Muḥammad left Mecca on 27 January 630 (6/x/8) and on the evening of the 30th camped at Ḥunayn close to the enemy. The next morning the Muslims moved forward down Wādi Ḥunayn in battle order; the vanguard, commanded by Khālid b. al-Walīd, included many men of Sulaym. The Muslims, who had been over-confident,[1] were somewhat dismayed at the huge mass of human beings and animals which they saw, for Hawāzin had brought all their women, children, and livestock, staking everything on the issue of the battle. Suddenly the enemy cavalry, posted overnight in the side valleys, attacked the Muslim van. Sulaym, though later they protested that they fought bravely,[2] are said to have fled almost at once, and their consternation affected a large part of Muḥammad's army. He himself stood firm, however, with a small body of Emigrants and Anṣār. This turned the tide, and before long the enemy were in full flight. Some Thaqīf fought bravely for a time, then fled to the safety of their walls. The chief of the confederacy, Mālik b. 'Awf, with his own tribe of Naṣr, held a pass to gain time for those on foot; and there seems to have been another stand in front of the enemy camp. In the end, however, all efforts proved unavailing. The fighting men were dispersed or taken prisoner or killed; the women, children, animals, and goods fell into the hands of the Muslims.

In the battle of Ḥunayn a larger number of men were involved than in any of Muḥammad's previous battles, with the possible exception of Mu'tah. It does not appear, however, to have been a stubbornly fought battle. The names of only four or five Muslim dead have been recorded, but these are all men with homes in Medina, and there must have been some loss—perhaps a considerable loss—among Muḥammad's nomadic allies.[3] This suggests that there was little hand-to-hand fighting. The victory, none the less, was notable and important. Ḥunayn was the major encounter during Muḥammad's lifetime between the Muslims and the nomadic tribes. The collection and concentration of 20,000 men was a notable feat for a nomadic chief, and after Mālik b. 'Awf's discomfiture none cared to repeat it against Muḥammad. Instead, so long as Muḥammad lived, and particularly in the year 9 of the Hijrah (April 630–

[1] Cf. Q. 9. 25. [2] IH, 850 f.
[3] IH, 857; WW, 368; Ṭab. 1669; cf. Caetani, ii/1. 166 f.

April 631), deputations came to Medina from all over Arabia to make agreements and alliances.

7. THE CONSOLIDATION OF VICTORY

From Ḥunayn Muḥammad went on at once to aṭ-Ṭā'if and set about besieging it. He had some siege-engines, probably adopted from the Byzantines, but even with these he made little headway. After some fifteen days he decided to abandon the siege. Thaqīf were resisting bravely and there had been casualties among the Muslims. If he allowed the siege to drag on, his men would become restive, blood would be shed and a final reconciliation with Thaqīf would be rendered more difficult; in the course of a long siege, too, much of the prestige gained at Ḥunayn would be dissipated. Besides he had Hawāzin and the booty of Ḥunayn to attend to. Thus, by abandoning the siege he lost nothing of importance, for he had other ways of influencing Thaqīf in his favour. Nevertheless he may have been disappointed or annoyed; this at any rate is a possible reason for his sharp treatment of a man who accidentally kicked him while they were riding back.

The booty had been left at al-Ji'rānah, not far from Ḥunayn, under the charge of Mas'ūd b. 'Amr al-Ghifārī. The prisoners were there also except that a few of the women had been given to the leading Companions. There was sufficient booty to give every man in the Muslim army four camels or the equivalent. There is said to have been trouble over the distribution and complaints at the delay. Some of the new recruits tried to keep pieces of booty they had picked up, while Muslims of longer standing scrupulously returned everything. Such stories, however, seem to be told mainly for the edification of the hearers, and may have been invented or developed long after Muḥammad's time.[1]

To some of the leading men among Quraysh and the recently allied tribes Muḥammad gave presents (either from the fifth or from the surplus).[2] The list is interesting as showing the importance of the various men.[3]

		Camels
Abū Sufyān	'Abd Shams	100 (300)
Yazīd b. Abī Sufyān	,,	100
Mu'āwiyah b. Abī Sufyān	,,	100

[1] IH, 880; WW, 366. [2] WW, 376.

[3] IH, 880–2; WW, 375 f.; Ṭab. 1679–81; cf. also the longer list, apparently not given by Ibn Is'ḥāq, but derived independently from az-Zuhrī by Ibn Hishām, IH, 882 f.

Ḥakīm b. Ḥizām	Asad	100 (?300)
an-Nuḍayr b. al-Ḥārith	'Abd ad-Dār	100
Usayd b. Ḥārithah	Zuhrah	100
al-'Alā' b. Jāriyah	Zuhrah (*ḥalīf*)	100 (50)
Makhramah b. Nawfal	Zuhrah	50
al-Ḥārith b. Hishām	Makhzūm	100
Sa'īd b. Yarbū'	"	50
Ṣafwān b. Umayyah	Jumaḥ	100 (or more)
'Uthmān ('Umayr) b. Wahb	"	50
Qays b. 'Adī	Sahm	50 (100)
Suhayl b. 'Amr	'Āmir	100
Ḥuwayṭib b. 'Abd al-'Uzzā	"	100
Hishām b. 'Amr	"	50
al-Aqra' b. Ḥābis	Tamīm	100
'Uyaynah b. Ḥiṣn	Ghaṭafān	100
al-'Abbās b. Mirdās	Sulaym	50 (100)
(Mālik b. 'Awf	Hawāzin	100)

These men came to be known as *al-mu'allafah qulūbu-hum*, 'those whose hearts are (or are to be) conciliated or united'. This is commonly taken to mean that the persons in question have just become Muslims and have to be strengthened in their attachment to Islam, or that they have to be induced to profess Islam. Presumably it was at al-Ji'rānah that most, if not all, of those in the list made their acknowledgement of Muḥammad as Messenger of God. The application of the name to all in the list, however, seems to be the work of political opponents during the Umayyad period. The Qur'ānic expression originally referred to a different set of people, since it occurs in a prescription for the use of *ṣadaqāt* or legal alms. In the case of the leaders of Quraysh the gifts had probably less to do with their conversion to Islam than Muḥammad's championship of the cause of Mecca against its enemies, Hawāzin and Thaqīf, while those with experience of leadership must have admired his skilful handling of difficult situations.

A hundred camels was probably regarded as a proper share for each of the leaders of Muḥammad's non-Muslim allies, in view of the fact that Muḥammad received the Fifth. Those in the list who did not come into this category of allied leaders, notably Mālik b. 'Awf and perhaps 'Uyaynah b. Ḥiṣn and al-Aqra', may have received gifts to reconcile their hearts. It is not impossible (though the sources are silent) that the leading men of the Aws, the Khazraj, and the Muslim tribes also received gifts; but they were in a different position from men like Abū Sufyān and Ṣafwān, since the latter were technically allies, whereas the Muslims were directly under Muḥammad's command. As Abū Sufyān and Ḥakīm

b. Ḥizām apparently received 300 each (for the mention of Abū Sufyān's sons is doubtless a device to conceal the favour shown to him by Muḥammad), whereas the others received at most 100, past services to Islam seem to have been rewarded, namely, their contribution to the peaceful surrender of Mecca.

While the siege of aṭ-Ṭā'if went on, Muḥammad was negotiating with Hawāzin, and about the time of the division of the spoil at al-Ji'rānah Mālik b. 'Awf and Hawāzin decided to accept Islam, but asked to have their women and children back. Ibn Isḥāq places the restoration of the women before the distribution of the animals, but it seems more likely that al-Wāqidī is correct in placing these events in the opposite order. The knowledge that the camels and sheep had been divided and that it was the turn of the women next would make Hawāzin more eager to achieve a settlement. As it was, the restoration of the women was treated as a favour, not as something to which Hawāzin had a right, nor even which Muḥammad could command; and they seem to have made a payment in return.[1]

Muḥammad remained at al-Ji'rānah from 24 February to 9 March 630 (5 to 18/xi/8). From there he set out to make the lesser pilgrimage (*'umrah*) at Mecca, then returned to Medina. In charge of his affairs in Mecca he left a young man of the clan of Umayyah b. 'Abd Shams, 'Attāb b. Asīd. His youth—he was under thirty—suggests that the functions cannot have been of first importance; but as he kept the position until his death in 634/13, he must have discharged his duties efficiently. The fact that he was of Abū Sufyān's clan shows that Muḥammad, though on good terms with most people in Mecca, tended to support Abū Sufyān and not the triumvirate, Ṣafwān, 'Ikrimah, and Suhayl.

For the rest of Muḥammad's life we hear practically nothing about Mecca directly, though something can be deduced from notices about his late opponents. Abū Sufyān helped with the destruction of the idol of al-Lāt at aṭ-Ṭā'if.[2] Muḥammad made him governor of Najrān, or part of it, and he is said to have been at the battle of the Yarmūk and to have lived on till about 652/32.[3] 'Ikrimah was put in charge of the *ṣadaqāt* of Hawāzin in 630/9, and in the revolt after Muḥammad's death known as the Riddah commanded a loyalist army in 'Umān; he died as a 'martyr' in the fighting in Syria. He apparently showed great zeal for Islam, and

[1] Cf. p. 101 below. [2] IH, 917 f.; WW, 384 f.
[3] *Usd*, v. 216; iii. 12 f.; cf. al-Balādhurī, *Futūḥ al-Buldān*, Leiden, 1866, 59.

remarks like the following are attributed to him: 'whatever money I spent fighting against you, I shall spend as much in the way of God'; 'I risked my life for al-Lāt and al-'Uzzā; shall I hold back from risking it for God?' Others mentioned as being killed in the fighting in Syria in 636–8 (15–17) are al-Ḥārith b. Hishām (Makhzūm) and an-Nuḍayr b. al-Ḥārith ('Abd ad-Dār).[1]

On the other hand, Ṣafwān b. Umayyah seems to have remained in Mecca and to have died there as an old man.[2] Suhayl b. 'Amr was apparently still in Mecca on Muḥammad's death, for he is credited with being the man chiefly responsible for keeping the Meccans loyal when there were signs of disaffection in some of the tribes and the 'governor' of Mecca did not give a lead. Later, however, he also went to Syria. He had the reputation of being the most pious of the group of leaders who came over to Islam after the conquest of Mecca; he had engaged in the religious exercise of *taḥannuth* in his pagan days.[3] Various others of the group do not seem to have left the Ḥijāz, but probably settled in Medina rather than Mecca; such were Makhramah b. Nawfal, Sa'īd b. Yarbū', Ḥuwayṭib b. 'Abd al-'Uzzā, and Ḥakīm b. Ḥizām.[4]

From such details it is clear that Mecca did not recover its position as a trading centre.[5] The increase of security over a wide area was advantageous to trade, but the new restrictions, like that on usury, imposed by Muḥammad stopped the old lucrative speculations in high finance. For the younger and more adaptable men war and administration gave a better promise of a career than commerce. Almost all the people of substance had left Mecca: and even for commerce Medina was now a better centre.[6]

With the events at al-Ji'rānah there ends what is perhaps the most brilliant phase of Muḥammad's career. With negligible exceptions (like Hubayrah) the men who a few months before had been implacable enemies had now come over to his side. They were ready not merely to become his partners, as they had been at Ḥunayn, but to acknowledge him as prophet; and this implied an acknowledgement of him as political superior, as chief of the

[1] *Usd*, iv. 5 (cf. WW, 345); i. 351 f.; v. 20 f.

[2] Ibid. iii. 22 f.

[3] Ibid. ii. 371–3; cf. F. Wüstenfeld, *Die Chroniken der Stadt Mekka*, Leipzig, 1858–61, iv. 118.

[4] *Usd*, iv. 337 f.; ii. 316 f., 75, 40–42.

[5] Cf. H. Lammens, art. 'Mekka' in EI (1).

[6] Cf. *Usd*, i. 352; WW, 61 f.

'super-tribe' to which they now belonged, without autocratic power indeed, but with various privileges which placed him above other men. Though some kept themselves to themselves, at least a few became enthusiasts for the propagation of their new faith.

IV

THE UNIFYING OF THE ARABS

1. THE TRIBAL SYSTEM CONFRONTING MUḤAMMAD

THE previous three chapters have surveyed in chronological order the course of Muḥammad's relations with the Meccans. The remaining two years or so of his life were occupied with extending his sway over some of the other tribes of the Arabian peninsula. These two years might also be dealt with chronologically. It will be more satisfactory, however, to divide up the tribes geographically, and, taking each tribe or group of tribes separately, to consider Muḥammad's relations to it both before and after the conquest of Mecca. In this way we shall be able to form an idea of Muḥammad's policy towards the tribes.

In the course of the present chapter the complexity of the tribal organization will become apparent.[1] The words 'tribe' and 'clan' will be used, but the application of them will be arbitrary. Ghaṭafān will be called a 'tribe', but Fazārah, which is a part of Ghaṭafān, will also be called a 'tribe'. What one finds is a bewildering multiplicity of groups within groups. The Arabs have half a dozen or more words for groups of different sizes, which later writers arranged in precise hierarchical order; but the usual practice was to call any group, whatever its size, 'Banū Fulān', 'the sons of so-and-so' (by European scholars sometimes contracted to 'B.', and sometimes omitted). Where the group was not known by the name of a real or supposed ancestor, but by some descriptive name, 'Banū' was inappropriate and not used; thus a section of the tribe of Thaqīf was known as the Aḥlāf or Confederates. Sometimes the same name is used for both a smaller and a larger group; thus a section of the tribe of Khuzā'ah became large enough to form itself into the separate tribe of Aslam, but the remainder continued to be known as Khuzā'ah; therefore in one sense Aslam is a part of Khuzā'ah and in another sense it is distinct from it. A further source of confusion, especially with the smaller groups, is that different groups have the same name; Banū Ka'b, for instance,

[1] Cf. W. Caskel, 'The Beduinization of Arabia', in *Studies in Islamic Cultural History*, ed. by G. E. von Grunebaum, Wisconsin (*The American Anthropologist*), 1954, 36–46.

may be B. Kaʿb b. ʿAmr of Khuzāʿah or B. Kaʿb b. Rabīʿah of Hawāzin, or even B. Kaʿb. b. Lu'ayy of Quraysh, but the sources may simply say 'B. Kaʿb' and assume that the reader knows which is intended.

The division and subdivision of the tribes is not just a matter of nomenclature but an important political fact. Within each group there were smaller groups intensely jealous of one another, and usually pursuing contrary policies. When we hear of a deputation from a tribe going to Muḥammad, the probability is that it represented only one faction in the tribe. Muḥammad must have had extensive knowledge of the internal politics of each group, and showed wisdom in deciding which faction to support. What has to be borne in mind is that he was always dealing with a very complex situation.

The traditional view of the last two years of Muḥammad's life is that during these two years most of the tribes of Arabia were converted to Islam. In particular, the year 9 of the Islamic era (April 630–April 631) is known as 'the year of deputations'. Each tribe is supposed to have sent its *wafd* or 'deputation' to Muḥammad, which professed Islam on behalf of the tribe; arrangements were made for giving instruction. Soon, however, some of the tribes became restive under the Islamic dispensation; they specially objected to the contributions they had to make to Medina, whether in money or in kind. As Muḥammad returned to Medina from the 'farewell pilgrimage' to Mecca in March 632 (xii/10) he was seen to be in poor health, and rumours spread. False prophets appeared as leaders of revolt against the Islamic state, first al-Aswad in the Yemen and Musaylimah in the Yamāmah, and then Ṭulayḥah among the tribe of Asad.[1] As his health continued to deteriorate (though he was still able to attend to business), disaffection grew. His death on 8 June 632 (13/iii/11) led to the outbreak of a series of rebellions in various quarters of Arabia. These are regarded as primarily religious, and are known collectively as the Riddah or 'apostasy'. The use of the Arabic name is convenient, but must not be taken to involve unquestioning acceptance of the underlying historical conception.

In opposition to this traditional view some European scholars have held that the extent of conversion has been greatly exaggerated, and that only a few tribes round Medina and Mecca became

[1] Ṭab. i. 1795.

Muslims. With some of the others there may have been political alliances; but some again had no connexion with Medina until after their defeat in the wars of the Riddah. Thus there was no apostasy, but at most political disloyalty. The supposed 'deputations' of all the tribes and their conversion are largely pious inventions to magnify the achievement of Muḥammad (and perhaps to minimize that of Abū Bakr).

This book is not the place for a full discussion of the Riddah, since it mostly falls in the caliphate of Abū Bakr. Nevertheless it has to be mentioned because it supplies information about the state of affairs during Muḥammad's lifetime and because its beginnings are then. In addition to Muḥammad's tribal policy, then, we are to give special consideration to two questions: firstly, to what extent the tribes were in alliance with Muḥammad (even if the relationship was purely political); and secondly, how far the motives of the tribes were social and political, and how far religious. For this investigation we have, in addition to the historical narratives of Ibn Hishām and al-Wāqidī, a collection of letters attributed to Muḥammad and accounts of 'deputations' to him, preserved by Ibn Saʿd.[1] According to the critical principle on which this book is based, these are to be accepted as genuine except when they contradict other early source material or well-established facts. Careful attention, however, has to be paid to the precise assertions of the sources about the 'deputations'. That a 'deputation' came from a certain tribe does not mean that the whole of that tribe became Muslim, for often the 'deputation' would represent nobody but themselves. An extreme case is that of the 'deputation' from Ghassān. The story is presumably the best that could be found to maintain the honour of the tribe; but it is so poor a story that we may safely infer that no members of the tribe became Muslims during Muḥammad's lifetime.[2]

The following are the main tribal groups mentioned in connexion with Muḥammad, showing some of their genealogical connexions and how they have been divided for purposes of discussion.

[1] IS, i/2. 15–86; also edited and commented on by J. Wellhausen, *Skizzen und Vorarbeiten*, Berlin, 1889, iv/3 (whose paragraph number is added in brackets after the references to IS, i/2), and by Caetani; little is added by Sperber, 'Die Schreiben Muhammeds an die Stämme Arabiens', *Mitteilungen des Seminars für orientalischen Sprachen* (Berlin), xix (1916), Westasiatische Studien, 1–93.

[2] Cf. p. 114 below.

Tribes to the west of Medina and Mecca (§ 2)

Khuzāʿah—
  Aslam; Kaʿb b. ʿAmr; al-Muṣṭaliq
Kinānah—
  Bakr b. ʿAbd Manāt—
    Ḍamrah (with Ghifār); Layth; ad-Du'il; Mudlij
  al-Ḥārith b. ʿAbd Manāt (part of Aḥābīsh)[1]
Muzaynah
Juhaynah
Azd Shanū'ah (with Daws).

Tribes to the east of Medina and Mecca (§ 3)

Khuzaymah (b. Mudrikah; Kinānah belonged to Khuzaymah)—
  Asad b. Khuzaymah; (ʿAḍal, al-Qārah)
Ṭayyi' (with Nabhān)
Hudhayl (b. Mudrikah)—
  Liḥyān
Muḥārib (b. Khaṣafah)
Ghaṭafān—
  Ashjaʿ; Fazārah; Murrah; Thaʿlabah (with Anmār, ʿUwāl)
Sulaym (with Riʿl, Shaybān)
Hawāzin—
  ʿĀmir b. Ṣaʿṣaʿah—
    al-Bakkā'; Hilāl; Kilāb (with al-Qurṭā, ʿUraynah); Rabīʿah
  Jusham; Naṣr; Saʿd b. Bakr; Thumālah
  Thaqīf (B. Mālik, Aḥlāf)
  (Bāhilah).

Tribes to the north (§ 4)

Saʿd Hudhaym; ʿUdhrah
Judhām
Quḍāʿah (with Jarm, al-Qayn, Salāmān)
Balī
Bahrā'
Lakhm (with Dār)

[1] The Aḥābīsh were a collection of small tribes or clans, including al-Muṣṭaliq (of Khuzāʿah) and al-Hūn b. Khuzaymah (with its subdivisions ʿAḍal and al-Qārah); the leading group was al-Ḥārith b. ʿAbd Manāt b. Kinānah. They were closely attached to Quraysh. Cf. IH, 245; IS, i/1. 81. 8; *M/Mecca*, 154 ff.; pp. 20, 57 above and 83, 88 below.

Ghassān
Kalb.

Tribes south of Mecca (§ 5)

Khathʿam (and near it Azd Shanūʾah)
Madhʾḥij—
  ʿAns; Juʿfī; Khawlān; an-Nakhaʿ; Ruhāʾ; Saʿd al-ʿAshīrah (with Zubayd); Ṣudāʾ
Bajīlah
Hamdān
al-Ḥārith b. Kaʿb (with Nahd)
Murād
Kindah (with Tujīb)
Himyar (and the Yemen) } perhaps not strictly tribal names
Ḥaḍramawt }
ʿAkk and Ashʿar.

Tribes in the rest of Arabia (§ 6)

Mahrah
Azd ʿUmān; ʿAbd al-Qays (in al-Baḥrayn)
Ḥanīfah
Tamīm
Wāʾil—
  Bakr (with Shaybān); Taghlib.

2. THE TRIBES TO THE WEST OF MEDINA AND MECCA

Muḥammad's earliest supporters, apart from the Emigrants and the Anṣār, were from the tribes roughly to the west and south-west of Medina. At his entry into Mecca in 630/8 he had in his army contingents from Sulaym, Ghifār, Aslam, Kaʿb b. ʿAmr, Muzaynah, Juhaynah, Layth, Ḍamrah, Saʿd b. Bakr, and Ashjaʿ;[1] and of these all except the first and the last came from the district we are now considering; some at least of Saʿd b. Bakr seem to have been close to Layth, Ḍamrah, and Ghifār in location, but it is genealogically a part of Hawāzin, and will be considered in § 3, as will also Ashjaʿ and Sulaym. Along with the remainder may be considered al-Ḥārith b. ʿAbd Manāt (the central part of the Aḥābīsh), Bakr b. ʿAbd Manāt with its subdivisions ad-Duʾil and Mudlij, al-Muṣṭaliq, and Azd Shanūʾah with its subdivision Daws. Several

[1] WW, 332.

of these groups were related to one another. Ghifār was part of Ḍamrah, while Ḍamrah and Layth were parts of Bakr b. ʿAbd Manāt. The latter, again, along with al-Ḥārith b. ʿAbd Manāt, belonged to Kinānah, of which Quraysh was reckoned a part. Another large group was Khuzāʿah, which included Aslam, Kaʿb b. ʿAmr, and al-Muṣṭaliq.

It is worth glancing at the past history of some of these tribes. Khuzāʿah had at one time been masters of Mecca, but, together with their allies Bakr b. ʿAbd Manāt, had been attacked and expelled by Quraysh.[1] Khuzāʿah fade into the background after this, but the hostility between Bakr and Quraysh continued until after the Hijrah. There was a war between them in which the Aḥābīsh supported Bakr, though in the later war of the Fijār the Aḥābīsh had gone over to the side of Quraysh.[2] The feeling between Bakr and Quraysh was stirred up again by the killing of the chief of Bakr to avenge a youth of Quraysh, and because of this Quraysh hesitated about going out to Badr until a prominent member of Bakr, Surāqah b. Juʿsham of Mudlij, said he would see that Bakr did not attack them in the rear.[3] At the same period Nawfal b. Muʿāwiyah of ad-Du'il (part of Bakr) received a large sum of money from certain men of Quraysh to provide arms and camels, presumably for poorer members of his own tribe. Subsequently this same Nawfal is frequently mentioned among the leaders of Quraysh. The closer relations between Quraysh and Bakr are perhaps mainly due to the threat from Muḥammad. In 630/8 Quraysh was ready to support Bakr when an old quarrel between Bakr and Khuzāʿah flared up; indeed Quraysh may have fanned the flames.[4]

All these subdivisions of Kinānah and Khuzāʿah (along with Saʿd b. Bakr of Hawāzin and Azd Shanūʿah) were within the sphere of the direct influence of Mecca. Juhaynah and Muzaynah were similarly within the sphere of influence of Medina. They seem to have been comparatively poor and weak, and incapable of independent action except on a small scale. They would not have dared to attack Medina as Ghaṭafān did. The only expeditions specifically directed against any of them were that against al-Muṣṭaliq in 627/5

[1] Cf. *M/Mecca*, 4 f.

[2] Al-Azraqī, in Wüstenfeld, *Mekka*, i. 71. 14; IS, i/1. 81. 8–11; quoted in *M/Mecca*, 155 f.

[3] IH, 430–2; WW, 43.

[4] IH, 802 ff.; WW, 319–21; cf. p. 62 above.

and one against a small section of Juhaynah in 629/8; the clan of Jadhīmah which Khālid was sent to 'summon to Islam' after the entry into Mecca is usually said to be Jadhīmah b. 'Āmir b. 'Abd Manāt b. Kinānah, but a Jadhīmah is also identified with al-Muṣṭaliq of Khuzā'ah.[1] Another mark of poverty might be the fact that members of Ghifār and Aslam looked after camels for Muḥammad, though this might also be due to the poverty of the individuals in question or to some other individual circumstances.[2] On the other hand some men of Ghifār seem to have had qualities of leadership—something which is not common among the tribes considered in this section; Sibā' b. 'Urfuṭah was left in charge of Medina during various absences of Muḥammad.[3]

In the first year or two after the Hijrah Muḥammad's chief aim must have been to gain friends, so that, when he and his followers went on expeditions, they could move about freely without fear of being molested. On an expedition in 623/2 he is said to have made a treaty with Mudlij and Ḍamrah.[4] These two parts of Kinānah were presumably disaffected towards the Meccans, and therefore ready to undertake not to attack the Muslims. They may also have helped Muḥammad by passing on information. The text of a treaty has been preserved, but it prescribes mutual help (*naṣr*), and that, unless it means less than it appears to mean, would be unlikely before Badr.[5] Another treaty with a section of Kinānah states that they are not to be required to help Muḥammad against Quraysh.[6]

In his relations with Kinānah, Khuzā'ah, and the other tribes in the neighbourhood of Mecca Muḥammad was taking advantage of the conflicts of interest within the Meccan sphere of influence, in which Quraysh had been unable to effect reconciliation. The clearest case of this was after the treaty of al-Ḥudaybiyah when Khuzā'ah allied themselves with Muḥammad while their enemies, Bakr b. 'Abd Manāt, allied themselves with Quraysh.[7] In his approaches to these tribes Muḥammad must have known or been able to discover which were dissatisfied with Quraysh. Until he

[1] For the usual view cf. Caetani, ii. 148; contrast IS, i/1. 46. 28.

[2] Abū Dharr, Abū Ruhm, &c., of Ghifār—WW, 227, 241; Salamah b. al-Akwa', Nājiyah b. Jundub, &c., of Aslam—WW, 227 f. (= IH, 719 f.), 241, 300, 416.

[3] IH, 668 (= WW, 174); WW, 265; IH, 896 (= WW, 393), 966.

[4] IS, ii/1. 5. 2, on the expedition of 'Ushayrah; cf. treaty with Ḍamrah alone during the expedition of al-Abwā' (WW, 34), which may or may not be the same.

[5] Cf. Excursus F, no. 1.

[6] Cf. ibid., no. 7.

[7] Cf. p. 49 above.

was strong enough, however, to protect them from Quraysh, he could not expect them to join in any act of open hostility against Quraysh. Thus his first aim must simply have been to establish friendly relations.

A second aim, however, gradually became evident, to gain supporters to join in his expeditions. To begin with he was more likely to find these in the Medinan sphere of influence. Juhaynah was confederate with the Khazraj at the battle of Buʿāth and Muzaynah with the Aws,[1] and the close relations continued. In this way Muḥammad may be said to have had an indirect alliance with these tribes from his first days in Medina. In the first expedition from Medina the Muslims were helped by Juhaynah and are said to have been in alliance with them, but Juhaynah was also in alliance with Quraysh, and the help consisted in acting somehow or other so as to avoid a conflict.[2] There is no record of any important group within Juhaynah joining Muḥammad as a group; the so-called 'deputation' (*wafd*) from Juhaynah seems to consist of two men speaking for themselves:[3] and the group with ʿAmr b. Murrah was probably small.[4] From an early period, however, individuals were attaching themselves to Muḥammad. A reconnoitring party before Badr consisted of two men from Juhaynah, while a third was killed at Uḥud.[5] There were also several men of Muzaynah at Uḥud, of whom one was killed.[6] Some of these, as confederates of Medinan clans, may have lived most of the time in Medina. At a slightly later date there was a district of Medina inhabited by Juhaynah, and they had a mosque of their own.[7] It is probable, however, that many of those who became followers of Muḥammad had hitherto been nomadic. A town-dweller, for example, would hardly have been put in charge of the pasturing of Muḥammad's war steeds, a duty given to a man of Muzaynah.[8] Very significant is a passage where a Juhanī who came to pledge

[1] A. P. Caussin de Perceval, *Essai sur l'Histoire des Arabes avant l'Islamisme*, Paris, 1847–8, ii. 681 ff.; cf. attachments of individual members of Juhaynah: Basbas b. ʿAmr was *ḥalīf* of B. Sāʿidah (*Usd*, i. 178 f.), ʿAdī b. Abī Zughbā' of B. Mālik b. an-Najjār (ibid. iii. 394), Ḍamrah al-Juhanī of B. Sāʿidah (WW, 139), ʿAbdallāh b. Unays of B. Salimah (*Usd*, iii. 119 f.). Sinān b. Wabr of B. Sālim of ʿAwf (IS, iv/2. 70 = WW, 179).

[2] IH, 419; WW, 33; cf. 44, where help is apparently given to Abū Sufyān.

[3] IS, i/2. 67. 21 ff.

[4] Ibid. 68. 3 ff.

[5] WW, 38, 44—Basbas b. ʿAmr and ʿAdī b. Abī Zughbā'; WW, 139—Ḍamrah al-Juhanī.

[6] WW, 128, 139.

[7] IS, iv/2. 67. 12 f., 69. 1; ibid. i/2. 68. 2.

[8] WW, 184.

himself to Muḥammad was asked whether he intended the bedouin pledge (*bay'ah 'arabīyah*) or the pledge of Hijrah (*bay'at hijrah*).[1]

A choice of this sort between continuing one's nomadic life and migrating to Medina (and taking part in expeditions) would be more critical for members of Kinānah and Khuzā'ah than for members of Juhaynah and Muzaynah. The men from Ghifār and Aslam who looked after Muḥammad's camels must have left their tribes. Moreover, such men would be direct adherents of Muḥammad himself, analogous to the Emigrants of Quraysh. Treaties are extant which speak of Aslam, Khuzā'ah, and Muzaynah being classed as Emigrants, even when they did not leave their home districts;[2] and, though this probably belongs to the later years of Muḥammad's life, it is an indication that individuals who had made the Hijrah or emigrated to Medina had the special status of Emigrants.

Whatever may have been the position with such Emigrants from Juhaynah and Muzaynah, the first loyalty of those from the Meccan sphere of influence would be to Muḥammad. Thus we find that the serious quarrel on the expedition to Muraysī' arose from a dispute between a Ghifārī and a Juhanī; the Emigrants of Quraysh took the side of the Ghifārī and the Anṣār that of the Juhanī.[3] Muḥammad no doubt recognized that the accession of such recruits not merely strengthened the Muslim cause but also strengthened his own position within the Medinan community. The terms of agreement with a 'mixed multitude' (*jummā'*) that was possibly little better than a robber band show Muḥammad anxious to gain adherents.[4] By the time of his death there were probably many persons from Kinānah and Khuzā'ah (and other tribes also) resident in Medina. 'Umar is said to have remarked that Abū Bakr would not have been acclaimed as caliph by the Anṣār had not a group of Aslam come on the scene at the critical moment; this is probably an exaggeration—the source of the information is a man of Khuzā'ah—but the tribesmen were a factor of the balance of power in Medina.

As might have been expected, then, the tribes in the surroundings of Medina and Mecca were among the foremost supporters

[1] IS, iv/2. 66. 3.

[2] IS, i/2. 24. 14–18 (§ 29), 25. 11–27 (§ 32), 38 f. (§ 76); cf. 41 f. (§ 79); see also Excursus F, nos. 5, 8.

[3] IH, 626; WW, 179.

[4] IS, i/2. 29. 13–22; cf. Excursus F, no. 6.

of Muḥammad after the Emigrants and the Anṣār. They supplied contingents for his army at the conquest of Mecca and the battle of Ḥunayn. Only Aslam seems to have been present as a tribe at the earlier expedition of al-Ḥudaybiyah, though, despite the refusal of the tribes of Juhaynah, Muzaynah, and Bakr to participate,[1] we find that many individuals from Juhaynah, for example, are said to have been present.[2] In later expeditions the same group of tribes were an important part of the Muslim forces. All remained faithful to Abū Bakr after Muḥammad's death and showed no sign of defection. Along with the Emigrants and the Anṣār, therefore, they constituted the core of the Islamic state, and were fittingly granted the status and privileges of Emigrants.

3. THE TRIBES TO THE EAST OF MEDINA AND MECCA

The tribes immediately east of Medina and Mecca may conveniently be treated together as a second group, since after Quraysh they claimed most of Muḥammad's attention in the years between Badr and Ḥunayn. There is an important division among these tribes. Some were sufficiently friendly to the Meccans to be willing to join them for a consideration; Ashjaʿ, Fazārah, and Murrah (of Ghaṭafān) together with Asad b. Khuzaymah and Sulaym sent contingents to the siege of Medina.[3] Others again—and notably Hawāzin—were hostile. More is known of the previous history of these tribes than of those in the last section, and a review of this contributes to the understanding of the position in Muḥammad's time.

Asad b. Khuzaymah was apparently closest to Quraysh. The eponymous ancestor is said to have been the *sādin* or priest of the Kaʿbah at one time;[4] and some close connexion seems to be presupposed by the large number of confederates of ʿAbd Shams (of Quraysh) from Asad b. Khuzaymah,[5] and by their alliance with Quraysh in the war of the Fijār.[6] The main part of the tribe, however, seems to have lived to the north and east of Ghaṭafān, where they were neighbours of Ṭayyi'. The latter had displaced them and constituted their main enemy.[7] There are several traces

[1] WW, 242.
[2] IS, iv/2. 66 ff.—Tamīm b. Rabīʿah, Rāfiʿ b. Mukayth, Jundub b. Mukayth, Abū Dubays, Suwayd b. Ṣakhr.
[3] WW, 191.
[4] Wüstenfeld, *Mekka*, ii. 139 f.
[5] Cf. *M/Mecca*, 174 f., where Khuzaymah is in fact Asad b. Khuzaymah.
[6] IS, i/1. 81. 8.
[7] Cf. H. Reckendorf in EI (1).

of this feud during Muḥammad's lifetime: it was a man of Ṭayyi' who brought the information in June 625 (i/4) that Ṭulayḥah b. Khuwaylid and his brother were trying to raise Asad against the Muslims; it was a man of Asad who guided the expedition to destroy the god of Ṭayyi'; and in a letter to Asad Muḥammad warns them against trespassing on the waters and lands of Ṭayyi'.[1] Similarly, in the wars following the death of Muḥammad the Muslims found it easy to detach Ṭayyi' from Ṭulayḥah.[2]

The main part of Asad was presumably at some considerable distance from Medina. Nevertheless the reports of Uḥud encouraged Ṭulayḥah and his brother to collect a force to raid Medina before the Muslims recovered; Muḥammad, however, forestalled him, and the Muslims by a lightning movement were able to capture some of the camels of Asad. This episode suggests that Ṭulayḥah was an opportunist, and the result doubtless discouraged him from further thoughts of this kind while Muḥammad lived. The only other expedition against Asad was some two years later, but was too small to be directed against Tulayḥah; it may have been due largely to some feud within the tribe, since the Muslim leader was from that section of Asad which had become confederates of 'Abd Shams. Opportunism may also mark the sending of a deputation to Muḥammad in the year 9 when there was a rush to 'get on the bandwaggon'. This would be especially the case if Ṭulayḥah was a member of the deputation;[3] some two years later he was leader of Asad and other tribes in a war against the Muslims, and must already have had wide influence. It is noteworthy, however, that there is a version which omits his name;[4] if this is correct, it means that only a section of Asad submitted in 9 and that Ṭulayḥah remained in independence, doubtless making preparations to resist Muslim expansion; this seems most likely, but the question is complex.

Little is heard of Khuzaymah apart from Asad. The small groups of 'Aḍal and al-Qārah belonged to al-Hūn b. Khuzaymah and were part of the Aḥābīsh, and so attached to Quraysh.[5] It was when they, allegedly in collusion with Sufyān al-Liḥyānī, asked

[1] WW, 151; ibid. 389; IS, i/2. 23; cf. also WW, 152.

[2] Caetani, ii/1. 131. The form Ṭulayḥah is not derisive; cf. p. 134, n. 3 below.

[3] IS, i/2. 39.

[4] *Usd*, ii. 29, on Ḥaḍramī b. 'Āmir, whose name comes first in the list in IS.

[5] *M/Mecca*, 154 (A), 155 (K); cf. IS, ii/1. 39. 11; WW, 155, 157, 199. There were men from al-Qārah in the *jummā'*, IS, i/2. 29. 15.

Muḥammad for men to instruct them in Islam that Sufyān was able to surprise the party.

Ṭayyi'. The main part of the tribe of Ṭayyi' (including the subtribe of Nabhān) was beyond Asad, and there were no expeditions from Medina against it apart from that led by ʿAlī in July/August 630 (iv/9) to destroy the god of the tribe, al-Fuls (or al-Fulus or al-Fils). Ṭayyi' is thus in a different position from the other tribes considered in this section, but it is convenient to mention it here in view of its feud with Asad. There were apparently some individual contacts between Ṭayyi' and Medina prior to Islam; the father of Kaʿb b. al-Ashraf (an opponent of Muḥammad, reckoned to the Jewish tribe of an-Naḍīr) belonged to B. Nabhān of Ṭayyi';[1] a man of Ṭayyi' is mentioned as acting along with the Medinan Hypocrites on the way back from Tabūk;[2] and two women of Ṭayyi' are recorded to have married into the Medinan clan of B. al-Ḥārith.[3] An early convert from Ṭayyi' was Rāfiʿ b. Abī Rāfiʿ (ʿUmayrah), who took part in the expedition of Dhāt as-Salāsil in October 629 (vi/8) as a Christian (or pagan), and accepted Islam soon afterwards.[4] In the two years following this many sections of the tribe seem to have professed Islam; letters have been preserved in which Muḥammad guarantees their security provided they perform the worship, pay the *zakāt*, hand over a fifth of any booty taken, obey his orders, and so on.[5] The most important convert was ʿAdī, son of the well-known Ḥātim aṭ-Ṭā'ī. When ʿAlī's expedition attacked the tribe, ʿAdī made his way to Syria where, as a Christian, he expected to be well received. Muḥammad, however, by means of his sister, persuaded him to come to Medina and become a Muslim; he was then put in charge of the *ṣadaqāt* of his tribe.[6] On Muḥammad's death the tribe was apparently at first uncertain what attitude to adopt, but, when Asad was seen to be in the opposite camp, there was little difficulty in persuading them to support the Muslims.

The behaviour of Ṭayyi' seems to be explained by the fact that it was largely Christian, but belonged to the Persian sphere of influence rather than the Byzantine. ʿAdī may have been the readier to become a Muslim because he found the Byzantines uncongenial.

[1] Cf. p. 210 below. [2] WW, 408.

[3] IS, iii/2. 89, wife of ʿAbdallāh b. ar-Rabīʿ; viii. 264, mother of Kabshah bint Wāqid. [4] IH, 985; WW, 315 f.

[5] IS, i/2. 23 (§ 23), 30 (§ 51), 59 f. (§ 103); also 22 (§ 21).

[6] IH, 947–50; IS, i/2. 60.

The Christian Arab tribes of the east and north-east willingly entered into political alliance with Muḥammad since both they and he were interested in raiding towards ʿIrāq; and after the breakdown of the Persian empire (in 628 and the following years) many became ready to accept Islam also.[1] Our information is so scanty, however, that it may well be that many members of Ṭayyi', though loyal to Medina during the Riddah, remained Christians till some time afterwards.

Hudhayl. The tribe of Hudhayl had been involved in the affairs of Mecca in pre-Islamic times. Their chief is said to have accompanied ʿAbd al-Muṭṭalib when he went to negotiate with Abrahah.[2] They had blood-feuds with Layth (Kinānah) and Aslam and Kaʿb (Khuzāʿah),[3] but these may have been temporary, for it was possible about the year 626/4 for a Medinan Muslim to win the confidence of the chief Sufyān by pretending to belong to Khuzāʿah.[4] This chief, Sufyān (or Ibn Sufyān) b. Khālid b. Nubayḥ of the sub-tribe of Liḥyān, was collecting a force to raid Medina, but ʿAbdallāh b. Unays was sent by Muḥammad and assassinated him. It was apparently in revenge for this that B. Liḥyān attacked the Muslim instructors asked for by their friends the clans of ʿAḍal and al-Qārah. Some were killed, but the prisoners were sold to Quraysh to sate their desire for revenge, an indication of the close ties between Hudhayl and Quraysh.[5] In view of this history it is not surprising that some of them offered active resistance at the conquest of Mecca.[6] They were probably incorporated in the Islamic state on similar terms to Quraysh, but the sources mention only their presence in Mecca and at the siege of aṭ-Ṭā'if, and the destruction of their idol by ʿAmr b. al-ʿĀṣ.[7]

Muḥārib. The small tribe of Muḥārib is obscure. It was attacked in the course of three expeditions in the years 624/3 and 627/6, and it sent a deputation to Muḥammad in 631/10.[8] It is presumably Muḥārib b. Khaṣafah (though there is also a minor clan of Quraysh called Muḥārib), but it seems to have become linked with Ghaṭafān, and in particular with Thaʿlabah; part of it is said to have lived among Thaʿlabah.[9] It is coupled with the latter in the accounts

[1] Cf. p. 131 below.
[2] IH, 34.
[3] WW, 369 and IS, iv/1. 32; WW, 341 f.
[4] Ibid. 225.
[5] IH, 981 f. = WW, 224 f. and Caetani, i. 577 f.; IH, 638–48 = WW, 156–60.
[6] WW, 333 f.
[7] Ibid. 342, 369, 350.
[8] Ibid. 99 f., 226, 233; IS, i/2. 43 (§ 83).
[9] *Aghānī*, xii. 124. 26; cf. Wellhausen's note on § 83.

of two of the Muslim expeditions, and the leader Du'thūr b. al-Ḥārith is sometimes called Ghaṭafānī.[1] Although genealogically distinct it seems to have become in practice a part of Ghaṭafān, and need not be further considered separately.

Ghaṭafān. In Muḥammad's time Ghaṭafān was a collection of tribes rather than a single tribe. To it belonged 'Abs and Dhubyān between whom the celebrated war of Dāhis had been fought. 'Abs plays little part in the events of Muḥammad's lifetime,[2] but much is heard of the subdivisions of Dhubyān, namely, Fazārah, Murrah, and Tha'labah.[3] Ashja' formed a distinct branch.

On the conclusion of the war of Dāhis there was a genuine reconciliation between 'Abs and Dhubyān, and we hear of little further strife within Ghaṭafān. Instead there is a series of wars with Hawāzin (Jusham, Naṣr, and 'Āmir) or rather with the wider group of Khaṣafah which also included Sulaym. Sometimes most of Ghaṭafān and Khaṣafah were involved, sometimes only one or two tribes on each side. We hear of fighting between Sulaym and Murrah, between Fazārah and 'Āmir, between 'Abs and 'Āmir, between Fazārah (with 'Abs) and Jusham, and so on. In some of these 'days' Fazārah was led by 'Uyaynah b. Ḥiṣn, the great-grandson of that Ḥudhayfah b. Badr who had successfully led Dhubyān in the war of Dāhis; thus he was the heir of a tradition of leadership.[4] A large part of the relations of Muḥammad with Ghaṭafān are those with 'Uyaynah. Since Hawāzin had been the chief enemy of Ghaṭafān for some decades and was also an enemy of Quraysh, we might expect a drawing closer of Ghaṭafān and Quraysh. The hostility of Ghaṭafān and Sulaym had not been so bitter, and the first Muslim expedition against these tribes is said to have been directed against a mixed group of the two; nevertheless there was rivalry between the two.

In September 624 (iii/3), about two months after the first expedition just mentioned, Muḥammad himself led a large force against Tha'labah and Muḥārib. Though there was no full-scale encounter with the enemy, the expedition seems to have had a deterrent effect, since no further trouble with Ghaṭafān is recorded until nearly two years later when they brought about 2,000 men to join in besieging

[1] *Usd*, ii, *s.v.*
[2] Cf. IS, i/2. 41, a convert from 'Abs.
[3] With Tha'labah are mentioned Anmār and 'Uwāl, otherwise obscure.
[4] Caussin de Perceval, ii. 424, 536–68, &c.

Medina (April 627 = xi/5). Mention is even made of a temporary truce with ʿUyaynah.[1] While it was doubtless the apparent strength of Muḥammad that induced ʿUyaynah to make such a truce, the prospect of a grand alliance against Muḥammad, coupled with the diplomatic pressure and bribes of the Jews from Khaybar (who included the exiles of an-Naḍīr from Medina), attracted him to active opposition. When Muḥammad's trench prevented the alliance from making full use of their numbers in attack and forced them to engage in a siege, ʿUyaynah was tempted to consider Muḥammad's offer of a third of the date-harvest of Medina in return for his immediate withdrawal. What exactly happened is not clear,[2] except that the parties in the alliance became more suspicious of one another and that ʿUyaynah did not get his dates from Medina. It was perhaps because he felt he had been unfairly treated in this matter that in August of the same year (iv/6) he raided Medina, causing great perturbation but getting the worst of the exchanges.

Meanwhile one of the results of the failure of the besiegers was that Ashjaʿ went over to Muḥammad. Nuʿaym b. Masʿūd of Ashjaʿ had become a Muslim about the beginning of the siege, but had not made the fact public, and so, as a secret agent for Muḥammad, had done much to increase the dissension between Quraysh, Ghaṭafān, and Qurayẓah (there may, however, be some exaggeration as the story comes from Nuʿaym himself through Ashjaʿī transmitters).[3] The deputation which came to Muḥammad after the siege is said to have been headed by Masʿūd b. Rukhaylah, the leader of the contingent from Ashjaʿ which had taken part in the siege.[4] The reasons they gave for coming to Muḥammad sound genuine; they were the section of their tribe (Ghaṭafān? or Ashjaʿ?) living closest to Muḥammad and smallest in number, and they were in distress through the war. They might have added that they had been allies of the Khazraj at Buʿāth.[5] It is doubtful, however, whether the whole tribe submitted to Muḥammad at this time. A secondary report in Ibn Saʿd gives the figure of 700 men, but the

[1] WW, 182 foot. [2] Cf. p. 38 above. [3] IH, 680–2; WW, 205 f.

[4] IS, i/2. 48. 26 f.; cf. iv/2. 19–24, biographies of ten early converts from Ashjaʿ.

[5] Caussin de Perceval, ii. 681; cf. 657, a Thaʿlabī as a client of Mālik b. al-ʿAjlān. WW, 233 mentions a Ghaṭafānī on the small expedition led by Muḥammad b. Maslamah in August 627 (iv/6), perhaps an old confederate of the latter's; Caetani (i. 694 n.) suggests he was not a Muslim.

main one gives only a hundred, while the contingent at the siege was said to number 400. Moreover there is some confusion of names. Nuʿaym b. Masʿūd is sometimes called Nuʿaym b. Masʿūd b. Rukhaylah, which would make him the son of the chief;[1] but it is more likely that the true version is that which gives his grandfather as ʿĀmir.[2] There is no further mention of Masʿūd b. Rukhaylah, but Nuʿaym b. Masʿūd appears frequently as one of the two leaders of Ashjaʿ among the Muslims. It seems probable, therefore, that he should be given as the leader of the 'deputation', especially as he is named in the text of an agreement with Muḥammad which looks as if it refers to this occasion.[3] There are said to have been 300 men from Ashjaʿ with Muḥammad at the conquest of Mecca, and there is no word of Ashjaʿ joining in the war against Abū Bakr.

After ʿUyaynah's raid on Medina in August 627 we hear nothing of him until the Khaybar campaign in May and June 628 (i/7).[4] In the interval there had been three small expeditions against Thaʿlabah and their neighbours, and one led by Zayd b. Ḥārithah against a section of Fazārah to take revenge for their ambushing him and his party. ʿUyaynah remained on friendly terms with the Jews at Khaybar. At least when they were attacked by Muḥammad he was prepared to bring 4,000 men to support them in return for half the date-harvest of Khaybar. His support, however, was not whole-hearted and consequently ineffective. What exactly happened is not clear, but ʿUyaynah certainly negotiated with Muḥammad. One account is that Ghaṭafān retired because they heard that the Muslims were attacking their families in their rear; this was perhaps a rumour spread by Muḥammad. Another account is that he offered them an equal or larger quantity of dates; and as the Jewish strongholds began to fall this would be more valuable than the similar Jewish promise. Yet another story says that ʿUyaynah received a part of Khaybar called Dhū 'r-Ruqaybah from Muḥammad. The three stories are not irreconcilable; it may be that Muḥammad refused to keep his offer of dates because ʿUyaynah had withdrawn (or Muḥammad alleged he had withdrawn) to meet a possible attack on the families in the rear, and that he gave him the piece of land as compensation.

[1] WW, 205; IS, i/2. 26. 19.
[2] IH, 680; *Usd* and *Iṣābah*, *s.v.*; IS, iv/2. 19–21.
[3] IS, i/2. 26. 18–20; cf. Excursus F, no. 10.
[4] IH, 755–81; WW, 264–96.

If this was how ʿUyaynah was treated, it would explain why in February 629 (x/7) he collected some men 'with hostile intentions'. These cannot have amounted to more than a raid, however, for only 300 men were sent against him. Perhaps the growing military reputation of the Muslims and his own lack of success were making the tribesmen reluctant to follow him. Al-Ḥārith b. ʿAwf, the leader of Murrah, who had been responsible for reconciling ʿAbs and Dhubyān, is said on this occasion to have counselled him to submit to Muḥammad; at Khaybar also he seems to have been unwilling to fight.[1] Moreover in December 628 and January 629 (viii, ix/7) sections of Murrah and Thaʿlabah had been roughly handled by Muslim expeditions. Apart from a very small expedition against Jusham in December 629 (viii/8) of which no further details are recorded, there was no further fighting between Ghaṭafān and the Muslims until after Muḥammad's death. They had learnt that there was no profit to be made by opposing Muḥammad.

It would seem that there must have been some agreement about this time between Muḥammad and ʿUyaynah, although there is no mention of any in the sources.[2] ʿUyaynah was with the Muslim army at the conquest of Mecca and the battle of Ḥunayn in January 630. Although he apparently did not have even a small detachment of his tribe with him,[3] he was treated honourably, was able to use his influence on behalf of a man of Ashjaʿ,[4] and received a hundred camels at al-Jiʿrānah. In April or May 630 (i/9) Muḥammad accepted his offer to punish a small part of Tamīm which had refused to pay their dues to Muḥammad's agent, and this is reckoned one of the Muslim expeditions.[5] Such agreement as ʿUyaynah may have made, however, need not have involved becoming a Muslim. There is no record of his having accepted Islam. About January 631 (x/9), after the expedition of Tabūk, there were 'deputations' to Medina from Murrah and Fazārah.[6] The former was led by the chief al-Ḥārith b. ʿAwf, and the latter by ʿUyaynah's brother and nephew, Khārijah b. Ḥiṣn and al-Ḥurr b. Qays b. Ḥiṣn. The absence of ʿUyaynah is noteworthy and together with his conduct in 630 presupposes an earlier agreement between him and Muḥammad. It may well be, as Caetani suggests, that this earlier agreement is passed over in silence because ʿUyaynah was allowed to remain

[1] WW, 299, 270. [2] Cf. Caetani, ii. 447.
[3] WW, 327. [4] Ibid. 366. [5] IH, 933–8; WW, 385–7.
[6] IS, i/2. 42; Thaʿlabah had accepted Islam about March 630, ibid. 43.

a heathen. When after an inglorious share in the Riddah he was captured and taunted by the boys of Medina with going back on his faith, he is said to have remarked, 'I never believed in God'.[1] There was probably no serious rift between 'Uyaynah and his brother Khārijah, and both took part in the Riddah. Yet 'Uyaynah may at times have acted separately in hopes of gaining some private advantage, and Khārijah seems to have been the independent commander of a section of the tribe.[2]

There is an amusing story which, whether literally true or not, is probably an excellent characterization of 'Uyaynah. At al-Ji'rānah he selected as his prize an old woman for whom a large ransom might be expected. Her son offered 100 camels for her but 'Uyaynah wanted more. Later, however, 'Uyaynah thought better of it and said he would accept 100, only to be presented with a reduced offer of 50, which he refused. Again he thought better of it, but the offer was now reduced to 25. The same thing happened again, and the offer sank to 10. By the time 'Uyaynah was ready to accept this, the woman's son was asking for her to be set free without ransom. Eventually, though with a bad grace, 'Uyaynah did so, only to be met with the request for the present of a dress; and in the end a dress he had to give.[3] Greed, which led him to try to drive too hard a bargain, coupled with lack of judgement, which often made him fare badly, are to be traced in all his relations with Muḥammad. It is not surprising that in the pages of the *sīrah* and the history of the Riddah, especially in al-Wāqidī, he is presented as something of a laughing-stock. By combining severity with kindness on appropriate occasions, Muḥammad was able to detach 'Uyaynah from Quraysh, but he did not manage to incorporate his tribe securely in the Islamic state.

Sulaym. The tribe of Sulaym, as has been noticed, sometimes joined with Hawāzin against Ghaṭafān. It was perhaps because of the memory of this alliance that Sulaym showed so little spirit against Hawāzin at Ḥunayn (if the report is unbiased).[4] Latterly, however, they had come to be closely linked with Quraysh, especially 'Abd Shams and Hāshim.[5] This was due above all to the

[1] Ṭab. i. 1897; further references in Caetani, ii/1. 622.

[2] Ibid. ii/1. 592 f.; *Iṣābah, s.v.* Khārijah; cf. W. Hoenerbach, *Waṯīma's Kitāb ar-Ridda aus Ibn Ḥağar's Iṣāba*, Wiesbaden, 1951, 83 f.

[3] WW, 378 f.

[4] Ibid. 358, &c.; but a Sulamī killed Durayd b. as-Simmah of Jusham (ibid. 63).

[5] H. Lammens, *La Mecque à la Veille de l'Hégire*, Beirut, 1924, 196–8;

fact that there were gold-mines in the territory of Sulaym and that Quraysh were able to help in their development.[1] Shortly before Sulaym became involved with the Muslims the leadership had been disputed by Khufāf b. Nadbah and al-ʿAbbās b. Mirdās, and by the award of an arbiter from Hawāzin the functions had been divided between them.

There were Muslim expeditions against Sulaym in July and October/November 624 (i, v/3), of 200 and 300 men respectively. Some Ghaṭafān are also said to have been involved in the first. On the second the enemy dispersed before contact was made. After this there does not seem to have been any widespread hostility to Muḥammad among Sulaym. Two clans of Sulaym were certainly responsible for the massacre of Bi'r Maʿūnah in July 625 (ii/4), and 700 men of Sulaym are said to have joined in besieging Medina as a result of Jewish bribes and intrigues. The other two expeditions mentioned in the sources cannot have been against Sulaym as a whole. One was a little-known expedition about September 627 (iv/6) led by Zayd b. Ḥārithah.[2] The other, led by a man of Sulaym in April 629 (xii/7), was probably a dispute within the tribe which was taken under the aegis of Islam.[3] For the conquest of Mecca and the battle of Ḥunayn in January 630 (ix/8) Sulaym provided 900 or 1,000 men. All this tends to show that there was a party favourable to Muḥammad in Sulaym, so that it was never necessary for him after 624 to keep the tribe quiet by a show of force. Among the Emigrants at Medina were a few confederates from Mecca belonging to Sulaym, and this may have helped. On Muḥammad's death only a few clans of Sulaym rebelled; the main part of the tribe remained loyal.[4]

How Sulaym came over to Islam is obscure, and also the precise part played by al-ʿAbbās b. Mirdās. In one story that occurs among the accounts of the 'deputations' credit for the conversion of the tribe is claimed by a member of the leading clan of ash-Sharīd, Qidr b. ʿAmmār.[5] (This is conceivably a mistaken form of the name of the well-known chief of the tribe, Ṣakhr b. ʿAmr, but

cf. *M/Mecca*, 175; the wife of ʿUthmān b. Maẓʿūn was of Sulaym, but her mother was of ʿAbd Shams (IS, iii/1. 286; WW, 372).

[1] The sanctuary of al-ʿUzzā at Nakhlah belonged to B. Shaybān of Sulaym, WW, 351, &c.

[2] Ṭab. 1555; cf. Caetani, i. 694 f. Not in IH and WW.

[3] WW, 303; not in IH.

[4] Cf. Caetani, ii/1. 579 f.

[5] IS, i/2. 50. 4.

he is thought to have died before the Hijrah.)[1] Qidr was alleged to have promised to help Muḥammad with 1,000 men. On his death he charged three men, al-ʿAbbās b. Mirdās, Jabbār b. al-Ḥakam, and al-Akhnas b. Yazīd[2] to carry out his promise, and this they did. In other accounts, however, Sulaym was summoned to join the expedition to Mecca by al-Ḥajjāj b. ʿIlāṭ and al-ʿIrbād b. Sāriyah, while the three standards at Ḥunayn were carried by al-ʿAbbās b. Mirdās, Khufāf b. Nadbah, and al-Ḥajjāj b. ʿIlāṭ.[3] It is also significant that on several occasions men of Sulaym appear under the leadership of Khālid b. al-Walīd and possibly suffer from the later tendency to blacken his name.[4] It seems certain, then, that there was no undisputed leader of Sulaym, and that for this reason Muḥammad originally gave al-ʿAbbās b. Mirdās an ordinary man's share of four camels, instead of the hundred camels given to chiefs.[5] This situation may have made it easier for Muḥammad to win over Sulaym, and his dealings with this tribe were certainly one of his successes.[6]

ʿĀmir b. Ṣaʿṣaʿah. The tribe of ʿĀmir b. Ṣaʿṣaʿah (not to be confused with B. ʿĀmir of Quraysh) was a part of Hawāzin, but is sufficiently important to be treated separately. In pre-Islamic times it had fought against various parts of Ghaṭafān and also against Tamīm. An incident between it and Quraysh (with Kinānah) is also recorded.[7] The chief for many years had been Abū 'l-Barā' ʿĀmir b. Mālik, but latterly, though he kept the name of chief, some of the power was in the hands of two younger men, ʿĀmir b. Ṭufayl and ʿAlqamah b. ʿUlāthah.[8] Some of the consequences of this divided rule are to be seen in the affair of Bi'r Maʿūnah; Abū 'l-Barā' had given a safe-conduct to the Muslim party, but this did not prevent ʿĀmir b. Ṭufayl from instigating two clans of Sulaym to attack them.[9]

There were practically no attacks on B. ʿĀmir by the Muslims. In June 627 (i/6) a small party of thirty men captured some booty

[1] Caussin de Perceval, ii. 556–63, &c.

[2] Presumably al-Akhnas b. Ḥabīb. Cf. IS, iv/2. 17. 16 and *Usd*, iv. 402 top (*s.v.* Maʿn b. Yazīd); but in *Usd*, i. 56 al-Akhnas b. Khabbāb.

[3] WW, 326, 358; for al-Ḥajjāj cf. ibid. 289.

[4] Ibid. 351 f., 358, 363.

[5] IH, 881 f.; WW, 376. Other references to al-ʿAbbās: IH, 832 (Caetani, ii/1. 147 f.); WW, 279, 378.

[6] Early converts from Sulaym, IS, iv/1. 157–60, iv/2. 14–19; cf. Ṣafwān b. al-Muʿaṭṭal, involved in the 'affair of the lie', IH, 732, WW, 185, &c. Letters about land rights: IS, i/2. 26, 34 (§ 34, 64, 65).

[7] Caussin de Perceval, i. 298 f.

[8] Ibid. ii. 564–8.

[9] Cf. p. 31 above.

from a section of Kilāb, and about three years later there was a raid on the same section under the leadership of aḍ-Ḍaḥḥāk b. Sufyān, himself of Kilāb. The small expedition to Sīy in July 629 (iii/8) was presumably against members of ʿĀmir, since Sīy was in the territory of ʿĀmir, but the sources say merely that the people attacked belonged to Hawāzin. That is all that is recorded. It may be that their high reputation as cavalry deterred the Muslims.[1] It is more probable, however, that Muslim policy was due rather to the readiness of at least a section of the tribe of ʿĀmir to be friendly with Muḥammad; this attitude may be partly the result of their hostility to the Meccans or of a friendship with the Medinans which is perhaps to be inferred from their alliance with an-Naḍīr.[2] Whatever the reasons on each side, there had been some agreement between Muḥammad and Abū 'l-Barā'; at the least this meant that each was to grant protection (*jiwār*) to the followers of the other. There is no word of B. ʿĀmir having joined in the siege of Medina, and, thanks to the son of Abū 'l-Barā' there were only a few (and these of Hilāl) with Hawāzin at the battle of Ḥunayn.[3]

After Bi'r Maʿūnah ʿĀmir b. Ṭufayl submitted to Abū 'l- Barā'; a son of the latter wounded him because he had disregarded the grant of protection, but he claimed no revenge for the wound, and so closed the incident; Muḥammad's payment of blood-money to him no doubt helped. He is also said to have asked Muḥammad, as a reward for becoming a Muslim, to grant him the succession to Muḥammad's position; when this was refused he turned away, and probably died soon afterwards, since nothing further is heard of him.[4] His rival ʿAlqamah b. ʿUlāthah, also went to Muḥammad; the report that he and his companions took the oath of allegiance on behalf of ʿIkrimah b. Khaṣafah (that is, a group of tribes including Hawāzin and Sulaym) perhaps indicates that they were hoping that Muḥammad would establish them as leaders of this group of tribes.[5] ʿAlqamah was evidently disappointed in Muḥammad, for after the siege of aṭ-Ṭā'if in February 630 (x–xi/8) he is said to have gone to Syria and only to have returned after the death of Muḥammad. He and Qurrah b. Hubayrah seem to have been the only men of note in ʿĀmir b. Ṣaʿṣaʿah who opposed Abū Bakr in the Riddah. When the military superiority of the Muslims became clear, they quickly surrendered or were captured, and were

[1] IS, i/2. 51. 22.
[2] IH, 652; WW, 160.
[3] WW, 355.
[4] IS, i/2. 51.
[5] Ibid. 52. 25; WW, 306.

pardoned by Abū Bakr; some of their followers were punished for war crimes according to the *lex talionis*.[1] The rest of the tribe—presumably the major part—is said to have avoided taking a definite attitude until the situation cleared. This probably is a mark of caution rather than of active disaffection to Islam.

On the whole, then, Muḥammad was successful in winning 'Āmir b. Ṣa'ṣa'ah to his side. They do not seem to have become Muslims, however, until comparatively late, and then only a few. Aḍ-Ḍaḥḥāk b. Sufyān is spoken of as having summoned Kilāb to Islam. His distribution of the alms (*ṣadaqah*) among the poor of his own tribe may be an indication that B. 'Āmir regarded themselves as equal allies of Muḥammad and not as subject to him.[2]

Hawāzin. Hawāzin properly includes 'Āmir b. Ṣa'ṣa'ah and Thaqīf, which are here being considered separately. The Arabic sources, however, sometimes seem to use the name when they are referring to the smaller group correctly known as 'Ujz Hawāzin, 'the rear of Hawāzin', which omitted 'Āmir and possibly Thaqīf, and comprised the sub-tribes of Naṣr, Jusham, Sa'd b. Bakr, and the smaller Thumālah.[3] Political alignments did not exactly follow

[1] Caetani, ii/1. 577, 603 f., 619–22.

[2] IS, i/2. 44. 16; 'deputations' from parts of 'Āmir, ibid. 44–47, 50–52. Aḍ-Ḍaḥḥāk b. Sufyān b. 'Awf al-Kilābī (IS, iv/1. 29. 5 and *Usd*) is usually distinguished from aḍ-Ḍaḥḥāk b. Sufyān b. al-Ḥārith as-Sulamī (IS, iv/2. 17 and *Usd*). But it is curious that the former has many connexions with Sulaym, while the second is said to have had a standard (*liwā'*) at the conquest of Mecca, although he is not mentioned among the standard-bearers of Sulaym. Perhaps the Kilābī had a standard, and, because there were no Kilāb present, some early scholar tried to explain the statements by inventing a Sulamī; or perhaps the Kilābī belonged to Sulaym on his mother's side.

Living with Kilāb was the small tribe of 'Uraynah. Some stole Muḥammad's camels about March 628 (x/6) and were punished. Later 'Abdallāh b. 'Awsajah al-'Uranī was used by Muḥammad as a messenger, WW, 388; but cf. IS, i/2. 31 (§ 52).

[3] Caetani, ii/1. 57; O. Loth in *Zeitschrift der Deutschen Morgenländischen Gesellschaft*, xxxv. 596; Buhl, *Muhammed*, 298 n. The tribe of Sa'd b. Bakr had apparently two sections. Some were present with Muḥammad at the conquest of Mecca, having been summoned through Ghifār (WW, 326, 332); at the battle of Ḥunayn there were 200 along with Ḍamrah and Layth. Others were with Hawāzin at Ḥunayn (IH, 840; WW, 364). The leader of the deputation to Muḥammad, Zuhayr b. Ṣurad (Abū Ṣurad or Abū Jarwal or Abū Tharwān) is curiously called al-Jushamī as-Sa'dī in *Usd*, ii. 208, though Sa'd was not genealogically part of Jusham. Perhaps some had become attached to Ḍamrah and some to Jusham. If al-Wāqidī is right in dating the 'deputation' of Ḍimām b. Tha'labah (IS, i/2. 44) in vii/5 (December 626), this would presumably be from the section attached to Ḍamrah; but the date is unduly early, and the story has the marks of later editing (cf. Caetani, i. 609 f.).

genealogy, and parts of 'Āmir such as Hilāl were sometimes found with 'Ujz Hawāzin though the rest of 'Āmir stood apart. In earlier times Hawāzin's great enemy had been Ghaṭafān. More recently it had fought two bitter wars with Quraysh and Kinānah, the wars of the Fijār, and the memory of these was doubtless still a factor of importance.

Until the campaign of Ḥunayn in January 630 (x/8), Muḥammad had had almost no contacts with Hawāzin, so far as our records go. Apart from those with 'Āmir mentioned above there had been only two expeditions about December 628 (viii/7), led respectively by Abū Bakr and 'Umar. These expeditions and the extension of Muḥammad's sway over Sulaym (manifested by the presence of a contingent at the conquest of Mecca) may have made Hawāzin aware that the growing Muslim strength was a threat to them. On the other hand, when they heard that Muḥammad was marching on Mecca, they may have expected a bloody and indecisive battle and may have hoped to have an easy victory over one or both of the exhausted combatants. Perhaps the two motives were combined. Muḥammad cannot have planned to attack them until they themselves massed their forces. With an unwieldy army such as he was then leading he could have accomplished little against a mobile and widely dispersed foe. Once they presented him with a target, however, he would gladly seize this opportunity of providing the booty which his army had not received in Mecca.

The battle of Ḥunayn, which has already been described, resulted in the defeat of Hawāzin and the capture of their families and animals, though their allies of Thaqīf managed to retreat safely to aṭ-Ṭā'if. Muḥammad entered into negotiations with Hawāzin, and eventually came to an agreement with them. The negotiations were apparently carried out to begin with by men of Sa'd b. Bakr, who had milk-relationship with Muḥammad since his wet-nurse Ḥalīmah had belonged to that tribe.[1] Through these men Muḥammad conveyed to the leader of Hawāzin, Mālik b. 'Awf an-Naṣrī, the generous terms on which he was prepared to make peace. Mālik thereupon escaped from aṭ-Ṭā'if and came to Muḥammad to express his acceptance. He was to receive back his family and property, and to be given a present of a hundred camels; he was also to be recognized as chief of those sections of his tribe which

[1] IH, 877; WW, 377; IS, i/1. 72.

had become Muslim.[1] The only obligation upon him that is explicitly stated is that he was himself to accept Islam. There is mention elsewhere, however, of a payment called *siʿāyah* made by Naṣr, Saʿd b. Bakr, Thumālah, and Hudhayl—Naṣr being Mālik's own tribe, and Thumālah one of the tribes or clans over which he was recognized as chief; since *siʿāyah* is used for the work done by a slave to earn his emancipation, the payment was probably not strictly a tax, but a payment for the liberation of the women.[2] Mālik in fact also attacked Thaqīf, but this may have been not as part of the agreement but from inclination, because he was annoyed with them for deserting him, and in order to make up for his tribe's loss of camels.

In the wars of the Riddah no part was taken by Hawāzin. They are said to have been uncertain for a time, and to have suspended paying the legal alms (*ṣadaqah*), but there is no mention of any of them taking up arms.[3] Mālik was no doubt genuinely reconciled to Muḥammad and the rule of Medina. Besides that, however, there was an important political reason. Hawāzin must have been comparatively weak after the loss of their property at Ḥunayn. The rebels nearest to them were Asad and Ghaṭafān, and to support these, their ancient rivals, would mean substituting their yoke for that of Quraysh and the Muslims. Self-interest thus helped to restrain Hawāzin from armed revolt. But self-interest would not have led them to decide in this way, since Quraysh recently had been bitter enemies, had not Muḥammad's careful handling of Mālik after Ḥunayn shown him and his tribe that they were likely to be better off within the Islamic community than as members of a confederacy headed by Ṭulayḥah of Asad. Muḥammad's conduct had made it clear that, even when he was fighting Mālik, he was hoping to win him over to support him, for he had arranged for Mālik's family not to be distributed as booty but to be kept together in safety in the house of a kinswoman in Mecca.[4] The reluctance of Hawāzin to combine with other tribes against Abū Bakr is a mark of the success of Muḥammad's policy towards them.

Thaqīf. The tribe of Thaqīf which inhabited the city of aṭ-Ṭā'if consisted of two sections known an Banū Mālik and the Aḥlāf. The name of the latter group means 'confederates' or 'confederacies',

[1] IH, 879; WW, 379.
[2] IS, i/2. 24. 5–14 (§ 28); for *siʿāyah* cf. Lane *s.v. saʿā*, 1, 10.
[3] Ṭab. 1871.
[4] WW, 379.

but does not indicate an inferior social or political *status*. The Aḥlāf may have been less influential in politics than the Banū Mālik, but that is a different matter. Their weakness they made up for by friendship with Quraysh. B. Mālik, on the other hand, were associated with Hawāzin. In the early years of Muḥammad (as has been noted more than once) the wars of the Fijār between Hawāzin and Thaqīf on the one hand and Quraysh and Kinānah on the other hand had resulted in the control by Quraysh of the commerce of aṭ-Ṭā'if. There was doubtless resentment among Thaqīf at this state of affairs, and Muḥammad may have hoped to profit by this when he visited them before the Hijrah.[1]

Whatever the past history of these two groups may have been, there is no doubt about their attitude towards Quraysh. When we hear that Thaqīf sent a hundred men to help Quraysh at Uḥud, we may safely assume that these were mainly from the Aḥlāf.[2] There were presumably some Thaqīf at the siege of Medina, though there is no record of this. The employment of 'Urwah b. Mas'ūd (of the Aḥlāf) in the early negotiations at al-Ḥudaybiyah was made possible by the presence of a detachment of Thaqīf with Quraysh there.[3] 'Urwah was presumably aware of the repercussions that the decline of Meccan power would have on the politics of aṭ-Ṭā'if and had been working to avoid a break with B. Mālik at this juncture. When al-Mughīrah b. Shu'bah of the Aḥlāf had killed thirteen of B. Mālik and then become a Muslim, that is, taken refuge with Muḥammad, 'Urwah had reached an understanding with Mas'ūd b. 'Amr of B. Mālik to avoid bloodshed and had himself accepted responsibility for paying the blood-wit of 1,300 camels.[4] It was presumably also the growing weakness of Quraysh that forced the Aḥlāf to acquiesce in the decision of the B. Mālik to join Hawāzin against Quraysh in January 630. Both parties had contingents at Ḥunayn, but it is not surprising to learn that, while B. Mālik fought stubbornly and lost a hundred men, the Aḥlāf took to flight when they saw the Muslims rallying and standing firm, and had only two casualties.

During the battle of Ḥunayn and the subsequent siege of aṭ-Ṭā'if 'Urwah had been in a city on the Byzantine frontier learning

[1] H. Lammens, *La Cité Arabe de Ṭāif à la Veille de l'Hégire*, Beirut, 1922 (from *Mélanges de la Faculté Orientale de Beyreuth*, viii), 104/216 ff., but not to be accepted without reserves; cf. *M/Mecca*, 139.

[2] WW, 102. [3] IH, 744. 2; cf. WW, 250–2. [4] Ibid.

about siege-engines and protective measures. On his return he directed the preparations for the defence of the city, but soon decided to become a Muslim. Perhaps the easy terms granted to Hawāzin had shown him that acceptance of Islam was more profitable than being constantly harried by the former allies whom Muḥammad had defeated so thoroughly. There was also the example of Quraysh to inspire him. Perhaps he wanted to forestall B. Mālik in gaining Muḥammad's favour. Perhaps he hoped to get himself recognized by Muḥammad as first man in aṭ-Ṭā'if. Certainly he was anxious that the whole city should go over. He returned from Medina to work for this end, but there was strong opposition and he was shot by a fellow citizen and died. The man who killed him is sometimes said to have been of B. Mālik and sometimes of the Aḥlāf; if the latter, the slayer was doubtless of one of the other clans of the Aḥlāf—there is some evidence that each of the main groups was divided into smaller groups at variance with one another. The latter point is in part confirmed by the flight of two prominent kinsmen of 'Urwah's to Medina.

The situation of aṭ-Ṭā'if became desperate, however. They were isolated, since the allies of both factions had joined Muḥammad; and the attacks of Hawāzin made it difficult for them to leave their stronghold. It was an astute move on Muḥammad's part to allow Hawāzin to do his work for him in blockading Thaqīf, while at the same time the rift between the two tribes became wider and a future combination of them against him more unlikely. The initiative was taken by two men of the Aḥlāf, 'Amr b. Umayyah of the clan of 'Ilāj and 'Abd Yālīl b. 'Amr, who had not been on good terms with one another but were brought together by the urgency of the position. It was decided to send to Muḥammad a deputation consisting of three men from each of the two main parties; 'Abd Yālīl was the leader. In this way it was hoped to avoid the suspicion that any individual or family was aiming at the control of the city—a suspicion which must, rightly or wrongly, have been attached to 'Urwah. Muḥammad insisted on the destruction without delay of the goddess, the Lady of aṭ-Ṭā'if, al-Lāt, but agreed that the task might be performed by al-Mughīrah and Abū Sufyān. He refused, too, to give any dispensation from observing the Worship or ritual prayers, and from avoiding usury, wine-drinking, and extra-marital relations with women. He seems, however, to have permitted a slight relaxation of the hours of the fast of Ramaḍān. The deputation eventually said they would try to induce the rest of Thaqīf to accept these terms. This they are said to have done by pretending that they had refused the conditions as too onerous; then, when the hopelessness of preparing to resist had sunk into the consciousness of their fellow citizens, they revealed that they had accepted.

One curious feature is that Muḥammad appointed as leader, primarily in the Worship, but perhaps in other respects also, the youngest member of the deputation, 'Uthmān b. al-'Āṣ, of the clan of Yasār of B. Mālik. He is said to have been the keenest Muslim of the party, but perhaps Muḥammad also had an eye on the relative position of the parties in aṭ-Ṭā'if; through al-Mughīrah the Aḥlāf had an influential place in the Islamic state, and it would not do to make B. Mālik inferior. Another curious point is that there is no mention of Thaqīf having to pay the *zakāt* or legal alms among Muḥammad's stipulations; and, so far as I have noticed, there is no mention of anyone being commissioned to collect any contribution or tax from Thaqīf. This might be a reason for the disappearance of the text of the treaty with aṭ-Ṭā'if. Such treatment of Thaqīf would be in line with Muḥammad's generosity to Hawāzin. While he specially wanted to have Quraysh on his side, he also wanted to win over the other Arabs. In cutting short the siege of aṭ-Ṭā'if he was probably trying to avoid bloodshed and harsh measures which would exacerbate feelings and make reconciliation difficult; once it was clear that Thaqīf were not ripe for surrender, such a decision was most in keeping with his strategy, even if his army had been more suited than it was for siege operations.

There is no whisper in the sources of any disaffection among Thaqīf during the Riddah. Perhaps, however, their attitude was not different from that of Hawāzin, who had stopped paying their legal alms. If Thaqīf had none to pay, then without taking any overt action their attitude might well be one of 'wait and see'. In view of their great reluctance to accept Muḥammad's terms, it is plausible to suppose that this was their motive rather than devout attachment to the Islamic faith. On the other hand, in the two years between the submission of Thaqīf and Muḥammad's death convinced supporters of the religio-political system of Islam like al-Mughīrah and 'Uthmān b. al-'Āṣ may have won a large following in the town. Even if this is so, however, the old attachment to the rest of Hawāzin and consequent opposition to Asad and Ghaṭafān probably played a large part in keeping them from military adventures.[1]

4. THE TRIBES TO THE NORTH

A study of the numbers involved in the various expeditions in the direction of Syria shows that the road north had a prominent place in Muḥammad's strategic thinking.[2] As early as August 626 (iii/5) he led 1,000 men to Dūmat al-Jandal, a larger number than he had hitherto collected, apart from the visit to Badr in April of that year (xi/4) when he had had 1,500. Again, the 3,000 of the expedition to Mu'tah in September 629 (v/8) was more than had ever gone on any distant expedition and equivalent to the number Muḥammad commanded at the siege of Medina; while the 30,000 of the expedition to Tabūk (October–December 630 = vii–ix/9), even if it is exaggerated, is far more than went on any other expedition during Muḥammad's lifetime. Unfortunately the sources, after giving us these suggestive figures, are tantalizingly reticent about details; and we are left to deduce from our general knowledge the reasons for this emphasis in strategy on the road to Syria.

It would be unrealistic to suppose that Muḥammad foresaw the later expansion of the Arabs in detail, and indeed no claim of this sort is made by the early Muslim sources. As has been hinted in previous chapters, however, there were factors within his ken which led him in this direction. From at least soon after Uḥud he seems to have been aspiring to become leader of all the Arabs. The Arabs, however, were constantly fighting one another, and this fighting helped to keep the population sufficiently small for the meagre resources of the desert to support. To keep the Arabs under his rule, he must stop inter-tribal fighting; but to do so, it was not enough to insist on the acceptance of blood-money instead of taking a life for a life; he must also provide some outlet for the warlike energies of the Arabs and for their excess population. This outlet he believed was to be found along the route to the north. Life in Byzantine Syria must always have seemed infinitely superior in material comforts to that of the desert or even of a town like

[1] Akin to Hawāzin was Bāhilah. It is mentioned as having helped 'Āmir b. Ṣa'ṣa'ah and Tamīm (Caussin de Perceval, ii. 467, 583). Two groups entered into agreement with Muḥammad after the conquest of Mecca (IS, i/2. 33 (§ 61), 49 (§ 93); cf. Caetani, ii/1. 221–3). The second group was exempted from payments.

[2] Cf. Excursus B.

Mecca. Perhaps there was a tradition of preying on the settled lands of the empire, though the buffer princedoms had tried to stop it. Certainly there would be no difficulty in moving the Arabs in this direction provided they were convinced that there was a reasonable hope of success. Whether Muḥammad was aware of the weakness of the Byzantine and Persian empires is a matter of conjecture. What he must have realized, however, before his death is that the Islamic state was now strong enough to detach the border tribes from the Byzantines, and that, once this was effected, the settled lands were open to Muslim raiders. He could not have been certain that the Arabs would be superior to the Byzantines in a pitched battle, though he must have known of the success of Arabs against the Persians at Dhū Qār a few years before this. Altogether he had solid reasons for a policy of expansion northwards.

In the case of the tribes nearer to Medina, it was necessary to pay attention to their relations to one another, but as one went north the primary question became that of a tribe's relations to the Byzantines. The chief problem came to be how to make them leave the Byzantine allegiance. The solution of this problem was rendered more difficult by the fact that most of the pro-Byzantine tribes were Christian and may have hesitated about accepting the religious aspects of Muḥammad's movement. In several cases he seems to have entered into an agreement with a tribe without requiring that the members should become Muslims.

The northern policy may have affected relations with some of the tribes considered in the previous sections. Thus Muzaynah seems to have been immediately north of Medina, while part of Fazārah was sometimes in Wādi 'l-Qurā on the usual road to Syria. The tribes now to be considered in detail, however, belong primarily to the northern route.

Saʿd Hudhaym and ʿUdhrah. According to the genealogists ʿUdhrah was the son of Saʿd Hudhaym, but in Muḥammad's time the names seem to have denoted two distinct tribes. We hear of a letter from Muḥammad to ʿUdhrah being intercepted by a man of Saʿd Hudhaym,[1] which suggests that the two groups were not on good terms. There are reports of some individuals becoming Muslims; the man who intercepted the letter to B. ʿUdhrah is said to have been killed as a Muslim in an expedition either in 624 (vi/3) or 627 (vii/6); another man is mentioned as becoming a Muslim

[1] IS, i/2. 33.

during the expedition to Tabūk.[1] The so-called 'deputation' to Muḥammad about the same time probably represented only a small section of the tribe.[2] There is also a report of a letter from Muḥammad to Saʿd Hudhaym and Judhām fixing the *ṣadaqah* or 'alms' and instructing that this is to be paid to his two commissioners or their agents; this presumably belongs to the negotiations with Judhām late in 627 (vii/6), and will be dealt with presently. All this gives the impression that Saʿd Hudhaym was small and weak, and closely associated with Judhām, or perhaps dependent on it. If we may assume that Saʿd Allāh is the Islamic form of Saʿd Hudhaym, then a section of them received (along with a section of Judhām) part of the payments made by a Jewish settlement in the north;[3] this would confirm to some extent the view that they were poor.

The tribe of ʿUdhrah was seemingly more important. In the distant past they had helped Quraysh to establish themselves in Mecca. One of the early converts from this tribe was a confederate of the clan of Zuhrah of Quraysh;[4] and some of Muḥammad's Medinan followers had mothers from ʿUdhrah.[5] Thus the tribe was in contact with Mecca and Medina. It appears to have been Christian, though the Christianity may have been nominal.[6] The account of the 'deputation' to Medina in May/June 630 (ii/9) implies that the bulk of the tribe was not Muslim then, and they probably did not become Muslim until after Muḥammad's death.[7] Some individual members of the tribe, however, became attached to Muḥammad at an early date, and we find him giving them responsible positions; one commanded the right wing at the battle of Mu'tah, and another had oversight of the relations between the tribes of Asad and Ṭayyi'.[8] He also used them as guides.[9] The letter already mentioned, that was intercepted by Saʿd Hudhaym, implies some understanding with the tribe or a part of it at an early period; and so also does the fact that one of the early converts brought *ṣadaqah* (Jamrah b. an-Nuʿmān), and that Muḥammad expected help from ʿUdhrah in an expedition in October 629 (vi/8).[10]

This is the gist of what we can learn about the relations between Muḥammad and ʿUdhrah, except that he made a grant of land to

[1] WW, 401.
[2] IS, i/2. 65; Ṭab. 1722. 11.
[3] WW, 405; cf. Caetani, ii/1. 255.
[4] Khālid b. ʿUrfuṭah, IS, iv/2. 74.
[5] Thābit b. Thaʿlabah, ibid. iii/2. 111; ʿAmrah bint Saʿd, viii. 271.
[6] Lammens, *La Mecque à la Veille de l'Hégire*, 257/353; cf. 264/360.
[7] IS, i/2. 66 f.; cf. Caetani, ii/1. 229.
[8] IH, 793; IS, i/2. 23. 22.
[9] WW, 175, 235.
[10] IS, i/2. 74; WW, 315.

Jamrah and perhaps to another man.[1] The probability is that Muḥammad had some sort of alliance with the tribe before they became Muslims. Even the phrase used about Jamrah is curious: 'he was chief of 'Udhrah, and he was the first of the people of the Ḥijāz who brought to the Prophet the *ṣadaqah* of B. 'Udhrah.' Could this originally have meant that Jamrah was the first of the non-Muslims of the Ḥijāz to bring a contribution to Muḥammad? Or does it distinguish the 'Udhrah of the Ḥijāz from those to the north of it? If 'Udhrah was receiving letters from Muḥammad at least by 626, they might have been early in sending *ṣadaqah*, even though many of them were still not Muslims when the 'deputation' came in 630. A solution of these problems is conjectural, and is bound up with a solution of the general problems involved.

Judhām. The problems concerning Judhām are similar to those just discussed. Judhām, or part of it, was in close relations with the Byzantines. The latter used individuals as agents, and employed the forces in the defence of the frontier.[2] They are mentioned in the sources of Muḥammad's life as attached to a Byzantine army;[3] and a man of Judhām, Farwah b. 'Amr, was commissioner (*'āmil*) for Caesar in 'Ammān and Ma'ān, and is said to have become a Muslim.[4] Quraysh also seem to have been on good terms with Judhām, for it was a man of Judhām who informed Abū Sufyān shortly before the battle of Badr about Muḥammad's attempt to attack him on the way north.[5]

The first mention of an agreement between Muḥammad and Judhām is about October 627 (vi/6), at or just before the time of the expedition of Zayd b. Ḥārithah to Ḥismā. The story is something like this. Diḥyah b. Khalīfah al-Kalbī, who had gone to Syria on an errand for Muḥammad, was returning to Medina with gifts, when he was robbed by a man of Judhām called al-Hunayd. Another clan of Judhām, however, or some men from another tribe, forced al-Hunayd to give the things back. Meanwhile a leader of Judhām, Rifā'ah b. Zayd, had been in Medina, had brought back to the tribe Muḥammad's terms for an alliance, and the tribe had accepted. Muḥammad had not been informed of this decision, however, and sent out Zayd b. Ḥārithah to avenge the insult to his messenger. There was a skirmish in which the Muslims

[1] IS, i/2. 26. 23, reading 'Udhrī for 'Adawī with *Usd, s.v.*

[2] Lammens, *Mecque*, 33/129 f.; id., *L'Arabie Occidentale avant l'Hégire*, Beirut, 1928, 315 n. 3; cf. IS, vii/2. 148 f.; *Usd*, iv. 178.

[3] IH, 792; WW, 311.

[4] IS, i/2. 18, 31, 83.

[5] WW, 40.

killed al-Hunayd and captured a number of women and animals. Rifāʿah was sent to Mecca again to protest, and the dispute was settled amicably. So run the sources.[1] The mention of negotiations between Muḥammad and Judhām about April 628 (xii/6), between al-Ḥudaybiyah and Khaybar,[2] must refer to the closing episodes of this incident.

Though the sources say that this agreement involved the acceptance of Islam, it is almost certain that this was not so. The clans of Judhām who joined together in the transaction included Wā'il, and there were also many members of the tribes of Salāmān and Saʿd Hudhaym. Yet late in 630 on the Tabūk expedition we hear of a man of the clan of Wā'il and another of Saʿd Hudhaym being converted, and apparently being rewarded for their conversion by the gift of some of the revenues from a Jewish settlement.[3] The simplest explanation of this is that the rest of Judhām had become allies of Muḥammad without becoming Muslims, and that he was now anxious to bring about their conversion. It is difficult to suppose that earlier converts from the tribe were less well treated, or that gifts to them have been passed over by the sources.

This hypothesis of alliance without conversion tends to be supported by the letter from Muḥammad to Rifāʿah which constitutes the first part of the account of the 'deputation' of Judhām.[4] The letter runs: 'This is a letter from Muḥammad, the Messenger of God, to Rifāʿah b. Zayd and to his tribe and to those who follow with them; he calls them to God; he who accepts is in the party of God (*ḥizb Allāh*); he who refuses has two months' security.' Muḥammad was surely not in a strong enough position in April 628 to make a demand for acceptance of Islam or withdrawal from the sphere of Muslim influence. It is not necessary, however, to take the words in the way that later practice suggests. The 'party of God' might be a 'united front' of Muslims and Christians,[5] and the letter might be a demand that the members of the group which Rifāʿah represented should state definitely to which side they belonged. The incident leading to the expedition of Ḥismā was probably due to some of them joining the group for certain purposes and not for others, and so trying to have the best of both worlds—the privileges of an alliance with Muḥammad without the responsibilities. The story suggests that Judhām was at fault,

[1] IH, 975; WW, 235 f.
[2] IS, i/2. 83. 1; cf. *Iṣābah*, i. 1060.
[3] WW, 405; and cf. above.
[4] IS, i/2. 82 f.
[5] Cf. Q. 5. 56/61; 58. 22.

and Muḥammad doubtless wanted to avoid further difficulties by having a clear distinction between friends and enemies.

If the argument so far holds, then the letter to Saʿd Hudhaym and Judhām about paying *ṣadaqah*[1] was sent to this same group. The payment may have been in part a punishment for their wrong attitude. If not, it must indicate that non-Muslims had to pay for the advantages of alliance with Muḥammad. The letter seems to refer to some specific occasion since the collectors of the *ṣadaqah* are named; just before the Tabūk expedition would be a possibility.

Muḥammad's treatment of Judhām shows the juxtaposition of severity and kindness which characterized much of his activity. He could be severe when men were not straight with him and tried to 'sit on the fence', but when a man stood out boldly for Islam he would be very generous.

Quḍāʿah. Strictly speaking, Quḍāʿah was a large group of tribes which included Juhaynah, ʿUdhrah, Balī, Bahrā', and Kalb. In the sources for the life of Muḥammad, however, the term appears to be used in a more restricted sense, probably in much the same way as Saʿd Hudhaym was distinguished from ʿUdhrah which was formally a part of it. Thus we hear of an expedition against Balī and Quḍāʿah.[2] Shortly before this Quḍāʿah had been responsible for killing Kaʿb b. ʿUmayr and his party,[3] and there were some men of Quḍāʿah, apparently Christians, among the opponents of the Muslims at Mu'tah.[4]

A number of small groups, reckoned by the genealogists as belonging to Quḍāʿah, may be mentioned here. Jarm, which had been involved in the fighting between Bakr and Tamīm in pre-Islamic times, is reported to have sent a 'deputation' to Muḥammad.[5] Al-Qayn—often in the form Ba'l-Qayn—was like many other tribes, divided. Some were with the opposing army at Mu'tah, yet Muḥammad expected help from the tribe against Balī and Quḍāʿah.[6] In pre-Islamic times a poet of the tribe, Abū 'ṭ-Ṭamaḥān, had been friendly with ʿAbdallāh b. Judʿān and az-Zubayr b. ʿAbd al-Muṭṭalib.[7] Salāmān sent a 'deputation' to Muḥammad in January 632, and is said to have become Muslim; some had earlier been associated with Judhām.[8]

[1] IS, i/2. 23 f. [2] IH, 984–6; WW, 315 f. [3] Ṭab. 1601. [4] WW, 314.
[5] Caussin de Perceval, ii. 582; IS, i/2. 69–71. [6] IH, 792; WW, 315.
[7] Ibn Qutaybah, *K. ash-Shiʿr wa-'sh-Shuʿarā'*, ed. M. J. De Goeje, Leiden, 1904, 229 f.; cf. Caussin de Perceval, i. 131; ii. 232.
[8] IS, i/2. 67; WW, 235.

Balī. Balī, like Judhām and other tribes, had members on both sides. The commander of the opposing Arab forces at Mu'tah was from Balī,[1] and we have just mentioned the expedition shortly after Mu'tah against Balī and Quḍā'ah. On the other hand, there were numerous confederates from Balī along with the Medinan Muslims at Badr; some clans like Unayf and Marthad had been at Medina before the arrival of the Jews and had become confederates of these.[2] Moreover, on the expedition against Balī and Quḍā'ah already mentioned, the Muslim leader was 'Amr b. al-'Āṣ, whose mother was of Balī, and it was hoped that a contingent from Balī would join him. When a 'deputation' came to Medina in June/July 630 (iii/9) and professed Islam, they lodged with one of the Medinan members of the tribe, already a Muslim.[3] Most interesting is the letter from Muḥammad to the clan of Ju'ayl, in which he acknowledges them as part of the clan of 'Abd Manāf of Quraysh and gives them the 'alms' (*ṣadaqāt*) from certain tribes; on these terms they profess Islam.[4] This was probably not due to mere respect for genealogy; the genealogy may rather have been an excuse for the generosity. Like similar grants to converts from Sa'd Allāh (Sa'd Hudhaym) and Judhām it suggests that Muḥammad realized the urgency of establishing his power along the road to the north and so securing an outlet for the more turbulent of his followers.

Bahrā'. Bahrā lived somewhere near Balī, to whom they were related. A contingent of them was in the 'Byzantine' army at Mu'tah. There is a report of a 'deputation' of thirteen coming to Medina and professing Islam, but there is no mention of the rest of the tribe doing the same. The story has been preserved in the family of al-Miqdād b. 'Amr, who was originally of Bahrā' but became a confederate and then adopted son of one of the leading men of Zuhrah at Mecca.[5] If this is all that can be said in glorification of Bahrā', one must conclude that very few of them became Muslims or even allies of Muḥammad. Distance from Medina is perhaps the explanation.

Lakhm. The part of Lakhm with which we are concerned also lived about the Syrian border; they were Christians, and co-operated with the Byzantines.[6] A letter has been preserved from

[1] IH, 792; WW, 311.
[2] IS, iii/2. 32–37, &c.; as-Samhūdī, i. 114 (= Wüstenfeld, 29; see p. 192 below); cf. also IS, iv/2. 73.
[3] IS, i/2. 65 f.; cf. ibid. iv/2. 73, Ruwayfi'.
[4] Ibid. i/2. 24.
[5] Ibid. 66; cf. iii/1. 114–16.
[6] IH, 792; WW, 311, 391; Caetani, ii/1. 288 ff.

Muḥammad to the Muslims of Ḥadas, a section of Lakhm; it promises protection to those who are clearly Muslims and warns those 'who go back from their religion' that they forfeit this protection.[1] This is the attitude of severity which has already been remarked on. The case of Tamīm ad-Dārī and other members of the clan of ad-Dār is interesting. Ten of them came to Muḥammad on his return from the Tabūk expedition with rich gifts and professed Islam. They were not a 'deputation' in the usual sense, however, for they did not return to their clan but remained in Medina, and were given a yearly allowance of dates from Khaybar.[2] This is unusual enough, but there is a curious sequel. Tamīm is said to have asked Muḥammad to give them two villages in Syria, Ḥibrā (or Hebron) and (Bayt) ʿAynūn, and there is extant the text of a letter from Muḥammad to Tamīm's brother Nuʿaym establishing their right to these.[3] European scholars have generally agreed that the letter cannot be authentic, and a medieval Ḥanafī jurisconsult, without impugning the authenticity, ventured to hold that even Muḥammad had no right to give away what was not his to dispose of! While we may join in doubting the authenticity of the text, it would not be surprising if Muḥammad had had some understanding with them, and indeed had been keeping them for use in the penetration of Syria. Another member of Lakhm had proved unreliable—Ḥāṭib b. Abī Baltaʿah. He was a confederate of the prominent Companion, az-Zubayr, and had fought at Badr and carried a letter to the Muqawqis of Egypt for Muḥammad; but just before the conquest of Mecca he was caught trying to give information to the enemy.[4] Perhaps Muḥammad's clemency to him on this occasion was with a view to gaining his assistance in dealing with Lakhm.

Ghassān. The chiefs of the tribe of Ghassān had for long been on friendly terms with the Byzantines and in return for a subsidy had defended the Byzantine frontier from the nomads. They were Christians but supported the monophysites and not the orthodox. Relations were disrupted by the Persian invasion of 613–14, and the old arrangements may not have been restored on the Byzantine victory in 629.[5]

[1] IS, i/2. 21.
[2] Ibid, 75; cf. IH, 777; WW, 287; Caetani, l.c.
[3] IS, i/2. 21; cf. Caetani, l.c.
[4] IS, iii/1. 80 f., i/2. 16; IH, 809 f.; WW, 325.
[5] Cf. Th. Nöldeke, *Die Ghassānischen Fürsten aus dem Hause Gafna's*, Berlin, 1887, 42 ff.

There are a number of notices of the passing of messengers between Muḥammad and various men on the frontier. Diḥyah b. Khalīfah al-Kalbī was sent to the governor (*ʿaẓīm*) of Bostra with a message for Caesar, probably in 627.[1] Shujāʿ b. Wahb of Asad b. Khuzaymah was sent to (al-Mundhir b.) al-Ḥārith b. Abī Shimr of Ghassān, and was badly received; this was perhaps in 628.[2] A letter was sent to Jabalah b. al-Ayham, 'king' of Ghassān, as a result of which he is said (wrongly) to have become a Muslim.[3] There is a report of ʿAmmār b. Yāsir being sent to al-Ayham b. an-Nuʿmān of Ghassān, though this may be a variant of the previous one.[4] Lastly, the expedition of Mu'tah in September 629 (v/8) was to punish Shuraḥbīl b. ʿAmr of Ghassān for executing al-Ḥārith b. ʿUmayr al-Azdī when carrying a letter from Muḥammad to the 'king' of Bostra.[5]

There is much in these notices that is to be rejected. That the letters contained appeals to these men to accept Islam is doubtless a later invention, as is the story of Jabalah's conversion. There may also be some confusion of names and dates. It seems certain, however, that Muḥammad was feeling his way by diplomacy towards Syria, and that he approached various important persons and used a number of messengers. It may well be that at one time, before the final victory of Heraclius was certain, Jabalah had a friendly understanding with Muḥammad. It is only to be expected that in these troubled years various leaders would be trying to get the better of one another, and that a man's attitude to Muḥammad might be different at different times. These notices, then, fit in well with what we know otherwise of Muḥammad's policy of northward expansion.

(It is perhaps worth mentioning some of the dates of the war between the Byzantines and the Persians. By 619 the Persians had overrun Egypt and all Asia Minor as well as Syria, and were encouraging barbarians to ravage the European provinces. From 622 to 625 Heraclius was campaigning in Asia Minor with some success, and in 626 a short siege of Constantinople by the Persians and their allies proved a failure. In 627 Heraclius invaded the Persian empire, and in December of that year won an important

1 IS, i/2. 16; cf. IH, 975 f.; WW. 234 f.; Caetani, i. 734.

2 IS, i/2. 17; cf. Caetani, i. 735.

3 IS, i/2. 20; cf. Caetani, ii/1. 69 and Nöldeke, o.c., 45 f.

4 Al-Yaʿqūbī, *Historiae* (ed. M. Th. Houtsma), Leiden, 1883, ii. 84; cf. Caetani, l.c.

5 WW, 309.

victory near ancient Nineveh, but had to retreat shortly afterwards. In February 628, however, the Persian emperor was assassinated, and the son who succeeded him desired peace. By about March 628 Heraclius could regard himself as victorious, but the negotiations for the evacuation of the Byzantine empire by the Persians were not completed until June 629. In September 629 Heraclius entered Constantinople as victor, and in March 630 restored the Holy Rood to Jerusalem.)[1]

The story of the 'deputation' from Ghassān to Muḥammad is evidence that Ghassān showed no signs of accepting Islam.[2] Even if it is true, it amounts to no more than that three unnamed members of the tribe came to Muḥammad in December 631 (ix/10), were convinced of the truth of his claims, but went home and did nothing about it; only one lived to make a public profession of Islam in 635. Other references show that Ghassān continued to oppose the Muslims for some years.[3] Thus Muḥammad had no success whatsoever in winning Ghassān over to his side. Some small settlements may have felt, when they saw the great expedition to Tabūk at the end of 630, that Muḥammad was a power to be reckoned with, but the great majority of the nomads of the Syrian border were unconvinced.

Kalb, &c. The tribe of Kalb had its territory slightly to the east of those just considered. This was as much on the route to al-'Irāq as on that to Syria.[4] Dūmat al-Jandal lay within this territory, but the settlement itself was in the hands of Ukaydir b. 'Abd al-Malik of the clan of as-Sakūn of Kindah. (The main body of Kindah lived in the south of Arabia.) An early convert from this tribe was Diḥyah b. Khalīfah, but we are told nothing about the circumstances of his conversion or the reason for it, though we hear much about his likeness to the angel Gabriel! Muḥammad used him as an envoy to places on the Byzantine frontier.[5]

Muḥammad's expedition to Dūmat al-Jandal in August and September 626 (iii–iv/5) may have been a punishment for attacks on caravans to Medina,[6] or perhaps merely a reconnaissance in

[1] Cf. Ch. Diehl and G. Marçais, *Le Monde Oriental de 395 à 1081* (Histoire Générale: Histoire du Moyen Age, iii), 2nd ed., Paris, 1944, 144–50.

[2] IS, i/2. 71 f.; cf. Caetani, ii/1. 328.

[3] WW, 391; cf. Ṭab. 2081.

[4] For al-'Irāq cf. Ṭab. 2065; for Syria WW, 175 n. 1.

[5] IS, iv/1. 184 f., cf. i/2. 16, 28, &c.

[6] Cf. al-Mas'ūdī, *K. at-Tanbīh wa'l-Ishrāt*, Leiden, 1894, 248.

force; it must have impressed the Arabs, but there is no record of any results apart from the capture of some animals. About the end of December 627 (viii/6), however, ʿAbd ar-Raḥmān led a force to the district, made some sort of agreement with the leader of Kalb there, al-Aṣyaʿ (or al-Aṣbagh) b. ʿAmr, and sealed it by marrying his daughter Tumāḍir.[1] One account says that al-Aṣyaʿ became a Muslim, but another speaks of ʿAbd ar-Raḥmān collecting *jizyah* or poll-tax, which would imply that he remained a Christian; the latter seems more likely. Finally, about October 630 (vii/9), Khālid b. al-Walīd was sent from Tabūk to Dūmat al-Jandal with 420 horsemen. By capturing the 'king', Ukaydir b. ʿAbd al-Malik al-Kindī, he secured the surrender of the stronghold. Apparently an immediate payment was to be made of 2,000 camels, 800 slaves, 400 coats of mail, and 400 lances, while for the future there was to be an annual *jizyah* or poll-tax.[2]

The letters to parts of Kalb and to Ukaydir, and the account of the 'deputation' from Kalb, add little to our knowledge.[3] It is almost certain that not all the persons mentioned became Muslims, but even if they did their number is negligible; on the whole Kalb did not become Muslim at this period. All that happened was that certain groups settled in or near Dūmat al-Jandal were forced to make payments to Muḥammad. Though these are often called *jizyah*, presumably to show that the persons making them were not Muslims, the regulations in the letters suggest that the payments were a fixed proportion of the herds and of the produce of the palms, and thus were formally similar to the *zakāt* paid by the Muslims. This is doubtless a source of the confusion.

Various settled communities. During the expedition to Tabūk agreements were also made with some settled communities in the south of Syria. The most important was probably the Christian community of Aylah (the biblical Elath and modern ʿAqabah) at the head of the Gulf of ʿAqabah.[4] The 'king' of Aylah, Yuḥannah b. Rūbah, came in person to negotiate with Muḥammad. The tribute for Aylah was fixed at 300 dīnārs annually. Near Aylah was Maqnā, a fishing town inhabited by Jews belonging to B. Janbah; they were required to pay annually a quarter of their produce of fruit and yarn (and perhaps also of fish).[5] Adhruḥ and Jarbā,

[1] WW, 236 f.; cf. Caetani, i. 700 f. For 'al-Aṣbagh' cf. IS, iii/1. 90. 15, &c.
[2] IH, 903 WW, 403–5.
[3] IS, i/2. 34, 36, 68 f.; cf. Excursus G.
[4] IH, 902; WW, 405; IS, i/2. 28 f. (§ 45), 37 (§ 74, 75); cf. Caetani, ii/1. 253 ff.
[5] WW, 405; IS, i/2. 28 (§ 44), 37 f. (§ 75).

apparently near 'Ammān, were also inhabited by Jews. According to one version the people of Adhruḥ were to pay 1,000 dīnārs; according to another the people of the two places were to pay 100.[1] It is clear, then, that by the late autumn of 630 Muḥammad had adopted the policy suggested by a verse of the Qur'ān (9. 29): 'Fight against those who . . . do not practise the religion of truth, of those who have been given the Book (Jews and Christians), until they pay the *jizyah*. . . .'

The northern policy. Muḥammad laid great emphasis on northward expansion. The motives were doubtless those already suggested. The review of the tribes does not support the belief that it was the extent of his success in the north that encouraged him to devote so much attention to this region. On the whole his successes were meagre, and when he died most of the tribes were still Christian and friendly to the Byzantines.

To begin with he seems to have been prepared to form alliances with Christian tribes. Perhaps he proposed a united front against the Persians, and followed this up with propaganda emphasizing what Muslims believed that was also held by Christians. Or perhaps he tried to gain the support of the Christian Arabs by siding with the monophysites among them against the orthodox. His letter to Bishop Ḍughāṭir is an example of this type of diplomatic approach.[2] So long as the Byzantine empire looked like breaking up, he probably found some men who were prepared to listen sympathetically to his envoys. By 630, however, it must have been clear that this policy was failing. Muḥammad must have heard of the great occasion at Jerusalem when the Holy Rood was restored, even if he had not heard of Heraclius' triumphant entry into Constantinople. Apart from this he would find the tribes becoming less sympathetic to himself, until one went so far as to murder his messenger. About this time, then, his policy towards the Christian tribes changed, in accordance with a Qur'ānic revelation. It may have changed by the time of the expedition to Mu'tah in September 629, but the details are obscure and we cannot be certain. It had certainly changed before he set out for Tabūk a year later.

By this new policy non-Muslim tribes were given a choice between accepting Islam and paying annual tribute. In either case they became members of the Islamic security system. If they refused that, they were killed or enslaved. Muḥammad had never

[1] WW, 405; IS, i/2. 37 f. (§ 75). [2] Ibid. 28 (§ 43); cf. Excursus F, no. 13.

tolerated double-dealing; now he made it more than ever necessary for a man to declare the side to which he belonged. Those who became subject to Muḥammad without conversion to Islam seem to have been given a heavy tribute in some cases. On the other hand, the clans which accepted Islam met with great generosity. It is worth noting the contrast between the people of Adhruḥ and the small groups from Saʿd Allāh and Judhām. The effect of this policy in the first place was to make the Christian tribes more eager to support the Byzantines until the tide of war was running very much against the latter and in favour of the Muslims. Ukaydir led an armed revolt, and the tribes, including Judhām, are mentioned as sending detachments to the Byzantine armies.[1] In the north during Muḥammad's lifetime there was no great battle comparable to the battle of Ḥunayn; nevertheless, the war with Syria may be said to have already begun. While Muḥammad could not have foreseen the subsequent expansion of the Arab empire in detail, his was the far-seeing mind which directed the Arabs' attention to the strategic importance of Syria for the new Islamic state.

5. THE TRIBES TO THE SOUTH OF MECCA

The tribes living to the south of Mecca differed in various ways from all those hitherto considered, and there was a corresponding difference in Muḥammad's policy with regard to them. One important point is that there were hardly any contacts between them and the Muslims until after the conquest of Mecca; and another is that at this critical period of their history no strong or statesmanlike leader appeared, for none of the men of whom we read had any inherited influence or innate ability comparable to that of Mālik b. ʿAwf of Hawāzin or even ʿUyaynah b. Ḥiṣn of Ghaṭafān. This lack of leadership may be due to a general decadence of the inhabitants of the region,[2] though the evidence is too slight to permit of certainty. The south-west corner of the Arabian peninsula was its most fertile part, owing to the plentiful rains, and had once had a flourishing civilization. The traditional accounts of the bursting of the dam of Ma'rib[3] must be based on memories of the breakdown of the irrigation system on which this civilization was founded, but modern scholarship regards this breakdown as a symptom of the

[1] Cf. Ṭab. 2065, 2081.

[2] Cf. Caetani, ii/1. 661–9, where the events up to Muḥammad's death are reviewed.

[3] IH, 8; cf. Q. 34. 16/15.

decline of the civilization and not as its cause. The latter is perhaps to be sought in some change of trade-routes. As the standard of living deteriorated some of the Arab tribes returned to nomadism, and most left the Yemen and made their way northwards. The groups with whom Muḥammad had to deal frequently contained both nomadic and settled members. The nomads seem to have been mostly pagan in religion, and the settlers Christian (or occasionally Jewish).

As the indigenous civilization weakened, foreign conquerors made their appearance. For some fifty years from about 525 the region was under the Abyssinians. They were succeeded by the Persians, and these retained the nominal sovereignty until the various districts were incorporated into the Islamic state; but owing to his poor communications with ʿIrāq the Persian governor was largely dependent on his own resources, and probably had little influence except in the neighbourhood of the seat of government at Ṣanʿāʾ. Indeed, he and the Abnāʾ (literally 'sons', that is, of Persian fathers and Arab mothers) merely constituted one of several groups contending for power in the Yemen. The presence of the Abyssinians and the Persians, however, probably helped to increase the divisive tendencies which were always latent. With the exception of al-Aswad (to be described presently) there are no signs of any attempt to combine against the Persians.

In the case of the southern tribes it seems best not to deal with them tribe by tribe, but to arrange the source material so as to illustrate the main aspects of Muḥammad's treatment of them. Such information as we have about inter-tribal relations in pre-Islamic times does not illuminate the early Islamic period, and our knowledge of the latter is often fragmentary. Despite the uncertainty of many details, however, it is possible to form a coherent picture of Muḥammad's policy.

The most important feature of this 'southern policy' is the extensive use of diplomatic methods. Before the conquest of Mecca, expeditions would of course have been impracticable; but even after that event Muḥammad made no great show of force in the south. The largest expedition in this direction had only 400 men. While this may in part be due to the weakness of the southern tribes, it also indicates that the road to the Yemen and the road to Syria had very different roles in Muḥammad's strategic thinking. In the south there was none of the sense of urgency which characterized his 'northern policy'; he seems to have been ready to allow matters to mature in their own time.

What he did was to support certain local factions when they were prepared to accept the minimum conditions which he named. Thus in a letter to Qays b. Salamah of al-Juʿfī Muḥammad says that he has made him agent (*istaʿmaltu-ka*) for a group of clans, 'those who perform the Worship, give the *zakāt*, and contribute (*ṣaddaqa*) of their wealth and purify it'; this particular plan was unsuccessful, for Qays eventually refused to play his part.[1] An early instance was that of two men, Arṭāh b. Sharāḥīl and al-Juhaysh of the tribe of an-Nakhaʿ, who received Muḥammad's blessing after explaining that in their tribe there was a group of seventy men of a superior class who controlled everything; Arṭāh is said to have led some of the tribe at the conquest of Mecca, and, even if these had gone to live in Medina, the leaven of Islam was working in the tribe, for the last 'deputation' to visit Muḥammad was one of 200 men from an-Nakhaʿ.[2]

The tribe of Murād had been defeated by Hamdān in a battle about the time of the Hijrah. They had also, perhaps after the battle, been in alliance with the 'kings' of Kindah, doubtless as inferiors. About 632/10 one of their leaders, Farwah b. Musayk, renounced the alliance with Kindah and came to Muḥammad. After he had been instructed in Islam, Muḥammad appointed him agent (*istaʿmala-hu*) for the tribes of Murād, Zubayd, and Madhḥij, and sent him back to his tribe in the company of an early Meccan Muslim, Khālid b. Saʿīd.[3] This apparently straightforward course of events is seen in a new light when we realize that there was another faction in Murād whose leader was Qays b. al-Makshūḥ (or, more fully, Qays b. Hubayrah b. ʿAbd Yaghūth al-Makshūḥ), that Qays was a friend of ʿAmr b. Maʿdīkarib of Zubayd, and that the two took the side of al-Aswad of ʿAns and received his support against Farwah.[4] Some of the details of these reports may be questioned: the alleged conversion of ʿAmr b. Maʿdīkarib[5] may in fact have been no more than a political alliance, though there is insufficient justification for regarding the whole incident as an invention; and Farwah may have claimed that Muḥammad gave him a position which he only received later as a reward for his

1 IS, i/2. 62 (§ 106).
2 Ibid. 77 (§ 129).
3 IH, 950 f.; IS, i/2. 63 f. (§ 108).
4 IH, 951 f.; Ṭab. 1732–4, 1796, 1996, &c.
5 IH, ibid.; IS, i/2. 64 (§ 109); Ṭab. 1732–4.

services against al-Aswad. There is no word of Qays having become a Muslim; the appearance of his name in the list of 'provincial governors' on the death of Muḥammad[1] need only mean that he had some share of power in Ṣanʿāʾ and that the leading man there, Fayrūz ad-Daylamī, was on friendly terms with Medina. Whatever view we take of the details, it is clear that the progress of Islam here was bound up with successful intervention in local quarrels.

Somewhat similar is the story of al-Ashʿath b. Qays of Kindah and Wāʾil b. Ḥujr, a *qayl* or prince of the Ḥaḍramawt.[2] Both claimed a certain valley, and Muḥammad supported Wāʾil; perhaps it was to placate al-Ashʿath that he arranged to marry his sister.[3] Not surprisingly al-Ashʿath tried to assert his independence of Medina on Muḥammad's death; but on the failure of his attempt he became a Muslim and was prominent in the conquests.

In the case of an-Nakhaʿ it was seen that Muḥammad apparently was ready to support the plebeians against the nobles. It is not clear whether there was a noble or patrician class elsewhere. It is possible that the 'kings' (*mulūk*) of Kindah and Hamdān and the 'princes' (*aqyāl*, plural of *qayl*) of Ḥimyar formed a separate class or caste, but it is also possible that they were simply the group of *de facto* rulers. They usually had a title beginning with Dhū or Lord, such as Dhū 'l-Kulāʿ, Lord of al-Kulāʿ. Muḥammad was frequently in contact with these men, and sometimes took the initiative. Some came to an agreement with him and were loyal during the Riddah.[4]

Sometimes Muḥammad encouraged energetic men to use force against their neighbours. One was Ṣurad b. ʿAbdallāh of the tribe of Azd Shanūʾah, who came to Muḥammad with a dozen or so men; Muḥammad put him in charge of these men and of any others of his tribe whom he could persuade to become Muslims, and gave them *carte blanche* to fight in the name of Islam against any non-Muslims in the region. Ṣurad chose to attack a fortified place called Jurash; after a month's siege he pretended to retire; the besiegers sallied out, hoping to take the withdrawing force at a disadvantage, but instead they found Ṣurad prepared for them

[1] Ṭab. 1983.
[2] IS, i/2. 71; cf. Caetani, ii/1. 326 f., with further references.
[3] Cf. p. 397 below, no. 2.
[4] Cf. IH, 955–7, 963 f.; IS, i/2. 20 (§ 11, 13), 21 (§ 15), 33 (§ 58), 64 (§ 110), 73 f. (§ 124a), 79 f. (§133), 84 (§ 142); Ṭab. 1989; *Usd*, iv. 147; *Iṣābah*, iii. p. 1004. Cf. also IS, iv/2. 115–19, early converts.

and fled with some loss. Eventually the men of Jurash came to make their peace with Muḥammad and to accept Islam.[1]

A more important example of such encouragement was Jarīr b. ʿAbdallāh of Bajīlah. Coming to Muḥammad with 150 men he accepted Islam. Then, at Muḥammad's suggestion, he attacked the town of Tabālah and destroyed the idol Dhū 'l-Khalaṣah, which was worshipped by Bajīlah, the related tribe of Khathʿam, and others. There was some fierce fighting, and much bloodshed, especially among Khathʿam, and not long afterwards the heads of Khathʿam came to offer their submission to Muḥammad.[2] Subsequently Muḥammad used Jarīr as an envoy to two of the Lords, and he was with them when Muḥammad died.[3] He was prominent among the Muslims during the Riddah and afterwards.

In various ways, then, Muḥammad was interfering 'by letter and by envoy' in the affairs of the southern tribes. Not merely factions within a tribe but whole clans and even tribes were becoming associated with Medina. This meant that they were being incorporated within what might be called the 'Medinan security system' or *Pax Islamica*. Again and again in the letters we find it stated that, if the persons addressed fulfil their obligations, they have the covenant or guarantee of security of God and His messenger (*dhimmah*, *dhimām*); this included security for their lives, goods, and rights to land.[4] Thus theoretically the whole strength of the Islamic state would be exerted against anyone who attacked those in alliance with Muḥammad. How this was accomplished in practice is not clear, since no Medinan troops were stationed in the region. We shall not be far wrong, however, in supposing that the many envoys whom Muḥammad sent to South Arabia, whatever else they may have done, saw to it that the various allies of Muḥammad helped one another against outsiders and avoided quarrels among themselves. By this means Muḥammad's guarantee of security may be presumed to have been in large measure effective.

It is worth mentioning here some accounts that have been preserved by aṭ-Ṭabarī.[5] According to these, when Bādhām, the Persian governor, and the people of the Yemen became Muslims, Muḥammad placed the whole administration of the Yemen under

[1] Ibid. i/2. 71; cf. Caetani, ii/1. 326 f., with further references.

[2] IS, i/2. 77 f.; Ibn al-Kalbī. *K. al-Aṣnām*, Cairo, 1914/1332, 34–36; IH, 56; Ṭab. 1763.

[3] IS, i/2. 20 (§ 13); Ṭab. 1989, letter from Abū Bakr.

[4] Cf. IH, 963 f.; *Usd*, iv. 147; IS, i/2, *passim*; p. 244 below.

[5] 1851–3; cf. Caetani, ii/1. 370 f.

Bādham. On the latter's death Muḥammad divided the administration among the following persons:

Shahr b. Bādhām	Ṣanʿā'.
ʿĀmir b. Shahr al-Hamdānī	Hamdān.
Abū Mūsā 'l-Ashʿarī	Ma'rib.
Khālid b. Saʿīd	between Najrān, Rimaʿ, and Zabīd.
aṭ-Ṭāhir b. Abī Hālah	ʿAkk and Ashʿar.
Yaʿlā b. Umayyah	al-Janad.
ʿAmr b. Ḥazm	Najrān.
Ziyād b. Labīd	Ḥaḍramawt.
ʿUkkāshah b. Thawr al-Ghawthī	as-Sakāsik and as-Sakūn.
al-Muhājir b. Abī Umayyah	Muʿāwiyah b. Kindah.
Muʿādh b. Jabal	Teacher of doctrine in the Yemen and Ḥaḍramawt.

These reports are not to be accepted without severe criticism, but neither are they to be rejected as valueless. The Persian governor may not have become a Muslim—a point to be discussed later—and was almost certainly not appointed by Muḥammad to govern the Yemen in his name. There are no serious objections, however, to holding that Muḥammad entered into an agreement with Bādhām and recognized him as governor of the Yemen; in this way Bādhām would come within the 'Medinan security system'. The reports of what happened on the death of Bādhām appear to be later compilations, but again, though in need of criticism, are far from worthless. The men, apart from those already in the south, were probably really sent there by Muḥammad, but on different occasions and with different functions. Family traditions would preserve the memory of the commissioning, but would be vague about the precise duties to be performed. Some later historian would then collect the items of information and systematize them according to his understanding of the period. Scattered through our sources are many variant and supplementary accounts. Thus Khālid b. Saʿīd is said to have been sent with Farwah b. Musayk of Murād, after his acceptance of Islam, in order to supervise the *ṣadaqāt* of the tribe.[1] Abū Bakr sent al-Muhājir b. Abī Umayyah to the Yemen as a military leader,[2] and this was possibly his first appearance there; the account of his

[1] IS, i/2. 64.

[2] Ṭab. 1880.

being sent by Muḥammad added that he was ill and could not go immediately, and the modern scholar will therefore suspect that this is an attempt by his family to glorify themselves by asserting that his commission was by the prophet himself and not by his successor. Abū Sufyān b. Ḥarb is not mentioned in the lists considered, though elsewhere he is said to have been in charge of Jurash or Najrān.[1]

However much dubiety there may be about some details, there is a sufficient body of material to make it reasonably certain that Muḥammad had a number of agents or residents among the southern tribes. In this way, though he could not have had so much influence as he had in Medina, he would exercise a measure of control over the affairs of the allied tribes and clans, especially their relations to one another. In some cases, however, he seems rather to have worked through an agreement with the man already in power, such as Bādhām's son Shahr and a chief of Hamdān, ʿĀmir b. Shahr.

It also seems clear that these men were agents or residents with at most a handful of troops under them. Muḥammad seems to have calculated that, if any military force was needed, it could be supplied by his allies on the spot. Only after the outbreak of disturbances upon the murder of Shahr b. Bādhām by al-Aswad al-ʿAnsī was a military commander sent, al-Muhājir, and he did not start from Medina with a large army—no men at all are mentioned—but collected his soldiers on the way, first at Mecca and aṭ-Ṭā'if, and then by attaching to himself local leaders like Jābir b. ʿAbdallāh and Farwah b. Musayk.[2]

It may seem contrary to Muḥammad's policy of using diplomacy in this southern region that he sent out even three expeditions against it (in addition to that against Ṣudā' which was prepared but not sent owing to the conversion of the tribe in question).[3] These expeditions were small, however, and should perhaps be regarded as intended to give a slight backing to diplomatic activities. The first was of twenty men only against some Khathʿam in the neighbourhood of Tabālah in May/June 630 (ii/9). It can hardly have been due to a private grievance, since the leader was Quṭbah b. ʿĀmir, an early Medinan Muslim and head of the clan of Salimah. There is no mention of negotiations, but only of booty captured, so it may have been an unsuccessful attempt to destroy the idol

[1] Al-Balādhurī, 59; *Usd*, v. 216, iii. 12 f.; al-Yaʿqūbī, ii. 81.
[2] Ṭab. 1998.
[3] IS, i/2. 63 (§ 107).

Dhū 'l-Khalaṣah.[1] The expedition of Khālid b. al-Walīd to Najrān with 400 men in July/August 631 (iii/10) does not seem to have involved any fighting, and is said to have resulted in the conversion of the tribe. In this expedition, then, the diplomatic activity was primary, and the show of force to support that.[2] The third expedition was of 300 men in December of the same year, was directed against Madh'ḥij and Zubayd, and was commanded by 'Alī. After a slight skirmish the opponents, who must have been merely a small part of Madh'ḥij, accepted Islam. This is not a clear case of the primacy of diplomacy, but that cannot be ruled out, especially when it is remembered that in the previous year, according to the same sources, Muḥammad had put 10,000 men in the field against Mecca and taken 30,000 with him to Tabūk. The booty is a difficulty, but it is unlikely at this period of Muḥammad's life that 'Alī would have been interested in raiding for booty.[3] Thus the accounts of the expeditions make it clear that Muḥammad did not regard the south as a suitable sphere for military activity.

In one or two cases Muḥammad may have backed up his diplomatic approaches by economic inducements. Qays b. Mālik of the clan of Arḥab of Hamdān is said to have been made chief and to have been given an annual grant of raisins and grain.[4] Again, several branches of the tribe of al-Ḥārith b. Ka'b are said to have been exempted from the tithe.[5] These facts are reminiscent of similar favours given to tribes on the road to the north, apparently as a reward for standing out openly as Muslims; but the information about the southern tribes is so slight that we cannot be sure that the preferential treatment of them was for the same reasons as that of the northern tribes, especially since there was nothing in the south corresponding to the Byzantine empire. Whatever Muḥammad's reasons in the above instances, his treatment of a group from the clan of Ruhā' (of the tribe of Madh'ḥij) is to be

[1] WW, 387.

[2] IH, 958–60; WW, 417 n.; IS, i/2. 72 (§ 123). The possibility of confusion between Khālid b. al-Walīd and Khālid b. Sa'īd should not be overlooked.

[3] IH, 967 f., 999; WW, 417–21; contrast Wellhausen, *Skizzen und Vorarbeiten*, Berlin, 1899, vi. 28 f. and Caetani, ii/1. 323. In IS, i/1. 108. 26 the reference is presumably to God.

[4] IS, i/2. 73 (§ 124a). In IH, 946 Musaylimah tries to twist complimentary remarks by Muḥammad into a recognition of his prophethood.

[5] Ibid. 22 (§ 22); cf. Caetani, ii/1. 314. Contrast the 'deputation' from Tujīb (a part of Kindah) which brought *ṣadaqah* in A.H. 9 (IS, i/2. 60 f.); Tujīb was loyal during the Riddah.

explained differently. This group was granted a hundred loads of Khaybar dates annually, but such a generous provision for them was doubtless due to their settling in Medina and attaching themselves directly to Muḥammad.[1] No names are mentioned in connexion with this 'deputation' of the Ruhāwīyūn, but it is probable that their leader was Mālik b. Murārah (or Murrah) ar-Ruhāwī, since he appears in various places as a trusted envoy of Muḥammad's to the southern tribes.[2]

Recent European scholars have tended to think that in his efforts to gain the support of tribes in the south and elsewhere Muḥammad was content with purely political alliances and did not make any religious demands. Many letters and treaties indeed say that the persons concerned are to perform the Worship and pay the *zakāt*; but these phrases might have been added by later editors of the text who, on the basis of their conception of the history of Muḥammad's lifetime, argued that these conditions must have been included. Though there can be no certainty about this explaining away of the wording of the texts, it is a ground for not basing any argument on these passages. On the other hand, there are passages which speak of the destruction of idols. Dhū 'l-Khalaṣah at Tabālah has already been mentioned. Others who were made to destroy their gods on accepting Islam were some men of Ḥimyar who worshipped sticks, the tribe of Khawlān, and Dhubāb of Sa'd al-'Ashīrah.[3] In certain cases, then, even if not in all, Muḥammad seems to have made religious demands.

An interesting variant is found in the story of Qays b. Salamah of the tribe of Ju'fī (a part of Madh'ḥij), a man whom Muḥammad had offered to recognize as a chief.[4] As it was the custom of these people to avoid eating the heart of animals, Muḥammad told them that their acceptance of Islam would not be perfect until they had eaten some heart. He therefore had a heart brought and roasted and despite their fears made them break this pagan taboo. Partly because of this demand and partly because the Muslims insisted that parents and ancestors who died as pagans were in Hell, Qays is said to have broken off relations with Muḥammad.

Some of the passages which have been thought to indicate that

[1] Ibid. 76 (§ 127).

[2] IH, 956 foot; IS, i/2. 20. 3. He may originally have been sent from the south to Muḥammad; cf. IH, 955; IS, i/2. 20. 8, 84. 4.

[3] Ibid. 32 (§ 56), 61 (§ 105), 74 (§ 124b).

[4] Ibid. 61 f. (§ 106, first part); cf. p. 119 above.

Muḥammad made agreements without demanding acceptance of Islam are inconclusive. In a letter to the clan of Bāriq they are to give three days' hospitality to needy Muslims passing through their lands, and a letter to the family of Dhū Marḥab speaks of the obligation of all Muslims to help them. The wording has been held to contrast the recipients with the Muslims and therefore to show that they were not Muslims.[1] The conclusion is not necessary, however. Even on the supposition that the recipients are Muslims, the letters read naturally; and there is also the possibility that they may have been Christians—and with Christians, we know, Muḥammad entered into agreements without making religious demands. These passages are thus no clear evidence of agreements with pagans where no religious demands were made. Again, the statement that at Muḥammad's death the two chiefs to whom Jarīr b. ʿAbdallāh was sent, Dhū ʿAmr and Dhū 'l-Kulāʿ, were not Muslims may merely be an inference from the fact that Jarīr was still there.[2]

With regard to the southern tribes, then, the case for holding that Muḥammad was ready to enter into alliances without making religious demands is weak. General considerations are also unfavourable to such a view. The contacts with the south were mostly during the last two years of Muḥammad's life. By that time he had broken with the Christians in the north, and was demanding, in return for the advantages of the *Pax Islamica*, either that they became Muslims or that they paid tribute. It is unlikely that he was content with something less in the south. Even if there was no Byzantine problem there to make him force a decision, there was a Persian problem, and there were many Christians. Careful scholarship, therefore, cannot sanction abandonment of the view of the earliest sources that in general those pagans who entered into agreements with Muḥammad became Muslims. The standard of performance demanded may have been low, but there was at least an attempt to root out idol-worship.

Muḥammad's treatment of the Christians of the south seems to have resembled what he did in the north; that is to say, they were allowed, while remaining Christians, to enter the sphere of the *Pax Islamica* provided they made certain payments, commonly referred to as the *jizyah* or poll-tax. There was probably a great difference, however, in the attitude of these southern Christians.

[1] Ibid. 35 (§ 70), 81 (§ 136), 21 (§ 15); Caetani, ii/1. 349, 302.
[2] Al-Bukhārī, *Maghāzī* (64), 64; cf. Wellhausen, *Skizzen*, iv. 106, n. 2.

In the north Christianity was linked with support of the Byzantine empire; but in the south the Christians, after half a century of support from the monophysite Christians of Abyssinia (from about 525 to 575), had fallen into the hands of Persians, and the Persian empire was officially Zoroastrian, had political ties with the Jews of the Yemen, and tended to support the East Syrian or Nestorian form of Christianity against the monophysite. Though the Christians of Najrān are thought to have been Nestorians by the beginning of the seventh century,[1] they could not have been so firmly attached to Persia as the northern Christians to Byzantium. Moreover, their negotiations with Muḥammad did not begin until 630; and in February 628 the Persian emperor had been assassinated and the empire, after the exhausting war with the Byzantines, had begun to show signs of collapse. There was thus no strong reason why the Christians of the south should not accept any fair offer made by Muḥammad.

We have a certain amount of information about the main group of Christians, those of the town of Najrān (who are themselves also sometimes called 'Najrān' as if it were a tribal name). They lived among the tribe of al-Ḥārith b. Kaʿb, most of whom were probably pagans, though Muḥammad addressed a letter to 'the bishop of Banū 'l-Ḥārith b. Kaʿb and the bishops of Najrān'.[2] A 'deputation' came to Muḥammad from the people of Najrān led by the three most important men of the community, the *ʿāqib* (or 'lieutenant', presumably the civil governor), who was of the tribe of Kindah and was called ʿAbd al-Masīḥ, the bishop, who was Abū 'l-Ḥārith b. ʿAlqamah of the tribe of Rabīʿah, and a third named as-Sayyid b. al-Ḥārith (though as-Sayyid, 'the master', may be a title, and the latter part may mean that he belonged to the tribe of al-Ḥārith). A treaty of peace was made in which it was agreed that Muḥammad would not interfere with their ecclesiastical affairs or property, that the people of Najrān would make an annual payment of 2,000 garments of stipulated value, and that they would become allies of the Muslims and receive protection.[3] In the case of war they were to lend the Muslims 30 suits of mail, 30 horses, and 30 camels,

[1] Tor Andrae, *Die Ursprung des Islams und das Christentum*, Upsala, 1926, ch. i, § 1 (p. 169 f. in *Kyrkohist. Årsskrift*, 1923).

[2] Cf. Excursus F, no. 16.

[3] IS, i/2, 84 f. (§ 143), 21 (§ 14), 35 f. (§ 72); the two latter are translated in Excursus F, nos. 16, 17. Cf. IH, 957. 1.

but there seems to be no question of their taking part themselves in fighting.

From a letter of Muḥammad's to some of the local rulers which tells them to pay *ṣadaqah* and *jizyah* to his agents, it may be concluded that there were Christians in the towns who did not become Muslims, but we have no means of estimating their numbers.[1] The instructions which Muḥammad is alleged to have given to ʿAmr b. Ḥazm when sending him to Najrān state that a Jew or Christian who becomes a Muslim is to have the full rights and duties of a believer, whereas those who retain their Christianity or Judaism are to be left alone but to be liable for a *jizyah* of a *dīnār* per person; for various reasons—the chief being the existence of a much shorter version—it is likely that these instructions have been greatly altered and expanded in the course of transmission, and now reflect the practice of a later period than Muḥammad's lifetime.[2] Many certainly remained Christians and were removed to ʿIrāq in the caliphate of ʿUmar b. al-Khaṭṭāb. Some, however, became Muslims; of the members of the 'deputation' from Najrān the *ʿāqib* and as-Sayyid are said to have returned to Medina shortly afterwards and made their profession of faith: and some at least of the last 'deputation' to come to Muḥammad, one of 200 men from an-Nakhaʿ, a branch of Madh'ḥij, appear to have been Christians.[3]

It remains to consider the attitude towards Muḥammad of the Persian element in the Yemen. This may best be done in connexion with the rising of al-Aswad b. Kaʿb of ʿAns (a part of the tribe of Madh'ḥij), known as Dhū 'l-Khimār, the 'man of the veil'. There are discrepancies in the sources, but the following may serve as a general account. On the death of the Persian governor in Ṣanʿā' about 631/10 al-Aswad took up arms against his son Shahr, who succeeded him, defeated him in battle, and killed him. Shortly afterwards he entered Ṣanʿā'. Though al-Aswad was supreme commander, he was in uneasy alliance with various other groups, and the leaders of these, notably Qays b. al-Makshūḥ of Murād and Dādhawayh who commanded the men of Persian descent, were partly independent and had considerable influence. Within a month or two, however, it was clear that al-Aswad was unable to

[1] IS, i/2. 20. 7; cf. IH, l.c.

[2] IH, 961 f.; cf. Abū Yūsuf, *K. al-Kharāj*, Bulāq (1885)/1302, 40 f. (tr. E. Fagnan, Paris, 1921, 108); and Caetani, ii/1. 317–19.

[3] IS, i/2. 77 (§ 129).

hold the alliance together. A plot was formed against him, and he was assassinated by Qays. These events are usually known as the first Riddah in the Yemen, and are distinguished from the second Riddah under the leadership of Qays.[1]

It is unlikely that the movement of al-Aswad had as its basis the (merely conjectural) local Arab feeling against the Persians, since under him, despite the death of Shahr, they were able to maintain themselves in Ṣanʿāʾ; only with the rise of Qays do they seem to have fled. Indeed the reports say nothing of any ideological foundation for al-Aswad's movement apart from his employing divinatory and magical practices, and he does not seem to have made a serious claim to be a prophet. Thus his activities are best interpreted as the attempts of one Arab chief to improve his position at the expense of his neighbours. The Persians, who in the sources are referred to as 'the sons', al-Abnāʾ, had Arab mothers and had doubtless become assimilated to the surrounding Arabs, so that for most purposes they could be regarded as being on an equal footing with the other groups contending for power. Whatever support they may have been receiving from Persia before 628, after that date there could be no hope of further reinforcements or subsidies. The knowledge of the internal weakness of the Persian empire may have prompted al-Aswad's attack.

The sources do not permit us to say whether the Abnāʾ had retained something of the official Zoroastrianism, or had adopted the Arab paganism of their mothers or even Nestorian Christianity. Whatever their religious views, however, they must have been perturbed at the downfall of the Persian empire, and ready to follow a leader who seemed able to give political and religious stability. Thus the Persians, more than anyone else in the Yemen, would be open to Muḥammad's propaganda. It is therefore not improbable that Bādhām, the Persian governor, and his son entered into agreements with Muḥammad, though these were doubtless of a purely political character. Nor is it improbable that, even before the rising of al-Aswad, a prominent member of the Abnāʾ, Fayrūz (b.) ad-Daylamī, should have been attracted to Islam. It seems to have been immediately obvious that al-Aswad was hostile to Islam. At least Muḥammad sent an agent or agents to the Abnāʾ, and these now came over to his side and made a formal profession of

[1] IH, 964; al-Balādhurī, 106 f.; Ṭab. 1745–99, 1853–68; Caetani, ii/1. 672–85; Wellhausen, *Skizzen*, vi. 26 ff.

faith as Muslims. It is difficult, however, to say to what extent Muḥammad's agents were responsible for the conspiracy which got rid of al-Aswad. Despite one or two statements in the sources which seem to imply the opposite, Qays b. al-Makshūḥ probably had no understanding with Muḥammad, since he is never explicitly said to have professed Islam, or even to have visited Medina until after his capture by the troops of Abū Bakr. The flight of the Abnā' from him would thus be due not to anti-Persian feeling on his part but to his opposition to Muḥammad and Islam. Fayrūz fled to the tribe of Khawlān, to which he was related, and which remained loyal to the Muslim cause throughout the Riddah.[1] The statement that al-Muhājir b. Abī Umayyah was sent 'to deal with the forces of (al-Aswad) al-ʿAnsī and to help the Abnā' against Qays b. al-Makshūḥ'[2] seems to indicate that the Abnā' had a key position in Muslim strategy in the Yemen.

The death of al-Aswad is said to have taken place a few days before that of Muḥammad. Qays, with the support of ʿAmr b. Maʿdīkarib of Zubayd, continued the anti-Muslim movement; but the two soon quarrelled with one another and fell into the hands of al-Muhājir. This collapse of the second Riddah on the appearance of a Muslim force that was not large and was perhaps mainly from the local tribes, shows that the greater part of the population apart from Christians and Jews was now Muslim, while the Christians and Jews were in alliance with Muḥammad. According to modern European ideas the conversions may have been nominal, but the religious element was present; and, to adapt the words of a Muslim tradition, we are unable to split open men's hearts to discover how far their belief in Islam was genuine.

6. THE TRIBES IN THE REST OF ARABIA

Mahrah. If we now consider the remaining tribes of Arabia geographically, starting in the south-east and moving northwards, we come first to the tribe of Mahrah. Here two groups seem to have become Muslims,[3] but they were probably small, for in the fighting of the Riddah we find that there were two factions in the tribe, neither of which was Muslim.[4] The persons who became Muslims

[1] Ṭab. 1991; but cf. al-Balādhurī, 100 and Caetani, ii/1. 604, expedition against Khawlān.

[2] Ṭab. 1880.

[3] IS, i/2. 34 (§ 67), 83 (§ 141).

[4] Ṭab. 1980–2.

are mentioned in connexion with the fighting. Remoteness from Medina doubtless explains the slightness of the contact.

Azd ʿUmān. Remoteness also helps to explain the form of the movement towards and away from Islam in ʿUmān and al-Baḥrayn. In ʿUmān, where a section of the tribe of Azd was dominant, the prince and his brother, Jayfar and ʿAbbād (or ʿAbd) sons of al-Julundā, seem to have approached Muḥammad of their own accord. He sent ʿAmr b. al-ʿĀṣ to negotiate with them. Jayfar hesitated to relinquish sovereignty to the extent demanded by Muḥammad, but was eventually persuaded by his brother to accept the terms offered. ʿAmr thereupon assumed certain judicial functions and control of the *ṣadaqah*, collecting this last from the rich and giving it to the poor.[1] This seems to show that there was social unrest in ʿUmān, though it is difficult to be certain about the precise form it took. The growing confusion in Persia may have had something to do with it. Even with the measures of ʿAmr b. al-ʿĀṣ, however, and the accession of other groups belonging to Azd ʿUmān,[2] the Muslim party was weak. On the death of Muḥammad, ʿAmr returned to Medina while Jayfar and ʿAbbād took to the mountains; the anti-Muslim forces—perhaps mainly the nomadic element[3]— found a leader in Laqīṭ b. Mālik, and were only defeated and brought into subjection when a Muslim army from outside ʿUmān was able to join the local Muslims.[4]

ʿAbd al-Qays. The Muslim party in al-Baḥrayn was relatively stronger than that in ʿUmān, if we may judge from the course of the Riddah in these two places. Most of the Arabs of al-Baḥrayn belonged to the tribe of ʿAbd al-Qays, but there were also some from Bakr b. Wāʾil and Tamīm. Moreover the population included Persians, Christians, and Jews. A number of separate groups were in touch with Medina, and some seem to have taken the lead in approaching Muḥammad.[5] Unfortunately many of the details that have been preserved are obscure. We do not know the relation of the settlement of Hajar to that of al-Baḥrayn, and thus do not understand the relation of the 'master' (*ṣāḥib*) of the one to the 'master' of the other. The most likely hypothesis is that these two and also al-Mundhir b. Sāwā, the chief local supporter of Muḥammad during his lifetime, were Arab rulers in the Persian interest

[1] IS, i/2. 18 (§ 8). [2] Ibid. 80 (§ 134); cf. 23 (§ 25), 30 (§ 49).
[3] Cf. Wellhausen, *Skizzen*, vi. 24–26. [4] Ṭab. 1976–80, &c.
[5] IS, i/2. 19 (§ 9), 27 (§ 41, 42), 32 f. (§ 57), 54 (§ 98); cf. Caetani, ii/1. 193–206; Wellhausen, *Skizzen*, vi.

and with support from Persia. They may have been Christians like the king of Ḥīrah who dealt with the Arabs on behalf of the Persian emperor; at least al-Jārūd b. Muʿallā, who rallied the loyal party during the Riddah, had been originally a Christian;[1] and a letter to al-Mundhir b. Sāwā telling him how to deal with Magians and Jews implies that arrangements had already been made for the Christians, and thus suggests that al-Mundhir himself was a Christian.[2] Once again it was probably the threatened break-up of the Persian empire that caused these men to appeal to Muḥammad, even though their distance from Medina made it difficult for him to give them any military help.

The 'deputation' from ʿAbd al-Qays is said to have come to Medina in the year of the conquest of Mecca, 630/8, and is thus one of the first 'deputations'.[3] In the two years or so between the coming of the 'deputation' and Muḥammad's death, things went far from smoothly in al-Baḥrayn; the pro-Muslim movement had its ups and downs, and there even seems to have been some apostasy. The absence of military support from Medina must have made things difficult for Muḥammad's agents in the area, of whom the chief was al-ʿAlā' b. al-Ḥaḍramī, a Meccan confederate. The difficulties came to a head with the death of al-Mundhir b. Sāwā, which occurred about the same time as that of Muḥammad. Muḥammad's death probably affected the politics of al-Baḥrayn only indirectly; with powerful anti-Muslim leaders between them and Medina the local anti-Muslim party thought the opportunity had come to set up an independent principality. The military leader was al-Ḥuṭam b. Ḍubayʿah of the tribe of Bakr b. Wā'il, but the plan was to set up a scion of the royal house of al-Ḥīrah as prince or king. The Muslim party was rallied by al-Jārūd, as already mentioned, but it was not strong enough to deal with its opponents until al-ʿAlā' brought an army from outside.

Ḥanīfah. More is recorded about the tribe of Ḥanīfah than about some other tribes, but it is difficult to wrest a coherent picture from the material. The crucial question is the relation to one another of the four individuals or groups who were in contact of some sort with Muḥammad, namely, Hawdhah, Thumāmah, the members of the 'deputation', and Musaylimah. One of the letters

[1] IS, i/2. 54. 21. [2] Ibid. 19 (§ 9).

[3] Ibid. 54 (§ 98); the group who came to Medina for corn in June 625 (i/4) were presumably not from al-Baḥrayn but from ar-Rawḥā' near Medina; IH, 590; WW, 150 f.; cf. ibid. 176 f.

which Muḥammad despatched on his return from al-Ḥudaybiyah was to Hawdhah b. ʿAlī of Ḥanīfah.[1] Hawdhah was possibly the strongest man in central Arabia at this time. He was allied to the Persians, and was responsible for the safety of their caravans on a certain section of the route from the Yemen to Persia. From the latter fact it may be inferred that, though most of Ḥanīfah lived by agriculture, Hawdhah belonged to the nomadic section of the tribe. He was hostile to Tamīm, especially to the sub-tribe of Saʿd. In religion he was probably a Christian like many members of Ḥanīfah.[2] The sources imply that Muḥammad's letter to him was a summons to become a Muslim, and he is said to have replied that, provided he was given a share in the control of affairs, he would become a Muslim. This may or may not have been the real tenor of the letters. Hawdhah apparently gave a friendly reception to Muḥammad's envoy but did not become a Muslim. He is said to have died in 630/8.

Of the second man, Thumāmah b. Uthāl, stories are told of how he was captured by the Muslims in an expedition and won to Islam by Muḥammad's kind treatment.[3] There seem to be no good grounds for denying that he was a Muslim, or at least favourably inclined towards Islam, by about 631/10. Shortly before his death, as portents of the coming storm became visible, Muḥammad sent out envoys to various friendly leaders; and one of these envoys was to Thumāmah.[4] Thumāmah thereupon became leader of the Muslims among Ḥanīfah and played a useful part in the Riddah.[5] What is puzzling is that Ibn Hishām speaks of Muḥammad writing to Thumāmah and Hawdhah, 'the two kings of the Yamāmah'.[6] If they were kings at the same time, but of different sections of the tribe, then Thumāmah was presumably much inferior in power. If, on the other hand, this is taken to imply that Thumāmah succeeded Hawdhah, then he was far from succeeding to all his influence, since most of the tribe followed Musaylimah. It is conceivable that Thumāmah was leader of the nomadic part of the tribe and would have inherited Hawdhah's position as Persian agent, had Persia not been in disintegration.

Thirdly, there are the members of the 'deputation' which went to Medina and made profession of Islam.[7] The leader was Salmā

[1] IS, i/2. 18 (§ 7); IH, 971.
[2] Caussin de Perceval, ii. 404–8, 575–8.
[3] IH, 996.
[4] Ṭab. 1798.
[5] Ibid. 1910 f., 1916, 1962, 1971.
[6] 971.
[7] IS, i/2. 55 (§ 101).

b. Ḥanẓalah, and one of the members was ar-Raḥḥāl (or Nahār ar-Rajjāl) b. ʿUnfuwah, who was later the most prominent supporter of Musaylimah. Musaylimah himself is said to have been one of the 'deputation', but to have looked after the camels and baggage and not to have seen Muḥammad; his name was perhaps included in the report because an alleged remark about him by Muḥammad was used by his followers to show that Muḥammad regarded him as a prophet;[1] it may be assumed, then, that Musaylimah was not one of the 'deputation'. We now come to the difficulties. Was the deputation sent by Hawdhah or Thumāmah? Or did they come of their own accord? The latter seems most likely, and the visit would presumably be after the death of Hawdhah; in this case these were probably the leading men of at least the non-nomadic part of the tribe. The situation about 631, with Hawdhah dead and Persia in decline, would incline them to seek support from Medina. Everything suggests that at the time of the 'deputation' Musaylimah had not yet set himself up as a prophet, or at least had not won any appreciable following.

In the fourth place comes Musaylimah himself, the so-called 'false prophet'. About the end of the year 10 (beginning of 632) Musaylimah is said to have written to Muḥammad as one prophet to another, and to have suggested that they divide the land between them; Muḥammad's alleged reply was a denial of Musaylimah's claim to be a prophet.[2] Even if this story has been touched up, there may well have been some attempt at negotiation. Certainly Musaylimah seems to have come forward before Muḥammad's death as leader of a political and religious movement. The religious aspect appears to have been genuine, and it is natural to suppose that Musaylimah had been interested in religious matters for many years, and had perhaps been some sort of preacher. It has been suggested[3] that Musaylimah was earlier than Muḥammad in his claim to prophethood. The opponents of Muḥammad are said to have alleged that he received his revelations from 'a man in the

[1] IS, i/2. 55 (§ 101); Ṭab. 1932, 1941; cf. IH, 946.

[2] IH, 965; IS, i/2. 25 f. (§ 33).

[3] D. G. Margoliouth, 'On the Origin and Import of the Names Muslim and Ḥanīf', *Journal of the Royal Asiatic Society*, 1903, esp. 485 ff.; contrast C. J. Lyall, 'The Words "Ḥanīf" and "Muslim"', ibid. 771–84; cf. F. Buhl, art. 'Musailima' in EI (1). There are no grounds for holding that the diminutive form is derisive; diminutives were regularly used as ordinary names, e.g. Khuwaylid, Khadījah's father. The same holds of Ṭulayḥah. In *M/Mecca*, 29. 1, the words 'Maslamah or' should be deleted.

Yamāmah called ar-Raḥmān';[1] and this presumably refers to Musaylimah who, though receiving revelations from ar-Raḥmān, the Merciful (that is, God), was himself called ar-Raḥmān.[2] General considerations, however, are against the view that Musaylimah was active during Muḥammad's Meccan period: had it been widely known that he was a prophet, the fact would have been used by Muḥammad's opponents as an argument against him. It seems more likely that the allegation that Muḥammad was taught by 'a man in the Yamāmah called ar-Raḥmān' and even the attribution of the name ar-Raḥmān to Musaylimah belong to the anti-Muslim propaganda of Musaylimah's followers, basing themselves on the use of the name in the Qur'ān and its special association with the Yamāmah.[3] Al-Wāqidī's story implying that Musaylimah was known as ar-Raḥmān before the Hijrah is doubtful since it contradicts other reports.[4] It is safest, then, to assume that, whatever Musaylimah's past religious practices and experiences may have been, he did not attain any wide public notice in his own tribe, still less beyond it, until after the death of Hawdhah.

The Muslim sources, though tending to blacken Musaylimah, have preserved some genuine details of his teaching. He employed *saj'*, rhythmic prose with rhyme or assonance, as in the earlier passages of the Qur'ān. He insisted on uprightness of life, and taught the doctrines of resurrection and Divine judgement based on what a man has done during his life. Formal prayers three times a day and fasting were prescribed. A sanctuary or sacred territory was instituted in the Yamāmah.[5] Most interesting is a passage in which, after an oath which refers to various operations of an agricultural people such as sowing, reaping, milling, and baking, he says, 'You are preferred to the people of the tents (*wabar*), and the people of the villages (*madar*) are not before you.'[6] The last two clauses simply mean 'no one is superior to you',[7] but the oath and the following injunction to defend their fields (*rīf*) seem to make it clear that Musaylimah's hearers consisted mainly of agriculturists.

[1] IH, 200.
[2] WW, 58; Ṭab. 1935. 14; cf. Caetani, ii/1. 641, n. 1.
[3] IS, i/1. 108. 26, as a name of God presumably.
[4] WW, 58 gives 'Abd ar-Raḥmān's original name as 'Abd 'Amr, whereas IS, i/1. 88 gives 'Abd Ka'bah.
[5] Ṭab. 1916 f., 1930–5; cf. Caetani, ii/1. 636–40.
[6] Ṭab. 1934.
[7] Cf. Lane, *s.v. madar* (p. 2698).

From the points just mentioned and some similar ones (like the use of the phrase 'kingdom of heaven', *mulk as-samā*),[1] and from the fact that there was much Christianity among Ḥanīfah, it is clear that Musaylimah had been largely influenced by Christianity, especially by some ascetic trends. If we remember that the rapid spread of his movement took place about 630 after the death of Hawdhah and when no more help from Persia could be looked for, it is further clear that Musaylimah's teaching was attempting to provide a religious and intellectual basis for a principality centred in the Yamāmah and independent of Persia, Byzantium, and Medina. A curious regulation to the effect that a man was not to have intercourse with any woman so long as he had a son alive was perhaps intended to deal with the economic basis of this principality;[2] the disappearance of the trade between the Yemen and Persia had perhaps affected the Yamāmah adversely.

Musaylimah was thus no mere imitator of Muḥammad, since he was dealing with a different problem, and in matters of detail was possibly more influenced by the local Christianity than by Muḥammad. The idea, however, of a state or political system whose head was a prophet does seem to have come from Medina; perhaps it suggested itself to ar-Raḥḥāl as he meditated on what he had seen during his visit to Medina with the 'deputation'. Whether the idea first came to ar-Raḥḥāl or to Musaylimah himself, the setting on foot of propaganda and the spread of the movement must have started soon after the return of the 'deputation'. Some members of the 'deputation', though probably not all, abandoned Islam for the new movement. We do not know sufficient about it to say whether, had it been successful in battle against the Muslims, it could have produced an organization of the Arabs comparable to that of Islam; there is no mention of the 'holy war' in the teaching of Musaylimah, and that was part of the necessary economic basis of Arab unity and the ideological ground for Arab expansion. Though Musaylimah is said to have been skilful in handling men, there is nothing to suggest that he was Muḥammad's equal in breadth of vision and far-sightedness; on the other hand, he was not unaware of the political realities of the time, and must not be regarded as a mere fanatic or visionary. The most serious challenge which the nascent caliphate had to face came from Musaylimah's movement. So far as concerns the life of Muḥammad, however,

[1] Ṭab. 1917. 2. [2] Ibid. 4 ff.

all that needs to be noted is the appearance of this movement and its attraction for most of Ḥanīfah.

Tamīm. The tribe of Tamīm was scattered over the region between the Yamāmah and the town of al-Ḥīrah, and some branches of it were in close relations with the latter. Many members of the tribe were Christians of the East Syrian (or Nestorian) church. Though there were settlements in this region, it has been suggested that these were peopled by other tribes and that Tamīm was mainly nomadic.[1]

The first convert from Tamīm was al-Aqraʿ b. Ḥābis, who with ten men joined Muḥammad on his way to the conquest of Mecca. Muḥammad treated him with great respect and gave him a hundred camels at al-Jiʿrānah. Later events give the impression that al-Aqraʿ was not one of the leading men of Tamīm; perhaps the respectful treatment was intended to make ʿUyaynah b. Ḥiṣn of Ghaṭafān jealous or to win over other members of Tamīm. The acceptance of Islam by al-Aqraʿ may not have been until some time after al-Jiʿrānah; it is sometimes connected with a curious story about a contest of eloquence and poetry to which some men of Tamīm challenged Muḥammad.[2]

The story of the contest is given separately in Ibn Hishām, but al-Wāqidī and Ibn Saʿd link it up with an expedition led by ʿUyaynah b. Ḥiṣn. In April 630 (the beginning of the year 9) Muḥammad sent out men to collect the *ṣadaqāt*. The envoy to B. Kaʿb of Khuzāʿah was well received by that tribe, but a small section of Tamīm who lived among them were refractory and refused to pay, and ʿUyaynah was allowed to go after them and punish them; some half-dozen men of Tamīm were killed, and about fifty men, women, and children taken captive to Medina. A 'deputation' of important men at Tamim came to ask for their release. This incident raises many questions. How did a section of Tamīm come to be so far from the usual haunts of the tribe? They must have been near Mecca, even if still to the north-east of it.[3]

[1] Caetani, ii/1. 218 f., &c.; WW, 386 n.; H. Charles, *Le Christianisme des arabes nomades sur le Limes et dans le désert syro-mésopotamien aux alentours de l'Hégire*, Paris, 1936, 55, 60 f.

[2] IH, 877–83 (expedition), 933–8 (contest), 985; WW, 327, 376, 385 f.; for the contest cf. IS, i/2. 40 (§ 78) and *Usd*, i. 119–22 (wrongly so numbered instead of 107–10).

[3] Various connexions of Tamīm with Quraysh are recorded: Asmā bint Mukharribah, the mother of Abū Jahl, ʿAyyāsh, &c. was of Tamīm, and also the mother of Firās b. an-Naḍr (IS, iv/1. *s.v.* ʿAyyāsh, Firās); Abū Jahl had a

Were they Muslims? If (as seems likely) they were not, why were they liable for the payment of camels to Medina? Was it because they were temporarily reckoned with Khuzāʿah, as being under their protection? Finally, did the poetical and rhetorical contest take place at the same time as the discussions concerning the captives?

The answer to the last question is probably in the negative, but it is not in itself important. What is important is to know which of the leading men of Tamīm became Muslims, if any. Ibn Hishām's list of those at the contest is practically identical with the list given by al-Wāqidī. The most important names are ʿUṭārid b. Ḥājib (the orator), az-Zibriqān b. Badr (the poet), Qays b. ʿĀṣim, and al-Aqraʿ b. Ḥābis. Of these only the last two appear in Ibn Hisham's list of those who came to negotiate about the prisoners; the others in this list are different from those in the previous list, the most influential being Sabrah b. ʿAmr. Apart from the names it is to be noted that while in Ibn Hishām the members of the 'deputation' at the contest become Muslims after it, in al-Wāqidī and Ibn Saʿd there is no mention of this; a late writer, Ibn al-Athīr, speaks of only al-Aqraʿ making the profession of faith.[1] Were this all, it might be possible to harmonize the different accounts as they stand; but another piece of evidence forces us to be very sceptical about the conversions. This is that towards the end of Muḥammad's life the persons responsible for the *ṣadaqāt* of Tamīm were Mālik b. Nuwayrah, az-Zibriqān b. Badr, Qays b. ʿĀṣim, and perhaps one or two others.[2] Now Mālik b. Nuwayrah is not mentioned as a member of any 'deputation' or as having become a Muslim, but it is not credible that he should have been omitted had he been present, as he seems to have been the leading man of the tribe; the collectors of *ṣadaqāt* for Tamīm are indeed no other than the chiefs of the various sections.[3] Since Mālik thus is almost certainly a non-

confederate, Yazīd b. ʿAbdallāh, from Tamīm (IH, 509; cf. WW, 82); the father of Saʿīd b. ʿAmr, a confederate of Sahm, was of Tamīm (IS, iv/1, 144). These do not explain the presence of some Tamīm near Mecca, though they may be the outcome of it.

[1] *Usd*, l.c.

[2] IH, 965; Ṭab. 1750, 1908 f.

[3] The following are named as leaders in Ṭab. 1910 f. (Caetani, ii/1. 628 ff.; variants in Caussin de Perceval, ii. 461–3):

Subdivisions of tribe		*Chief leader*	*Other leaders*
ar-Ribāb	—Ḍabbah:	az-Zibriqān b. Badr	ʿAbdallāh b. Ṣafwān
	—ʿAbd Manāt:	„	ʿIṣmah b. Ubayr

Muslim, the same must be true of az-Zibriqān and Qays b. 'Āṣim. From this we may conclude that, if they took part in a 'deputation' to Medina, they did not become Muslims but only reached some understanding with Muḥammad, presumably an alliance and an agreement that they were to pay *ṣadaqāt*.

What exactly happened during the Riddah among Tamīm is obscure, partly because one of the chief authorities, Sayf b. 'Umar, belonged to Tamīm and is thought to have covered up the extent of his tribe's apostasy, and partly because the enemies of Khālid b. al-Walīd have twisted the stories to blacken him. The focus is a woman called Sajāḥ who claimed to be a prophetess. Her father was of Tamīm, but her mother came from the largely Christian tribe of Taghlib farther to the north; Sajāḥ may have lived for some time among Taghlib, and in any case was probably a Christian. Her claim to receive revelations was probably subsequent to that of Musaylimah and Ṭulayḥah, but may have been advanced before Muḥammad's death. She had military support from followers not of Tamīm, and at first many of the chiefs of her own tribe, such as Mālik b. Nuwayrah, were friendly towards her. The main result of her appearance, however, was to stir up strife between the various subdivisions of Tamīm. Some of the parts of which she had fallen foul met her private army in battle and defeated it. After this her star rapidly waned. She moved towards the Yamāmah, perhaps seeking protection rather than a fresh world to conquer, while Tamīm soon made its peace with the Muslims. Mālik b. Nuwayrah was put to death by Khālid b. al-Walīd, justly, it would seem, for he was the most compromised in the affair of Sajāḥ; the other leaders retained their positions.[1]

So far as Muḥammad's lifetime is concerned, then, there were probably few Muslims from Tamīm, and these not the most

Subdivisions of tribe		*Chief leader*	*Other leaders*
Sa'd b. Zayd Manāt	—'Awf:	az-Zibriqān b. Badr	'Awf b. Bilād (Jushamī)
	—al-Abnā'	,,	,,
	—Muqā'is:	Qays b. 'Āṣim	(?)'Amr b. al-Ahtam
	—al-Buṭūn:	,,	Si'r b. Khufāf
'Amr b. Tamīm	—Bahdā	Ṣafwān b. Ṣafwān	al-Ḥuṣayn b. Niyār (also over ar-Ribāb)
	—Khaḍḍam	Sabrah b. 'Amr	
Ḥanẓalah	—Mālik:	Wakī' b. Mālik (+'Uṭārid)	
	—Yarbū':	Mālik b. Nuwayrah.	

[1] Ṭab. 1908–15, 1925 f., &c.; cf. Caetani, ii/1. 626–35, 651–61.

important men—perhaps al-Aqraʿ b. Ḥābis, an otherwise unknown Sufyān b. al-ʿUdhayl and his family, and certainly al-Ḥutāt b. Yazīd, whom Muḥammad made a 'brother' of Muʿāwiyah b. Abī Sufyān.[1] On the other hand, nearly the whole of Tamīm seems to have entered into alliance with Muḥammad and agreed to pay *ṣadaqāt*. This state of affairs is not surprising in view of the swift growth of Muḥammad's reputation and the weakness of Persia and al-Ḥīrah. The fact that the old tribal leaders were responsible for collecting the *ṣadaqāt* confirms the belief that Tamīm was not Muslim, for this was the usual arrangement with the non-Muslim communities in later times; in this case, however, the *ṣadaqāt* may have been retained for the poor of the tribe. The tribe was not necessarily all of one religion. Christianity was probably nearest to being the official religion, but acceptance of it must have been largely nominal, and it had done little to modify the outlook and ideals of the tribesmen, which were still those of the average nomadic Arab.[2] There may have been some Magians (Zoroastrians). The presence of a vague monotheism and the absence of idol-worship were doubtless felt by Muḥammad to justify an alliance with this tribe. Their religion, whatever it may have been, did not bind them to Persia as the Christianity of the north-western tribes made them loyal to the Byzantines. On the contrary they were ready to raid the Persian domains, and thus were most suitable allies for the Muslims.

There is no mention of any distinctive teaching by Sajāḥ. Presumably the current—mainly Christian—beliefs of the tribe were taken for granted, and guidance given in practical, that is, political affairs. It is not impossible that there was an attempt to replace the Nestorian doctrines of Tamīm by the monophysite doctrines of Taghlib;[3] but we have no information about this. In any case little would be said about connexions with other Christians elsewhere, since the point of having a prophetess was to be religiously independent. While the changing social situation, with the rise of Medina and decline of Persia, favoured the progress of such a movement, Sajāḥ does not seem to have attempted to deal with social problems. In arguing from the silence of the records we perhaps do injustice to these shadowy figures. Nevertheless the impression we

[1] IS, i/2. 41 (§ 78); IH, 933 f., &c.

[2] Cf. fighting within the tribe; also IS, i/2. 56–59 (§ 192), esp. 58 foot, apparent matriarchy.

[3] Cf. Charles, op. cit. 64, 76, &c.

are given by the sources is that the affair of Sajāḥ was no more than a slight variation on the age-old intrigue of the desert. She hoped to gain some power for herself; Mālik b. Nuwayrah hoped to use her to increase his own influence. He is said to have encouraged her not to attack the Muslims but to deal with the internal affairs of the tribe; he does not seem, however, to have fought for her.

Bakr b. Wā'il and Taghlib. These two related tribes are famous in pre-Islamic history for many exploits, and especially for the fratricidal war they carried on for many years. By the time of the conquest of Mecca they were both largely monophysite Christian, at least in name.[1] Bakr had been in alliance with the kings of al-Ḥīrah for a time, but they had also been victorious against the Persians in the notable battle of Dhū Qār (about 611)[2]. The forces involved in this battle may not have been large and it may have been a skirmish rather than a regular engagement; yet it profoundly affected the attitude of the Arab tribes towards the Persians, and made them realize that in Persia there was a possible field for raids and booty. Some parts of Bakr seem to have lived sufficiently far west to be attached to the Byzantines.[3]

Records have been preserved of 'deputations' to Muḥammad from Bakr and Taghlib, and also from Shaybān, an important sub-tribe of Bakr, mainly responsible for the victory of Dhū Qār.[4] Of those mentioned by name in these records, however, none appears to have been influential. It is therefore to be concluded that no major section of Bakr or Taghlib became Muslim. All the more surprising in the light of this conclusion is the appeal of al-'Alā' b. al-Ḥaḍramī, after the initial defeat of al-Ḥuṭam in al-Baḥrayn, to 'those who remained loyal Muslims' (*man aqāma 'alā islāmi-hi*) of Bakr b. Wā'il to intercept the fugitives. These fugitives were, of course, of their own tribe; but only a small fragment of Bakr can have been involved with al-Ḥuṭam in the Riddah in al-Baḥrayn. The chiefs named as having been appealed to were 'Utaybah b. an-Nahhās, 'Āmir b. 'Abd al-Aswad, Misma', Khaṣafah at-Taymī, and al-Muthannā b. Ḥārithah ash-Shaybānī.[5] These were doubtless the chiefs of various sections of Bakr. Probably the most important already, and certainly the most important as time went on, was al-Muthannā, who played a leading part in the

[1] Charles, op. cit. 3 f.; cf. Wellhausen, *Skizzen*, iv. 156n.; Caetani, ii/1. 299.
[2] Ibid. i. 237 f.
[3] WW, 311.
[4] IS, i/2. 31 (§ 54), 55 (§ 99, 100), 56–59 (§ 102); cf. WW, 100, conversion of a man from 'Ijl, a branch of Bakr b. Wā'il.
[5] Ṭab. 1971.

conquest of 'Irāq. The silence of the earliest sources about conversion must be taken to imply that these men were not Muslims; but the appeal to them by al-'Alā' implies that they were on friendly terms with the Muslims. The statement that they 'remained loyal Muslims' is a misreading of the situation by a later historian; but the underlying fact is that they were in alliance with Medina and remained loyal to the alliance.

To go beyond this is to venture into the realms of conjecture, with little evidence to guide one. Yet the venture must be made, for the question has been raised about the relative positions of the Muslims and the eastern tribes in the alliance between them and in the advance against Persia. Were the tribes (and al-Muthannā as heir of the victors at Dhū Qār) already moving against Persia, and did Muḥammad (or Khālid after settling the Yamāmah) humbly ask to be allowed to join them? Or did the Muslims call the attention of al-Muthannā and the others to the possibilities of invading Persia? The answer lies somewhere between the two extremes. Bakr and Taghlib were in a strong position for bargaining; they were far from Medina and militarily strong. The initiative in forming the alliance must have been taken by the Muslims, presumably by Muḥammad himself towards the close of his life; and the Muslims seem to have been content with an alliance according to which Bakr and Taghlib paid no *ṣadaqah*—at least there is no mention of any payment in the earliest period. It is unlikely, however, that Bakr and Taghlib thought of more than brief raids on Persia. On the other hand, if what has been said in this chapter about Muḥammad's northern policy is sound, he had been concerned to find an outlet for the energies of the Arabs to prevent them rending one another. He had paid most attention to the route to Syria, since this was the easiest line of expansion from Medina. During the last two years of his life, however, with the great increase in the number of tribes in alliance with him or dependent on him, a second line of expansion towards 'Irāq became practicable. Doubtless it was Muḥammad who sought alliance with Bakr and Taghlib, but it was mainly his strategic conception which guided later developments.

7. THE SUCCESS OF MUḤAMMAD'S POLICY

For the historian, contemplating the events described in this chapter from his lofty eyrie, it is natural to regard as their most prominent feature the large measure of unification of the Arab tribes. It does not follow that Muḥammad and his advisers saw things in this light. The idea that the Arabs constituted a unity existed, but only in a rudimentary form. It was through the achievements of Muḥammad himself that it became more explicitly held. The word 'Arabs' is hardly to be found in pre-Islamic poetry, and the adjective 'Arabic' is said to occur first in the Qur'ān.[1] There the reference is essentially linguistic: in three passages the clear Arabic speech of the Qur'ān is contrasted with the indistinct or 'chewed' speech of the 'barbarian' or foreigner (*'ajamī*);[2] in the remaining passages where *'arabī* is used it is an attribute of the Qur'ān or refers to it.[3] Though there is no word for 'Arabs' in the Qur'ān and the form *al-a'rāb*, which does occur in some later passages, means the nomadic tribes as distinct from the Medinans and other town-dwellers, the conception of 'Arabs' as a separate ethnological or cultural unit is implicit in the use of the word 'Arabic'. The phrase 'an Arabic Qur'ān' indicates that this revelation is intended for the 'clear-speakers', and the contrast suggested to the hearers was doubtless with Abyssinians, Byzantines, Persians, and perhaps Jews. Thus, at least from about the middle of the Meccan period, the religion founded on the Qur'ān was regarded as an alternative to any of the religions of these foreigners; anti-foreign feeling had much to do with its acceptance in preference to Christianity or Judaism.

To begin with, Muḥammad thought of himself as sent to his own tribe (*qawm*), which presumably means Quraysh; but gradually, by steps which are not clearly marked in the Qur'ān, he came to see his mission as a wider one. Before the Hijrah he had summoned some members of nomadic tribes to believe in God, in addition to negotiating with the people of Medina. With the Hijrah the notion of an *ummah* or community with a religious basis became prominent. The most urgent problem of this community was the establishment of peace between the various clans of Medina. This was a problem, however, not merely in Medina but throughout Arabia, and, as Muḥammad showed himself successful in establishing the *Pax Islamica* at Medina and among the surrounding tribes, it was

[1] O. A. Farrūkh, *Das Bild des Frühislam in der arabischen Dichtung von der Hiǧra bis zum Tode des Kalifen 'Umar*, Leipzig, 1937, 128.

[2] 16. 103/105 E or D; 26. 195, 198 C; 41. 44 C?

[3] 12. 2 C; 20. 113/112 ? D; 39. 28/29 E; 41. 32 E +; 42. 7/5 E; 43. 3/2 ? C; 13. 37 DE (*ḥūkm*); 46. 12/11 DE (*lisān*).

natural that other tribes would want to take advantage of the new system. Muḥammad, too, would not be averse to extending his security system, since, if details were satisfactorily arranged, extension would lead to greater security. Presumably, then, in Muḥammad's explicit thought about what he was doing, he conceived himself as extending the Islamic community, that is, the body of those who professed Islam or who without professing Islam believed in God and had placed themselves under His protection and that of His messenger.

The whole of Muḥammad's work may be regarded as the building on religious foundations of a political, social, and economic system; and his tribal policy was merely an aspect of this. The Medinan clans which joined with the Emigrants to form the new community already had confederates both from among the Jews of Medina and from among the surrounding nomads; and from the beginning these confederates shared at least partially in the benefits of the new political system and the *Pax Islamica*. In the early years of the Medinan period Muḥammad seems to have contracted alliances with other tribes in the neighbourhood on a purely secular basis. Gradually, however, as the sphere of the *Pax Islamica* became wider and Muḥammad grew stronger, he began to demand, as conditions of alliance, belief in God and recognition of himself as prophet. After his disappointment with the nomads who failed to join the expedition of al-Ḥudaybiyah, there was a tightening up, and, from this time on, acceptance of Islam presumably also meant acknowledgement of the prophet's right to give orders to all Muslims.

It is important to realize that, when Muḥammad began to demand acceptance of Islam from some would-be allies, he did not cease to make alliances with other groups without any religious demand. No demand was made of the Meccans when he marched into their city in triumph, and many of them took part in the battle of Ḥunayn without being Muslims. The survey of tribes in this chapter has shown or suggested that, even up to the time of his death and after, there were many alliances with non-Muslims. This was normally so in the case of distant and powerful tribes. Though such allies were merely secular allies, they belonged in a sense to the *Pax Islamica* in view of current Arab ideas about alliances; they shared in its benefits and helped to maintain it.

As the new social and political system expanded, Muḥammad

must have given some thought to its economic basis. The problem thrust itself upon him with full force during the last two years of his life, but he had seen it coming. In so far as tribes entered into the *Pax Islamica* and stopped raiding one another, the population would be larger, since there would be no deaths or other losses in raids; and it would no longer be possible for a tribe, temporarily in need, to make good its deficiencies by attacking its neighbour. From the psychological standpoint also, some outlet was required for the energies which would otherwise have been spent in the razzia. If the *Pax Islamica* was to be permanent, the standard of living must be maintained; and for that a new source of wealth was required.

For a time Muḥammad may have looked to increased trade as a solution. There was some trade between Medina and Syria, but so little is said about it in the sources that it can hardly have been important. When Mecca came under his rule, even if its former trade had been restored and extended, it would not have been sufficient to satisfy the demands of the multitudes who now looked to Muḥammad as leader. Besides there was the danger that trade would foster the false religious attitude that had been the fault of the pagan Meccans. So Muḥammad felt that trade was not the solution.

Another possibility was booty from non-Muslims. In the early Medinan years this meant a lot to the Muslims, especially the Emigrants; just how much it meant to them is difficult to say. It was doubtless love of booty that made many men come to Medina and attach themselves to Muḥammad. In a sense this was the solution Muḥammad chose, but a further refinement was necessary. As the numbers of Muslims grew, and the number of prosperous non-Muslims within easy reach decreased, raiding of the traditional type became more difficult. If the whole of Arabia were to become Muslim, only on the northern frontier would raiding be possible. It is one of the great statesmanlike insights of Muḥammad that at a comparatively early period he conceived of the *Pax Islamica* as embracing all or most of the Arabs, and consequently being forced to expand northward. This insight governed his tribal policy. His first aim was to see that the members of his community and those in alliance with them enjoyed a high degree of security for life and property both from enemies without and enemies within. After that, however, his chief effort was to increase his influence along the road to Syria. In the closing years he also seems to have cultivated the friendship of the tribes in the direction of ʿIrāq. In contrast with this he seems to have done little to spread Islam in the south and south-east of Arabia. Though he did not refuse any prospective Muslims there, he may have looked on them more as an embarrassment than an asset—more people to provide for!

Such, then, are the general lines of Muḥammad's tribal policy. It remains to consider the two questions about the extent of political relationship to Medina and the relative importance of political and religious aspects. Let us start with the second question.

If we are to understand the relative importance of religious and non-religious motives in the conversion of seventh-century Arabs to Islam, we must get rid of the current Western idea that politics and religion exist in separate compartments, and we must not expect emotional conversions of the type described by William James. From the exodus of the Israelites from Egypt, through Old Testament times, through New Testament times, through the patristic period with its sects, and down to the present day, religion and politics in the Middle East have always been closely linked with one another. And even if the Muslim had had abnormal experiences at his conversion (as some perhaps had), he would have lacked words in Arabic to describe his inner states, and would not have been sufficiently interested in them to make the effort to describe them.

Islam provided an economic, social, and political system, the *Pax Islamica*. Of this system religion was an integral part; it may be called the ideological aspect of the system. The peace and security given by the system were 'the security of God and of His messenger'. We have just seen how, latterly, in appropriate cases Muḥammad insisted on acceptance of the religious basis. This became specially necessary in the north-west when the Christian tribes there showed clearly that they preferred to remain allies of the Byzantines. Now the Islamic system attracted men of the nomadic tribes in various ways. It offered an adequate livelihood, mainly by booty. It did not involve subjection to a distant potentate; all Muslims were in principle equal, and the prophet treated his followers with the courtesy and respect shown by a nomadic chief to his fellow tribesmen. And when the Byzantine and Persian empires showed signs of disintegrating and men needed 'something firm to hold on to', the Islamic community promised to have the requisite stability.

The nomads who felt attracted to the new system did not ask themselves how far their motives were religious and how far secular. For the most part they thought of the system as a whole and did not analyse it. They were no doubt ready, however, to bargain with Muḥammad to try to get him to remit some of the more irksome conditions. Contributions to Medina, under whatever name, were one disagreeable item. But to some at least it was disagreeable to acknowledge Muḥammad as prophet for the non-religious reason that this was tantamount to promising to obey him. Thus, apart from details of one's treaty with Muḥammad, the essential question came to be whether to enter the Islamic system or to remain outside it. Moreover, after the battle of Ḥunayn the necessity for a decision on this question was thrust upon most of the Arabs; and with that came a material reason for accepting Islam quickly—early application for admission to the system gave some advantage over one's rivals. It is not surprising, then, that after the conquest of Mecca and victory over Hawāzin there should have been a 'mass-movement' towards Islam. In the religious sphere it often happens that seed which has apparently been lying dormant in men's hearts suddenly by a change of circumstances finds conditions suitable for its germination; and when the circumstances are common to many men, conversions are widespread.[1] In politics there is the familiar phenomenon of 'the rush to get on the band-wagon'.

There is thus nothing surprising or impossible about a mass movement into the Islamic community in the ninth and tenth years of the Hijrah; and consequently there is no justification for rejecting outright the statements in the sources because they tend to glorify Muḥammad. It may, in European analytical terms, be primarily a political movement, but in the integral reality of the events the religious and political factors were inseparable. To this movement the Riddah was a reaction. It was not the mere revival of anything old, whether paganism or pro-Byzantine or pro-Persian Christianity. It doubtless had roots in these religious systems, but

[1] Cf. R. Oliver, *The Missionary Factor in East Africa*, London, 1952, 182–90, an instance of how a religious movement with political and other secular consequences, after a period of slow growth, rapidly expanded in a year or two.

the reaction of pagan or Christian Arabs to the new circumstances created by the growth of the Islamic community produced something new. Moreover, as in the movement towards Islam, so in the Riddah religious and political factors were inseparably mixed with one another.[1] The Muslim historians were therefore right in regarding it as a religious movement; it was European scholars who erred by taking 'religion' in a European and not an Arab sense. The Riddah was a movement away from the religious, social, economic, and political system of Islam, and so was anti-Islamic.

It is worth remarking that, although we speak of *the* Riddah, there were over half a dozen separate movements. One may have got some ideas from another, but they were essentially distinct. They have their unity from being all parts of the reaction of Arabia to Muḥammad, but each had its peculiar character. In al-Baḥrayn and 'Umān there seems to have been little mention of religion; but elsewhere the special feature of the Riddah was the appearance of 'false prophets', each preaching a new religion with himself as centre. Our sources are too meagre for us to be certain about the background of these prophets, how far it was pagan and how far Christian, how far inspired by Islam and how far a similar but independent reaction to similar circumstances. We do not know whether their supporters were mainly nomads or mainly agriculturists. If the supporters were settled, then the movements might be responses to the challenge from which Islam arose—the change from a nomadic to a settled economy; if the supporters were nomads, the challenge might be the destructive effect of constant feuds. The impression given is that only Musaylimah was trying to deal with the social and economic problems of his locality; but this may be due to lack of evidence about the others.

In this diversity the one thing that is clear is that the Riddahs were movements of a new type. The appeal was not to something old, except at al-Baḥrayn, where there was an attempt to restore an old dynasty. The inference thus seems to be justified that they were reactions to a *new* situation. Now the new situation might be either the rise of a new religious movement in Arabia, or the rise of a new political power there at a time when the Byzantine and

[1] The connexion between religion and politics in pre-Islamic Arabia is emphasized by J. Ryckmans, *L'Institution Monarchique en Arabie avant l'Islam*, Louvain, 1951, 329 ff.

Persian empires were in decline. In so far, however, as Islam is a religious and political system there is, between these alternatives, a distinction but no difference.

Finally, we have to ask to what extent the tribes were in at least political alliance with Muḥammad. Those in the neighbourhood of Medina and Mecca were all firmly united to him. So also were those of the centre and along the route to ʿIrāq, but there were some exceptions. In the Yemen and the rest of the south-west there were numerous groups in alliance, but they may not have been more than half the population. In the south-east the proportion was probably less. Along the route to Syria there had been little success in detaching tribes from the Byzantine emperor.

Thus Muḥammad had not altogether succeeded in unifying Arabia, but he had done more than sceptical European scholars have allowed. Moreover, his personal influence doubtless gave him power and authority beyond that conferred by formal agreements, for example, in the affairs of tribes which were in alliance with him on an equal footing. There were certainly gaps, but except in the north-west they were inconsiderable. The framework of unity had been built. A political system with strong foundations had been erected, into which the tribes could be brought. Many had come in; others could easily be added. The economic basis of the system was sound. The quarrels and rivalries of the tribes had not been removed, but they had been subdued. Indeed they had been used to strengthen the system; the chief motive of tribes like Ṭayyi' and Hawāzin for being loyal during the Riddah may have been that their chief rivals were opposed to Medina.

Religious conversion, as has been seen in our survey, did not extend as far as political alliance. It is not easy to find exact details. Where a man is said to have made profession of Islam, this was probably the case; but, where the sources are silent, it is more likely that he did not become a Muslim until later. There must always have been a tendency for Christian Arabs in political alliance with Muḥammad or the caliphs to become Muslims. In the great upheavals of the age, many men were in need of the support given by religion. The 'false prophets' tried to meet this need, but had little success. The Christian tribes must have found it difficult to 'stand on their own legs' in matters of religion after they had been cut off from the Byzantine empire and had seen the Christians of ʿIrāq suffer from the decline in prestige of the Persian empire.

For those who had allied themselves politically with Medina, the new religion of this rapidly expanding state must have had a great fascination and must have seemed the answer to their religious needs. Only a deeply rooted Christianity could withstand such fascination.

V

THE INTERNAL POLITICS OF MEDINA

1. SOCIAL AND POLITICAL GROUPINGS BEFORE MUḤAMMAD

In *Muḥammad at Mecca* the various clans of Quraysh were named and briefly described. Unfortunately, before a similar description can be given of the social and political groupings at Medina, there are various difficulties to be surmounted.

The first difficulty concerns the reliability of our sources. Those for Medina are indeed more ample than those for Mecca; Ibn Saʿd, in the second part of his third volume, deals with more than 200 Medinans who fought at Badr, and in many cases names their mothers and wives, while in the eighth volume the women who became Muslims—to the number of about 400—are similarly dealt with. Apart from the children who are also named, we have the complete genealogies of perhaps nearly a thousand Medinans of Muḥammad's time, and know something about their marriages. The difficulty is that these genealogies are entirely patrilineal, whereas a number of points in the sources make it clear that matrilineal descent counted for something in Medina. Tribes and individuals are known as the 'son of such and such a woman'; it is noted that a man is the son of the maternal aunt of another man; men marry their kinswomen in the female line; and so on. These matters will be considered in greater detail subsequently.[1] Our information about them is scantier than could be wished, and some points are obscure. Sufficient is clear, however, to make us doubt whether the neatly arranged patrilineal clans of the later genealogists coincide altogether with the actual social units of Muḥammad's time.

On the other hand, it is also clear that patrilineal descent counted for much, and there are no grounds for supposing a general system of matrilineal clans. At the time of the Hijrah patrilineal descent seems to have been the main principle of organization of the social subdivisions of Medina, but within this general framework there may have been a number of small groups in which matrilineal descent was dominant, although we are seldom able to identify these. In practice this means that we accept the patrilineal

[1] Cf. below, p. 378.

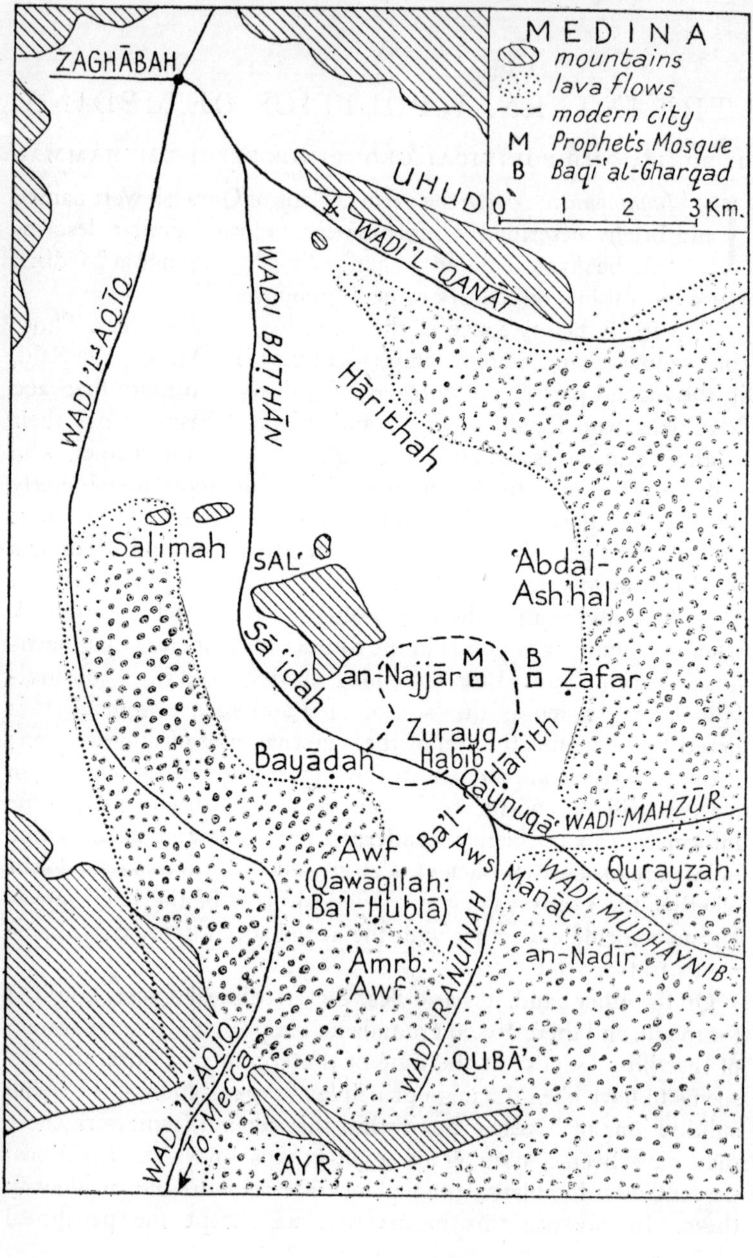
MEDINA
mountains
lava flows
modern city
M Prophet's Mosque
B Baqī'al-Gharqad
0 1 2 3 Km.
ZAGHĀBAH
UHUD
WADI 'L-QANĀT
WADI 'L-'AQĪQ
WADI BAṬHĀN
Hārithah
Salimah
SAL'
'Abdal-Ash'hal
Sā'idah
an-Najjār
M
B
Ẓafar
Zurayq
Ḥabīb
Ḥārith
Bayāḍah
Ba'l-Qaynuqā'
WADI MAHZŪR
Aws Manāt
'Awf
(Qawāqilah
Ba'l-Ḥublā)
Qurayẓah
WADI MUDHAYNIB
an-Naḍīr
'Amr b.
'Awf
WADI RANŪNAH
QUBĀ'
To Mecca
WADI 'L-'AQĪQ
'AYR

groupings as generally reliable for Muḥammad's time, whatever may have been the position earlier, but are on the look-out for individuals who tend to side with their mother's kin rather than with their father's. As Medina was in a state of transition from nomadic practices to those of a settled agricultural community, it is safer to assume some lack of homogeneity.

Even after we have formed a working rule on this point, we have still to decide which were the effective groups in the Medinan Arab community. There are at least three sets of names to be considered. There are the two great tribes, the Aws and the Khazraj; there are the eight clans mentioned in the constitution; and there are the thirty-three smaller groups found in Ibn Saʿd's list of the Anṣār who were at Badr.

Some doubts may justifiably be entertained whether the Aws and the Khazraj, as important social units, are not the invention of the genealogists. For present purposes it is unnecessary to go into this question and to try to discover how the genealogists manipulated the genuine material which they presumably had. It may be that the theory of common descent was invented to explain or justify the fact that certain clans usually acted together, but it may also have some basis either in blood relationship or in religious practice. Yet, even if there really is common descent, this was not a strong motive for action in Muḥammad's time. There was intermarriage between the two alleged tribes, and sometimes a clan of one tribe seems to have been more friendly with a clan of the other tribe than with the fellow members of its own tribe. In the constitution of Medina the groups responsible for blood-money are not the two tribes but eight smaller units, and indeed the two tribes play no part in that constitution. Moreover, in some cases at least the effective units seem to have been smaller than the eight clans of the constitution; for example, the constitution speaks of an-Nabīt, but one of the subdivisions of an-Nabīt, B. Ḥārithah, was frequently on the opposite side from another, B. ʿAbd al-Ash'hal. On the other hand, not all the thirty-three groups of Ibn Saʿd were active as independent political units. The accompanying diagrams show the relationships of the clans according to Ibn Saʿd, while the map gives their approximate locations.[1]

[1] The map is based in part on as-Samhūdī's indications and in part on that of the Khandaq in Hamidullah, *Battlefields of Muhammad*, 26 (also the earlier version in *Bulletin des Études Islamiques*, 1939, and that in *Muḥammad al-Qā'id*, by M. ʿAbd al-Fattāḥ Ibrāhīm).

THE CLANS OF THE ANṢĀR

I

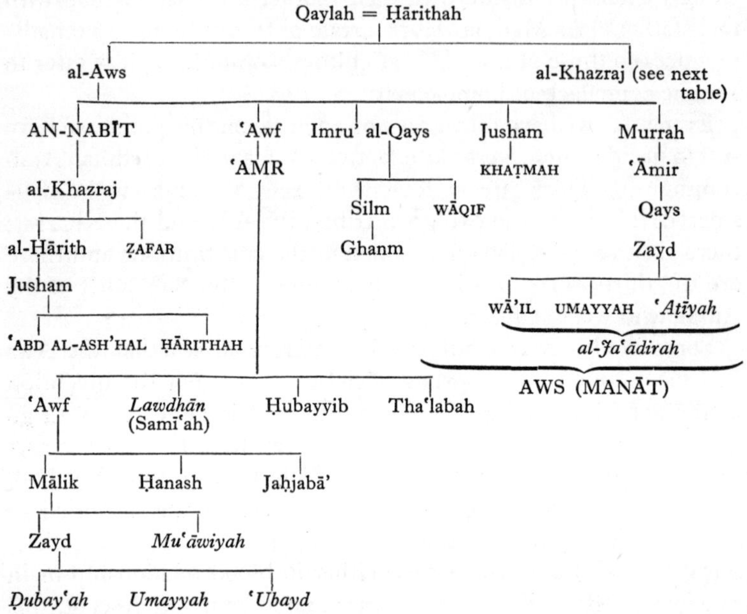

II

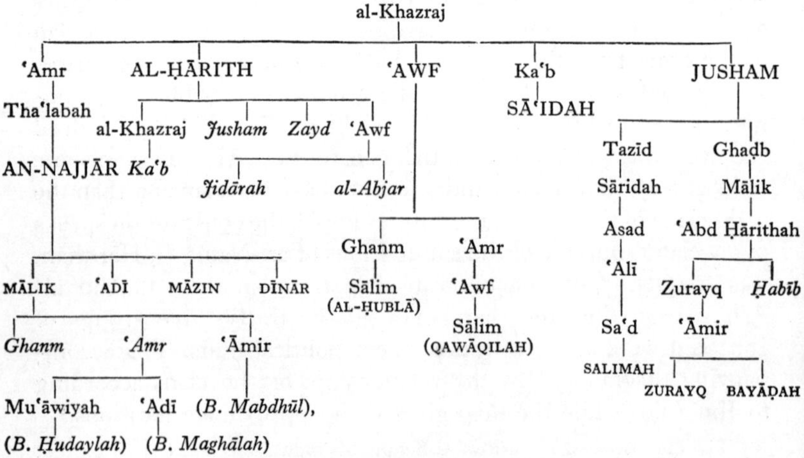

'AWF —clans mentioned in the Constitution.
SALIMAH —clans commonly mentioned as such.
al-Abjar —minor clans or sub-clans.

(a) *The pre-Islamic feuds*

A survey of the pre-Islamic fighting between the clans will give some idea of the important units. For many years before the Hijrah —traditionally for over a hundred, but according to existing records for only fifty years or so—there had been a series of feuds and battles, gradually increasing in numbers involved and in ferocity. Originally, like nomadic blood-feuds, they seem to have been directed mainly against the persons of the hostile clan and possibly against their animals. As time passed, however, the aim became more and more the expulsion of the rival group from their lands and homesteads, and sometimes even their extermination. An economic motive is thus making its appearance, but it is difficult to assess its importance accurately. It seems clear that virgin land was available even to Umayyad times,[1] but doubtless the labour of bringing it under cultivation was considerable and the yield at first comparatively poor. Certainly, wherever a clan was strong enough to seize old cultivated land it did so, and only those who had been expelled from their former lands broke fresh ground. We may assume, then, that as the population grew more land was required and that the development of new land was a disagreeable task. In this sense there was economic pressure. The tendency to self-aggrandizement, however, whether in individual or in clan, was possibly also not without importance, notably in the career of ʿAmr b. an-Nuʿmān of Bayāḍah, about whom more will be said presently. The impression one receives is that he was moved, not by sheer economic necessity, but by the realization that in extending the lands of his clan and of other groups who acknowledged him as leader he was increasing his own power.

The sources separate fighting between an Aws clan and a Khazraj clan from fighting between two clans of the same tribe. There is little justification, however, for this distinction, and study of the events suggests that the conception of two rival tribes was at most only being elaborated during this period and had not won general acceptance. Fighting was usually between adjacent clans, but the fact that neighbours were of the same tribe did not prevent a strong clan from attacking them and improving its position at their expense. If, as seems to be the case, expropriation of lands from

[1] Cf. J. Wellhausen, 'Medina vor dem Islam' (= *Skizzen und Vorarbeiten* IV/1), 21 n.

members of the same tribe took place at an earlier date than expropriation from the other tribe, that may be due to the fact that, for example, Zurayq (of the Khazraj) when attacked by Bayāḍah (also of the Khazraj) was in a weaker position and less able to gain strong allies than ʿAmr b. ʿAwf (of the Aws) when attacked by Bayāḍah.[1]

The first recorded fighting between the two tribes was in the south-west between B. Sālim (later identified with Qawāqilah) and B. Jaḥjabā'. Their respective leaders were Mālik b. al-ʿAjlān (the first of the Aws and the Khazraj to assert his independence of the Jews) and Uḥayḥah b. al-Julāḥ, but these two, whose mothers were sisters, do not seem personally to have fought one another. In the interval between this dispute and the War of Ḥāṭib we hear of four 'wars': one was between ʿAmr b. ʿAwf (led by Ḥuḍayr b. Simāk) and al-Ḥārith (led by ʿAbdallāh b. Ubayy); in another Māzin put to flight Wā'il (led by Abū Qays b. al-Aslat); while in the remaining two the clans of Ẓafar and ʿAbd al-Ash'hal (the latter under Muʿādh b. an-Nuʿmān) got the better of certain sections of an-Najjār. About the same time ʿAbd al-Ash'hal was expanding northwards and pushing Ḥārithah into fresh lands to the west, and Bayāḍah was expanding at the expense of Zurayq.

The War of Ḥāṭib is the name of a series of incidents which culminated in the great battle of Buʿāth shortly before the Hijrah.

The quarrel began between one Ḥāṭib b. Qays (of a branch of ʿAmr b. ʿAwf) and Yazīd b. Fus'ḥum (of al-Ḥārith). Words led to blows and then to bloodshed, and others became involved. The quarrel may in part be a continuation of the one mentioned in the last paragraph, but it is interesting to note that, while ʿAmr b. ʿAwf are still led by Ḥuḍayr b. Simāk, al-Ḥārith are no longer led by ʿAbdallāh b. Ubayy (who belonged not to them but to B. al-Ḥublā) but by ʿAmr b. an-Nuʿmān of Bayāḍah. It may be conjectured that, after the successful expansion of Bayāḍah against Zurayq, ʿAmr b. an-Nuʿmān welcomed an opportunity for further expansionist adventures. He was victorious in the first two battles, though in the second, in which he had also some of an-Najjār on his side, there was great loss of life on both sides. In the next conflict Abū Qays b. al-Aslat and ʿAbdallāh b. Ubayy had joined in on opposite sides; Abū Qays seems to have brought with him not merely his own clan of Wā'il but the group of clans known as Aws Manāt (or later Aws Allāh); though he was the senior leader on the side of

[1] Contrast ibid. 29 and n.

ʿAmr b. ʿAwf, he allowed Ḥuḍayr b. Simāk to command. Ḥuḍayr was victorious, but, as his side had lost three more men, they received three hostages. For reasons not given these hostages were killed, and as a result there was some apparently localized, but stubborn, fighting between Abū Qays and ʿAbdallāh b. Ubayy.

Up to this stage in the war ʿAbd al-Ash'hal had apparently not been involved, for Ḥuḍayr seems to be reckoned to ʿAmr b. ʿAwf, although according to the later patrilineal genealogies he was of ʿAbd al-Ash'hal, and his son Usayd shared the leadership of ʿAbd al-Ash'hal with Saʿd b. Muʿādh b. an-Nuʿmān. Now, however, the local quarrel of ʿAbd al-Ash'hal with their neighbours Salimah became linked with the wider quarrel, and they entered on opposite sides. In a battle known as the 'day of Muʿabbis and Mudarris' the allied clans of the Aws were defeated. ʿAmr b. ʿAwf and Aws Manāt made peace, presumably on disadvantageous terms. The curious complexity of relationships is shown by the fact that, after Salimah had raided the lands of ʿAbd al-Ash'hal, the leader of the former, ʿAmr b. al-Jamūḥ, took under his protection both the person and the stronghold of the wounded leader of the latter, Saʿd b. Muʿādh. ʿAbd al-Ash'hal and Ẓafar, however, refused to submit and left Medina (though this possibly means not the whole clan, but only the most important men). A deputation went to Mecca, but whether with the aim of settling there, or merely in the hope of getting military help from Quraysh, is not clear; and in any case they were unsuccessful. Eventually they made an alliance with the Jewish tribes of Qurayẓah and an-Naḍīr, whose lands—some of the best in Medina—were coveted by ʿAmr b. an-Nuʿmān and Bayāḍah. When ʿAmr b. an-Nuʿmān heard of the intrigues, he demanded hostages from Qurayẓah and an-Naḍīr; and when the intrigues continued, he had those of the hostages in his immediate power put to death. ʿAbdallāh b. Ubayy, however, disapproved of his policy in this matter, and set his hostages free. In the ensuing struggle, for which both sides were energetically preparing, he and ʿAmr b. al-Jamūḥ remained neutral, as did B. Ḥārithah of the Aws. At the battle of Buʿāth ʿAmr b. an-Nuʿmān had not merely Bayāḍah and an-Najjār but also some men from the nomadic tribes of Juhaynah and Ashjaʿ, while Ḥuḍayr b. Simāk had a detachment from the nomadic Muzaynah as well as the Medinan clans of ʿAmr b. ʿAwf, Aws Manāt, ʿAbd al-Ash'hal, Ẓafar, Qurayẓah, and an-Naḍīr. The battle was fiercely contested, but at length went in favour of Ḥuḍayr's side, though both the leaders lost their lives.

No formal peace was made after Buʿāth, but the combatants were too exhausted to continue the struggle actively. For the most part the enemy groups avoided one another, but there was a state of hostility, and, if a man was careless and gave his opponents an opportunity, he was liable to be murdered. This was the uneasy position in Medina when negotiations with Muḥammad commenced.[1]

(b) *Description of the individual clans*

Against this background of pre-Islamic history let us try to say something about the individual clans as they were in Muḥammad's time. The following notes are based mainly on the biographical details given by Ibn Saʿd and the geographical information of as-Samhūdī.[2]

ʿAbd al-Ash'hal. This clan comes first in the normal order of the sources, and it is convenient to describe it first as there is much information about it and it is of more than ordinary complexity. The leader of the clan in Muḥammad's time was Saʿd b. Muʿādh, who succeeded to the position of his father, Muʿādh b. an-Nuʿmān. This is one of the very few instances in Medina of an important man having a son of comparable importance, and, along with the fact that Saʿd and his brother Aws had both married Hind bint Simāk, suggests that patrilineal descent was more esteemed in this clan than in others. With this, however, must be contrasted the case of al-Ḥuḍayr b. Simāk, whose son Usayd appears to have been almost as important in the clan about the time of the Hijrah as Saʿd b. Muʿādh. It has been seen how al-Ḥuḍayr played a leading role in Medinan affairs up to his death at Buʿāth, but did so apparently as the leader of ʿAmr b. ʿAwf. We know that al-Ḥuḍayr's sister Hind, who has just been mentioned, had a mother from ʿAmr

[1] For the pre-Islamic history of Medina see Ibn al-Athīr, *al-Kāmil*, Cairo (1929)/1348, &c., i. 400–20; as-Samhūdī, *Kitāb Wafāʾ al-Wafāʾ*, Cairo, 1908–9, esp. i. 152 ff.; F. Wüstenfeld, *Geschichte der Stadt Medina*, Göttingen, 1860 (extracted from *Abhandlungen der Königlichen Gesellschaft der Wissenschaften*, ix; it consists of a summary of as-Samhūdī); Wellhausen, *Medina*.

[2] IS, iii/2; iv/2. 79–95 (nos. 118 ff); viii. 230–337; as-Samhūdī, op. cit. i. 109–16, 134–52; cf. Ibn Durayd, *K. al-Ishtiqāq* ('Genealogisch-etymologisch Handbuch'), ed. F. Wüstenfeld, Göttingen, 1854, 259 ff.

b. ʿAwf;[1] and the same must have been true of al-Ḥuḍayr. Presumably it was the same woman, Umm Jundub bint Rifāʿah b. Zanbar. Moreover al-Ḥuḍayr seems to have been specially connected with those sections of ʿAmr b. ʿAwf which were settled near Ẓafar and ʿAbd al-Ash'hal, and latterly at least his *uṭum* or stronghold was in the territory of ʿAbd al-Ash'hal, and he is said to have led ʿAbd al-Ash'hal when they expelled Ḥārithah and occupied their lands. As Usayd's mother was also of ʿAbd al-Ash'hal, it was natural for him to identify himself with that clan.

The names in the lists of men and women belonging to the clan fall into several distinct groups. Apart from what may be regarded as the clan proper, there is an important sub-clan which traces its descent from a man called Zaʿūrā'. Sometimes the genealogy runs Zaʿūrā' b. ʿAbd al-Ash'hal b. Jusham, sometimes Zaʿūrā' b. Jusham, but there is no justification for assuming two distinct persons. More primitive appears to be the description of Zaʿūrā' as 'brother of ʿAbd al-Ash'hal', which is presumably a way of indicating that Zaʿūrā' was a group of persons permitted to live alongside and to intermarry with the group at that time known as ʿAbd al-Ash'hal. At one point as-Samhūdī says there is some doubt whether Zaʿūrā' belonged to the Aws, and at another point he lists a group called B. Zaʿūrā' among the Jewish clans, though this may merely mean that they were Arabs who had settled in Medina before the Aws and the Khazraj and had become subordinated to one of the Jewish tribes or clans.[2] The name also occurs in a genealogy of B. ʿAdī b. an-Najjār of the Khazraj,[3] that of Qays b. as-Sakan, his wife and his daughter; and this may indicate another fragment of the primitive group. Of those in ʿAbd al-Ash'hal one of the chief seems to have been Abū 'l-Haytham b. at-Tayyihān,[4] but it was his mother who was of Zaʿūrā', as according to Ibn Saʿd his father was either of Balī or of ʿAmr b. Jusham, a group to be mentioned shortly.

Among those mentioned as confederates of ʿAbd al-Ash'hal are one or two members of the rival clan of Ḥārithah, whose lands ʿAbd al-Ash'hal had seized. We can only guess at the reasons for this behaviour, but it is clear that the group were not poor and

[1] IS, viii. 231.

[2] As-Samhūdī, i. 136, 115; cf. Wellhausen, *Medina*, 12; *Aghānī*, xix. 95; Ibn Durayd, op. cit. 263; J. Horovitz, *Koranische Untersuchungen*, 158.

[3] IS, iii/2. 70. 14–17; viii. 319. 20.

[4] As-Samhūdī, i. 136.

down-trodden, since one of them, Muḥammad b. Maslamah, was prominent as a Muslim. They all belonged to the sub-clan, B. Majdaʿah, of Ḥārithah.

Finally, if we neglect a solitary confederate from the Qawāqilah of the Khazraj about whom we have little information, there is a curious group known not as 'the sons of so-and-so' but as 'the people of Rātij', which is either a stronghold (*uṭum*) or a locality. As-Samhūdī mentions them among the Jewish groups, and Ibn Saʿd has some interesting remarks about them.[1] Salamah b. Salāmah of Zaʿūrā' married a woman who was one 'of the Jaʿādirah of the inhabitants of Rātij of the Aws, confederates of B. Zaʿūrā' b. Jusham'; while of the descendants of ʿAmr b. Jusham, ostensibly a brother of ʿAbd al-Ash'hal, it is said that 'these are the people of Rātij, except that among the people of Rātij are a group from Ghassān from the descendants of ʿUlbah b. Jafnah'. (The Jaʿādirah are B. Wā'il and some related clans from Aws Manāt; B. Jafnah appear as a minor group in the Constitution of Medina.) From this we see that 'the people of Rātij' were composed of several small groups, drawn together for mutual protection, and until shortly before the Hijrah probably subordinate to a Jewish clan.

The genealogies also give us information about the marriages of the clan. In roughly half the cases both parties are members of the clan, and the different sections enumerated intermarry. About half, however, are with other clans, and it is interesting to note which these are. The marriages may be divided roughly into earlier and later. For the earlier, partners come from al-Abjar, an-Najjār, and Sāʿidah of the Khazraj and Wāqif and ʿAmr b. ʿAwf of the Aws. The later matches are less adventurous, and are confined to their allies, Ẓafar, and to the adjacent Khazrajī clans of an-Najjār and Salimah. Finally, there is an interesting case; one woman, Amāmah bint Bishr, married a Jew of B. Qurayẓah, Asad b. ʿUbayd al-Hadlī.[2]

Altogether this is an illuminating picture of a society in transition from a basis of blood to a basis of locality, but it will be best to defer remarks of a general nature until the other clans have been described.

Ḥārithah. Reference has already been made to the expulsion of Ḥārithah from their lands by ʿAbd al-Ash'hal. Strictly speaking, this was not accomplished by force, but followed on the decision

[1] As-Samhūdī, i. 116; IS, iii/2. 16. 6, 21. 10.

[2] IS, viii. 236.

of mediators. The account of as-Samhūdī[1] suggests that it was only the *uṭum* or stronghold of Musayyir that was forfeited. The clan had other strongholds, but Musayyir may have been the main one. After a year at Khaybar the main body returned to a site west of the later memorial to Ḥamzah at the battlefield of Uḥud. It was probably at this time that Muḥammad b. Maslamah and others became confederates of ʿAbd al-Ash'hal, doubtless retaining their lands. There is much obscurity, however, about the relations of Ḥārithah to ʿAbd al-Ash'hal. On the one hand, some bitter feeling continued; at Buʿāth Ḥārithah refused to fight under al-Ḥuḍayr b. Simāk, who had been chiefly responsible for their expulsion; as the Muslims marched to Uḥud just before the battle, there was nearly a quarrel between Mirbaʿ b. Qayẓi of Ḥārithah and Usayd b. al-Ḥuḍayr, and in the confusion of the battle it was perhaps not altogether an accident that Usayd was wounded by a confederate of Ḥārithah.[2] Despite this bitterness, however, the main clan seems to have continued to intermarry with the section that had become confederates of ʿAbd al-Ash'hal and even with some parts of ʿAbd al-Ash'hal.

Apart from this little is to be learnt from the list of genealogies. Among the mothers of the men and women who became Muslims were women from the clans of an-Najjār, Bayāḍah, Sāʿidah, Salimah, Khaṭmah, and ʿAmr b. ʿAwf, as well as one from the Qawāqilah who were confederates of ʿAbd al-Ash'hal. The Muslims themselves, however, married within the clan or with ʿAbd al-Ash'hal (including the allied Ẓafar); only two marriages with other clans are recorded—Muʿāwiyah, a sub-clan of ʿAmr b. ʿAwf, and Mabdhūl of an-Najjār. Ḥārithah must have been poor after their forced move, and this may have restricted the matches open to them. With three clansmen present, they were well represented at the convention of ʿAqabah, but only the same number at Badr was poor. Among the absentees from Badr was al-Barā' b. ʿĀzib, apparently chief man of the clan after the Hijrah.

Ẓafar. The three clans of ʿAbd al-Ash'hal, Ḥārithah, and Ẓafar were held to constitute together an-Nabīt, but that did not prevent the third joining the first in the attack on the second. In general Ẓafar appears to have been dependent on ʿAbd al-Ash'hal. Marriages outside the clan were chiefly with members of an-Najjār,

[1] i. 135–6.

[2] WW, 107, 112.

Salimah and the other two clans of an-Nabīt. The leading man of the clan under Muḥammad was Qatādah b. an-Nuʿmān.

ʿAmr b. ʿAwf. This, like ʿAbd al-Ash'hal, was a composite group, but there is a difference between the two. ʿAbd al-Ash'hal gives the impression of being a young group with centripetal tendencies, whereas ʿAmr b. ʿAwf is old and centrifugal. Their lands are scattered—the sub-clan Jaḥjabā' is to the west of Qubā' in the south-west, while Muʿāwiyah b. Mālik is 'behind' (? east of) Baqīʿ al-Gharqad in the east—and consequently they did not have the political influence their numbers warranted.

Of the subdivisions of the clan some appear to have been more closely-knit groups than others. Moreover, there are grounds for suspecting that in some cases kinship through females (which is not fully recorded in our sources) may have determined the composition of the groups; e.g. al-Ḥuḍayr b. Simāk, who led the clan although only his mother belonged to it. One such closely-knit group is B. Jaḥjabā'. A generation or two before Muḥammad it had been strong, for Uḥayḥah b. al-Julāḥ who belonged to it was regarded by some as the leading man among the Arabs of Medina.[1] A member of this group, however—perhaps Uḥayḥah himself—was responsible for killing an important member of the clan, Rifāʿah b. Zanbar, and B. Jaḥjabā' are said to have given up at least two strongholds as the blood-price, which doubtless weakened them considerably. Nevertheless they held together as a group and mostly married within the group. Attached to them as confederates were some remnants of B. Unayf of the older stratum of Arab inhabitants of Medina.

Another group that appears to have functioned as a group some time before the Hijrah was Muʿāwiyah, which settled in the east beside Baqīʿ al-Gharqad (later a great Muslim cemetery) and near Ẓafar. There is probably some confusion between this group and a similarly named group belonging to an-Najjār. The genealogies as given in the sources are quite distinct, but the Western historian may wonder whether these are not two fragments of an older group which have formed different associations. As-Samhūdī mentions B. Muʿāwiyah among the Arabs in Medina before the coming of the Aws and the Khazraj, and also among the Jewish groups.[2] The former of these, of course, is quite distinct genealogically from the

[1] Cf. the war of Ṣumayr, Ibn al-Athīr, op. cit. 402 f., &c.

[2] 114, 115.

groups among ʿAmr b. ʿAwf and an-Najjār, but the constructions of the later genealogists need not be followed closely. No genealogy is given for the 'Jewish' group, but they are probably meant to be identified with the primitive group. It is stated, however, that they lived among B. Umayyah b. Zayd, and these are presumably B. Umayyah b. Zayd of ʿAmr b. ʿAwf, not of Murrah. As Ḥāṭib b. Qays, from whom the war of Ḥāṭib takes its name, is sometimes attributed to Muʿāwiyah and sometimes to Umayyah b. Zayd, it seems probable that the 'Jewish' group is to be identified with that belonging to ʿAmr b. ʿAwf. Of the few marriages of Muʿāwiyah which have been recorded, several are with Ḥārithah. To Muʿāwiyah also are assigned confederates from Muzaynah and Balī. It thus appears to be a mixed group, not unlike B. Zaʿūrā' and the 'people of Rātij' in the clan of ʿAbd al-Ash'hal.

Umayyah b. Zayd, which has just been mentioned, is a name which also appears in the genealogies as that of a brother of Wā'il (and hence a descendant of Murrah b. al-Aws), and one may suspect some lost connexion between the two. In ʿAmr b. ʿAwf the group of Umayyah b. Zayd is less closely knit than Jaḥjabā', but still has a definite unity. To it belonged Rifāʿah b. Zanbar, and in Muḥammad's time his grandson, Abū Lubābah b. ʿAbd al-Mundhir b. Rifāʿah, was important. If, as is almost certain, the mother of al-Ḥūḍayr b. Simāk was the same as that of his sister Hind, then she was a daughter of this Rifāʿah and it was to this section of ʿAmr b. ʿAwf that al-Ḥuḍayr was primarily attached. To it also belonged Abū ʿĀmir who went to Mecca rather than submit to Muḥammad.

Umayyah b. Zayd is supposed to have had two brothers, Ḍubayʿah and ʿUbayd, and after these also the genealogists name groups. Ḍubayʿah is comparatively well defined. Many of its marriages are within the group; it also married with Wāqif and, in Islamic times, with the clan of ʿAdī of Quraysh, as well as with other parts of ʿAmr b. ʿAwf. Of ʿUbayd little is recorded, though Kulthūm b. Hidm belonged to it, who was prominent in the early days of Islam in Medina.

There are also one or two less important groups, notably Ḥanash, Ḥubayyib, Samīʿah (or Lawdhān), and Thaʿlabah. There is a group of confederates, B. al-ʿAjlān of Balī, who are attached to Zayd, that is, presumably, to Umayyah, Ḍubayʿah, and ʿUbayd jointly. The sub-clan of B. Silm or B. Ghanm b. Silm, to which belonged

Sa'd b. Khaythamah, though it sprang from a completely different branch of the Aws genealogically, had left its kinsmen and joined 'Amr b. 'Awf.

Thus the clan of 'Amr b. 'Awf consists of a number of sections, of which some had a distinct existence as groups, while others were more nebulous. All the different sections seem to have intermarried with one another, to judge from our meagre information. They married occasionally with Khaṭmah and Wāqif of Aws Manāt, with an-Najjār, and with Bayāḍah and other parts of Jusham of the Khazraj. Apart, however, from the marriage at an early date of Simāk to a woman of 'Amr b. 'Awf, and the marriages of B. Mu'āwiyah with B. Ḥārithah, we have no record of any marriage between 'Amr b. 'Awf and any of the three clans forming the Nabīt.[1]

Aws Manāt—Wāqif, Khaṭmah, Wā'il, &c. The remaining clans of the Aws are best considered together. The name Aws Manāt became in Islamic times Aws Allāh, or sometimes, as in the constitution of Medina, simply al-Aws. There was some dispute about the precise application of the name, which is not surprising since it is essentially that of the tribe of the Aws. In the constitution, however, it appears to mean those clans belonging to the tribe of the Aws (according to later genealogists) which we have not yet considered. The same group without Wāqif and Khaṭmah was apparently called al-Ja'ādirah.

The most important clan, in Islamic times at least, was Khaṭmah. As-Samhūdī says that before Islam they were scattered but afterwards they gained a centre and multiplied greatly.[2] Ibn Sa'd has biographies of fifteen men and women of the clan. Most of the marriages recorded are within the clan, but there are also others with Wāqif, Wā'il, 'Amr b. 'Awf, and Ḥārithah of the Aws, and Qawāqilah and al-Ḥārith of the Khazraj. On the whole, however, they were not important in the affairs of Medina.

About the remaining clans we have less information, since with one exception Ibn Sa'd has no biographical notes on any members of them. It may be that this is because they tended to be opposed to Islam, but it is possible that after the battle of Bu'āth they were few in numbers. A group of the Ja'ādirah—whether all or some we cannot say—had become attached to 'Abd al-Ash'hal. Others

[1] The marriage of Thābit b. Wadī'ah to a woman of Rātij (presumably after the Hijrah) should perhaps be added; IS, iv/2. 86. [2] 140.

may similarly have become more closely connected with the Jewish tribes after the battle of Buʿāth, for Aws Manāt seem to have been interspersed among the Jews. Prior to Buʿāth, Abū Qays b. al-Aslat of Wā'il had been one of the leaders of the Aws, senior to al-Ḥuḍayr b. Simāk, but apparently not so influential. When he died, less than a year after the Hijrah, he had not become a Muslim, though he had been a *ḥanīf* or monotheist previously and is said to have thought of acknowledging Muḥammad. Nothing of importance is recorded of his son Miḥṣan.

It has been suggested that there may be some connexion between Umayyah b. Zayd of ʿAmr b. ʿAwf and Umayyah b. Zayd of Aws Manāt which the later patrilineal genealogies have obscured. As-Samhūdī also mentions a small related group called ʿAṭīyah b. Zayd. The general impression given by Aws Manāt is that it is a heterogeneous collection of old groups whose strength was declining. They lacked both genealogical and geographical unity, though they were all towards the south of the Medinan oasis. Whatever may be the reason, they carried little weight in the Medina that Muḥammad found.

An-Najjār. The most numerous clan or clan-group among the Khazraj, and indeed among the Anṣār as a whole, was an-Najjār. This was an amorphous body, somewhat like ʿAmr b. ʿAwf, but not so scattered. The genealogists arrange the subdivisions under the four sons of an-Najjār, who is also known as Taym Allāt, later Taym Allāh.[1] Of these B. Māzin b. an-Najjār seems to have been a distinct entity. There is a record of a blood-feud between Māzin and Wā'il, in which Abū Qays b. al-Aslat of Wā'il was put to flight;[2] and the relative adjective Māzinī is frequently used, whereas members of the other sections are usually called just Najjārī. Most of the marriages recorded are within B. Māzin; there are also several with other sections of an-Najjār, and only one or two with other clans.

The largest part of an-Najjār was B. Mālik b. an-Najjār, but within this are several curious groups, B. Ḥudaylah (or Muʿāwiyah), B. Maghālah, and B. Mabdhūl. Ḥudaylah and Maghālah were women. Few members of these groups are given biographical notices by Ibn Saʿd. Of Ḥudaylah the only man of note is Ubayy b. Kaʿb, one of Muḥammad's secretaries. To Maghālah belonged Ḥassān b. Thābit the poet. Many of the marriages noted are within B.

[1] Wellhausen, *Medina*, 6.

[2] Ibn al-Athīr, i. 407 f.

Mālik b. an-Najjār, but very few are restricted to the smaller group. There is no obvious peculiarity about the groups named after women, and they appear to be based on patrilineal descent at the time of the Hijrah. It is curious, however, that there is said to have been a dispute whether ʿAbdallāh b. Ubayy belonged to Ba'l-Ḥublā (as is commonly said) or to B. Maghālah;[1] the only connexion seems to have been that he married a woman of Maghālah, and it therefore looks as if he lived with his wife's group for a time.

B. ʿAdī b. an-Najjār were also numerous, but had little distinctive character; indeed through intermarriage they were much mixed with Mālik b. an-Najjār. They included some persons who had the name Zaʿūrā' in their genealogy, which suggests some connexion with the B. Zaʿūrā' of ʿAbd al-Ash'hal, though, apart from the fact that the unusual name as-Sakan occurs in both groups, there is no confirmatory evidence. B. Dīnār b. an-Najjār is smaller but more compact; that is to say, there is more intermarriage within the group; some of this intermarriage appears to be between those who are related on the female side.

Thus an-Najjār is a clan or clan-group, into which several smaller groups are in process of being absorbed so that they cease to exist as distinct entities. The large group has as its basis patrilineal kinship, but in some of the smaller groups matrilineal kinship may have played a part, though our evidence is insufficient to show whether it ever was the main basis of these groups. More and more the smaller groups seem to have been intermarrying, and there was a slight amount of intermarriage with most of the other clans of Medina except those of Aws Manāt. The lands of an-Najjār became the site of the Muslim city, doubtless owing to the presence of the house of Muḥammad, which became the central mosque of Medina; but prior to the Hijrah the point of greatest density of population was probably farther south. Whatever the reason may be, an-Najjār, despite its numbers, came behind some other clans in political importance—at least it did not produce a leader of the first rank. Asʿad b. Zurārah came nearest to this description, but unfortunately died a few months after the Hijrah. After him the most important were Muʿādh b. al-Ḥārith and his brothers Muʿawwidh and ʿAwf, commonly called the sons of ʿAfrā' after their mother. Those just named were all of B. Mālik b. an-Najjār.

[1] As-Samhūdī, 142.

Al-Ḥārith. The descendants of al-Ḥārith, often known by a contracted form Ba'l-Ḥārith, were not a vigorous clan. We hear of them ceding a stronghold to a clan of the Aws, probably Wāqif, and of sections of them going off to Syria. Apart from this they present some of the features of an-Najjār, but on a smaller scale. One of the small groups which is being absorbed by the clan is said to be descended from twin sons of al-Ḥārith, Jusham and Zayd. This is doubtless a device to effect the integration of two families, or else to explain something of this sort. As the group is also known as 'the people of as-Sunḥ' (a place), its unity is possibly based on the fact of common habitation and not on blood. Other two small groups are B. al-Jidārah and B. al-Abjar. The latter are said to be 'brothers' of the former, and are also known as B. Khudrah from the mother of al-Abjar (with the relative adjective Khudrī). B. al-Abjar, to judge from our scanty information, was a completely exogamous group—apparently the only example in Medina. Apart from Abū Sa'īd al-Khudrī, from whom many traditions are narrated, no man of note came from B. al-Abjar, but the mothers of Sa'd b. Mu'ādh and As'ad b. Zurārah were sisters belonging to it. Two important men from what may be called the main section of the clan were Sa'd b. ar-Rabī' and 'Abdallāh b. Rawāḥah.

'Awf: Ba'l-Ḥublā and Qawāqilah. This is one of the points at which the fictitious character of the earlier parts of the genealogies becomes obvious. Two or three generations before the Hijrah it was usual to speak of a clan of Sālim, and to this belonged the leader who made the Arabs independent of the Jews, Mālik b. al-'Ajlān. The probability is that there was only a single clan of this name, but it seems to have split up into three, and the genealogists have conveniently produced three men of the name of Sālim. From these are descended three clans commonly known as Ba'l-Ḥublā, the Qawāqilah, and Wāqif. The two former are most closely connected, since according to the genealogists both are descended from 'Awf b. al-Khazraj; moreover, in both, Sālim is connected with a man called Ghanm, but there is doubt about the precise relationship. Wāqif is one of the clans of Aws Manāt, and therefore far removed genealogically from B. 'Awf of the Khazraj; but he is also known as Sālim, and he had a brother Silm (or Salm) who had a son Ghanm. Wāqif intermarried with both the others; so far as our records go, it was the only section of Aws Manāt to do so.

These facts together tend to show that there was a close relationship between these three clans which the patrilineal genealogies do not reveal.

At the time of the Hijrah Ba'l-Ḥublā and al-Qawāqilah were not greatly different in character from several other small clans. The majority of marriages were within the clan or with confederates or members of the other clans known as Sālim. In addition there were a few marriages between Ba'l-Ḥublā and B. Maghālah of an-Najjār, Ba'l-Ḥārith, Sā'idah, Zurayq, and 'Amr b. 'Awf. Al-Qawāqilah intermarried with other parts of an-Najjār and with Ba'l-Ḥārith, Bayāḍah, 'Amr b. 'Awf, 'Abd al-Ash'hal, and Ẓafar. These facts link up with others. It has already been noticed that a section of al-Qawāqilah—how large we cannot tell—had become confederates of 'Abd al-Ash'hal (with whom Ẓafar were in alliance). Again, in pre-Islamic times there was great rivalry between 'Abdallāh b. Ubayy of Ba'l-Ḥublā and the chief of Bayāḍah; and it is therefore interesting to note that, while al-Qawāqilah intermarries with Bayāḍah, Ba'l-Ḥublā intermarries with its enemy, Zurayq. Ba'l-Ḥublā was presumably the stronger in view of the influential position of 'Abdallāh b. Ubayy in Medina, though the latter may have been largely due to his personal qualities. The leading man of al-Qawāqilah, 'Ubādah b. aṣ-Ṣāmit, was not without importance. (It may further be noted that there is much disagreement about the meaning and origin of the name al-Qawāqilah; Wellhausen suggests that it comes from the name of a place, but the sources look for men called Qawqal.)[1]

Sā'idah. The clan of Sā'idah, so far as we can tell, was small, and it is not mentioned in the pre-Islamic fighting. Yet at the time of Muḥammad's death its chief, Sa'd b. 'Ubādah, was the leading man not merely of the Khazraj but of the Anṣār as a whole. As-Samhūdī speaks of four subdivisions in separate localities; but these were presumably adjacent, and all were near the *sūq* or marketplace of the Muslim city. Among the records are marriages with Maghālah, Salimah, Ba'l-Ḥārith, Ba'l-Ḥublā, 'Abd al-Ash'hal, and Ẓafar. From an early time Muḥammad seems to have been aware of the actual or potential importance of this clan, for, although only two members of it were present at the great convention at 'Aqabah, both of these became *nuqabā'* or representatives.

[1] Wellhausen, *Medina*, 18 n.; IS, iii/2. 95; as-Samhūdī, i. 141, &c.

Salimah. The clan of Salimah along with Zurayq, Bayāḍah, and some small fragments belonged to B. Jusham b. al-Khazraj. It was a large clan, but in Ibn Saʿd its proportionate strength may seem greater than it really was, since its members were outstanding for their enthusiasm for Islam. It seems to have played little part in pre-Islamic politics, though it had some skirmishes with its neighbours on the east, ʿAbd al-Ash'hal. Some families of Salimah were on friendly terms with some families of ʿAbd al-Ash'hal, and these protected one another from their fellow clansmen. An unusually large percentage of the marriages recorded in Ibn Saʿd are within the clan, especially if nomadic confederates are included. There was also intermarriage with the other parts of B. Jusham, and with an-Najjār, Sāʿidah, Ḥārithah, ʿAbd al-Ash'hal, Ẓafar, and ʿAmr b. ʿAwf. As-Samhūdī speaks of several distinct localities occupied by this clan, adjacent to one another, and near the foot of mount Salʿ. The chief of Salimah was al-Jadd b. Qays, but Muḥammad at some point caused him to be replaced by al-Barā' b. Maʿrūr.[1] The latter, on pilgrimage to Mecca before the Hijrah, had refused to turn his back on the Kaʿbah until told by Muḥammad to face Jerusalem, and, appropriately, it was in the territory of Salimah that the change in *qiblah* was announced. This suggests that in some sections at least of Salimah there was no friendship for the Jews.

Zurayq. Zurayq, Bayāḍah, and a small group called B. Ḥabīb b. ʿAbd Ḥārithah had once been friendly with one another, but a quarrel developed and Ḥabīb sided with Bayāḍah against Zurayq. Zurayq was forced to evacuate its lands, perhaps more than once, and these were occupied by Ḥabīb. Some of Zurayq eventually emigrated to Syria. The matter was complicated by the fact that one family of Zurayq remained among Bayāḍah for a time, though at last it decided that life was better among its own clan; and one family of Ḥabīb, becoming involved in a blood-feud with Zurayq, settled it by abandoning the *ḥilf* or alliance of Bayāḍah for that of the latter. Another blood-feud caused a small part of Jusham, B. Ghudārah, to attach itself to Zurayq, because the other fragments of Jusham with which it was in collision received the support of Bayāḍah. The antagonism between these two clans links up with various points. As just seen, Ba'l-Ḥublā, who under ʿAbdallāh b.

[1] Cp. p. 234 below. For the spelling of the clan name see as-Suyūṭī, *Lubb al-Lubāb*, ed. P. J. Veth, Leiden, 1840–2, i. 138.

Ubayy were opposed to Bayāḍah under ʿAmr b. an-Nuʿmān, intermarry with Zurayq and not with Bayāḍah, while their rivals the Qawāqilah do the opposite (unless the mother of Rāfiʿ b. Mālik is a real as well as an apparent exception). Ḥārithah intermarry with Bayāḍah, and the enemies of both, ʿAbd al-Ash'hal, with Zurayq. According to a report in as-Samhūdī Bayāḍah and Zurayq along with Ẓafar were the best of the Anṣār in war, and this, if there is any substance in it, may have attracted small groups to them. Unfortunately, in the years round about the Hijrah, Zurayq did not produce any great leader. To it belonged Rāfiʿ b. Mālik, one of the twelve *nuqabā'* or representatives appointed at al-ʿAqabah, but he was not outstanding.

Bayāḍah. Something has already been said about the ruthlessly aggressive policy of Bayāḍah under ʿAmr b. an-Nuʿmān. With his death at Buʿāth expansion stopped. One gets the impression that alliances were gladly made with aggrieved parties, such as Ḥabīb and Ḥārithah, in order to have grounds for aggression. The smallness of the number of men and women of the clan given notices by Ibn Saʿd may be due to great losses at Buʿāth or to lack of enthusiasm for Islam; or perhaps the clan had never been large. Its possession of nineteen *uṭums* or strongholds, however, according to as-Samhūdī, indicates considerable military strength. Its territory, along with the territory of confederates like Ḥabīb and the other fragments of Jusham, formed a solid block, and this also made for strength. Apart from the other sections of Jusham and the clans just mentioned, Bayāḍah, like Zurayq, intermarried with B'al-Ḥārith, an-Najjār, Sāʿidah, and ʿAmr b. ʿAwf.

It is convenient at this point to introduce the following table, although the figures in it refer to Muslims. But, except where a clan had a special reason for tending to accept or to reject Islam, we may, in default of better evidence, take these figures as a rough guide to the relative strength of the clans. For this purpose the last column is perhaps best, namely, the number of women to whom, as having sworn allegiance to Muḥammad, a notice is given in Ibn Saʿd's eighth volume. In that column seven of those whom Ibn Saʿd classifies as Ḥārithah have been transferred to ʿAbd al-Ash'hal, since they appear to belong to the part of their clan which had become confederates of the latter.

Clan	*First Muslims*[1]	*'Aqabah 1*[2]	*'Aqabah 2*[3]	*Nuqabā'*[4]	*At Badr*[5]	*Killed at Uḥud*[6]	*In IS viii*
'Abd al-Ash'hal	..	1	3	1	15	13	35
Ẓafar	..	..	..	..	5	..	23
Ḥārithah	..	..	3	..	3	..	23
'Amr b. 'Awf	..	1	5	2	40	7	28
Aws Manāt (Khaṭmah)	..	..	..	..	..	..	12
an-Najjār	2	3	11	1	56	12	83
al-Ḥārith	..	..	7	2	19	5	30
Ba'l-Ḥublā and al-Qawāqilah	..	3	6	1	25	6	21
Sā'idah	..	..	2	2	9	6	12
Salimah	3	3	29	2	43	3	54
Zurayq	1	2	4	1	16	1	16
Bayāḍah	..	..	3	..	7	1	12

(c) *Forces and tendencies in Medinan society*

This survey of the Medinan clans is precarious in that we do not know how complete our information is. If a serious gap has escaped notice or not been properly appreciated, a false and misleading emphasis may have been given at that point. Despite this possibility the basis of factual information is sufficiently wide to give a reliable general picture of the social forces and tendencies present in Meccan society.

There are some instances of the tendency, constantly found in nomadic society, for large groups to disintegrate. One instance would be the quarrel of Zurayq with Ḥabīb and then with Bayāḍah, another the separation of Silm from Wāqif, and a third, as seems likely, the splitting up of the old clan of Sālim. Under agricultural conditions the groups that attempt to live independently are smaller than would be the case in the desert.

The main tendency, however, is a contrary one towards the formation of larger groups. In a society such as that of Medina, where there were numerous small groups in close contact with one another, it was always possible, if two had a quarrel, to appeal to third parties for help; and ambitious families and clans were

1 IH, 287; cf. Caetani, Ann. i, p. 314.
2 IH, 288–9; cf. Caetani, l. c.
3 IH, 305–12; cf. Caetani, ibid. 321–2.
4 IH, 297–8; cf. Caetani, ibid. 319.
5 IS, iii/2; cf. IH, 495–506; WW, 86–90; Caetani, ibid. 497–510.
6 WW, 138–41; cf. IH, 607–10; Caetani, ibid. 563–4.

usually ready to respond to such appeals. Normally, however, they had some definite grounds for their interference in other people's affairs. To a pre-Islamic Arab the most obvious of such grounds was kinship, even though kinsmen tended to have bitter quarrels with one another; and the genealogical theory of the two great tribes of the Aws and the Khazraj seems to have been worked out, whether with or without a genuine basis of fact, in order to justify and unify the two alliances which were splitting Medina. In the course of the survey there have been several examples of how genealogy seems to have been invoked to strengthen the ties which held together several small groups. It is possible that what was originally known to be a fiction—for example, that Zaʿūrāʾ was a 'brother' of ʿAbd al-Ash'hal—in course of time came to be accepted as a genealogical fact. Allegations were also made about the eponymous ancestors in order to justify the existing relationship of the clans; the father of Zurayq and Bayāḍah was said to have entrusted the former to the latter, and Zurayq was said on his death-bed to have given charge of his sons to Ḥabīb, who treated them harshly. In general, then, we have the curious position that kinship, though it was proving unable to prevent fratricidal strife, was in certain ways being developed as a principle of unity.

The pre-Islamic Arabs were also familar with various forms of contractual agreement which bound men together. Chief among these were the mutual alliance (*ḥilf*, *taḥāluf*) between groups and individuals, by which they became confederates (*ḥulafāʾ*) of one another, and the *jiwār* or temporary protection of a 'neighbour' (*jār*)—in the Old Testament phrase, the 'sojourner within thy gates'. This method was employed in Medina. Thus we are told that B. al-Muʿallā broke off their *ḥilf* with Bayāḍah and formed one with Zurayq, while B. Ghudārah made a *ḥilf* with ʿAmr b. ʿAwf but then quarrelled with them and came to Zurayq. When, too, it is said that Zaʿūrāʾ was 'brother' of ʿAbd al-Ash'hal, I take this to mean that he had some such status as that of 'neighbour' and was allowed to intermarry. At the same time, it is possible that the later genealogists to whom we owe our information, when they were unable to link a man patrilineally with the clan to which they knew he belonged, assumed he was a confederate, whereas he may have been linked to the clan in the female line at some point. Statements about confederates should therefore be treated with a certain care.

In the growth of larger units the influence of physical or geographical neighbourhood was important. For defensive purposes it became usual in Medina to employ the *uṭum* or stronghold, and in order to build and maintain a stronghold a certain minimum number of persons was presumably required. Groups smaller than this minimum would therefore be compelled to join with other small groups, and so we find units like the 'people of Rātij' which was an amalgamation of fragments joined together for mutual defence, and becoming in course of time also linked by blood. In larger units, also, locality was important. Each of the main clans was in a sense a minute state, for it was an independent political entity. Within the territory of this state there was a measure of security, since to shed the blood of one's fellow clansman was an unpardonable offence. Outside the territory of one's clan and its confederates there was little security and, in the period of 'cold war' after Buʿāth, positive danger. It is noteworthy that most of the cases recorded of intermarriage between clans are between adjacent clans. A man might venture a little way into the territory of another clan where he knew he had some friends; but to go right across another clan's lands to those of a third was a risky matter.

In the development of larger units the personality of the leader played a great part. We are more likely to understand the history of the decade or two before the Hijrah if we concentrate not on the supposed hostility between the Aws and the Khazraj, but on the relations between the individual leaders who commanded in the main battles. These leaders must have seen that the existing state of affairs—practically a war of all against all—was intolerable, and that there were opportunities for a strong man to gain control over a large section of Medina, perhaps even over the whole. This was the issue at stake at Buʿāth. Had ʿAmr b. an-Nuʿmān won there, no one in Medina would have been able to stand up to him. He had proved himself, however, to be little better than the leader of a robber band, ready, as far as possible, to meet the claims of the members of the band, but ruthless and unprincipled in his conduct towards those outside his band. He could promise his followers the rich lands of the Jewish clans of Qurayẓah and an-Naḍīr before—so far as we can tell—any *casus belli* had appeared; and he could kill the Jewish hostages for a dubious reason. Such acts show that he was not sufficient of a statesman to look beyond his immediate advantage and, since the unification of Medina was almost inevitable, to consider on what principles the would-be ruler of the whole must act. ʿAmr's lack of principle was sowing the seeds of future conflicts and may well have lost him the support of men like ʿAbdallāh b. Ubayy, who would feel that under such a leader there was little security.

One wonders whether Ibn Ubayy had a wider vision. All we know is that he disagreed with ʿAmr b. an-Nuʿmān on the question of the Jewish hostages, since he set free those in his own hands, and that he remained neutral at Buʿāth. He may simply have been afraid of ʿAmr; but it is probable that he realized the need for a single ruler in Medina (since his supporters are said to have been preparing to crown him when Muḥammad arrived), and saw that this ruler must not lightly cause discontent in any section of the community, but must attempt to treat all parties fairly. Perhaps through his Jewish friends he had been influenced by Old Testament ideals of social justice.

Al-Ḥuḍayr b. Simāk, the other commander at Buʿāth, may not have been much better than ʿAmr, since he had driven out Ḥārithah from its lands. Yet there is nothing to make one suppose that he equalled ʿAmr in ruthlessness, and the heterogeneous character of his supporters suggests that he was fair in his dealings with them. The degree of unity between diverse elements attained in the clan of ʿAbd al-Ash'hal provided a pattern and was a good augury for the unification of Medina as a whole.

Finally, it should be noticed that the clans which, according to the incomplete figures just quoted, were strongest numerically did not produce the strongest leaders. Ba'l-Ḥublā and Bayāḍah, the clans of Ibn Ubayy and ʿAmr, were not large, and those that *were* large like an-Najjār and Salimah did not produce a great leader; even as Asʿad b. Zurārah of an-Najjār was not on the same level as those mentioned. Al-Ḥuḍayr b. Simāk was perhaps in a different position, since ʿAbd al-Ash'hal was fairly numerous, but his relation to it is obscure. This is a curious point and attention will have to be paid to it later.

2. MUḤAMMAD'S SUPPORTERS

The three lists of names given by Ibn Isḥāq, from which are derived the figures in the above table under the headings 'First Muslims', 'ʿAqabah 1', and 'ʿAqabah 2', may be taken to reflect three stages in the conversion of the Medinans to Islam, or, if one likes, in their conversion to the policy of bringing Muḥammad to Medina.[1] When these figures are examined from the standpoint of clan relationships, some interesting facts come to light. The original approach—for the alleged previous contacts and conversions did not lead to anything—was made by men of an-Najjār, Zurayq, and Salimah, the foremost probably being As'ad b. Zurārah of an-Najjār. For the next stage, which is known as the first meeting of al-'Aqabah, these were joined by men from al-Qawāqilah, 'Abd al-Ash'hal, and 'Amr b. 'Awf. The second or great meeting at al-'Aqabah was attended by men from all the clans of the Aws and the Khazraj with the exception of Aws Manāt (since, for this purpose, Ẓafar may be regarded as one with 'Abd al-Ash'hal). The noteworthy features are that, whereas the representation of most clans seems to be roughly in accordance with their strength, Salimah has proportionately three or four times as many representatives, and that 'Abd al-Ash'hal and Ba'l-Ḥublā, the clans of Sa'd b. Mu'ādh, and 'Abdallāh b. Ubayy, seem to be under-represented. Sa'd had become a Muslim prior to this, and so, presumably, had Ibn Ubayy, though in view of his later record we are told little about him. These two were the chief remaining leaders from the days before Bu'āth, and, though both became Muslims, neither deigned to be present at al-'Aqabah. It is to be noted that Ibn Ubayy and his like, who later came to be known as the Hypocrites, were for the first year or two after the Hijrah just as much Muslims in outward conduct as any one else. In this Ibn Ubayy is contrasted with Abū Qays b. al-Aslat of Wā'il who did not become a Muslim, and with Abū 'Āmir ar-Rāhib of 'Amr b. 'Awf who retired to Mecca.

These facts and figures give an idea of the groups which supported Muḥammad most vigorously in the early days of Islam in Medina. In particular the part played by Salimah is remarkable. Is it possible to discover why these clans and not the others were first attracted to Islam? One feature common to nearly all the men in the first two lists is that they came from clans which had not produced great leaders themselves but which had suffered from warlike leaders belonging to other clans. An-Najjār and Salimah had been involved in fighting, but no military commanders from them are named. The sufferings of Zurayq have been mentioned. Al-Qawāqilah had produced the great leader, Mālik b. al-'Ajlān,

[1] *M/Mecca*, 144–7.

but that was several generations earlier, and now they seemed to be weaker than Ba'l-Ḥublā and to be making friends with the latter's enemies. The clans of ʿAmr b. ʿAwf and ʿAbd al-Ash'hal are in a different position, but the two men at the first ʿAqabah seem to have been confederates and so probably did not represent the feeling of the leading groups within each clan.

It is easy to see how clans and sub-clans in this position would be attracted by the prospect of an outsider coming to hold the balance in the affairs of Medina. They may have felt that unification was bound to come sooner or later, but have disliked being under a ruler from Ba'l-Ḥublā or Bayāḍah. A member of any of the Medinan clans would already have his friends and his enemies among the other clans, and was unlikely to be fair to all. The fact that Muḥammad was an outsider and the trust his character inspired in them gave a promise that he would be more satisfactory. Moreover, under Muḥammad unification would be effected without first having a disastrous civil war. Since Salimah showed anti-Jewish tendencies, one may also wonder whether they were afraid that Ibn Ubayy, who was friendly with the Jewish clans, might rely on them to a great extent and so allow them to regain their influence in Medina. It is tempting to suppose that the clans represented at the first ʿAqabah were proletarian in constitution and the remainder aristocratic, but there is not sufficient evidence for such a view.

It remains to account for the conduct of the leaders. But for the conversion of Saʿd b. Muʿādh the course of the Islamic community would not have been so successful as in fact it was. His relation to al-Ḥuḍayr b. Simāk, the victor of Buʿāth, is not clear, but he seems to have succeeded to some of his power, and, according to our sources at least, al-Ḥuḍayr's son Usayd worked harmoniously with Saʿd as his second in command. Yet this duality in the leadership of ʿAbd al-Ash'hal may have been felt by Saʿd as a weakness, and it is perhaps significant that even in Ibn Isḥāq's pleasantly romanticized story of his conversion, it is made to follow soon after that of Usayd. This factor, however, was by no means the only one. Saʿd must be credited at the least with some awareness of what this new movement was going to mean in Medina, and at the most with a genuine belief in the message proclaimed by Muḥammad. He was a kinsman of Asʿad b. Zurārah and was friendly with ʿAmr b. al-Jamūḥ of Salimah, so that he had good opportunities of estimating the hold Islam had gained on members of these clans, and of hearing the case for Islam presented by men towards whom he was sympathetically disposed. When he decided to become a Muslim, he entered Islam whole-heartedly; he had no hesitation in going on the expedition to Badr, from which Ibn Ubayy and even Usayd b. al-Ḥuḍayr stayed away (though the latter subsequently apologized to Muḥammad). As Saʿd b. ʿUbādah was also absent from Badr, allegedly suffering from snake-bite, Saʿd b. Muʿādh was the leading man among the Anṣār there present and contributed much to the Muslim victory.

The attitude of Ibn Ubayy has to be surmised from the scant accounts of his behaviour. He must have realized that the movement towards Islam had become so strong that it could not be checked, and that to withstand it would simply cause him to lose influence. He probably also hoped to rule all Medina, and may even have seen in Islam a means towards his end; if Islam provided a religious basis for unity, he could exercise the political control. Had the Jews been converted to Islam, this dream might have come true in part. But the Jews rejected Islam, Muḥammad proved to be an expert in handling political affairs, and Ibn Ubayy showed too little fervour for the cause he had nominally espoused to have a position of importance within the religious movement. This is admittedly conjectural, but some such line of thought is required to explain why Ibn Ubayy became a Muslim, and then, without outwardly ceasing to be a Muslim, became an opponent of Islam.

It may well be, as Ibn Isḥāq says, that it was the conversion of Saʿd b. Muʿādh which led to the general acceptance of Islam by the Medinans. Study of the available evidence gives the impression that, apart from the exceptions about to be mentioned, the acceptance was really general, and that all the leading men and women in all the clans became at least nominally Muslims. We hear of no person of even a moderate degree of importance who became a Muslim only after, say, the victory of Badr or the breaking of the siege. In other words we have justification for assuming that there is no important person of whom we are uninformed, though it is likely that there are many mediocrities of whom we know nothing.

The clans from whom before the Hijrah there were no converts of standing were those of Aws Manāt, namely, Umayyah b. Zayd (of Murrah b. Mālik b. al-Aws), Khaṭmah, Wā'il, and Wāqif. The

Jewish clans also kept aloof from Islam, though in the course of time there were a few converts from them. None of the Arab clans mentioned seems to have been strong, though there was among them in Abū Qays b. al-Aslat of Wā'il a leader who at one time had been in the first rank. The sources do not give any reason for the refusal of these clans to join the new movement. Abū Qays is said to have thought of becoming a Muslim, but to have died before he put his thought into effect; such thoughts without actions, however, make one suspect an attempt to save the face of the clan, for the one solid fact which is not denied is that Abū Qays did *not* become a Muslim. The most probable explanation of this lack of response to Muḥammad is that these clans were closely linked with the Jews. Their lands were apparently not in a solid block, but mixed among Jewish lands. Their position was thus weak, and it is understandable that they were not ready, without further observation at close quarters, to commit themselves irrevocably to a movement that was looked on with disfavour by their Jewish neighbours.

It is convenient at this point to narrate the subsequent history of this 'pagan opposition', since it never was of prime importance in the affairs of Medina. Abū Qays died before Badr, and the other leading men also held aloof from Muḥammad, though there were some converts among the rank and file, presumably some younger men. Those who remained pagans were bitter about the advance of Islam. In particular, ʿAṣmā' bint Marwān (of Umayyah b. Zayd of Aws Manāt), the wife of a man of Khaṭmah, composed verses taunting and insulting some of the Muslims.[1] If those quoted by Ibn Isḥāq are genuine, the chief point was that the persons addressed were dishonouring themselves by submitting to a stranger not of their blood. Shortly after Badr (according to the most probable version) a man of Khaṭmah called ʿUmayr b. ʿAdī (or ʿUdayy) went to the house of ʿAṣmā' by night and killed her. Muḥammad did not disapprove, no one dared take vengeance on ʿUmayr, and many of the clan (and perhaps of the rest of Aws Manāt) now professed Islam openly; some of these are said to have been secret believers previously. The assassination of Abū ʿAfak of ʿAmr b. ʿAwf about the same time[2] by a man of his clan had similar motives and probably similar effects, since some

[1] IH, 995–6; WW, 90–91.
[2] IH, 994–5; WW, 91–92. WW's dating is to be preferred.

sections of 'Amr b. 'Awf were close to Aws Manāt both in outlook and in physical situation. Abū 'Afak had taunted his hearers with allowing an outsider to control their affairs, a man who confused right and wrong and who aimed at kingship. After these events we may assume that there was little overt opposition to Muḥammad among the pagans. If any still refused to become Muslims, they must have been relying on Jewish support, and can hardly have continued in their refusal after the expulsion of the chief Jewish clans. By the time of the campaign of Ḥunayn we find among the Muslim forces contingents from Wāqif, Khaṭmah, and Umayyah.[1] Thus, because of the bankruptcy of paganism confronted with the gloomy situation in Medina, the pagan opposition with its appeal to old ideas of honour and blood-relationship gradually died out. The sons of the pagans became Muslims, the idols of the clans were destroyed,[2] and Aws Manāt came to be known as Aws Allāh.

The case of Abū 'Āmir ar-Rāhib is mysterious, but may be dealt with here since he was neither Jew nor Muslim.[3] His name was 'Abd 'Amr b. Ṣayfī, and he belonged to the sub-clan Ḍubay'ah of 'Amr b. 'Awf. For many years before the Hijrah he had been a monotheist, and by his ascetic practices had gained the nickname of ar-Rāhib, the monk, although his asceticism did not include celibacy. When Muḥammad came to Medina, Abū 'Āmir, rather than submit to him like his maternal cousin Ibn Ubayy, migrated to Mecca. With fifteen (or perhaps fifty) Medinan followers he fought against the Muslims at Uḥud. He seems to have been at Khaybar for a time. On the fall of Mecca he retired to aṭ-Ṭā'if, and when that also submitted took refuge in Syria. Of his outlook we can know only what is to be inferred from his actions. He is important, however, as a sign that Muḥammad's claim to be a prophet was a stumbling-block to some who on general grounds might have been expected to welcome the new religion; and presumably this was so because they were aware of the political implications of the claim and disliked them.

Thus, with the exception of Abū Qays and Abū 'Āmir and their meagre following, Muḥammad, when he went to Medina, had the support for one reason or another of all the most influential men among the Arabs; and, apart from Sa'd b. Mu'ādh and Ibn Ubayy,

[1] WW, 358 and n.
[2] IS, iv/2. 94–95, 90.
[3] IH, 411–12, 561; WK, 205–6; WW, 103, 190, &c.; IS, viii. 251–2 (daughters).

they all came to the great convention of al-ʿAqabah. It is worth giving the names of the twelve *nuqabā'* or representatives who were appointed there, for they were leading men in their clans and in the new Islamic community as a whole.

Usayd b. al-Ḥuḍayr	ʿAbd al-Ash'hal.
(Abū 'l-Haytham b. at-Tayyihān) .	,,
Saʿd b. Khaythamah	ʿAmr b. ʿAwf.
Rifāʿah b. ʿAbd al-Mundhir . .	ʿAmr b. ʿAwf.
Saʿd b. ar-Rabīʿ	Ba'l-Ḥārith.
ʿAbdallāh b. Rawāḥah . . .	,,
Saʿd b. ʿUbādah	Sāʿidah.
al-Mundhir b. ʿAmr	,,
al-Barā' b. Maʿrūr	Salimah.
ʿAbdallāh b. ʿAmr b. Ḥaram . .	,,
ʿUbādah b. aṣ-Ṣāmit	al-Qawāqilah.
Rāfiʿ b. Mālik	Zurayq.
Asʿad b. Zurārah	an-Najjār.

3. THE MUSLIM OPPOSITION

The opponents of Muḥammad among those who had formally professed Islam are commonly spoken of as the *munāfiqūn* or Hypocrites, and the usage has Qur'anic sanction. A more useful term in the present connexion, however, is the 'Muslim opposition' since this name distinguishes the object of study from the pagan opposition (just mentioned) and the Jewish opposition (to be dealt with later), and does not restrict the historian to those persons branded as Hypocrites. There were occasional disagreements with Muḥammad's policy even among those Muslims loyal to him, but the sources tend to minimize the disagreements within the community and to suggest that it was more united than in fact it was. Only in the case of those stigmatized as Hypocrites are we given accounts of what they said and did against Muḥammad, and even these are meagre. There is consequently a scarcity of information about the internal politics of Medina, and at many points we have to rely on conjectures and probabilities.

(a) *The first five years*

The setting out of the expedition which humbled the Meccans at Badr was the first occasion on which the Anṣār were faced with an important decision. Were they to respond to Muḥammad's summons? One who did not respond was Usayd b. al-Ḥuḍayr; but on the return of the victorious army he apologized to Muḥammad, saying that he thought it was only a raid for booty, and that had he known there was to have been fighting he would certainly have been present. This conduct could be explained easily as a reaction to Muḥammad's success. We might suppose that Usayd, learning that Saʿd b. Muʿādh (his rival for leadership within the clan of ʿAbd al-Ash'hal) was high in Muḥammad's counsels, dallied with the idea of gaining an advantage by not identifying himself with what probably seemed to be a losing cause; when it was made clear that the cause was not a losing one, he hurriedly dropped this idea and resigned himself to second place within the clan on the side of Muḥammad.[1]

This explanation, even if mainly sound, probably has a false emphasis, laying too much stress on the personal rivalry. Up to this time, some eighteen months after the Hijrah, Muḥammad had apparently accomplished nothing of moment. Others also stayed away—Ibn Ubayy, and even Saʿd b. ʿUbādah; the latter indeed is said to have been suffering from snake-bite, but that may be merely his excuse.[2] If there was a movement away from Muḥammad, his notable victory and his gentle handling of the truants put a stop to it. Usayd and Saʿd b. ʿUbādah continued to stand high in his favour, and even Ibn Ubayy did not refuse outright to help at Uḥud. The man who gave the lead in loyal devotion to Muḥammad was Saʿd b. Muʿādh, and he continued to be foremost of the Anṣār as a whole until his death, when Saʿd b. ʿUbādah (Sāʿidah) took his place. The leader of the Khazraj at Badr was al-Ḥubāb b. al-Mundhir (Salimah), but he was not specially prominent in later events.

If there was an incipient movement away from Muḥammad among the Muslims, probably encouraged by the Jews, it is conceivable that the attack on the Qaynuqāʿ was intended by Muḥammad not merely to weaken the Jews but to reward his supporters and to teach a lesson to the lukewarm Muslims like Ibn Ubayy. It is noteworthy that Qaynuqāʿ were confederates of Ibn Ubayy, who had fought by his side on several occasions before the Hijrah. Among those prominent in the attack on Qaynuqāʿ were Saʿd b. Muʿādh, who must be reckoned a rival of Ibn Ubayy, and ʿUbādah b. aṣ-Ṣāmit of al-Qawāqilah, which, as has been seen, was

[1] IH, 428; WW, 37 f., 72.
[2] WW, 66.

apparently jealous of Ibn Ubayy and Ba'l-Ḥublā. 'Ubādah had also been a confederate of the Jews (doubtless because he and Ibn Ubayy were both members of the old B. Sālim), but, instead of pleading for them like Ibn Ubayy, he declared that he renounced his relationship to them.[1]

Ibn Ubayy appears to have used the argument to Muḥammad that the Meccans were likely to march against Medina to exact revenge, and that in such a case the support of the 300 armed men of Qaynuqā' would be an asset, and that therefore they should not be expelled. According to a tradition which may be accepted, the following Qur'anic passage refers to this occasion:

> O ye who have believed, do not take Jews and Christians as friends (or patrons); they are friends to each other; whoever of you makes friends of them is one of them; verily God doth not guide the wrong-doing people. Yet one sees those in whose hearts is disease hastening (*sc.* to speak to Muḥammad) about them, saying: 'We fear a turn of fortune may befall us.' But possibly God will bring the Issue (or final deliverance) or some affair from Himself (*sc.* direct intervention), and they will become remorseful on account of what they concealed within themselves. . . .[2]

The following verses, which exhort the believers to 'take as friend (or patron) God and His messenger and those who have believed', are traditionally connected with the action of 'Ubādah in renouncing his league with non-Muslims.

This passage from the Qur'ān tends to prove what general considerations made a probability, namely, that this incipient opposition to Muḥammad among Medinan Muslims was strongest among those friendly with the Jews. Other passages corroborate. The phrase 'those in whose hearts is disease' is the Qur'ānic term at this period for the Muslim opposition. This group is accused of criticizing the Qur'ān, especially some of the more recently revealed passages.[3] In particular they made difficulties over the matter of abrogation.[4] To begin with, their main effort seems to have been to weaken Muḥammad's position by verbal arguments.[5] When it became clear, however, that Muḥammad's policy was to provoke the Meccans by raids on their caravans which might, like that to Nakhlah, involve bloodshed, they became seriously alarmed.

[1] IH, 545–7; WW, 92–93.
[2] Q. 5. 51 f./57 f.
[3] Q. 9. 124–7/125–8 E; cf. 74. 31 E+.
[4] Q. 22. 52/51–54/53 E.
[5] Q. 2. 8/7–15/14 FG.

Some time before Badr the Muslims had received by revelation the command: 'when ye meet those who have disbelieved (let there be) slaughter . . . until war lays down its burdens'.[1] We may surmise that the Anṣār had not been enthusiastic about the matter until this revelation came, for it is probably in this connexion that the Qur'ān reports them as saying: 'Why has not a sūrah been sent down?'[2] The loyal Muslims now accepted the policy of provoking Quraysh, but the opposition became more alarmed; 'when a clearly formulated sūrah is sent down and fighting is mentioned in it, thou seest those in whose hearts is disease looking at thee with the look of one already faint in death'.[3] About the same time (or perhaps a little later) there was a movement to avoid bringing disputes to Muḥammad for settlement.[4]

The Qur'ān and the biographical sources thus give complementary pictures of the discontent in Medina with Muḥammad's policy. His success at Badr and against Qaynuqā', however, and his firm but gentle handling of the opposition prevented any serious attempt to leave his camp for that of the Meccans, and when Quraysh advanced against Medina in the campaign of Uḥud, the Islamic community was intact, if not altogether united. Ibn Ubayy had an honoured place in the discussions of strategy. He supported Muḥammad's original suggestion, that they should remain in the strongly fortified central settlements; but it may well be that Muḥammad made the suggestion because he knew that such a policy of playing for safety was most likely to be acceptable to men like Ibn Ubayy. The young men, eager for battle, protested, and found some responsible men to support them on the grounds that to do nothing while their crops were being ruined would cause a serious loss of prestige. This group opposed to Ibn Ubayy included Ḥamzah (Muḥammad's uncle), Sa'd b. 'Ubādah (Sā'idah), an-Nu'mān b. Mālik (al-Qawāqilah), Iyās b. Aws ('Abd al-Ash'hal), and Khaythamah and Anas b. Qatādah ('Amr b. 'Awf). This list of names is not large, and it is possible that many Muslims favoured the first course. Sa'd b. Mu'ādh and Usayd b. al-Ḥuḍayr may have done so, for, when Muḥammad decided on the second course, they seemed to think that he had been unduly influenced by the pressure of the second group, and proposed that the decision should be reviewed and left entirely in his hands.

[1] Q. 47. 4 EF.
[2] Q. 47. 20/22 EF; cf. 35/37.
[3] Ibid. 20/22.
[4] Q. 24, 47/46–52/51 G.

What subsequently happened has already been narrated. Muḥammad adhered to the decision already taken, and Ibn Ubayy, after marching out part of the way, retired with his party to their strongholds. With reference to this and to Ibn Ubayy's remarks to his wounded son after the battle, the Qur'ān says:

What befell you on the day when the two hosts met was by the permission of God, and in order that He might know the believers and in order that He might know those who played the hypocrite; they were asked to come and fight in the way of God, or to defend (themselves), but they said: 'If we knew aught of fighting (*sc.* with a chance of success; or else, if we thought there would actually be fighting), we would follow you.' They were that day nearer to unbelief than to belief, saying with their mouths what was not in their hearts; but God knoweth what they conceal—those who, having stayed behind, say regarding their brethren: 'If they had obeyed us, they would not have been killed.'[1]

The word here translated 'played the hypocrite' properly means 'crept to their holes' like moles or mice. In this passage it is probably used for the first time with regard to Ibn Ubayy and his party, and used in its literal sense; later, of course, the participle *munāfiqūn* became the regular description of the 'Muslim opposition' and is commonly translated Hypocrites; but the derived sense is probably due to this Qur'anic passage, and we might perhaps convey more of the original feel of the word by speaking of the Creepers or the Moles.[2]

It is noteworthy that the Qur'ān here speaks only of the cowardice of the Hypocrites, and does not accuse them of disobedience. From this it is to be inferred that Ibn Ubayy was within his rights in acting as he did, and did not formally break his league with Muḥammad (which was presumably in the terms of the Constitution).[3] Previously he had gone out of his way to be condescending towards Muḥammad in public; now he made it clear that he was not a wholehearted supporter of Muḥammad like Sa'd b. Mu'ādh, but insisted on being regarded as at least an equal. Since he was still nominally a Muslim and had committed no punishable offence, Muḥammad, who was occupied with promoting public security, could take no violent measures against him, much as his followers desired this; but when he rose in the mosque after the Friday

[1] Q. 3. 166/160–168/162 G; cf. WW, 145.

[2] But cf. A. Jeffery, *The Foreign Vocabulary of the Qur'ān*, Baroda, 1938, *s.v.*; Horovitz, *Koranische Untersuchungen*, 64, with further references.

[3] Cf. p. 221 below.

Worship, and tried to make his usual condescending speech, he was roughly handled by men of Mālik b. an-Najjār and al-Qawāqilah.[1]

Up to this point Ibn Ubayy and his friends had been grumbling and criticizing Muḥammad and his revelations, but their position had essentially been that of 'sitting on the fence'. It is presumably they who are described in these words of the Qur'ān: 'Those who have believed and then disbelieved, then believed and then disbelieved again, . . . vacillating between (this and) that, are neither one thing nor the other.'[2] His treatment after Uḥud, however, seems to have infuriated him, and for the next two years he was seeking opportunities of injuring or even destroying Muḥammad. Five months after Uḥud the Muslims sent an ultimatum to the Jewish clan of an-Naḍīr. Ibn Ubayy and some fellow clansmen did all they could to persuade the Jews to resist, even promising military support. Some of the Jews found this to their liking, but the cooler and wiser heads were aware of the emptiness of the promises, and an-Naḍīr soon submitted. Their departure was a further defeat for Ibn Ubayy. His actions are described in Sūrat al-Ḥashr:

> Hast thou not seen those who have played the hypocrite saying to their brethren the People of the Book who have disbelieved: 'Surely, if ye are expelled, we shall go out with you, we shall never obey anyone in regard to you, and if ye are attacked in war, we shall help you'? God testifieth that they are lying. If they are expelled, they (the Hypocrites) will assuredly not go out with them, and if they are attacked in war, they will not help them, and if they help them, they will certainly turn their backs (in flight), and then they will not be helped.[3]

The next opportunity for action, so far as our records go, was over a year later during the expedition of Muraysī'. A quarrel between two men over a bucket of water rapidly developed into a fight between the Anṣār and the Emigrants, and the results might have been serious had it not been as rapidly quelled by the loyal Muslims. Ibn Ubayy seems to have used the occasion to say to any who would listen that this man who came ostensibly to keep the peace was merely involving them in brawls; and he also seems to have muttered something about the stronger driving out the weaker when they returned to Medina. As Sūrat al-Munāfiqīn puts it, it is the Hypocrites 'who say: "If we return to the city, the highest in dignity in it will assuredly expel the most abased," though dignity

[1] IH, 591 f.; WW, 145. [2] Q. 4. 137/136, 142/141 F; cf. 141/140.
[3] Q. 59. 11 f.; IH, 652 f.; WW, 162–5.

belongs to God and His messenger and the believers'. Muḥammad was informed of Ibn Ubayy's words, but refused to take any violent action, though Ibn Ubayy's son ʿAbdallāh, who was devoted to Muḥammad, said he would himself kill his father if Muḥammad wanted that done. Muḥammad preferred to tire out the participants in the expedition by an exceptionally long march.[1]

Ibn Ubayy, however, had not learnt his lesson. Before the party arrived back in Medina, Muḥammad's young wife ʿĀ'ishah, who had accompanied them, was somehow left behind after the last halt, and eventually entered Medina after the others attended by a handsome young man. Tongues wagged, and Ibn Ubayy did what he could to magnify the scandal. In this he had some strange helpers, the son of a cousin of Abū Bakr, the poet Ḥassān b. Thābit and the sister of Muḥammad's wife Zaynab, each of whom must have been moved by some personal animosity against ʿĀ'ishah or by sympathy for Ibn Ubayy or by dislike for the Emigrants. The scandal kept growing for weeks before matters came to a head. The question of fact was decided by Muḥammad in favour of ʿĀ'ishah, since there was no solid evidence against her; and the incident is commonly referred to as 'the affair of the lie' (*ʿifk*). The lesser scandal-mongers are said to have been flogged. With Ibn Ubayy Muḥammad had a 'show-down'. He summoned a meeting of the leading men among the Anṣār, and asked for permission to take punitive measures against one of them who was attacking his family; violence towards a man without the consent of his clan or tribe would lead to reprisals by the *lex talionis*. Muḥammad's request was followed by an angry scene in which the Aws and the Khazraj nearly came to blows—a state of affairs perhaps deliberately provoked to make them forget their common grievance against the Emigrants. It was not long before the quarrel was made up.[2]

Ibn Ubayy was probably not punished in any way (though some authorities said he was flogged). From this point onwards, however, there are no records of his taking any active steps against Muḥammad, and it may be assumed that he now realized that his following was so small that he could not hope to achieve anything. He was too old to become an enthusiastic Muslim, and he may sometimes

[1] Q. 63. 8; IH, 726–8; WW, 179–83.

[2] IH, 731–40; WW, 184–9; al-Bukhārī, *Maghāzī* (64), 34; Nabia Abbott, *Aishah the Beloved of Mohammed*, Chicago, 1942, 29–38.

have grumbled,[1] but he was sufficiently a Muslim at al-Ḥudaybiyah in 628/6 to refuse the privilege of making the pilgrimage, which Quraysh, while denying it to the other Muslims, offered to him as a special favour.[2] That he did not remain unreconciled to Muḥammad is further shown by his presence at al-Ḥudaybiyah and by the fact that Muḥammad himself conducted his funeral rites.[3]

The weakness of the position of Ibn Ubayy was that it had no ideological basis. As one of the leaders of an-Naḍīr is alleged to have put it, Ibn Ubayy did not know what he wanted; he was whole-heartedly committed neither to Islam nor to Judaism nor to the old religion of his people.[4] He was probably moved chiefly by personal ambition, and lacked the statesmanship to see all the vaster issues involved and the vision to propound a way of dealing with them that would attract men. He must have seen the need for peace in Medina, but his attempts to meet it were along conservative lines that were already discredited. His opposition to Muḥammad may be said to be due to a failure to move with the times; and it is significant that one source remarks that there was only one young man among the Hypocrites.[5]

Perhaps there were similar reasons for the refusal of some men of 'Amr b. 'Awf to help with the defence of Medina when it was besieged.[6] Such people might be nominally Muslims, but they evidently did not regard membership of the Islamic community as a primary fact in their lives. Another whose attitude was presumably similar was al-Jadd b. Qays, whom Muḥammad deposed from the leadership of the clan of Salimah.[7] The Qur'ān charges the Hypocrites with unbelief at the time of the siege, and gives the impression that their attitude was more dangerous than is indicated by the narrative sources, which were not written down until long after the great triumphs of Islam.

The Hypocrites and those in whose hearts is disease were saying: 'God and His messenger have promised us nothing but illusion.' A party of them said: 'O people of Yathrib, there is no abiding place for you, so return'; and a part of them were asking leave of the prophet, saying: 'Our houses are a weak point'; they were not a weak point, they were only wishing to flee. If an entrance had been made upon them from that side (*sc.* on which their houses stood), and they had been asked to

[1] Cf. WW, 247. [2] Ibid. 255. [3] IH, 927; WW, 414 f.
[4] WW, 162. [5] IH, 363. [6] WW, 194.
[7] IH, 309; IS, iii/2. 112; for his conduct cf. IH, 746, 894; WW, 248, 392; cf. p. 234 below.

join in sedition, they would have joined in it and would have hesitated but slightly. Yet they had covenanted with God previously that they would not turn their backs. . . .[1]

(b) *The last five years*

The treachery of Abū Lubābah in connexion with Banū Qurayẓah may be said to mark the transition to the second phase of the opposition in Medina, when its efforts were directed not against the Islamic community as such but against particular aspects of Muḥammad's policy. Unfortunately the affair of Abū Lubābah is obscure. The following is Ibn Isḥāq's version.

Then they (B. Qurayẓah) sent to the Messenger of God (God bless and preserve him) the request, 'Send to us Abū Lubābah . . . that we may consult him about our course of action.' The Messenger of God (God bless and preserve him) sent him to them, and when they saw him . . . they said to him, 'O Abū Lubābah, do you think that we should surrender at the discretion of Muḥammad?' He said, 'Yes,' and pointed with his hand to his neck, indicating that it would be slaughter. (Subsequently) Abū Lubābah said, 'By God, my foot had not moved from the spot beforeI realized that I had betrayed God and His messenger.' Then he departed. He did not go, however, to the Messenger of God (God bless and preserve him), but bound himself to one of the pillars in the mosque and said, 'I shall not leave my place here until God pardons me for what I have done,' and he swore to God, 'I shall never again go to Banū Qurayẓah, and I shall never again go to a district in which I betrayed God and His messenger. . . . When news of this reached the Messenger of God (God bless and preserve him)—he had been surprised at the delay—he said, 'Had he come to me, I would have forgiven him; but since he has done as he has done, it is not for me to loose him from his place until God pardons him.'[2]

Abū Lubābah then remained bound to the pillar except during the times of prayer when his wife (or daughter) untied him. After six days Muḥammad announced that God had pardoned him, and at Abū Lubābah's request himself untied him.

The story as we have it must have been manipulated. The only obvious 'treachery' in it is the betrayal of Muḥammad's intention of putting the men to death, for this might be supposed to have made Qurayẓah less ready to surrender. Actually, however, it does not appear to have done so; and the offence is not commensurate with the punishment. Nor is the mystery explained by the further

[1] Q. 33. 12–15. [2] IH, 686 f.; cf. WW, 213–15.

details in al-Wāqidī of how Abū Lubābah tried to persuade the main body of Qurayẓah to abandon Ḥuyayy, who had been mainly responsible for the resistance to Muḥammad. The explanation is probably to be looked for in some undertaking given by Abū Lubābah to stand faithful to his clan's alliance with Qurayẓah. This would have led to a grave split in the Islamic community, had any attempt been made to punish Qurayẓah. In this or some similar form the question at issue must have been the continuation of pre-Islamic relationships with non-Muslims. There is no suggestion that Abū Lubābah was other than a faithful member of the Islamic community; he had no thought of leaving that community, but on a certain matter of policy he differed from Muḥammad. This, then, is the characteristic of the Muslim opposition to Muḥammad during the last few years of his life. It accepts the community as a fact but disagrees with particular lines of policy, usually for selfish reasons.

The next case of this is the refusal of some of the nomadic tribes to take part in the expedition of al-Ḥudaybiyah in 628/6, doubtless because they failed to see any immediate gain to be derived from it.[1] Muḥammad's grasp of events was so much wider than that of the majority of his followers that it must often have been difficult to bring them to accept his policies when these involved hardship. The crisis came with the expedition to Tabūk in 630/9. Arabia was now rushing to enter into alliance with Muḥammad, and some of the worthy farmers of Medina thought it was time to have a little rest from their labours and enjoy their hard-won prosperity. Not so Muḥammad. He realized that the internal peace of Arabia could only be maintained if its excess energies were directed outwards. The expeditions to the north were thus of primary importance in the creation of a stable Arab state. But this was a long-term policy whose advantages were not obvious to the multitude. In particular, some of the well-to-do men of Medina objected both to the discomfort of personal participation in an expedition and to the contributions (*ṣadaqāt*) they were expected to give. They kept their hands tight shut, and jeered at those who gave generously.[2] When the summons came to march to Tabūk, a number of the Anṣār remained at home.[3]

Three incidents connected with this expedition throw light on

[1] IH, 740; WW, 242.
[2] Q. 9. 75/76–80/81.
[3] IH, 897, 907–13; WW, 393, 411–13.

the state of feeling among some of the Muslims. There is said to have been a plot against Muḥammad; something was to happen on a dangerous bit of road on a dark night, and it would have looked like an accident.[1] Then there was the 'mosque of dissension' (*masjid aḍ-ḍirār*). Just before the expedition set out Muḥammad had been asked to honour by his presence a mosque at Qubā' which some Muslims had built, but he postponed the matter till his return. On the journey, however, he somehow realized that an intrigue against himself was involved, and as soon as he returned to Medina he sent two men to destroy the mosque. The mosque-builders were of the clan of ʿAmr b. ʿAwf and apparently supporters of Abū ʿĀmir ar-Rāhib (who may even himself have been in Medina at this time), and the new mosque was to give them a convenient meeting-place where they could hatch their plots without interruption. Abū Lubābah had made a gift for the mosque but was clear of the intrigues.[2]

About the same time the men who had stayed at home from the expedition to Tabūk were being cross-examined and their excuses scrutinized. Three who were not involved in the intrigue of the mosque-builders but had no good excuse were 'sent to Coventry' for fifty days. The severity of the punishment shows the importance of the matter, and several Qur'ānic verses indicate that about this time those now called 'Hypocrites' were practically excluded from the community; they were to be treated roughly and threatened with Hell as apostates.[3] A little reflection makes it clear that, if the Islamic community was to engage in expeditions into Syria which would involve the absence of most of its fighting men for long periods, it could not allow a body of dissidents to ensconce themselves in a suburb of Medina. Moreover, for the spiritual health of the community it was desirable that all its able-bodied men should share in the campaigns. Thus it would seem that about this time there was a definite change of policy towards the opposition; but the Hypocrites who are now attacked and denounced are not identical with the previous ones, and may be entirely different. Ibn Ubayy was not at Tabūk, but his excuse (presumably ill-health) was apparently accepted, and he was not 'excommunicated', since Muḥammad attended his funeral shortly afterwards.

This series of events may well be regarded as the final crisis

[1] WW, 409.
[2] IH, 906 f.; WW, 410 f.
[3] Q. 9. 73/74 f.; cf. 66. 9.

during Muḥammad's lifetime in the internal politics of Medina. Medina was now prosperous, and some of the Anṣār hoped for a lazy enjoyment of their prosperity. Muḥammad, however, either persuaded them to accept his policy of continued expansion or showed them that his demands were not lightly to be rejected, since his will could be made effective by overwhelming force. In this way he established the Islamic community on foundations sufficiently solid to permit its expansion into an empire.

There were other tensions in Medina, of course, notably those between Emigrants and Anṣār[1] and between the Aws and the Khazraj, but the sources give little information about them during Muḥammad's lifetime. It is sometimes only years afterwards that the cleavages become apparent.

[1] Cf. IH, 912; WW, 413; of the Emigrants only Ṭalḥah and az-Zubayr showed friendship to Ka'b b. Mālik.

VI

MUḤAMMAD AND THE JEWS

1. THE JEWS OF YATHRIB

THAT there were Jews in Medina when Muḥammad went there is clear,[1] but how they came to be there and whether they were of Hebrew stock is not clear. Were they the descendants of fugitives from Palestine—perhaps after the rising of Bar Kokhba? Were they mainly Arabs who had adopted the Jewish faith? Such questions have been much discussed first by Muslim and then by Western scholars, but no general agreement has been reached.[2] The Jewish tribes had many customs identical with those of their pagan Arab neighbours and intermarried with them,[3] but they adhered firmly to the Jewish religion, or at least to a form of it, and maintained their distinct existence.

When the Aws and the Khazraj came to Yathrib from the south, they found it dominated by Jews, though there were also a few Arabs in a subordinate position to the Jews. The dividing line between Arabs of this earlier stratum and Jews is confused. The Arabs were weaker than the Jews—thirteen Arab strongholds (*āṭām*) to fifty-nine Jewish ones is one figure[4]—and were in relations of *jiwār* or *ḥilf* to them, that is, were protected by them, either as 'neighbours' or as confederates. They probably intermarried, and marriage was presumably uxorilocal.[5] They may have adopted the Jewish religion. Not surprisingly, then, certain Arab clans are sometimes reckoned as Jewish clans; thus as-Samhūdī's list of Jewish clans includes B. Marthad, B. Muʿāwiyah, B. Jadhmā', B. Nāghiṣah, B. Zaʿūrā', and B. Thaʿlabah, although the first of

[1] General sources for the section: as-Samhūdī, 109–16, 152 ff. (= Wüstenfeld, *Medina*, 25–31); Ibn al-Athīr, i. 400–20; Wellhausen, *Medina*, 7–15; H. Hirschfeld, 'Essai sur l'histoire des Juifs de Médine', *Revue des Études Juives*, vii. 167–93; x. 10–31; A. J. Wensinck, *Mohammed en de Joden te Medina*, Leiden, 1928, 33–53 (part of this has been translated by G. H. Bousquet and G. W. Bousquet-Mirandolle as 'L'Influence Juive sur les Origines du Culte Musulman', in *Revue Africaine*, xcviii (1954), 85–112).

[2] Cf. Wellhausen, l.c.; Caetani, *Ann.* i. 383; C. C. Torrey, *The Jewish Foundation of Islam*, New York, 1933, ch. 1; D. G. Margoliouth, *The Relations between Arabs and Israelites prior to the Rise of Islam*, London, 1924, lecture 3.

[3] E.g. IH, 351 (parents of Kaʿb b. al-Ashraf); IS, viii. 236. 23 ff. (Umāmah bint Bishr and Asad b. 'Ubayd).

[4] As-Samhūdī, 116 (= Wüstenfeld, 31).

[5] Cf. p. 379 below.

these is properly a part of the Arab tribe of Balī, the second a part of Sulaym, the third and fourth Arabs of the Yemen, and the last two Arabs of Ghassān.[1]

The authentic Jewish tribes or clans are commonly said to be three, Qurayẓah, an-Nadīr, and Qaynuqāʿ. This is a simplification, however. As-Samhūdī has a list of about a dozen clans in addition to those already mentioned as being clearly of Arab extraction.[2] The most important was B. Hadl, closely associated with Qurayẓah, unless the clan of Thaʿlabah to which Fiṭyawn belonged is to be distinguished from the Ghassānid Thaʿlabah. Of the three main tribes Qaynuqāʿ possessed no agricultural land but had a compact settlement where they conducted a market and practised crafts such as that of the goldsmith. Qurayẓah and an-Naḍīr, on the other hand, had some of the richest lands in the oasis, situated in the higher part towards the south and mostly given over to growing palms. Here, as in several other fertile spots in western Arabia such as Khaybar, the Jews appear to have been pioneers in agricultural development.

The Aws and the Khazraj were allowed to settle, presumably on lands that had not yet been brought under cultivation, and were under the protection of some of the Jewish tribes. One of the marks of their subordinate position was the *ius primae noctis* exercised by Fiṭyawn of B. Thaʿlabah. Mālik b. al-ʿAjlān (of B. ʿAwf of the Khazraj) is said to have been instigated to revolt against Fiṭyawn by his sister who wanted to avoid having to spend her first night as a bride with Fiṭyawn. Either because he had outside help, or because the Jews were temporarily weak owing to outside interference, Mālik was able to make himself independent. It is difficult, however, to estimate accurately the extent of his success. It is commonly suggested that the Aws and the Khazraj became rulers of Yathrib with all the Jews in subjection to them; but the sources do not support such a view.[3] All that we can be certain about is that some of the Khazraj became independent; it is probable, however, that nearly all the Khazraj and many of the Aws became independent, and doubtless acquired strongholds. Indeed, as time went on, they seem to have become stronger than the Jews, since

[1] As-Samhūdī, 114–16; Wellhausen, op. cit. 12; *Aghānī*, xv. 162. 16; xix. 95. 13 f.

[2] Cf. *Aghānī*, xix. 95. 9 ff.

[3] The general impression is that the Jews were independent. Some of the Khazraj are said to be *mawālī 'l-yahūd* in Ṭab., *Tafsīr*, iv. 22, but this is doubtful.

they were able to indulge in the luxury of fighting among themselves. On the other hand, those clans of the Aws which at first refused to become Muslim presumably did so because they were in close relations with Jewish neighbours. Any estimate of strength, of course, must allow for the fact that there were probably serious cleavages among both the Arabs and the Jews; it was improbable that there would be a league of all the Jews or all the Arabs.

Various changes, however, seem to have been taking place in the Jewish community which indicate that they were becoming relatively weaker. Several Arab clans of the early stratum instead of being subordinate to the Jews (doubtless as confederates) became confederates of Arab clans. Thus B. Unayf became attached to B. Jaḥjabā' (of ʿAmr b. ʿAwf), and B. Ghusaynah to B. Qawāqilah,[1] while B. Zaʿūrā' had become recognized as members of the clan of ʿAbd al-Ash'hal b. Jusham, or at least of Jusham, and, as confederates of Zaʿūrā', the group known as 'the people of Rātij' had become attached to ʿAbd al-Ash'hal.[2] By about the time of the Hijrah all the lesser Jewish clans or groups in as-Samhūdī's list had lost their identity, or at least had ceased to be of political importance. They are not mentioned in the primary sources for the career of Muḥammad. When the Constitution of Medina deals with them they are simply 'the Jews of an-Najjār', 'the Jews of al-Ḥārith', and so on.[3] The nearest to being an exception is Hadl; it had become very closely connected with Qurayẓah, but we find three members of it becoming Muslims and escaping the fate of Qurayẓah.[4] From these facts it seems likely that the clan system had largely broken down, and that the groups which became attached to the various clans of the Anṣār were not small clans or sub-clans but groups containing people of varying origin.

The four Jewish clans which feature as clans in the life of Muḥammad are Qurayẓah, an-Naḍīr, Qaynuqāʿ, and Thaʿlabah. The last must be counted as a Jewish clan, since it seems to appear as such in the Constitution of Medina, but it is said to be of Arab origin.[5] Qaynuqāʿ were confederates of ʿAbdallāh b. Ubayy, and, as they supplied him with 700 men (of whom 300 had armour) in earlier battles, the parties to the alliance may have regarded one another as equals.[6] The other two tribes, an-Naḍīr and Qurayẓah,

[1] Cf. IS, iii/2. 41, 98, &c.
[2] Cf. also the list of Muḥammad's opponents in IH, 350 f., and see below, p. 227.
[3] See above, p. 160.
[4] IH, 135, cf. 387.
[5] Cf. Wellhausen, *Medina*, 12, &c.
[6] IH, 546; WW, 92.

were not attacked by Muḥammad until after his success against Qaynuqāʿ, either because they were stronger, or, more probably, because he was more dependent on the support of their Arab confederates. The fact that before the battle of Buʿāth they had given hostages to the Khazraj suggests that they felt themselves at least temporarily weaker than ʿAmr b. an-Nuʿmān al-Bayāḍī and his allies. The affair of the hostages, however, together with the rupture between ʿAmr b. an-Nuʿmān and ʿAbdallāh b. Ubayy, is obscure, and does not provide a foundation for a strong argument. The incident seems to show the existence among certain of the Arabs of a desire to expel the Jews and seize their lands. The two clans decided to deal with this threat by exchanging their existing alliance for one with the Aws (especially ʿAbd al-Ash'hal), even at the cost of the lives of some of their hostages; thereby they made possible the victory of the Aws at Buʿāth. In all this these two clans seem to be acting as sovereign bodies, making alliances with Arab clans as equals, not politically subordinate to any of them, but perhaps tending to become relatively weaker.

Thus there was little unity among the Jews of Yathrib. In their political relationships they behaved in much the same way as Arab clans and smaller groups. All had some form of alliance with Arab clans, but at least in the case of the stronger Jewish clans this did not involve any subordination. By themselves the Jews did not constitute a threat to the Arabs, but as supporters of ʿAbdallāh b. Ubayy they might have had considerable influence, and he seems to have tried to gain their support.

2. THE JEWS AT THE HIJRAH

There is no mention of any direct negotiations between Muḥammad and the Jews before the Hijrah. He must, however, have been aware of their importance in Medinan politics, and have considered, at least provisionally, the attitude he should adopt towards them. He believed that the revelation which was coming to him was identical with that which had previously been given to Jews and Christians.[1] It was natural for him to suppose that this would be as obvious to the Jews as it was to him, and that they would therefore accept him as a prophet. Presumably some of Muḥammad's agents made an approach to the Jews before he left Mecca, and their answer may not have been wholly unsatisfactory; they

[1] Cf. Q. 10. 38 C–E+; 46. 10/9 ff. DE, &c.

may have been ready to enter a political agreement, but not to accept Muḥammad's religious claims. Whatever may have happened before the Hijrah, he hoped in his first months at Medina to win them over by personal contact.

The precise status of the Jews in Muḥammad's community is not clear. They certainly had an indirect relationship to it as confederates of Arab clans which belonged to it. Whether there was something more than this it is difficult to say. There is some mention of a treaty or covenant in the traditional sources. In one passage al-Wāqidī says that when Muḥammad came to Medina all the Jews made an agreement with him, of which one condition was 'that they were not to support an enemy against him'; elsewhere he says that the agreement was to the effect that 'they were to be neither for him nor against him', and a document was signed by Ka'b b. Asad on behalf of Qurayẓah, and retained by him until the siege of Medina, when it was torn up.[1] In Ibn Isḥāq's parallel to the latter passage a treaty with Qurayẓah is mentioned, but not with the other Jews, and nothing that is said implies an actual document.[2] A little later the clan says it has no treaty with Muḥammad, but this might mean either that it had broken its treaty or that there never was any.[3] This gives the impression that the story has grown in the telling. Ibn Isḥāq does not name his source; al-Wāqidī has two, a grandson of the poet Ka'b b. Mālik of the clan of Salimah, and Muḥammad b. Ka'b (d. 735–8/117–20), the Muslim son of a member of Qurayẓah who escaped death on the surrender of the clan since he was only a child; as Salimah was hostile to the Jews, and as converts are often bitter against the group they have abandoned, both have reasons for making the case against Qurayẓah as black as possible. Despite some such heightening of the melodrama, however, there may be a basis of truth in the reports, especially since the terms of the alleged agreement are modest and do not imply any close alliance, indeed little more than was involved in their being confederates of the Anṣār. Such understanding as there was between Muḥammad and the Jews may have been embodied in a formal document, but it is more likely that the Jews were merely mentioned in his agreement with the Anṣār (as in § 16 of the extant form of the Constitution); the statement in al-Wāqidī's first account above that Muḥammad 'joined each clan to its confederates' (*sc.* of the Anṣār) would bear this out. This

[1] WK, 177 (= WW, 92); WW, 196. [2] IH, 674. [3] Ibid. 675.

would also be sufficient to explain the remark of Abū Bakr in his quarrel with Finḥāṣ (of Qaynuqā'), 'If it were not for the treaty (*'ahd*) between us and you, I would have cut off your head.'[1] It is in accordance with this, too, that the Jews who came to fight at Uḥud (with the exception of the convert Mukhayrīq) are specifically said to have done so as confederates of 'Abdallāh b. Ubayy.[2]

By way of exception a small number of Jews accepted Muḥammad as prophet and became Muslims. The chief of these was apparently 'Abdallāh (originally al-Ḥuṣayn) b. Sallām (of Qaynuqā'), and he was in consequence much maligned by the other Jews.[3] There was also a group of eight, mainly from Qaynuqā', but they seem to have been friends of Ibn Ubayy and became Munāfiqūn.[4] Others mentioned by name were converted at a later period, e.g. on the day of Uḥud,[5] or at the time of the attacks on an-Naḍīr[6] and Qurayẓah.[7] The numbers were sufficient to warrant references to them in the Qur'ān (at least on the most probable interpretation of the passages); thus

among the People of the Book are some who believe in God and in what has been sent down to you and in what has been sent down to them, humbling themselves to God. . . .[8]

Another passage seems to speak of the Jews who had accepted Muḥammad as if they were not completely merged with the Muslims but formed a separate community (*ummah*):

They are not all alike; there is a community of the People of the Book, which is steadfast reciting the signs of God at the drawing on of night, prostrating themselves, Believing in God and the Last Day, . . . and vying in good deeds.[9]

In any case, however, the great majority of the Jews not merely did not accept Muḥammad, but became increasingly hostile. The numerous appeals to the Jews in the Qur'ān almost all imply that they might be expected to reject the appeals. Very soon after the

1 IH, 388.
2 WW, 106 (and 124).
3 IH, 353 f., 387 (quoting Q. 3. 113/109 as referring to converts); cf. *Usd*, iii. 176 f.
4 IH, 361 f.
5 Mukhayrīq (Tha'labah): IH, 354; WW, 124.
6 Benyamīn b. 'Umayr, Abū Sa'd b. Wahb: WW, 164, cf. 98 f.
7 Asad b. 'Ubayd, &c.: IH, 387, 687; (?) Rifā'ah b. Simwāl, *Usd*, ii. 181 (cf. IS, viii. 335 f., Ibn Ḥanbal, *Musnad*, Cairo, (1895)/1313, vi. 37. 26, 193. 5). Cf. also WW, 349; IS, i/1. 123. 5–15.
8 Q, 3. 199/198; cf. 28. 52–55.
9 3. 113/109 f.

Hijrah it must have become clear that few Jews were likely to accept the Gentile prophet.[1]

3. MUḤAMMAD'S ATTEMPTS TO RECONCILE THE JEWS

Early in his career Muḥammad must have become aware of the similarity between the message that was being revealed to him and the teachings of Judaism and Christianity; indeed, according to tradition, shortly after the first revelations Waraqah told him that what had come to him was identical with the *nāmūs*, presumably the Jewish scriptures. Especially after it seemed likely that he would go to Medina Muḥammad appears to have tried to model Islam on the older religion. In the year before the Hijrah, when Muṣʿab b. ʿUmayr was acting as Muḥammad's emissary in Medina, he asked permission to hold a meeting of the believers, and was told he might do so provided he observed the day on which the Jews prepared for the Sabbath (that is, Friday, the *paraskeue* or preparation).[2] Thus the Friday worship, which became a distinctive feature of Islam, was somehow connected with Judaism. Muḥammad himself does not seem to have observed it until his first Friday in Medina.[3]

Another point in which Muḥammad may have followed the Jewish practice while still in Mecca was in facing towards Jerusalem while worshipping, or, to use the technical term, in taking Jerusalem as his *qiblah*. It is certain that in the early Medinan period Jerusalem was the *qiblah* of the Muslims, but it is doubtful whether in Mecca they had this *qiblah* or another one or none at all. The view that even before the Hijrah Jerusalem was the *qiblah* of at least the Medinan Muslims is supported by a story about al-Barā' b. Maʿrūr, the leading Muslim of B. Salimah. During the expedition to Mecca shortly before the Hijrah he refused to turn his back on the Kaʿbah, though his companions expostulated. In Mecca Muḥammad was consulted, and told him to return to his previous *qiblah*, Syria (that is, Jerusalem).[4] Muḥammad himself may have had no *qiblah* at this time but may have been

[1] For *ummī* as 'Gentile' see Horovitz, *Koranische Untersuchungen*, 51–53; R. Paret, art. 'Ummī' in EI(S), with references; also H. L. Fischer, *Kleinere Schriften*, Leipzig, 1888, ii. 115–17.

[2] IS, iii/1. 83. 23 ff., reading *yatajahhazu*—cf. C. H. Becker in *Der Islam*, iii. 379; Wensinck, op. cit. 111–14; Buhl, *Mohammed*, 214.

[3] Ṭab. 1256. 20; cf. Caetani, i. 375 f. (writing without access to IS, iii/1).

[4] IH, 294 f.; Ṭab. 1218 f.

keen to assimilate his religion to that of the Jews in this respect. If in his Meccan period Muḥammad faced towards Jerusalem, this would not necessarily indicate Jewish influence or a desire to be like the Jews, since the practice was apparently common among Christians.[1] By 624/2, however, he was aware that there were differences between Jews and Christians.[2] On the whole it seems most likely that the Jerusalem *qiblah* was adopted by Muḥammad from the Medinan Muslims, especially since the main point in the story about al-Barā' is confirmed by the Qur'ān (2. 150/145).[3]

There is less uncertainty about the institution of a fast on the Jewish Day of Atonement, the Fast of 'Āshūrā.[4] Muḥammad certainly commanded the Muslims to observe this fast when the 10th of the Jewish month of Tishri came round, though it is not certain in which of the Muslim months this fell. Perhaps some of the Medinan Muslims had already been in the habit of observing it, for, when the fast of Ramaḍān was instituted, that of the 'Āshūrā was not forbidden, though it ceased to be obligatory. Similarly, in accordance with Jewish practice, midday worship (*ṣalāt*) was instituted. In Mecca there had apparently been only morning and evening worship, apart from nocturnal vigils;[5] but at Medina the Qur'ān commands, 'Remember the Worship, the middle Worship included' (or, 'especially the middle Worship').[6] Further, it has been suggested that in building the mosque at Medina Muḥammad had in mind the Jewish synagogue; but what became the mosque was primarily his own house and courtyard, and there are strong grounds for doubting any imitation of an ecclesiastical building.[7] Apart from this, however, there is evident in Muḥammad, shortly before and shortly after the Hijrah, a tendency to make his religion similar to that of the Jews and to encourage his Medinan followers to continue Jewish practices which they had adopted.

The same aim of reconciling the Jews probably underlies the verse which permits Muslims to eat the food of the People of the

[1] Tor Andrae, *Ursprung des Islams*, 4; Buhl, 218.

[2] Q. 2. 145/140; cf. Bell, *Origin of Islam*, 144.

[3] Cf. discussions of the whole question by Wensinck, op. cit. 108–10, and Buhl, 216–18; also D. G. Margoliouth, in *Journal of the Royal Asiatic Society*, 1925, 437.

[4] Q. 2. 183/179; Ṭab. 1281; cf. Wensinck, 122–5; Buhl, 214; Caetani, *Ann.* i. 431 f., 470 f.

[5] Cf. Q. 11. 114/116; Buhl, 215; Wensinck, 106–8.

[6] 2. 238/239.

[7] Buhl, 204 f.; Caetani, i. 432 ff.; Wensinck, 116; C. H. Becker, *Islamstudien*, Leipzig, 1924, i. 450 (= *Nöldeke-Festschrift*, Giessen, 1906, 331).

Book and to marry women from them (5. 5/7). This presumably refers to the Jews. It may be that the Meccan Muslims did not at first realize that the Jews had numerous restrictions, and thought that only the things mentioned in the Qur'ān were forbidden, namely blood, pork, and animals that had died naturally or been strangled or sacrificed to idols.[1] (It is curious that this list, apart from the mention of pork, should be so like that in Acts xv. 18; and one wonders whether this represents a common level of observance among monotheists in the Arabian peninsula, both Jews of Arab descent and Christians.) At any rate, there is no record of Muḥammad ever expecting his followers to observe all the Jewish restrictions; and after his break with the Jews we find in the Qur'ān denials that these are part of the revelation to the Jews from God, and the suggestion that they are intended as a punishment for the Jews.[2] Some of the phrases of the Qur'ān, however, might imply that Muslims had been following Jewish practice.[3]

All such ordering of the new religion to make it conform more closely to the older one was probably inspired by two motives, the desire for a reconciliation with the Jews and the desire to substantiate the reality of Muḥammad's prophethood by showing the essential identity of his revelation with the preceding one. Latterly the second motive may have become dominant, but to begin with the other must also have been prominent. Indeed, there are slight traces of Muḥammad's being ready to make far-reaching concessions to Jewish feeling. In the first section of this chapter it was assumed (as Western scholars have usually assumed) that Muḥammad's appeal to the Jews was an appeal to become Muslims or rather 'believers' on exactly the same footing as his Arab followers. It was noticed, however, that he could also speak of certain Jews who had apparently responded to his appeal as forming a distinct community. When this latter point is linked up with others about to be mentioned, there is some justification for thinking that at some period during the first year or so at Medina (not necessarily in the first months) Muḥammad contemplated a religious and political arrangement which would give a measure of unity but would not demand from the Jews any renunciation of their faith or acceptance of Muḥammad as prophet with a message for them. Such an

[1] Q. 5. 3/4; cf. 16. 115/116.
[2] 3. 78/72 F; 4. 160/158 F; 6. 146/147 E+; 10. 59/60 C–E+; 16. 118/119 E.
[3] 16. 116/117 E, &c. (apparently addressed to *believers*).

arrangement would be in accordance with the general idea that each prophet was sent to a particular community, and that the community to which he was sent was the Arabs. There seems to be such an appeal for reconciliation on the basis of monotheism and nothing else in a verse (possibly revealed in A.H. 2):

> Say: 'O People of the Book, come to a word (which is) fair between us and you, (to wit) that we serve no one but God, that we associate nothing with Him, and that none of us take others as Lords beside God.[1]

Moreover the verse permitting Muslims to eat the food of the People of the Book (5. 5/7) takes on a different colour if it is regulating the relations of two religious groups within a single political community. This would explain how it comes about that it appears to legislate for the Jews by making Muslim food permissible for them—an act which the Jews would regard as one of presumption. There is no mention in extant records of Jews marrying Muslim women, either because there were not sufficient Muslim women, or because there was a mention but it dropped out when the practice ceased. If there was thus a Jewish *ummah* as well as a Muslim *ummah* within the one political entity, it is conceivable, though not probable, that in the phrase of the Constitution about the Emigrants and the Anṣār forming an *ummah* 'distinct from the (other) people' (*dūn an-nās*), the word *nās* or 'people' refers not to people in general but to the People *par excellence*.[2]

Despite the concessions Muḥammad was prepared to make and his attempt to render his religion similar to that of the Jews, the latter did not become any friendlier towards him as time went on. On the contrary, they became hostile, and broadcast adverse criticism of Muḥammad's claims to be a prophet. Their reasons for this may have been partly religious—the obvious contradiction between what Muḥammad claimed or asserted and some of their fundamental dogmatic attitudes. There is no way, however, of measuring the strength of this motive, for the matter had a political aspect, and this also, one may suspect, was of importance. If Muḥammad succeeded with his plan, the Jews would have no chance of supreme power; they may have realized already that the Emigrants would generally have more influence on

[1] 3. 64/57; for the last clause cf. 9. 31.
[2] Constitution, § 1; cf. § 15.

Muḥammad than the Anṣār. On the other hand, until the battle of Badr Muḥammad's prospects of success were poor, and they may have thought that they would be better off if there was a return to the *status quo*; for some of them hopes may have been set on a league with Ibn Ubayy. They were, of course, far from being united, and their motives doubtless varied from clan to clan. All, however, with the few exceptions noted above, rejected Muḥammad's appeals.

Muḥammad remained outwardly patient for some time. Then there was a sudden change in his attitude—at least if we may believe a story not found in the earliest sources. One day while engaged in the Worship at the prayer-place in the quarter of B. Salimah, he received a revelation bidding him turn from facing Syria and face the Ka'bah instead. He did so, followed by the other participants, and the spot became the site of the Mosque of the Two Qiblahs.[1] A less colourful but more likely version is that he received the revelation of 2. 144/139 by night, and communicated it to the believers the following day.[2] The date is usually given as about the 15th of Sha'bān, A.H. 2 (= 11 February 624).[3] On the other hand, the verses referring to a change of *qiblah* (2. 142/136–152/147) show different strands and must have been revealed at different times. Richard Bell in his *Translation* therefore suggests that there may have been an interval between dropping the Jerusalem *qiblah* and adopting the Meccan. Certainly there seems to have been a period of hesitation. There is a report that the Jews taunted the Muslims that they did not know where to turn in worship until they (the Jews) told them, and that this made Muḥammad desirous of the change.[4] The Muslims, too, may have been divided among themselves. It is significant (though perhaps only for the criticism of sources) that the change of *qiblah* is said to have taken place among B. Salimah, for this was the tribe of al-Barā' b. Ma'rūr, who before the Hijrah was an advocate of the Ka'bah as *qiblah*. If the traditional date is correct, the change must have been made about the time of the raid of Nakhlah by which a challenge was issued to Quraysh; it was also just before Badr.

About the same time—traditionally in the same month of Sha'bān (viii), but more probably in the following month of

[1] Ad-Diyārbakrī, *al-Khamīs*, i. 414. 17–20.

[2] Al-Bukhārī, *Ṣalāt* (8), 32; *Tafsīr* (65), on 2. 144/139.

[3] IH, 427, contrast 381; Ṭab. 1279 f.

[4] Ibid. 1281.

Ramaḍān (ix) after Badr, about the 19th (= 15 March)—Muḥammad instituted the fast of Ramaḍān and declared that of the ʿĀshūrā no longer obligatory.[1] Various suggestions have been given for the source of this new practice, from the Christian Lent to customs of Manichaeans and pre-Islamic Arabs.[2] Most light on its significance for Muḥammad is thrown by Bell's view that the victory at Badr was the *Furqān*, that is, the coming of the promised calamity upon the unbelievers and the deliverance of the believers, analogous to the deliverance of Moses at the Red Sea, and that in commemoration of this *Furqān* the month's fast was instituted.[3] There is some confirmation for this view in the account of aṭ-Ṭabarī:[4]

> In this year, according to report, the fast of the month of Ramaḍān was instituted; the institution is said to have been in Shaʿbān; when the Prophet (God bless and preserve him) came to Medina, he observed the Jews fasting on the day of ʿĀshūrā, and questioned them; they informed him that it is the day on which God caused the drowning of the host of Pharaoh and delivered Moses and those of them who were with him; Muḥammad remarked, We have more right than they, and both fasted himself and bade the people fast on that day; when the fast of the month of Ramaḍān was instituted, he neither commanded them to fast on the day of ʿĀshūrā nor forbade them.

No *isnād* is given for this, but it may nevertheless contain in a slightly distorted form the memory of how Muḥammad had originally connected the fast with the victory on the analogy of a supposed connexion between the Jewish fast and the deliverance of Moses from the Egyptians. The chief difficulty about Bell's view is the date. Aṭ-Ṭabarī's mention of Shaʿbān, however, is hesitating, and is presumably an inference from the fact that the fast would have to be proclaimed before it was due to begin. Muḥammad is said to have fasted a day or two on the way to Badr, though it was permitted to those on a journey not to fast.[5] As this was the first occasion of the fast, however, one would expect the matter to be treated more explicitly. It is difficult to resist the conclusion that the fast of Ramaḍān was not fully observed before A.H. 3.

[1] Ibid.
[2] Caetani, i. 470 f.; Wensinck, 137; Buhl, 227, with further references.
[3] *Origin of Islam*, 124 f.
[4] Ṭab. 1281 (not referred to explicitly by Bell), omitting the words 'to Moses' after 'right', following one manuscript.
[5] WW, 46.

These marks of 'the break with the Jews' are in fact indications of a completely new orientation both politically and religiously.[1] The Medinan state now began a series of attacks on the Jews in the physical sphere, and at the same time the Qur'ān carried on polemics against their religion in the intellectual sphere.

The reasons for the new policy are not far to seek. So long as Muḥammad claimed to be receiving revelations identical in essence with the revelation in the hands of the Jews, they were in a strong position, and could either support Muḥammad by acknowledging the similarity or hinder his cause by drawing attention to differences. It was mostly the latter that they chose to do, and consequently they threatened to undermine the intellectual foundations of his political and religious position. Muḥammad was always very sensitive to such ideological attacks, and, for example, dealt severely with poets who opposed him. His stern attitude towards the Jews when they rejected his appeals was not simply pique at this rejection, but the reaction of a man in danger to those whose ill will is causing this danger.

4. THE INTELLECTUAL ATTACK ON THE JEWS

In the polemics of the Qur'ān against the Jews a prominent place is taken by the conception of the religion of Abraham. This is an idea which is not found in the Meccan revelations and is presumably not based on pre-Islamic Arab legends. During the Meccan period more prominence was given to Moses than to Abraham among the prophets as a forerunner of Muḥammad. Abraham is simply one of many prophets, and the people to whom he is sent are not specified; indeed, it seems to be implied that he was *not* sent to the Arabs, since Muḥammad is said to be sent to a people who had never had a warner.[2] Likewise there is no mention of any connexion of Abraham and Ishmael with the Ka'bah; Ishmael is named in lists of prophets, but no details are given about him.[3] The presumption is that at first the Muslims did not know

[1] Cf. Buhl, 228; and for further points of detail, D. G. Margoliouth, *Mohammed and the Rise of Islam*, London, 1905, 250.

[2] 32. 3/2 E+; 34. 44/43 D–E; 36. 6/5 C. The argument is a repetition of that of C. Snouck Hurgronje, *Verspreide Geschriften*, Bonn, &c., 1923–7, i. 22–29, 334–8; cf. Buhl, 229–31; Bell, *Origin*, 129–31; contrast E. Beck in *Muséon*, lxv (1952), 73–94. (The first passage from Snouck Hurgronje has been translated into French and annotated by G.-H. Bousquet, *Revue Africaine*, xcv (1951), 273–88.)

[3] 6. 86 ? C–E+; 21. 85 ? D; 38. 48 CD.

about the connexion of Ishmael with Abraham and (according to the Old Testament) with the Arabs. At Medina, however, in closer contact with the Jews they gained knowledge of such matters. When it came to a break with the Jews, Abraham had two great advantages: he was in a physical sense the father of the Arabs as well as of the Jews; and he lived before the Torah had been revealed to Moses and the Gospel to Jesus (as the Jews had to admit), and was therefore neither a Jew nor a Christian.

The Qur'ān therefore instructs Muḥammad and the believers to regard themselves as neither Jews nor Christians, but a community distinct from both, followers of the 'creed of Abraham' (*millat Ibrāhīm*); and Abraham is described as a *ḥanīf*, a *muslim* (that is, one surrendered to God), not one of the idolaters.[1] The religion of Abraham is simply the pure religion of God, since all the prophets have received in essentials the same revelation. Judaism and Christianity, however, now come to be looked on as imperfect manifestations of this religion of God, and therefore a distinctive name has to be found for it. First *ḥanīf* and later also *muslim* are used in the Qur'ān for the adherent of the true religion; *ḥanīf* had apparently been used previously by Jews and Christians either for 'pagan' or for 'a follower of the Hellenized Syro-Arabian religion', and is thus given a completely new turn of meaning by the Qur'ān;[2] *muslim* is presumably a new coinage. Moreover, Abraham is now said to have founded the Meccan sanctuary with the help of Ishmael, and to have prayed for a prophet for the Meccans from among his descendants,[3] while in addressing the believers the phrase 'your father Abraham' is used.[4] In these ways the practice of facing Mecca during the Worship comes to be supported by a vast ideological structure.

The corollary of the conception of the religion of Abraham is that the religion of the Jews is not the pure religion of Abraham. This idea is implicit in a number of passages, and becomes explicit in certain specific points. One of these is that the Jews have broken their covenant with God, made at Sinai, by worshipping a calf instead.[5] Another is that they disbelieve in part of the Book which has been given to them, and act wickedly in disobedience to the

[1] 2. 130/124–141/135; 3. 65/58–71/64; 5. 44/48 f.; 6. 159/160–165; 14. 35/38; 16. 120/121–123/124.

[2] Cf. *M/Mecca*, 162 ff. and references.

[3] 2. 125/119–129/123.

[4] 22. 78/77.

[5] 2. 27/25, 40/38, 83/77; 4. 154/153 f.; 5. 12/15 f.; &c.

commands of God.[1] The taking of usury is an instance of such disobedience.[2] In all this they show their worldliness.[3] Moreover all that they allege to belong to the Book revealed to them is not in fact part of that Book; such statements apparently refer to the Jewish oral law, and they would serve to explain the absence of corresponding regulations in the revelation to Muḥammad.[4] Not dissimilar to this is the charge of 'altering words from their proper meanings' (*yuḥarrifūna 'l-kalim 'an mawāḍi'i-hi*);[5] in the Qur'ān this need mean nothing more than deliberately interpreting passages to suit oneself, and neglecting the plain and straightforward meaning; but later Muslim apologetic took this to mean that the Jewish and Christian scriptures were textually corrupt.

The repeated assertions that the Jews conceal part of the truth revealed to them point to the corruption of individual Jews and not of their religion, but there may be a close connexion with the charge of 'altering' or 'making oblique' (commonly referred to as *taḥrīf*, this being the noun corresponding to *yuḥarrifūna*). Thus in 2. 76/71, immediately after some Jews have been accused of *taḥrīf*, there is a description of how some who feign to be believers (that is, to accept Muḥammad) say to one another in privacy that it is foolish to tell the Muslims what has been revealed to them (the Jews) since the Muslims will be able to produce it as proof against them in the presence of God. In certain other passages the reference might be to the concealing of such facts as that Abraham was the father of the Arabs and was not a Jew, but there can be little doubt that what is concealed in the verse under discussion is the fact that Muḥammad and his prophetic mission are foretold and described in the Torah (as stated elsewhere in the Qur'ān).[6] In this verse, then, the Jews are represented as knowing that Muḥammad fulfils the scriptural description of the prophet who is to come (as did the convert 'Abdallāh b. Sallām, according to Ibn Isḥāq);[7] but these Jews, though they profess to believe, are not prepared to act accordingly and become whole-hearted followers of Muḥammad, and they will therefore be severely treated on the Last Day—though of course,

[1] 2. 85/79; 5. 78/82 f.; 62. 5.
[2] 4. 161/159.
[3] 2. 86/80, &c.
[4] 3. 78/72, 93/87.
[5] 4. 46/48; 5. 13/16; cf. 5. 41/45; 2. 75/70; and Lane, *s.v. ḥarafa*.
[6] 7. 157/156; cf. 4. 37/41 (with Ṭab., *Tafsīr*, v. 51); IH, 388. For the main point cf. comment of 'Abd al-Qādir in Wherry (Sale) on 2. 76/71 (i. 317).
[7] IH, 353; contrast Kinānah b. Ṣūriyā' in WW, 161.

as the next verse states, God knows what they are keeping secret and does not require to be informed about it by the Muslims. In other verses of the Qur'ān the Jews are simply said to conceal truth,[1] but no doubt the reference is mostly to the description of Muḥammad as prophet. (Ibn Isḥāq's story of how some Jews tried to conceal the verse in the Torah which made stoning the punishment for adultery belongs rather to later controversies and cannot be used uncritically to determine the meaning of the Qur'ān.)[2]

So long as the Muslims knew little about the Jewish scriptures, it was possible for the Jews to get the better of most arguments. But, with growing knowledge, the Muslims were able to use the scriptures against the Jews. The point that Abraham was not a Jew has already been mentioned. In particular, the Torah provided excellent material for countering the Jewish rejection of Muḥammad. Some of his followers had probably been perturbed when they saw how the Jews, whom they respected in religious matters as People of the Book, did not acknowledge him. The force of this consideration, however, was greatly weakened by showing that this was no new feature of Jewish history, but that their sacred record was full of instances of their rejection of those who came to them from God.

> If then they count thee false, messengers have already before thy time been counted false who came with the Evidences and the Psalms and the illuminating Book.[3]

It was further suggested that the Jews' rejection of Muḥammad was not based on their scriptures but was due to base motives such as envy or jealousy.[4]

Much of the Jewish strength presumably lay in their absolute conviction that they were God's chosen people. Some of the more presumptuous forms of this conviction are described in the Qur'ān. They hold that they are 'justified', and that they alone will be in Paradise; if they go to Hell at all, they will only be a limited time there.[5] To such claims, which were tantamount to a dismissal of Islam as completely false, the Qur'ān had various forms of reply. It could deny directly, as when it insisted that the judgement

[1] 2. 42/39, 146/141, 159/154, 174/169; 3. 71/64; 5. 15/18; 6. 91.
[2] IH, 394 f.
[3] 3. 184/181; cf. 2. 61/58, 87/81, 91/85 f.; 3. 181/177; 4. 155/154; 5. 70/74 f.
[4] 2. 105/99, 109/103; cf. 2. 90/84; 4. 54/57.
[5] 4. 49/52; 2. 94/88, 80/74; 3. 24/23.

passed on the Last Day depended on a man's righteousness and obedience to God's commands.[1] It could deny by implication, as when it asked why the Jews (and Christians) were punished, if, as they held, they were the sons of God.[2] In accordance with old Arab custom they could be challenged to take an oath to the effect that they were the friends of God and that they alone would be in Paradise.[3] But perhaps the trump card was that Jews and Christians denied one another's exclusive claims. The two claims were similar and therefore could not both be true; but there was little to choose between them, and it was thus not unreasonable from the Muslim standpoint to suppose that both went beyond what their revealed scriptures justified. This point had the more force in that Jews and Christians were apparently regarded by the Arabs as being two branches of the Children of Israel. With regard to the matters about which they differed the decision had been postponed by God until the Last Day.[4] As against the exclusive claims of the two older religions there was a show of broadmindedness and tolerance in the Muslim claim to acknowledge all earlier prophets,[5] and the idea of a covenant between God and the prophets, in which they promised to believe in and help any subsequent prophet with a message confirming the existing revelation, might be regarded as setting forth an important truth in mythic form.[6]

Such are the main points of the Qur'ānic attack upon the Jews. There were also some minor matters, but sufficient has been said to show that the Muslim attitude towards the Jews was well developed. This degree of elaboration is an index of the great importance of the Jewish question for the Muslims. In the thoughts of their leaders it must have bulked at least as largely as the struggle with Mecca. This has to be kept in mind in considering the actual hostilities between Muḥammad and the Jews.

5. THE PHYSICAL ATTACK ON THE JEWS

During the months and years that followed the change of the *qiblah* there were a number of hostile encounters between the Muslims and the Jews. While it is convenient to group these together, it should not be assumed without examination that all these events spring from a deliberate policy—presumably adopted in

[1] 2. 80/74 ff.; 3. 24/23 f. [2] 5. 18/21. [3] 2. 94/88; 62. 6 ff.
[4] 2. 111/105 ff.; cf. 10. 93; 27. 76/78; 42. 14/13 f.; 45. 16/15 ff.; 98. 4/3.
[5] Cf. 4. 150/149 ff.; 2. 136/130. [6] 3. 81/75.

623/2 before Badr—of subduing or getting rid of the Jews. Whether this is so is a question that must be discussed, but it may be postponed until the events themselves have been briefly described.

The first event of note was the siege and expulsion of the clan of Qaynuqā'.[1] On his return from Badr Muḥammad is said to have renewed his appeals to the Jews, pointing to the Meccan losses as an example of the fate of those who did not respond to God's message. The Jews, however, were no readier than before to become followers of Muḥammad. A few days later an incident occurred. Some Jews played a trick on an Arab woman.[2] While she was sitting doing business in the market of the Qaynuqā', one of them contrived to fasten her skirt in such a way that when she stood up a considerable portion of her person was revealed. A Muslim who happened to be present regarded this act and the ensuing laughter as an insult, and killed the Jew, who was at once avenged by his fellows. The Jews then retired to their strongholds. Muḥammad regarded the matter as a *casus belli*, and collected a force to besiege the clan. There were doubtless some negotiations, but no record has been preserved. After a siege of fifteen days the Jews surrendered. They were forced to leave Medina, taking their wives and children with them. Three days were granted to them to collect money owing to them, but they had to leave behind their arms and perhaps some of their other goods, such as their goldsmith tools (though one might conjecture that by the latter are meant the tools used in making weapons and armour). The usual account is that they went to the Jewish colony at Wadi 'l-Qurā, and after a month proceeded to 'Adhra'āt in Syria.

It is important to notice the part played by various Arabs in these happenings. Ibn Ubayy receives most prominence, since he spoke to Muḥammad on behalf of Qaynuqā'; and they are said to have become reconciled to exile only after they saw that Ibn Ubayy, their confederate, on whose support they were counting, had little influence in Medinan affairs; when he tried to force his way into Muḥammad's presence the man on guard pushed him so violently against the wall that his face bled, and Ibn Ubayy was apparently incapable of exacting revenge or compensation. Others, however, are also mentioned as prominent in the operations on the Muslim side, namely, 'Ubādah b. aṣ-Ṣāmit, al-Mundhir b. Qudāmah,

[1] IH, 545–7; WK, 177–81; WW, 92–94; Ṭab. 1360–2.
[2] For a similar trick, cf. Caussin de Perceval, i. 297 f.

Muḥammad b. Maslamah, and Sa'd b. Mu'ādh. The first two belonged to branches of the old clan of Sālim,[1] al-Qawāqilah and Ghanm b. Silm respectively. Ibn Ubayy was of Ba'l-Ḥublā, another branch of Sālim. As 'Ubādah also had had a confederacy with Qaynuqā' but had publicly denounced it when tension began to grow, it may be inferred that Qaynuqā' had originally been confederates of the whole of Sālim. The other two Arabs were of the clan of 'Abd al-Ash'hal which had formed an alliance with an-Naḍīr and Qurayẓah just before the battle of Bu'āth and may therefore have had some relationship to Qaynuqā' also. Alternatively, if there was no such relationship, Sa'd b. Mu'ādh's contribution may have been to keep the other Jewish clans from interfering. Qaynuqā' are said to have had 700 fighting men, of whom 400 wore armour, and Muḥammad could not have been successful against them without the whole-hearted support of many of their confederates among the Arabs. His high prestige after Badr no doubt made it easier for him to gain such support.

Four months or so later (early September, 624 = the middle of iii/3), there occurred the assassination of Ka'b b. al-Ashraf.[2] Ka'b was the son of an Arab of the distant tribe of Ṭayyi', but he behaved as if he belonged to his mother's clan of an-Naḍīr. After Badr he went to Mecca and composed anti-Muslim verses which had a wide circulation. At Muḥammad's instigation the Muslim poet, al-Ḥassān b. Thābit, satirized Ka'b's Meccan hosts and so forced him to return to Medina, where he continued his propagandist activities. Muḥammad apparently let it be known that he would gladly be rid of Ka'b and, when five men hatched a plot against him, gave them permission to say what they liked about himself. Two, Muḥammad b. Maslamah of the section of Ḥārithah attached to 'Abd al-Ash'hal and Abū Nā'ilah of the sub-clan Za'ūrā of the same clan, were milk-brothers of Ka'b and one or other of them secured his confidence by complaining of the hardships they had to suffer under Muḥammad's régime, and in particular of the lack of food. Ka'b agreed to give them a loan and to accept arms as a pledge. To receive the arms he left his house in the middle of the night. All five set upon him at a quiet spot and not without some difficulty killed him. On their return to within earshot of Muḥammad, who was watching for their return, they announced their success by

[1] Cf. p. 167 above.

[2] IH, 548–53; WK, 115–17, 184–90; WW, 74, 95–99; Ṭab. 1368–72.

a shout of *Allāh akbar*, 'God is very great'. It is noteworthy that the five conspirators were all members of 'Abd al-Ash'hal or the closely connected Ḥārithah. As an-Naḍīr were confederates of 'Abd al-Ash'hal, no blood-feud would be created. The Jews are said to have been greatly perturbed at the assassination, to have complained to Muḥammad, and to have entered into a treaty with him.

Almost exactly a year after Ka'b's death, in iii/4 (= late August or early September 625), a second Jewish clan, Banū 'n-Naḍīr, were expelled from Medina.[1] The story is that Muḥammad went to the settlement of an-Naḍīr to demand a contribution towards the blood-money due to B. 'Āmir b. Ṣa'ṣa'ah for the two men killed by the survivor of Bi'r Ma'ūnah.[2] As an-Naḍīr were in alliance with 'Āmir, there may have been complications, though the sources say nothing of these; Muḥammad may have thought that the Jews ought to do more than the average of the inhabitants of Medina, and they may have thought they ought to do less. Whatever the precise point was, an-Naḍīr professed themselves ready to give a satisfactory answer, but bade Muḥammad make himself comfortable while they prepared a meal. He and his companions seated themselves with their backs to the wall of one of the houses. Presently Muḥammad slipped quietly away and did not return, and his companions also eventually left. When they found him at his house, he explained that he had had a Divine warning that an-Naḍīr were planning a treacherous attack on him—they could easily have rolled a stone onto his head and killed him as he sat by the house. He therefore at once dispatched Muḥammad b. Maslamah to an-Naḍīr with an ultimatum; they were to leave Medina within ten days on pain of death, though they would still be regarded as owners of their palm-trees and receive part of the produce. Such an ultimatum seems out of proportion to the offence, or rather to the apparently flimsy grounds for supposing that treachery was meditated. Yet perhaps the grounds were not so flimsy as they appear at first sight to the Westerner of today. Both parties knew how some Muslims had treated Ka'b b. al-Ashraf, and, in accordance with the ideas of the Arabia of that day, Muḥammad was bound to expect that, if he gave his opponents an opportunity, they would kill him. An-Naḍīr's postponement of

[1] IH, 652–6; WK, 353–62; WW, 160–7; Ṭab. 1448–53.

[2] For Abū Rāfi' see IH, 714–16, 981; WW, 170–2; Ṭab. 1375–83; Caetani, i. 590–2. For Usayr cf. IH, 980 f.; WW, 239 f.; Caetani, i. 702 f.

a reply created such an opportunity, and was therefore tantamount to a hostile act.

The Jews at first were inclined to submit to the demand, especially when they saw that it was carried by a leading member of the clan on which they were primarily dependent for support. They were divided among themselves, however. Ḥuyayy b. Akhṭab, apparently chief of the clan, was less inclined to submit than other men such as Sallām b. Mishkam. While Ḥuyayy hesitated, Ibn Ubayy sent messages to him promising support and speaking of the readiness of some of the allied nomads to attack Muḥammad. The Jews therefore refused to comply with Muḥammad's demand, and he set about besieging them. The siege lasted about fifteen days. An-Naḍīr lost heart when the Muslims began to destroy their palms, for Ibn Ubayy was doing nothing to help them and they realized that, even if they were able to keep their foothold in Medina, their livelihood would be gone. They expressed their readiness to fulfil the original demand, but Muḥammad now imposed less favourable terms on them. They were to leave their weapons and to have nothing from the palms. To this perforce they agreed, and departed proudly with a train of 600 camels for Khaybar, where they had estates. The swords, cuirasses, and helmets all went to Muḥammad, doubtless with a view to his next encounter with Quraysh. The Anṣār agreed that the houses and palm-gardens should be allotted to the Emigrants, so that they might be able to support themselves and be no longer dependent on the hospitality of the Anṣār. Among the Muslims mentioned in connexion with the affair, Muḥammad b. Maslamah and Saʿd b. Maʿādh are prominent, but it is significant that Saʿd b. ʿUbādah provided a specially fine tent for Muḥammad and dates for the whole army. This may indicate that he was coming forward as leader of all the Khazraj in opposition to Ibn Ubayy. Of the two poor Anṣārīs who shared with the Emigrants in the distribution of the confiscated property, one was Abū Dujānah from Saʿd b. ʿUbādah's clan of Sāʿidah.

The expulsion of an-Naḍīr from Medina was not the end of their dealings with Muḥammad. From Khaybar some of them continued to intrigue assiduously against Medina, and they played a considerable part in the formation of the great confederacy to besiege Medina in April 627 (xi/5). It is not surprising, therefore, that two of their leaders, Abū Rāfiʿ Sallām b. Abī 'l-Ḥuqayq and Usayr (or

Yusayr) b. Rāzim, were assassinated by Muslims. The dates adopted by al-Wāqidī are respectively xii/4 (=May 626) and x/6 (= February–March 628), but there are variants, notably some which place the former after the siege of Medina and the attack on Qurayẓah.[1] This later date seems to be slightly more probable.[2] Al-Wāqidī[3] states that Usayr b. Rāzim became leader in war of an-Naḍīr after the death of Abū Rāfi'. If this position is identical with that occupied by Ḥuyayy b. Akhṭab, then Abū Rāfi' could not have assumed it until after the death of Ḥuyayy along with Qurayẓah, and could not have been assassinated until after that. The reason for the assassination of Abū Rāfi' as for that of Usayr was intrigues with Ghaṭafān against the Muslims, and this would fit either date.

The attack on Abū Rāfi' was the work of five men of B. Salimah. They are said to have been moved to it by the desire to show that the dispatching of Ka'b b. al-Ashraf by the Aws could be rivalled by the Khazraj. A prominent part was played by 'Abdallāh b. 'Atīq, who spoke Hebrew and had a Jewish foster-mother in Khaybar (perhaps a woman of an-Naḍīr); but the leader and person chiefly responsible for the actual assassination appears to have been 'Abdallāh b. Unays. The party managed to gain admittance to the house of Abū Rāfi', and had little difficulty in mortally wounding the old man. They hid until the pursuit died down and then returned safely to Medina.

'Abdallāh b. Unays seems to have been responsible for the killing of Usayr also, though the leader of the party of thirty was 'Abdallāh b. Rawāḥah (of Ba'l-Ḥārith). They went openly to Khaybar as representatives of Muḥammad with talk of honours to be bestowed on Usayr and an invitation to a parley in Medina. Despite warnings from some of his friends, Usayr and thirty companions set off for Medina, each mounted behind one of the Muslims. On the way 'Abdallāh b. Unays became suspicious of Usayr, who was behind him and seemed once or twice to be feeling for 'Abdallāh's sword, presumably regretting his decision; from this and from the fact that later he used the branch of a tree it is to be inferred that the Jews were unarmed. 'Abdallāh contrived that his camel lagged behind the others and when they were alone killed Usayr. Subsequently the other Jews were also killed with one exception.

[1] For Abū Rāfi' see IH, 714–16, 981; WW, 170–2; Tab. 1375–83; Caetani, i. 590–2. For Usayr cf. IH, 980 f.; WW, 239 f.; Caetani, i. 702 f.

[2] Cf. Buhl, 277, n. 48.

[3] WK, 4. 17; WW, 239 n.

There were still a number of Jewish groups in Medina, but the only one of any importance was the clan of Qurayẓah. During the siege of Medina this clan had probably preserved neutrality so far as outward acts were concerned, but they had engaged in negotiations with Muḥammad's enemies, and, could they have trusted Quraysh and their bedouin allies, would have turned against Muḥammad. Immediately upon the withdrawal of his opponents Muḥammad attacked Qurayẓah,[1] to show that the rising Islamic state was not prepared to tolerate such 'sitting on the fence'. Qurayẓah retired to their stronghold, but did not fight back with much vigour. Soon they sent and asked to be allowed to surrender on the same terms as an-Naḍīr, but were told they must surrender unconditionally. They then requested to be allowed to consult Abū Lubābah, and he went to them. What exactly happened is mysterious.[2] Abū Lubābah must have committed some grave fault not mentioned in our sources. Probably he did not repudiate the old alliance of his clan ('Amr b. 'Awf) with Qurayẓah, but used his influence somehow or other in their favour.

After the unconditional surrender of Qurayẓah, Muḥammad b. Maslamah was in charge of the men and 'Abdallāh b. Sallām of the women and children. Some of the Aws are said to have appealed to Muḥammad to forgive Qurayẓah for the sake of the Aws as he had pardoned Qaynuqā' for the sake of Ibn Ubayy and the Khazraj. Those who made this approach are not named, but subsequently four persons are said to have been gravely concerned at the fate of Qurayẓah, namely, aḍ-Ḍaḥḥāk b. Khalīfah and Salamah b. Salāmah (both of 'Abd al-Ash'hal), Mu'attib b. Qushayr (Ḍubay'ah of 'Amr b. 'Awf), and Ḥāṭib b. Umayyah (Ẓafar). This seems to indicate a wide-spread tendency in the Aws to honour the old alliance with Qurayẓah. Muḥammad met their request by suggesting that the fate of the Jews should be decided by one of their confederates, and to this they agreed. Muḥammad therefore appointed as judge Sa'd b. Mu'ādh, the leading man of the Aws, who had been gravely wounded during the siege and died soon after his sentence on Qurayẓah. When he was brought to where Muḥammad was, all the Aws and the others present swore to abide by his decision. He decreed that all the men of Qurayẓah should be put to death and the women and children sold as slaves. This sentence was duly carried out, apparently on the following day.

[1] IH, 684–99; WW, 210–24; Ṭab. 1485–98.

[2] Cf. p. 188 above.

Some European writers have criticized this sentence for what they call its savage and inhuman character. The general question involved will be dealt with later.[1] Here it is to be noticed that the participants in the events (and likewise the transmitters of the material) do not seem to have been concerned with the alleged harshness of the sentence.[2] The point at issue was whether allegiance to the Islamic community was to be set above and before all other alliances and attachments. In this connexion it must be remembered that the old Arab tradition was that you supported your confederate whatever his conduct towards other people might be, provided only that he remained faithful to you. It would seem then that those of the Aws who wanted leniency for Qurayẓah regarded them as having been unfaithful not to the Aws but only to Muḥammad; that means that they still regarded themselves as being primarily members of the Aws (or of some subdivision of it) and not of the Islamic community. It is thus unnecessary to suppose that Muḥammad brought any pressure to bear on Saʿd b. Muʿādh to punish Qurayẓah as he did. A far-sighted man like Saʿd must have realized that to allow tribal or clan allegiance to come before Islamic allegiance would lead to a renewal of the fratricidal strife from which they hoped the coming of Muḥammad had saved Medina. As he was being led to the presence of Muḥammad to pronounce his sentence, he is said to have remarked to those urging him to remember the old alliance that 'the time has come for Saʿd that no one's blame should touch him in respect of God', presumably meaning that, in view of the approach of death, he must perform his duty towards God and set the Islamic community above the old confederacy; and it is noteworthy that the phrase rendered 'no one's blame' (*lawmat lā'im*) occurs in a verse of the Qur'ān warning the believers against 'drawing back' from their religion.[3]

We are given a glimpse of the potential dangers of the situation by the report of al-Wāqidī that Saʿd b. ʿUbādah and al-Ḥubāb b. al-Mundhir, leaders of the Khazraj, remarked to Muḥammad that the Aws were not in agreement with the execution of the men of

[1] Cf. p. 328 below.

[2] Cf. 'The Condemnation of the Jews of Banū Qurayẓah', *Muslim World*, xlii (1952), 160–71, esp. 171. (N.B. The second paragraph on p. 160 is entirely a quotation from Caetani.)

[3] IH, 689. 1; Q. 5. 54/59. Cf. IS, iii/2. 4. 8, 'the time has come for me that no one's blame matters to me in respect of God'; also WW, 215.

Qurayẓah. This served, however, to put the Aws on their mettle, and Saʿd b. Muʿādh assured Muḥammad that all the devout believers among the Aws concurred in it. Thereupon two of the condemned were given to each of the clans or sub-clans involved (ʿAbd al-Ash'hal, Ḥārithah, Ẓafar, Muʿāwiyah, ʿAmr b. ʿAwf, and Umayyah b. Zayd), and these were duly executed, so that all the clans were involved in the blood of Qurayẓah. As the execution is said to have been organized by ʿAlī and az-Zubayr, the majority of the Jews (said to have numbered 600) were probably killed by Emigrants, though the Khazraj may also have helped, since apart perhaps from Ibn Ubayy they had no longer any alliance with Qurayẓah. In the division of the palms there is no mention of any being given to B. ʿAwf of the Khazraj, to which Ibn Ubayy belonged.[1] On the other hand, Saʿd b. ʿUbādah certainly took part in the affair, and his clan of Sāʿidah is also omitted from the division of palms; this may be an error in the recorded list, but it may also be due to Sāʿidah having numerous palms already—Saʿd b. ʿUbādah had sometimes supplied the whole of Muḥammad's forces with dates.[2] If the latter alternative is the true one, the absence of ʿAwf and also Bayāḍah from the list of recipients of palms may be because they did not take any part in the fighting. Whatever the truth of the last detail, there must still have been much vigour in clan attachments and in the old ideas connected with them. The appointment of Saʿd b. Muʿādh as judge over Qurayẓah was not an attempt by Muḥammad to conceal his alleged dictatorial power, since in fact at this period he had none; it was the only tactful way open to him of dealing with a difficult situation.

After the elimination of Qurayẓah there remained no important group of Jews in Medina. There were still some Jews there, however, and perhaps quite a number. One such was Abū 'sh-Shaḥm, who was attached to B. Ẓafar; he was a merchant and money-lender, and even bought some of the women and children of Qurayẓah![3] If the view of the dating of the Constitution to be propounded in the next chapter is sound, there must have been several small groups of Jews scattered about Medina.

The continuing presence of at least a few Jews in Medina is an

1 WW, 220.

2 WW, 150, 163, 212; cf. 189, gift of a palm garden.

3 IS, i/2. 173. 14; WW, 221; cf. WW, 174, 264 f., 278.

argument against the view sometimes put forward by European scholars that in the second year after the Hijrah Muḥammad adopted a policy of clearing all Jews out of Medina just because they were Jews, and that he carried out this policy with ever-increasing severity. In general it was not Muḥammad's way to have definite policies of such a kind. What he did have was a balanced view of the fundamentals of the contemporary situation and of his long-term aims, and in the light of this he moulded his day-to-day plans in accordance with the changing factors in current events. The occasions of the attacks on Qaynuqāʿ and an-Naḍīr are no more than occasions (though they may well be genuine), and the historian is justified in looking for deeper underlying reasons. These are not far to seek. In Muḥammad's first two years at Medina the Jews were the most dangerous critics of his claim to be a prophet, and the religious fervour of his followers, on which so much depended, was liable to be greatly reduced unless Jewish criticisms could be silenced or rendered impotent. It was difficult, however, for Muḥammad to share with the rank and file of his followers his own appreciation of the importance of the Jews in the total religious-cum-political situation. When circumstances in general were favourable (e.g. when his own prestige was high and Ibn Ubayy's low) and an occasion of hostilities presented itself of the type familiar to the Arabs, then Muḥammad acted. In a sense, therefore, his actions were spontaneous and not premeditated. Moreover, in so far as the Jews changed their attitude and ceased to be actively hostile, they were unmolested, as the case of Abū 'sh-Shaḥm indicates. After the first incidents we may suppose that verbal criticisms of the Qur'ānic revelation ceased except in strict privacy. This was replaced, however, by another form of hostile activity, diplomatic intrigue against Muḥammad. With the fate of Qurayẓah before their eyes the remaining Jews of Medina were presumably very circumspect and avoided all compromising relationships, though at the time of the expedition to Khaybar their sympathies seem naturally to have been with their co-religionists.[1]

Though the Jews of Medina had become quiescent, those at Khaybar, among whom the leaders of an-Naḍīr were the most prominent, were still anxious to avenge themselves on Muḥammad. They made lavish, though no doubt judicious, use of their wealth to induce the neighbouring Arabs and especially the strong tribe

[1] Cf. WW, 264, also 266; contrast 283, Jews with Muḥammad.

of Ghaṭafān to join them against the Muslims. Muḥammad had thus a straightforward reason for attacking Khaybar. The moment he chose for the attack—May/June 628 (i/7) shortly after his return from the expedition of al-Ḥudaybiyah—was one when it was also convenient for him to have booty to distribute to his followers whose expectations had recently been disappointed. The people of Khaybar had had some word of Muḥammad's preparations, but his march to Khaybar was executed swiftly and secretly and they were taken by surprise with inadequate dispositions to resist a siege. Khaybar comprised several groups of strongholds, many built on the tops of hills and virtually impregnable. The Muslims attacked them piecemeal, beginning with the group known as an-Naṭāt. There was much shooting from a distance and apparently some single combats. When the besieged made a sally, the Muslims fought back vigorously, and on at least one occasion followed them inside the gates. Several of the Muslim successes, however, were due to help they received from Jews who wanted in this way to ensure the safety of themselves and their families. When the strongholds of an-Naṭāt and those of ash-Shiqq had fallen there was little further resistance, and terms of surrender were speedily arranged for the remaining groups of strongholds, al-Katībah, al-Waṭīḥ, and Sulālim. The principle was adopted that the Jews should continue to cultivate the land, but should hand over half the produce to the Muslim owners—the 1,600 participants in the expedition, or those to whom they had sold their shares. Several of the prominent men of Khaybar had been killed in single combat, and Kinānah b. Abī 'l-Ḥuqayq, apparently the chief leader, together with a brother, was put to death after the surrender because he had concealed the family treasure. Khaybar was thus reduced to a position of subservience and rendered innocuous.[1]

About the same time treaties were forced upon the colonies of Jews at Fadak, Wādi 'l-Qurā, and Taymā'. After the news of the fall of even a few of the strongholds of Khaybar there was no will to resist. The two former received similar terms to the men of Khaybar, but the impost on the latter is called *jizyah*. It may be that they were treated differently because the two former had been actively hostile to Muḥammad and had stirred up the neighbouring Arab tribes of Sa'd and possibly Badr b. Fazārah against him.[2]

[1] IH, 756–81; WW, 264–96; Ṭab. 1575–90.
[2] Fadak: IH, 975; WW, 237 f. Wādi 'l-Qurā: IH, 979 f.; WW, 236 n.

Various factors contributed to this Muslim success. The Jews were over-confident in the strength of their positions in Khaybar, and failed to lay in supplies of water sufficient for even a short siege. Man for man the Muslims were the better fighters, but this did not count for much in a siege except in so far as the besieged were forced to leave their strongholds through lack of water or other supplies. The Muslims seem to have been short of food for a time until they captured one of the strongholds with ample provisions. The lack of fundamental unity among the Jews was a weakness which meant that it was easy for Muḥammad to find Jews ready to help him. Moreover, the Arab allies of the Jews were attached to them chiefly by bribes, and were therefore easily detached, partly by fear of Muslim reprisals and partly by Muḥammad's diplomatic skill. At Fadak B. Sa'd had been raided by 'Alī some months earlier, and Ghaṭafān, despite a show of support, made no effective intervention during the operations at Khaybar.

6. CONCLUSION

The fall of Khaybar and surrender of the other Jewish colonies may be said to mark the end of the Jewish question during Muḥammad's lifetime, and this is not the place to discuss the expulsion of the Jews from the Ḥijāz by the caliph 'Umar. The Jews had opposed Muḥammad to the utmost of their ability, and they had been utterly crushed. Many of them still remained in their former homes in Medina and elsewhere, but they had ceased to count in Arabian politics, and had lost much of their wealth.

It is interesting to speculate on what would have happened had the Jews come to terms with Muḥammad instead of opposing him. At certain periods they could have secured very favourable terms from him, including religious autonomy, and on that basis the Jews might have become partners in the Arab empire and Islam a sect of Jewry. How different the face of the world would be now, had that happened! In the early months at Medina the seeds were sown of a great tragedy; a great opportunity was lost. On the purely theological issues there would appear to be fewer difficulties in Islam for Jews than for Christians. But Muḥammad's claim to receive messages from God conflicted with the cherished belief that the Jews were the chosen people through whom alone God revealed Himself to men. It was altogether in keeping with the traditional outlook of Jewry that the Jews of Medina should reject Muḥammad. Even men more far-sighted than their actual leaders would have acted similarly. It was perhaps not necessary for the Jews to indulge in mocking criticism of Islam as they did; but, once they had decided to reject Muḥammad, they had to justify this action at least to themselves. Their criticism was a threat to the whole social and political experiment in which he was engaged, and could not be ignored. Thus the whole sorry train of events was set in motion.

To suggest that Muḥammad was unaware of the wealth of the Jews would be a serious underestimate of his intelligence. To make this the sole reason, however, for his attacks on the Jews is to be unduly materialistic. The wealth of the Jews was certainly of great benefit to him and considerably eased his financial position, and the prospect of financial betterment may have influenced the timing of his attacks on the Jews. But the fundamental reason for the quarrel was theological on both sides. The Jews believed that God had chosen them specially, Muḥammad realized that his prophethood was the only possible basis of Arab unity. As so often in the history of the Middle East, theology and politics were intermingled.

VII

THE CHARACTER OF THE ISLAMIC STATE

I. THE CONSTITUTION OF MEDINA

IBN ISḤĀQ has preserved an ancient document commonly known as the 'Constitution of Medina'. Apart from the introductory words, however, he tells us nothing about it, neither how he came by it nor when and how it was brought into force. On the latter points he must be presumed ignorant; its place near the beginning of his account of the Medinan period is simply that called for by logic.

(a) *The text of the document*[1]

Ibn Isḥāq said: The Messenger of God (God bless and preserve him) wrote a writing (*kitāb*) between the Emigrants and the Anṣār, in which he made a treaty and covenant with the Jews, confirmed them in their religion and possessions, and gave them certain duties and rights:

In the name of God, the Merciful, the Compassionate!

This is a writing of Muḥammad the prophet between the believers and Muslims of Quraysh and Yathrib and those who follow them and are attached to them and who crusade (*jāhadū*) along with them.

1. They are a single community (*ummah*) distinct from (other) people.[2]

2. The Emigrants of Quraysh, according to their former condition,[3] pay jointly the blood-money between them, and they (as a group) ransom their captive(s), (doing so) with uprightness and justice between the believers.

[1] IH, 341–4. The numbering of the paragraphs follows Wensinck, *Mohammed en de Joden*, 74–81, except that the closing sentence of § 19 has been moved there from the beginning of § 20. Cf. also Wellhausen, *Skizzen*, iv. 65–83, and Caetani, i. 391–408.

[2] The literal translation of the last phrase is 'from the people', which might refer to the Jews; but on the whole this is unlikely.

[3] Lane, *s.v.*, makes it clear that the phrase *'alā rib'ati-him* means 'according to their former or good condition'. There is no reason to suppose any reference to 'quarter'. The interpretation is either that each group remains distinct or that it follows its previous practice. The last clause prescribes a fair apportionment between the various groups within the clan.

3. Banū ʿAwf, according to their former condition, pay jointly the previous blood-wits, and each sub-clan (*ṭā'ifah*) ransoms its captive(s), (doing so) with uprightness and justice between the believers.[1]

4. Banū 'l-Ḥārith, according to their former condition, pay jointly . . . (as 3).

5. Banū Sāʿidah . . . (as 3).

6. Banū Jusham . . . (as 3).

7. Banū 'n-Najjār . . . (as 3).

8. Banū ʿAmr b. ʿAwf . . . (as 3).

9. Banū 'n-Nabīt . . . (as 3).

10. Banū 'l-Aws . . . (as 3).

11. The believers do not forsake a debtor among them, but give him (help), according to what is fair, for ransom or blood-wit.

12. A believer does not take as confederate (*ḥalīf*) the client (*mawlā*) of a believer without his (the latter's) consent.

13. The God-fearing believers are against whoever of them acts wrongfully or seeks (? plans) an act that is unjust or treacherous or hostile or corrupt among the believers; their hands are all against him, even if he is the son of one of them.

14. A believer does not kill a believer because of an unbeliever, and does not help an unbeliever against a believer.

15. The security (*dhimmah*) of God is one; the granting of 'neighbourly protection' (*yujīr*) by the least of them (the believers) is binding on them; the believers are patrons (or clients—*mawālī*) of one another to the exclusion of (other) people.

16. Whoever of the Jews follows us has the (same) help and support (*naṣr, iswah*) (as the believers), so long as they are not wronged (by him) and he does not help (others) against them.

17. The peace (*silm*) of the believers is one; no believer makes peace apart from another believer, where there is fighting in the way of God, except in so far as equality and justice between them (is maintained).

18. In every expedition made with us the parties take turns with one another.[2]

19. The believers exact vengeance for one another where a man

[1] 'The previous blood-wits' (*al-maʿāqil al-ūlā*) are those according to the principles previously in force. The words 'between the believers' may be intended to exclude unbelievers belonging to B. ʿAwf.

[2] This may apply to taking turns at riding a camel (Wellhausen; cf. IH, 433, &c.), or to all military duties (Caetani).

gives his blood in the way of God. The God-fearing believers are under the best and most correct guidance.

20. No idolater (*mushrik*) gives 'neighbourly protection' (*yujīr*) for goods or person to Quraysh, nor intervenes in his (a Qurashī's) favour against a believer.

21. When anyone wrongfully kills a believer, the evidence being clear, then he is liable to be killed in retaliation for him, unless the representative of the murdered man is satisfied (with a payment). The believers are against him (the murderer) entirely; nothing is permissible to them except to oppose him.

22. It is not permissible for a believer who has agreed to what is in this document (*ṣaḥīfah*) and believed in God and the last day to help a wrong-doer[1] or give him lodging. If anyone helps him or gives him lodging, then upon this man is the curse of God and His wrath on the day of resurrection, and from him nothing will be accepted to make up for it or take its place.

23. Wherever there is anything about which you differ, it is to be referred to God and to Muḥammad (peace be upon him).

24. The Jews bear expenses along with the believers so long as they continue at war.

25. The Jews of Banū 'Awf are a community (*ummah*) along with the believers. To the Jews their religion (*dīn*) and to the Muslims their religion. (This applies) both to their clients and to themselves, with the exception of anyone who has done wrong or acted treacherously; he brings evil only on himself and on his household.

26. For the Jews of Banū 'n-Najjār the like of what is for the Jews of Banū 'Awf.

27. For the Jews of Banū 'l-Ḥārith the like . . .

28. For the Jews of Banū Sā'idah the like . . .

29. For the Jews of Banū Jusham the like . . .

30. For the Jews of Banū 'l-Aws the like . . .

31. For the Jews of Banū Tha'labah the like of what is for the Jews of Banū 'Awf, with the exception of anyone who has done wrong or acted treacherously; he brings evil only on himself and his household.

32. Jafnah, a subdivision (*baṭn*) of Tha'labah, are like them.

[1] *Muḥdith*, literally 'innovator', means one who disturbs the existing state of affairs in any way.

33. For Banū 'sh-Shuṭaybah[1] the like of what is for the Jews of Banū ʿAwf; honourable dealing (comes) before treachery.[2]

34. The clients of Thaʿlabah are like them.

35. The *biṭānah*[3] of (particular) Jews are as themselves.

36. No one of them (? those belonging to the *ummah*) may go out (to war) without the permission of Muḥammad (peace be upon him), but he is not restrained from taking vengeance for wounds. Whoever acts rashly (*fataka*), it (involves) only himself and his household, except where a man has been wronged. God is the truest (fulfiller) of this (document).[4]

37. It is for the Jews to bear their expenses and for the Muslims to bear their expenses. Between them (that is, to one another) there is help (*naṣr*) against whoever wars against the people of this document. Between them is sincere friendship (*naṣ'ḥ wa-naṣīḥah*), and honourable dealing, not treachery. A man is not guilty of treachery through (the act of) his confederate. There is help for (or, help is to be given to) the person wronged.

38. The Jews bear expenses along with the believers so long as they continue at war.

39. The valley of Yathrib is sacred for the people of this document.

40. The 'protected neighbour' (*jār*) is as the man himself so long as he does no harm and does not act treacherously.

41. No woman is given 'neighbourly protection' (*tujār*) without the consent of her people.

42. Whenever among the people of this document there occurs any incident (disturbance) or quarrel from which disaster for it (the people) is to be feared, it is to be referred to God and to Muḥammad, the Messenger of God (God bless and preserve him). God is the most scrupulous and truest (fulfiller) of what is in this document.

43. No 'neighbourly protection' is given (*lā tujār*) to Quraysh and those who help them.

[1] Wensinck, *Joden*, 79, corrects to Banū 'sh-Shuṭbah; cf. as-Samhūdī, 151.

[2] Or 'honourable dealing without treachery (is demanded)'.

[3] The meaning of *biṭānah* is obscure. It probably means those who were closely connected with some Medinan Jews by ties of friendship, not of blood; cf. Q. 3. 118/114; IH, 519. 4; *Aghānī*, xvii. 56. 22. Wensinck, 78, with some likelihood thinks they may be those Arabs who had been associated with the Jews before the coming of the Aws and the Khazraj.

[4] The second half of this article, and especially the last sentence are uncertain in meaning. The last sentence might mean 'God is very far from this.'

44. Between them (? the people of this document) is help against whoever suddenly attacks Yathrib.

45. Whenever they are summoned to conclude and accept a treaty, they conclude and accept it; when they in turn summon to the like of that, it is for them upon the believers,[1] except whoever wars about religion; for (? = incumbent on) each man is his share from their side which is towards them.

46. The Jews of al-Aws, both their clients and themselves, are in the same position as belongs to the people of this document while they are thoroughly honourable in their dealings with the people of this document. Honourable dealing (comes) before treachery.

47. A person acquiring (? guilt)[2] acquires it only against himself. God is the most upright and truest (fulfiller) of what is in this document. This writing does not intervene to protect a wrong-doer or traitor. He who goes out is safe, and he who sits still is safe in Medina, except whoever does wrong and acts treacherously. God is 'protecting neighbour' (*jār*) of him who acts honourably and fears God, and Muḥammad is the Messenger of God (God bless and preserve him).

(b) *The authenticity, date, and unity of the document*

This document has generally been regarded as authentic, though it has not always been given the prominence appropriate to an authentic document of this sort. The reasons for its authenticity have been succinctly stated by Wellhausen.[3] No later falsifier, writing under the Umayyads or 'Abbāsids, would have included non-Muslims in the *ummah*, would have retained the articles against Quraysh, and would have given Muḥammad so insignificant a place. Moreover the style is archaic, and certain points, such as the use of 'believers' instead of 'Muslims' in most articles, belong to the earlier Medinan period.

There has been some discussion, however, whether the document is to be dated before or after the battle of Badr. Wellhausen placed it before Badr. Hubert Grimme,[4] however, argued for a date

[1] This may mean 'it is a debt owed to them by the believers' (cf. W. Wright, *Arabic Grammar*³, Cambridge, 1896–8, ii. 169 a), or 'it is for them to conclude without taking notice of the believers' (cf. ibid. 172 a). The interpretation of this article is obscure.

[2] Cf. Q. 4. 111, cited by Wensinck.

[3] *Skizzen*, iv. 80; cf. Caetani, i. 403.

[4] *Muhammed*, Munster, 1892, i. 76.

after Badr on the following grounds: the functions attributed to Muḥammad in §§ 23 and 36 show that his authority was generally recognized; the references to fighting for the faith (*fī sabīl Allāh*, §§ 17, 19; *fī 'd-dīn*, § 45) imply that some fighting had taken place; the hostile attitude towards Quraysh could have been demanded of Medinan believers only after Badr. Caetani[1] shows that these arguments are not so strong as Grimme thought, and prefers a date prior to Badr.

This discussion of the date has assumed that the document is a unity; but that is the point that ought to be examined first. There are reasons for thinking that articles which originated at different dates have been collected.[2] Thus there are certain linguistic variations: the believers are mostly spoken of in the third person, but sometimes they are 'you' and sometimes 'we' (as in §§ 23, 16, 18); mostly they are 'believers', but twice they are 'Muslims' (§§ 25, 37). Again, certain articles come near to being repetitions of other articles; they deal with the same problem but may have slight alterations. Both §§ 23 and 42 say that disputes are to be referred to Muḥammad, though § 42 is more precise. Both §§ 20 and 43 are directed against Quraysh. The points about Jews in §§ 16 and 24 are similar to those in §§ 37 and 38; and indeed §§ 24 and 38 are identical. Finally both §§ 30 and 46 deal with the Jews of the Aws. It is to be noted that the articles which are similar do not occur together, as one would expect where articles dealt with different aspects of the same point. On the contrary one set is spread between §§ 16 and 30 and another set between §§ 37 and 46. This is sufficient to justify an examination of the possibility that the document as we have it contains articles from two or more different dates.

With this possibility in mind let us turn to what is said about the Jews. The inclusion of the Jews in the *ummah* is an important argument for dating the document before Badr.[3] The omission of the names of the three great Jewish tribes or clans is surprising. One way of explaining it, however, is to suppose that Muḥammad grouped the Jews according to the Arab clans in whose districts they lived; an-Naḍīr and Qurayẓah would then be included among the Jews of al-Aws and Thaʿlabah, since they lived between

[1] Op. cit. 404.

[2] I am here indebted to the late Richard Bell, who, by his insistence on this point in conversation, led me to examine it carefully.

[3] Cf. Wellhausen, ibid. 80.

Awsallāh and Thaʿlabah b. ʿAmr b. ʿAwf.[1] There are strong reasons, however, for thinking that the three main Jewish groups are not included in the document. For one thing it is most likely that a phrase like 'the Jews of the Banū ʿAwf' means the Jews who were confederates of that clan. Small groups of Jews, like those at Rātij,[2] doubtless became confederates of the Arab clan surrounding them; but an-Naḍīr and Qurayẓah had their own territories, and were latterly confederates of ʿAbd al-Ash'hal, who lived some distance away, and who were part of the clan of an-Nabīt which is not mentioned in §§ 25–35 among the clans with Jews attached. Secondly, Ibn Isḥāq[3] has a list of sixty-seven Jewish opponents of Muḥammad and arranges them under the following heads: B. an-Naḍīr (12), B. Thaʿlabah b. Fiṭyawn (3), B. Qaynuqāʿ (31), B. Qurayẓah (17), Jews of B. Zurayq (1), Jews of B. Ḥārithah (1), Jews of B. ʿAmr b. ʿAwf (1), Jews of B. an-Najjār (1). This makes it probable that 'the Jews of B. Thaʿlabah' of § 31 are those whom Ibn Isḥāq and as-Samhūdī[4] reckon as a Jewish clan, and shows that at some period small groups of Jews, distinct from the three main clans, were known as 'the Jews of such-and-such an Arab clan'.

It seems probable, then, that the three main Jewish groups are not mentioned in the document. If that is so, the document in its present form might belong to the period after the elimination of Qurayẓah. The difficulty that much attention is given to Jewish affairs at a time when there were few Jews in Medina could be explained by the hypothesis that the document in its final form was intended as a charter for the Jews remaining in Medina and included all relevant articles from earlier forms of the Constitution of the city.

The history of the document might be reconstructed conjecturally somewhat as follows. The earlier articles (up to §§ 15 or 16 or 19 or 23) may have been the original terms of agreement between Muḥammad and the Medinan clans at al-ʿAqabah, or they may have been drawn up by the 'representatives' (*nuqabā'*) shortly after the Hijrah. They mostly deal with problems involved in keeping peace between the Arab clans. To these from time to time as need arose other articles were added, while articles which became inoperative would be dropped, e.g., articles about Qurayẓah and

[1] Cf. ibid. 75.
[2] Cf. above, pp. 160, 194.
[3] IH, 351 f.
[4] i. 115.

an-Naḍīr. The word *ṣaḥīfah* (translated 'document'), which occurs from §§ 22 to 47 implies a written document formally accepted by different parties. The phrase 'the people of this document' is doubtless used so as to cover both Jews and Muslims. To the 'document' in this special sense belongs the solid body of articles dealing with Jews, §§ 24 to 35 (or, if § 36 is interpreted as referring to the Jews, to § 38). § 16 is perhaps part of the 'Aqabah agreement with the Aws and the Khazraj, and prior to the formal agreement with the Jews in the *ṣaḥīfah* or 'document'.

While scholars may come to approve some such view of the existing text of the Constitution of Medina, there is much that is bound to remain conjectural and obscure. Thus, is § 44 an earlier version of the middle clause of § 37? Are the Jews of Banū 'Awf given a special place because 'Abdallāh b. Ubayy first obtained good terms for them? Why are the Jews of Banū 'l-Aws mentioned twice? Is Banū 'l-Aws here and in § 30 identical with Banū 'l-Aws in § 10 (which is commonly taken to be the group usually known as Awsallāh), or is it the whole tribe of the Aws? This is not the place to pursue such queries further. This study of the text of the Constitution, however, is sufficient to justify the use of it as a source for the ideas underlying the Islamic state in the early formative years, while at the same time it warns us not to base an argument solely on the supposed date of any article of the Constitution.

2. THE POSITION OF MUḤAMMAD

The Constitution of Medina is not certain evidence of the position taken by Muḥammad in Medina when he arrived there in September 622 (iii/1), but his powers under the Constitution are so slight that they cannot have been much less at the beginning of his residence in Medina. All that the Constitution explicitly states is that disputes are to be referred to Muḥammad (§§ 23, 42). In addition the phrase 'Muḥammad the prophet' occurs in the preamble; and the appearance of the Muhājirūn or Emigrants on the same level as one of the Medinan clans implies that Muḥammad as chief of the Emigrants was on a level with the chiefs of the various clans. As the Emigrants are mentioned first, perhaps Muḥammad had a primacy of honour among the chiefs of the clans. He is very far, however, from being autocratic ruler of Medina. He is merely one among a number of important men. During his first year in Medina several others were probably more influential than Muḥammad. The provision that disputes were to be referred to him would not in itself increase his power, unless he had sufficient tact and diplomacy to find a settlement that would command general agreement.

Various incidents of the first half of the Medinan period show the theoretical weakness of Muḥammad's position. After the 'affair of the lie' against 'Ā'ishah's chastity, in which Ibn Ubayy had been active in spreading the calumny, Muḥammad could not take direct action against him, but had to call a meeting of the Anṣār and ask permission of those who might have felt that it was obligatory for them to avenge any injury to Ibn Ubayy. In this case Muḥammad easily gained his point, for, whether by design or accident, the enmity of the Aws and the Khazraj was fanned into flame, and the great decline in Ibn Ubayy's influence became apparent.[1] Similarly, when the question of punishing B. Qurayẓah for their disloyalty arose, Muḥammad did not venture to pronounce any judgement himself, since, had he decreed any shedding of blood, honour might have impelled some confederates of B. Qurayẓah to avenge it, even though they were Muslims. The decision about the punishment was left to the chief of the clan of which they had been confederates.[2]

These are clear examples of how the Medinan clan-chiefs retained much of their power and thereby limited Muḥammad's authority. They are not isolated examples, however. The whole story of his physical attacks on Jews presupposes the old background of clan-relationships, and shows how these had always to be considered in choosing agents.[3] Muḥammad is seen to be the chief of one of several co-operating groups, with little to mark him out from the others.

The referring of disputes to Muḥammad is closely connected with the recognition of him as prophet. The wording of the Constitution is that disputes are to be referred *to God and to Muḥammad.* The idea that one of the functions of a prophet is to mete out justice occurs in a Meccan passage of the Qur'ān: 'each community has a messenger, and when their messenger comes, judgement is given between them with justice, and they are not wronged'.[4] This point was doubtless realized by the Medinans when they recognized Muḥammad as prophet; part of what attracted them to him was

[1] Cf. above, p. 186.
[2] Cf. above, p. 214.
[3] Cf. above, pp. 181 f., &c.
[4] 10. 47/48 c.

the hope that he would be able to put an end to the internal disputes that made life in Medina intolerable.[1] If the Medinans did not explicitly admit this right to judge disputes when they acknowledged Muḥammad as prophet and arranged for him to come to their city, they must soon have been forced to do so, since a revelation came commanding the reference of disputes to God.[2] This should properly mean that disputes were to be settled by a specific revelation from God to Muḥammad; but doubtless in practice Muḥammad was held to have the best knowledge of what God's decision would be on a case where there was no specific revelation. The opening words of this verse, 'wherever there is anything about which you differ', are identical with those of § 23 of the Constitution; this suggests that the connexion is close. The phrase is a vague one and could be applied to far-reaching differences on policy as well as to petty quarrels between neighbours.

Such, then, is the position of Muḥammad as stated in the Constitution and portrayed in the history of his early years in Medina. How far this position was agreed upon in the meetings at al-ʿAqabah it is impossible to say. The 'pledge of the women' (*bayʿat an-nisā'*) follows the text of a verse of the Qur'ān revealed after al-Ḥudaybiyah, and cannot be accepted as evidence of the content of a promise made to Muḥammad.[3] According to the traditional account of the second meeting of al-ʿAqabah, a further pledge was made there, known as the 'pledge of war' (*bayʿat al-ḥarb*). In Ibn Isḥāq's version the important words are those spoken by al-Barā' b. Maʿrūr, 'By Him who sent thee a prophet with the truth, we shall defend thee from that from which we defend ourselves' (or 'our wives and families').[4] Apart from the reference to Muḥammad's prophethood, there is nothing in these words to suggest that this alliance between Muḥammad and the Medinans is different from any other alliance. The same holds of Muḥammad's reply to a question about the possibility of his receiving a revelation commanding him to return to Mecca; he said he regarded himself and the Medinans as belonging to one another, and that he would fight those against whom they fought, and make peace with those with whom they made peace. This is

[1] Cf. T. Nöldeke, *Geschichte des Qorāns*, ed. F. Schwally, Leipzig, 1909, i. 165.

[2] 42. 10/8 E; cf. 4. 59/62 G; 24. 47/46–52/51 G may refer to a later attempt to reverse the argument.

[3] 60. 12 G; IH, 289; cf. *M/Mecca*, 146; G. H. Stern in *Bulletin of the School of Oriental Studies*, x. 185–97.

[4] IH, 296.

just a military alliance. The accounts tell us nothing about Muḥammad's position in the Medinan polity, apart from the fact that he was acknowledged as prophet; and this we would in any case have presumed. It may well be that, until he went to Medina, Muḥammad was content with the recognition of his prophethood and asked for no further privileges (unless something is implicit in his request for *nuqabā'* or representatives to confer with him). In so far as his prophethood was recognized he would have a starting-point from which he could begin to build up his power.[1]

The most mysterious aspect of Muḥammad's position when he went to Medina is the military one. The words of the 'pledge of war' speak of defensive action only; they say nothing about offensive operations, and even in the case of defence they do not say anything about who was to lead. What happened was that the first expeditions were offensive—expeditions from Medina in the hope of ambushing a Meccan caravan. It is not certain that the Medinans took part in these expeditions, but the probability is that they did.[2] In every case the leader was either Muḥammad himself or one of the Emigrants appointed by him. This was doubtless not because of any unrecorded agreement that the Emigrants were to lead in war, but because the organizers of these expeditions were the Emigrants, while the Anṣār were merely invited to join. It is expressly stated that Muḥammad called for volunteers for the expedition of 'Ushayrah.[3] As these expeditions, even that to Badr, were razzias, where the aim was to capture booty without undue danger to oneself, the Anṣār presumably did not think that they would provoke a great expedition against Medina, such as that of the Meccans to Uḥud. Muḥammad seems to have done what he could to collect men for Badr, but apparently not even all who sincerely believed in his prophethood joined in; and we are told that those who did not join were not blamed. It must therefore have been by invitation and exhortation that Muḥammad obtained his 300 or so men.

The booty captured at Badr was apparently disposed of by Muḥammad as he pleased, and this confirms the view that the expedition was, as it were, a private one organized by him, which he invited others to join. Before the battle he is said to have promised certain rewards to those who killed or captured an

[1] Cf. E. E. Evans-Prichard, *The Sanusi of Cyrenaica*, Oxford, 1949, 59 f.

[2] Cf. p. 3 above.

[3] WW, 34.

enemy; and apparently, after fulfilling these promises (and presumably retaining some for his own use), the rest of the spoil was divided equally among the participants. Muḥammad may subsequently have felt, however, that this way both of fighting and of dividing the spoil was unsatisfactory; or the repercussions of Badr in Medina may have necessitated changes. At any rate, by the time of the expedition against Qaynuqā' in the month after Badr, it had been decreed that a fifth (*khums*) of all spoils taken on a Muslim expedition was to go to Muḥammad. This change, moreover, implies several other changes. For one thing it implies that Muḥammad had been recognized as in some sense chief of the *ummah*. It was customary in Arabia for the chief of a tribe to receive a quarter of the spoils, partly for his own use, but partly in order to perform certain functions on behalf of the tribe, such as looking after the poor and giving hospitality.[1] The change from a quarter to a fifth marks off the head of the *ummah* from tribal chiefs; yet the verse prescribing the fifth[2] (which was perhaps revealed immediately after Badr) indicates that the fifth was in part to be used by Muḥammad for these communal purposes.

Such arrangements, again, together with the recognition of Muḥammad as head of the *ummah*, show that he had managed, in the enthusiasm after the victory, to persuade most of the *ummah* to accept the consequences of Badr. All must have realized that the Meccans would try to avenge the bloodshed; and the more level-headed may have suspected that they might not defeat the Meccans so easily another time. Despite the anxious future, however, the Anṣār in general resolved to support Muḥammad more fully. To strengthen their resolution there were revelations bidding them to fight the Meccans till 'there is no more persecution and the religion is entirely God's'.[3] This, too, is the most likely period for the inclusion in the Constitution of articles directed against Quraysh, and also of others emphasizing the unity of the *ummah* in war and peace. It is not easy to see how the Anṣār could have been brought to accept such articles earlier while there was still no break with Mecca.

As it was, there was some opposition in which Ibn Ubayy was no

[1] Abū Tammām, *Hamāsah*, ed. G. Freytag, Bonn, 1828–47, i. 458; *Aghānī* xvi. 50; Lane, *s.v. rub'*; Buhl, *Mohammed*, 31 n.

[2] 8 41/42 F; cf. Lammens, *Mecque*, 153/249.

[3] 8. 39/40 F; 47. 4 is probably later than Badr, if the fighting there was unpremeditated.

doubt prominent. The question asked by this party, 'Why has not a sūrah been sent down?', implies that they professed themselves ready to act on a revelation from God, but not on the mere word of Muḥammad; but, when 'a clearly formulated sūrah' did come, their misgivings were not allayed.[1] The period between Badr and the siege of Medina must have been a difficult one for Muḥammad, when he was endeavouring to establish his ascendancy in Medina. The words 'obey God and His messenger' and various equivalents occur about forty times in the Qur'ān, and are to be dated mostly in the months before and after the battle of Uḥud. There is a series of stories of earlier prophets where these are made to say to their hearers 'fear God and obey me'.[2] There are passages where those who obey God and His messenger are promised the delights of Paradise,[3] while those who have not obeyed repent at leisure in the Fire (that is, Hell).[4] Some passages refer to particular points (such as the disposal of spoils,[5] and the prohibition of wine and the game of *maysir*)[6] where there is no obvious connexion with circumstances about the time of Uḥud. A few seem to be later.[7] Many, however, refer to the opposition which Muḥammad's policy encountered after Badr, either in general[8] or over some particular point, such as fighting the Meccans or bringing disputes to Muḥammad.[9] This shows that it was becoming necessary for Muḥammad to insist on his own special position. He appears, however, to have regarded such passages as exhortations and not as commands. The Constitution does not prescribe obedience; and it is not for disobedience but for faintheartedness that Ibn Ubayy and his supporters are reproached after Uḥud.[10] We must therefore conclude that at this period general obedience to Muḥammad (as distinct from obedience to specific precepts of the Qur'ān) was not formally prescribed.

This state of affairs must be presumed to have continued at least

[1] Q. 47. 20/22, 33/35 ff.; cf. p. 183 above.

[2] 26. 108–79, eight instances, added in Medina according to Bell; cf. 43. 63 E; 71. 3 E+; 3. 50/44 FG.

[3] 4. 13/17 G, 69/71 G; 33. 71; 48. 16 f. HI; 49. 14 HI.

[4] 33. 66 f. E.

[5] 8. 1 F, almost certainly revealed at Badr; for a discussion of the meaning of *anfāl*, cf. Ṭab., *Tafsīr*, ix. 106–12.

[6] 5. 91/93 G.

[7] 9. 71/72 ? HI; 48. 16 f. HI; 49. 14 HI; and perhaps others.

[8] 24. 54/53 G; 3. 32/29 G; cf. 4. 80/82 G; &c.

[9] 47. 33/35 ff. FG; 24. 47/46 ff. G; 4. 59/62 GH.

[10] Cf. p. 184 above.

until the expedition of al-Ḥudaybiyah in March 628 (xi/6). The punishment of Abū Lubābah in May 627 (xii/5) was inflicted not by Muḥammad but by himself; and he appears to have been released not by an order from Muḥammad but by a revelation from God (though none of the suggested verses of the Qur'ān fits the occasion). It may well be, therefore, that 'the pledge of good pleasure', as suggested above, was a pledge to do whatever Muḥammad commanded, that is, to obey him.[1] Whether obedience was expected of all Muslims or only of those who pledged themselves is not clear; but, even if for a time those who did not pledge themselves were not formally bound to obey Muḥammad, it would be increasingly difficult for them to oppose him. He was growing stronger, and, when weak tribes asked for alliance, was demanding a promise to obey. A Qur'ānic verse denouncing those who oppose the decisions of Muḥammad (33. 36) possibly belongs to the year 628; most of the sūrah can be dated in 627 (5–6), but Richard Bell regards this verse as a later addition.[2]

A matter which might have thrown light on the extent of Muḥammad's authority after al-Ḥudaybiyah is unfortunately obscure. He is said to have remarked to some men of the Medinan clan of Salimah, 'Who is your chief (*sayyid*)?' When they replied 'al-Jadd b. Qays', Muḥammad said, 'No, it is Bishr b. al-Barā' b. Ma'rūr'.[3] This might be the formal deposition of a clan chief, but it might also be merely a hint to clansmen loyal to Muḥammad that they ought to depose al-Jadd (or perhaps even just a compliment to Bishr). Though this seems a curious way to depose a chief formally, yet it is conceivable that it was something like a formal deposition. If so, it was an exercise of Muḥammad's authority following on 'the pledge of good pleasure'. Indeed the incident is closely connected with the pledge, and probably occurred almost immediately afterwards. Al-Jadd was the one man in Muḥammad's party at al-Ḥudaybiyah who refused to make the pledge, while Bishr was a suitable person for chief, being the son of al-Barā' b. Ma'rūr, the chief of Salimah who first made 'the pledge of war' at al-'Aqabah but died about the time of the Hijrah. Bishr ate of the poisoned fish at Khaybar, two months after al-Ḥudaybiyah. All we can say, then, is that this may be an instance of Muḥammad using his autocratic power and is then to be dated immediately

[1] Cf. p. 50 above.
[2] *Translation, ad loc.*
[3] IS, iii/2, 112; cf. WW, 248.

after the pledge at al-Ḥudaybiyah. If it is merely a hint to the loyal clansmen, it is an interesting example of how Muḥammad obtained the decision he wanted in matters where he had no formal authority.

An incident from early 631 (late 9) shows that by that time Muḥammad was being obeyed. When Kaʿb b. Mālik and two other men stayed away from the expedition to Tabūk without any reasonable excuse, they were 'sent to Coventry' by the Muslims, and this was done by Muḥammad's order. Even here, however, it is interesting to note that Muḥammad insisted that the repeal of the sentence came not from himself but from God (probably in Qur'ān 9. 118/119).[1] The excommunication of the 'hypocrites' of this period was probably based on revelation and not on Muḥammad's order.[2]

The treaties and letters whose text is given by Ibn Saʿd (i/2) mostly come from the closing years of Muḥammad's life. It is not surprising, then, to find Muḥammad's name coupled with that of God in such phrases as 'the security-guarantee (*dhimmah*) of God and of Muḥammad b. ʿAbdallāh' and 'secure with the security (*āmin bi-amān*) of God and the security of Muḥammad'.[3] The obligation to obey Muḥammad is not mentioned except in a few documents;[4] but, though it is not mentioned, it is often implicit. The extant documents thus confirm the view that from a date not later than the conquest of Mecca Muḥammad was acting as undisputed head of the Muslim community in political as well as religious matters. If Muḥammad wrote letters to the heads of neighbouring states after al-Ḥudaybiyah (though the traditional account of the contents may be regarded as incorrect), that would suggest that it was about this time that he became conscious of having overcome all serious opposition.[5] It may also be that, in accordance with pre-Islamic custom, the use of titles like 'Muḥammad the Prophet' and 'the Messenger of God' involved a claim to political leadership.[6]

The extent of Muḥammad's autocratic powers in his last two or three years is further illustrated by his appointment of 'agents' to act on his behalf in various areas, and indeed by the whole

[1] IH, 907/13; WW, 411–14. [2] Cf. p. 190 above.
[3] IS, i/2. 23. 26 (§ 25); 25. 2 (§ 30 d); &c.
[4] Ibid. 23. 10 (§ 23); 25. 1 (§ 30 d); &c. [5] Cf. p. 41 above.
[6] Cf. J. Ryckmans, *L'Institution Monarchique en Arabie Méridionale avant l'Islam*, 327–9; inscriptions show the importance of the royal epithet and the ceremony of taking it.

matter of administrative appointments. From the beginning Muḥammad had appointed men to perform various functions for which he was responsible. Thus he appointed commanders for the expeditions where he was not present in person. Until Badr he may have done so as head of the Emigrants, but latterly he was acting on behalf of the Muslim community as a whole, since some of the leaders were from the Anṣār or even from nomadic tribes.[1] It may sometimes have happened that a man who had a private feud against an enemy of Muḥammad's was allowed to organize an expedition in the name of the community; the leader thus recognized doubtless agreed to pay Muḥammad the 'fifth' of the booty. 'Uyaynah even seems to have led such an expedition against Tamīm before he was a Muslim.[2] Another regular appointment from the earliest times was that of a deputy in Medina when Muḥammad was absent from the city. During the Badr expedition there was another deputy in the suburb of Qubā', perhaps because this district was still mainly non-Muslim.[3] Other appointments from an early date were of men to supervise the booty and the prisoners.[4] All these were in spheres where Muḥammad's right to order matters was accepted. The Constitution (§ 36) states that warlike expeditions required Muḥammad's permission.

As Muḥammad's influence expanded, further appointments were needed. Thus, even after the spoils of Khaybar had been divided out, it was necessary to have an inspector to estimate and receive half of the annual harvest.[5] We hear of governors of the neighbouring Jewish settlements of Wādi 'l-Qurā and Taymā'.[6] In his dealings with tribes in the neighbourhood of Medina Muḥammad made use of the leading men of the tribe in so far as these were friendly to him. One of the earliest functions entrusted to these men was that of summoning their fellow tribesmen for Muḥammad's expeditions, such as those of the conquest of Mecca and of Tabūk;[7] those who summoned the tribes were also to a large extent their

[1] E.g. Muḥammad b. Maslamah, Ghālib b. 'Abdallāh al-Laythī; cf. Excursus B.

[2] IH, 933–8, &c.; cf. p. 94 above.

[3] 'Āṣim b. 'Adī—IS, iii/2. 36; WW, 66; cf. IH, 494.

[4] 'Abdallāh b. Ka'b al-Māzinī was *'āmil* for *maghānim* at Badr—IH, 457; WW, 70; IS, iii/2. 73. Budayl b. Warqā' (Khuzā'ah) was in charge of prisoners after Ḥunayn—WW, 368.

[5] 'Abdallāh b. Rawāḥah—IH, 177; WW, 286.

[6] 'Amr b. Sa'īd b. al-'Āṣ and Yazīd b. Abī Sufyān—Caetani, ii. 50 f. (from al-Balādhurī, 34), 358, nos. 11, 13 (from al-Ya'qūbī, ii. 81, where 'Amr is said to be over *qurā 'arabīyah*).

[7] WW, 326, 391; &c.

leaders in battle.[1] When it came to the matter of collecting the tax (or legal alms) from these tribes, it was to the summoners that Muḥammad turned, or at least to the most responsible of them.[2] This happened in the case of the tribes of Aslam, Juhaynah, and Kaʿb; and the collector for Aslam also collected for the related tribe of Ghifār. Certain tribes which had not been in alliance with Muḥammad for a long time had collectors sent to them belonging to Quraysh or the Anṣār; for example, Sulaym, Fazārah, al-Muṣṭaliq. The sending of one of the Anṣār to Muzaynah is probably different, since he was of the Aws, and so an old confederate; the reason may have been that no man of Muzaynah was capable of taking the responsibility, since even their leading man, Bilāl b. al-Ḥārith, could be given the comparatively menial task of looking after the grazing land for Muḥammad's war-horses.[3] The general picture is thus one of Muḥammad making use of capable men from the friendly tribes—men who already had a high standing in their tribes—and in the case of other tribes appointing as his agents men of administrative ability from Mecca and Medina.

The stronger tribes in the centre and north-east of Arabia, in so far as they entered into alliance with Muḥammad, negotiated through their chiefs, or at least through men who aspired to be chiefs. To begin with they probably made no contributions to Muḥammad's exchequer, so that the question of tax collection did not arise. Where it did, the chief was responsible.[4] It was therefore only in east-central and south-west Arabia that there was scope for establishing a system of provincial administration. Muḥammad had there to deal with a large number of small units, some friendly and some unfriendly. He made some use of local men of influence, but for the most part he preferred to employ Meccan or Medinan 'agents'. Some of these were apparently responsible for maintaining order and collecting money due to Muḥammad, each in a definite area. At least one, however, Muʿādh b. Jabal, had duties throughout the Yemen and Ḥadramawt in the regions assigned to other agents; these duties included the giving of instruction in the religion of Islam and, at least in some areas, the collection of taxes, but there is no mention of supervising the local agents.[5] During

[1] Cf. WW, 358. [2] WW, 385; Excursus H.
[3] WW, 184; cf. poverty of 'Amr b. 'Awf al-Muzanī, WW, 392.
[4] Cf. cases of Ṭayyi' and Tamīm in Excursus H.
[5] Ṭab. 1852 f.; IS, i/2. 20.

the wars of the Riddah these 'agents' commanded armies of which at least the nucleus came from Medina. Prior to this, however, they normally had no military support beyond that of a dozen or score of their fellow citizens of Medina or Mecca. If necessary, they could presumably appeal for help to the pro-Medinan party in each district.

Mecca was in a special position. As already noticed, Muḥammad appointed as his representative there a young man of the clan of ʿAbd Shams, ʿAttāb d. Asīd, but we can only guess at his functions.[1] There are also references to some subordinate posts in Mecca: one man was inspector of markets, another was charged with delimiting the sacred area, and a third had some unspecified functions.[2]

Thus Muḥammad's administrative appointments illustrate the nature and extent of his power. In theory he is simply the foremost of a number of equal allies. His primacy comes from his office of prophet and from the fact that many of the allies undertook to obey him. The men whom he sends to perform various functions are not officials of an impersonal state, but 'agents' of Muḥammad, doing what he was formally entitled to do or what his personal influence allowed him to do. They probably worked more by persuasion than by coercion. So long as Muḥammad lived, his personal influence must have seemed to contemporaries to be the cement which held the structure together. Yet the building was more firmly constructed than appeared and less dependent on Muḥammad's person; and later events showed that it was capable of being expanded into the administration of an empire.

3. THE CHARACTER OF THE *UMMAH*

The political thinking of the Arabs of Muḥammad's time had as its centre the conception of the tribe. The tribe was essentially a group based on blood-kinship, though in practice this might be modified in various ways. Several tribes might take an oath and form a confederation; but this was usually only for a limited purpose, such as fighting against a similar confederation of tribes. Again, an individual or a family might for practical purposes become a member of a tribe to which he (or it) was not related by

[1] Cf. p. 75 above.

[2] Saʿīd b. Saʿīd b. al-ʿĀṣ (Ibn Ḥajar al-ʿAsqalānī. *Al-Iṣābah*, Calcutta, 1856, &c., ii. no. 5083; *Usd*, ii. 309; cf. IH, 875, killed at aṭ-Ṭā'if); Tamīm b. Asad al-Khuzāʿī (WW, 341); al-Ḥārith b. Nawfal (IS, iv/1. 39).

blood, as a confederate (*ḥalīf*) or a 'protected neighbour' (*jār*) or a client (*mawlā*). These modifications, however, did not lessen the dominance of the conception of the tribe. The tribe was the basis of such social security as there was. Only through membership of a tribe did life become tolerable for a man, and in return the tribe demanded his supreme loyalty. The main tribes were sovereign and independent political entities. The Arabs certainly had some superficial knowledge of the Byzantine, Abyssinian, and Persian empires, and they had some idea of kingship and disliked it.[1] This did not affect their political thinking, however; instead they conceived the empires in terms of their own tribal system, and, for example, made Heraclius, in the story of Muḥammad's letter to him, act as if he were the chief of an Arab tribe.[2] Thus in studying the character of the state and community created by Muḥammad—which for simplicity will be called the *ummah*—we shall keep in mind the question how far the *ummah* is similar to a tribe in conception, and how far different.[3]

The outstanding difference is that the *ummah* was based on religion and not on kinship. This idea is nowhere given theoretical expression, but it is everywhere implied or assumed. It was implied when the Anṣār accepted Muḥammad as a messenger from God. If Muḥammad is a messenger, there must be a message; and a message in turn implies that God is giving directions to the *ummah* in the practical affairs of life. In many matters of principle Muḥammad does not act of his own accord, but merely announces what God commands. Thus God is the head and director of the *ummah*. In the Constitution (§ 15) the security enjoyed by members of the *ummah* and groups attached to it is regarded as coming from the *dhimmah* of God, that is, His compact or guarantee of security. In the letters and treaties collected by Ibn Sa'd Muḥammad's name is coupled with that of God. Many groups are given or offered the *dhimmah* of God and of Muḥammad;[4] some are said to have the security (*amān*) of God and Muḥammad;[5] and a few (apparently all Christian) have merely 'neighbourly protection' (*jiwār*), but in the same two names.[6] This usage continued long in certain spheres;

[1] Cf. *M/Mecca*, 15 f.; also Ryckmans, *Institution Monarchique*, for South Arabia.

[2] IS, 1/2. 16 (§ 2).

[3] Cf. Bertram Thomas, *The Arabs*, London, 1937, 125, 'super-tribe'.

[4] IS, 1/2. 21 (§§ 16, 17), 23 (§§ 24, 25), 28 (§ 44), 29 (§ 45), 34 (§ 67), 37 (§ 74).

[5] Ibid. 23 (§ 23c), 25 (§ 30 d), 32 (§ 57), 33 (§ 61 a, b), 37 (§ 75).

[6] Ibid. 21 (§§ 14, 15), 29 (§ 45), 36 (§ 72, *jiwār Allāh wa-dhimmat an-nabī*).

the public treasury, for example, was known as 'the wealth of God' (*māl Allāh*).[1]

The idea of this theocratic polity is probably not derived directly from the Old Testament. It is rather an independent Arabian elaboration of certain basic ideas from the Old Testament, such as God, revelation, and prophethood. The *ummah* is not very like the Israelite theocracy of the judges. It is closer to the theocracy under Moses. The Qur'ān, however, shows no detailed knowledge of the theocratic government of the Israelites under Moses; though there are many stories about Moses, they tell little about the political organization. The *ummah*, therefore, is not consciously based on the community of Moses. The position is rather that the Qur'ān gives a picture of the relation of prophet and community, in which an Old Testament pattern is vaguely to be traced, but whose specific colouring is Arabian. We have already noticed one Arabian feature of Muḥammad's position—the parallel between the 'fifth' which he received and the quarter share usually given to tribal chiefs.

In the Qur'ān a development can be observed in the meaning of *ummah*. The word is not from the Arabic root found in *umm*, mother, but is ultimately derived from Sumerian. It appears to have come into Arabic at an early period, but whether directly from Sumerian or indirectly through Hebrew or Aramaic is not certain.[2] According to Nöldeke's dating of the *sūrahs*, most of the usages of *ummah* in the Qur'ān are in the Meccan period. Richard Bell, on the other hand, only regards three instances as certainly Meccan,[3] though there are a number of others which he describes as 'Meccan (?)' and 'late Meccan or early Medinan'. It may be therefore that this word was introduced only after the founding of a new type of community at Medina was envisaged. *Ummah* was the sort of word that could be given a new shade of meaning; and it also was capable of further development subsequently. Hitherto it had been said that a prophet was sent to his *qawm*, but *qawm*, which may be translated 'tribe', had for long been associated with the kinship-group, which was the only form of social and political organization known in Arabia. When *ummah* is first used in the

[1] Cf. Q. 24. 33.

[2] Cf. Rudi Paret, art. 'Umma' in EI (1); A. Jeffery, *Vocabulary*, *s.v.*; J. Horovitz, *Koranische Untersuchungen*, 52.

[3] 6. 38 C; 10. 47/48 C; 13. 30/29 D.

Qur'ān it is hardly to be distinguished from *qawm*; every beast and bird is even said to be an *ummah*.[1] Mostly, however, the *ummah* is a community to which a prophet is sent; 'each *ummah* has a messenger'.[2] Gradually, however, *ummah* comes to mean more and more a religious community, until in the latest instances (none much after Uḥud according to Bell) *ummah* is applied almost exclusively to the Muslim, Jewish, and Christian communities, or some section of them. Thus the Muslims are told that they have been made 'an *ummah* in the middle',[3] and that they 'have become the best community';[4] while it is said that among the People of the Book is 'an *ummah* which aims at doing right'.[5] There is a marked difference between this later usage and the earlier one according to which it could be said that a whole community might reject its messenger.[6]

What we thus learn from the Qur'ān may be supplemented from the Constitution of Medina. There in § 1 it is stated that the believers and Muslims of Quraysh and Yathrib are one *ummah*; and this community presumably includes also 'those who follow them . . .'. The *ummah* is thus the complex community at Medina to which Muḥammad believed himself to be sent. The later article (§ 25) which affirms that certain Jews 'are an *ummah* along with the believers', though it could conceivably mean that they constituted a community parallel to that of the believers, presumably means that they are included in the one *ummah*. As they are specifically allowed to practise their own religion, however, this suggests that the *ummah* is no longer a purely religious community. If, however, the last use of *ummah* in the Qur'ān is to be dated a little after Uḥud while this article is subsequent to the execution of Banū Qurayẓah (as has been suggested), there is no contradiction but only a development dictated by circumstances.

This development points to a third possible basis for a community distinct from kinship and religion, namely, locality. This is indeed, if not the whole basis, at least a prominent factor in the basis of most settled communities. In the examination of the various clans of Medina it was seen that in some cases, like that of the 'people of Rātij', organization by kinship appeared to be giving place to organization by locality. To the external observer it is clear

[1] 6. 38 C. [2] 10. 47/48 C. [3] 2. 143/137 EF.
[4] 3. 110/106 G. [5] 5. 66/70 FG.
[6] 40. 5 ? C; 28. 18/17 E+ ?; cf. 27. 83/85 E+.

that the *ummah* as described in the Constitution of Medina in fact has a territorial basis; but it is also clear that this territorial basis was not officially recognized by the members of the *ummah*. The *ummah* has as its core the Muslims now living in Yathrib, but it is thought of as a group of clans together with their confederates and other 'followers'. The basis could never have been purely territorial, of course, for nomadic confederates of the Anṣār like Juhaynah and Muzaynah were presumably included. The territorial factor appeared again in the caliphate of ʿUmar when he made all non-Muslims leave Arabia, but, for example, allowed the Jews of Wadi 'l-Qurā to remain since they were not in the Ḥijāz but in Syria.[1] Thus in practice the element or factor of locality helps to constitute the *ummah*, but no recognition is given to this in theory where everything is interpreted in terms of the kinship-group.

Something of the same kind happens to the conception of *hijrah* or 'emigration'. To the European it suggests primarily change of location, but the Arab seems to have thought of it rather as a change of relationship to one's tribe—to make the *hijrah* was to leave one's tribe and attach oneself to the *ummah*.[2] Two points involving the idea of *hijrah* fall to be considered here. The first is the application of the word to members of nomadic tribes who came and settled in Medina. There were many of these, and when they pledged themselves to Muḥammad a distinction seems to have been made between the 'nomadic pledge' and the 'pledge of migration' (*bayʿah ʿarabīyah, bayʿat hijrah*).[3] There is no mention of these persons in the Constitution, though it is carefully worded and says merely 'emigrants of Quraysh'; they may have ranked as 'protected neighbours' of Muḥammad. In the second place the status of 'Emigrants' or *Muhājirūn* is given by treaty to the tribes of Aslam, Khuzāʿah, and Muzaynah.[4] We cannot be certain exactly what this involved. For Muzaynah it probably meant that they belonged to the core of the *ummah* in their own right and were not merely confederates of the Aws. There is no record of any signal service by Muzaynah to justify this reward, but Aslam and Khuzāʿah had

[1] Cf. WW, 292.

[2] Cf. C. Snouck Hurgronje, *Verspreide Geschriften*, i. 297–305, 'Twee populaire Dwalingen verbeterd. I, De hidjra.'

[3] IS, iv/2. 66. 3; cf. p. 86 above; for *bayʿah* cf. *M/Mecca*, 112.

[4] IS, i/2. 24. 17, 25. 14, 38. 13 (§§ 29, 32 a, 76); p. 86 above.

served Muḥammad well. As explained above,[1] the conferment of this status probably also attached these tribes specially to Muḥammad and so strengthened his position in Medina relatively to the Anṣār.

When we turn from these reflections on the basis of the *ummah* to consider its relations to other groups, we find the conception of the tribe very influential. The enemies of the *ummah* are essentially the unbelievers and the idolaters, in accordance with the religious basis; but the attitude towards them was that appropriate towards hostile tribes. There were few conventions to restrain a tribe in its dealings with a hostile tribe, and the individual stranger in Arabia in pre-Islamic times had few rights unless someone voluntarily gave him protection. But the Muslims disregarded even the existing rights and conventions where these were connected with the old religion, and some of their behaviour seemed outrageous to their pagan opponents.[2] Thus the conduct of the Muslims to their enemies was that of one tribe to another, but with some of the conventions disregarded. Indeed, there was nothing in common between the two, no positive relationship, and there was no reason for observing any decencies except where non-observance debased oneself (like mutilating corpses)[3] or might incur unpleasant retaliation from one's enemies.

The prohibition of intermarriage with pagans is probably an indication of this complete separation from idolatry and its adherents. Soon after al-Ḥudaybiyah there came a revelation interpreted as forbidding Muslim women to remain married to pagan husbands and Muslim men to continue to have pagan wives. On being informed of this command ʿUmar divorced two pagan women to whom he was still married (though they were probably not in Medina).[4] The order doubtless had its place in the total strategy. Coming after al-Ḥudaybiyah it emphasized the impossibility of being on good terms with Muḥammad without accepting his claims. It also removed possible sources of false doctrine, and got rid of attachments which might have made the prosecution of war to the uttermost more difficult. It presumably did not imply the prohibition of relations other than marriage with pagan women.

[1] Cf. p. 86 above. The importance of the status is shown by the list of women classified as *muhājirāt* in IS, viii.

[2] Cf. I. Goldziher, *Muhammedanische Studien*, Halle, 1888, i. 69.

[3] Cf. IH, 463, 585; WW, 69, 135; &c.

[4] Q. 60. 10; cf. IH, 755; WW, 263. IS, iii/1. 190 does not mention the first of the two divorced by ʿUmar.

The *ummah* entered into positive relations with tribes in much the same way as a strong tribe did. 'Neighbourly protection' (*jiwār*) was given in the name of God and of Muḥammad.[1] What came, however, to be the main conception of the relation of the *ummah* to other groups is that contained in the word *dhimmah*. This is an obscure word in some ways. Its primary meaning seems to be 'compact' or 'covenant' though this is remote from the meaning of the verb *dhamma*, 'to blame'. It is used twice in the Qur'ān in the sense of 'compact'.[2] The meaning broadens out, however, to that of a compact giving a guarantee of security, and so it comes to mean 'guarantee of security' and even 'protection'. Perhaps the truth is that our Western minds have failed to seize the essence of *dhimmah*, and so it seems to us that it vacillates between two meanings. The best we can do is to look at some examples.

When it says in § 15 of the Constitution that 'the *dhimmah* of God is one', the meaning is presumably that the 'compact guaranteeing security' is one; and this implies (as is shown in the following clauses) that all members of the *ummah* are equally protected, that all are equally capable of giving protection which the whole *ummah* is obliged to make effective, and that they all stand to one another in the relation of protector and protected, while none is to be protected, except temporarily, by anyone outside the community. In the letters and treaties of Muḥammad collected by Ibn Sa'd there is frequent mention of 'the *dhimmah* of God and the *dhimmah* of Muḥammad'. In many cases the translation 'protection' would suit. Sometimes it even seems to be required, as, for example, when it is said that 'the Prophet covenants (*'ahada*) to them (Ghifār) the *dhimmah* of God and the *dhimmah* of His Messenger'.[3] On the other hand, there is sometimes also present the idea of a compact or of an obligation binding on God and Muḥammad. In the letter to the clan Ḥadas of Lakhm it is said that the Muslim who performs his duties is secure 'by the *dhimmah* of God and the *dhimmah* of Muḥammad', but, if he apostasizes, 'the *dhimmah* of God and the *dhimmah* of Muhammad, His Messenger' is 'free of (responsibility towards) him' (*barī'ah min-hu*); and there is the curious addition that the man whose *islām* is attested by a Muslim is secure 'by the

[1] IS, i/2. 21. 4, 14; 29. 10; 36. 7, 13 (§§ 14, 15, 45, 72); the last has *jiwār Allāh wa-dhimmat (Muḥammad) an-nabī*. Cf. also IH, 986. 10.

[2] 9. 8, 10.

[3] IS, i/2. 26. 28 (§ 39) = Excursus G, no. 2.

dhimmah of Muḥammad' alone.[1] The reason for the omission of God's name here is not clear; there may have been a slight distinction present in the mind of Muḥammad since in another letter he speaks of 'the *jiwār* of God and the *dhimmah* of the prophet'.[2] A common expression is that certain people 'have (*la-hum*) the *dhimmah*',[3] but in at least one case it is said to be 'upon them' or 'over them' (*ʿalay-him*).[4] The translation 'guarantee of security' fits most of these passages, except that, where the *dhimmah* of Muḥammad is said to be free of responsibility towards (*barīʾah min*) someone, it seems to be regarded almost as a part of his personal being.

The explanation of this difficulty in giving a precise meaning to *dhimmah* is perhaps to be found in the fact that the conception was a fluid one. One of the chief functions of the tribe or kinship-group was to guarantee the security of its members; this was a matter of universally recognized custom. Muḥammad's problem was to find something for his religiously based community that would take the place of this customary obligation. He solved his problem by developing the pre-Islamic practice of forming an alliance or confederacy. The old word *ḥālafa*, 'formed a confederacy', is used in Muḥammad's letter to Nuʿaym b. Masʿūd;[5] but it seems to have been replaced by phrases including *amān*, 'security' or *dhimmah*; the reason for this change will appear presently. The 'pledge of war' at al-ʿAqabah was presumably an act establishing a confederacy or at least something analogous. The confederacy (if we may call it so) thus founded could be joined by others, as, for example, Nuʿaym b. Masʿūd. Even where no word from the root *ḥilf* was used, the conditions were those of a confederacy, namely, mutual help and succour. In the early years there seem to have been agreements with non-Muslims, presumably pagans;[6] in the expedition of Ḥamzah to Sīf al-Baḥr, perhaps the first of all, the tribe of Juhaynah acted as confederates of the Muslims; and the letters to the tribes of Ḍamrah and Ghifār assuring them of the *dhimmah* of God and Muḥammad, though stating their obligation to help Muḥammad, do not imply in any

[1] Ibid, 21. 14–19 (§ 16) = Excursus G, no. 10; cf. 23. 21 (§ 24), the *dhimmah* of Muḥammad is *barīʾah* from whoever disobeys him.

[2] Ibid. 36. 13 (§ 72).

[3] Ibid. 29. 21 (§ 46; Excursus G, 5).

[4] Ibid. 27. 6 (§ 40); Excursus G, 1).

[5] Ibid. 26. 19 (§ 35; Excursus G, 8).

[6] *Mīthāq* in Q. 8. 72/73 seems to be with non-Muslims.

way that they were Muslims; the presumption therefore is that they were not. Muḥammad may have wondered for a time whether non-Muslims could have the *dhimmah* of God, and this may explain why in some places we find the *dhimmah* of Muḥammad only. But in the end he seems to have extended the *dhimmah* of God to all who belonged to his security system; in later times it was precisely the non-Muslim member of an Islamic state who was known as a *dhimmī* or one of the *ahl adh-dhimmah* (people of the *dhimmah*). Muḥammad's hesitation, of course, was only about the propriety of God's *dhimmah* being extended beyond the community of Muslims, for he had no hesitation about accepting non-Muslims as allies. Moreover, apart from the pagan Meccans at Ḥunayn, there are several instances of men fighting under Muḥammad before they became Muslims.[1]

In the old Arab idea of confederacy it was assumed that the contracting parties were equal in status, though one of them might be stronger than the other. In some of the earlier treaties this appears in the form that help (*naṣr*) is due from each to the other. In so far as God was mentioned, however, and after Muḥammad had become the strongest man in Arabia, there was no equality. Consequently in the later treaties what is demanded as a condition for the granting of the *dhimmah* of God and Muḥammad is the fulfilment of the religious duties of Muslims, and in particular the payment of *zakāt*; there are also special demands in certain cases. For non-Muslims who make a treaty with Muḥammad the demand is for what is usually called *jizyah*. Whatever the name, this payment by non-Muslims was regarded as being in return for the protection given. It was apparently common in pre-Islamic times for weak tribes or settled communities to make payments for protection to strong nomadic tribes. Where protection could not be given, payment was not accepted; when an individual or tribe refused to pay an assessment, protection was withdrawn.[2] When, in the caliphate of 'Umar, the Muslims had on one occasion to retire from Ḥims they refunded the tax (*kharāj*) which had been paid.[3]

[1] Cf. p. 89 above; also Abū Ruhm al-Ghifārī, WW, 56 f., &c.; Jews, WW, 283.

[2] Cf. D. C. Dennett, jr., *Conversion and the Poll-tax in Early Islam*, Cambridge, U.S.A., 1950, 117.

[3] Al-Balādhurī, 131. 6–9, and Dennett, op. cit. 55–57; the matter is not wholly clear, however.

There does not seem to be any standard term to designate the Islamic community after Mecca had been incorporated and many tribes had become confederates. *Ummah* is no longer used in the Qur'ān or in the treaties. In the latter one occasionally finds terms like *jamā'ah*[1] or *ḥizb Allāh*.[2] An official term was perhaps unnecessary, since diplomacy was carried out in the name of God and Muḥammad. Presumably members of Muslim tribes in alliance with Muḥammad were regarded as full members of the community (in contrast to non-Muslims). We cannot say at what point this change took place and what it involved. After the fixing of stipends by 'Umar in 636/15 all full members of the community received a stipend; and presumably some such arrangement was in force earlier, though nothing is known of details. It would seem that, in order to be a member of the community, a man must be a member of some group which had had a treaty or confederacy with Muḥammad—either of one of the clans mentioned in the Constitution of Medina, or of a tribe which had later made a treaty. This would explain why there was such eagerness to show that every tribe had sent a deputation to Muḥammad. It would also explain why non-Arabs, on becoming Muslims, had to become *mawālī* of Arab tribes.[3] The population of the conquered countries as a whole had no treaties with Muḥammad or his successors, while towns that had treaties had them as non-Muslims. (We have already noticed how individuals who left their tribes and came to settle in Medina were classed as Muhājirūn or Emigrants.)

From these points it follows that the Islamic community was never thought of as a collection of individuals, but as a collection of groups who were in various forms of alliance or confederacy with Muḥammad. The retention of these groups was perhaps for administrative convenience;[4] in the Constitution of Medina the clans are responsible for blood-money, ransoms, &c., and later the clans and tribes may have been useful, not merely in the administration of justice, but as subdivisions of the stipend roll. Nevertheless there was a strong tendency in Islam to get rid of such subdivisions. Every Muslim was to be equally protected by all,

[1] IS, i/2. 27. 9 (§ 41). [2] Ibid. 83. 4 (§ 140 a); cf. Q. 5. 56/61; 58. 22.
[3] Cf. Dennett, op. cit., 58.
[4] Cf. IH, 345 f., where 'Umar inscribes Bilāl and all Abyssinian Muslims under Khath'am because Bilāl was originally 'brothered' with a man of Khath'am.

said the Constitution, and none was to be protected by others from being punished for wrong acts. Thus these subdivisions were redundant in theory, and perhaps undesirable in themselves. It was a principle attributed—probably rightly—to Muḥammad that 'there is no confederacy (*ḥilf*) in Islam'; that is, no two groups within the community were to establish a specially close relationship.[1] Such a confederacy or special relationship would be tantamount to a denial of Islam, since it would imply that the protection given by Muḥammad or his successors was incomplete. (In the confederacy of a small group with Muḥammad[2] there is of course no contradiction; but it was clearly advisable not to use the term *ḥilf* for the relationship of a group to Muḥammad in view of the prohibition of *ḥilf* in other forms.)

The institution of the *nuqabā'* (sing. *naqīb*) or 'representatives' at the second ʿAqabah is so obscure that it adds little to our knowledge of the nature of the *ummah*, but it at least confirms that it was thought of as a group of clans. The *nuqabā'* were not just twelve men representing the Anṣār, but were representatives of clans; thus Asʿad b. Zurārah was the *naqīb* of an-Najjār, and, when he died, soon after the Hijrah, the clan set about appointing a successor, but were persuaded to accept Muḥammad, who was related to them through his paternal great-grandmother. The distribution of the 'representatives' among the clans[3] was based on the numbers and quality of the members of the clan present at al-ʿAqabah. No clan had more than two 'representatives'; but, while Bayāḍah with three men present had no *naqīb*, Sāʿidah with only two men present had two. The *nuqabā'* were the leading man or men in each clan at al-ʿAqabah, and were of course all Muslims. A weakness of the institution was that some of the leading men of Medina were excluded—not merely uncertain supporters of Muḥammad like Ibn Ubayy, but even Saʿd b. Muʿādh, who from Badr until his death was the most important of the Anṣār. This failure to include the real leaders probably explains why we hear nothing of the workings of the system of *nuqabā'*; it did not work!

The practice of what may be called 'brothering' (*mu'ākhāh*) does not help in the understanding of the nature of the community, but

[1] Cf. Goldziher, op. cit. i. 69; cf. Constitution, § 12; also al-Bukhārī, *Adab* (78), 67; Ibn Ḥanbal, *Musnad*, i. 190. [2] Cf. p. 245 above.
[3] Cf. table on p. 180; for the institution of *nuqabā'* v. *M/Mecca*, 145–8.

it may be mentioned here. The main instance of 'brothering' was before Badr, and probably just immediately before it; each Emigrant was paired with one of the Anṣār, and the pair who thus became brothers were supposed not to leave one another during the battle. The purpose of the device was doubtless to prevent the different sections of the force from reacting differently to the onset of the enemy. If one 'brother' was killed, the other was supposed to inherit. Sa'd b. ar-Rabī' (Ba'l-Ḥārith), with whom 'Abd ar-Raḥmān b. 'Awf was paired, offered his 'brother' half of his wealth and one of his two wives.[1] Perhaps owing to the difficulties about inheritance, the practice of 'brothering' was abrogated, but it is not clear whether this happened soon after Badr or later.[2] Though even Ibn Isḥāq[3] speaks as if the 'brothering' before Badr was the only instance of the practice, this was not so. Muḥammad also 'brothered' some of his Meccan followers with one another, as we learn from the individual biographies in Ibn Sa'd, and this presumably happened before the Hijrah; thus 'Abd ar-Raḥmān b. 'Awf was 'brother' of Sa'd b. Abī Waqqāṣ as well as of Sa'd b. ar-Rabī'.[4] There must also have been some 'brothering' later in the Medinan period, since there are cases involving men who were not in Medina until after Badr.[5] Further, on two occasions the leader of an expedition is said by al-Wāqidī to have 'brothered' his men to prevent them following the enemy too far; the 'brothers' were told not to separate from one another, but in both cases one was disobedient and pursued the enemy some distance.[6] These latter cases make it probable that the early 'brothering' in Medina of Emigrants and Anṣār aimed at securing greater cohesion in battle. The practice may be regarded as an adaptation of the pre-Islamic confederacy to lessen the disadvantages from the continuing influence of the kinship-group.[7]

[1] IS, iii/1. 89; cf. Q. 4. 33/37, abrogated by 33. 6, according to Ṭab., *Tafsīr*, v. 31–35; also C. van Arendonk, art. 'Ḥilf' in EI (1)

[2] Ibid. 100. 19–25, iv/1. 23. 27; cf. Q. 8. 75/76, 33. 6, and Abū Ja'far an-Naḥḥās, *K. an-Nāsikh wa-'l-Mansūkh*, 159 (on Q. 8. 75/76).

[3] IH, 344–6; cf. phrase *min ahl Badr* in IS, iii/2. 23. 13, 24. 7.

[4] IS, iii/1. 89; but cf. also IH, 934. 1, 'brothered' with 'Uthmān b. 'Affān.

[5] IH, 933 f., Mu'āwiyah and al-Ḥutāt b. Yazīd (Tamīm); cf. IS, iv/1. 12. 12, al-'Abbās and his nephew, Nawfal b. al-Ḥārith.

[6] WW, 297, 318, in 628/7 and 629/8 respectively.

[7] Cf. J. Schacht, art. 'Mīrāth' in EI(S); also J. Wellhausen, 'Die Ehe bei den Arabern' in *Nachrichten der kgl. Gesellschaft der Wissenschaften zu Göttingen*, 1893, 461; and I. Lichtenstädter in *Islamic Culture*, xvi (1942), 47–52.

4. FINANCE

The finances of the Islamic community are worthy of some consideration in detail. During the Meccan period the community had nothing resembling public finance, though Abū Bakr and perhaps others spent money in freeing slaves who became Muslims.[1] Several of the articles of the Constitution of Medina deal with financial matters, but all except one exemplify the principle that each group was responsible for its own expenses and not for those of other groups united with it in the *ummah*; this applies to the paying of blood-money and ransoming of captives,[2] and also to the expenses incurred in campaigns.[3] The exceptional article is 11 which states that the believers in general give a debtor help towards the payment of ransom or blood-money. How this worked in practice is not clear; perhaps it was left to some of the richer Muslims to give help, and, if they were unwilling, Muḥammad himself may have stepped in. When ʿAbdallāh b. ʿAmr (Salimah) was killed at Uḥud, he left debts equivalent to two years' produce of his date-palms; when the son explained the difficulty to Muḥammad, the latter helped him to meet his creditors (though as the story stands it does not concern public finance, since Muḥammad's method was the miraculous multiplication of the stock of dates).[4] Even if money had been given in this case, it would still show a rudimentary financial organization.

It is not clear how any of the Emigrants made a living in the period between the Hijrah and the battle of Badr, far less contributed to a common purse. They presumably did not take up agriculture, and they presumably did not plan to live indefinitely off the hospitality of the Anṣār. It has been suggested that they must have had in view either raids on Meccan caravans or long-distance trading, and both courses would lead to conflict with Mecca.[5] There is some evidence that the Emigrants engaged in commercial operations. ʿAbd ar-Raḥmān b. ʿAwf rejected the offer of half the wealth of his Medinan 'brother', and asked instead to be shown the market (*sc.* that among B. Qaynuqāʿ); he soon returned with a skin of butter and a cheese that he had gained by his superior business acumen.[6] This presumably happened soon

[1] IS, iii/1. 122; cf. *M/Mecca*, 118.
[2] §§ 2–10.
[3] § 37; § 24(= § 38) is doubtless to be interpreted in the light of § 37.
[4] IS, iii/2. 107.
[5] *M/Mecca*, 148.
[6] IS, iii/1. 88; al-Bukhārī, *Buyūʿ* (34), 1.

after the Hijrah and certainly before the expulsion of B. Qaynuqā'; the next two pieces of evidence to be mentioned cannot be dated certainly, but both of them are probably to be referred to this early period. 'Umar did not hear an instruction given by Muḥammad because he was engaged in a market transaction.[1] 'Alī obtained rushes from one of the Anṣār in order to sell them.[2] 'Uthmān and 'Abd ar-Raḥmān b. 'Awf traded in the captives of B. Qurayẓah.[3] In general the Emigrants are said to have spent their time in the markets while the Anṣār were in their fields,[4] though commerce was not unknown among the Anṣār.[5] At a later period the Muslims, presumably both Emigrants and Anṣār, did some trading on the expedition of Badr al-Maw'id in 626/4;[6] Zayd b. Ḥārithah attempted to take a trading caravan to Syria in 627/6, but was ambushed;[7] Diḥyah b. Khalīfah al-Kalbī had merchandise with him when Muḥammad sent him to 'Caesar'.[8]

From all this it may be concluded that the Emigrants gained what they could by trading, both before Badr and after. It must not be supposed that every Emigrant could earn his supper as easily as 'Abd ar-Raḥmān; he was the merchant *par excellence* among the Muslims, and became extremely wealthy under the caliphs. With the clan of Qaynuqā' already, at least in part, devoted to trade, there cannot have been a livelihood for seventy Muslims in the early months, though things would be easier after the expulsion of Qaynuqā'. At least until Badr, then, the Emigrants must have been partly supported by the Muslims of Medina. Indeed, one of the complaints made to Ka'b b. al-Ashraf by the men who assassinated him, to persuade him that they were not Muslims, was that Muḥammad and his Meccan followers were burdensome to the people of Medina.[9] Presumably Muḥammad made no specific demands on the Anṣār, but merely exhorted them to 'contribute' what they could. The process seems to be described in a verse of the Qur'ān:[10]

> The good which ye contribute is . . . for the poor, who have been restricted (? fighting) in the way of God, and are therefore unable to knock about in the land (to trade); the ignorant think them rich because of their self-restraint; but one may recognise them by their mark; they ask not importunately of the people.

1 Al-Bukhārī, ibid. 9.
2 Ibid. *Sharb* (42), 13. 3.
3 WW, 221.
4 Al-Bukhārī, *Buyū'* (34), 1.
5 E.g. ibid. 9.
6 WW, 168.
7 Ibid. 238.
8 IH, 976. 2.
9 Cf. p. 210 above.
10 2. 273/274 E.

The Qur'ān has ample evidence of the importance of voluntary 'contributions' in the plans for the young community at Medina. Men are commanded to believe in God and His messenger and contribute of their wealth.[1] Their contributions are a loan they lend to God; He knows what they do; He will repay them the double and more.[2] They are to contribute what they can spare.[3] From the very first the Qur'ān had insisted on generosity;[4] but it is apparently only in the early Medinan period that the requests for contributions commence. Though they were voluntary, and though men were encouraged to give them by the promise of a reward from God, yet there must have been some pressure or obligation on the richer Muslims to contribute, since the withholding of contributions (*bukhl*, &c.) is criticized and threatened with Divine punishment.[5] There is also mention of some persons, presumably Hypocrites or Jews, who made contributions but in other ways did not act as true believers.[6] In the difficult period after Uḥud some of the opponents tried to stop the contributions (*ṣadaqāt*) by mockery.[7]

One or two incidents are recorded which show the kind of thing which happened. On the expedition to Sīf al-Baḥr in November 629 (vii/8) when food was scarce, Qays, the son of Sa'd b. 'Ubādah, on three successive days bought a camel (by promising to pay in dates on his return to Medina) and had it slaughtered for the party.[8] About a year later Muḥammad asked for gifts towards the fitting out of the great expedition to Tabūk with arms, camels, and provisions, and the leading Muslims responded generously.[9] A note has been preserved of large sums which 'Abd ar-Rahmān b. 'Awf contributed (*taṣaddaqa*) during Muḥammad's lifetime.[10] A man of the clan of an-Najjār presented (*taṣaddaqa*) a stronghold (*qaṣr*) to Muḥammad.[11] These are no doubt some of the 'high-lights' among the contributions, but they show how the early Muslim community lived. Those who had anything to spare were expected to give to those in need, but there was no regimentation. Gradually

[1] 2. 195/191 ?; 2. 254/255 E; 57. 7 E.

[2] 2. 245/246 E; 5. 12/15 F; 57. 11, 19/18 E—; 64. 17 G; 73. 20 E+; 2. 261/263 ? FG; &c.

[3] 2. 219/216 f. ? FG.

[4] Cf. *M/Mecca*, 68 ff.

[5] 3. 180/175 G; 4. 37/41 ff. G, rejecting the interpretation in IH, 389 f. in favour of that of some commentators in Ṭab., *Tafsīr*, *ad loc.* (v. 51).

[6] 2. 262/264 ff. ? FG; cf. 9. 53 f. I.

[7] 9. 75/76 ff. GH; cf. 4. 37/41 G.

[8] WW, 317 f.

[9] Ibid. 391.

[10] *Usd*, iii. 316. 3 ff.

[11] Ṭab. i. 1528. 4.

the force of public opinion must have compelled the meaner among the men of affluence to make some contributions. Where necessary, Muḥammad may have dropped a hint, as he is said to have done on one occasion to ʿAbd ar-Raḥmān b. ʿAwf,[1] and as he did before the expedition to Tabūk.

What has been said so far is based mainly on those Qur'anic verses which contain the word *nafaqah* or phrases such as *mā anfaqtum*; these must be translated 'contribution', 'what you contribute', &c., although the common meaning is 'expenditure' and 'what you spend'. Some verses with *ṣadaqah* (alms) have also been used, since there are passages where both roots occur without any apparent difference of meaning. In the early Medinan period the word *zakāt* also seems to refer to contributions or voluntary almsgiving; at least there is no evidence to show that at this period the *zakāt*, which later became the 'legal alms', was a fixed proportion of a man's property or income. An examination of the use of this word in the Qur'ān[2] reveals that it was in some way closely connected with the Jews, though not used exclusively with respect to them. One inference from this is that the Jews of Medina were also expected to make contributions. For the most part these were presumably to take the form of alms to the poorer members of the community, among whom Emigrants would be prominent. Shortly before their expulsion an-Naḍīr were asked to contribute to a payment of blood-money.[3]

The problem of how *zakāt* came to have its technical meaning of 'legal alms' lies outside the scope of a life of Muḥammad, since the change came about later. What must be considered, however, is the extent to which there was a transition from voluntary contributions to fixed 'alms' during Muḥammad's lifetime. Definite proportions of property or income to be paid as 'alms' to Muḥammad or one of his agents are mentioned in some of the treaties from the last two years or so of his life. The usual word, if there is any at all, is *ṣadaqah*, and the collector of these amounts is consequently known as *muṣaddiq*. This, according to available evidence, is the beginning of the system of 'legal alms', for which *zakāt* became the usual name, while *ṣadaqah* came to be reserved for voluntary or supererogatory almsgiving. There are no grounds, however, for thinking that the fixed proportions were made obligatory for all

[1] IS, iii/1. 93.
[2] Cf. Excursus I.
[3] IH, 652; WW, 161; cf. p. 211 above.

Muslims during Muḥammad's lifetime. Not even all the nomadic tribes in alliance with him are said to have given *ṣadaqāt*. On the contrary, the presumption is that completely voluntary almsgiving remained the rule for those Muslims for whom no fixed *ṣadaqah* was prescribed by agreement. This presumption is supported by the appeal for contributions before the expedition to Tabūk. After the battle of Ḥunayn the major part of the income of most of the Emigrants and Anṣār probably came from sharing in the spoils and booty of the various expeditions, and was not therefore liable to 'legal alms'. (The same consideration would apply even more widely during the caliphates of Abū Bakr and 'Umar.) Thus, in a sense, there is no transition from voluntary contributions to legal alms. The older Muslims continued to act as they had been doing; but fixed sums were prescribed for the later additions to Muḥammad's security system.

The question of gifts is relevant to this matter of voluntary or stipulated alms. As early as the expedition of al-Ḥudaybiyah Muḥammad is said to have refused to accept milk as a gift from some pagans, but to have paid for it.[1] At al-Ji'rānah a man of Aslam presented some sheep to Muḥammad, who made to refuse them, until the man assured him that he was a Muslim and had paid his tax to the collector for his tribe.[2] The latter point is significant. It suggests that Muḥammad was not prepared to accept voluntary alms in cases where a man might claim that this exempted him from the fixed 'legal alms', which was doubtless heavier. On another occasion, presumably after Ḥunayn (though placed earlier by al-Wāqidī because of the connexion with 'Uyaynah b. Ḥiṣn), Muḥammad stated publicly that he would accept gifts only from Quraysh and Anṣār.[3] This further suggests that only these two groups were permitted to continue giving voluntary contributions.

It is also possible that there was little difference between the obligatory payments made to Muḥammad by Muslims and those made by Christian Arabs. At least in some cases, however, a special name was given to the latter, *jizyah*, derived from a Qur'anic verse (9. 29), which bids the Muslims fight against the Christians until they are subdued and pay the *jizyah*. The word is thought to have come from a similar Syriac word meaning 'poll-tax', either directly or through Persian, but it might also be an Arabic formation meaning 'due' or 'satisfaction', and something of this was doubtless

[1] WW, 242. [2] Ibid. 374. [3] Ibid. 232.

suggested when it was used in the Qur'ān.[1] Despite the different name, however, the same men often collected both *ṣadaqāt* and *jizyah*.[2] It is also possible that in the early days some Christian groups had to pay a tax levied on the herds or fields like the 'legal alms', and not on the heads like the *jizyah*.[3]

Other names are also occasionally used for the fixed sums of money or goods which had to be paid to Muḥammad. In one passage a man is empowered to collect *'ushūr*, 'tithes', as well as *ṣadaqah*; this may have been a pre-existing tax that was continued under Muslim administration, but it is impossible to be certain.[4] Another word found is *si'āyah*.[5] Its precise significance is 'money earned by a slave which counts towards buying his freedom'. It occurs in connexion with some of the tribes defeated at Ḥunayn, and probably implies that they were required to pay a fixed sum for a number of years by way of ransom, but not in perpetuity.

In voluntary almsgiving the gift presumably went direct to the recipient, since secret almsgiving is regarded as possible. The fixed *ṣadaqah*, however, and other taxes and dues were paid to Muḥammad, and thus belong to public finance. From an early period Muḥammad had been holding public money or goods, namely, the *khums* or 'fifth' of the spoils or booty captured on campaign. The standard account is that the 'fifth' was not instituted until after Badr, and was first applied in the campaign against B. Qaynuqā'.[6] At Badr there was a dispute about the division of the spoil, and a verse (8. 1) is said to have been revealed giving Muḥammad power to dispose of the whole as he pleased. After this it seems to have been agreed that a fifth of the total should go to Muḥammad for public purposes, and that the remainder should be divided equally among the participants; a horseman received two shares for his horse in addition to his own share. The 'fifth' was parallel to the fourth part that it had been customary for the chief of a tribe to receive.[7] Again like the chief of a tribe Muḥammad was entitled to have a 'first pick' (*ṣafī*) before the general distribution; in pre-Islamic times this usually was some object such as a she-camel, horse, sword, or girl, and Muḥammad is said to have chosen a sword at Badr.[8] Muḥammad also received a share of the booty

[1] Jeffery, *Vocabulary*, *s.v.*; Lane, *s.v.*; cf. IS, i/2. 28. 2, *jizyat arḍi-hā*.

[2] IS, 1/2. 20, 28, &c.

[3] Excursus G.

[4] WW, 65, 93; cf. Bell on Q. 59. 7 F; he connects vv. 6, 8–10 with an-Naḍīr; cf. also Dennett, op. cit. 21.

[5] Cf. p. 101.

[6] Cf. p. 232.

[7] Abū Tammām, *Ḥamāsah*, i. 458; *Aghānī*, xvi. 50.

[8] Lane, *s.v. ṣafī*; WW, 67.

(presumably three if he was on horseback) along with the others. In his negotiations with nomadic tribes Muḥammad regularly insisted that they should pay the 'fifth', and his share (*sahm*) and the *ṣafī* are often mentioned as well.[1]

The actual division of the spoil was efficiently carried out, as was to be expected in a capable commercial community. When the booty consisted of sheep and camels, it was a simple matter to give so many to each man, reckoning ten sheep equal to one camel.[2] When the booty was more varied, as after Ḥunayn, it was divided into lots regarded as equal in value. Each man received a particular object or objects, but there were usually dealers about, and he had no difficulty in exchanging his goods for cash;[3] at Khaybar the booty was auctioned to the campaigners and (presumably) dealers.[4] Thus the commercial transactions resulting from the division of booty must latterly have employed many men, apart from those entrusted by Muḥammad with guarding and dividing it. Muḥammad had a special agent for the 'fifth', Maḥmiyah b. Jaz' az-Zubaydī, a brother-in-law of Muḥammad's uncle al-ʿAbbās.[5]

When the Muslims gained booty not in actual fighting but through an agreement, Muḥammad claimed the whole. This happened in the case of the Medinan Jewish clan of an-Naḍīr. By arrangement with the heads of the Anṣār the lands of an-Naḍīr were not divided equally among all the Muslims, but were given to the Emigrants (along with two of the poorest of the Anṣār); the Anṣār, however, insisted on the Emigrants continuing to live with them, perhaps to avoid dispersing their forces and thereby weakening them.[6] There is no mention earlier of any use of the habitations of Qaynuqāʿ; perhaps Arabs shared the strongholds with them. There is also no mention of how the lands of an-Naḍīr were cultivated by the Emigrants. Some sources imply that at Khaybar and Fadak also the lands fell entirely to Muḥammad.[7] Whatever the precise legal position, a new system was instituted at Khaybar, which was followed in the conquests after Muḥammad's death. The previous owners were allowed to remain in occupation but had to hand over half of the produce to the Muslims.

1 IS, i/2. 30. 7 (§ 48); contrast ibid. 25. 1, 2 (§ 30 d).
2 WW, 226, 387, &c.
3 Ibid. 282, 284.
4 Ibid. 275, 281; there are apparent contradictions in the accounts of Khaybar.
5 IH, 783; WW, 177, 221, &c.; IS, iv/1. 146. 5.
6 WW, 166.
7 Ibid., but cf. 286, mention of 'fifth'.

The assessment and collection of the half was the work of an overseer, presumably appointed by Muḥammad. From the 'fifth', or perhaps rather third, of the lands retained by Muḥammad he assigned so many loads of dates and grain annually to his wives and to members of the clans of Hāshim, al-Muṭṭalib, &c. The quantities varied from five to two hundred loads. The remainder of the lands of Khaybar was divided into eighteen lots and assigned to Emigrants and Anṣār. The lands of Wadī 'l-Qurā were also divided.[1] The capture of Khaybar thus made a vast difference to Muḥammad's financial position; his responsibilities, of course, were also growing. (An interesting measure of Muḥammad's growing wealth is the number of horses on his expeditions; at Badr in 624/2 there were over 300 men and only 2 horses; at Badr al-Maw'id in 626/4 there were 1,500 men and 10 horses; at Khaybar in 628/7 there was about the same number of men, but 200 horses; at Ḥunayn in 630/8 700 Emigrants alone had 300 horses, and 4,000 Anṣār had another 500; finally on the great expedition of Tabūk in 630/9 there are said to have been 30,000 men and 10,000 horses.[2] The military importance of these figures can be seen from the fact that at Uḥud the Meccan cavalry, which played a decisive part in the battle, numbered only 200 in a force of 2,000.)[3]

Other miscellaneous sources of revenue may be briefly listed. A Jew called Mukhayrīq fought with the Muslims at Uḥud and fell, having previously willed his property to Muḥammad.[4] Muḥammad seems to have had sole disposal of the temple treasure from aṭ-Ṭā'if; this was perhaps specified in the treaty when the inhabitants consented to the destruction of the goddess.[5] Finally, after the conquest of Mecca Muḥammad demanded 'loans' from some of the rich Meccans; part of the money was used to pay the damages due to B. Jadhīmah.[6] As there had been no plundering in Mecca, this was no doubt considered a fair arrangement.

These, then, so far as our records go, are the various sources of the income which came to Muḥammad to be spent for the public weal.[7] The spending does not require much discussion.

The Qur'ān contains several sets of directions for the spending

[1] IH, 773–6; WW, 285–96.
[2] WW, 39, 168, 285, 358, 395.
[3] Ibid. 102.
[4] IH, 354; WW, 124.
[5] WW, 384 f.
[6] Ibid. 348, 353.
[7] For the name *māl Allāh*, 'wealth of God', applied to the public treasury, cf. H. Lammens, in *Mélanges de la Faculté Orientale de Beyrouth*, vi (1913), 403 f.

of money, which resemble one another although they apply to different things. Some are instructions to individuals about the use of their private wealth; they are to bestow it on relatives, on orphans (who are probably also relatives), on the poor, on the 'son of the way', and, in one passage, on beggars and for the ransoming of captives.[1] One of these passages deals explicitly with contributions, but it is not concerned exclusively with the needs of the Emigrants, for it mentions parents as recipients; thus the system of voluntary contributions would seem to have grown out of general principles for the use of wealth. What is curious, however, is that when regulations for the use of the 'fifth' appear in the Qur'ān, the groups mentioned are the same—relatives, orphans, the poor, and the 'son of the way'.[2] Finally, when at a comparatively late period, regulations are given for the use of the *ṣadaqāt* fixed by treaty, the poor (and destitute) and the 'son of the way' are again named, though they are now accompanied by the agents for the *ṣadaqāt*, 'those whose hearts are reconciled', slaves (for their liberation), debtors, and expenditure 'in the way of God'.[3]

These instructions and regulations are an impressive witness to the continuity of the Qur'anic message. From the very first it had been implied that at the root of many of the social evils of the day was a false attitude to wealth.[4] Generosity had been urged on the believers, and niggardliness had been denounced as leading to Hell. By reading between the lines it can be seen that the evils of the time are linked with the growth of individualism. Men think of themselves primarily as individuals and not as members of a tribe or clan. Consequently they become selfish and neglect their traditional obligations to fellow tribesmen and clansmen, even to members of their own family. The classes on whom a man is to bestow his wealth are presumably those that were the chief sufferers from the breakdown of the tribal system. Orphans are prominent because men frequently died young and left small children, and it was easy for the guardian to appropriate any property the father had left. Relatives, other than orphans, are indigent members of the same clan, who under the old system would have been cared for by the chief or some wealthy clansman, but were now left to fend for themselves. The poor were probably at first those inhabitants of Mecca or Medina who had no clear connexion with any clan, or

[1] 2. 177/172 F; 2. 215/211 FG; 4. 36/40 E—; 17. 26/28 C—E+.
[2] 8. 41/42 F+. [3] 9. 60 I. [4] *M/Mecca* 68–71, 72 ff.

whose clan was too poor itself to do much for them; this class would thus only come into being in so far as groups based on locality replaced kinship-groups. The mention of the (two) parents may be due to cases where strong men neglected their parents when they became old and weak; but it is more likely that its aim was to correct some anomaly of the obsolescent family and kinship system (to be considered in the next chapter).

The 'son of the way' is a problem. It is natural to interpret the phrase to mean 'traveller', but it is difficult to see why there should be so much insistence on helping travellers. Inhospitality can hardly have been a great social evil in Medina, where all or most of the passages with the phrase were revealed. Another suggestion is that it means 'guest' (*ḍayf*), and that, when a guest stayed more than the three days during which it was obligatory to look after him, his entertainment became a *ṣadaqah*.[1] On this interpretation the hospitality given to Emigrants by the Anṣār could be counted as fulfilling the religious obligation to be generous with one's wealth. It is unlikely that any more precise group should have been meant and that all memory of this should have been lost.[2]

The latest regulations—those for the *ṣadaqāt*—show how Muḥammad's responsibilities had grown. He now requires agents to collect the *ṣadaqāt* from his 'allies', and these agents have to be paid. Affairs of state also require the spending of money, and, since the state is a theocracy, this may simply be described as 'expenditure in the way of God'. The primary reference is doubtless to military expenditure, since 'fighting in the way of God' was a common phrase. 'Those whose hearts are reconciled' seem originally to have been the members of the deputations which came to Medina in a stream after the battle of Ḥunayn; Muḥammad was in the habit of giving each man a present of several ounces of silver.[3]

Scattered in the sources are various illustrations of Muḥammad's practice. He had some of the booty and captives from B. Qurayẓah sold in Syria and the proceeds used to buy arms and horses;[4] and, as already noticed, contributions were requested to equip the expedition to Tabūk. Again, besides his gifts to members of deputations, to women who accompanied expeditions and others—

[1] Ṭab., *Tafsīr*, ii. 55, on Q. 2. 177/172.
[2] But cf. Bell, *Translation*, i. 24, n. 3.
[3] Cf. below, p. 349, and IS, i/2 *passim*.
[4] IH, 693; WW, 221.

all probably regarded as obligatory under Arabian conditions—we find him giving large subsidies to certain tribes. B. Juʿayl (of Balī) received the *siʿāyah* or liberation payment Muḥammad had imposed on tribes defeated at Ḥunayn, and the tribute from the Jews of Maqnā was assigned to men of Saʿd Allāh and Judhām. The aim must have been to strengthen these tribes and to ensure their allegiance to Islam.[1] In respect of blood-money, too, Muḥammad seems to have been responsible where Muslims on an expedition killed or injured someone in alliance with him;[2] this is not necessarily contrary to what is said in the Constitution about blood-money as a clan responsibility. He may also have paid blood-money or debts himself, where to leave them to those responsible might have occasioned quarrels.

The provision for his wives and relatives which Muḥammad made out of the annual tribute from Khaybar might seem to indicate partiality. It must be remembered, however, that Muḥammad stood in a special relation to the clans of Hāshim and al-Muṭṭalib; he was their leader among the Muslims. According to the principles of the Qur'ān, therefore, it was above all to him that the poor and needy members of these clans must look for help. Moreover, while the leaders of other clans of the Emigrants, such as ʿAbd ar-Raḥmān b. ʿAwf, might spend their time in the market making money, some of which they would give to their relatives, Muḥammad had to devote all his time to political duties, and it was thus no more than fair that he should use on their behalf some of the money that came to him. As we have seen, the kinship-group had still a part to play in the Islamic community, and, where a man had wealth to bestow, his relatives had a strong claim on it. It would thus not be too much to assert that Muḥammad's treatment of this wives and relatives at Khaybar is intended to exemplify the Qur'ānic ideal of generosity towards one's kith and kin.

[1] IS, i/2. 24; WW, 405; cf. p. 117 above.

[2] WW, 160, for B. ʿĀmir; ibid. 353, B. Jadhīmah.

VIII

THE REFORM OF THE SOCIAL STRUCTURE

It was suggested in *Muhammad at Mecca* that the proclamation of a new religion was a response to the malaise of the times, and that this malaise was at bottom due to the transition from a nomadic to a settled economy. From the point of view of social structure there was a tendency to replace tribal solidarity by individualism. Individualism fostered selfishness, and selfishness knew very well how to twist nomadic ideals and practices to the private advantage of those who found themselves with a measure of power. There was a corresponding growth of discontent among those who found themselves at a disadvantage in the struggle for wealth and power.

The purpose of the present chapter is to describe the social reforms instituted by Muḥammad.[1] It is not enough, however, simply to describe them in isolation. An attempt must be made to see them as an adequate response to the needs of the times. Moreover, they will be found to be no sheer novelty but an adaptation of existing ideas and practices. The relation of the new social institutions to the background must therefore be given special consideration.

1. SECURITY OF LIFE AND PROPERTY

Prior to Muḥammad security of life, in so far as it was maintained, was maintained by the principle of the blood-feud and the *lex talionis*. It must be insisted that this is not a barbarous practice to be abolished as quickly as possible, but a form of justice, or at least of the prevention of indiscriminate killing. From the standpoint of modern society it seems barbarous, but that is because it belongs to a level of social organization we have outgrown.

[1] Cf. Robert Roberts, *The Social Laws of the Qorān*, London, 1925, where most of the relevant Qur'ānic passages are collected; they are discussed in the light of later practice. (The author published an earlier form of this work in German in 1908.)

Moreover the process of outgrowing it does not consist in uprooting it, but in transforming it.

The blood-feud belongs essentially to a society consisting of groups, normally groups of kinsmen. When a member of one group is killed or injured by a member of another group, the first group is in theory entitled to exact an eye for an eye, a tooth for a tooth, and a life for a life. The duty of exacting this vengeance rests specially on the next-of-kin (of mature age), but he has the support of his clan or tribe. Though it is preferable to inflict the penalty on the person responsible for the death or injury, it may be inflicted on any member of his clan or tribe instead of him. It is thus clear that ultimately the responsibility both for the original act and for exacting vengeance is communal.

These points are illustrated by many stories of pre-Islamic days, and also by the behaviour of the pagan Meccans and other opponents of the Muslim community at Medina. As an example there may be cited the gruesome account of what happened to two Muslims captured at ar-Rajīʿ in 625/4. Their nomadic captors took them to Mecca, and they were readily purchased by the families of men killed at Badr. They remained in captivity until the end of the sacred month, and were then killed in cold blood. Against one, Khubayb b. ʿAdī,[1] the first blow was struck by a son of al-Ḥārith b. ʿAmr (Jumaḥ), but as he was a mere child he was unable to inflict a mortal wound.[2] Though Khubayb and his companion were probably present at Badr, neither seems to have killed anyone there. Thus they were paying for the deeds of the Muslims.

When a member of the offending group had been killed, vengeance was satisfied and the two groups were supposed to live in peace. There was, of course, no binding law about this, and, even if there had been, no authority to enforce such a law. It was merely a generally recognized custom. There was no punishment for not observing it, only the disadvantage (if it was a disadvantage) of continuing in a state of war with another tribe. In practice the two parties frequently disputed about what constituted a fair requital. In the well-known story of the war of Basūs, the trouble began when the chief Kulayb—perhaps the most powerful man in central Arabia in his day—by his pride provoked his brother-in-law Jassās to kill him. Kulayb's brother one day ran into a well-born

[1] Apparently sometimes confused with Khubayb b. Asāf (or Yasāf); see IH, Index, also *Usd*, and Ibn Ḥajar, *Iṣābah*.

[2] IH, 640 ff.; WW, 158 ff.

youth of Jassās's tribe and killed him. An influential kinsman of Jassās, who had hitherto stood aside from the quarrel, made it known that, if the youth's life was accepted as an equivalent for that of Kulayb, he would count the matter settled. The insolent answer was given, however, that the youth was equivalent only to Kulayb's shoe-latchet. Things then went from bad to worse, and much blood was shed on both sides over a period of many years.

Such developments are perhaps inevitable where there is no supreme authority but each tribe is a sovereign political body. The best hope of peace lay in the good offices of men friendly to both parties. If both could accept someone as arbiter, there was some hope of peace. This is how the war of Basūs was brought to an end. Usually the number of dead on each side was reckoned up, and the tribe with the surplus of losses received from the other tribe so many camels for every man of this surplus. The older view, however, was that it was dishonourable and a sign of weakness to accept camels in lieu of blood, and it was not extinct in Muḥammad's time. One of the Anṣār, Hishām b. Ṣubābah, was accidentally killed by another. His brother Miqyas came to Muḥammad and asked for blood-wit (*diyah*), which was duly paid. Evidently this did not satisfy his sense of honour, however, for, when there was an opportunity, he killed the man responsible for his brother's death, and fled to Mecca.[1] Nevertheless, the wiser and more progressive men of the time seem to have recognized the advantages of substituting a blood-wit for the actual taking of a life. An unreliable story about 'Abd al-Muṭṭalib, Muḥammad's grandfather, claims that an action of his in redeeming his son for a hundred camels led to the general recognition of a hundred camels instead of ten as a proper blood-wit for a man.[2] This may be taken as evidence, even if the figures are not accurate, of a tendency to raise the blood-wit in order to make the acceptance of it the more attractive course. Just before the battle of Badr some Meccan opponents of Abū Jahl urged 'Utbah b. Rabī'ah of 'Abd Shams to declare that he would be responsible for the blood-wit of his confederate 'Amr b. al-Ḥaḍramī who had been killed at Nakhlah; in this way a battle might have been avoided, for according to the

[1] IH, 728, 819; WW, 176. For the idea of the blood-wit as dishonourable, cf. R. A. Nicholson, *A Literary History of the Arabs*, Cambridge, 1930, 93.

[2] IS, i/1. 54; cf. T. H. Weir, art. 'Diya' in EI (1).

traditional view this blood was the only valid cause of quarrel between the Meccans and the Muslims.[1]

Such, then, was the system of social security in Arabia as it existed at the time of the Hijrah. In Mecca it worked well, for Quraysh were noted for the quality of *ḥilm*, a combination of wisdom, concern for material prosperity, and self-control. In Medina it worked badly, and indeed had broken down. In two respects the basis of the system was communal and not individualistic. Firstly, the system rested on the principle of communal responsibility for crimes. Where there is a strong sense of group loyalty it is always possible for the tribe to hide an individual offender, especially in the desert with only camel transport available, but it is not easy for a whole tribe to remain in hiding indefinitely. Under such circumstances the only way to maintain order is to hold the group responsible for the misdoings of members of it, and this is in fact done by modern civilized governments in circumstances of this kind. Secondly, the system apparently aims at maintaining or restoring the relative strength of the tribes involved in a quarrel. If a member of one tribe is killed, then the tribe responsible for his death must be weakened to the same extent. This idea recurs in some of Muḥammad's regulations.

The system as a whole had deep roots in Arabian society, and there could be no question of replacing it by anything else or even of radically altering it. Muḥammad may be said to have accepted in general the principles underlying the system, and to have set himself to reform the most serious abuses.

In a certain sense Muḥammad's greatest innovation was not an innovation at all. This was the establishment of a new type of group, the Islamic community or *ummah*, which was based not on blood-relationship, but on a common religious allegiance. As has been noted in the previous chapter, the *ummah* was conceived as a kind of tribe. The incident just quoted of the killing of Muslim captives in Mecca as retaliation for men killed at Badr suggests that for purposes such as this the *ummah* was regarded as a tribe even by its enemies. This inference is not certain, however, since the two men for whom vengeance was taken seem to have been killed by members of the Anṣār, and the two captives also belonged to the Anṣār; consequently the Anṣār and not the whole *ummah* may have been regarded as the group responsible. The case of the

[1] WW, 50 f.

two men of B. ʿĀmir killed by a Muslim fugitive from Bi'r Maʿūnah, for whom Muḥammad felt obliged to pay blood-money, shows that he accepted responsibility for the acts of members of the *ummah*, at least towards tribes with whom he was in alliance.[1] In exacting vengeance the *ummah* certainly functioned as a tribe. According to the Constitution (§ 19) 'the believers exact vengeance for one another where a man gives his blood in the way of God'. The Qur'ānic verse (2. 177/173 E—) prescribing retaliation (*qiṣāṣ*) for the slain doubtless applied to non-Muslim groups, even if, supposing the second half *not* to be a later addition, it also applied from the first to killing within the *ummah*. The following assertion that 'in retaliation is life for you, O ye of insight; mayhap ye will show piety', is a reminder that the taking of vengeance was a duty, and the performance of this duty the mark of a virtuous man.

It was probably only to tribes with whom he had some alliance or agreement that Muḥammad would have considered paying blood-money. With regard to other tribes it is not clear whether he regarded the *ummah* as bound by the rule that held in internal cases, namely, not to exact more than the equivalent by way of vengeance. The verse just quoted suggests that the rule also held in external cases, for it speaks of 'the free for the free, the slave for the slave, and the female for the female'. Where Muḥammad was not in alliance with a tribe, however, he was presumably either actually or potentially at war; and in war almost anything was permissible. For the military prestige of the *ummah* it was essential in Arabian conditions that no Muslim should go unavenged, but the more non-Muslims whom their tribes could not avenge, the greater the prestige of the *ummah*. The execution of B. Qurayẓah would probably not have been regarded as an act of war against an enemy by Muḥammad and his contemporaries, but as the punishment of an ally which had acted treacherously. Such an action would, of course, have involved the *ummah* in a blood-feud, had there been any representative of Qurayẓah strong enough to take revenge. Thus as Muḥammad became stronger, there was no longer any question of 'normal relations' of the old type between the *ummah* and non-Muslim tribes. If they were pagan, they had a choice between submission to Islam and perpetual warfare; if they were Christian or Jewish, they might submit to Muḥammad but retain their faith and pay tribute (*jizyah*).

[1] Cf. p. 32 above.

An interesting corollary of the conception of the *ummah* as a new type of group or tribe, is that existing liabilities under the *lex talionis* were cancelled. Some such course was necessary if peace was to be restored in Medina. Old scores were to be wiped out. This is probably the point of the ruling of the Constitution (§ 14) that 'a believer does not kill a believer because of an unbeliever', though it may also have had other applications. The point is frequently mentioned. In his letter to a 'mixed multitude'(*jummāʿ*) in the Tihāmah Muḥammad promised that, if they became Muslims, any liability for blood would cease.[1] Muḥammad's remark to al-Mughīrah b. Shuʿbah when he became a Muslim, that 'conversion cuts off what was before it' (*al-islām yajubbu mā kāna qabla-hu*), is to be taken in a similar sense.[2] And one of the points of the declaration to the Meccans on the submission of their city was that claims for usury, blood, and blood-money were cancelled.[3] While practical needs may first have led Muḥammad to formulate this principle, there was probably also present the idea that Islam was not simply a confederation of previously existing tribes and clans, but a new entity, and that entry into it involved a break with the past.

In the relation of the *ummah* to other groups, then, there are no great novelties. It was within the *ummah* that Muḥammad had a chance to introduce reforms. What he did, when the record of it is read, seems to be very little, but in the circumstances of the time it was effective and achieved its aim of securing a large measure of peace within the community.

There are certain indications that murder and other crimes were to be regarded as matters affecting the whole community. Thus the Constitution (§ 13) states:

> The God-fearing believers are against whoever of them acts wrongfully or seeks (? plans) an act that is unjust or treacherous or hostile or corrupt among the believers; their hands are all against him, even if he is the son of one of them.

Another article (§ 21) says that, when a believer is killed (*sc.* by another believer), 'the believers are against (the murderer) entirely; nothing is permissible to them except to oppose him'. With these regulations we may compare a verse of the Qur'ān where it is recorded that God enjoined on the Children of Israel 'that whoever

[1] IS, 1/2. 29. 19 (§ 46); translated p. 356 below. [2] Ibid. iv/2. 26.
[3] WW, 338; cf. speech at Pilgrimage of Farewell, IH, 968 (= WW, 430).

kills a person otherwise than (in retaliation) for another person, or for causing corruption in the land, shall be as if he had killed the people in a body (*an-nās jamīʿan*)'.[1] Bell thinks that this was 'perhaps early Medinan' and that another passage was substituted for it afterwards.

On the basis of these references the hypothesis might be propounded that Muḥammad originally attempted to eliminate the old kinship-groups from his system of social security, but that he found the principle of blood-relationship so strong that he had to bring it back. We shall see that it was an integral part of the system of security finally elaborated at Medina; in the Qur'ān the next-of-kin of a man wrongfully murdered is explicitly authorized to take life in revenge.[2] Though this hypothesis is attractive, however, it cannot be accepted, since it leaves some facts out of account. The early articles of the Constitution show that the old clans of Medina were part of the security system; they were responsible for blood-money. The presumption is that this did not merely refer to relations with groups outside the *ummah*, and also that there had been no previous way of organizing the *ummah* where the clans were not responsible for blood-money. The view that is to be preferred to the suggested hypothesis is that articles 13 and 21 of the Constitution are to be interpreted negatively and positively; that is to say, they do not prescribe any method for the execution of justice, but forbid believers, on grounds of loyalty to kin, to interfere with the execution of justice. Since Muḥammad had no police force which could punish offenders, the exaction of a penalty must always have been left to the next of kin.

From the first, then, we conclude, the system of security at Medina was based on the principle of blood-revenge by the kinship-group. Two rules, however, were stated, or restated; and the observance of these would prevent the cumulative tendencies of the blood-feud from gaining momentum and wrecking the system.

The first of these rules was that the penalty exacted was not to be greater than the action for which it was a penalty. There was to be no question of a life for a shoe-latchet. No more than a life was to be taken for a life.[3] On the contrary, it was proclaimed to be virtuous to be satisfied with a penalty that was less than the act

[1] 5. 32/35 ? E.
[2] 17. 33/35 E+; cf. reaffirmation of blood-ties in 8. 75/76; 33. 6.
[3] Q. 5. 45/49; 16. 126/127; 17. 33/35; 42. 39/37.

penalized, or to forgive altogether.[1] On this point the Islamic ideal was in opposition to that of pre-Islamic Arabia. Moreover, there is implicit in the Islamic ideal a recognition of the equality of all members of the community. This is illustrated by the story of how in the caliphate of 'Umar a haughty scion of the desert nobility, Jabalah b. al-Ayham, was struck in the face by a humble member of the humble tribe of Muzaynah; Jabalah expected that, because of his importance, a severe penalty would be imposed, and when he was merely given the opportunity of striking the man on the face, he was so disgusted that he abandoned Islam and returned to the Christian faith and the Byzantine allegiance.[2]

The second rule was that, once revenge had been taken (up to the equivalent but not more), the matter was to be considered at an end. No penalty could justly be taken for the killing of a man where that was itself the exaction of a just penalty.[3] This may be said to be an early form of the principle that the executioner is not guilty of murder. The growing influence of individualism in the Islamic community is shown by the later view that only the murderer himself could justly be put to death, and by the interpretation of the Qur'ān to this effect;[4] the words of the Qur'ān in their obvious sense, however, permit the taking of an equivalent life from the murderer's tribe. This second rule was known in pre-Islamic times; a case is mentioned by al-Wāqidī, for example, where Quraysh as a whole were satisfied that a quarrel was at an end but the dead man's family insisted on taking further revenge.[5] Indeed, both rules are old Arab rules which are restated by the Qur'ān. Though they appear limited in scope, they effectively brought internal peace to Medina. This was possible after the Hijrah, as it was not before, because in Muḥammad there was a permanent arbiter to whom disputes could be referred. The presence of Muḥammad in Medina was the novel factor in the situation which enabled the rules to function properly.

The Qur'ānic exhortations to forgiveness which have just been mentioned do not necessarily imply complete remission of the penalty. In a world in which blood cried out for blood, to substitute camels for blood—'milk for blood' as the Arabs tauntingly put it—

[1] Q. 5. 45/49; 16. 126/127; 42. 39/37.
[2] Nicholson, *Lit. Hist*. 51; IS, i/2. 20; &c.
[3] Q. 2. 173/177 ff.; 42. 39/37; cf. 22. 60/59.
[4] Cf. J. Schacht, arts. 'Ḳiṣāṣ' and 'Ḳatl' in EI (S).
[5] WW, 43.

was already a measure of forgiveness, and is perhaps what is implied by 'forgiveness' in these passages of the Qur'ān. Where a blood-wit was paid, there was no excuse for further shedding of blood. It is to be assumed that Muḥammad's interest in the internal peace of Medina led him to encourage the acceptance of blood-money. As we have seen, the figure of 100 camels as the blood-wit for a man appears to have been known before Muḥammad's time, but he gave official recognition both to this figure and to equivalents of it in other animals and in goods.[1] So far as one can tell, 100 camels or 2,000 sheep is a high price, and the material inducement to accept this price must have been strong. Nevertheless, there was no absolute command to take money instead of blood in all cases. The Qur'ān makes it clear that those who exact a life for a life are within their rights and that no judicial action can be taken against them.[2] If we accept the reported address of Muḥammad on the day after the capture of Mecca, the kinsmen of a man who had been killed were given a choice between blood and money.[3] This may have been the practice of Muḥammad's later years, when many nomadic tribes were entering Muḥammad's security system for political rather than religious reasons; it does not easily harmonize, however, with a Qur'ānic passage which must now be considered.

This passage[4] distinguishes several different cases. If a believer deliberately kills another believer, he will be punished in Hell. If a believer kills another believer involuntarily or accidentally, then he must pay blood-money to the family of the man killed, unless, though the man was a Muslim, his family are unbelievers. Further, in all cases of involuntary killing of a believer, the person responsible, where he has the means to do so, has to pay for the freeing of a believing slave. This last clause is interesting, for it seems to be analogous to the aim of the pre-Islamic system of maintaining the relative strength of the two tribes involved; in the Islamic form the number of believing freemen is kept constant. The fate of the man who deliberately kills a believer is reminiscent of the original inexpiability of the blood of a kinsman under the old dispensation.[5] The distinction between deliberate and involuntary killing is

[1] Ibid. 420; cf. 338.

[2] 42. 41/39; but in WW, 366 f. the acceptance of blood-money is enforced, perhaps because 'Uyaynah was only a non-Muslim ally.

[3] WW, 342.

[4] 4. 92/94 f.

[5] W. Robertson Smith, *Kinship and Marriage in Early Arabia*, Cambridge, 1885, 161; for an instance of commutation, cf. Lane, *s.v.* *'aqqa* (*bi 's-sahm*).

perhaps novel, but its range of application is limited, for the blood-wit has still to be paid. (At the present day in certain Muslim countries, a taxi-driver who runs over and kills a child has to pay blood-money, even although everyone agrees that the fault was entirely the child's.) In Muḥammad's lifetime there were cases of Muslims being killed by other Muslims because the latter did not realize or credit the fact that they were Muslims.[1] In such cases the killing was deliberate, but not the killing-of-a-Muslim. The general impression given by the passage is that these regulations belong to the earlier Medinan period. In the last two or three years some of the details may have been allowed to lapse. There was much discussion in later times of how to interpret the statement that Hell was the punishment for the deliberate killing of a Muslim.[2] When the passage was revealed, the community was no doubt small and the words interpreted literally.

Female infanticide may be mentioned here, though to the Arabs it had little connexion with murder. It was an old custom among them (as it was in many other parts of the world) to kill a certain number of female children.[3] The underlying reason was poverty,[4] coupled with the need to maintain a due balance of age and sex in the tribe. The strength of a tribe lay in the number of its adult males; though as mothers of sons the women could add to the strength of the tribe, the period between the birth of a girl and her sons' coming of age was long, and there was a limit to the number of women, children, and animals whom the fighting men could effectively protect. Moreover girl babies seem to have been hardier than boys; of Muḥammad's seven children by Khadījah, the three boys died very young, whereas the girls all reached the age of marriage.[5] The practice of female infanticide had also a sanction in the old religion.[6] The Qur'ān denounces the practice as a great sin, and exhorts men to trust in God to provide for their needs.[7] In the optimistic atmosphere of political and economic expansion there would be much less need to avoid an increase of population.

[1] Q. 4. 94/96; WW, 235 f. —B. Judhām; IS, iv/2. 22 f. (= WW, 325, 366 f.)—'Āmir b. al-Aḍbaṭ (Ashja').

[2] Cf. an-Naḥḥās, *K. an-Nāsikh wa 'l-Mansūkh*, 112 ff.

[3] Q. 81. 9; cf. Robertson Smith, 153 ff.; Roberts, 94 ff.

[4] Q. 6. 151/152 E+; 17. 31/33 E+; cf. 16. 58/60 f. C—.

[5] Cf. *M/Mecca*, 38; IS, i/1. 85; &c.

[6] Q. 6. 137/138 ? C—E+; cf. sacrifice of children in the Old Testament.

[7] 17. 31/33; &c.

Unless Muḥammad proclaimed the Divine command without considering the economic consequences, his opposition to female infanticide is another indication that he had far-seeing plans for expansion. Unfortunately it does not seem possible to assign an exact date to the passages from the Qur'ān.

Apart from these rules to stop or modify criminal and anti-social conduct, we may be sure that in various ways Muḥammad was constantly doing many small things that made positive contributions to the maintenance of peace and security. Where the solution of a difficulty was not quite clear (as when there was right on both sides), he would cut the knot by paying the blood-wit himself,[1] thus following the example of the great *sayyids* of the Jāhilīyah.[2] The declaration that Medina was a sacred area (*ḥaram*) doubtless made wrongdoers more hesitant about shedding blood there.[3] A severe penalty was prescribed for theft.[4] Charters were given defining land rights, which no doubt made it easier in the future to deal with land disputes.[5]

In these questions of the security of life and property, the reforms introduced by Muḥammad appear to be slight. Yet they were by no means negligible. Indeed they were fully effective, and for the uneasy lulls between raids to which the nomads were accustomed, substituted a system of social security which enabled the Arabs to work together for a century in the administration of large provinces—until blood once more asserted itself over religion. In the conditions of Muḥammad's Arabia nothing better was possible. He had no police force. The very idea of such a thing was probably unknown among the Arabs. All men were potential policemen or potential resisters of police. Muḥammad could only have punished wrongdoers had he had superlative force; but for most of the Medinan period he had no strength to spare. In questions of blood, too, the old solidarity of tribe and clan was still a powerful force. As things were, Muḥammad's combination of new and old appealed sufficiently to the Arabs to fire them with enthusiasm for the new system. Thus his treatment of these questions, without being revolutionary, had the revolutionary effect of achieving security.

[1] Cf. WW, 188 f. (Ḥassān b. Thābit), 293 f., 342 (Khuzā'ah).

[2] Cf. WW, 50 f. (suggestion to 'Utbah); as-Samhūdī, 146 (for political advantages B. Zurayq paid blood-wit when a Zuraqī was killed by B. Mu'allā).

[3] Constitution, § 39; p. 224 above.

[4] Q. 5. 38/42; cf. Roberts, 90–94; EI(1).

[5] IS, i/2. 21 f. (§ 19 ff.).

2. MARRIAGE AND THE FAMILY

(a) *The existing situation*

Many facts have been recorded in Arabic literature about marriage and the family in the Jāhilīyah. It is difficult, however, to see the wood for the trees, and consequently there is no generally accepted view of the nature of the wood. In order to understand and to estimate aright the contribution in this sphere made by Qur'ānic legislation and Muḥammad's administrative practice, it is necessary to have some view of what existed previously. What follows is a tentative suggestion, though not without justification.[1] Even if this view is at fault in many details and in much of the general picture, yet it enables us to make a better assessment of Muḥammad's achievements than is otherwise possible.

In the recorded facts about pre-Islamic Arabia there is much evidence that the social system was on a matrilineal basis. Thus we find that men and women are reckoned as belonging to their mother's groups. Tribes and individuals are known as sons of females. Property belongs communally to the matrilineal group, and is normally administered by the woman's uterine brother (or her mother's). Marriage is uxorilocal, that is, the women remain in their family house, and their husbands visit them. A woman often had several such visiting husbands, some of them probably concurrently. Indeed, one type of marriage,[2] or temporary union, is hardly distinguishable from prostitution. On the other hand, some of the marriages must have been relatively stable, since women bore half a dozen or more children to one man.[3] Divorce was also common, however, and many of the early Muslim women of whom we have biographical notices seem to have had two or more husbands in succession.

While this matrilineal system was predominant over most of Arabia, there is also evidence of practices which have a patrilineal basis. The patrilineal system was strongest in Mecca, though not to the exclusion of all matrilineal practices, and there are also traces of it at Medina and elsewhere. In the patrilineal system the family consisted of the relatives in the male line; individuals were named after their fathers, and tribes were known as the sons of

[1] Grounds for holding the view and illustrative details are given in Excursus J, pp. 373 ff. below.

[2] The fourth in al-Bukhārī's tradition; cf. p. 379 below.

[3] e.g. Kabshah bint Rāfi' to Mu'ādh b. an-Nu'mān, IS, viii. 269.

males. Property, if communal, belonged to the patriclan; if owned by an individual, it was inherited by his sons or consanguine brothers (there being no rule of primogeniture in Arabia). Marriage may have continued to be uxorilocal and may not have become virilocal, but presumably a woman had only one husband at a time. (It must always be remembered that the material on which we are dependent was written down at a time when the patrilineal system had superseded the matrilineal, and that the writers therefore tend to exaggerate the patrilineal features already present in Muḥammad's lifetime; thus they always give patrilineal genealogies, but omit information about descent in the female line, or relegate it to second place.)

About the time of the Hijrah, then, matrilineal and patrilineal features were found in Arabian society side by side, and often intermingled. This much is fact. The explanation of this fact, which is to be adopted here as a working hypothesis, is that the matrilineal system had been prevalent in Arabia for a long period, whereas the appearance of the patrilineal was comparatively recent and was bound up with the growth of individualism. It was argued in *Muhammad at Mecca* that the Qur'ān presupposes a breakdown of tribal solidarity and the rise of an individualistic outlook. This fits in well with the appearance of patrilineal features in the social system. Individualism means, among other things, that a man appropriates to his personal use what had hitherto been regarded as communal, though administered by him for the common good. It would be natural for him at the same time to become specially interested in *his own* children,[1] and to want them to succeed to the wealth he had appropriated. In a matrilineal family the control of the family property would normally pass from a man to his sister's son.

At the time of the Hijrah, then, Arabian society was in transition. Individualism was growing, and along with it there was a tendency for matrilineal features to be replaced by patrilineal. In the transitional stage, too, there were many opportunities for unscrupulous men to take unfair advantage of weaker relatives and 'feather their own nests'. This is the background against which the Qur'ānic reforms must be seen.

(*b*) *The recognition of physical paternity*

Under the matrilineal system a woman's child belonged to her

[1] Cf. Q. 68. 14, 74. 12 f., &c.

family, and it was therefore comparatively unimportant to know who was father of a child in the physical sense.[1] Once men became interested in their own children, however, they would want to have definite knowledge of the physical paternity of their wives' children. The Qur'ānic reform encourages this tendency. One of its central points is insistence on the *'iddah* or *tarabbus*, the waiting-period after a woman has been widowed or divorced before she can re-marry. The purpose of the waiting-period, which was normally of three or four months, was to discover whether the woman was pregnant by her previous husband. In the case of divorce the man, if he was a 'gentleman', would do nothing during the waiting-period that would prevent cancellation of the divorce should his wife present him with a son.[2] Where a marriage had not been consummated, there was no need to observe a waiting-period on divorce.[3] If, however, a woman was pregnant, the waiting-period was until after the birth of the child; after that the father, if he divorced her, had to provide food and clothing for her while she was suckling the child, and this was to be for two years unless they agreed to make it shorter or to give the child to a wet-nurse.[4]

(c) *Plurality of wives*

It has commonly been held in Christendom that the distinctive feature of Islamic marriage is the permission to have four wives. The practice is based on a curious verse of the Qur'ān (4. 3):

> If ye fear that ye may not act with equity in regard to the orphans, marry such of the women as seem good to you, two or three or four —but if ye fear that ye may not be fair (to several wives), then one (only) or what your right hands possess. . . .

The interesting point is that the verse is not placing a limit on a previous practice of unlimited polygyny. It is not saying to men who had had six or ten wives 'You shall not marry more than four'. On the contrary it is encouraging men who had had only one wife (or perhaps two) to marry up to four. It is not the restriction of an old practice but the introduction of something new.

The verse says nothing about where the spouses are to live. Presumably, however, virilocal marriage was intended. There would have been little novelty in a man having a number of wives

[1] Cf. p. 383 below.
[2] Q. 2. 226–32, 234 f.; 65. 1–4.
[3] 2. 236/237 f.; 33. 49/48.
[4] 2. 233; 65. 6.

whom he merely 'visited'. Muḥammad's own marriages were virilocal, though each of his wives had her own apartment. Some extra-Qur'ānic regulations also imply virilocality. A divorced woman had to wait with her husband's people until her waiting-period was over;[1] and even in the case of a woman whose husband died without leaving her a house of her own or any money, the ruling was that she must remain where she was and not return to her brothers until the fourth month.[2] This evidence is late and might reflect later conditions, but it must always have been difficult in an uxorilocal society for a man to have several marriages at once. It may be assumed, then, that the verse is primarily encouraging men to establish multiple virilocal families, though, if other arrangements could be made, it would not exclude these.[3]

European scholars have recognized that this verse of the Qur'ān is an exhortation and not a restriction, and have further asserted that there are no clear cases of polygyny at Medina before Islam.[4] Ibn Saʿd's biographies, of course, have numerous examples of men who had more than one wife; but this is balanced by the examples of women with more than one husband. We generally have no information whether the marriages were contemporary or not; in the case of the women one husband is usually said to have 'followed' another, but this way of putting things might be due to the environment of Islamic practice when the facts were written down. In some cases it looks as if a man and woman of the same tribe married and lived in the same house, while the man sometimes 'visited' a woman of another tribe, and the woman perhaps received 'visits' from a strange man; thus in the sub-clan of Dīnār b. Mālik of an-Najjār, of four women who had two (or in one case three) husbands, all had one husband from their own sub-clan of Dīnār, one had a second husband from Dīnār, and the others had second (and third) husbands from neighbouring clans.[5] There are a few examples (including some from Medina) of a man marrying two sisters,[6] and this may be a step towards polygyny, even though the marriage was still uxorilocal. Abū Uḥayḥah Saʿīd b. al-ʿĀṣ (of ʿAbd Shams of Quraysh) is said to have been the first to join together

[1] 65. 6.
[2] IS, viii. 267 f.
[3] Cf. J. Wellhausen, 'Die Ehe bei den Arabern', 469.
[4] Gertrude H. Stern, *Marriage in Early Islam*, London, 1939, 62, 81; cf. Snouck Hurgronje, *Verspreide Geschriften*, i. 233.
[5] IS, viii. 320 f., omitting Huzaylah.
[6] Cf. p. 387, n. 1 below.

two sisters;[1] as this was at Mecca his household may have been virilocal but we cannot be certain. A man of aṭ-Ṭā'if is said to have had ten wives, apparently at once;[2] but we really know nothing about the social system in which this occurred, and it would be rash to generalize from it. There seem, therefore, to be good grounds for holding that in pre-Islamic Arabia, and especially in Medina, it was unusual for a man to have more than one wife living with him in his house.

Such a view is in harmony with the traditional account that the verse about plurality of wives was revealed shortly after the battle of Uḥud. In that battle some seventy Muslims, mostly Medinans, were killed, so that the number of widows for whom the Islamic community had to care must have been considerable. It was doubtless in order to meet this sudden increase in the number of unattached women that encouragement was given to polygyny. It has also to be noted, however, that the Qur'ān connects the matter with just conduct towards 'orphans' (*yatāmā*). This suggests that the crux of the problem of excess women was not the widows but the unmarried girls who now came under the guardianship of uncles, cousins, and other kinsmen. With some hints from the sources[3] we can imagine the treatment women and girls might receive from selfish and unsympathetic guardians; they would be kept unmarried so that the guardian could have unrestricted control of their property, and it would be difficult for them to obtain legal redress against their legal protectors. The matter would be specially irksome in matrilineal Medina if, as seems likely, guardianship now went in the male line. This, then, is the situation the Qur'ān tries to meet by encouraging polygyny. It probably did not intend that the guardians should themselves marry their wards, though, where the wards were outside the forbidden degrees, this would be possible. The idea seems rather to be that, if the Muslims generally adopt polygyny, it will be possible for all girls to be properly married as soon as they reach marriageable age.

The excess of women which this practice of polygyny presupposes is sufficiently accounted for by the battle of Uḥud and the other Muslim expeditions. It may be, however, that an excess of women was a regular feature of Medina and Arabia about this

[1] Ash-Shahrastānī, *Kitāb al-Milal wa 'n-Niḥal*, ed. W. Cureton, London, 1846, 440.

[2] *Usd*, *s.v.* Ghaylān b. Salamah, &c.

[3] Cf. case of Kubayshah bint Ma'n, Robertson Smith, 84, 268 ff.

time. The number of men killed in forays and the greater chances of survival of girl babies would tend to cause a surplus of females, but it would partly be offset by female infanticide and the sale of women captives out of the country as slaves.[1] Yet, whatever the position before Muḥammad's time, there must have been some excess of women after Uḥud. Moreover, the Qur'ān encourages marriage and the procreation of children.[2] This is a corollary of confidence in the goodness and the success of Muḥammad's movement. Because God will provide, poverty need no longer deter men from marriage, just as it should no longer cause them to kill female infants. The first successes of Islam infused confidence into the Muslims, though, so long as the issue was not certain, in having large families they were staking all on Muḥammad's victory. He himself, with far-seeing plans for expansion beyond Arabia, may have been aware of the need for increased manpower. It should also be mentioned that the Arabs knew how to avoid conception by *coitus interruptus* (*'azl*), and Muḥammad is said to have sanctioned this; even if the reports are true, however,—and they are open to doubt—he would seem to have permitted the practice only on occasions when there was some special reason for it.[3]

We conclude, then, that virilocal polygyny, or the multiple virilocal family, which for long was the distinctive feature of Islamic society in the eyes of Christendom, was an innovation of Muḥammad's. There may have been some instances of it before his time, but it was not widespread, and it was particularly foreign to the outlook of the Medinans. It remedied some of the abuses due to the growth of individualism. It provided honourable marriage for the excess women, and checked the oppression of women by their guardians; and it thereby lessened the temptation to enter into the loose unions allowed in the matrilineal society of Arabia. In view of some of the practices hitherto current, this reform must be regarded as an important advance in social organization.

(d) *The attitude to looser forms of union*

The Arabic word *nikāḥ*, usually translated 'marriage', is wider in meaning than its European equivalents. Its sense in Islamic law has been defined as 'a contract for the legalization of intercourse and the procreation of children'.[4] Forms of union sanctioned by

[1] Cf. p. 270 above.
[2] Q. 24. 32; cf. 2. 223.
[3] Al-Bukhārī, *Nikāḥ* (67), 96; WW, 366.
[4] A. A. A. Fyzee, *Outlines of Muhammadan Law*, London, 1949, 74.

custom in pre-Islamic Arabia are called types of *nikāḥ* in Arabic, though in European languages some of them are nearer to prostitution than to marriage.[1] It is not necessary here to discuss the types of polyandry in detail, but merely to notice that the Qur'ān presupposes a distinction between those women who kept themselves to one man at a time and those who—apparently with the full sanction of custom—did not. These two classes of women may be called 'monandric and 'polyandric' respectively. Such polyandry was contrary to the Qur'ān's insistence on the recognition of physical paternity, and accordingly we find the Qur'ān attempting to lessen polyandry and to promote monandry (in the senses indicated).[2]

Thus in 5. 5/7 the believers are given permission to contract marriages with women of both the Anṣār and the Jews of Medina, subject only to the provision that the women should observe monandry; this was doubtless during Muḥammad's first year in Medina. The financial difficulties of establishing monandry, in view of the large 'dowers' required, are shown by the exhortation to continence until God provides sufficient wealth (in 24. 33). The same verse also refers to another aspect of the financial problem, namely, the vested interests of those under whose control 'polyandric' women found themselves. If these women want to become 'monandric', the believers are not out of greed to force them to engage in polyandric practices. It is impossible to say what precisely is involved in this last situation.

Temporary unions with 'polyandric' women appear to have been sanctioned by 4. 24/28. Several early Muslim scholars took the verse as permitting *mut'ah*, but held that it had been abrogated.[3] The words added in some texts, 'up to a fixed date', would confirm this interpretation. The practice of *mut'ah* is usually referred to as 'temporary marriage' in books on Islamic law, though it is hardly marriage at all and the name of 'wife' is not properly applied to the woman contracted in *mut'ah*.[4] The practice is only permitted among a small section of the Shī'ah. It is a union for a fixed period, the period being explicitly stated in the contract. At the end of the period the union automatically ceases without any divorce, and the woman has to observe an *'iddah* or waiting period of only two courses. As part of the contract the woman receives a specified

[1] Cf. p. 379 below.
[2] For a justification of what follows cf. Excursus K.
[3] Cf. an-Naḥḥās, *K. an-Nāsikh wa'l-Mansūkh*, 105 f.
[4] Cf. Fyzee, 102.

'dower'.[1] The practice of *mut'ah* according to this description is not the continuance of a pre-Islamic custom, but a modification of such a custom by Islamic ideas, notably the *'iddah*. The most objectionable features are the possibility of complete secrecy and the fact that the *mut'ah* need last no longer than one day. Thus it would be easy for a woman who was attached to the old ways or who regarded paternity as unimportant to slip into polyandry. Why after a union of a day or two should she wait two months before accepting the advances of another suitor? It may well be, then, that the practice of forming temporary unions was tolerated during at least part of Muḥammad's lifetime, perhaps even without an *'iddah*.[2] It would in any case have been difficult to stop a widespread social custom of this kind all at once. The tradition that 'Umar I prohibited *mut'ah* is evidence that until his time irregular uxorilocal unions were formed;[3] and they may have continued later.

While the Qur'ān thus appears for a time to have sanctioned temporary unions with 'polyandric' women, the following verse, 4. 25/29, which may be of the same date or later, facilitates the passage of 'polyandric' women to the practice of monandry, as well as making a regular marriage possible for those who had not enough wealth to marry a 'monandric' wife. Marriages with these 'polyandric' women were to be made with the consent of their people (*ahl*), and the women were to observe monandry. Nothing is said about a limited duration; but there is the provision that, if the woman slipped into her old ways, her punishment was to be only half that of a 'monandric' woman. Thus an attempt was made to get Muslim men and women to abandon old Medinan practices in so far as these involved neglect of paternity.

As was to be expected, the attempt did not meet with complete success. The Qur'ān shows that a number of persons must have clung to the old ways. With regard to them, therefore, it proposes a policy of segregation. A man and woman convicted of 'adultery' (*zinā*), which perhaps means people who have formed a union secretly and perhaps also without observing the *'iddah*, are to be

[1] W. Heffening, art. 'Mut'a' in EI (1); Fyzee, 100–2; J. Schacht, *The Origins of Muhammadan Jurisprudence*, Oxford, 1950, 266 f. *Nikāḥ as-sirr* is discussed by I. Goldziher, 'Geheimehen bei den Arabern', *Globus*, 68. 32 f. (ref. from S. Kohn, *Die Eheschliessung im Koran*, London, 1934, 83).

[2] No *'iddah* according to an-Naḥḥās, l. c.

[3] Muslim, *Ṣaḥīḥ*, Nikāḥ, 16–18 (see EI).

flogged and forbidden to marry believers.[1] A little later in the same sūrah there comes the phrase, 'bad women to bad men and bad men to bad women, good women to good men and good men to good women'; and in this we may suppose that 'bad' is equivalent to 'adhering to the old customs' and 'good' the opposite.[2] By thus making those who held to the old ways a class apart, it was doubtless hoped that in time all would adopt the new principles.

(e) *The forbidden degrees*

In Islamic law, on the basis of the Qur'ānic verses 4. 22/26 f., a man may not marry his mother, his daughter, his sister (including half-sister, consanguine or uterine), his aunt (paternal or maternal), his brother's or sister's daughter, his wife's mother or daughter, or his father's or son's wife. Milk-relationship has a similar effect to blood-relationship, and marriage with foster-mother or foster-sister is expressly forbidden. Mother is taken to include grandmother, and so on. Marriage to two sisters at the same time is also prohibited.

From the Qur'ān itself we learn that until this time marriage with the father's wife and marriage with two sisters together had been practised. It has been argued that there was no bar to marriage in the male line, except that a man could not marry his daughter;[3] and this conclusion may be accepted with the proviso that it does not necessarily hold of all sections of Arabian society. On the other hand, it seems to be the case that 'on the mother's side all relations nearer than cousinship barred marriage'.[4] Consequently the Qur'ānic law of forbidden degrees of consanguinity amounts to the application to the father's side of the rules already applicable to the mother's side. In respect of affinity, the prohibition of marriage with a step-daughter and probably also that with a daughter-in-law was novel, as well as that with a step-mother.

This account of the element of novelty in the forbidden degrees of the Qur'ān fits in well with our general picture of the reorganization of marriage and the family instituted by Muḥammad. One noticeable feature is the prominence given to paternity and patrilineal descent. The rules about bars to marriage insist that blood-

[1] 24. 2 f.; cf. 4. 15/19 f.

[2] 24. 26.

[3] Robertson Smith, 163 ff.; with his instance of half-sister contrast IS. iii/1. 87.

[4] Ibid.

relationship on the father's side counts equally with that on the mother's. Thus, without any rejection of matrilineal principles in this sphere, patrilineal ones are added to them, and we have a sort of compromise. The retention—and indeed extension—of the principle that milk-relationship is on the same level as blood-relationship may be regarded as a concession to matrilineal groups. Possibly some of those which practised forms of polyandry avoided undue endogamy by making certain degrees of milk-relationship a barrier to marriage. It is significant that it is a Meccan woman, 'Ā'ishah, who finds it strange that she is allowed to appear unveiled before her paternal uncle by fosterage, remarking that it was a woman and not a man who suckled her.[1]

Another concession to the practice of matrilineal groups which may be mentioned here is that of *khul'* or 'divorce by mutual consent'. This is probably a relic of pre-Islamic uxorilocal marriages where the woman or her brother had power to dismiss the husband. In Islamic law this power of dismissal is transformed, but the initiative still rests with the woman. She may ask her husband to divorce her, mentioning some compensation she will give him (such as abandoning her 'dower' to him or undertaking the suckling of his child); but the husband is within his rights in refusing to divorce her.[2]

Perhaps the most important trend to be noticed in the rules about forbidden degrees is that they attempt to uproot all practices in which the individual is not treated as an independent person. In this category would come the prohibition of marriage with a step-mother, since in certain groups in pre-Islamic times a son on his father's death had the right to marry the widow, apart from any consent on her part. Indeed, more generally, a man's heirs had a right to marry the women under his guardianship, including his wife and daughters.[3] Under the old system, where the new guardian was in a position to marry a woman in his care, she had no means of redress against him if he chose to abuse his position. The Qur'ān shows great concern for this problem which is the chief one underlying its frequent references to orphans; the believers are not to inherit women against their will.[4] The sources do

[1] Al-Bukhārī, *Nikāḥ* (67), 117; cf. Stern, op. cit. 100.

[2] Robertson Smith, 92; Stern, 129 ff.; Fyzee, 139–42; G. H. Bousquet and L. Bercher, *Le Statut Personnel en Droit Musulman Hanefite*, Tunis, n.d., 118 ff.

[3] Robertson Smith, 86 ff.

[4] Q. 4. 19/23; contrast Bell's note.

not make it clear whether in early Islam a woman's consent was needed for marriage, but there are several cases in which Muḥammad intervened when a woman was married against her will.[1] It seems probable, therefore, that the prohibition of marriage with a niece—a practice of which several pre-Islamic instances have been recorded[2]—was directed towards increasing a woman's freedom from customary restraints. Perhaps something the same was true of the rule forbidding marriage to two sisters simultaneously.

Little is known about the practice of adoption in pre-Islamic times, and we can only guess why Muḥammad stopped it. Perhaps, when a man married the chief woman in a household, he automatically became 'father' of any sons and daughters living with her, and of any persons reckoned as sons or daughters.[3] Zayd b. Ḥārithah may have become Muḥammad's 'son' when Muḥammad married Khadījah, rather than when he freed him. He was apparently known as Zayd b. Muḥammad. In one of the verses dealing with Muḥammad's marriage to Zayd's divorced wife, Zaynab, the words occur 'ascribe them to their (real) fathers . . . if you do not know their fathers, then (let them be) your brethren in religion and your clients'; these may refer to a matrilineal household where the physical paternity of a woman's children was known but for social purposes her husband was reckoned as their 'father'.[4] Among the meanings given for *daʿī* (the word commonly translated 'adopted son') are 'one who claims the relationship of a son to one who is not his father' and 'one who is claimed as a son by one who is not his father'.[5] All this suggests that we are dealing with social customs and not with formal acts of adoption; and these social customs are features of the old family organization that are undesirable and to be eradicated.

It has often been alleged that permission to marry the former wife of an adopted son was proclaimed only because Muḥammad wanted to marry Zaynab. This allegation is an unjustified inference. It is not only in this case that actual physical relationship is insisted on. In the verse of which a part has been quoted, the practice of *ẓihār*, or divorcing a wife irrevocably by swearing you regard her as your mother, is condemned on the grounds that this does not make her really your mother. More illuminating, however, is the rule which permits marriage with a step-daughter provided

[1] Stern, 32–36; IS, viii. 334 f., &c.
[2] Stern, 62, 173 f.
[3] Cf. Robertson Smith, 112 f.
[4] Q. 33. 4.
[5] Lane, *s.v.*

the marriage with her mother has not been consummated.[1] There seems to have been a general attack on fictitious—or should we say 'merely social'?—relationships which placed restraints on the individual.

Some ideas about forbidden degrees may have come to Muḥammad from the Jews, but he differs from the Jewish practice in forbidding marriage with nieces.[2] Thus, while he was no doubt anxious that the revelation through him should be in agreement with previous revelations, he was also well aware of the problems of his own milieu. There was no blind adoption of Jewish rules for the sake of conformity, but those adopted were in fact appropriate to Medinan conditions. The similarity of the needs of Medina to the needs of the Israelites for whom the Levitical rules were written down—both were settled communities with a nomadic background—may have contributed to the similarity of the result, independently of deliberate imitation.

In passing, another point may be noted at which woman is treated in Islam as an individual, namely, that she personally receives the 'dower' paid by the bridegroom. ('Dower' is the usual translation of *mahr* in books on Islamic law, though the term used by anthropologists is 'bridewealth'.) The evidence for the pre-Islamic situation is fragmentary, and it may be that Islam merely consolidated a social trend that was already dominant. In uxorilocal marriages the 'dower' was sometimes given to the father or guardian of the bride, though there is a pre-Islamic instance of virilocal marriage where a gift of 'estates' was made to the bride.[3] In Islam it is assumed rather than enacted that the 'dower' is the woman's. The Qur'ān mentions 'dower' only incidentally in connexion with divorce; the hire (*ujūr*) to be given to women (4. 24/28 f.) is probably something different. Tradition tells us, too, that Muḥammad forbade the practice of *shighār* whereby two males or groups of males *without any 'dower'* exchanged daughters or sisters for matrimonial purposes.[4]

Little need be said about other aspects of the marriage provisions of early Islam. Concubinage with slaves or captive women was permitted and regulated. Divorce, which had been of frequent

[1] Q. 4. 23/27.

[2] Robertson Smith, 166; *Leviticus*, xviii; cf. Q. 24. 31.

[3] Robertson Smith, 102, quoted on p. 385 below.

[4] Al-Bukhārī, *Nikāḥ* (67), 28; Robertson Smith, 91; cf. Lane, *s.v. shāghara*.

occurrence in pre-Islamic times (unless one prefers to say that most unions had been temporary), was likewise brought under regulation. The rule that after a man has divorced his wife three times he cannot take her back until she has had sexual intercourse with another man is possibly made in the interests of the woman, either to prevent husbands pronouncing divorces lightly, or to prevent a man in effect breaking off marital relations without giving the woman freedom to remarry.

(f) *The social aspects of Muḥammad's marriages*

While the personal aspect of Muḥammad's marriages is best linked with a discussion of his character, the social aspect may conveniently be mentioned here, since it both illustrates what has been said and is illuminated by it.[1]

The most noticeable feature of Muḥammad's matrimonial practice is his establishment of a plural virilocal family. This was apparently done in the early Medinan period. At the Hijrah Muḥammad had only one wife, Sawdah, and on the building of his residence in Medina—called 'the mosque' in the sources—she was assigned an apartment there. Other apartments were added for the other wives. It is usually assumed that 'Ā'ishah, the first to be married at Medina, went at once to her apartment in 'the mosque'; but one account says that the marriage was consummated in her father's house.[2] In view of 'Ā'ishah's youth she may well have remained with her mother for some time; but the housing of Muḥammad's wives in his residence can hardly have been much later than the revelation of the verse about plurality of wives, probably in 625/3. The tradition is that Muḥammad slept in the apartment of each of his wives in turn.

There is some evidence that, besides his regular marriages and his unions with concubines, Muḥammad had relations with women in accordance with the older matrilineal customs. The relevant verse of the Qur'ān (33. 50/49) permits him to marry believing women who 'offer themselves to him'. Some seem to have done this, but the evidence is not clear.[3]

Another important feature is the superior status that is gradually given to Muḥammad's wives. The first stage in marking them off from other women is the institution of the *ḥijāb*, usually translated

[1] Cf. p. 329 below; for details see Excursus L, pp. 393 ff.
[2] Ṭab. i. 1263.
[3] Cf. Excursus L.

'veil', though originally it was rather a 'curtain'[1] The verse prescribing it deals also with other matters.

O ye who have believed, do not enter the houses of the prophet . . . without observing when he is ready, and without announcing yourselves for an interview; verily that has been insulting to the prophet. . . . When ye ask them (his wives) for any article, ask them from behind a curtain; that is purer for your hearts and for theirs.[2]

The following regulation probably belongs to the same time.

O prophet, say to thy wives, and thy daughters, and the womenfolk of the believers, that they let down some (part) of their mantles over them (? cover their faces); that is more suitable for their being recognised and not insulted.[3]

There are various stories giving reasons for these rules.[4] At the wedding-feast of Zaynab bint Jaḥsh some of the guests stayed too long and were a nuisance. At this meal or some other the hands of men guests touched the hands of Muḥammad's wives. In the absence of indoor sanitation the women had to go out at night, and were sometimes insulted by Hypocrites; the insults may have been deliberate, but the perpetrators could give the excuse that they had mistaken Muḥammad's wives for slaves.

The fundamental reason was doubtless that with Muḥammad's growing importance his residence was more and more a place of public resort. There would always be people in the courtyard round which were the apartments of his wives. One way in which a man could obtain favours from Muḥammad would be to find one of the wives to make the request. The society of Medina looked with suspicion on any private interview between a woman and a man not closely related to her, and consequently some protection was necessary for Muḥammad's wives if scandals were to be avoided. The 'affair of the lie', in which hostile tongues in Medina made the most of an unfortunate incident involving 'Ā'ishah, and which occurred shortly after the introduction of the 'veil', shows how careful Muḥammad had to be. One of the rumours spread to discredit 'Ā'ishah was that in the days before the 'veil' she had had several friendly conversations with the young man who rescued her.[5]

[1] Cf. Stern, 111 ff.; Cl. Huart, art. 'Ḥidjāb' in EI (1); Snouck Hurgronje, *Verspreide Geschriften*, i. 309 f., &c.

[2] 33. 53.

[3] 33. 59.

[4] IS, viii. 124 ff.; cf. N. Abbott, *Aishah*, 20–29, with further references.

[5] Cf. EI (1), art. ''Ā'ishah'; Abbott, 32, &c.

Regulations prescribing modesty for all believing women were revealed a little later; they were to cast down their eyes, guard their private parts, throw their scarves over their bosoms and not show their ornaments except to near relatives.[1] Likewise no one was to enter another man's house without receiving permission.[2] Even if this shows that the general moral level was low and needed to be raised, it also marks the growth of individualism in insisting on respect for privacy.

A further stage in the separating of Muḥammad's wives from other women is connected with 'the verse of the choice' (33. 28 f.), usually assigned to 630/9, though it may be earlier.[3] The underlying reason was perhaps that Muḥammad's rapidly increasing wealth was leading to increasing jealousy between his wives. They kept pestering him for clothes and articles of luxury. Zaynab bint Jaḥsh became annoyed when she thought 'Ā'ishah had given her less than her fair share of something. 'Ā'ishah and Ḥafṣah were jealous of Māriyah the Copt.[4] Whatever the precise incident which led to it, there was a crisis. Muḥammad withdrew from all his wives for a month and apparently threatened to divorce them all. At length he received the command:

> O prophet, say to thy wives: 'If ye desire the life of this world and its adornment, then come, I shall make a provision for you and send you forth elegantly; but if ye desire God and His messenger and the future abode, then God has prepared for those of you who do well a mighty reward.'

This was in effect a choice between divorce and continuation of their marriages on any terms dictated by Muḥammad. Some further verses indicated in general terms the sort of conduct expected of them (33. 30 ff.):

> O wives of the prophet, whoever of you commits a manifest indecency, for her the punishment will be doubled twice over. . . . But to whoever of you is obedient to God and His messenger, and acts uprightly, We shall give her reward twice over, and We have prepared for her a noble provision. O wives of the prophet, ye are not like any ordinary woman; if ye show piety, do not wheedle in your speech, so that one in whose heart is disease grow lustful, but speak in reputable fashion. Remain in your houses (or 'sit with dignity'), and do not swagger about in the manner of the former paganism. . . .

[1] 24. 32/31. [2] 24. 28/27 f. [3] IS, viii. 129 ff.; cf. Abbott, 49–59.
[4] Cf. Q. 66. 1–5 and commentaries; Abbott, 50, 59.

ʿĀʾishah and eight other wives are said to have chosen God and His messenger. Perhaps it was on this occasion that Muḥammad divorced some of the women classed as 'married to Muḥammad and divorced'; a wife from the tribe of ʿĀmir is said to have chosen to be sent away, but her identity is uncertain.[1]

From now on Muḥammad's wives had an honoured and important place in the community. He had probably no intention of imitating the monarchs of Persia and other oriental countries, who increased their own dignity by special arrangements for their wives. Nevertheless the regulations did have an effect of this kind. The believers were forbidden to marry Muḥammad's wives after him.[2] Permission to do so would have increased the disunity in the community. Perhaps it was by way of compensation for this restriction that the wives came to be known as 'mothers of the believers'.

The last feature to be noted about Muḥammad's marriages is that he used both his own and those of the closest Companions to further political ends. This was doubtless a continuation of older Arabian practice. All Muḥammad's own marriages can be seen to have a tendency to promote friendly relations in the political sphere. Khadījah brought him wealth, and the beginnings of influence in Meccan politics. In the case of Sawdah, whom he married at Mecca, the chief aim may have been to provide for the widow of a faithful Muslim, as also in the later marriage with Zaynab bint Khuzaymah; but Sawdah's husband was the brother of a man whom Muḥammad perhaps wanted to keep from becoming an extreme opponent;[3] and Zaynab's husband belonged to the clan of al-Muṭṭalib, for which Muḥammad had a special responsibility, while he was also cultivating good relations with her own tribe of ʿĀmir b. Ṣaʿṣaʿah. His first wives at Medina, ʿĀʾishah and Ḥafṣah, were the daughters of the men on whom he leaned most, Abū Bakr and ʿUmar; and ʿUmar also married Muḥammad's grand-daughter, Umm Kulthūm bint ʿAlī. Umm Salamah was not merely a deserving widow, but a close relative of the leading man of the Meccan clan of Makhzūm. Juwayriyah was the daughter of the chief of the tribe of al-Muṣṭaliq, with whom Muḥammad had been having special trouble. Zaynab bint Jaḥsh, besides being Muḥammad's cousin, was a confederate of the Meccan clan of ʿAbd Shams, but a social motive may have outweighed the political one in her case—

[1] IS, viii. 138.

[2] Q. 33. 53.

[3] Suhayl b. ʿAmr; cf. *M/Mecca*, 140; also pp. 56–64 above.

to demonstrate that Muḥammad had broken with old taboos. Nevertheless the clan of ʿAbd Shams, and Abū Sufyān b. Ḥarb in particular, were in his thoughts, for Abū Sufyān had a Muslim daughter, Umm Ḥabībah, married to a brother of Zaynab bint Jaḥsh; and when the husband died in Abyssinia, Muḥammad sent a messenger there to arrange a marriage with her. The marriage with Maymūnah would similarly help to cement relations with her brother-in-law, Muḥammad's uncle, al-ʿAbbās. There may also have been political motives in the unions with the Jewesses, Ṣafīyah and Rayḥanah. In so far as there are any solid grounds in the accounts of his marriages or proposed marriages with women in the 'supplementary list', the dominant motive was presumably political. They nearly all came from nomadic tribes or places at a distance.

It is noteworthy that Muḥammad had no Medinan wife. Laylā bint al-Khaṭīm (Ẓafar) is said herself to have arranged a marriage with Muḥammad, but to have been forced by her people (*qawm*) to give up the project.[1] Likewise Muḥammad is said to have thought of marrying Ḥabībah bint Sahl (Mālik b. an-Najjār), but to have refrained because of the Anṣār.[2] Clearly he could only be successful in Medina if he was impartial, and his impartiality would be seriously infringed by such marriages. Abū Bakr married a woman of the Khazraj, apparently towards the end of his life (the uterine sister of Saʿd b. ar-Rabīʿ), and ʿUmar had a wife from the Aws. On the whole, however, there was very little intermarriage at Medina between the Meccans and the Medinans, perhaps because of the differences in the social systems.

Other two important Companions, ʿAlī and ʿUthmān b. ʿAffān, were bound to Muḥammad by marriages with his daughters, Fāṭimah and Ruqayyah (followed by Umm Kulthūm); ʿAlī also married Muḥammad's grand-daughter (by Zaynab), Umāmah bint Abī 'l-ʿĀṣ.[3] Az-Zubayr b. al-ʿAwwām was married to Abū Bakr's daughter Asmāʾ. ʿAbd ar-Raḥmān b. ʿAwf, on being sent in command of an expedition to Dūmat al-Jandal in 627/6, was told to marry the daughter of the chief if he submitted. Thus it was by no means only Muḥammad's own marriages that were political, though in his case, as head of the community, there were special reasons for taking political considerations into account.

[1] IS, viii. 107 f.
[2] Ibid. 326 f.
[3] Ibid. 169.

(g) *Conclusion*

In the sphere of marriage and family relations Muḥammad effected a profound and far-reaching reorganization of the structure of society. Before his time new individualistic tendencies were certainly present, but their presence was leading more to the breakdown of the old structure than to the building up of a new one. Muḥammad's essential work here was to use these individualistic tendencies in the raising of a new structure. The customs and practices of the communal (tribal) stage of society, to vary the metaphor, had suffered shipwreck; Muḥammad salvaged what was valuable from them, and carried it over to the new individualistic society. In this way he produced a family structure that in many respects has proved attractive and satisfactory for societies emerging from the communal stage and passing into an individualistic one.

Both by European Christian standards and by those of Islam, many of the old practices were immoral, and Muḥammad's reorganization was therefore a moral advance. The old nomadic system may have been satisfactory in desert circumstances so long as it remained intact. Once disintegration commenced, however, it became unsatisfactory and had to go. It is to Muḥammad's credit that he produced a viable substitute.

3. INHERITANCE

A few verses of the Qur'ān[1] state succinctly but in some detail the rules for the division of an inheritance on a man's death, and these have been elaborated into a complex system by later jurists. It would be confusing rather than illuminating to discuss the matter fully here, but it is important to try to understand the fundamental principles.[2] It will be found that Muḥammad's enactments are aimed at eliminating the abuses which arose in the change from a communal system of ownership to an individualistic one.

There is much that is obscure about the existing practice in regard to inheritance at the time of the Hijrah, but certain general features are clear. In Medina, where society was mainly matrilineal,

[1] Q. 4. 11/12–14/18, 176/175.

[2] Cf. S. Vesey-Fitzgerald, *Muhammadan Law*, London, 1931, 111 ff.; Fyzee, *Outlines of Muhammadan Law*, 331 ff.; F. Peltier and G.-H. Bousquet, *Les Successions Agnatiques Mitigées*, Paris, 1935.

a woman could not own property; this possibly only means that under the communal system it was administered by her maternal uncle, uterine brother, or son; when an administrator died, he would be succeeded by the next most eligible person in the matrilineal group. If there were patrilineal groups where property was held in common, then something similar would hold good; a man would be succeeded by one of his brothers or sons, who would administer on behalf of the group; if the group was large, the property might be divided between several administrators; and the same might happen if several 'heirs' were of approximately equal standing and ability. Where effective administration was the chief consideration, there could be no question of considering as 'heirs' anyone who was not living and above the age of puberty.

With the infiltration of individualistic ideas it was easy to pass imperceptibly from administration to individual ownership. In practice this meant that the strong took everything and the weak had nothing. When Muḥammad's grandfather died, Muḥammad's father was already dead, and Muḥammad was a minor; consequently he received nothing. The dead had no share, and Muḥammad was too young to share in his own right along with his uncles. This is doubtless part of the reason for the Qur'ān's insisting on good treatment for orphans. But the principle that the dead do not inherit and that the living cannot represent the dead must have been deeply rooted, for the Qur'ān does not attempt to make any change on this point.

This is the situation with which the Qur'ān had to deal. The new tendencies and the corresponding abuses had already appeared. The Qur'ān accepts the tendencies and sets out to remedy the abuses. It does not state that property is to belong to individuals, but assumes that it does in fact so belong. Further, it assumes that property may belong to women as well as to men. The case of Khadījah, despite its obscurities, shows that this had been the practice in Mecca. In Medina, however, it was apparently a novelty, and there may have been some conservative opposition at first.[1]

The main aim of the Qur'ānic rules was to ensure that no relative towards whom a man had some obligations was defrauded of his fair share of the inheritance. Consequently they prescribe that,

[1] Cf. Q. 4. 127/126, 'the female orphans to whom ye do not give what is prescribed for them'.

before the inheritance is handed over to the normal or agnatic heirs (ʿ*aṣabāt*—often misleadingly translated in English as 'residuaries'), fixed shares are to be given to certain persons in certain circumstances. These persons are known as 'sharers' (*aṣḥāb al-farāʾiḍ*, &c.) or 'Qurʾānic heirs'. The main 'sharers' are the widower or widow(s), the parents, the daughters, and in certain cases a son's daughters, and the man's sisters and uterine brothers. After the prescribed shares have been paid, the 'residue' (normally the main part of the estate) goes to the sons, father, and brothers, in that order. For the sake of completeness the essential part of the Qurʾānic rules may be quoted:

In regard to your children God charges you (as follows): The male receives the portion of two females; if they be women, more than two, then they receive two-thirds of what a man has left, but if they be only one she receives a half. His parents receive each of them a sixth of what he has left, if he have children; but if he have no children and his parents heir him, then his mother receives a third; if, however, he have brothers, his mother receives a sixth—(this) after any bequests he may have made or debts (have been paid). . . .

A half of what your wives leave belongs to you if they have no children; if they have children, a fourth of what they leave belongs to you. . . . To them belongs a fourth of what ye leave, if ye have no children; if ye have children, an eighth. . . .

If a man or a woman whose property falls to be inherited have no direct heirs (*sc.* agnates), but have a (*sc.* uterine) brother or sister, each of the two receives a sixth; if there be more than that, they share in the third. . . .

If a man perishes and has no children but a sister, the half of what he leaves belongs to her; and he is her heir if she have no children; if there be two (sisters), the two-thirds of what he leaves belongs to them; if there be brothers and sisters, a share equal to the portion of two females belongs to the male.

Instead of showing how these rules are applied in Islamic law, it will be more useful to give some examples of the distribution of property in the type of case which frequently occurs.

Wife, son: receive respectively 1/8, 7/8.
Wife, son, daughter: 1/8, 7/12, 7/24.
Wife, two sons, two daughters: 1/8, 7/24 (2), 7/48 (2).
Husband, two sons, two daughters: 1/4, 1/4 (2), 1/8 (2).
Two daughters, father or distant agnates: 1/3 (2), 1/3.
Two daughters, father, mother: 1/3 (2), 1/6, 1/6.

Father, mother: 2/3, 1/3.
Father, mother, brother: 5/6, 1/6, nil.
Father, mother, wife, two sons, two daughters: 1/6, 1/6, 1/8, 13/72 (2), 13/144 (2).
Husband, son: 1/4, 3/4.
Husband, father: 1/2, 1/2.
Father's father, two brothers: 2/3, 1/6 (2).
Sister, no children: 1/2.
Brother, sister, no children: 1/3, 1/6.

There are certain further points which may be noticed. The system is fundamentally patrilineal. The normal heirs are the sons, father, and brothers. A daughter's sons do not inherit, since they are not members of the patrilineal clan. Even if there are no sons and father to be considered, a man's daughters do not get more than two-thirds of his estate; the remainder goes to more distant agnates. Nevertheless there seems to be a concession to matrilineal practice in the provision that, where a man has no direct heirs (usually taken to be child, son's child, father or father's father), his uterine brothers and sisters (if more than one) inherit a third between them. It is also significant that in this case males and females have equal shares, whereas males mostly have twice the portion of a female. (The above statements are based primarily on the interpretation of the Qur'ān according to the Ḥanafī type of Sunnī law; there are slight differences in other types of Islamic law; e.g. relations through females fare better in the law of the Ithnā ʿAsharī branch of the Shīʿah, the underlying principle apparently being that relations through females and relations through males were equally close to a man.)[1]

The effect of the Qur'ānic rules was to subdivide property within the simple family, and also occasionally within a slightly wider family group. The system to which the rules lead bears the marks of its origin in an environment of caravan-city and desert. It is easy to subdivide a herd of camels or sheep, or a quantity of merchandise which can be valued in money. The subdivision of land in this way is not so satisfactory, and tends to retard agricultural improvements. At the same time, the rules of inheritance and the subdivision they bring about show that individualism had by no means driven out all communal ideas from the outlook of the Arabs. The individual may have his precise share in the property of his father

[1] Cf. Fyzee, 381–406, esp. 403 ff.

or brother, but the family has a certain claim on the property of every member of it. This is seen, not only in the precise fixing of shares, but in the fact that the right to make bequests outside the family was restricted to a third of the estate,[1] while no bequests were allowed to persons who were heirs in any case.[2] These two rules are based on Tradition and not on the Qur'ān, but they are in accordance with the spirit of the latter. They give expression to the conception that, though a man is owner of his property during his lifetime and may dispose of it as he pleases, he is also in a sense a steward of it on behalf of his family. Thus the Qur'ān goes far to meet the individualism of the times, and yet is not completely individualistic.

4. MISCELLANEOUS REFORMS

The topics that have been dealt with so far, social security, marriage, and inheritance, are the only ones on which Muḥammad carried out extensive reforms. There are a few minor matters, however, which ought to be mentioned.

(a) *Slavery*

The attitude of the Qur'ān to slavery is not unlike that of the New Testament. Both accept the fact of slavery and do something to mitigate it. The commonest source of slavery in pre-Islamic times was presumably the warfare between the Arab tribes.[3] In such raiding and fighting women and children were often carried off. Where their tribe could afford it, they would probably be ransomed; but frequently they were sold as slaves. Zayd b. Ḥārithah was thus carried off as a stripling and sold at ʿUkāẓ.[4] Out of the 86 Emigrants named by Ibn Saʿd as fighting at Badr at least another 10 were freedmen or slaves; there were also 4 freedmen and perhaps 1 slave among the Anṣār.[5] Of most of the Emigrants we are told either that they were captured when mere boys or else that they were born in slavery (*muwallad*). Most of them were of Arab descent, but there were at least one Persian and two Abyssinians, these foreigners being apparently born in slavery. There were also slaves fighting for the Meccan pagans, but the hypothesis that Meccan military strength rested on Abyssinian slaves is

1 Fyzee, §71.
2 Ibid. §72.
3 Roberts, *Social Laws*, 53 ff.
4 IS, iii/1. 26.
5 See Excursus C, p. 344 below.

unwarranted and to be rejected.[1] If the Emigrants are a fair sample, the majority of slaves were Arab and not foreign.[2]

There was no objection in principle to the selling of adult males, as is shown by the sale of Muslim prisoners by B. Liḥyān to the Meccans in 625/4. In practice, however, it would be difficult usefully to retain an adult male who had been captured, since he would presumably try to escape whenever there was an opportunity. A man who had been born into slavery, on the other hand, would normally have no tribe to which to flee. There were obvious advantages in removing slaves far from their original region. On the whole, however, slaves seem to have been well treated. Despite their inferior status they had a recognized position in the family and clan, and shared to a large extent in its good fortune and bad fortune. Muḥammad's slave, Ṣāliḥ Shuqrān, fought at Badr for the Muslims while still a slave, and there are said to have been two other slaves among the Muslims.[3] The freedmen (*mawālī*) also stuck closely to their patrons, on whom they were dependent for protection according to the pre-Islamic security system. Zayd b. Ḥārithah, after receiving his freedom, chose to remain with Muḥammad rather than return to his own family.[4]

The inferior status of the slave did not prevent his becoming a Muslim. A few did so in the early days. Abū Bakr bought some and freed them; and it was always regarded as a pious act to free a slave.[5] The freeing of a believing slave was prescribed by way of compensation to the community in cases where one believer had killed another unintentionally.[6] Provision is also made in the Qur'ān for the manumission of slaves by a method which presumably had pre-Islamic antecedents.[7] A contract is made between the master and the slave that the slave is to pay a certain sum for his freedom, and the slave was able, while still a slave, to earn money for this purpose. It was not compulsory, however, to set even believing slaves free, as is shown by the presence of Muḥammad's slave Ṣāliḥ Shuqrān at Badr. Muḥammad's concubine Māriyah, a Christian, was apparently not set free; and, to judge from Ibn Saʿd's accounts of the Badr fighters, the same was true of many of

[1] *M/Mecca*, 154–7.
[2] Contrast R. Brunschvig, art. ''Abd' in EI (2), apparently following H. Lammens.
[3] IS, iii/1. 34. [4] Ibid. 28. [5] Cf. Q. 2. 177/172; 90. 13.
[6] Q. 4. 92/94; for perjury, 5. 89/91; 58. 3/4.
[7] 24. 33; cf. Lane, *s.v. kātaba*.

their concubines. On the contrary, the rules about the marriage of slaves in the Qur'ān show that slavery was regarded as continuing.[1] In 4. 36/40 they are one of several classes of dependent, weak, or needy persons to whom kindness is to be shown.

The critics may say that, in view of his political power towards the end of his life, Muḥammad could have done more to alleviate the lot of the slaves. Such a criticism rests on a false appreciation of the situation in which he found himself. There were many things which urgently required to be set right but this was not one of them. On the whole the slaves were not too badly treated. The chief disability in being a slave was that one could not of one's own will leave the group to which one was attached. In the Arabia of the early seventh century, however, this was much less of a disadvantage than it would be in a more individualistic society. Though the connexion of Islam with the rise of individualism has been emphasized throughout this study of the life of Muḥammad, it should also be realized that individualism was only at its beginnings. The family and the clan still counted far more than they do in Western Europe in the twentieth century. For protection and even livelihood the ordinary man or woman was dependent on the group to which he or she belonged. A strong man might break away from his group to the extent of making himself head of a sub-group. For the ordinary individual, however, the question of leaving the group could hardly arise. Even when a woman married and went to live with her husband's family, she was still to a large extent dependent on her own family. When it is remembered that the slaves were either women or men born in slavery or men taken away from their kinship group when young, it is clear that in their inability to leave the group they differed from other dependent members of the group only in a slight degree. Freedom would only be valuable for them if it meant attachment to a group in which they would have more privileges, or an increase in privilege within the group in which they were slaves. In practice it was usually the latter which occurred at manumission. The slave did not leave the group to which he belonged as slave, but certain relationships within it were changed; the head of the group, instead of being his 'master', became his 'patron'.

Moreover there are two ways in which Muḥammad may be said

[1] 24. 32; cf. 2. 221/220; but for the *fatayāt* of 4. 25/29 and 24. 33 cf. Excursus K, p. 391 below.

to have done something to improve the position in Arabia with regard to slavery. The institution was deeply rooted in the military customs of the time and region. When a defeated tribe was too weak to retaliate or even to ransom its captives, the victors would kill the men and sell the women and children into slavery. The treatment of the Jewish clan of Qurayẓah by the Muslims was simply the regular Arab practice, but on a larger scale than usual, since the Muslims were stronger than even the average strong tribe. Nevertheless the extension of the *Pax Islamica*, by reducing warfare and raiding, reduced the opportunities for making slaves. Indeed it became impossible for a Muslim to make a slave of another Muslim. This was an implication of the conception of the *ummah*, and it is explicitly stated in Tradition.[1] In the second place, this effective reduction of slavery in Arabia through Muḥammad's activity was supported by the conception, implicit in the Qur'ān and in many of his sayings, and sometimes also explicit, that all Muslims are brothers. The recognition that inequalities between men belong to the nature of things has been something of a counterpoise.[2] Nevertheless the idea of 'brotherhood' has been a powerful one in Islam and has aided the movement for the mitigation and abolition of slavery.

(b) *Usury*

It might be thought that the prohibition of usury (*ribā*) in Islam was due to the wrong attitude to wealth among the rich merchants of Mecca. A careful examination of the Qur'ān, however, makes it clear that this is not so, but that the prohibition was first made in the early years at Medina and was directed primarily against the Jews.[3] Richard Bell's dating of the passages referring to usury is unfortunately not so precise as one would desire. None is Meccan in his view; and for the other limit his statements might be taken to imply that none is later than about the siege of Medina. The passage which clinches the matter is the following:

> So for wrong-doing on the part of those who have judaized We have made (certain) good things forbidden to them which had (formerly) been allowable for them, . . . and for their taking usury though they had been forbidden to do so.[4]

[1] Cf. A. J. Wensinck, *A Handbook of Early Muhammadan Tradition*, Leiden, 1927, *s.v.* 'Slave'.

[2] Cf. Q. 16. 75/77.

[3] Cf. J. Schacht, art. 'Ribā' in EI (1).

[4] 4. 160/158 f. F—? G.

There may be a reference to usury in another passage about the Jews.[1] Once this connexion between usury and the Jews has been established, it is natural to regard the threat of war against believers who take usury as directed against Jews.[2] The remaining passages suggest that those who take usury are in danger of Hell or assert that usury leads to no increase from God whereas *zakāt* does.[3]

A reconstruction of the situation would be somewhat as follows. In his first years at Medina Muḥammad was nominally in alliance with the Jews. In course of time he had to appeal for contributions, either to support the poorer Emigrants until booty began to come in, or—as is more likely—for military preparations, especially in the period between Badr and the siege of Medina when Meccan attacks were expected. This appeal was made to the Jews as well as to the Muslims. Most of the Jews refused, but said they were ready to lend money at interest.[4] Muḥammad, however, came to realize that it was contrary to the Jewish law to lend money at interest to a co-religionist. In his eyes Jews and Muslims were co-religionists, and therefore the Jews ought to make outright contributions to his cause, or at least to lend money without interest. In this way the question of usury becomes an aspect of his quarrel with the Jews about recognition of his prophethood.

Though the prohibition of usury was directed against the Jews in the first place, some Arabs also may have been involved at Medina. The later development of both practice and theory, however, is very obscure.[5] There was much discussion of the precise meaning of *ribā* and of what transactions were prohibited, for the general idea in the word is roughly 'getting more than you give'. The nature of the jurists' discussions suggests that *ribā* was comparatively limited in Muḥammad's time. He is said to have mentioned the point in his proclamation after the conquest of Mecca;[6] and in a letter to B. Juhaynah he specifies that they are to abandon the interest on sums owing to them and claim only the capital.[7] On the other hand, there is no evidence of any attempt by Muḥammad to stop commercial dealings at Mecca. The caravan trade of Mecca and Medina continued for some time, and in the end

[1] 5. 62/67 ? FG. [2] 2. 278–81 ? FG.

[3] 2. 275/276 f. E—, E+; 3. 130/125 f. GH; 30. 39/38 ? F.

[4] Cf. WW, 164—80 dīnārs lent by a Jew to one of the Anṣār for a year at 50 per cent. interest; al-Bukhārī *Buyū'* (34), 14—Muḥammad bought grain from a Jew and had to give a coat of mail as a pledge till he paid for it.

[5] Cf. Schacht, l.c. [6] IH, 821; WW, 338. [7] IS i/2. 25. 3.

probably died a natural death. The energies of the entrepreneurs were absorbed in administering the conquests and making fortunes elsewhere; and the occupation of ʿIrāq and Syria brought an easier route from the Indies under Muslim control. Perhaps Muḥammad himself only tried to stop lending for consumption as distinct from lending for productive purposes. The later elaborations which in the modern age have hindered the financing of productive commercial and industrial enterprises are possibly the work of theoreticians remote from any thriving commerce.

This is no place, however, to discuss these later developments. In Muḥammad himself there seems to have been no intention of hindering legitimate trade or of revolutionizing the financial practices of Mecca, despite the Qur'ānic criticisms of the pagan Meccans' attitude to money. The idea underlying the prohibition of usury was that all believers were brothers and therefore ought to help one another financially as well as in other ways.

There is hardly anything that could be called reform in the other rules of the Qur'ān dealing with commerce and finance. They exhort to upright dealing, and in certain cases prescribe that the matter should be put in writing—presumably an innovation.

(c) *Wine-drinking*

The prohibition of intoxicating drinks is one of the well-known features of Islamic civilization, and has its basis in certain verses of the Qur'ān:

> They will ask thee about wine and *maysir*; say: 'In both of them there is great guilt, and also uses for the people, but their guilt is greater than their usefulness.'
>
> O ye who have believed, wine, *maysir*, stone altars (or images), and divining arrows are simply an abomination, some of Satan's work; so avoid it, mayhap ye will prosper. Satan simply wishes to cause enmity and hatred to fall out amongst you in the matter of wine and *maysir*, and to turn you away from the remembrance of God and from the Worship, so are ye going to refrain?[1]

At the conquest of Mecca Muḥammad is said to have refused a present of wine, and to have had the wine poured out.[2]

The only point to be discussed is that of the reason for this prohibition of wine-drinking. The tenor of the Qur'ānic passages, especially if, with later Muslims, *maysir* is taken to include all

[1] 2. 219/216; 5. 90/92 f.
[2] WW, 348.

forms of gambling, suggests that the attitude of the early Muslim community was not unlike that in certain pietistic circles in Europe today. Some other facts support this suggestion. There is an ascetic strain in the Semitic temperament, and even before Muḥammad began to preach there were men in Mecca, like ʿUthmān b. Maẓʿūn,[1] who avoided wine. There are also stories of the unpleasant effects of drunkenness, even among prominent Companions.[2]

On the other hand, there are reasons for thinking that such a view is not the whole truth of the matter. The meaning of *khamr* was much discussed by later jurists, and we cannot be sure whether it originally meant any intoxicating drink or wine in the strict sense (the fermented juice of the grape). If it meant the latter, then political considerations may have come in, for grape-wine was normally imported from Syria and ʿIrāq. Thus wine-drinking would imply trading with the enemy. This point, however, is not so weighty as another, namely, the connexion of wine with *maysir* in the verses quoted from the Qur'ān. *Maysir* was a practice by which ten men bought a camel, slaughtered it, and then drew lots for the portions by means of arrows; three arrows had no portions assigned to them, and the men to whom these fell had to pay for the whole camel. The Qur'ānic objection to the passage is presumably not that it was a form of gambling, but that it was closely connected with the pagan religion, since the arrows were kept by the guardian of the Kaʿbah at Mecca.[3] It seems likely, therefore, that the main reason for the prohibition of wine may have been some connexion with pagan religion of which we are not aware.[4]

(d) *The calendar*

The abolition of intercalary months is a slight change introduced under Muḥammad which has given a definite stamp to Islamic civilization. The pre-Islamic Arabs observed the lunar months, but kept their calendar in line with the solar year by introducing intercalary months where necessary. The matter is referred to in a passage of the Qur'ān:

Twelve is the number of the months with God, (written) in God's Book on the day when He created the heavens and the earth; of these

[1] IS, iii/1. 286.
[2] Al-Bukhārī, *Sharb* (42), 13; for further references cf. A. J. Wensinck, art. 'Khamr' in EI (S).
[3] Cf. B. Carra de Vaux, art. 'Maisir' in EI (S).
[4] Cf. J. Wellhausen, *Reste Arabischen Heidentums*, 2nd ed., Berlin, 1897, 114.

four are sacred; that is the eternal religion; so do not wrong each other in them; but fight the polytheists continuously, as they fight you continuously, and know that God is with those who act piously. The postponement (the intercalary month—*nasī*) is simply an increase of unbelief, in which those who have disbelieved go astray; they make it free (not-sacred) one year and sacred another, that they may make adaptable the number of what God hath made sacred, and may make free (not-sacred) what God hath made sacred. . . .[1]

Muḥammad is said to have made public these verses during the address he gave during the Pilgrimage of Farewell.[2]

There are so many obscurities in the whole question of the intercalary month that it is difficult to say what were the underlying reasons for the adoption of a lunar year.[3] The Qur'ān implies that intercalation was in some respect a human activity infringing God's law, and contrasts the fixity of the latter with variability of the human device. This makes it almost certain that, despite some of the accounts, the Arabs had no *fixed* system of intercalation. As reason for the prohibition of intercalation there are two main possibilities. The method of settling when a month was to be intercalated may have been connected with paganism in some way of which we are not aware; it was certainly linked with the observance of the sacred months.[4] Or else there may have been a risk that the uncertainty about which months were sacred would cause disputes and endanger the *Pax Islamica*. Whatever the reason for it, this adoption of the lunar year shows again the non-agrarian character of Islam; Islam is often said to mould or influence every department of life, but it has not penetrated the agricultural life of the millions of peasants who are good Muslims. Their farming practices—and some of the religious ideas connected with them—continue in the traditional way regardless of Islam. A work like the *Georgics* is inconceivable in any Islamic literature.

5. CONCLUSION

The prohibition of usury, wine, and intercalated months has done much to give Islamic countries the appearance they present to the traveller; but the other matters dealt with in this chapter

[1] 9. 36 f.

[2] IH, 968 f.; WW, 430 f.

[3] Cf. Caetani, i. 356 ff.; Buhl, *Muhammed*, 350 f.; M. Plessner, art. 'Muḥarram' in EI (1), with further references.

[4] Cf. p. 8 above. Contrast H. Winckler in *Arabisch-Semitisch-Orientalisch*, 85–90 (Berlin, Mitteilungen der Vorderasiatischen Gesellschaft, 1901, 4).

are more important in a consideration of the reform of the social structure. It remains to say a word about the relation of these reforms to the social aspect of the malaise of the times.

The root of the social troubles of the Ḥijāz in the early seventh century A.D. was that the communal (tribal) system of the desert was breaking down in the settled life of Mecca and Medina. The precise reasons were different in the two places. In Mecca a mercantile economy had fostered the growth of individualism. In Medina the autonomy of each tribe and clan, appropriate to desert conditions, led in the confined space of an oasis to an insecurity of life that had become intolerable. Individualism meant that the strong oppressed the weak and neglected their traditional duties to clan and family. It was present at Medina, but not so noticeable there as at Mecca. The characteristic of the social structure of Medina was a tendency towards the formation of larger groupings, either as alliances or on the basis of kinship, real or artificial. In all this social disintegration most individuals were doubtless painfully aware of their insecurity and isolation.

Among the nomadic tribes there does not appear to have been any social crisis apart from the menace to their autonomy arising from Muḥammad's successes. There were, of course, the perennial problems of nomadic life—constant raiding and blood-feuds and the recurring risk of famine.

Against this background it is interesting to see how individualism and communalism were combined by Muḥammad. The *ummah* or new community of Islam has as its first aim the preservation of peace between its members, and Muḥammad, as executive head of the community, had to see to it that this aim was realized. But the *ummah* was much more than a method of preserving peace. In one respect it was a community of individuals, for Islam accepted the tendency towards individualism, and even encouraged it (as in the new family structure). The ultimate moral sanction in Islam, punishment in Hell, applies to the individual for his conduct as an individual. On the other hand, the individual was taken out of his isolation and insecurity and made to feel that he belonged to the *ummah*. The early practice of 'brothering' may seem artificial, but the sense of brotherhood between Muslims has become very deep; witness such a title in our own days as 'the Muslim Brotherhood' (*al-Ikhwān al-Muslimīn*—literally 'the brothers, the Muslims'). The *ummah* was a closely-knit community, thought of on the lines of a tribe, and much of the old mystique attaching to the kinship group has become attached to it.

At the same time, however, these kinship groups continued to play a part in the structure of Islamic society. The *ummah* was essentially a body of clans and tribes in alliance. These still had a part to play in maintaining the security of life and property. In the regulations for inheritance, too, the claims of a man's family are fully acknowledged, while a check is placed on the abuses proceeding from individualism. With the rapid increase in the number of Muslims after the conquest of Mecca and battle of Ḥunayn the sense of community between them must have decreased. Muḥammad himself, doubtless for political and strategic reasons above all, wanted to be on good terms with his former opponents from Quraysh. Thus old ties of kinship came to have an increased importance within the *ummah*.[1] Later, as is well known, the deep hostility to one another of certain Arab tribes was a major factor in the downfall of the Umayyad dynasty.

In the structure of Islamic society both individualism and communalism have thus a part. The kinship groups remain important for social and administrative purposes, but in the religious sphere membership of the clan or tribe has been replaced by membership of the Islamic community, and 'tribal humanism'[2] by the religion of Islam.

[1] Cf. Q. 8. 75/76; 33. 6; but note Bell's dating.

[2] Cf. *M/Mecca*, 24 f., and further Bichr Farès, *L'Honneur chez les Arabes avant l'Islam*, Paris, 1932.

IX

THE NEW RELIGION

1. THE RELIGIOUS INSTITUTIONS OF ISLAM

IN the course of examining Muḥammad's statesmanship and his political and social reforms it is easy to forget that he was first and foremost a religious leader. A study of his life would be incomplete without some account of the religion which he founded. Unfortunately the early history of the religious institutions of Islam is an obscure and difficult subject. It is therefore most suitable here to leave aside the details, and to describe only the general features of the institutions.

The Hijrah brought Muḥammad into closer contact with the Jews, and thereafter his relations to the Jews determined in large measure the line of development taken by the Islamic religion. First there was a period of assimilation to Judaism, then a period of opposition.[1] To begin with, the thought was that, if the Jews fasted, so must the Muslims; but later it came to be that, if the Jews fasted in a certain way, the Muslims must fast in another way. Thus we find both similarities to Judaism and dissimilarities; and in a sense both are deliberate. Indeed this bipolar attitude towards the older monotheistic religions, though most apparent in the Medinan period, had been present from the earliest days. Both religions had political implications which were distasteful to Muḥammad. His aim was therefore to produce a religion parallel to these religions, but specially for the Arabs. The effect of the Jewish refusal to recognize Muḥammad's religion as in some way parallel to their own was that it came to be, not merely a religion specially for the Arabs, but also one that was distinctively Arabian.

The name of Muḥammad's religion was not always Islam. In the Meccan period one name for it seems to have been *tazakkī*, 'righteousness',[2] but the religion and its adherents are seldom explicitly mentioned. After the Hijrah there are many references to 'believers' (*mu'minūn*), 'those who believe', and so forth; in some cases these terms include the Jews. On Muḥammad's break with the Jews he claimed to be following the religion of Abraham, the

[1] Cf. pp. 198 ff. above. [2] *M/Mecca*, 165–9.

ḥanīf; and for some time Muḥammad's religion must have been known as the Ḥanīfīyah. This word was read instead of 'Islam' by Ibn Mas'ūd in Qur'ān, 3. 19/17,[1] and was presumably the original reading. It also occurs in sayings of Muḥammad to the effect that the religion he took to Medina was the Ḥanīfīyah.[2] This name must have had a wide currency, for a Christian writing in Egypt in the thirteenth century A.D. can still speak of the time when 'the Hanifite nation appeared and humbled the Romans'.[3] It is difficult to say at what period *ḥanīf* and Ḥanīfīyah were replaced by *muslim* and Islam. Richard Bell says that the latter do not occur before A.H. 2,[4] and even after their occurrence they may not have immediately replaced the others. The variant in the codex of Ibn Mas'ūd, too, is a reminder that early Medinan passages of the Qur'ān may have been revised to bring them into line with the later nomenclature. 'Islam' is undoubtedly the better designation, with a profounder religious content, probably meaning 'resignation or submission to God'. It has been suggested that the usage has been developed from the account of Abraham's sacrifice of his son in the Qur'ān, where the two are said to 'resign themselves' (*aslamā*).[5] If this is so, then there would be an easy transition from 'the religion of Abraham' to 'Islam'.[6]

Of the main institutions of Islam, the so-called 'five pillars', the most important is the *ṣalāt*, the Worship or formal Prayer. The usual translation of *ṣalāt* is 'prayers', but this corresponds rather to *du'ā*.[7] The Worship had been a feature of Muḥammad's religion from the earliest times, and attempts to stop his followers from worshipping were the first open signs of opposition.[8] The Worship did not consist in asking God for favours, but was essentially an acknowledgement of His might and majesty.[9] It was adoration, and

[1] A. Jeffery, *Materials for the History of the Text of the Qur'ān*, Leiden, 1937, 32.

[2] IH, 411 foot; IS, i/1. 128. 13. Cf. WW, 161 foot, 91 foot (= IH, 995. 11).

[3] Abū Ṣāliḥ, *The Churches and Monasteries of Egypt*, ed. and tr. B. T. A. Evetts, 230 f. (quoted from L. E. Browne, *The Eclipse of Christianity in Asia*, Cambridge, 1933, p. 40).

[4] *Introduction to the Qur'ān*, Edinburgh, 1953, 108; contrast J. Horovitz, *Koranische Untersuchungen*, 54 f., following the older dating.

[5] 37. 103. Cf. H. Ringgren, 'Islam, 'aslama and muslim', *Horae Soderblomianae*, ii (Upsala, 1949), 27, &c.; J. Robson, '"Islam" as a term', *Muslim World*, xliv (1954), 101–9.

[6] Q. 9. 29 I has 'the religion of truth' (*dīn al-ḥaqq*).

[7] Cf. E. E. Calverley, *Worship in Islam*, Madras, 1925, 3.

[8] Q. 96. 10.

[9] Cf. Snouck Hurgronje, *Verspreide Geschriften*, i. 213.

the fundamental expression of this adoration was a cycle of physical acts, repeated twice or oftener, and culminating in the prostration (*sujūd*) where the worshipper touched the ground with his forehead. There were forms of words to be repeated along with the physical acts—at the prostration, for example, something like 'Praise be to God'—but the physical acts were primary and the words secondary. This whole conception of worship is very strange to the Western European, but in its emphasis on acknowledging God the Almighty it is in full harmony with Muḥammad's early prophetic proclamation.

When the Worship was stabilized by the later jurists, it became obligatory for every Muslim to perform it five times daily. It is doubtful, however, whether the five daily hours were regularly observed even during Muḥammad's closing years. The night-vigil, popular with his followers at Mecca, was abrogated at Medina:[1] and a phrase in the Qur'ān shows that there must have been at least three hours of prayer daily.[2] Beyond that nothing certain can be said. The call to the Worship was given by the human voice, and the Abyssinian freedman, Bilāl, was Muḥammad's first muezzin (*mu'adhdhin*). The Worship was performed facing in a certain direction, the *qiblah*; at first, as explained above, the worshippers probably faced Jerusalem, but after the break with the Jews they turned to Mecca.[3] The Worship was preceded by ablutions,[4] and the timing for the physical acts was given by a leader (*imām*) who stood in front of the ranks. Performing the physical acts of adoration along with one's fellow believers must have fostered a strong sense of community.

The Worship might be performed anywhere. It was not necessary to go to a special place of worship. For the mid-day Worship on Fridays, however, there was a strong recommendation that the Muslims should gather together in some public place.[5] In Medina it became usual to hold this Worship in the courtyard of Muḥammad's house; and at other times of the day and week also there were probably always a number of the Companions who came to join in the Worship with Muḥammad. It may be noted in passing that, while strangers may sometimes have lodged in the portico (*ṣuffah*, *ẓillah*) in this courtyard, the later accounts of a company

[1] Q. 73. 20 and commentaries.
[2] Cf. p. 199 above; also Caetani, *Ann.* i. 452 f.
[3] Cf. pp. 198, 202 above. [4] Q. 4. 43/46. [5] Cf. Q. 62. 9.

of poor and pious Muslims, known as Ahl aṣ-Ṣuffah, who lived there permanently, are not historical.[1] In constructing his residence Muḥammad probably tried to make it suitable for gatherings of the Muslims, religious or secular; but during his lifetime it was almost certainly not regarded as a sacred place or sanctuary, like the courtyard of the Kaʿbah at Mecca.[2] For special occasions Muḥammad went to the *muṣallā* or 'chapel' (?) in the district of B. Salimah; and it may be that this is the 'place of worship (*masjid*) founded upon piety' to which the Qur'ān refers.[3] When Muḥammad had died, however, and had been buried in ʿĀ'ishah's apartment in his residence, it was natural for the residence to become the mosque of Medina. Muḥammad is also said to have founded a mosque among B. ʿAmr b. ʿAwf at Qubā',[4] while the story of the 'mosque of dissension' has already been told.[5]

The second of the five pillars of Islam is the *zakāt* or 'legal alms'. The Qur'ān frequently employs the phrase 'performing the Worship and paying the *zakāt*', and thus indicates that these were the distinguishing marks of a good Muslim. Much has already been said about the financial aspect of the *zakāt* and its place in Muḥammad's budget. It remains to say something of its religious character, though this also has been touched on in a discussion of the word *tazakkā*.[6] There must be some connexion of thought between *tazakkā* and *zakāt*, but it is difficult to say precisely what it is. *Zakāt*, however, was not simply the paying of a tax, though it may have appeared in this light to the more secular-minded. It always had a religious significance. It took up into itself old Semitic ideas of sacrifice, and provided deep feelings with a form of expression. Because of this, *zakāt* has remained one of the pillars of Islam even where it ceased to be part of the financial arrangements of the state; and in Muslim countries alms-giving is regarded as a pious duty.

The third of the pillars of Islam is the fast (*ṣawm*) of the month of Ramaḍān. As already related,[7] the practice of fasting was adopted

[1] Cf. art. 'Ahl al-Ṣuffah' in EI (2).

[2] IH, 333–7; Ṭab. i. 1259 f.; Caetani, i. 376–80, 432–47; Buhl, *Muhammed*, 204 f.

[3] 9. 108/109; A. J. Wensinck, art. 'Muṣallā' in EI (1); C. H. Becker, 'Zur Geschichte des islamischen Kultus', *Der Islam*, iii (1912), 374–99 (= *Islamstudien*, i. 472–500).

[4] IH, 335; J. Pedersen, art. 'Masdjid', I (a), in EI (S).

[5] Cf. p. 190 above.

[6] *M/Mecca*, 165–9.

[7] Cf. p. 199 above.

during the Medinan period so that the Muslims might be like the Jews, but when the break with the Jews came the Jewish fast of the ʿĀshūrā was replaced by the fast of Ramaḍān.

The fourth pillar is the pilgrimage (*ḥajj*), sometimes called the 'greater pilgrimage' to distinguish it from the *ʿumrah* or 'lesser pilgrimage'.[1] In pre-Islamic times the *ʿumrah* seems to have been connected specially with the Kaʿbah, while the *ḥajj* was rather associated with other sacred sites in the neighbourhood of Mecca. Under Islam the *ḥajj* came to be more closely related to the Kaʿbah, while the *ʿumrah* may be said to consist now of certain supererogatory works which may be added to the performance of the *ḥajj*. The verse of the Qur'ān enjoining pilgrimage (2. 196/192a) is dated by Bell before Badr; and this adoption of an Arabian custom into Islam would suitably occur about the time of Muḥammad's break with the Jews. Nevertheless something of the kind had long been implicit in Islam. An early Meccan revelation (106. 3) recognized the Kaʿbah as a 'house' of God; and some at least of the Muslims who pledged themselves to Muḥammad at al-ʿAqabah regarded the pilgrimage to Mecca as a religious act, and not simply as a convenient excuse for visiting Muḥammad.[2] Saʿd b. Muʿādh is said to have made the pilgrimage in the first pilgrimage-month after the Hijrah, and to have been the guest of Umayyah b. Khalaf.[3] Before the next occasion, however, the battle of Badr had occurred, and access to Mecca was presumably impossible for all Muslims.

Nevertheless Muḥammad continued to be interested in the pilgrimage. The ostensible purpose of the expedition to al-Ḥudaybiyah in 628/6 was the performance of the *ʿumrah*, and there is no reason to doubt a genuine desire on Muḥammad's part to perform this religious act, even if he also had political aims in mind. He performed the *ʿumrah* a year later according to the treaty, as already related, and again in the following year after the battle of Ḥunayn. In 631/9 there was held the first truly Muslim pilgrimage; Abū Bakr was the leader, and idolaters were prohibited from taking part.[4] A year later in March 632 (xii/10) Muḥammad himself

[1] A. J. Wensinck, art. 'Ḥadjdj' in EI (1); R. Paret, art. "ʿUmra', ibid.; C. Snouck Hurgronje, *Het mekkaansche Feest*, Leiden, 1880 (in *Verspreide Geschriften*, i. 1–124); M. Gaudefroy-Demombynes, *Le Pèlerinage à la Mekke*, Paris, 1923.

[2] Cf. refusal of al-Barā' b. Maʿrūr to turn his back on the Kaʿbah, IH, 294 and p. 169 above.

[3] Al-Bukhārī, *Maghāzī* (64), 2; cf. Caetani, i. 425 f.

[4] IH, 919–29; WW, 416 f. Snouck Hurgronje, op. cit., i. 45, suggests that

led the pilgrimage, 'the pilgrimage of farewell', and established the course and form of the ceremonies in general outline; many details of what he did, however, were later disputed between the various schools of jurists.

The pilgrimage may be said to focus on one point in space and time the whole Islamic world's acknowledgement of the might and majesty of God. The recognition of the Kaʿbah as the house of God *par excellence* in Arabia (though without any denial of the sanctity of Jerusalem) and the adoption of it as *qiblah* meant that, so far as Arabia was concerned, the worship of God was focused on one point in space. By retaining the pilgrimage in Islam, albeit in a modified form. Muḥammad further focused the worship of God in time, since the main events of the pilgrimage occur on specified days of the pilgrimage-month (*Dhū 'l-Ḥijjah*). The expansion of Islam, and the consequent impossibility for the majority of Muslims of ever making the pilgrimage, have not led to its becoming any less central in the Muslim's religious year. The departure and return of the pilgrims are great events in many Muslim towns. Those who remain at home nevertheless may and do participate in one of the ceremonies, the 'festival of the sacrifice' (*ʿīd al-aḍḥā*); in this they follow the example of Muḥammad who, during the period when he was debarred from Mecca, annually celebrated this feast at the 'place of worship' (*muṣallā*) of B. Salimah.[1] The climax of the pilgrimage is the 'standing on ʿArafāt', a hill and plain some four hours' journey east of Mecca by camel. This takes place on the 9th of the month from midday to sunset. In recent years there have sometimes been half a million people present here. The pilgrimage thus makes an important contribution to the awareness of Islam as a community, a powerful band of brothers.

The remaining one of the five pillars of Islam is the confession of faith (*shahādah*), that is, the repetition of the words, 'There is no god but God, and Muḥammad is the Messenger of God'. The precise formula does not occur in the Qur'ān, though the sense is omnipresent. The two points were those on which latterly Muḥammad insisted in his dealings with would-be followers, and the formula was doubtless used in his closing years. Repetition of it made a man a Muslim.

this measure led by economic pressure to the conversion of the pagans *en masse*.

[1] Ṭab. i. 1362; Caetani, i. 525; EI (1), art. 'Muṣallā', &c.

In concluding this review of the religious institutions of Islam attention may be drawn to the individualism which pervades them.[1] Worship for the Muslim is essentially something which concerns God and the individual only. Where several Muslims are together it is appropriate that they, for example, perform the Worship together; but when a man is by himself and performs the Worship by himself, what he does is just as much a fulfilment of God's requirements as what he did in a crowd. In short, all the strict obligations of Islamic worship could be carried out even if there was only one Muslim in the world. This is a corollary of the belief that it is as an individual that man is judged by God on the Last Day. Nevertheless, as we have seen, there is also a complementary tendency to emphasize the unity of the Islamic community, and to develop ceremonies which impress this on the worshipper. Perhaps the sum of the matter is that Islam is a community of individuals or band of brothers, joined together by common duties, but in the last resort not necessary to one another.

2. ISLAM AND ARAB PAGANISM

It is interesting to look more closely at the attitude of Muḥammad and the Qur'ān to the existing paganism of Arabia, since that attitude was more complex than might at first sight appear. As has been maintained elsewhere, the vital religious force in the lives of most of the Arabs was 'tribal humanism',[2] and the old paganism was almost dead. All that remained of it was some magical practices and some ceremonies whose meaning had been forgotten.

In *Muhammad at Mecca* it was argued that the earliest parts of the Qur'ān did not contain any attack on paganism, but rather assumed in the audience a 'vague monotheism'.[3] Later, however, the unity of God was strictly insisted on, and a critique of increasing severity was directed against idolatry.[4] This has remained a feature of Islam ever since. During Muḥammad's Medinan period it led to the destruction of idols both in the Medinan clans as some members became converted, and in all the chief sanctuaries of the

[1] G. H. Bousquet, *Les grandes Pratiques rituelles de l'Islam*, Paris, 1949, 116–20.

[2] *M/Mecca*, 24 f.

[3] Cf. further C. Brockelmann, 'Allah und die Götzen, der Ursprung des islamischen Monotheismus', *Archiv für Religionswissenshaft*, xxi (1922), 99–121.

[4] P. 63 f., 158.

Ḥijāz. Sometimes special raiding parties were sent out; sometimes, as in the case of aṭ-Ṭā'if, the destruction of an idol by its worshippers was made a condition of their acceptance within the Islamic community.[1] In various other ways, too, all vestiges of idolatry were removed. Pagan theophoric names were changed; thus 'Abd ar-Raḥmān b. 'Awf had originally been 'Abd 'Amr or 'Abd al-Ka'bah;[2] another 'Abd ar-Raḥmān had been 'Abd al-'Uzzā;[3] and so on with many an 'Abdallāh.[4] Perhaps the comparative disuse of the name 'ar-Raḥmān', 'the Merciful', was due to the danger of it encouraging idolatry. For a time in the later part of the Meccan period it was being used more frequently than 'Allāh' in references to the Deity (possibly because increased emphasis was being laid on the Divine mercy and goodness);[5] then it passed almost entirely out of use, apart from the heading of the sūrahs. The use of 'ar-Raḥmān' as a name and not merely an epithet could easily cause confusion for simple-minded people, especially in view of the association of this name with certain localities, such as South Arabia and the Yamāmah.[6]

Despite this extirpation of idolatry, many old pagan ideas and practices were retained. Though the possibility of the corruption of the sources cannot be excluded, it is probable that Muḥammad himself believed in omens from names. He derived omens of success, for example, from the names of the strongholds at Khaybar;[7] and in many instances he is said to have changed inauspicious names to the opposite, 'disobedient' to 'obedient', and so on.[8] The Qur'ān implies belief in the efficacy of cursing, though chiefly, it must be admitted, the curse of God.[9] Oaths also were regarded as transactions which created a special relation between man and God. Even where an oath was part of a practice forbidden by Islam, it

[1] Cf. pp. 69, 103 above.

[2] IS, iii/1. 87 f.; *Usd*, iii. 313.

[3] IS, iii/2. 41. 18.

[4] e.g. 'Abdallāh Dhū 'l-Bijādayn, originally 'Abd al-'Uzzā (*Usd*, iii. 122).

[5] H. Grimme, *Muhammed*, ii. 39 f.; R. Bell, *Introduction*, 143.

[6] For the latter cf. p. 135 above; Q. 17. 110 presupposes some confusion.

[7] WW, 272; cf. 266, choice of route.

[8] 'Āṣiyah to Muṭī'ah ('disobedient' to 'obedient'), IS, viii. 257. 2; B. aṣ-Ṣammā' to B. as-Samī'ah ('deaf' to 'hearing'), as-Samhūdī, i. 138; Khurbā to Ṣāliḥah, &c. ('waste' to 'prosperous', of a *dār*), ibid. 142; al-'Abir to al-Yusayrah, Barrah to Juwayriyah, Ju'āl to 'Amr, WW, 152, 178, 193.

[9] 2. 89/83, &c.; for human curses cf. 7. 38/36, 2. 155/154; cf. also use of a curse in a legal document, IS, i/2. 22. 2 (§ 19), 'the curse of God and the angels and the people altogether'.

had to be expiated when broken;[1] and at al-Ḥudaybiyah the vow Muḥammad had made to sacrifice the horse of Abū Jahl is said to have made it impossible for him to exchange the horse for a hundred camels.[2]

The Qur'ān also makes it clear that the Muslims continued to believe in supernatural beings below the rank of divinity, namely, angels, jinn, and demons (*shayāṭīn*).[3] The precise nature of the jinn and their relation to the demons is obscure, but need not be further discussed here. On the rejection of the pagan deities, the first suggestion was that they were among these lesser supernatural beings, but later they were said to be mere names.[4] The forbidding of recourse to soothsayers (*kuhhān*) was doubtless bound up with their inspiration by jinn.[5]

The old Semitic idea that certain places were sacred was preserved, at least in a modified form. The sacredness of the Ka'bah, apparently recognized in the early revelation (106. 3) where God is called 'the Lord of this House', was confirmed by the taking of it as *qiblah* or direction in worship and by the acknowledgement of the duty of pilgrimage. The sacredness of the 'sacred mosque' (*al-masjid al-ḥarām*), however, is based by the Qur'ān (22. 26/27) on a revelation of God to Abraham, telling him to purify it for worship; likewise it is God who makes the neighbourhood of Mecca a 'sacred area' (*ḥaram*).[6] On the contrary, there is nothing sacred about the sanctuaries of the pagan deities, and, when the sacred objects are destroyed by Muslims and the sites desecrated, nothing bad happens to those who do this; thus the nothingness of the alleged deities is evident. We see then that although the idea has been retained that certain places are sacred, there has been a subtle change in it. Places are not intrinsically sacred, and they are not made sacred by any of the alleged pagan deities; they only

[1] Q. 58. 3/4, according to the usual interpretation.

[2] WW, 258.

[3] Cf. I. Goldziher, *Abhandlungen zur arabischen Philologie*, Leiden, 1896, i. 106–17, &c.; W. Eickmann, *Die Angelologie und Dämonologie des Korans*, New York, Leipzig, 1908; P. A. Eichler, *Die Dschinn, Teufel und Engel im Koran*, Leipzig, 1928; S. Zwemer, 'The Worship of Adam by Angels', *Moslem World*, xxvii (1937), 115–27. For the connected idea of 'spirit', cf. D. B. Macdonald, 'The Development of the Idea of Spirit in Islam', *Acta Orientalia*, ix (1931), 6–15; T. O'Shaughnessy, *The Development of the Meaning of Spirit in the Koran*, Rome, 1953.

[4] Cf. *M/Mecca*, 107 f.; Q. 53. 23.

[5] WW, 348.

[6] Q. 28. 57; 29. 67; for the Ka'bah cf. 8. 98, &c.

become sacred through the act of God. In § 39 of the Constitution there is apparently an extension of this principle, for the valley of Yathrib (or Medina) is declared sacred (*ḥarām*) by the Messenger of God and the Islamic community.[1]

The question of food-restrictions belongs in part to the domain of Islam's relationship with paganism. There are several injunctions to the Muslims to eat what is good and not to regard as forbidden what God had made allowable.[2] Some commentators said that this was directed against ascetic practices.[3] The context in which several of the passages occur, however, makes it clear that they were directed in the first place against pagan taboos.[4] The existence of the Jewish food laws led to difficulties, in view of the claim that Muḥammad's revelation was identical with the Jewish; but the difficulties were met partly by insisting that most of the Jewish regulations had been instituted as a punishment for them,[5] and partly by introducing a modified set of restrictions, namely, prohibition of what was found dead, of blood, of pork, and of animals sacrificed to idols.[6] This list, especially when strangling is added,[7] is reminiscent of that adopted by the Christians at Jerusalem in the early days of the church—meats offered to idols, blood, and things strangled[8]—and suggests that in this matter what was common to Christianity and Judaism was regarded as authentic revelation.

There is no convincing evidence that any *belief* in magical practices was retained in the Qur'ān or by Muḥammad himself. Islam certainly retained rites that had been magical in origin, but the Qur'ān does not show any signs of belief in their magical efficacy. Many Muslims, of course, continued to believe in magic, and stories of magical practices have found their way into the traditions about Muḥammad. One such is about the battle of Badr. Muḥammad is said to have taken a handful of pebbles, to have turned towards Quraysh expressing a wish for evil on them, and then to have thrown the pebbles at them;[9] at his word his followers attacked fiercely and Quraysh were routed. This story would not

[1] Contrast the attitude to the 'sacred month', p. 299 above.
[2] Q. 2. 168/163 E; 5. 86/89 f. E; cf. 6. 118 f. E—.
[3] Cf. Wherry (Sale) on 5. 86/89.
[4] 6. 141/142 ff. C—E+; 116 E; ? 148/149 ff. E.
[5] 6. 146/147 E+; 16. 118/119 f.
[6] 2. 172/167 f. ? F; 6. 145/146 E+; 16. 114/115ff.
[7] As in 5.3/4 ? H.
[8] Acts, xv. 20, 29.
[9] *Nafaḥa-hum bi-hā*, IH, 445; cf. WW, 58.

deserve much credence apart from the fact that the Qur'ān is said to refer to the incident in the words:

> Ye did not kill them, but God killed them, and thou threwest not, when thou threwest, but God threw.[1]

This passage, however, need not refer to the story of the pebbles; the word for 'throw' here (*ramayta*) is different from that in the story (*nafaḥa*) and could easily be applied to shooting with arrows.[2] Moreover, many of the commentators whose views are recorded by aṭ-Ṭabarī appear to be ignorant of the story.[3] This verse, therefore, is no proof of a belief in magic.

If an attempt is now made to say on what principles pagan ideas and practices are retained or rejected, the following conclusions may be suggested. Pagan ideas, such as belief in angels, jinn, and demons, are retained where they are deep-rooted and do not obviously contradict God's oneness. In the case of the idea that certain places are sacred, there is also great social utility in the idea and in the practices dependent on it—the opportunities that it provided for the Arabs to meet together in peace, with the resultant feeling that they were a single community. These two points of deep-rootedness and social utility appear to account for most of the beliefs and practices retained. Where neither was present, old practices were rejected, such as those connected with camels in 5. 103/102.

It is further interesting to note that these pagan survivals, when incorporated in Islam, were nearly always transformed. Whatever may have been the pagan justification for belief in the sacredness of places, the Qur'ān made it dependent on God's appointment. The angels became servants of God's purposes. The effectiveness of curses was probably held to be due to God's activity. The lapidation of stone pillars (a rite included in the pilgrimage) was interpreted as stoning the devils. Old ideas of sacrifice, as retained in the practice of *zakāt* or 'legal alms', were directed into socially useful channels, namely, the relief of the poor or the financing of the Islamic state. The actual sacrifice of victims as retained in Islam (during the pilgrimage and on one or two other occasions) does not have the ideas of atonement and propitiation associated with it as in Judaism and Christianity; it is always socially useful, however,

[1] Q. 8. 17.
[2] Cf. Lane, *s.v.*; also WW, 116, where Muḥammad himself used a bow.
[3] *Tafsīr*, ix. 127 f.

for in theory the sacrificial animal is consumed.[1] There are slight traces of these ideas attached to alms-giving,[2] but the later emphasis is rather on the reward given by God in the life to come.[3]

Oaths and vows are in a curious position. Although, as already seen, they are real transactions and, if broken, have to be expiated, yet the final effect of Islam was to render them negligible. An oath is essentially the removal of oneself from the protection of one's patron deity or exposure of oneself to punishment by this deity. But God as conceived by the Muslims cannot be influenced in this way by a man's words and deeds. If it becomes clear to a man that something he has sworn to do is contrary to God's will or command, then it is right to break his oath; the breaking of the oath does not separate him from God (or make him liable to punishment) to the same extent as disobedience towards God.[4]

On the whole Islam has regarded the outward expression as the more important aspect. Where an idea—such as belief in the gods of paganism—had to be renounced, an outward act committing a man to the opposite course was demanded or at least encouraged. Idols had to be destroyed, both those of the clans and families and those in the great sanctuaries. New converts had to take part publicly in Islamic worship. On one occasion the leader of a tribe which on religious grounds did not eat the heart of animals was told that he would only be recognized as chief by Muḥammad and the Muslims if he ate a heart in their presence.[5] Muḥammad's own marriage with Zaynab, the divorced wife of his adopted son Zayd, was perhaps in part an attempt to demonstrate that such a marriage, though contrary to pre-Islamic taboos, led to no evil consequences.

At the same time, where a pagan practice had nothing obviously idolatrous in its outward form, it was comparatively easy for Islam to retain it. The typical act of *islām* or 'resigning oneself to God' was that of Abraham preparing to sacrifice his son in obedience to God though the act had no obvious utility.[6] Consequently, in accordance with this conception, it was possible for Islam to take over practices from pre-Islamic times with little modification, since

[1] Cf. Bousquet, op. cit. 114 f.; a Muslim friend, however, tells me that in practice nowadays most of the meat of the pilgrimage sacrifices is not consumed.

[2] 2. 271/273, 196/192; cf. *M/Mecca*, 168.

[3] Cf. Q. 2. 276/277; 30. 39/38; &c.

[4] Cf. J. Pedersen, *Der Eid bei den Semiten*, Strassburg, 1914, 194 ff., esp. 196; also Q. 2. 225; but cf. p. 328 below.

[5] IS, i/2. 62, &c.

[6] Esp. 37. 103, *aslamā*.

in order to become Islamic they did not require to have any meaning attached to them but only to be regarded as commands of God.

3. ISLAM AND CHRISTIANITY

The attitude of Islam to the two earlier monotheistic religions of the area was closely linked with practical questions. Relations with Jews and the Jewish religion have been sufficiently studied in Chapter VI. Something has also been said in Chapter IV about Muḥammad's dealings with Christian tribes, but the question of the Islamic attitude to Christianity, especially as it appears in the Qur'ān, is worthy of further consideration.

It is interesting to ask why Muḥammad did not become a Christian, for the attempt to answer this question brings to light important points that are liable to be overlooked. It might seem that if, as I have maintained, Muḥammad was concerned with the social and moral malaise of his time, and looked on the cause of this malaise as fundamentally religious, the simplest thing for him to do would have been to become a Christian or a Jew. Why did he not do this? The first part of the answer is that in one sense he did adopt the religion of Jews and Christians. He originally regarded the monotheism which he believed and preached as identical with the existing Jewish and Christian monotheism.[1] The creed of the Meccan prophet was not new in itself, but only in respect of its adoption and practice at Mecca. This conception of his relation to Judaism and Christianity was possible because direct contacts were few. There were a few Christians in Mecca, of whom one, Khadījah's cousin, Waraqah b. Nawfal, may have influenced Muḥammad considerably; but the majority were probably Abyssinian slaves and not well instructed in the faith.[2] Muḥammad would also have seen something of Christianity while trading in Syria. Until he went to Medina he may have had practically no contacts with Jews. In his first months at Medina he still hoped that the Medinan Jews would recognize his prophethood. His

[1] The account of the birth of Jesus in 19. 16–33/34 is in accordance with this conception.

[2] Cf. H. Lammens, 'Les Chrétiens à la Mecque à la veille de l'Hégire' in *L'Arabie occidentale à la veille de l'Hégire*, Beyrouth, 1928, 1–49; C. A. Nallino, *Raccolta di Scritti*, Rome, 1941, iii. 87–156, 'Ebrei e Cristiani nell' Arabia preislamica'; R. Devreesse, 'Le Christianisme dans la Province d'Arabie', *Vivre et Penser*, 2e série, Paris, 1942, 110–46.

approaches to Christian Arab tribes before the Hijrah[1] may have been based on a similar hope for recognition from them.

Thus for Muḥammad the question 'Should I become a Christian?' did not arise. If during his Meccan period, after he came forward publicly as a prophet, the matter had been raised, he would have said, 'I acknowledge Jesus the Messiah as a prophet, but my business is to preach a similar message to the people of Mecca and Arabia.' Before Muḥammad received any revelations the question might have arisen in the form, 'Should I go to some Christian teacher to learn more about God?' There is no reason for supposing that Muḥammad did not try to learn as much as possible from conversation with Christians such as Waraqah; but a prolonged visit to a seminary in Syria or to an outstanding bishop was impossible. Apart from any financial difficulties, such a visit would have had political implications; at the very least the person who acted in such a way would have become politically suspect to his fellows.[2] For the Arab of the Ḥijāz Christianity was above all the religion of the Abyssinians and the Byzantines. To ask formally for instruction and baptism would have been to open a channel to these foreign influences. It is significant that the opposition to Islam about the time of Muḥammad's death had as its religious focus several Arab prophets who were apparently independent of all foreign hierarchies.[3]

Once Muḥammad had received a number of revelations, it was impossible for him to accept in full the teaching of Christians and Jews without denying the truth of his own revelations.[4] Nevertheless he remained for long in friendly relations with Christians. The Negus of Abyssinia gave help and protection to the Muslims who 'emigrated' to his country. This friendship is reflected in the Qur'ān (5. 82/85 ff. F):

> Assuredly thou wilt find that the most violent of the people in enmity against the believers are the Jews and the idolaters, and thou wilt find the nearest in love to the believers to be those who say, 'We are Naṣārā (Christians)'; that is because there are amongst them priests and monks, and because they count not themselves great. When they hear what has been sent down (revealed) to the messenger (*sc.* Muḥammad), one sees their eyes overflowing with tears because of the truth which they recognize; they say, 'O our Lord, we believe, so write us

[1] Cf. *M/Mecca*, 140 f.
[2] Cf. ibid. 28.
[3] Cf. p. 148 above.
[4] Cf. Q. 2. 120/114; &c.

down among those who bear witness. Why should we not believe in God and the truth which has come to us, and crave that our Lord should cause us to enter with the upright folk?' So for what they have said, God has rewarded them with Gardens through which rivers flow, therein to abide; that is the recompense of those who do well.

While most of the Jews refused to acknowledge Muḥammad's prophethood, a mixed group of Christians is said to have accepted it shortly after Khaybar, and to have been the occasion for the revelation of 28. 52–54;[1] while Christians may well have accepted Muḥammad at that period, it is more likely that the verse is earlier and refers to some of the Jewish converts to Islam.[2]

The usual view expressed in the Qur'ān in the first few years after the Hijrah is that Christianity is a distinct religion parallel to Judaism and Islam.[3] The growth of hostility, however, between Muslims and Jews did not involve a deterioration of relations between Muslims and Christians. On the contrary, we find that stories of Jesus the Messiah ('Isā 'l-Masīḥ) are used in the Qur'ān as part of the intellectual attack on the Jews. He is represented as having gone to the children of Israel with a message from God confirmed by 'evidences' (*bayyināt*) and having been rejected by many of them.[4] It is significant that the twelve apostles are called the *anṣār* or 'helpers' of Jesus[5]—the name applied to the Arabs of Medina who supported Muḥammad and opposed the Jews; speakers of Arabic probably felt a connexion between this word and the Qur'ānic word for 'Christians', Naṣārā. Moreover a careful reading of the passage about the crucifixion of Jesus shows that it is not intended as a denial of Christian doctrine, but as a denial of a Jewish claim to have triumphed over the Christians, and it goes on to assert the superiority of the Christian hope.[6]

And for their (the Jews') saying, 'We killed the Messiah, Jesus the son of Mary, the messenger of God', though they did not kill him and did not crucify him, but he was counterfeited for them; verily those who have gone different ways in regard to him are in doubt about him; they have no (revealed) knowledge of him and only follow opinion; and certainly they did not kill him, but God raised him to Himself; God

[1] Al-Bayḍāwī, *ad. loc.*; not in aṭ-Ṭabarī.

[2] Ṭab., *Tafsīr*, xx. 51 f. mentions one Rifā'ah al-Quraẓī (perhaps b. Simwāl, cf. *Usd*, ii. 181), and also 'Abdallāh b. Sallām.

[3] 5. 46/50 f. EF; cf. 5. 69/73.

[4] 43. 63–65 E; 61.6 E; 5. 110/109–111 F.

[5] 3. 52/45–54/47 F—.

[6] 4. 157/156 f. F—; cf. 3. 55/48.

is sublime, wise. There is not one of the People of the Book but will surely believe in him before his death, and on the day of resurrection he will be a witness against (or regarding) them.

In the light of this favourable attitude to the Christians at a time when the Muslims were hostile to the Jews, we must conclude that many of the apparently early Medinan passages criticizing Jews and Christians were originally directed only against the Jews.[1] In 2. 135/129–141/135, for example, the reference to the Christians could be removed by the omission of a few words, and there is therefore a strong presumption that the passage was later 'revised' to make it apply to Christians as well as Jews. There are, of course, criticisms in the Qur'ān of doctrines specifically held by Christians (at least according to Arab ideas). The main point made in the Qur'ān is that Jesus and his mother are not gods,[2] since Jesus is in fact a created being.[3] The view rejected is that Jesus is 'a god' or 'God'; in the passages referred to there is no mention of Jesus as 'son of God'. The latter idea is also criticized in the Qur'ān, but it is given a minor place. The counter-assertion is made that God does not beget offspring.[4] This point was first developed as a criticism of the term 'daughters of God' applied to the pagan deities; and in passages denying that God has offspring the presumption is that the primary reference is to paganism unless there is a clear mention of Jesus.[5]

The dating of these passages in criticism of the Christians is uncertain. Part of the difficulty is that we do not know how far the Muslims were acquainted with Christian beliefs prior to the conquest of Mecca. They may not have realized that views resembling those mentioned were held by Christians; or they may have thought that such views were the aberrations of a minority, and that the great body of Christians regarded Jesus merely as a prophet. In a sense, indeed, it is true that the doctrines refuted by the Qur'ān, namely those of tritheism and of the physical sonship of Jesus, are aberrations and not Christian orthodoxy. Thus even if the passages criticizing these Christian views are early, they cannot be taken as evidence of a generally hostile attitude towards Christians. On the contrary, the presumption is that Muḥammad maintained friendly

[1] 2. 111/105, 120/114; 3. 67/60; 5. 18/21, 51/56.
[2] 5. 116–20; cf. 17/19.
[3] 3. 59/52 ff.; 43. 59.
[4] 19. 35/36; 4. 171/169.
[5] e.g. 10. 68/69; 37. 149 ff.; 39. 3/5 ff.; 43. 16/15 ff., 81 ff.

relations with the Negus of Abyssinia, at least until the return of the Muslims at the time of the expedition to Khaybar.

After the conquest of Mecca and battle of Ḥunayn the situation changed. Muḥammad began to have dealings with political groups which were wholly or mainly Christian. A letter from him to a a certain bishop Ḍughāṭir has been preserved,[1] and it looks like an attempt to state the tenets of Islam in such a way as to gain the bishop's support. It must soon have become clear, however, that some Christians, while ready to submit to Muḥammad's political demands, would never acknowledge him as a prophet to be followed. The criticisms of supposed Christian doctrines would be most relevant at this period. Political considerations, however, must have dominated Muḥammad's attitude to Christians. In southern and central Arabia the Christian tribes and clans made treaties with Muḥammad, and at least the weaker among them paid tribute to Medina. Along the route to Syria, however, there had been a resurgence of Byzantine influence and Muḥammad gained hardly any adherents here, although expansion into Syria and 'Irāq was a strategic necessity for him. The general attitude of Islam to Christians came to be determined largely by the attitude to these northern tribes, who were nearly all Christian, and friendship was replaced by hostility. A revelation came commanding war on them until they submitted.[2]

> Fight against those who do not . . . practice the religion of truth, of those who have been given the Book, until they pay the tribute (*jizyah*) off-hand, being subdued. The Jews say that 'Uzayr (Ezra) is the son of God, and the Christians say that the Messiah is the son of God; that is what they say with their mouths, conforming to what was formerly said by those who disbelieved; God fight them! How they are involved in lies! They take their scholars and their monks as Lords apart from God, as well as the Messiah, son of Mary, though they were only commanded to serve one God, besides Whom there is no god, glory be to Him above whatever they associate (with Him)! They would fain extinguish the light of God with their mouths, but God refuses to do otherwise than perfect His light, though the unbelievers are averse.

While parts of this passage were probably revealed on several different occasions, the passage as a whole marks the transition to a policy of hostility to the Christians. This policy found its expression

[1] IS, i/2. 28 (§ 43); translated on p. 358 below.
[2] 9. 29–35.

in the great expedition to Tabūk in 630/9,[1] and was continued not merely for the rest of Muḥammad's lifetime but also afterwards, at least until Syria had been completely subjugated. In so far as the passage prescribes hostility to the Byzantine empire and to Christians in general, it long continued to influence the Muslim attitude to the Christian church.

One of the remarkable features of the relationship between Muslims and Christians is that neither Muḥammad nor any of the Companions seems to have been aware of some of the fundamental Christian doctrines. Apart from the reference to the crucifixion (which is primarily a denial of a Jewish claim), and the mention of the twelve apostles as the 'helpers' of Jesus, and of miracles of healing and raising the dead, there is nothing in the Qur'ān about the adult life and teaching of Jesus as recorded in the New Testament. The early Muslims gave Jesus the title of Messiah (*Masīḥ*) but did not appreciate that it involved a claim to be 'God's anointed'. They did not understand the distinctive work of Jesus in redeeming the world and atoning for its sins. They did not realize that the Holy Spirit was regarded by Christians as the third person in the Godhead. It is indeed remarkable that there should have been among the Muslims over such a wide area this absence of knowledge of Christianity. The blame for this state of affairs probably rests on those Christians with whom Muḥammad and his Companions were in contact, who may themselves have had little appreciation of the doctrines mentioned. Nevertheless the 'absence of knowledge' remains, and in the thirteen centuries since Muḥammad's time few Muslims have done anything to fill in the lacuna.

[1] Cf. p. 116 above.

X

THE MAN AND HIS GREATNESS

1. APPEARANCE AND MANNER

SEVERAL accounts have been preserved of the appearance of Muḥammad, and, as they largely agree, they are perhaps near the truth, though there is a tendency in some of them to paint a picture of the ideal man.[1] According to these accounts Muḥammad was of average height or a little above the average. His chest and shoulders were broad, and altogether he was of a sturdy build. His arms, or perhaps rather forearms, were long, and his hands and feet rough. His forehead was large and prominent, and he had a hooked nose and large black eyes with a touch of brown. The hair of his head was long and thick, straight or slightly curled. His beard also was thick, and he had a thin line of fine hair on his neck and chest. His cheeks were spare, his mouth large, and he had a pleasant smile. In complexion he was fair. He always walked as if he were rushing downhill, and others had difficulty in keeping up with him. When he turned in any direction, he did so with his whole body.

He was given to sadness, and there were long periods of silence when he was deep in thought; yet he never rested but was always busy with something. He never spoke unnecessarily. What he said was always to the point and sufficient to make his meaning clear, but there was no padding. From first to last he spoke rapidly. Over his feelings he had a firm control.[2] When he was annoyed he would turn aside; when he was pleased, he lowered his eyes. His time was carefully apportioned according to the various demands on him. In his dealings with people he was above all tactful. He could be severe at times, but in the main he was not rough but gentle. His laugh was mostly a smile.[3]

[1] IS, i/2, 120–31; cf. WW, 349 f.

[2] But cf. WW, 373 f., where he strikes a man, perhaps because he was overstrained, and later gives him a present.

[3] The accounts of his aversion to poetry and inability to scan it may contain some truth but are suspect because of their 'tendency' to enhance the miraculous character of the Qur'ān. Cf. Q. 36. 69; IH, 882; WW. 376; Ibn Ḥanbal, *Musnad*, i. 134, 148, 189; &c. He certainly disliked hostile poets, but he encouraged favourable ones like Ḥassān b. Thābit, Ka'b b. Mālik, 'Abdallāh b. Rawāhah (IS, iii/1. 80 f.).

There are many stories illustrating his gentleness and tenderness of feeling. Even if some of them are not true, the probability is that the general picture is sound. There seems to be no reason, for instance, for doubting the truth of the story of how he broke the news of the death of Ja'far b. Abī Ṭālib to his widow Asmā' bint 'Umays; the story is said to have been told by Asmā' herself to her grand-daughter.[1] She had been busy one morning with her household duties, which had included tanning forty hides and kneading dough, when Muḥammad called. She collected her children—she had three sons by Ja'far—washed their faces and anointed them. When Muḥammad entered, he asked for the sons of Ja'far. She brought them, and Muḥammad put his arms round them and smelt them (as a mother would a baby). Then his eyes filled with tears and he burst out weeping. 'Have you heard something about Ja'far?', she asked, and he told her that he had been killed. Later he instructed some of his people to prepare food for Ja'far's household, 'for they are too busy today to think about themselves'. About the same time the little daughter of Zayd b. Ḥārithah (who had been killed along with Ja'far) came to him in tears to be comforted, and he wept along with her; afterwards, when questioned about this, he said it was because of the great love between Zayd and himself.[2] The memory of his first wife Khadījah could also soften his heart. After Badr the husband of his daughter Zaynab was among the prisoners taken by the Muslims, and Zaynab sent a necklace of Khadījah's to Muḥammad for a ransom, but he was so moved at the sight of it that he set the man free without payment.[3]

Muḥammad seems to have felt especial tenderness towards children, and to have got on well with them.[4] Perhaps it was an expression of the yearning of a man who had seen all his sons die in infancy. Much of his paternal affection went to his adopted son Zayd, who has just been mentioned. He was also attached to his nephew 'Alī b. Abī Ṭālib, who had been a member of his household for a time, but he doubtless realized that 'Alī had not the makings of a successful statesman. Among the stories showing his affection for children are some about his grand-daughter, Umāmah bint Abī 'l-'Āṣ (the daughter of Zaynab). He sometimes carried her on his shoulder during the Worship, setting her down when he bowed or prostrated, then picking her up again. On one occasion

[1] IS, viii. 206. [2] IS, iii/1. 32. 5. [3] WW, 77.
[4] I am indebted to Sir H. A. R. Gibb for calling my attention to this point.

he teased his wives by showing them a necklace and saying he would give it to the one who was dearest to him; when he thought their feelings were sufficiently agitated, he presented it not to any of them but to Umāmah.[1] He was also fond of Zayd's son Usāmah and took him on his camel for a bit when he returned from the battle of Badr.[2]

He was able to enter into the spirit of childish games and had many friends among children. 'Ā'ishah was still a child when he married her, and she continued to play with her toys. He would ask her what they were. 'Solomon's horses', she replied, and Muḥammad smiled.[3] He is even said to have had a game of 'spitting' with a child.[4] He had fun with the children who came back from Abyssinia and spoke Abyssinian.[5] We hear of a house in Medina where there was a small boy with whom he was accustomed to have jokes, for it is recorded that once he found the small boy looking very sad; when he asked what was the matter, he was told that his pet nightingale had died, and he did what he could to comfort him.[6] In view of all this kindness and liking for children, the following story may be true, even though it has a legal import. A baby was once brought to Muḥammad; he took it in his arms, and in due course it wet him. When the mother slapped it, he reproached her saying 'You have hurt my son', and—this is the legal point—refused to change his clothes to have them washed, since this was not necessary in the case of a boy baby.[7] His kindness extended even to animals, and this is something remarkable for Muḥammad's century and part of the world. As his men marched towards Mecca just before the conquest they passed a bitch with puppies, and Muḥammad not merely gave orders that they were not to be disturbed, but posted a man to see that the orders were carried out.[8]

These are interesting sidelights on the personality of Muḥammad, and fill out the picture of him we form from his conduct of public affairs. He gained men's respect and confidence by the religious basis of his activity and by such qualities as courage, resoluteness, impartiality, firmness inclining to severity but tempered by generosity. In addition to these, however, he had a

[1] IS, viii. 26 f.
[2] WW, 72.
[3] IS, viii. 42. 16; further references in N. Abbott, *Aishah*, 8.
[4] *Usd*, v. 393. 6 from foot.
[5] IS, iv/1. 72.
[6] IS, iii/2. 65. 12.
[7] IS, viii. 204.
[8] WW, 327.

charm of manner which won their affection and secured their devotion.

2. THE ALLEGED MORAL FAILURES

Of all the world's great men none has been so much maligned as Muḥammad. It is easy to see how this has come about. For centuries Islam was the great enemy of Christendom, for Christendom was in direct contact with no other organized states comparable in power to the Muslims. The Byzantine empire, after losing its provinces in Syria and Egypt, was being attacked in Asia Minor, while Western Europe was threatened through Spain and Sicily. Even before the Crusades focused attention on the expulsion of the Saracens from the Holy Land, medieval war-propaganda, free from the restraints of factuality, was building up a conception of 'the great enemy'. At one point Muḥammad was transformed into Mahound, the prince of darkness. By the eleventh century the ideas about Islam and Muslims current in the crusading armies were such travesties that they had a bad effect on morale. The crusaders had been led to expect the worst of their enemies, and, when they found many chivalrous knights among them, they were filled with distrust for the authorities of their own religion. It was to deal with this situation that Peter the Venerable started the process of disseminating more accurate information about Muḥammad and his religion. Since then much has been achieved, especially during the last two centuries or so, but many of the old prejudices linger on.[1]

In the modern world, where there are closer contacts than ever before between Christians and Muslims, it is urgent that both should strive to reach an objective view of Muḥammad's character. The denigration of him by European writers has too often been followed by romantic idealizations of his figure by other Europeans and by Muslims. The aim of the present discussion is to work towards a more objective attitude with regard to the moral criticisms inherited from medieval times The main points are three. Muḥammad has been alleged to be insincere, to be sensual, and to be treacherous.

[1] Cf. G. Pfannmüller, *Handbuch der Islamliteratur*, Berlin, 1923, 133–97; Montgomery Watt, 'Carlyle and Muhammad', *Hibbert Journal*, liii (1954–5), 247 ff.; the views of Islam taken by Latin writers from the twelfth to fourteenth centuries are studied by N. A. Daniel in an Edinburgh Ph.D. thesis.

The allegation of insincerity or imposture was vigorously attacked by Thomas Carlyle over a hundred years ago, has been increasingly opposed by scholarly opinion since then, and yet is still sometimes made. The extreme form of the view was that Muḥammad did not believe in his revelations and did not in any sense receive them from 'outside himself', but deliberately composed them, and then published them in such a way as to deceive people into following him, so gaining power to satisfy his ambition and his lust. Such a view is incredible. Above all it gives no satisfying explanation of Muḥammad's readiness to endure hardship in his Meccan days, of the respect in which he was held by men of high intelligence and upright character, and of his success in founding a world religion which has produced men of undoubted saintliness. These matters can only be satisfactorily explained and understood on the assumption that Muḥammad was sincere, that is, that he genuinely believed that what we now know as the Qur'ān was not the product of his own mind, but came to him from God and was true.

This conception of Muḥammad's sincerity, however, is open to possible misunderstandings and requires to be made more precise. Thus, to say that Muḥammad was sincere does not imply acceptance of the Qur'ān as a genuine revelation from God; a man may without contradiction hold that Muḥammad truly believed that he was receiving revelations from God but that he was mistaken in this belief. Further, once this point is grasped, it should be clear that, even if true, the alleged fact that the revelations fitted in with Muḥammad's desires and pandered to his selfish pleasure would not prove him insincere; it would merely show him to be capable of self-deception. The verses usually quoted in this connexion are 33. 37 f., justifying his marriage with Zaynab bint Jaḥsh, and 33. 50/49, granting him special marriage privileges. The affair of Zaynab will be considered presently, and it will be shown that Muḥammad was not merely yielding to selfish desires In connexion with the other verse 'Ā'ishah is said to have made the remark, 'God is in a hurry to satisfy your desires'.[1] Even if she really said this (and it is not a later invention), it would only show that she was suspicious of the correspondence between the revelation and Muḥammad's desires; but, as the remark itself suggests that she was

[1] IS, viii. 112. 5, 141. 2; Ibn Ḥanbal, vi. 134, 158; al-Bukhārī, *Tafsīr* (65) on Q. 33. 50/49.

jealous, she cannot be taken as an impartial witness On the contrary, if a remark like this could be made to Muḥammad without disturbing his belief in himself, that tends to confirm the view that he was sincere.

Again, the theory held by Richard Bell and others, that Muḥammad 'revised' passages of the Qur'ān, is not necessarily at variance with a belief in his sincerity. The revision, if it may be so called, consists in the addition or omission of words, phrases, and longer passages. Muḥammad may be presumed to have regarded these changes as emendations communicated to him by God to meet fresh circumstances. A certain amount of revision is admitted by Muslim orthodoxy in its doctrine that some verses have been abrogated, that is, have ceased to be applicable to the Muslims. Additions could be justified in a similar way; for example, God could reveal to Muḥammad that the words 'and Christians' were to be added to a verse about Jews, and the justification for the change would be that, whereas the Muslims had at first to deal only with Jews, latterly they had to deal with Christians also; the words 'and Christians' might simply have been confusing if included in the original revelation at a time when they had no practical application. Muḥammad had possibly some technique of 'listening' or 'waiting' for an emending revelation, and he may have employed this also when there was a topic on which he felt that a revelation was desirable. Whatever his technique, however, when words 'came to him' he had some means of knowing when they were from God. To say he was sincere is simply to hold that, when he had thus recognized words as being from God, he really believed that they were so, and did not confuse them with his own thoughts.

There are no sufficient grounds, then, for regarding Muḥammad as an impostor. On the contrary, the case for his sincerity is strong. A high degree of certainty is attainable here, since the discussion, unlike that of the other two moral criticisms, is at a factual level and does not involve any dispute about moral standards. In other words, if it could be shown that Muḥammad, in full knowledge that the contents of the Qur'ān were the product of his own mind, gave out that they were revelations to him from God, that would be imposture and would be generally recognized as a serious moral defect.

When we come to the other two allegations, however, namely,

that Muḥammad was morally defective in that he was treacherous and sensual, the discussion has to embrace not merely factual points, but also the question of the standard by which the acts have to be judged. On the factual side, there is agreement on such acts as his breaking of the treaty of al-Ḥudaybiyah and his marriage to Zaynab, the divorced wife of his adopted son, but there is ample room for dispute about circumstances and motives. With regard to standards there are two main possibilities: we may ask, 'Was Muḥammad a good man according to the standards of the Arabia of his day?', or we may ask, 'Was he a good man according to the standards of, say, the best people in Europe about the year 1950?' Let us begin, then, by trying to answer the first of these questions with special reference to the two points of criticism.

The allegation of treachery may be taken to cover a number of criticisms made by European writers. It applies most clearly to such acts as the breaking of his agreements with the Jews and his one-sided denunciation of the treaty of al-Ḥudaybiyah with the Meccans.[1] It may also, however, be taken to include the infringement either of the sacred month or of the sacred territory on the expedition to Nakhlah when the first Meccan blood was shed, the mass execution of the Jewish clan of Qurayẓah, and the orders or encouragement given to his followers to remove dangerous opponents by assassination.[2]

In all these actions there was nothing which disturbed the conscience of Muḥammad's followers apart from the events at Nakhlah. This may seem incredible to the European, but that is in itself a measure of the remoteness of the moral ideals of ancient Arabia from our own. In some respects the nomadic Arabs had a high ideal of conduct, but they had no idea whatsoever of a minimum standard of decent behaviour towards all men, simply because they were men. They had no conception of a universal moral law of the Kantian type. There were customary duties and obligations within the tribe (and this included those attached to the tribe as confederates, clients, or slaves); related to these matters was an ideal of honourable conduct. Outside the tribe, however, there were no duties or obligations. You could do what you liked with an unprotected stranger. When you were at war with another tribe, it was a case of 'nothing barred'. The only restraints on your

[1] Cf. pp. 208 ff., 63 above.
[2] Cf. pp. 8, 214, 15 above.

behaviour towards an enemy or even a stranger were those set by fear of retaliation or fear of supernatural powers.

Now the Islamic community or *ummah* was thought of as a tribe. Towards tribes with which it had agreements, it had duties and obligations, and these were scrupulously observed according to the standards of the day; Muḥammad even paid blood-money to a man who was really but not technically responsible for the death of several Muslims.[1] Where a tribe was at war with the Muslims, however, or had no agreement, they had no obligations towards it even of what we would call common decency. If contemporaries showed some surprise at the execution of all the males of Qurayẓah, it was because Muḥammad was not afraid of any consequences of such an act; the behaviour of Qurayẓah during the siege of Medina was regarded as having cancelled their agreement with Muḥammad. Similarly, the terms of the treaty of al-Ḥudaybiyah had been broken by the Meccans before Muḥammad denounced it, and the individuals who were assassinated had forfeited any claim to friendly treatment by Muḥammad through their propaganda against him. So far were the Muslims who killed them from feeling any qualms that one of them, describing the return from the deed, wrote that they returned with the head of their victim 'five honourable men, steady and true, and God was the sixth with us'.[2] This is so much in keeping with the spirit of pre-Islamic times that it is almost certainly authentic; but, even if not, it shows the attitude of the early Muslims.

One point at which the actions of Muḥammad or the Muslims were disapproved for no merely selfish reasons was the expedition to Nakhlah. The disapproval, however, was not on moral but on religious grounds; something sacred had been violated, and those who disapproved were presumably afraid of supernatural punishment. In this instance Muḥammad deliberately decided in the end to oppose public opinion, believing that he was thereby following God's command and attacking a pagan superstition. In the circumstances, then, Muḥammad's conduct is that of a moral reformer and not of a wicked man. Similarly, in respect of oaths, the religious aspect was probably more important than the purely moral one. The Qur'ān (66. 2) permits the annulling of oaths, and for reasons already suggested oaths came to have little importance in Islam.[3]

[1] Cf. p. 32 above.

[2] WK, 190; WW, 97; cf. Q. 58. 7/8.

[3] Cf. p. 314 and n. 4 above.

In so far as the keeping of one's word in pre-Islamic times had been associated with pagan deities, and since oaths by God did not fully take the place of pagan oaths, there may have been a vacuum in which there were no effective sanctions for keeping one's word.

Again, the common European and Christian criticism that Muḥammad was a sensualist or, in the blunter language of the seventeenth century, an 'old lecher', fades away when examined in the light of the standards of Muḥammad's time. There was a strain in early Muslim thought which tended to magnify the common—or perhaps we should say 'superhuman'—humanity of their prophet. There is even a tradition to the effect that his virility was such that he was able to satisfy all his wives in a single night.[1] This looks like an invention, for the usual account is that he gave his wives a night each in turn, but it shows the outlook of some at least of his followers. The early Muslims looked askance at celibacy and checked any movements towards it, and even rigorous ascetics in Islam have commonly been married. Compared with the late king ʿAbd al-ʿAzīz of Arabia, known as Ibn Saʿūd, Muḥammad was temperate in the matter of wives. His contemporaries thought none the less of him for the multiplicity of his marital relations; to them it would be no more than what was befitting a man of his political power. These contemporaries or their immediate successors even seem to have touched up the stories about his relations with women, such as those about the jealousies in his hareem and his 'love at first sight' for Zaynab.

The one point of this kind on which Muḥammad was criticized by his contemporaries was his marriage with Zaynab bint Jaḥsh. Zaynab was Muḥammad's cousin, being the daughter of his father's sister. At the time of the Hijrah she was either unmarried or (more probably) a widow, and she went to Medina, presumably with her brothers. Muḥammad made her, against her will, marry his adopted son, Zayd b. Ḥārithah. Some time afterwards, about the year 626/4 Muḥammad called at Zayd's house to talk to him; Zayd was out, but he saw Zaynab in disarray, and is supposed to have been smitten by love for her. He went away saying to himself, 'Praise be to God, praise to the Manager of Hearts!' Zaynab told Zayd about Muḥammad's visit, his refusal to enter, and his cryptic utterance. Zayd at once went to Muḥammad and offered to divorce Zaynab, but Muḥammad told him to keep his wife. After this,

[1] IS, i/2. 96.

however, life with Zaynab became unbearable for Zayd, and he divorced her. After her waiting-period (*'iddah*) had been observed, a marriage with Muḥammad was arranged, and justified by a revelation.[1]

About the main outline of the story there can be little dispute, but the significance of the various actions is a matter for discussion. One point is tolerably certain, and that is the reason for the criticism of Muḥammad's action by his contemporaries. They were not moved in the slightest by what some Europeans have regarded as the sensual and voluptuous character of his behaviour. They were opposed to the marriage because in their eyes it was incestuous. This view of the marriage was doubtless based on the Qur'ān,[2] in conjunction with the old principle that an adopted son counted as a real son. We cannot be certain of all that is involved, but the most natural explanation of the Qur'ānic passages is to suppose that there was something objectionable about the equating of adoptive sons with real sons, and that it was desirable that there should be a complete break with the past in this respect.[3] The Qur'ān implies that Muḥammad had originally been unwilling to marry Zaynab and afraid of public opinion, but had come to acknowledge the marriage as a duty imposed on him by God; his marriage demonstrated to the believers that there was no blame in marrying the divorced wife of an adoptive son.[4] The criticism of Muḥammad, then, was based on a pre-Islamic idea that was rejected by Islam, and one aim of Muḥammad in contracting the marriage was to break the hold of the old idea over men's conduct. How important was this aim compared with others which he might have had?

It is not too much to say that *all* Muḥammad's marriages had a political aspect.[5] There is therefore a strong presumption that in the case of Zaynab bint Jaḥsh Muḥammad was not carried away by passion but was looking at the political implications of the match.

[1] IH, 1002; IS, viii. 71, 81; Q. 33. 37; Caetani, i. 610 f.; Abbott, *Aishah*, 16–18.

[2] 4. 23/27; cf. p. 280 above. Cf. also Wellhausen, 'Die Ehe bei den Arabern', 441, n. 3.

[3] 33. 4 f. S. Kohn, *Die Eheschließung im Koran*, 12, notes that if Muḥammad had merely wanted to marry Zaynab, he could have made this a *khāliṣah*, special privilege, for himself; since he made it a general rule, other points must be involved. Cf. G. H. Bousquet, in *Studia Islamica*, ii. 78.

[4] 33. 37.

[5] Cf. p. 287 above.

There are two points of importance: Zaynab was a close relative of Muḥammad's, and her family were, or had been, confederates of Abū Sufyān's father. As Zaynab's marriage took place long before that with Abū Sufyān's daughter and at a time when Abū Sufyān was directing the Meccan campaign against Muḥammad, this aspect of the match cannot have escaped Muḥammad. It is also clear, however, from the records that he used the marriages of his cousins, like those of his daughters, for political ends. Just as Fāṭimah was married to ʿAlī, and Ruqayyah and later Umm Kulthum to ʿUthmān b. ʿAffān, so Ḥamnah bint Jaḥsh was married after Uḥud to Ṭalḥah b. ʿUbaydallāh and Ḥabībah bint Jaḥsh to ʿAbd ar-Raḥmān b. ʿAwf. There can therefore be no doubt that the marriage of Zaynab to Zayd was part of this scheme of alliances, since Zayd was a prominent man in the community, in some ways as prominent as Abū Bakr.

Beyond this point doubts increase. Why was Zaynab unwilling to marry Zayd? She can hardly have thought that he was not good enough. She was an ambitious woman, however, and may already have hoped to marry Muḥammad; or she may have wanted to marry someone with whom Muḥammad did not want his family to be so closely allied. After the incident of Muḥammad's visit to Zayd's house, Zaynab clearly worked for marriage with Muḥammad. What of Muḥammad's reasons for marrying her at this particular time? It cannot be that Zayd was declining in his favour, because in 627/6 and subsequent years Zayd led several expeditions, including the large one to Mu'tah on which he met his death. Perhaps he realized that she was tired of Zayd, and had no follower worthy of becoming her husband. Perhaps he felt that the time had come when he was strong enough to go against public opinion and contract this marriage that was politically and socially desirable. Despite the stories, then, it is unlikely that he was swept off his feet by the physical attractiveness of Zaynab. The other wives are said to have feared her beauty; but her age when she married Muḥammad was thirty-five, or perhaps rather thirty-eight, which is fairly advanced for an Arab woman.[1] The only one of his wives who was older at marriage was Khadījah.

In general, then, there was nothing in Muḥammad's marital

[1] IS, viii. 81 f.; she is said to have been 35 when she married Muḥammad in A.H. 5, but she is also said to have been 'thirty odd' at the Hijrah and 53 when she died in A.H. 20.

relationships which his contemporaries regarded as incompatible with his prophethood. They did not consider him a voluptuary any more than they considered him a scoundrel. The sources record criticisms of him, but these are based on no moral criterion, but on a conservatism which was akin to superstition. Though later Muslims might produce colourful stories of Muḥammad's susceptibility to feminine charm, and though there is no reason to suppose that he disregarded the factor of physical attraction, it is practically certain that he had his feelings towards the fair sex well under control, and that he did not enter into marriages except when they were politically and socially desirable.

It is possible, too, to go further and, while restricting oneself to the standpoint of Muḥammad's time, to turn the alleged instances of treachery and sensuality into matter for praise. In his day and generation Muḥammad was a social reformer, indeed a reformer even in the sphere of morals. He created a new system of social security and a new family structure, both of which were a vast improvement on what went before. In this way he adapted for settled communities all that was best in the morality of the nomad, and established a religious and social framework for the life of a sixth of the human race today. That is not the work of a traitor or a lecher.

It may be remarked at this point that there are no solid grounds for thinking that Muḥammad's character declined after the Hijrah. Too facile a use has been made of the principle that all power corrupts and that absolute power corrupts absolutely. The allegations of moral defects are attached to incidents belonging to the Medinan and not the Meccan period; yet, if the exposition just given of these incidents is sound, they marked no failure in Muḥammad to live up to his ideals but were in accordance with his moral principles. As the ruler of Medina was a man of his time, so also was the persecuted preacher of Mecca. If nothing is recorded of the preacher to show us how different his attitude was from that of nineteenth-century Europe, it does not follow that his ideals were any loftier than those of the reforming ruler. The opposite is more likely to be the case in so far as the preacher was nearer to the pagan background. In both Meccan and Medinan periods Muḥammad's contemporaries looked on him as a good and upright man, and in the eyes of history he is a moral and social reformer.

Up to this point Muḥammad has been considered only in relation to the moral standards of his time, but there is also another way of judging him, namely, by a universal moral standard. I do not propose here to attempt any judgement of this sort, but shall be content if I have fairly presented the evidence on which such a judgement must be based. The readers of this book will presumably include Christians and Muslims of many different shades of opinion, as well as persons who are neither, and, even if there is a wide area of agreement between them, there are also differences which make it impossible in a book like this adequately to meet all the objections that any such judgement would arouse. There is one thing, however, which may be said in this connexion.

The world is becoming increasingly one world, and in this one world there is a tendency towards unification and uniformity. Because of this tendency the day will doubtless come when there will be a set of moral principles which not merely claim universal validity but are actually accepted almost universally throughout the one world. Now Muslims claim that Muḥammad is a model of conduct and character for all mankind. In so doing they invite world opinion to pass judgement upon him. Up till now the matter has received scant attention from world opinion, but, because of the strength of Islam, it will eventually have to be given serious consideration. Are any principles to be learnt from the life and teaching of Muḥammad that will contribute to the one morality of the future?

To this question the world has not yet given a final answer. What has been said so far by Muslims in support of their claims for Muḥammad can be regarded as no more than a preliminary statement of the case, and few non-Muslims have been convinced by it. Nevertheless the issue still remains open. How the world answers the question about Muḥammad depends to some extent on what the Muslims of today do. They still have an opportunity to give a fuller and better presentation of their case to the rest of the world. Will they be able to turn to the life of Muḥammad and by sifting the universal in it from the particular discover moral principles which make a creative contribution to the present world situation? Or, if this is too much to expect, will they at least be able to show that Muḥammad's life is one possible exemplification of the ideal man in the unified world morality? If they make a good case, there are some Christians who will be ready to listen to them and to learn whatever is to be learned.

The difficulties confronting Muslims, however, are immense. A combination of sound scholarship and deep moral insight is essential, and this combination is rare. I will not conceal my personal view that Muslims are unlikely to be successful in their attempt to influence world opinion, at least in the sphere of morals. In the wider sphere of religion they have probably something to contribute to the world, for they have retained emphases—on the reality of God, for example—which have been neglected or forgotten in important sections of the other monotheistic religions; and I for one gladly acknowledge my indebtedness to the writings of a man like al-Ghazālī. Towards convincing Christian Europe that Muḥammad is a moral exemplar, however, little, indeed nothing, has so far been accomplished.

3. THE FOUNDATIONS OF GREATNESS

Circumstances of place and time favoured Muḥammad. Various forces combined to set the stage for his life-work and for the subsequent expansion of Islam. There was the social unrest in Mecca and Medina, the movement towards monotheism, the reaction against Hellenism in Syria and Egypt, the decline of the Persian and Byzantine empires, and a growing realization by the nomadic Arabs of the opportunities for plunder in the settled lands round them. Yet these forces, and others like them which might be added, would not in themselves account for the rise of the empire known as the Umayyad caliphate nor for the development of Islam into a world religion. There was nothing inevitable or automatic about the spread of the Arabs and the growth of the Islamic community. But for a remarkable combination of qualities in Muḥammad it is improbable that the expansion would have taken place, and these vast forces might easily have spent themselves in raids on Syria and ʿIrāq without any lasting consequences. In particular we may distinguish three great gifts Muḥammad had, each of which was indispensable to the total achievement.

First there is what may be called his gift as a seer. Through him —or, on the orthodox Muslim view, through the revelations made to him—the Arab world was given an ideological framework within which the resolution of its social tensions became possible. The provision of such a framework involved both insight into the fundamental causes of the social malaise of the time, and the genius to express this insight in a form which would stir the hearer to the depths of his being. The European reader may be 'put off' by the Qur'ān, but it was admirably suited to the needs and conditions of the day.

Secondly, there is Muḥammad's wisdom as a statesman. The conceptual structure found in the Qur'ān was merely a framework. The framework had to support a building of concrete policies and concrete institutions. In the course of this book much has been said about Muḥammad's far-sighted political strategy and his social reforms. His wisdom in these matters is shown by the rapid expansion of his small state to a world-empire and by the adaptation of his social institutions to many different environments and their continuance for thirteen centuries.

Thirdly, there is his skill and tact as an administrator and his wisdom in the choice of men to whom to delegate administrative details. Sound institutions and a sound policy will not go far if the execution of affairs is faulty and fumbling. When Muḥammad died, the state he had founded was a 'going concern', able to withstand the shock of his removal and, once it had recovered from this shock, to expand at prodigious speed.

The more one reflects on the history of Muḥammad and of early Islam, the more one is amazed at the vastness of his achievement. Circumstances presented him with an opportunity such as few men have had, but the man was fully matched with the hour. Had it not been for his gifts as seer, statesman, and administrator and, behind these, his trust in God and firm belief that God had sent him, a notable chapter in the history of mankind would have remained unwritten. It is my hope that this study of his life may contribute to a fresh appraisal and appreciation of one of the greatest of the 'sons of Adam'.

EXCURSUS A

Further Remarks on the Sources

LITTLE need be added to what was said about the sources in the Introduction to *Muhammad at Mecca.*[1] There are one or two points, however, which will bear further emphasis.

The first point is the relation of the Qur'ān to the other source-material. I have made use of the Qur'ān wherever possible, but the small proportion of references to it will make it clear that the historian has to rely mainly on other material. Nevertheless, so far as it goes, the Qur'ān is a first-hand witness, especially to the contemporary feelings of the Muslim community about various events. It is also the main witness for the reform of the social system. The passages revealed at Medina can frequently be dated on the basis of internal evidence. The most complete and satisfactory attempt to do this is that of Richard Bell in his translation of the Qur'ān. In several places where the dating was not obvious the investigations involved in writing this book have confirmed Bell's results (which were presumably reached along different lines); and I have therefore adopted the position that in general his dating is to be regarded as authoritative.[2]

The sources other than the Qur'ān may be termed collectively 'the traditional historical material'. In *Muhammad at Mecca*[3] the attitude taken towards this material was that in general it is to be accepted; only where there is internal contradiction is it to be rejected; where 'tendential shaping' is suspected it is as far as possible to be corrected. Perhaps the coherence of the resulting account of Muḥammad's career will be accepted as an additional argument for the soundness of this procedure. An important application of the principle adopted is the acceptance as genuine of Muḥammad's letters and treaties (with the exception of the first seven) as reproduced by Ibn Saʿd (i/2).

While, then, the traditional historical material is to be regarded as in general sound, a distinction must be made within it between material concerning disputed points and material where there is no reference to any disputed point. This distinction may be roughly

[1] pp. xi–xvi.

[2] For the system of indicating it see p. xiii above.

[3] p. xiv.

described as one between legal material and historical material. Where an anecdote about Muḥammad involved legal issues disputed between rival schools, it was liable to be twisted a little by each to make it support their views. This has happened very often in traditions with a legal bearing, but it is also found where the point at issue is rather theological or political. Thus in the story of Muḥammad's call[1] he is stated to have used the words *mā aqra'u* which may mean either 'I cannot read' or 'What am I to recite?' The latter is probably the original meaning, but certain later theologians insisted on Muḥammad's inability to read as a confirmation of the doctrine of the miraculous nature of the Qur'ān, and versions are found where words have been substituted which can only mean 'I cannot read' (viz. *mā anā bi-qārin*). The story has thus been given a little twist in order to make a theological point. At the same time rival theologians have given it a little twist in the other direction by replacing *mā* by *mādhā*, so that it can only mean 'What shall I recite?' Again, the remark of Muḥammad about Sa'd b. Mu'ādh when he was about to judge the case of Banū Qurayẓah, 'Stand for your chief' (*sayyid*), could be taken to justify the view that the Anṣār were capable of ruling over Quraysh, and the story was therefore twisted in various ways to remove this implication.[2]

On the other hand, where a story involved no disputed point of this sort, the presumption is that it was not twisted, or at least not twisted to the same extent. Details of how an ancestor behaved during Muḥammad's lifetime would often be preserved in a clan or family, and naturally they would dwell on what glorified the descendants and omit anything of an opposite character. Such exaggerations and omissions, however, are much easier to correct than the twists given to stories in legal and other disputes. The critique of Islamic traditions by European scholars, notably Ignaz Goldziher in his *Muhammedanische Studien* and Joseph Schacht in his *Origins of Muḥammadan Jurisprudence*, has been based mainly on the legal traditions found in the standard collections by al-Bukhārī, Muslim and others, that is, on the section of the traditional historical material where distortion is most to be expected. It is thus not surprising if sceptical views about the

[1] *M/Mecca*, 46.

[2] Cf. Montgomery Watt, 'The Condemnation of the Jews of Banū Qurayẓah' *Muslim World*, xlii, 1952, 164.

traditions have resulted. If, however, one considers the undisputed or purely historical section of the traditional historical material, it is apparent that there is a solid core of fact.[1]

The process of transmission may be conceived somewhat as follows. To begin with the stories would be handed down informally in families and clans, and from the older men and women to younger acquaintances. Before the end of the first Islamic century, however, a few persons had begun to collect all the information they could about the life and campaigns of Muḥammad, and some at least wrote down what they had collected. These early collectors of information, however, though they seem to have scrutinized their sources carefully and sometimes stated what they were, did not in every case give a complete *isnād* or chain of authorities going back to an eye-witness of the events. It was only gradually that the complete *isnād* became *de rigueur*. Ibn Isḥāq, working in the second quarter of the second Islamic century (middle of the eighth century A.D.), usually gives his authorities, but not always a complete chain, and he does not always repeat the words of the authority verbatim. Al-Wāqidī, half a century later, is similar in method, but his secretary and follower, Ibn Saʿd, some twenty years younger, always attempts to quote exactly and to give a complete chain of authorities. The insistence on complete chains is to be associated with the teaching of ash-Shāfiʿī,[2] who was roughly a contemporary of al-Wāqidī. Once it became fashionable to give complete *isnāds*, scholars must have been tempted to extend their chains backwards to contemporaries of Muḥammad. Even when they thus added to the chains, however, their additions may have been sound, since they probably knew in a general way where their predecessors had obtained information. This means only that we cannot rely so fully on the early links of a chain as on the later ones.[3]

[1] Cf. Montgomery Watt, op. cit. 171. The distinction was noted by J. Horovitz, 'Alter und Ursprung des Isnad', *Der Islam*, viii (1918), 39.

[2] Cf. Schacht, op. cit.

[3] Cf. *Muslim World*, l.c. For earlier discussion of the sources cf. J. Fück, *Muḥammad b. Isḥaq*, Frankfürt, 1925; J. Horovitz, 'The Earliest Biographies of the Prophet and their Authors', *Islamic Culture*, i (1927), 535–59; J. Schacht on Mūsā b. 'Uqbah in *Acta Orientalia*, xxi (1953), 288–300; A. Guillaume in a forthcoming volume on Ibn Isḥāq.

EXCURSUS B

List of Expeditions and Dates

No independent chronological investigations have been undertaken in connexion with this study of the life of Muḥammad, since the disputed points hardly affect the general picture. The first main point in dispute is whether the Muslims observed intercalary months during the first ten years at Medina. Intercalation was forbidden at the pilgrimage at the end of the year 10, and therefore it may be taken as certain that the first day of the year 11 corresponded to 29 March 632. Without intercalation, then, the beginning of the era of the Hijrah (that is, the first day of the year in which Muḥammad migrated to Medina) would be on 16 July 622. Even if the Muslims observed intercalary months (presumably three) during the ten years, it is almost certain that statements in the sources are made on the basis of orthodox Muslim reckoning, with no intercalation, since scholars in the second Islamic century would overlook intercalation or deliberately reject it. Orthodox reckoning also fits in best with a number of statements in the sources.[1]

The order and dating of some of the separate expeditions is the other main point of dispute. Ibn Isḥāq gives a number of dates, but the first complete chronology is that in al-Wāqidī. The best course is that adopted by Leone Caetani, namely, to follow al-Wāqidī as a general rule where there are discrepancies between him and Ibn Isḥāq.[2] The Shīʿite leanings of al-Wāqidī presumably do not affect his chronology.

A	B	C	D	E	F	G	H	I
Date[3]		*Destination or Name*	*Opponents*	*Leader*	*Number of participants*	*Result*	*References*	
A.H.	A.D.						*IH*	*WW*
1	**622**							
1/1	16/7	Beginning of era of Hijrah		..	..	..	..	
12/3	24/9	Hijrah, arrival in Qubā'			..	..	..	..
—	**623**							
9	3	Sīf al-Baḥr	Quraysh	Ḥamzah	30	no fighting	419–21	33

[1] For a defence of this position see Caetani, *Ann.* i. 345–60. The position is apparently admitted by H. Amīr 'Alī, 'The First Decade in Islam', *Muslim World*, xliv. 136.

[2] The discrepancies are discussed by Caetani, *Ann.* i. 466, 519 f., 575, 577, ii. 509 f., &c. The following list is based on his *Annali*; cf. his *Chronographia Islamica*, Paris, 1912, i.

[3] Heavier type indicates years and normal type months. The day of the month

A	B	C	D	E	F	G	H	I
Date							*References*	
A.H.	A.D.	*Destination or Name*	*Opponents*	*Leader*	*Number of participants*	*Result*	*IH*	*WW*
10	4	Rābigh	Quraysh	'Ubaydah	60–80	no fighting	416–18	33
11	5	al-Kharrār	,,	Sa'd b. Abī Waqqāṣ	20 (or 8)	no contact	422 f.	33 f.
2	—							
2	8	al-Abwā'	,,	Muḥammad	60	no contact	415 f.	34
3	9	Buwāṭ	,,	,,	200	no contact	421	34
3	9	Safwān	Kurz al-Fihrī	,,	..	failed to overtake	423	34
6	12	al-'Ushayrah	Quraysh	,,	150–200	no contact	421 f.	34
—	**624**							
7	1	Nakhlah	,,	'Abdallāh b. Jaḥsh	7–12	one enemy killed	423–7	34–37
19/9	15/3	Badr	,,	Muḥammad	c. 315	victory	427–539	37–90
9	3	..	'Aṣmā'	'Umayr	1	successful	995 f.	90 f.
10	4	..	Abū 'Afak	Sālim	1	,,	994 f.	91 f.
10	4	..	Qaynuqā'	Muḥammad	..	expelled	545–7	92–94
1/2	5–6	(Sawīq)	Quraysh	,,	200 or 400	enemy retreated	543 f.	94
3	—							
1	7	al-Kudr	Sulaym, Ghaṭafān	,,	200	some booty	539 f.	94 f.
3	8-9	..	Ka'b b. al-Ashraf	Muḥammad b. Maslamah?	5	successful	548–55	95–99
3	9	Dhū Amarr	Tha'labah, Muḥārib	Muḥammad	450	? no contact but converts	544	99 f.
5	10–11	Buḥrān	Sulaym	,,	300	enemy dispersed	544	100
6	11	al-Qaradah	Quraysh	Zayd b. Ḥārithah	100	caravan captured	547 f.	100 f.
—	**625**							
7/10	23/3	Uḥud	,,	Muḥammad	1,000	battle	555–638	101–48
10	3	Ḥamrā' al-Asad	,,	,,	c. 900	enemy retreated	588–90	149–51
4	—							
1	6	Qaṭan	Asad	Abū Salamah	150	booty	975	151–3
(?) 1	6	..	Sufyān al-Liḥyānī	'Abdallāh b. Unays	1	successful	981–3	224 f.
2	7	Bi'r Ma'ūnah	Sulaym ('Āmir)	al-Mundhir b. 'Amr	40–70	Muslims killed	648–52	153–6
2	7	ar-Rajī'	Liḥyān (Khuzaymah)	Marthad al-Ghanawī	7–10	Muslims ambushed	638–48	156–60
3	8	..	an-Naḍīr	Muḥammad	..	expelled	652–61	160–7
—	**626**							
11	4	Badr al-Maw'id	Quraysh	,,	1,500	no contact	666–8	167–70
12	5	..	Abū Rāfi'	'Abdallāh b. Unays	5	successful	981	170–2

is occasionally placed before a stroke; thus 16/7 means the 16th day of the seventh month (that is, in Christian dates, July). Where the disagreement between the Muslim and Christian months was slight, it has been neglected.

A	B	C	D	E	F	G	H	I
Date							*References*	
A.H.	A.D.	*Destination or Name*	*Opponents*	*Leader*	*Number of participants*	*Result*	*IH*	*WW*
5	—							
1	6	Dhāt ar-Riqā'	Anmār, Tha'labah	Muḥammad	400–800	no contact	661–5	172–4
3–4	8–9	Dūmat al-Jandal	tribes towards Syria	,,	1,000	some booty	668	174 f.
—	**627**							
8	1	al-Muraysī'	al-Muṣṭaliq	,,	..	much booty	725–40	175–90
11	4	al-Khandaq (siege)	Quraysh	,,	3,000	besiegers retreated	668–713	190–210
11–12	5	..	Qurayẓah	,,	3,000	surrendered	684–93	210–21
6	—							
1	6	al-Qurṭā	Muḥārib?	Muḥammad b. Maslamah	30	booty	975	226
3	7	..	Liḥyān	Muḥammad	200	no contact	718 f.	226 f.
4	8	al-Ghābah (Dhū Qarad)	Ghaṭafān	,,	500–700	slight fighting	719–25	227–32
4	8–9	al-Ghamr	Asad	'Ukkāshah	40	booty	975	232
4	8–9	Dhū'l-Qaṣṣah	Tha'labah, &c.	Muḥammad b. Maslamah	10	Muslims surprised	..	232 f.
4	8–9	,,	,,	Abū 'Ubaydah	40	enemy dispersed	973	233
(?) 4	9	al-Jamūm[1]	Sulaym	Zayd b. Ḥārithah	..	booty	..	..
5	9–10	al-'Īṣ	Quraysh	,,	170	caravan taken	469 f.	233 f.
6	10–11	aṭ-Ṭaraf	Tha'labah	,,	*c.* 15	booty	979	234
6	10–11	Ḥismā	Judhām	,,	500	booty (later returned)	975–9	234–6
7	11–12	Wādi 'l-Qurā	(Badr b. Fazārah)	,,	..	Muslims ambushed	..	(236)
8	12–1	Dūmat al-Jandal	Kalb	'Abd ar-Raḥman b. 'Awf	700	Kalb submitted	..	236 f.
8	12–1	Fadak	Sa'd	'Alī	100	booty	975	237 f.
—	**628**							
9	1–2	(Umm Qirfah)	Badr b. Fazārah	Zayd b. Ḥārithah	..	Badr punished	980	238 f.
10	2–3	Khaybar	Usayr b. Rāzim	'Abdallāh b. Rawāḥah	30	successful	980–7	239 f.
10	2–3	(al-Ḥarrah)	'Uraynah	Kurz al-Fihrī (?)	20	robbers punished	999	240 f.
?	?	..	Madyan[2]	Zayd b. Ḥārithah	..	booty	..	..
11	3	al-Ḥudaybiyah	Quraysh	Muḥammad	700–1,600	treaty	740–55	241–64
7	—							
(?) 1	5–6	Khaybar	Jews	,,	? 1,600	captured	755–81	264–96
1	5–6	Najd[3]	..	Abān b. Sa'īd	..	..	..	..

[1] Cf. Caetani, i. 694 f. [2] Ibid. 705. [3] Ibid. ii. 56.

A	B	C	D	E	F	G	H	I
Date		*Destination or Name*	*Opponents*	*Leader*	*Number of participants*	*Result*	*References*	
A.H.	A.D.						*IH*	*WW*
8	12	Turbah	Hawāzin	ʿUmar	..	no contact	788, 973	297
8	12	Najd	„	Abū Bakr	..	raided enemy	..	297
8	12	Fadak	Murrah	Bashīr b. Saʿd	30	mostly killed	975	297
8	12	„	„	Ghālib b. ʿAbdallāh	200	revenge taken	..	297 f.
—	629							
9	1	Mayfaʿah	Thaʿlabah	„	130	successful	..	298
10	2	Jināb, Yumn	Ghaṭafān	Bashīr b. Saʿd	300	successful	975	298–9
11	3	Mecca	..	Muḥammad	2,000	pilgrimage	788–91	300–3
12	4	..	Sulaym	Ibn Abī 'l-ʿAwjā' (Sulamī)	50	mostly killed	..	303
8	—							
2	6	al-Kadīd	Mulawwiḥ (Layth)	Ghālib b. ʿAbdallāh (Laythī)	10	successful	973–5	307 f.
3	7	Dhāt Aṭlāḥ (Syria)	? Quḍāʿah	Kaʿb al-Ghifārī	15	all but one killed	983	308
3	7	Siy	Hawāzin	Shujāʿ	24	successful	..	308 f.
5	9	Mu'tah	Ghassān?	Zayd b. Ḥārithah	3,000	leaders killed	791–802	301–15
6	10	Dhāt as-Salāsil	Balī, Quḍāʿah	ʿAmr b. al-ʿĀṣ	500	enemy dispersed	984–6	315 f.
7	11	Sīf al-Bahr (Khabaṭ)	part of Juhaynah	Abū ʿUbaydah	300	did not see enemy	992	317 f.
8	12	Khaḍirah (al-Ghābah)	Ghaṭafān (Jusham)	?	16	..	989–91	318f.
? 9	12	Baṭn Iḍam	to north	Abū Qatādah ar-Ribʿī	8	no contact	808	325
—	630							
9	1	Mecca	Quraysh	Muḥammad	10,000	conquered Mecca	802–40	319–51
9	1	Yalamlam	?	Hishām b. al-ʿĀṣ	200	?	..	350
9	1	ʿUranah	?	Khālid b. Saʿīd	300	?	..	351
9	1	..	Jadhīmah	Khālid b. al-Walīd	350	successful	833–6	351–4
9	1	(various expeditions from Mecca to destroy shrines)					839 f.	350 f.
10	1	Ḥunayn	Hawāzin	Muḥammad	12,000	victory	840–69	354–68
10–11	2	aṭ-Ṭā'if	Thaqīf	„	„	siege failed	869–76	368–73
11	2–3	al-Jiʿrānah	..	„	„	distribution of booty	876–86	373–81
9	—							
1	4–5	(al-ʿArj, &c.)	Tamīm	ʿUyaynah b. Ḥiṣn	50	submitted	933–8	385–7
2	5–6	(Maṣhab)	Khathʿam	Quṭbah b. ʿĀmir	20	booty	..	387
3	6–7	(Zujj)	al-Qurṭā	aḍ-Ḍaḥḥāk b. Sufyān	..	successful	..	388
4	7–8	Shuʿaybah	Abysinnians	ʿAlqamah b. Mujazzaz	300	successful?	998	388 f.

A	B	C	D	E	F	G	H	I
Date							*References*	
A.H.	A.D.	*Destination or Name*	*Opponents*	*Leader*	*Number of participants*	*Result*	*IH*	*WW*
4	7–8	(al-Fuls)	Ṭayyiʾ	ʿAlī	150	destroyed idol	947–50	389 f.
..	..	al-Ḥubāb[1]	ʿUdhrah?	ʿUkkāshah	..	..	..	..
7–9	10–12	Tabūk	Ghassān	Muḥam-mad	30,000	indecisive?	893–906	390–416
7	10	Dūmat al-Jandal	Kindah	Khālid b. al-Walīd	420	surren-dered	903	403–5
—	**631**							
12	3–4	Pilgrimage	..	Abū Bakr	..	..	919–22	416 f.
10	—							
3	6–7	al-Yaman (Najrān)	al-Ḥārith b. Kaʿb	Khālid b. al-Walīd	400	sub-missions	(958-60)	(417 n.)
9	12	al-Yaman	Madhḥij	ʿAli	300	,,	967 f., 999	417–21
	632							
12	3	Pilgrimage	..	Muḥam-mad	..	..	966–70	421–33
11	—							
4	6–7	Mu'tah	Ghassān?	Usāmah b. Zayd	3,000	a success-ful raid	970	433–7
13/3	8/6	death of Muḥammad					999–1013	..

[1] Cf. Caetani, ii. 235.

EXCURSUS C

Slaves and Freedmen among the Emigrants at Badr

1. Zayd b. Ḥārithah (261):[1] an Arab, captured when young and sold into slavery; freed by Muḥammad.

2. Anasah (33): freedman of Muḥammad, born in slavery, said to be of Persian father and Abyssinian mother.[2]

3. Abū Kabshah (33): freedman of Muḥammad, born in slavery, presumably Arab.

4. Ṣāliḥ Shuqrān (34): an Abyssinian slave, bought by Muḥammad from ʿAbd ar-Raḥmān b. ʿAwf and given positions of trust. (The notice says that there were other slaves at Badr belonging to ʿAbd ar-Raḥmān, Ḥāṭib b. Abī Baltaʿah and, from the Anṣār, Saʿd b. Muʿādh.)

5. Sālim (60): freedman and adopted son of Abū Ḥudhayfah, of Persian descent.

6. Saʿd (81): freedman of Ḥāṭib b. Abī Baltaʿah, said to be Saʿd b. Khawlayy, of the tribe of Kalb or Madhḥij, and to have been enslaved on capture.

7. Khabbāb b. al-Aratt (116): born free but sold at Mecca after capture.

8. Ṣuhayb b. Sinān (161): an Arab but captured by Byzantines; either sold to Kalb and by them to ʿAbdallāh b. Judʿān who freed him, or escaped to Mecca and put himself under the protection of ʿAbdallāh b. Judʿān.

9. ʿĀmir b. Fuhayrah (164): born in slavery (according to *Usd*, iii. 90); bought by Abū Bakr and freed.

10. Bilāl b. Rabāḥ (165): of Abyssinian descent, born in slavery, freed by Abū Bakr.

11. Mihjaʿ b. Ṣāliḥ (285): from the Yemen (presumably Arab); fell into captivity; freed by ʿUmar b. al-Khaṭṭāb.

[1] The details are from Ibn Saʿd, iii/1, and the number in brackets after each name is a reference to the page there.

[2] Ṭab. i. 1780, 7.

EXCURSUS D

Muḥammad's Letters to the Princes

THE position has been adopted[1] that the material collected by Ibn Sa'd in volume i/2, pp. 15–86 is in general to be regarded as authentic. An exception must be made, however, of the story with which the collection opens, that in May 628 (i/7) on his return from al-Ḥudaybiyah Muḥammad sent six messengers to the rulers of the surrounding countries summoning them to accept Islam. The messengers were 'Amr b. Umayyah aḍ-Ḍamrī, Diḥyah b. Khalīfah al-Kalbī, 'Abdallāh b. Ḥudhāfah as-Sahmī, Ḥāṭib b. Abī Balta'ah, Shujā' b. Wahb al-Asadī, and Salīṭ b. 'Amr al-'Āmirī; and they were sent respectively to the Najāshī or Negus of Abyssinia, the governor of Bostra (Buṣrā) as representative of the Byzantine emperor, the Persian emperor, the Muqawqis or ruler of Alexandria, a Ghassānid prince called al-Ḥārith b. Abī Shimr, and Hawdhah b. 'Alī of the tribe of Ḥanīfah in the Yamāmah.[2]

This story cannot be accepted as it stands.[3] Muḥammad was a wise and far-seeing statesman, and he did not 'lose his head' after the measure of success he obtained at al-Ḥudaybiyah. To appeal to these princes at this period to accept Islam would have done more harm than good. Moreover, close examination shows that the sending of some of the envoys was prior to al-Ḥudaybiyah. The mission of Diḥyah to Bostra must have been in the summer of 627, since he was plundered by Judhām on his return and a punitive expedition was sent against them about October 627 (vi/6).[4] The two slave-girls brought back by the envoy to the Muqawqis appear to have been in Medina soon after January 627 (viii/5), since Muḥammad presented one of them to Ḥassān b. Thābit at the conclusion of 'the affair of the lie'.[5] Further, it is possible to discern a theological motive for the alteration of the stories. Ibn Isḥāq makes Muḥammad himself refer to the sending out of the apostles by Jesus, and with this connects the gift of languages at Pentecost.

[1] Cf. p. 336 above.

[2] The story of Farwah b. 'Amr must be a later intrusion, since Muḥammad did not take the initiative in his case; cf. below. J. Wellhausen, *Skizzen*, iv. 102 noted the break after the seventh.

[3] Cf. Caetani, i. 725–39; Buhl, *Muhammed*, 294–8.

[4] Cf. p. 43 above.

[5] Cf. p. 186 above.

This appears to be intended to substantiate the claim that Muḥammad was a prophet to all nations and not simply to the Arabs.[1]

The conclusion to be drawn is not that the stories of the six envoys are worthless, but that they contain a kernel of fact which has become distorted in the course of transmission because of the theological interest. This factual basis is clearly discerned in the case of the envoy to Abyssinia; he had to arrange for the marriage of Muḥammad to Umm Ḥabībah and perhaps also for the return to Arabia of Jaʿfar b. Abī Ṭālib and the other Meccans who still remained there. In the case of the others it is practically certain that the aim of the embassy was to conclude a friendly agreement between Muḥammad and the ruler in question. Such agreements would be primarily political, though there would probably also be some mention of religion similar to that in the letter to Bishop Ḍughāṭir.[2] There is difficulty about the identification of the Muqawqis and of al-Ḥārith b. Abī Shimr,[3] but this is not surprising since this was about the time of the Persian withdrawal from Egypt and before the Byzantines had regained full control. It is also doubtful whether any envoy went to the court of the Persian emperor; the kernel of fact in this story is the agreement with the Persian governor in the Yemen.[4]

It would be interesting to study in detail all the early material for these embassies contained in Ibn Hishām, Ibn Saʿd and aṭ-Ṭabarī. These extant sources raise questions about the circles responsible for the theological manipulation of the original accounts and about the relationship between the recensions of Ibn Isḥāq by Ibn Hishām and aṭ-Ṭabarī respectively. Here it must suffice to indicate the general course of the 'tendential shaping' of the material. Ibn Isḥāq appears to have made a list of the envoys Muḥammad 'sent in different directions to the princes (*mulūk*) of the Arabs and the non-Arabs, summoning them to God, in the period between al-Ḥudaybiyah and his death'.[5] This list included the six named above, and also the names of three sent to ʿUmān, al-Baḥrayn, and the Yemen.[6] Ibn Isḥāq was also aware of the

[1] IH, 971 f.; Ṭab. i. 1560; Buhl, 295, with a further reference to his art. 'Faßte Muhammed seine Verkündigung als eine universale, auch für Nichtaraber bestimmte Religion auf?' in the Festschrift for A. Fischer (*Islamica*, ii).

[2] Cf. p. 358 below.

[3] Cf. Caetani, i. 730, 735; Buhl, 296 f., nn., with further references.

[4] Cf. 122 above.

[5] Ṭab. 1560. 5 f.

[6] IH, 971; all except the one to the Yemen are mentioned in Ṭab. 1560–71.

parallel with Jesus, but does not seem to have emphasized it or brought the stories into accordance with it. Al-Wāqidī either reduced the list to six, or had an independent list.[1] The three omitted—the envoys to 'Umān, al-Baḥrayn, and the Yemen—were to minor Arabic-speaking princes and were known not to have been sent until after Ḥunayn. Ibn Hishām seems to have shortened Ibn Isḥāq's narrative, to have corrected one or two slips, and to have brought out more clearly the parallel with Jesus. The story of Farwah, first included by Ibn Sa'd (or possibly al-Wāqidī) is probably intended to replace that of the mission of Salīṭ to Hawdhah, since the latter ruled in east-central Arabia (and so was hardly a foreign potentate), while Farwah was in the Byzantine empire.[2]

[1] Ṭab. 1559. 13–1560. 3; cf. IS, i/2. 15 ff.
[2] Ibid. 18. 1 (§ 6); cf. 31 (§ 53).

EXCURSUS E

'Those whose hearts are reconciled'

The phrase from Q. 9. 60, *al-mu'allafah qulūbu-hum*, 'those whose hearts are reconciled', is commonly applied to the leading Meccans (along with one or two others), either still pagans or recent converts to Islam, who received 50 or 100 camels from Muḥammad during the distribution of spoils at al-Jiʿrānah. This use of the phrase is at least as early as Ibn Isḥāq, who writes: 'The Messenger of God made gifts to the *mu'allafah qulūbu-hum*, who were some of the leaders of the people, reconciling them (*yata'allafu-hum*) and through them reconciling their tribe.'[1] The suggestion is that it was only this substantial gift that made these men accept Islam; Ṣafwān b. Umayyah is alleged (probably falsely) to have said, 'Muḥammad was the most hateful of men to me, but he made me a gift, and at once he was the dearest of men to me.'[2]

Study of the Qur'ānic passage, however, shows that it cannot apply to the men of al-Jiʿrānah. The normal meaning of *mu'allafah* would be 'are reconciled', that is, 'are already reconciled'; the meaning 'are to be reconciled', though perhaps possible, is unusual. Further, if the Qur'ān referred to persons who were wavering, it would not refer to them by any term with a suggestion of disparagement; this would have defeated the purpose of winning them over. The decisive point, however, is that the Qur'ān is dealing with the *ṣadaqāt* or contributions of the Muslims, whereas the gifts made to the men of al-Jiʿrānah were admittedly made either from the fifth of the spoils, which was Muḥammad's share, or from the *farā'iʿ*, what remained over after four camels or their equivalent had been given to every man in the army. This is stated by al-Wāqidī, and al-Bukhārī deals with the matter under the heading of *Khums*.[3] Aṭ-Ṭabarī in his commentary takes the view that the phrase refers to the men of al-Jiʿrānah, but the traditions that he quotes do not all support him, since the first, sixth, seventh, and eighth run as follows:

(1) Ibn 'Abbās said . . . these are some people who used to come to Muḥammad, having been converted, and he would make a little gift

[1] IH, 880; cf. IS, ii/1. 110. 10.
[2] Ṭab., *Tafsīr*, on the phrase (x. 98–99), third tradition.
[3] WW, 367; al-Bukhārī, *Khums* (57), 19.

to them (*rakhaḍa*, which implies something much smaller than 100 camels) from the *ṣadaqāt*; when he did this and they obtained something good from the *ṣadaqāt*, they said, This is a right religion; otherwise they would have spoken ill of it and left it. (6) People of the Bedouin and others whom Muḥammad used to reconcile with gifts so that they believed. (7) Jewish and Christian converts . . . even if rich. (8) Jews or Christians.[1]

This divergence of view shows that the Qur'ānic verse did not refer clearly and unambiguously to the gifts made at al-Ji'rānah. The first tradition would fit in better with the gifts that Muḥammad made to the various 'deputations' which came to him from the year 8 onwards. Whatever the original application of the phrase, it cannot have been a justification of Muḥammad's conduct towards Abū Sufyān and the others at al-Ji'rānah.

Can any further light be thrown on how it came about that the men of al-Ji'rānah are normally described as 'those whose hearts are reconciled'? The matter is not clear, but some stages seem traceable. In particular 'Uyaynah b. Ḥiṣn and al-Aqra' b. Ḥābis, two nomadic chiefs, have special prominence. Writing in the thirteenth/seventeenth century with marks of judicious scholarship, al-Bayḍāwī comments thus:

Al-mu'allafah qulūbu-hum. Some people who had become Muslims but whose resolve was weak, so (Muḥammad) tried to reconcile their hearts. Or else: leading men to whom gifts were given and regard shown in the expectation of the conversion of their fellows; it was for that purpose that Muḥammad had made gifts to 'Uyaynah and al-Aqra' and al-'Abbās b. Mirdās. Another view is: leading men whom he tried to reconcile so that they became Muslims, for Muḥammad used to make gifts to such men. But the truth is rather that these gifts were made (not from the *ṣadaqāt* but) from that fifth which was his private property.

With this may be compared aṭ-Ṭabarī's statement of his own views on the phrase:

These are some people who were reconciled to Islam, but to whom it was not right to give anything in order to improve their condition or that of their tribe (*sc.* since they were not needy); for example, Abū Sufyān, 'Uyaynah, al-Aqra' and their fellows among the chiefs of tribes.

The special prominence of 'Uyaynah and al-Aqra' (along with al-'Abbās b. Mirdās) is to be connected with a story told by both Ibn Isḥāq and al-Wāqidī.[2] 'Uyaynah b. Ḥiṣn (of Fazārah) had long

[1] Ṭab., *Tafsīr*, *ad loc.*

[2] IH, 881; WW, 376.

been a thorn in the flesh to Muḥammad. Both he and al-Aqraʿ b. Ḥābis (of Tamīm), who now appears for the first time, accompanied Muḥammad on his expedition to Mecca and Ḥunayn, but perhaps as observers rather than as allies, since they did not have their tribesmen with them. Nevertheless at al-Jiʿrānah Muḥammad treated them like the chiefs of the Meccan clans and gave them 100 camels each. Upon this al-ʿAbbās b. Mirdās of Sulaym, whose tribe had sent over 900 men, complained that he had received only four camels, though his ancestry was no less noble than that of ʿUyaynah and al-Aqraʿ. The point may have been that he had been treated as an ordinary man and not as a chief, or (if we suppose that 100 camels was the recognized share of the leader of a non-Muslim group allied to Muḥammad) it may have been that Sulaym was to be reckoned as an allied group. The memory of a recent war between Ghaṭafān (to which Fazārah belonged) and Sulaym would make al-ʿAbbās feel the supposed slight more keenly.[1] He expressed his dissatisfaction in verse. When this was reported to Muḥammad, he gave orders for the docking of his tongue, which was understood to mean presenting him with 100 camels.

This story may well have a basis in fact, though the point does not affect the present argument. Al-Bukhārī has a tradition which seems to refer to this incident, though without naming al-ʿAbbās. ʿAbdallāh (b. Masʿūd), after remarking how the Prophet showed special favour to al-Aqraʿ and ʿUyaynah and others (unnamed), told how a man came and accused him of being unjust, and how Muḥammad exclaimed, 'Who is just, if not God and His Messenger?' It is noteworthy that one of the important links in the *isnād* is a Sulamī, Manṣūr b. al-Muʿtamir (d. 132), who also had leanings towards the Shīʿah.[2]

There is another story in which the same two chiefs are singled out for mention.[3] Someone asked Muḥammad why he made gifts to those two, and did nothing for Juʿayl (or Juʿāl) b. Surāqah (of Ḍamrah). He replied that Juʿayl was much better than fellows like these, 'but I treated them well (*ta'allaftu-humā*) that they might become Muslims, whereas I trusted Juʿayl to his faith'. (Juʿayl was given lodging, at least for a time, within the mosque at Medina (that is, Muḥammad's house), and performed various errands for

[1] Caussin de Perceval, ii. 556–64.
[2] *Khums*, 19. 8.
[3] IH, 883 (= Ṭab. 1681 f.); IS, iv/1. 181, from al-Wāqidī.

him;[1] he may have lived in Medina before he became a Muslim, though his tribe was one of the first to make an alliance with Muḥammad; he was apparently of low morale at the battle of Uḥud, for he told Muḥammad of a dream in which he had seen him killed, and later, perhaps because of the dream, he was thought to have raised the shout that Muḥammad was killed.) Ibn Isḥāq reports this story on the authority of Muḥammad b. Ibrāhīm b. al-Ḥārith (b. 119–21), a Medinan lawyer or jurisconsult, belonging to the clan of Taym of Quraysh, and grandson of one of the early Muslims who had migrated to Abyssinia. Such a man doubtless belonged to the 'pious opposition' in Medina, and the point of the story and the selection of Juʿayl may be to emphasize the superiority of faith to worldly goods. Some of the other stories about the dissatisfaction of the Anṣār with the distribution of spoil at al-Jiʿrānah have the same point. The fact that the same words—'with them I treated a group of people well, that they might become Muslims, but I trusted you to your faith'—are applied to the Anṣār as a whole in another story,[2] suggests that at least one of the stories is an invention. Nevertheless it is probably true that Muḥammad's gifts to ʿUyaynah and al-Aqraʿ (as distinct from those to Abū Sufyān and Ḥakīm b. Ḥizām and perhaps others) were intended to win them to accept Islam. To this extent Mujāhid is justified in interpreting the Qur'ānic phrase as meaning 'people whom he reconciled by gifts, ʿUyaynah and those with him'.[3]

A complicating factor is the story of how Muḥammad, from some gold sent to him by ʿAlī from the Yemen, made presents to four chiefs, al-Aqraʿ, ʿUyaynah, Zayd aṭ-Ṭā'ī, and ʿAlqamah b. ʿUlāthah al-ʿĀmirī, and, when Quraysh and the Anṣār complained, said, 'I am reconciling them (*ata'allafu-hum*).'[4] With this is joined a version of the story of how Muḥammad was accused of being unjust. The latter is suspect, since there are many forms of it and it was developed as propaganda against the sect of Khawārij; but the distribution of the gold may be largely true.

The next stage in the process we are trying to disentangle is the connexion of the two desert chiefs with Abū Sufyān and other Quraysh who received 50 or 100 camels at al-Jiʿrānah. We have already seen how aṭ-Ṭabarī in his summing-up mentioned only

[1] WW, 204, 272, 407; cf. IS, l.c.
[2] IH, 886. 8.
[3] Ṭab., *Tafsīr*, *ad. loc.*, fourth tradition.
[4] Al-Bukhārī, *Anbiyā'* (60), 6; cf. Muslim, *Zakāt*, 143.

Abū Sufyān along with 'Uyaynah and al-Aqra'. In the *Ṣaḥīḥ* of Muslim there are earlier instances of a similar character.[1] One version says that Muḥammad gave 100 camels to Abū Sufyān, Ṣafwān b. Umayyah, 'Uyaynah and al-Aqra', and fewer to al-'Abbās b. Mirdās; other versions omit Ṣafwān or add 'Alqamah. The *isnād* of some is Kūfan, with 'Umar b. Sa'īd b. Masrūq, brother of Sufyān ath-Thawrī, as principal figure. One version has a Medinan *isnād* which includes 'Amr b. Yaḥyā b. 'Umārah (d. 757/140); this version alone has the words 'and he made gifts to the *mu'allafah qulūbu-hum*'.

Finally, there are the (more or less) complete lists. There are two in Ibn Hishām.[2] One is on the authority of Ibn Isḥāq alone; the other came to Ibn Hishām from an unnamed informant, who had it from Ibn Shihāb az-Zuhrī, from 'Ubaydallāh b. 'Abdallāh b. 'Utbah, from Ibn 'Abbās. The second of the traditions in aṭ-Ṭabarī's commentary on the phrase, which gives a list of thirteen names, is traced back to Ma'mar (b. Rāshid) (d. 769–71/152–4) and Yaḥyā b. Abī Kathīr (d. 746–50/129–32). Al-Wāqidī does not give any authority for his whole list, but certain details have come through az-Zuhrī.[3] Thus everything points to the conclusion that the identification of 'those reconciled in heart' with the men who received gifts at al-Ji'rānah was made in Medina among the 'pious opposition' not later than the early years of the second century A.H. Ma'mar is noted as one of the best exponents of the views of az-Zuhrī, and Yaḥyā must have belonged to the same circle.

It need not be seriously doubted that az-Zuhrī and his friends, many of whom had been supporters of the revolt of 'Abdallāh b. az-Zubayr and were still hostile to the Umayyads, should have found great delight in spreading stories which put the ancestors of the Umayyads and their supporters in an unpleasant light. It was almost certainly anti-Umayyad feeling which brought about the change of interpretation of the phrase *al-mu'allafah qulūbu-hum*. While blackening the Umayyads, az-Zuhrī did his best to avoid blackening his own friends. He could not deny that Ḥakīm b. Ḥizām, now head of the clan of Asad (the clan of az-Zubayr), had received 300 camels, but he continued by telling how, as a result of Muḥammad's words on this occasion, he came so to despise worldly goods that he never again accepted the slightest gift; in the

[1] *Zakāt*, 137–9.
[2] 880–1, 882–3.
[3] WW, 375–6.

case of Makhramah b. Nawfal of his own clan of Zuhrah, he denied that he received any gift on this occasion.[1]

The course of development suggested by this study of the traditions may be outlined as follows. At an early period two stories were in circulation; whether true or not, we need not ask, though it seems probable that they were true. One was about the complaint made by al-ʿAbbās b. Mirdās against ʿUyaynah and al-Aqraʿ at al-Jiʿrānah, and the other was about a gift of gold to these chiefs and some others, presumably not at al-Jiʿrānah. As part of this second story, or perhaps at first independently of it, Muḥammad was said to have made a remark using the word *ta'allaftu*, 'I reconciled'. There was some conflation of the stories. The word *ta'allaftu* came to be applied to ʿUyaynah and al-Aqraʿ in connexion with al-Jiʿrānah, and was then extended to all those who received a large gift there, though for some it was not suitable and led to lexicographical difficulties. From this, as *mu'allafah* comes from the same root, it was a short step to the assumption that the Qur'ānic phrase meant the men of al-Jiʿrānah, especially since, presumably, it no longer had any practical application.

In all this it is not denied that Muḥammad was well aware of the importance of material inducements in attracting men to Islam and frequently made use of them. This was probably so in the case of many of the recipients at al-Jiʿrānah. What is mischievous, however, is the suggestion that this was the dominant factor in the submission of the leaders of Quraysh. It keeps one from appreciating one aspect of Muḥammad's achievement, the fact that, leading an army which included these Meccans, he had triumphantly averted a threat, with apparently overwhelming force, from the old enemy of Mecca.

[1] Ibid.; cf. al-Bukhārī, *Khums*, 19. 1.

EXCURSUS F

Text of Selected Treaties

THE following are translations of some of the more interesting treaties and letters preserved by Ibn Saʿd.[1] All the treaties and letters in this volume were edited and translated into German by Julius Wellhausen in *Skizzen und Vorarbeiten*, iv, section 3 (Berlin, 1889). His interpretation has usually been followed.

1. The Messenger of God (God bless and preserve him) wrote to B. Ḍamrah b. Bakr b. ʿAbd Manāt b. Kinānah that they have a guarantee for (*āminūn ʿalā*) their goods and persons, and that succour (*naṣr*) is due to them against whoever wrongfully oppresses them; the succour of the prophet (God bless and preserve him) is (incumbent) on them so long as water wets a piece of wool, unless they are (already) fighting about God's religion;[2] when the prophet summons them, they are to respond to him. On that condition, there is over them the *dhimmah*[3] of God and His messenger, and they have succour, for whoever of them is just and pious (*man barra wa-'ttaqā*).[4]

2. The Messenger of God (God bless and preserve him) wrote to B. Ghifār that they are of the Muslims, with the privileges of the Muslims and the obligations of the Muslims; and that the prophet covenants to them the *dhimmah* of God and the *dhimmah* of His messenger, for their goods and persons; succour is due to them against whoever begins wrong against them; when the prophet summons them to succour him, they are to respond to him; (incumbent) on them is his succour,[5] except (on) those who are fighting about religion, so long as the sea wets a piece of wool;

[1] i/2. 15–86; in the references the page and (sometimes) line of the standard edition is given, followed in brackets by the number of the paragraph in Wellhausen's text and translation (*Skizzen und Vorarbeiten*, iv/3).

[2] This translation of a difficult passage seems to make sense without violence to the text; on this view the clause excludes from the duty of answering a summons those who are already engaged in an expedition 'on behalf of the religion of God'. Wellhausen differs. Cf. the similar passage in the following letter, and also Excursus G, I (*j*) and II (*j*). Another possible rendering is: 'the succour of the prophet is *against* them (*sc.* Ḍamrah) unless they fight *for* God's religion.'

[3] i.e. guarantee of security, protection; cf. p. 244 above.

[4] IS, i/2. 27. 3–7 (§ 40).

[5] i.e. giving succour to him; an alternative rendering is: 'against them is his succour, except him who fights for religion.'

this writing does not come in front of (and protect from the penalties of) crime.[1]

3. The Messenger of God (God bless and preserve him) wrote to B. Zurʿah and B. ar-Rabʿah of Juhaynah that they have a guarantee for their persons and their goods; and that there is due to them succour against whoever wrongs them or fights them, except about religion and family (*ahl*);[2] there is due to the people of their nomadic part, who are just and pious, what is due to their settled part; and God is the one appealed to for help.[3]

4. The Messenger of God (God bless and preserve him) wrote to ʿAmr b. Maʿbad al-Juhanī and B. al-Ḥuraqah of Juhaynah and B. al-Jurmuz—if any of them becomes a Muslim and performs the Worship and gives the *zakāt* and obeys God and His messenger and gives of his spoils the fifth and the share of the prophet and the *ṣafī* ('first pick'),[4] and if he professes Islam openly and keeps apart from the idolators, then he is secure by the guarantee (*āmin bi-amān*) of God and the guarantee of Muḥammad; where a debt is owing to any Muslim, (the repayment of) the capital is prescribed for him, but the interest on the pledge is void. The tax (*ṣadaqah*) on fruits is the tenth. He who joins them has the same rights as they have.[5]

5. The Messenger of God (God bless and preserve him) wrote to Budayl and Busr and the heads (*sarawāt*) of B. ʿAmr. '. . . I have not betrayed your rights, nor injured your reputation.[6] The most honoured to me of the people of Tihāmah, and the nearest of them to me in kin are yourselves, and those of the Muṭayyabūn[7] who follow you.' '. . . I have taken (or adopted, *sc.* as rights or privileges) for him of you who migrates (*hājara*) the like of what I have taken for myself, even if he migrates in his own land, except the dweller in Mecca, apart from him who makes the lesser or greater pilgrimage (*muʿtamir*, *ḥājj*). I have not done away with (anything) in respect

[1] 26. 26 ff. (§ 39).

[2] Perhaps *ahl* ought to be omitted; the following word, translated 'people', is also *ahl*.

[3] 24. 2–4 (§ 27); Wellhausen thinks this and the two preceding treaties are with non-Muslims (p. 112 n.).

[4] Cf. p. 255 above. Add *wa* before *aṣ-ṣafī*.

[5] 24. 27–25. 5 (§ 30 d).

[6] Or 'done away with what is due to you'. Wellhausen's translation would require *ʿalā*; cf. instances of the meaning 'instigate' in R. Dozy, *Supplément aux Dictionnaires Arabes*², Leiden, 1927, ii.

[7] Cf. *M/Mecca*, 5 f., &c.

of you since I made agreement. You have nothing to fear from my part and you are not oppressed.'[1]

6. The Messenger of God (God bless and preserve him) wrote to a mixed band (*jummāʿ*),[2] who were in the mountainous part of Tihāmah and had used violence on the passing (travellers), (the band being men) from Kinānah, Muzaynah, al-Ḥakam, and al-Qārah, together with slaves who followed them. When the Messenger of God (God bless and preserve him) triumphed, a deputation came from them to the prophet (God bless and preserve him), and the Messenger of God (God bless and preserve him) wrote to them: 'In the name of God, the Merciful, the Compassionate. This is a writing from Muḥammad the Prophet, the Messenger of God, to the servants of God, the freedmen (*ʿutaqā'*); if they believe and perform the worship and give the *zakāt*, then the slave among them is free (*ḥurr*), and their patron is Muḥammad; he among them who is from a tribe is not handed back to it; whatever there is among them of blood they have shed or wealth they have taken is (given) to them (and blood-wit or repayment will not be exacted); whatever debt is (owing) to them among the people, will be repaid to them; there will be no wrong (done) to them and no hostility (shown); on these terms they have the *dhimmah* of God and the *dhimmah* of Muḥammad. Peace be upon you. Ubayy b. Kaʿb wrote it.'[3]

7. There came before the Messenger of God (God bless and preserve him) the deputation of B. ʿAbd b. ʿAdī (of Kinānah), among them al-Ḥārith b. Uhbān, ʿUwaymir b. al-Akhram, and Ḥabīb and Rabīʿah the sons of Mullah, and along with them a number of their tribe. They said, 'O Muḥammad, we are the people of the sacred area (*ḥaram*—? of Mecca), and the dwellers there and the strongest of those in it; and we do not want to fight you; if you are fighting against others than Quraysh, we will fight with you, but we will not fight against Quraysh; we love you and those from whom you are (? Muslims); if you strike one of us by mistake, blood-wit for him is obligatory for you, and if we strike one of your companions, blood-wit for him is obligatory for us.' He said 'Yes', and they became Muslims.[4]

8. The first of (the tribal group of) Muḍar to come as a deputation to the Messenger of God (God bless and preserve him) were

[1] 25. 11–16 (§ 32 a).
[2] Cf. p. 61 above, affair of Abū Baṣīr.
[3] 29. 13–22 (§ 46).
[4] 48. 19–24 (§ 91 b).

400 men of Muzaynah. That was in Rajab (vii) of the year 5 (December 626). The Messenger of God (God bless and preserve him) gave them (the dignity of) the *hijrah* in their own home. He said, 'You are Emigrants (*muhājirūn*), wherever you are; so return to your property (*sc.* herds)'. They returned to their country.[1]

9. The Messenger of God (God bless and preserve him) wrote: In the name of God, the Merciful, the Compassionate. From Muḥammad the prophet to B. Asad. Peace be upon you. I praise God to you, besides whom there is no god. Furthermore, do not approach the watering-places and the land of Ṭayyi', for their watering-places are not lawful for you. Let no one enter their land except him whom they cause to enter. The *dhimmah* of Muḥammad is not responsible for him who disobeys him. Let Quḍā'ī b. 'Amr see to this. Khālid b. Sa'īd wrote it.[2]

10. The Messenger of God (God bless and preserve him) wrote: In the name of God, the Merciful, the Compassionate; these are (the terms) on which Nu'aym b. Mas'ūd b. Rukhaylah al-Ashja'ī made confederacy (*ḥālafa*); he made confederacy with him on the basis of help and counsel (*naṣr, naṣīḥah*), so long as Uḥud is in its place and so long as the sea wets a piece of wool. 'Alī wrote it.[3]

11. (After the conversion of Rifā'ah b. Zayd of Judhām, Muḥammad gave him a letter to his tribe.) 'This is a letter from Muḥammad, the Messenger of God, for Rifā'ah b. Zayd (to take) to his tribe, and whoever enters along with them; he calls them to God; whoever accepts is in the party of God (*ḥizb Allāh*), and whoever rejects has safety for two months.' His tribe responded to him (favourably) and became Muslims.[4]

12. The Messenger of God (God bless and preserve him) wrote to whoever of Ḥadas of Lakhm became Muslim, performed the worship, paid the *zakāt*, gave the share (*ḥazz*) of God and the share of His messenger and separated from the idolaters—he is secure (*āmin*) by the *dhimmah* of God and the *dhimmah* of Muḥammad; in the case of him who goes back from his religion, the *dhimmah* of God and the *dhimmah* of Muḥammad, His messenger, is free of (responsibility towards) him; he whose *islām* is attested by a Muslim is secure by the *dhimmah* of Muḥammad, and is of the Muslims. 'Abdallāh b. Zayd wrote it.[5]

[1] 38. 11–14 (§ 76 a).
[2] 23. 18–22 (§ 24).
[3] 26. 18–20 (§ 35).
[4] 83. 2–4 (§ 140 a).
[5] 21. 14–19 (§ 16).

13. The Messenger of God (God bless and preserve him) wrote to Ḍughāṭir the bishop. 'Peace to him who believes. Furthermore, Jesus son of Mary is the spirit of God and His word; He placed it in Mary the pure. I believe in God and what was revealed to us and what was revealed to Abraham, Ishmael, Isaac and Jacob, and to the Israelites (*asbāṭ*), and what was given to Moses and Jesus, and what was given to the prophets from their Lord. We do not distinguish between any of them (*sc.* count some superior to others). We are surrendered (*muslimūn*) to Him. Peace be upon him who follows the guidance.' He sent this by Diḥyah b. Khalīfah al-Kalbī.[1]

14. The Messenger of God (God bless and preserve him) wrote to B. Janbah, who were Jews in Maqnā, and to the people of Maqnā. Maqnā is a town of Aylah. 'Furthermore, your envoys have come to see me as they returned to your town. When this letter of mine comes to you, you are in security. You have the *dhimmah* of God and the *dhimmah* of His messenger. The Messenger of God pardons you your evil deeds, and all your faults. You have the *dhimmah* of God and the *dhimmah* of His messenger. Towards you there is no wrong and no enmity. The Messenger of God is your neighbour (*jār*), (protecting you) from what he protects himself from. To the Messenger of God belong all the fine cloth and all the slaves among you, and all the horses and the armour, except what is not required by the Messenger of God or the messenger of the Messenger of God. In addition, there is due from you a quarter of what your palm-trees produce, a quarter of what your fishing-rafts (or fishermen) catch, and a quarter of what your women weave. Thereafter you are free from all tax (*jizyah*) or forced labour (*sukhrah*). If you hear and obey, it will be incumbent on the Messenger of God to honour the honourable man of you, and to pardon the wrong-doer.

Furthermore, to the believers and Muslims (it is said): He who does good to the people of Maqnā, it will be good for him, and he who does evil to them, it will be evil for him. There is over you no ruler (*amīr*) except from yourselves or from the people of the Messenger of God. Peace.'[2]

15. In the name of God, the Merciful, the Compassionate. From Muḥammad the prophet to B. Zuhayr b. Uqaysh, a clan of 'Ukl.

[1] 28. 6–11 (§ 43).

[2] 28. 12–23 (§ 44); the closing paragraph might be from a separate letter.

If they confess that there is no god but God, and that Muḥammad is His messenger, and keep apart from the idolaters, and agree to give the fifth of their spoils and the share of the prophet and his *ṣafī* ('first pick'), then they are secure by the guarantee (*amān*) of God and of His messenger.[1]

16. The Messenger of God (God bless and preserve him) wrote to the bishop of B. al-Ḥārith b. Kaʿb and the bishops of Najrān and their priests and those who followed them and their monks, that for all their churches, services and monastic practices, few or many, they had the protection (*jiwār*) of God and His messenger. No bishop will be moved from his episcopate, no monk from his monastic state, no priest from his priesthood. There will be no alteration of any right or authority or circumstance, so long as they are loyal and perform their obligations well, they not being burdened by wrong (? suffered) and not doing wrong. Written by al-Mughīrah.[2]

17. This is a letter from Muḥammad the prophet, the Messenger of God, to the people of Najrān. To him belonged the decision upon them in respect of every fruit, yellow, white, or black, and every slave; but he was gracious to them and left (them) all that for the payment of 2,000 suits of clothes, namely, suits of ounces, of which a thousand are to be handed over each (year in) Rajab (vii) and a thousand in Ṣafar (ii), each suit worth one ounce (*ūqīyah*). Where these tribute suits exceed or fall short of the ounce, that is taken into account. Whatever was taken from them of the coats of mail and horses and riding-camels and equipment they possessed is taken into account. Najrān is to give lodging to my messengers for 20 days or less, but my messengers are not to be kept more than a month. It is obligatory for them to lend 30 coats of mail, 30 horses, and 30 camels if there is war (*kayd*) in the Yemen. Whatever is destroyed of the coats of mail or horses or camels they lend my messengers is guaranteed by my messengers until they repay it. Najrān and their followers have protection (*jiwār*) of God and the *dhimmah* of Muḥammad the prophet, the Messenger of God, for themselves, their community, their land, and their goods, both those who are absent and those who are present, and for their churches and services (no bishop will be moved from his episcopate, and no monk from his monastic position, and no church-warden[3]

[1] 30. 5–8 (§ 48).

[2] 21 (§ 14).

[3] Reading *wāfih* for *wāqif* with C. A. Nallino, *Raccolta di Scritti*, iii. 128 n.

from his church-wardenship) and for all, great or little, that is under their hands. There is no usury, and no blood-revenge from pre-Islamic times (*lā damm al-Jāhilīyah*). If any of them asks for a right, justice is among them (*sc.* in their own hands) (to see that they are) not doing wrong and not suffering wrong; it belongs to Najrān. If any one takes usury after this, my *dhimmah* is free from (responsibility for) him. No one of them is punished for the wrong-doing of another. On the terms stated in this document (they have) protection (*jiwār*) of God and *dhimmah* of the prophet for ever, until God comes with His command, if they are loyal and perform their obligations well, not being burdened by wrong. Witnessed by Abū Sufyān b. Ḥarb, Ghaylān b. ʿAmr, Mālik b. ʿAwf an-Naṣrī, al-Aqraʿ b. Ḥābis, al-Mustawrid b. ʿAmr, a brother of Balī, al-Mughīrah b. Shuʿbah and ʿĀmir, client of Abū Bakr.[1]

18. The Messenger of God (God bless and preserve him) wrote to Khālid b. Ḍimād al-Azdī, that to him belongs the land he had when he became a Muslim, on condition that he believes in God—He has no partner—and confesses that Muḥammad is His servant and His messenger, and on condition that he performs the Worship, pays the *zakāt*, fasts the month of Ramaḍān, makes pilgrimage to the house (*sc.* the Kaʿbah), does not give shelter to any rebel (or disturber of the peace) and does not waver, and on condition that he deals uprightly with God and His messenger and that he loves the friends of God and hates the enemies of God. On Muḥammad the prophet it is incumbent to protect him (Khālid) and his property and family from what he protects himself from. Khālid al-Azdī has the *dhimmah* of God and the *dhimmah* of Muḥammad the prophet, if he fulfils this. Ubayy wrote it.[2]

19. The Messenger of God (God bless and preserve him) wrote to al-Hilāl, the master of al-Baḥrayn: Peace to you. I praise to you God, besides whom there is no god, and who has no partner; and I summon you to God alone, that you believe in God, and obey, and enter into the community (*jamāʿah*). That is better for you. Peace be upon whoever follows the guidance.[3]

20. The Messenger of God (God bless and preserve him), on leaving al-Jiʿrānah, sent al-ʿAlāʾ b. al-Ḥaḍramī to al-Mundhir b. Sāwā al-ʿAbdī, who was in al-Baḥrayn, summoning him to Islam, and he wrote a letter to him. He (al-Mundhir) wrote to the

[1] 35 f. (§ 72); see also Abū Yūsuf, *Kharāj*, 44 (tr. 108), and al-Balādhurī, 63 f.
[2] IS, i/2. 21. 19–25 (§ 17).
[3] 27. 7–10 (§ 41).

Messenger of God (God bless and preserve him) announcing his acceptance of Islam and his belief in him (or it): 'I have read your letter to the people of Hajar. Some of them like Islam and admire it and have entered it; and some dislike it. In my country are Magians and Jews. Tell me your command about that.'

The Messenger of God (God bless and preserve him) wrote to him: In so far as you act well, we shall not remove you from your position as ruler. He who remains a Jew or a Magian is obliged to pay the tax (*jizyah*).

The Messenger of God (God bless and preserve him) wrote to the Magians of Hajar, presenting Islam to them. If they refuse, there is taken from them the *jizyah*; and their women are not to be married (by men of other religions) and their sacrifices are not to be eaten.[1]

21. The Messenger of God (God bless and preserve him) wrote to al-Mundhir b. Sāwā. 'Furthermore, my messengers have praised you. In so far as you act well, I shall act well towards you, and reward you for your work; and you shall deal uprightly with God and His messenger. Peace be upon you.' He sent it by al-ʿAlā b. al-Ḥaḍramī.[2]

[1] 19. 1–8 (§ 9).

[2] 27. 25–28 (§ 42).

EXCURSUS G

The Treaties with Dūmat al-Jandal

SEVERAL accounts have been preserved of negotiations between Muḥammad and various groups among the inhabitants of Dūmat al-Jandal.[1] Some of these require no special discussion, but two documents are worthy of detailed examination, since their authenticity has been questioned, while, if they are authentic or mainly authentic, they raise interesting questions. The text of the documents may be given in full (divided into sentences to bring out the parallelism and for convenience of reference).[2]

I

(*a*) This is a letter from Muḥammad, the Messenger of God, to Ukaydir, when he agreed to become a Muslim (or 'to submit', *sc.* to God and to Muḥammad) and repudiated the gods and idols, along with Khālid b. al-Walīd, the Sword of God, in respect of Dūmat al-Jandal and its neighbourhood (or 'removed the gods . . . which were in . . .').

(*b*) To him (*sc.* Muḥammad) belongs the outer part where there is little water, what is uncultivated, what is not marked off and what is not appropriated of the land; and the armour, the arms, the horses and the stronghold.

(*c*) To you belong the inner palm-trees, and the cultivated land watered by springs (= or 'appropriated').

(*d*) And far distant is the fifth (meaning that the fifth is not to be exacted; or 'and after the fifth', meaning that it is to be paid before possession is established, or before the following clause applies).

(*f*) Your pasturing beast is not to be turned away (from the pasture; ? before tithing); your segregated beast is not to be reckoned (as liable for tithe).

(*g*) You are not to be debarred from the pasture (lit. 'plants', presumably in the outer area).

(*h*) The tithe is not to be taken from you except on the established (*thabāt*, *sc.* palms).[3]

(*i*) You are to perform the Worship (*ṣalāt*) at its (proper) time, and to give the *zakāt* as is due.

[1] IS, i/2. 34 (§ 66), 36 (§ 73), 68 f. (§ 119); cf. Caetani, ii/1. 259–70.

[2] IS, i/2. 36, 69; cf. IH, 903 (and ii. 205); WW, 403 f.; Ṭab. 1702 f.; al-Balādhurī, 61 ff.

[3] IH, ii. 205 has v. l. *nabāt*, plants, as in (*g*).

(*j*) On those terms you have an agreement and covenant, and thereby you have (to expect from us) uprightness and performance of duties.

(*k*) Witnessed by God and those of the Muslims who were present.

II

(*a*) This is a letter from Muḥammad, the Messenger of God, to the people of Dūmat al-Jandal and those who follow them of the clans (*ṭawā'if*) of Kalb, along with (? sent by) Ḥārithah b. Qaṭan.

(*b*) To us belongs the outer rain-watered (or unwatered) part.

(*c*) To you belong the inner palm-trees.

(*e*) Where there is running water a tenth is due; where there is spring-water half a tenth is due.

(*f*) Your pasturing beasts are not to be joined together; your segregated beasts are not to be turned away.

(*i*) You are to perform the Worship at its (proper) time, and to give the *zakāt* as is due.

(*g*) You are not to be debarred from the pasture.

(*h*) The tithe is not to be taken from you on household goods (*batāt*).

(*j*) On those terms you have an agreement and covenant, and we owe you (? you owe us) sincerity and fulfilment, and the *dhimmah* of God and His messenger.

(*k*) Witnessed by God and those of the Muslims who were present.

The first comment to be made on these documents is that there are several places where the text is uncertain and the meaning obscure. The most notable is (*h*) where there are three readings, *thabāt*, *nabāt*, and *batāt*, which could easily be confused with one another in Arabic script; moreover the word 'except' (*illā*) seems to have fallen out in II. The precise meaning of clauses (*f*) and (*g*) is also obscure, but it is not specially relevant to the present discussion.

The next point to notice is that there are no cogent reasons for thinking that I is a later invention based on II. Ukaydir is a well-attested historical character. Our ignorance of his relation to the other inhabitants of Dūmat al-Jandal and its neighbourhood is not a ground for denying his existence. There was presumably room for several distinct groups. It may well be, as Caetani suggests at one point, that Ukaydir (who was from the South Arabian tribe of Kindah) ruled over the town-dwelling immigrants from 'Irāq, while the tribesmen of Kalb were partly agricultural and partly nomadic; the distinction cannot have been sharp, however, since Ukaydir's letter speaks of herds and Ḥārithah's of palms. Once the existence of different groups in the oasis is admitted, there is no improbability in two letters being similar. Moreover, such a variation as the addition of the closing words of (*b*) in I is appropriate to what we know of Ukaydir's situation.

The question whether Ukaydir and Ḥārithah's group are Christians or Muslims leads us to the heart of the problem. There is evidence elsewhere that Ukaydir remained a Christian.[1] The tenor of the documents, too, implies the surrender of non-Muslims to Muslims. Note the contrast between 'us' and 'you' in II (*b*, *c*) and the mention of 'the Muslims' in (*k*). The case of Hawāzin, who became Muslims and yet had to make a liberation-payment (*si'āyah*),[2] is not an exact parallel; had there been something similar at Dūmat al-Jandal we should presumably have heard more about it. It is almost certain, therefore, that the persons to whom these letters were written were not Muslims; and we have next to explain how the texts contain passages which seem to imply that they were —(*i*) and I (*a*).

There are two possible explanations. Firstly it might be held that (*a*) in I is a later editorial heading, and that (*i*) has also been added in both—in different positions, be it noted—at some later period; the phrase 'repudiated the gods and idols' is not altogether suitable for a Christian. Secondly it might be held that *islām* in I (*a*) does not have the technical sense of 'becoming a Muslim', but means 'submitting' merely; again, 'performing the Worship' might perhaps refer to Christian rites and *zakāt* might be applied to the payments made to Muḥammad by monotheistic subject groups.

Of these two possibilities the former is the more probable, but it is not necessary here to make a final decision between them. On either explanation the problem remains. These persons (we have argued) are not Muslims; yet they have to make payments which are identical in principle and in manner of calculation with the *zakāt* paid by Muslims. Indeed, document II appears in Ibn al-Athīr's *Usd al-Ghābah*[3] reduced to clause (*e*); and this suggests that this document was an important source for the principle that the *zakāt* on naturally and artificially irrigated land is a tithe and a half-tithe respectively. There is here a potent reason for the insertion of (*i*) and I (*a*). These people were paying something that was materially identical with *zakāt*; therefore, the early scholars would argue, they must have been Muslims. Finally, if this train of reasoning is

[1] e.g. mention of *jizyah* in IH, 903 and WW, 404. [2] Cf. p. 101 above.
[3] i. 357, *s.v.* Ḥārithah b. Qaṭan; cf. al-Bukhārī, *Zakāt* (24), 55.

sound, it leads to an important conclusion, namely, that for a time—presumably before the revelation of the verse about *jizyah*,[1] or at least before its general application—some allied or subject non-Muslim groups made payments to Medina that were identical with those made by Muslim groups. Such a conclusion, of course, is at the same time the setting of a problem for future research.

[1] 9. 29; cf. pp. 115, 255 above.

EXCURSUS H

List of Administrators sent out by Muḥammad

(This list merely contains the main references from Ibn Hishām and aṭ-Ṭabarī, along with one or two others, and does not claim to be complete.)

(a) *Sent to the south*

1. al-Muhājir b. Abī Umayyah (Quraysh–Makhzūm); sent to Ṣanʿāʾ (IH, 965 = Ṭab. i. 1750; cf. IH, 971 foot); to B. Muʿāwiyah b. Kindah, but did not go until the caliphate of Abū Bakr (Ṭab. 1853).

2. Ziyād b. Labīd (Anṣār–Bayāḍah); to Ḥaḍramawt (IH, 965 = Ṭab. 1750); was also set over the district of al-Muhājir (B. Muʿāwiyah?) (Ṭab. 1852 f.).

3. ʿAlī b. Abī Ṭālib (Quraysh–Hāshim); sent to Najrān to collect *ṣadaqāt* and *jizyah* (IH, 965 = Ṭab. 1750).

4. Muʿādh b. Jabal (Anṣār–Salimah); to Ḥimyar (IH, 956); to the Yemen (IS, i/2. 20); to teach in the Yemen and Ḥaḍramawt in districts that were under various 'agents', *ʿummāl* (Ṭab. 1852 f.).

5. ʿAbdallāh b. Zayd (Anṣār–Ba 'l-Ḥārith); to Ḥimyar (IH, 956; ? also in Ṭab. 1853).

6. Mālik b. ʿUbādah (Hamdān); sent to Ḥimyar (IH, 956).

7. ʿUqbah b. Namir (Hamdān); to Ḥimyar (IH, 956).

8. Mālik b. Murrah (or Murārah) ar-Ruhāwī (Madhḥij); to Ḥimyar (IH, 956; cf. IS, i/2. 20).

9. Shahr b. Bādhām (Persian); recognized as governor of Ṣanʿāʾ (Ṭab. 1852 f.).

10. ʿĀmir b. Shahr al-Hamdānī; to Hamdān (Ṭab. 1852).

11. Abū Mūsā (ʿAbdallāh b. Qays) al-Ashʿarī; to Maʾrib (Ṭab. 1852).

12. Khālid b. Saʿīd b. al-ʿĀṣ (Quraysh–ʿAbd Shams); to region between Najrān, Rimaʿ and Zabīd (Ṭab. 1852; cf. al-Yaʿqūbī, ii. 81, to Ṣanʿāʾ).

13. aṭ-Ṭāhir b. Abī Hālah (Tamīm, confederate of ʿAbd ad-Dār of Quraysh); to ʿAkk and Ashʿar (Ṭab. 1852).

14. Yaʿlā b. Umayyah (Tamīm, confederate of Nawfal of Quraysh); to al-Janad (Ṭab. 1852).

15. ʿAmr b. Ḥazm (Anṣār–an-Najjār); to Najrān (Ṭab. 1852); sent to the Yemen (perhaps to B. al-Ḥārith b. Kaʿb) (IH, 961 f. = IS, i/2. 2).

16. ʿUkkāshah b. Thawr al-Ghawthī; to Sakāsik, Sakūn and (?) Muʿāwiyah b. Kindah (Ṭab. 1852 f.). (N.B. Most of the names mentioned in Ṭab, 1852 f. also occur on 1952 f.).

17. Abū Sufyān b. Ḥarb (Quraysh–ʿAbd Shams); in Jurash of the Yemen (al-Balādhurī, 59); in Najrān (*Usd, s.v.*; p. 75 above).

(b) *To the east*

18. al-ʿAlā' b. al-Ḥaḍramī (confederate of Quraysh—ʿAbd Shams); to al-Baḥrayn (IH, 945, 965; Ṭab. 1750; IS, i/2. 19; cf. al-Yaʿqūbī, ii. 81, al-Ghutayf bi 'l-Baḥrayn).

19. al-Aqraʿ (? b. Ḥābis) (Tamīm); *muṣaddiq* for Hajar (al-Baḥrayn).

(c) *In the neighbourhood of Medina*

20. al-Walīd b. ʿUqbah b. Abī Muʿayṭ (Quraysh–ʿAbd Shams); to al-Musṭaliq, repulsed (IH, 730 f.; WW, 387).

21. ʿAdī b. Ḥāṭim (Ṭayyi'); to Ṭayyi' and Asad (IH, 965 = Ṭab. 1750).

22. Mālik b. Nuwayrah (Tamīm); to collect *ṣadaqāt* of B. Ḥanẓalah of Tamīm (IH, 965 = Ṭab. 1750).

23. az-Zibriqān b. Badr (Tamīm); to half of B. Saʿd of Tamīm (IH, 965); cf. p. 139 above.

24. Qays b. ʿĀṣim (Tamīm–Minqar); to half of B. Saʿd of Tamīm (IH, 965); cf. p. 139 above.

25. Buraydah b. al-Ḥusayb (Aslam); collected tax of Aslam and Ghifār (WW, 385); summoned Aslam for Tabūk (ibid. 391).

26. Kaʿb b. Mālik (Anṣār–Salimah); variant for above (ibid. 385).

27. ʿAbbād b. Bishr (Anṣār–ʿAbd al-Ash'hal); collected tax of Sulaym and Muzaynah (WW, 385); and of al-Musṭaliq after al-Walīd b. ʿUqbah (ibid. 387); summoned Aslam (ibid. 391).

28. Rāfiʿ b. Makīth (Juhaynah) collected tax of Juhaynah (WW, 385); summoned tribe along with brother (ibid. 326, 391).

29. ʿAmr b. al-ʿĀṣ (Quraysh–Sahm); tax of Fazārah (WW, 385).

30. aḍ-Ḍaḥḥāk b. Sufyān (Kilāb); tax of Kilāb (WW, 385).

31. Busr b. Sufyān (Kaʿb); tax of Kaʿb (WW, 385); summoned Kaʿb, along with Budayl b. Warqāʾ and ʿAmr b. Sālim (ibid. 326, 391).

32. Nuʿaym b. ʿAbdallāh an-Naḥḥām (Quraysh–ʿAdī); variant for collector from Kaʿb (WW, 385).

33. Ibn al-Lutbīyah (Azd); tax of Dhubyān (WW, 385).

34. ʿUyaynah b. Ḥiṣn (Fazārah): sent to collect tax of Tamīm in April–May 630 = i/9 (IS, ii/1. 115. 19, presumably referring to the expedition to al-ʿArj; the list in WW, 385 is repeated here).

35. Quḍāʿī b. ʿAmr (ʿUdhrah); over Asad, &c. (IS, i/2. 23. 22 f.; cf. p. 357 above).

EXCURSUS I

Zakāt and Ṣadaqah

As is well known *ṣadaqah* in later Islamic usage commonly means 'voluntary alms', while *zakāt* means the prescribed 'legal alms', whose amount is fixed, though in practice the giving of it may be voluntary. It is in this sense that *zakāt* is one of the five 'pillars of Islam'. The use of the word *zakāt* in the Qur'ān, however, raises serious difficulties. There are thirty-one instances of it, and in nearly all of them we have some form of the phrase 'observing the Worship and giving the *zakāt*'.[1] This is evidently, then, a technical phrase. We should consequently expect to find it used chiefly towards the end of the Medinan period, when the nomadic tribes were making treaties with Muḥammad, and he was fixing the amount of *zakāt* for them. According to Richard Bell's dating, however, though all the uses of the word are Medinan (with the possible exception of 18. 81/80 and 19. 13/14 where the meaning is different in any case), several of them fall early in the Medinan period. How is this to be explained? Was the *zakāt* exactly prescribed at an early time? Or was the word *zakāt* used in the meaning of 'voluntary contribution'? If the latter, was there any distinction from *nafaqah*, *mā tunfiqū*, and the like, which is commonly translated 'contribution'?

Part of the explanation is perhaps to be found in the fact that many of the earliest passages where *zakāt* occurs refer to the Jews or to disaffected Medinan Arabs, who may be presumed to have been friendly with the Jews. The point is sufficiently important for it to be illustrated in detail.

7. 156/155 E—. In reply to Moses at Sinai, God promises mercy to those who are pious, give the *zakāt* and believe in His signs.

5. 12/15 F. God (at Sinai) made a covenant with the Israelites and promised a reward if they observed the Worship, gave the *zakāt*, believed and supported His messengers and lent to Him a good loan.

2. 83/77 FG. God made a covenant with the Israelites and

[1] *Aqāmū 'ṣ-ṣalāt wa-ātaw 'z-zakāt*. Exceptions: 18. 81/80; 19. 13/14, where the meaning is probably 'purity'; 23. 4 has perhaps the same meaning, but *ṣalāt* is mentioned in the context; 7. 156/155; 30. 39/38; 41. 7/6.

commanded them, among other things, to observe the Worship and give the *zakāt*.

21. 73 EI. God revealed to Isaac and Jacob the doing of good, observing of the Worship and giving of *zakāt*. (Cf. 19. 31/32, 55/56 EI where Jesus is charged with the Worship and *zakāt* (? for himself), and Ishmael enjoins them on his people.)

98. 5/4 F. The people of the Book were commanded to serve God alone, as *ḥanīfs*, to observe the Worship and give the *zakāt*.

2. 43/40 ? F. An appeal to the Jews to observe the Worship and give *zakāt*.

4. 162/160 ? GH. Some Jews believe in God and the Last Day, observe the Worship and give *zakāt*; they will be rewarded.

30. 39/38 EI. *Zakāt* is rewarded by God, but not money given for usury (the reference to usury is probably to the Jews).[1]

24. 37 ? H. Men who are not diverted by trade and bargaining from remembering God, observing the Worship and giving *zakāt*. (Bell apparently interprets of the Meccan merchants and thinks that the mention of Worship and *zakāt* was added later; but it might refer to the Jews and be early Medinan, especially as places of worship are mentioned in the previous verse.)

2. 110/104 ? FG. An exhortation to observe the Worship and give *zakāt*. (This occurs as part of a warning against Jewish influence, and hence is primarily addressed to friends of the Jews.)

24. 56/55 G. A command to observe the Worship, give the *zakāt* and obey Muḥammad. (This occurs in a passage addressed to disaffected persons, but does not fit the context, and was perhaps revealed separately.)

22. 41/42 ? G. God will support those who, among other things, observe the Worship and give *zakāt*.

5. 55/60 FG. The believers are to be friends (not with the Jews) but with God, His messenger, and those who believe, observe the Worship and give *zakāt* (presumably addressed to friends of the Jews).

4. 77/79 ? E (or G). Some of those who were told to restrain their hands, observe the Worship and give the *zakāt*, are afraid of fighting. (Presumably friends of the Jews; the surrounding verses are from the time after Uḥud, and suggest

[1] Cf. p. 297 above.

that this verse is of the same date, but Bell thinks it is possibly early Medinan.)

Of the remaining usages of the word six (9. 5, 11, 18, 71/72; 33. 3; 58. 13/14) are definitely late. One (23. 4 E) is dated early Medinan, but might conceivably have the meaning of 'purity', though 'the Worship' occurs in a neighbouring verse (according to a tradition this was the last sūrah revealed before Muḥammad left Mecca). Two (2. 177/172 F—; 22. 78 F) seem to be about the time of the change of *qiblah*, which is perhaps significant; in the first Bell thinks the mention of *zakāt* has been added by way of revision, but this may be an unnecessary supposition in view of the connexion with the Jews we are now studying. Four others (2. 276/277; 31. 4/3; 41. 7/6; 73. 20) are described generally as 'Medinan', and may or may not be early.

The results of this examination are most surprising. One would have expected *zakāt* to acquire its 'technical' sense in the late Medinan period, when alliances were being formed with nomadic tribes. But only six instances clearly belong to this period. A larger number belong to the early period when Muḥammad was in close touch with the Jews and trying to gain their support. The conception of *zakāt* appears to have been adopted and developed in the Qur'ān because it was already familiar to the Jews[1] and to those who had been influenced by them. That seems to be the point of the references to the covenant at Sinai. Muḥammad must have been insisting that the Jews should give *zakāt* (whatever that may have implied). The Qur'ān supports his demand by showing that it is in accordance with what God had previously demanded of them and they had agreed to.

In the light of this strong connexion of *zakāt* with the Jews, it is probable that the cognate word *yuzakkī*, used of a messenger towards a people,[2] means 'to appoint *zakāt* for', though the thought of it as a means of purification is not necessarily absent.[3]

An examination of the use of *ṣadaqah* (plural *ṣadaqāt*) in the Qur'ān leads to a similar result. There are not so many instances as of *zakāt*, and the word is not coupled with 'the Worship'. One instance (2. 276/277 ? E) contrasts *ṣadaqāt* with usury,[4] in the same

[1] Cf. its probable origin in Aramaic; Jeffery, *Vocabulary*, &c.

[2] Cf. *M/Mecca*, 165, 'second group'.

[3] Cf. IS, iii/1. 93. 16—works of charity by 'Abd ar-Raḥmān b. 'Awf will be a 'purification of what he has' (*tazkiyat mā huwa fī-hi*).

[4] Cf. also 2. 280 E.

way as *zakāt* had been contrasted. The other four early instances (2. 263/265, 264/266, 271/273 all ? FG; 4. 114 GH), with the possible exception of the third, have the Jews or hypocrites in view. There are also some later instances. In Muḥammad's letters and treaties reproduced by Ibn Saʿd (i/2) *ṣadaqah* is preferred to *zakāt* for what may now be called 'legal alms'.

There remains much that is obscure. Why should the Qur'ān sometimes speak of *az-zakāt*, sometimes of *ṣadaqah*, and sometimes of *nafaqah* or *mā anfaqtum*? Was there any difference (in the early Medinan period) in the thing to which they refer, or are they merely directed to different groups of people? It might be suggested that *nafaqah*, &c. were contributions to war purposes; but the passage 2. 261/263 ff. identifies *ṣadaqāt* and contributions, and speaks of *ṣadaqāt* being given secretly; 2. 215/211 says that contributions are for parents, relatives, the poor, &c. Thus there is no evidence of any fixed levy on any section of Muḥammad's followers. Those who had something to spare were required to help those in need, and presumably most of the Emigrants were in this category at first. If for the early period *zakāt* is identified with *ṣadaqah*, there would have been no tax on the Jews, but they would have been expected to help people in difficulties by gifts, and not by lending money at interest.[1]

[1] Cf. p. 297 above, esp. n. 4.

EXCURSUS J

Marriage and the Family in pre-Islamic Times

NINETEENTH-CENTURY scholars, notably W. Robertson Smith and G. A. Wilken, following the anthropological ideas of their day, explained the phenomena of Muḥammad's Arabia by the hypothesis of an age in which matriarchy was dominant. It is now widely recognized, however, that to posit some previous historical situation for which there is no direct evidence does little to explain the observed or recorded facts of social anthropology, and that it is better to analyse the phenomena with a view to discovering the structural or functional principles actually present. For pre-Islamic Arabia there is a great mass of material available, though most of it is found only in Arabic. Most of it, too, can only be satisfactorily interpreted by someone well versed in anthropology. A thorough examination of the material is clearly out of place in a biography of Muḥammad. In the body of this work I have said only enough to make possible an intelligible account of the reform of the system, while the present Excursus sets out some facts which justify what was said above.

(a) *Patrilineal features*

In most primitive societies both patrilineal and matrilineal principles are to be found at work. In pre-Islamic Arabia Mecca is the clearest example of a system that is predominantly patrilineal. We have to remember, of course, that our material was not written down till at least a century after Muḥammad's death, and that in the interval the patrilineal system had ousted most traces of the matrilineal from Islamic society, so that the men who wrote down the material may have misunderstood some of the old practices they tried to describe. Nevertheless patrilineal relationships must have been important in Mecca. For one thing the chief social units were patrilineal clans, named after male ancestors only. Moreover, from about the time of Quṣayy at least, these ancestors appear to be real figures and not mere names in a genealogy. This is in contrast to Medina where, until shortly before the Hijrah, the genealogies consist of names about which nothing is known. In accordance with this naming of the clans in Mecca, both men and women are known there almost exclusively by paternal descent, that is, as the sons and daughters of males, not of females. In the *kunyah*, too, at Mecca—the honorific title, 'father of X' or 'mother of Y' (Abū X, Umm Y)—X and Y are always sons.

Among the exceptions is the name sometimes given to Muḥammad, Ibn Abī Kabshah, but it is the kind of exception which proves the rule. Kabshah was a common feminine name at Medina, as may be seen from Ibn Saʿd (especially iii/2, viii, and the Index), but apparently does not occur at Mecca. As there are other instances at Medina of a *kunyah* from a female (for example, Abū Lubābah), the probability is that this name is connected with Medina. There is nothing to show that it indicates any relationship with Muḥammad's freedman, Abū Kabshah, who fought as a Muslim at Badr. The use of this name for Muḥammad would mean, then, that either his father or one of his ancestors through his grandfather's mother had the *kunyah* Abū Kabshah. The rudeness in the use of the appellation by Abū Uḥayḥah and other opponents (if there was any) would consist in reminding Muḥammad of his connexion with Medina and its queer ways.[1] A tribesman, presumably from a matrilineal background, seems to have used it with a perfect courtesy.[2]

There are also one or two examples among Quraysh of men being known by their mothers' names. ʿAlī had a son known as Muḥammad b. al-Ḥanafīyah, but this was probably to distinguish him from two other sons of ʿAlī also called Muḥammad.[3] An example that cannot thus be explained away is that of Muḥammad's opponent, Abū Jahl, who was sometimes known as Ibn al-Ḥanẓalīyah after his mother, Asmā' bint Mukharribah of the tribe of Ḥanẓalah, a branch of Tamīm.[4] Asmā' later appears as a merchant in perfumes on her own account, and that further supports the belief that matrilineal ideas were still strong in this household. Moreover, Umm al-Julās bint Mukharribah, described as *khālah* (maternal aunt) of Abū Jahl, is sometimes said to have been the person with whom the written agreement for the boycotting of B. Hāshim was deposited;[5] but elsewhere Umm al-Julās is said to have been the *kunyah* of Asmā'. (There is also confusion between

[1] IS, iv/1. 69. 3; WW, 48, 137; Ṭab. i. 1565; *M/Mecca*, 103.
[2] Ibid. i/2. 145. 27.
[3] Ibid. iii/1. 11 f.
[4] IH, 441; IS, viii. 220; *Usd*, v. 393 f., *s.v.* Asmā' bint Salamah (*sic*); WW, 61.
[5] IS, i/1. 40. 1.

the mother of Abū Jahl and her niece, married to her son ʿAyyāsh, Asmā' bint Salāmah b. Mukharribah; and in some texts Mukharribah is corrupted to Makhramah.)

Patrilineal features can also be observed in connexion with inheritance, blood-revenge, and the place of marriage. Inheritance in the male line seems to have been common at Mecca, though without any rule of primogeniture. The power of Quṣayy passed to his sons, grandsons, and so on; and it is to be presumed that to some extent this succession to power was based on inherited wealth. Similarly in the clan of Makhẓūm the power of al-Mughīrah went to his son al-Walīd and then to the latter's nephew Abū Jahl. Again, the duty of avenging blood lay primarily on the next-of-kin in the male line. This was perhaps the case even in groups that were mainly matrilineal. The son of Kulayb, the great chief of Taghlib, avenged his father's death by killing his mother's brother, Jassās; but the close proximity of Jassās and Kulayb shows that Kulayb had gone to live with his wife's people, whose property was under the control of Jassās, and so the system may have been mainly matrilineal.[1] The groups responsible for blood-money according to the Constitution of Medina appear to have had a patrilineal basis.

About the place of residence of husband and wife there is little clear information for Mecca. The impression that marriage was often virilocal is supported by names like 'the *shiʿb* (quarter) of Abū Ṭālib', 'the house of al-Arqam', and by the fact that some of the Muslims who emigrated to Abyssinia were accompanied by their wives (not all of whom can have been accompanying male relatives). There are also several cases of uxorilocal marriage, though of course this is a feature that may occur in mainly patrilineal societies. Muḥammad's mother remained among her own kin, and ʿAbdallāh merely visited her there; Muḥammad was with her, apart from his time in the desert, until her death, and only then went to the house of his paternal grandfather, ʿAbd al-Muṭṭalib.[2] It is interesting that in connexion with Muḥammad's birth it was said that there was 'prophethood in the clan of Zuhrah' (his mother's clan); from the fact that the first transmitters of this tradition belonged to Zuhrah it may be inferred that, apart from the practice of uxorilocality, matrilineal ideas were strong in this clan.[3] Muḥammad's own marriage with Khadījah was presumably

[1] Caussin de Perceval, ii. 336; *Aghānī*, iv. 150 f.; Robertson Smith, *Kinship*, 155 f. [2] IS, i/1. 58. 17, 74. [3] Ibid. 51. 23.

uxorilocal. Khadījah must have been a woman with some power and wealth, and may have married Muḥammad on her own initiative. There are stories about her father or her uncle giving her in marriage, but the discrepancies in the stories make it probable that neither did so, and that the stories reflect later practice.[1] How Khadījah came to have her special position is very obscure. Apart from the growth of individualism it would presumably have been impossible for Khadījah and Asmā' bint Mukharribah to trade in their own name.

In general, as we shall see, there appears to be a connexion between the growth of individualism and the extension of the patrilineal system. Yet there are some pre-Islamic practices in which the emphasis on paternity is associated not with individualism but with the unity of the group of agnate males. The essential unity of a man and his consanguine brother (and presumably, by extension, of the whole patriclan) is expressed in an Arab saying, 'the paternal uncle is as the *ṣinw* of the father'. The word *ṣinw* means one of a pair or triad, and is used especially of palms growing from a single root. It can mean either consanguine or uterine brother, or even son. The application to palm-trees (which may be the original use) shows that the word emphasizes the unity of stock.[2]

Among the practices based on this idea is the marriage of brothers to the same woman, of which there are several examples from Medina.[3] It is presumably a form of the levirate. There is also at least one instance from Mecca, Asmā' bint Mukharribah, the mother of Abū Jahl, who married Abū Jahl's father Hishām b. al-Mughīrah and also the latter's brother Abū Rabī'ah.[4] There

[1] IS, i/1. 58 f.; cf. Robertson Smith, 274 f. and 99.

[2] Lane, *s.v.*; cf. Ibn Ḥajar al-'Asqalānī, *Tahdhīb at-Tahdhīb*, Hyderabad, (1907)/1325, &c., viii. 119 on 'Amr b. Yaḥyā b. 'Ammārah.

[3] Hind bint Simāk (Balī, confederates of Qawāqilah)—Sa'd and Aws bb. Mu'ādh ('Abd al-Ash'hal); IS, iii/2. 99. 16, viii. 231.

Suhaymah (Wāqif)—Salāmah and Rūmī bb. Waqsh ('Abd al-Ash'hal); IS, viii. 235. 19 f., 236. 7 f.

Buraydah bint Bishr (Ẓafar)—'Abbād and Abū Ma'qil bb. Nahīk (Ḥārithah); IS, viii. 251.

An-Nawār bint Qays (Ḥārithah)—Ṣayfī and Zayd bb. 'Amr (Ḥārithah); IS, viii. 240. 11–14.

Umm al-Ḥārith bint Mālik (Salimah)—Jabbār and Thābit bb. Ṣakhr (Salimah); IS, viii. 292. 23, 297. 5 f.

Laylā bint Abī Sufyān (Ḍubay'ah)—Mu'ādh and Bakīr bb. 'Āmir b. Jāriyah? (Ḍubay'ah); IS, 253. 6–10.

(Cf. G. H. Stern, *Marriage in Early Islam*, 172 f.)

[4] IS, viii. 220.

are also examples of the marriage of father and son to the same woman, that is, of a man to his stepmother; and these are from Mecca, Medina and elsewhere.[1] The underlying idea was perhaps that the woman's child-bearing capacity belonged to this patriclan (a suitable compensation having been given to her own patriclan), and the son or brother of the deceased has the right or duty of actualizing the potentialities.[2] Muḥammad b. Ka'b al-Quraẓī (d. *c.* 736/118) is reported to have said that 'when a man died leaving a widow, his son was the person with the best right to marry her (*aḥaqq bi-hā an yankiḥa-hā*, presumably not *yunakkiḥa*), if he wanted to do so, provided she was not his mother'.[3]

Another obscure matter may be mentioned at this point, since there seems to have been a difference between Mecca and Medina. This is the attitude towards *ghīlah* or *ghayl*, that is, having sexual intercourse with a woman while she is suckling a child. The Meccans apparently thought that this was harmful to the child and objected to the practice, but there does not seem to have been the same objection to it at Medina.[4] There is a tradition to the effect that Muḥammad had intended to forbid *al-ghīlah* until he remembered that the Persians and Greeks practised it without injury to their children.[5] Despite this tradition, however, Muḥammad did

[1] Sukhtā bint Ḥārithah (Sā'idah)—al-Mundhir b. Ḥarām, Thābit b. al-Mundhir (Maghālah); IS, iii/2. 63.

Hind bint Aws (Khaṭmah)—an-Nu'mān b. Umayyah, Thābit b. an-Nu'mān ('Amr b. 'Awf); IS, iii/2. 44. 25, 45. 5.

Mulaykah bint Khārijah (a wife of 'Alī) married a Fazārī and his son; Robertson Smith, 89, 271; cf. *Aghānī*, xxi. 261 (quoted by Farrūkh, *Das Bild des Frühislam*, 116); the names are variously spelt.

'Āminah (mother of Abū Mu'ayṭ) married Umayyah b. 'Abd Shams and his son Abū 'Amr; Robertson Smith, 89.

Nufayl (grandfather of 'Umar) left a Fahmī widow who was married by his son; Robertson Smith, 89.

Kubayshah bint Ma'n—Abū Qays, Ḥiṣn b. Abī Qays; Robertson Smith, 271 from al-Wāḥidī on Q. 4. 26.

Umm 'Ubayd bint Ḍamrah—al-Aslat, Abū Qays b. al-Aslat; Robertson Smith, 271 from aṭ-Ṭabarī on Q. 4. 26.

Bint Abī Ṭalḥah ('Abd ad-Dār)—Khalaf, al-Aswad b. Khalaf (Jumaḥ); Robertson Smith, 271 f. from al-Wāḥidī and aṭ-Ṭabarī.

Fākhitah bint al-Aswad (Asad)—Umayyah b. Khalaf, Ṣafwān b. Umayyah (Jumaḥ); Robertson Smith, 271 f. from the same sources.

[2] Cf. A. R. Radcliffe-Brown and C. Daryll Forde, *African Systems of Kinship and Marriage*, London, 1950, 50 f., &c.; Robertson Smith, 87.

[3] IS, iv/2. 95. 27 f.

[4] G. H. Stern, *Marriage in Early Islam*, 96 f.: Lane, *s.v. ghīlah.*

[5] Lane, ibid., IS, viii. 177. 16.

not consummate his marriage with Umm Salamah until she had stopped suckling Zaynab, her daughter by Abū Salamah;[1] and another woman refused to marry Muḥammad because she had two children by a former husband to nurse.[2] The examples are of avoiding intercourse with a woman while she is suckling another man's child. It is not clear, however, what the underlying idea is and whether there would have been the same objection when the woman was suckling the man's own child or his brother's child. After the Hijrah there was a strong feeling against intercourse with a woman pregnant by another man, and it was spoken of as 'irrigating another man's crop'; but whether there was much of this feeling before the Hijrah we cannot tell.[3]

(b) *Matrilineal features*

Despite the dominance of patrilineal ideas at the time when our sources were written down, many points of matrilineal organization have been recorded. Descent in the female line was relatively more important at Medina than at Mecca. Some clans, such as Banū Ḥudaylah and Banū Maghālah, took the name of a woman; and the Aws and the Khazraj together, before they became the Anṣār on conversion to Islam, could be called Banū Qaylah after a common ancestress. Individuals also were known by their mothers. Among the best-known examples are Muʿādh, Muʿawwidh, and ʿAwf, the sons of ʿAfrā', while ʿAbdallāh b. Ubayy is sometimes called Ibn Salūl after Ubayy's mother. An interesting case is that of Kaʿb b. al-Ashraf, who was reckoned as belonging to his Jewish mother's clan of an-Naḍīr, although his father was of a nomadic Arab tribe.[4] Frequently, too, in dealing with the Medinan 'companions', Ibn Saʿd remarks that two men were *ibn khālah* of one another, that is, sons of sisters; e.g. ʿAbdallāh b. Ubayy and Abū ʿĀmir ar-Rāhib, Saʿd b. Muʿādh and Asʿad b. Zurārah.

As a prelude to a discussion of the form of the marriage relationship and the place of residence of the spouses, it will be convenient to quote the account of pre-Islamic marriage recorded by al-Bukhārī:[5]

Ibn Shihāb (az-Zuhrī) said: ʿUrwah b. az-Zubayr informed him that ʿĀ'ishah, the wife of the Prophet (God bless and preserve him), informed him that marriage in the Jāhilīyah was of four types. (1) One was the

[1] IS, viii. 63–66.
[2] Ibid. 109. 3.
[3] IH, 759; WW, 282.
[4] IH, 548; cf. 351.
[5] 67. 37. 1.

marriage of people as it is today, where a man betroths his ward or his daughter to another man, and the latter assigns a dower (bridewealth) to her and then marries her. (2) Another type was where a man said to his wife when she was purified from her menses, Send to N. and ask to have intercourse with him; her husband then stays away from her and does not touch her at all until it is clear that she is pregnant from that (other) man with whom she sought intercourse. When it is clear that she is pregnant, her husband has intercourse with her if he wants. He acts thus simply from the desire for a noble child. This type of marriage was (known as) *nikāh al-istibḍāʿ*, the marriage of seeking intercourse. (3) Another type was where a group (*rahṭ*) of less than ten used to visit the same woman and all of them to have intercourse with her. If she became pregnant and bore a child, when some nights had passed after the birth she sent for them, and not a man of them might refuse. When they had come together in her presence, she would say to them, 'You (pl.) know the result of your acts; I have borne a child and he is your (sing.) child, N.'—naming whoever she will by his name. Her child is attached to him, and the man may not refuse. (4) The fourth type is where many men frequent a woman, and she does not keep herself from any who comes to her. These women are the *baghāyā* (? = prostitutes). They used to set up at their doors banners forming a sign. Whoever wanted them went in to them. If one of them conceived and bore a child, they gathered together to her and summoned the physiognomists. Then they attached her child to the man whom they thought (the father), and the child remained attached to him and was called his son, no objection to this course being possible. When Muḥammad (God bless and preserve him) came preaching the truth, he destroyed all the types of marriage of the Jāhilīyah except that which people practise today.

This description may be taken as accurate so far as it goes, but there are certainly gaps in it. It does not tell us, for instance, whether in the first type the marriage is virilocal or uxorilocal. Nevertheless it is useful to have this classification in mind as we consider the various aspects of the question.

The place of marriage may be dealt with first. In al-Bukhārī's third and fourth types it is uxorilocal, and probably also in the second. This is in accordance with the picture given by pre-Islamic poetry. The normal way to begin an ode is to speak of a lost love, and one is given the impression of passionate amours, carried on with ardour so long as the tribes of the couple are near one another, and then ceasing abruptly when the encampments are moved. In the most romantic cases the man would only visit the woman at night and by stealth; in others he might reside with her tribe for a considerable period. This would presumably be a marriage of the third type, but we cannot tell whether the other men in it were also of a strange tribe or were of the woman's tribe. The second type would also provide an opportunity for a noble stranger. The marriage of Hāshim in Medina seems to have been akin to the desert unions. He spent only a short time with his wife, and the son, Muḥammad's grandfather, ʿAbd al-Muṭṭalib, remained in Medina and was only with difficulty restored to his father's tribe in Mecca.[1] Where a man settled more or less permanently with his wife's tribe, he would often become attached to it as a confederate. It is doubtless along this line that we must look for the explanation of how al-Akhnas b. Sharīq, a confederate from aṭ-Ṭā'if, became head of the clan of Zuhrah at Mecca; as has been seen, there are other reasons for thinking that matrilineal descent was esteemed in this clan.[2]

It is from Mecca that we have the clearest example of a matrilineal household. In connexion with Muḥammad's marriage to Maymūnah at the 'pilgrimage of fulfilment' in 629/7, we are informed that Ḥamzah's daughter ʿAmmārah (or Umāmah) was taken to Medina. Up to this time she had been in Mecca with her mother, Salmā bint ʿUmays. There is no obvious reason for connecting the two happenings, but a little investigation reveals that Maymūnah bint al-Ḥārith and Salmā bint ʿUmays were uterine sisters, being daughters of a Ḥimyarite woman, Hind bint ʿAwf; and both Maymūnah and Salmā seem to have been living in the household of Muḥammad's uncle al-ʿAbbās, who was the husband of Maymūnah's full sister, Umm al-Faḍl. Thus al-ʿAbbās had a household consisting of his wife and her children, together with her two sisters and their children. If the sources are right in saying that he gave Maymūnah in marriage to Muḥammad, then he was presumably in charge of the household, though in matrilineal systems it is normal for the control to be in the hands of the woman's uterine brother or maternal uncle. Moreover not all the children of Hind were in this household. A son, Maḥmiyah b. Jaz', early became a Muslim and went to Abyssinia; there he may have been in the household of Asmā', the wife of Jaʿfar b. Abī Ṭālib, but he returned to Medina at least two years before Jaʿfar and was given a position of trust by Muḥammad. Another sister was the mother of Khālid b. al-Walīd and presumably

[1] IH, 88; cf. Robertson Smith, 69 f.

[2] Cf. p. 375 above.

resided with her husband. When Ḥamzah's daughter ʿAmmārah came to Medina there was a dispute who should be her guardian; Muḥammad placed her under Jaʿfar, less because he was her father's brother than because he was husband of her mother's full sister. In giving this decision Muḥammad quoted a principle expressing the unity of a matrilineal group, namely, 'the maternal aunt is a mother' (*al-khālah wālidah*). We may conclude, then, that this was a group which was largely matrilineal in organization, but not entirely so.[1]

Where marriage was uxorilocal and matrilineal ideas predominated, a woman of character would have much authority. According to *Kitāb al-Aghānī*,

> the women in the Jāhilīyah, or some of them, had the right to dismiss their husbands, and the form of dismissal was this. If they lived in a tent, they turned it round, so that if the door had faced east it now faced west, and when the man saw this he knew that he was dismissed and did not enter.

This implies that the tent belonged to the woman or the woman's family, and that she allowed him to live in it only so long as she pleased.[2] Salmā bint ʿAmr, the Medinan woman whom Hāshim married, would only unite with a man on condition that she could dissolve the union when she chose.[3] Indeed the women of Medina in general were noted for pride and for jealousy of their honour and position—summarized in the word *ghayr*. Muḥammad is said to have remarked that, because of their *ghayr* he would not marry a woman of the Anṣār, since she would not have sufficient patience to endure fellow-wives;[4] and, even if this is not the whole reason for Muḥammad's not marrying a Medinan woman, there is doubtless something in it, and the contrast between the social attitudes in Mecca and Medina may explain why there was hardly any intermarriage between the Emigrants and the Anṣār. A saying of the caliph ʿUmar's is recorded:

> we of Quraysh used to dominate (our) women; but when we came

[1] IS, viii. 33, 113, 94–98, 202–9; WW, 302. For Maḥmiyah cf. IS, iv/1. 145 f.; WW, 177, &c. (disagreeing with IH, 783); also IS, iv/1. 40. 26, iv/2. 8. 20, 37. 17. For Khālid cf. IS, viii. 209. 18, and *Usd, s.v.*

[2] Robertson Smith, 65; based on *Aghānī*, xvi. 106, where Māwiyah dismisses Ḥāṭim.

[3] IH, 88; but cf. her apparently virilocal marriage with Uḥayḥah b. al-Julāḥ in Ibn al-Athīr, *Kāmil*, i. 404 f., &c.

[4] IS, viii. 148. 20; Stern, op. cit. 76 f.

among the Anṣār, they proved to be a people whose women dominated them; and our women began to copy the habits of the women of the Anṣār.[1]

Despite their great influence, the women of Medina are commonly said to have been unable to own property. This presumably means that the property belonged to the matrilineal family and was administered by a woman's uterine brothers or maternal uncles or sons. This arrangement would not be disadvantageous for the woman so long as communal ideas prevailed; but with the growth of individualism the men would sometimes claim that the property belonged to them as individuals. As already suggested, the greater individualism at Mecca probably helped to make it possible for outstanding women like Khadījah and Asmā' bint Mukharribah to own property and trade in their own name.

While many matters of detail are to be gleaned from the stories of the Jāhilīyah and biographies of early Muslims, little is said about the underlying ideas. It may be helpful, therefore, to quote an African parallel. Among certain 'matrilineal' tribes of the central Bantu

> there is a remarkable degree of uniformity as to the principles governing descent and succession and the various ideologies by which people explain their adherence to the mother's rather than to the father's line, and stress their community of interests with their maternal relatives. Blood is believed to be passed through the woman and not through the man. The metaphors of kinship stress the ties between people 'born from the same womb' or 'suckled at the same breast', and in some tribes the physical role of the father is believed to be limited to the quickening of the foetus already formed in the uterus.[2]

It cannot be assumed that exactly these ideas were found in Arabia, especially if revenge for blood was a matter for the patriclan. Nevertheless there are some close parallels. In the sphere of language there is the use of *raḥim*, which properly means 'womb', for 'kinship', and of *batn* or 'belly' for a subdivision of a tribe.[3] In later Islamic law there are the same forbidden degrees in milk-relationship or foster-relationship as in blood-relationship, and this justifies an inference to the importance of milk-relationship in earlier times among the groups which were chiefly matrilineal, since it is essentially a relationship through females.

[1] Al-Bukhārī, 67. 83.
[2] Radcliffe Brown and Forde, op. cit. 207.
[3] Cf. Robertson Smith, 28–34, but for *ummah* see Jeffery, *Vocabulary*, *s.v.*

We cannot tell whether the Arabs believed, like some of the Bantu tribes, that the contribution of the father to the heredity of the child was slight or negligible, but certainly in some circles little attention was paid to the fact of physical paternity. The insistence of the Qur'an on the *'iddah* or waiting period before remarriage (to ensure that the woman has not conceived by her previous husband) argues that it was often not observed. That was certainly the case in al-Bukhārī's third and fourth types of pre-Islamic marriage; and even in the second type the precautions to make sure that the child was procreated by the stranger sound like an Islamic rewriting of an old custom. This would be in accordance with the widely accepted principle of 'the child to the bed' (*al-walad li 'l-firāsh*). In other cases also a woman's child was reckoned the son of the man who was her husband when the child was born, even when it was known that he was not physically the father.[1] Similarly in Islamic practice the owner of a slave-woman was the pater of her child, even when another man was known to be the genitor.[2] Where matrilineal ideas prevailed there was apparently a strong feeling that the child belonged to the mother's group. A man called 'Ijl b. Lujaym, on marrying a pregnant woman, agreed with her previous husband to bring up the child and eventually restore it to its father's tribe; but when it came to sending away the child, feeling in 'Ijl's tribe about the wrongness of this procedure was so violent that he and the father agreed to abandon the arrangement.[3]

Forms of marriage where little attention is paid to paternity sometimes come very near to promiscuity or prostitution, though in other cases they may lead to lasting unions. We are so ignorant, however, of many of the points involved in Arabian practices, and of the interpretation of some of the points which have been recorded, that it is unwise to be dogmatic. Though there is no direct evidence, for example, we might suppose that women with infants in a matrilineal group made a regular practice of exchanging them for the purposes of suckling; the effect of forbidden degrees based on milk-relationship would be to make extreme endogamy impossible. Again, a poet's use of the word *kannah* to denote his own wife, whereas it usually means his sister-in-law or daughter-in-law is possibly to be explained as referring to a polyandric group where

[1] Robertson Smith, 109–11. [2] Stern, 93.

[3] Robertson Smith, 115, based on al-Maydānī, *Majma' al-Amthāl*, Būlāq, (1867)/1284, i. 160 (= ed. G. Freytag, Bonn, 1838–43, i. 321).

brothers cohabited with the same woman; but we cannot be certain.[1]

It is difficult, again, to know what was meant by 'adultery' in pre-Islamic times. When Hind bint 'Utbah, the wife of Abū Sufyān, made her submission to Muḥammad along with some other women, they were told not to commit adultery, and she indignantly replied, 'Does a free woman commit adultery?'[2] To a European the natural interpretation of these words would be that free women were too proud or too chaste to do such a thing; but it is possible that Hind meant that no union a free woman was likely to contract was such as to have the term *zinā* applied to it, presumably because she had the right to dismiss or at least to separate from any husband of whom she tired. In Islamic times *zinā* meant 'adultery' in a wide sense, but it is not clear what it meant previously. Like other Islamic terms for sexual misconduct, it may originally have designated a normal practice in the pre-existing social system. The men of aṭ-Ṭā'if complained to Muḥammad that *zinā* was necessary for them since they were merchants.[3] For them it must have been a practice to which no stigma attached, perhaps temporary unions with strangers.

The loose polyandry which al-Bukhārī describes as his fourth type of pre-Islamic marriage was another primitive practice which a higher civilization was bound to condemn. The word *bighā* in Sūrat an-Nūr (24), 33, is usually translated 'prostitution', and the passage is said to refer to certain men—Ibn Ubayy is one who is named—who had control over a number of women and profited from their earnings as prostitutes.[4] As they stand, however, the stories command little respect. The probability is that *bighā* refers to some form of temporary union with neglect of paternity, in which the male head of the household to which the woman belonged shared in the presents given to her—possibly al-Bukhārī's fourth type. This differs from prostitution as understood in the West or in modern Islam in that there is no clear line of demarcation between such unions and others which, according to the

[1] Abū Tammām, *Ḥamāsah*, Būlāq, (1879)/1296, ii. 33 (= ed. G. Freytag, Bonn, 1828–47, i. 252).

[2] IS, viii. 4. 17, 172. 17; cf. Robertson Smith, 106; Stern, 73.

[3] Stern, ibid.; cf. *Usd*, v. 282—story told of Abū Kabīr al-Hudhalī in explanation of verses in IH, 646; further references in Farrukh, *Das Bild des Frühislam in der arabischen Dichtung*, 113; cf. Wellhausen, 'Die Ehe bei den Arabern' 472 n.

[4] Ṭab., *Tafsīr*, xviii. 93; Wherry (Sale), *ad loc.*; &c.

principles of the matrilineal system of pre-Islamic Arabia, were thoroughly respectable. In dealing with all such questions we must remember that what is right and proper in one social system may be a heinous crime in another.

(c) *Signs of transition*

In pre-Islamic Arabia we not merely find what may be called patrilineal and matrilineal groups; there are also indications that patrilineal principles were sometimes replacing matrilineal principles. The Islamic religion encouraged patrilineal principles,[1] and a century later these were dominant among the Arabs. Nevertheless, the transition had begun before the time of Muḥammad. Some of the cases already discussed have shown a mixture of the two kinds of principle, and others may now be given.

A story is quoted by Robertson Smith[2]

> where to a suitor proposing for a girl's hand the father says, 'Yes, if I may give names to all her sons and give all her daughters in marriage.' 'Nay', says the suitor, 'our sons we will name after our fathers and uncles, and our daughters we will give in marriage to chieftains of their own rank, but I will settle on your daughter estates in Kindah and promise to refuse her no request that she makes on behalf of her people.'

The suitor here represents patrilineal principles, the father matrilineal—but not purely matrilineal, since we should then have expected the marriage to be arranged by the maternal uncle of the girl. A contrasting story from Islamic times is that of Khansā' bint Khidhām (or Khudhām), apparently of the nomadic tribe of Asad, whose first husband was killed at Uḥud; her father then tried to marry her to another man, but she objected, saying that the paternal uncle of her child was preferable, and Muḥammad allowed her to marry whom she pleased; the man she chose was a kinsman of her first husband, but not actually a brother (though the Arabic word *'amm*, rendered by 'paternal uncle' would include this).[3] Here the woman herself seems to prefer patrilineal principles, and once again it is her father who gives her in marriage and who objects to patriliny; but presumably personal matters about which we are not informed were also involved.

[1] Cf. ch. VIII, § 2, above.

[2] *Kinship*, 102, based on Ibn 'Abd Rabbi-hi, *Al-'Iqd al-Farīd*, Būlāq, (1876)/1293, iii. 272.

[3] IS, viii. 334 f., iii/2. 35. 1 (Asadīyah); *Usd*, v. 440 f. (Anṣārīyah), ii. 115 f.

Another aspect of the problem of transition is to be seen in the complaint made to Muḥammad by the women of Medina that they were under the domination of their paternal cousins.[1] Somewhat similar is the case of the widow of Saʿd b. ar-Rabīʿ; on his death his brother (*sc.* ʿAbd ar-Raḥmān b. ʿAwf who had been 'brothered' with him by Muḥammad) assumed control of his property, and Saʿd's widow complained to Muḥammad that her rights and those of her daughters were being infringed and that it would be difficult for her daughters to find husbands.[2] Both complaints show that patrilineal ideas were gaining ground at Medina. In particular cases relatives in the male line (and ʿAbd ar-Raḥmān would count as such) may have taken over administration of communal property which was normally inherited in the female line, because of the absence of suitable maternal relatives. The great slaughter at Buʿāth and elsewhere would contribute to this absence. For the woman, however, control by husband or paternal relatives would mean that the property had passed from the control of the matrilineal family with which she primarily identified herself. For the proud, 'managing' women of Medina this would mean a loss of wealth, prestige, and influence, and, even with the rights conferred on them by Islam, they (or the most fortunate of them) would not be so secure as they were previously.

In this connexion the case of Qays b. al-Khaṭīm may be mentioned, though the interpretation of it is obscure. Qays, who was a poet of the Medinan clan of Ẓafar and died before the Hijrah,[3] married both ʿIqrab and her daughter (by another man) Ḥawwāʾ.[4] He apparently also looked after his mother, for, when setting out to avenge his father, he left a palm-garden to a kinsman on condition that, if Qays died, the kinsman would provide for Qays's mother (Qarībah bint Qays of Salimah)[5] from it.[6] There may be no connexion between these two facts, but, if so, it is strange that his mother was not looked after by his heir (matrilineally) in the usual way. If Qays administered the property of her family and lived

[1] Quoted by Robertson Smith, 84, from a manuscript of al-Wāḥidī on Q. 4. 19/23.

[2] IS, iii/2. 78, viii. 261 f.; WK, 320–3; WW, 146 f.; cf. Robertson Smith, 96 f.; Stern, 165; Caetani, i. 569.

[3] *Usd*, i. 229, *s.v.* Thābit b. Qays; cf. IH, Index; Ibn Qutaybah, *Kitāb ash-Shiʿr wa-'sh-Shuʿarāʾ*, ed. de Goeje, Index; &c.

[4] IS, viii. 231, 237.

[5] Ibid. 246. 22.

[6] *Aghānī*, ii. 160; cf. Robertson Smith, 96; Stern, 165.

in her household, then he must have been afraid that his successor as administrator would use the property for his private ends and would not treat Qarībah properly. On the other hand, if Qays lived with his wives in their household, and looked after his mother there, she clearly could not remain in it after his death. In the latter case, if Qays was administering the property of his wives, this is an instance of the transition to a patrilineal system. There may have been patrilineal tendencies in the wives' family, since 'Iqrab's brother Sa'd seems to have inherited the power of his father, Mu'ādh b. an-Nu'mān.

One wonders to what extent cases where a man married two women of the same matrilineal household are signs of a movement towards patriliny. There are some examples of marriage with two sisters from both Mecca and Medina,[1] though we are not informed whether they were contemporary or successive. Such a position would presumably give a strong man much influence, especially if the women's relatives on the female side were weak. It is also not clear whether quarrels between a woman's husband and her brother are specially connected with the transition from matriliny to patriliny, or whether such quarrels are always to be found in a matrilineal society. The instances of Jassās killing his sister's husband Kulayb,[2] and of Salmā bint 'Amr (mother of 'Abd al-Muṭṭalib) helping her brothers against her husband,[3] are considerably before the Hijrah.

(d) *Conclusions*

A little investigation of pre-Islamic ideas about marriage and the family shows how much remains obscure and requires further study. Unfortunately, in order to assess Muḥammad's achievement in this sphere, it is necessary to adopt some view of the nature of what he found. The view is therefore suggested here by way of

[1] Abū Uḥayḥah Sa'īd b. al-'Āṣ ('Abd Shams)—Hind bint al-Mughīrah, Ṣafīyah (Makhzūm); ash-Shahrastānī, *Kitāb al-Milal wa 'n-Niḥal*, ed. Cureton, p. 440.

Qays b. Makhramah (al-Muṭṭalib)—Waddah, Umm Sa'd ('Abd al-Ash'hal); IS, viii. 232.

'Amr b. Ḥarām (Salimah)—ar-Ribāb bint Qays, Hind (Salimah); IS, iii/2. 105, 119. 2, viii. 288. 11.

Mu'ādh b. 'Āmir (Ḍubay'ah);—Laylā bint Abī Sufyān, 'A'ishah (Ḍubay'ah); IS, viii. 253 (?).

[2] Cf. Caussin de Perceval, ii. 276–8; Nicholson, *Literary History*, 56.

[3] Ibn al-Athīr, *Kāmil*, i. 404 f.

hypothesis that a transition was in progress from a matrilineal system to one that was wholly or largely patrilineal, and that this transition was linked with the growth of individualism. This seems more likely in itself than the alternative view that from time immemorial some tribes had been matrilineal and some tribes patrilineal, and it also fits in with the standpoint of this book which sees in the growth of individualism from perhaps about the middle of the sixth century an important cause of the malaise with which the religion of Islam dealt. No strict proof can be given of the view adopted, but it is not improbable as an explanation of the facts, and it leads to a reasonable account of the reforms achieved by Muḥammad.

The important question is not where the marriage takes place, for uxorilocality can exist in a patrilineal system, and may have continued for some time after Muḥammad's reforms. The essential point is the composition of the group which owns and inherits property. Until the later sixth century, we assume, the group was a matrilineal one, and the property was held communally, or at least as a trust for the common good. It would normally be administered by the uterine brothers of the women concerned. When individualism appeared, however, and men began to think of themselves more as individuals than as members of a group, and to set private interests above the interests of the group, there would be a tendency for a man to appropriate for personal use as much as he could of the communal property he administered. This would still be within the matrilineal system, of course. A transition to the patrilineal system would come, however, if a man tried to hand on this property he had appropriated not to his sister's son but to his own son. There are no doubt also other ways in which the transition could come about. When there were many deaths (as had been the case in Medina just before the Hijrah), one man might have to look after the property of several families; and as many marriages were between closely related families, people would often stand in several different relations to one another, and the strong man would know how to benefit from this confusion.

While we can only conjecture about the precise manner in which the change from a matrilineal to a patrilineal system was effected, it is certain that it was in progress before the Hijrah, and that in the century after the Hijrah the matrilineal system largely disappeared.

EXCURSUS K

The Technical Terms in Sūrahs 4. 24/28, 5. 5/7, and 24. 33

THESE three passages are important for the understanding of Muḥammad's attitude to some of the uxorilocal marriage customs of Medina, but the original meaning of the terms in them has been lost owing to centuries of reinterpretation to make them fit later Muslim practice. Even the dictionaries are of little help, since the meanings they give are those attributed to the words after this process of reinterpretation. The passages, with the crucial words merely transliterated, are as follows:[1]

(4. 24/28) (Forbidden to you are) . . . and the *muḥṣināt* among the women [except what your right hands obtained—the rescript of God for you]. Allowable for you with regard to what is beyond that is the seeking them by your wealth, but *muḥṣinīn* and not *musāfiḥīn*. And for what you enjoy from these women (*v. l.* adds 'up to a fixed term') pay them their hire as stipulated (or 'at the stipulated time'). But with regard to what you mutually agree on after the stipulated time, no sin is attributed to you; God is knowing, wise.

(4. 25/29) And he of you who has not a superabundance so as to marry believing *muḥṣināt*, (may take) [of what your right hands possess] of your believing *fatayāt*—God knows your faith, that you are one of another. Marry them with the consent of their people, and give them their hire reputably, they being *muḥṣināt*, not *musāfiḥāt* and not taking *akhdān*. (25 cont./30) And when, after *iḥṣān* (? = becoming *muḥṣināt*), they commit *fāḥishah*, their penalty is half that of the *muḥṣināt*. . . .

(5. 5/7) Today there are made allowable for you the good things; . . . also the *muḥṣināt* of the believers and the *muḥṣināt* of those who were given the Book before you, if you give them their hire, *muḥṣinīn*, not *musāfiḥīn* and not taking *akhdān*.

(24. 33) Let those who do not find (means) to marry be continent until God enriches them of His bounty. For those your right hand possesses who desire the writing (of manumission) write it if you know any good in them, and give them of God's wealth He has given you. Do not compel your *fatayāt* to *bighā'* if they want *taḥaṣṣun*, in order that you may seek the gain of this present life. . . .

The first word to attract attention is *muḥṣināt*. The usual text is

[1] Round brackets indicate additions made in translation to elucidate the meaning; square brackets indicate portions of the actual text which I take to be later additions to the original text.

muḥṣanāt, this being the passive participle, whereas the other is the active participle. There would seem, however, to be a close parallel between '*muḥṣināt*, not *musāfiḥāt*' and '*muḥṣinīn*, not *musāfiḥīn*'; but in the latter phrase it is always the active of the masculine which is found, and it is therefore most likely that this would be the form of the feminine also. Lane gives such meanings as the following: continent, chaste, abstaining from what is not lawful nor decorous, married, having a husband, emancipated, having become a Muslim woman; the passive form would indicate that it is her husband who has caused her to be continent, chaste, &c. The basic meaning of the root is to be inaccessible or unapproachable, as a fortress, and this perhaps links up with the idea of chastity. The meaning of 'married' is probably derived from the beginning of the first Qur'ānic quotation.

Now the act or state expressed by *muḥṣinīn* or *muḥṣināt* is approved by the Qur'ān, for both men and women apparently, while the opposite is disapproved. In the light of what we know about the existing situation and the Islamic reforms the most satisfactory meaning would be 'observing purity of paternity'. This would mean that a woman observed an *'iddah* or waiting-period after separating from a 'husband' before having intercourse with another man; where the woman was pregnant the *'iddah* would last until after the birth of the child at least, and perhaps until she had stopped suckling it. In short, this is the restriction of a woman to one man at a time, and may be referred to as monandry, while in some contexts *muḥṣināt* could be rendered as 'monandric'. In the first instance of the word above it must be taken as involving not merely the general practice of monandry, but a marriage actually in force. There is no difficulty about applying this conception of monandry to the other instances both of the participles and of the noun *taḥaṣṣun*. A precise meaning of this kind is more likely to be the original meaning than one of the vaguer meanings commonly given to the words. Other precise meanings are conceivable —perhaps linking up with virilocal marriage—but the one given best fits all the instances.[1]

The opposing types of action, represented by *musāfiḥīn* and *musāfiḥāt*, may be described as 'polyandric', though of course there

[1] For the modern legal meaning cf. Snouck Hurgronje in *Zeitschrift der deutschen morgenländischen Gesellschaft*, 53. 161 f. = *Verspreide Geschriften*, ii. 407–9.

are other sorts of polyandry. In Medina this would mean that a woman had intercourse with a number of men without observing any *ʿiddah*, so that there could be no certainty about the father of any child she had. In the dictionaries *sāfaḥa* is given the vague meaning of committing fornication. The basic meaning of the first stem of the word is to pour out (a liquid) or to spread (as a camel spreads itself on the ground). Thus *sāfaḥa* is not inappropriate as a description of the 'unlimited' polyandry mentioned by al-Bukhārī. The complementary phrase, 'not taking *akhdān*', confirms this, for *akhdān* are 'secret or private friends', and after 'visits' from such persons a woman would be unlikely to observe an *ʿiddah*. In its outward aspect the practice is hardly distinguishable from prostitution (at least in extreme cases), but it differs in its social setting and in the underlying ideas. The word *bighā'* in 24. 33 presumably refers to the same practice.

The *fatayāt* in 4. 25/29 and 24. 33 are commonly said to be slaves, and the word certainly can refer to female slaves, though its primary meaning is young women. But the command to 'marry them with the consent of their people' (*ahl*) would imply that they belong to someone else, and regular marriage (*nikāḥ*) with another man's slave at this period is most unlikely. The words 'of what your right hands possess', which support the traditional interpretation, seem to be an addition made some time after the original revelation of the passage, presumably when female captives were plentiful; but the original remark about 'consent of their people' was not expunged. It would be more satisfactory to regard the *fatayāt* as a class of women in matrilineal households, possibly younger sisters and more distant kinswomen of the leading woman, who were not allowed to have a permanent husband resident in the household, but were allowed to receive 'visits' from men as they pleased. That they were a distinct class seems clear from the lighter punishment prescribed in 4. 25/30. Since a marriage with one of these women was to cost less, the man presumably went to live (? for a time only) in the woman's household, and while she was married to him she was not to have intercourse with any other men; he may indeed have paid only a series of 'visits' to her. The lighter penalty may be due either to the woman's recent change of status from 'polyandric' to 'monandric', or to her continued residence in her old home with the temptation to revert to the old ways. The word *fāḥishah*, meaning something like 'an abominable thing', appears to be applied not to adultery specifically but to any practice which was formerly normal but is now regarded as objectionable by Islam; in 4. 22/26 marriage with one's stepmother is *fāḥishah*.

If this treatment of the technical terms is sound, the passages under discussion may be interpreted somewhat as follows. The first (4. 24/28) gives permission to contract a temporary alliance with a 'polyandric' woman, provided she gives up her polyandry. The following verse is similar, but the alliance is not necessarily temporary and the woman's people must consent—so that it cannot be secret; this seems to be a little later than the previous verse. The next passage is perhaps earliest of the four, since it speaks of 'people of the Book', presumably Jews, and permits marriage with 'monandric' women from these and from the believers generally. The last passage illustrates how vested interests try to perpetuate the existing system.

EXCURSUS L

Muḥammad's Marriages

THE classification of Muḥammad's marriages has been influenced by a verse of the Qur'ān, 33. 50/49. Unfortunately there is some difficulty in the interpretation and even the translation of this verse. In the century after Muḥammad's death conditions changed so much that men had ceased to be aware of many of the facts of the social system to which this verse was relevant. It must therefore be examined in detail. A rough translation is as follows (the clauses being numbered for convenience):

O prophet, We have made allowable for thee (1) thy wives whose hires (*ujūr*) thou hast given, (2) and what thy right hand has possessed of the booty God has bestowed on thee, (3) and the daughters of thy paternal and maternal uncles and aunts, (4) those who emigrated with thee, (5) and a believing woman, if she gives herself to the prophet, if the prophet wants to marry her, (6) being special for thee apart from the believers.

The first group (1) consists of Muḥammad's wives in the strict sense. The word 'hires' (*ujūr*) is usually interpreted as 'dowers' (sing. *mahr*). It must be either *mahr* or something which took the place of *mahr* in the early days. It might perhaps be the annual supply of provisions from Khaybar.

The second group (2) are the slave-concubines, women who had been captured in war and not set free (like Juwayriyah). Rayḥānah is sometimes said to have belonged to this group. So presumably did Māriyah the Copt, though she was not captured but presented.

The third group (3) is of cousins. It is not clear whether the following clause (4), 'those who emigrated with thee', is a limitation on the right to marry cousins or signifies a fourth group. ʿAbdallāh b. Masʿūd read 'and' before the phrase and thus made it clear that this was a distinct class; to such a class one might assign Zaynab bint Khuzaymah, who presumably emigrated to Medina with her husband, ʿUbaydah b. al-Ḥārith of the clan of al-Muṭṭalib. A story is told about Muḥammad's cousin, Umm Hāni', a daughter of Abū Ṭālib, which presupposes that clauses (3) and (4) indicate only one class; she refused a proposal of marriage on the grounds that she had not emigrated with Muḥammad.[1] This is not infallible evidence, however, since there are other accounts of her refusal to marry Muḥammad which do not mention this point. The solution of the problem of clauses (3) and (4) depends on the view adopted of the purpose of the rule stated in them. The most likely view is that these women, whether two groups or one, did not receive *ujūr* like the first class; and the reason for this would presumably be either that Muḥammad had already provided for them (as his cousins or as widows of his community),[2] or that he was their official male representative and did not hand over property to himself. The marriage of cousins was not prohibited in Islam, and the verse could not be a prohibition to Muḥammad to marry further wives,[3] since at the time of his death he was in the process of arranging a marriage with Qutaylah bint Qays.[4]

The last group (5) is that of believing women who gave themselves to Muḥammad. These are doubtless women who contracted a union with Muḥammad according to the old principles (perhaps as modified in Q. 4. 25/29).[5] Various women are mentioned as belonging to this category. With the exception of Maymūnah none of them seems to have had an apartment in Muḥammad's residence in Medina. It is interesting that Maymūnah is included in this group, since she came of a matrilineal family.[6] In some accounts al-ʿAbbās is said to have arranged her marriage, but the alternative report, that she 'entrusted her affair' to Muḥammad may mean that al-ʿAbbās had only a secondary part in the arrangements.[7] One wonders whether when she first went to Medina along with her niece, Ḥamzah's daughter, the two of them lived in the household of her sister and Jaʿfar b. Abī Ṭālib. When her marriage to Muḥammad was consummated during his return journey to Medina from the 'pilgrimage of fulfilment' (*ʿumrat al-qaḍīyah*) she had her own tent (*qubbah*);[8] but this was perhaps usual in the case of Muḥammad's wives and may not signify that the marriage was uxorilocal. Apart from Maymūnah, however, Muḥammad's unions with 'believing women who gave themselves to him' were

1 IS, viii. 109. 9–12; cf. 15–19.
2 As for Umm Hāni', ibid. 32. 13.
3 Contrast Ṭab., *Tafsīr*, xxii. 15 top.
4 IS, viii. 105.
5 Cf. p. 391 above.
6 Cf. p. 380 above; for her giving herself cf. IS, viii. 98. 3.
7 IS, viii. 95. 3; for the phrase *jaʿalat amra-hā ilā* cf. ibid. 95. 6 (Maymūnah to al-ʿAbbās), 82. 15 (Zaynab bint Khuzaymah to Muḥammad).
8 IS, viii. 100. 1.

presumably uxorilocal. This would be in line with the current practice in those sections of Arabian society where matrilineal principles were dominant.

There remains the interpretation of the last clause (6), *khāliṣatan la-ka min dūn al-mu'minīn*. These words are now always taken to mean '(this is a) special (privilege) for you as distinct from the believers'; the special privilege is often held to be marriage with a woman who gives herself to Muḥammad without a *walī* and without a 'dower'.[1] This interpretation is in harmony with the attempt by 'Umar and others to stop *mut'ah* unions, and could be a device to bolster up the prohibition of *mut'ah*. While this interpretation is not impossible, a more natural one would be to take *khāliṣatan* as an adjective qualifying 'woman', so that the clause would mean '(keeping herself) special for you and not (having sexual relations with other) believers'. This would be in line with the insistence on women becoming 'monandric'.

The categories of women named in this verse have had some influence on the later accounts of the wives of the prophet. The phrases 'bestowed by God as booty' and 'gave herself to the prophet' frequently occur. In his eighth volume Ibn Sa'd, in addition to the 'wives of the prophet', has lists of 'women whom the Messenger of God married without consummating the marriage, and those whom he divorced' and 'women to whom the Prophet made a proposal without completing the marriage, and women who gave themselves to the Messenger of God'. Some of the subsumed cases do not fit the headings. Thus there is no word of Muḥammad wanting to marry Umāmah bint Ḥamzah; someone else suggested the match, and Muḥammad said that it was impossible since Ḥamzah was his brother by fosterage.[2]

Muḥammad is usually said to have had fourteen wives in the strict sense, of whom nine survived him; but there is some dispute about the identity of the fourteen.[3] The following is a list of the women whom he married or with whom he contemplated marriage.

1. Khadījah bint Khuwaylid (Quraysh—Asad), married about 595 when she was aged 40.[4]

2. Sawdah bint Zam'ah (Quraysh—'Āmir), married about 620, aged about 30 (?); widow of as-Sakrān b. 'Amr, an early Muslim,

[1] Cf. Qatādah ap. Ṭab., *Tafsīr*, xxii. 14. 24 f.

[2] IS, viii. 113 f.

[3] Ibid. 156–9; IH, 1001–5 names those in the first list together with Asmā', 'Amrah, and Umm Sharīk.

[4] IS, viii. 7–11, i/1. 85; Ṭab. i. 1766 f.; Caetani, i. 166–73.

with whom she made the *hijrah* to Abyssinia and returned to Mecca; his brother was a prominent pagan, and her own brother remained in Abyssinia.[1]

3. 'Ā'ishah bint Abī Bakr (Quraysh—Taym), married in 623/1 aged 9;[2] the only virgin Muḥammad married.

4. Ḥafṣah bint 'Umar b. al-Khaṭṭāb (Quraysh—'Adī), married in 625/3 aged 18; widow of a Muslim killed at Badr.[3]

5. Umm Salamah (Hind) bint al-Mughīrah (Quraysh—Makhzūm), married 626/4 aged 29; her husband Abū Salamah had died of wounds received at Uḥud.[4]

6. Zaynab bint Khuzaymah ('Āmir b. Ṣa'ṣa'ah), married 626/4 or the previous year, aged about 30, and died a few months later; after a divorce from aṭ-Ṭufayl b. al-Ḥārith (Quraysh—al-Muṭṭalib) she had married his brother 'Ubaydah who was killed at Badr.[5]

7. Juwayriyah (al-Muṣṭaliq of Khuzā'ah), daughter of the chief of the tribe, captured in the attack on it in January 627 (viii/5), married by Muḥammad on her profession of Islam and set free; aged 20 at marriage; perhaps only a concubine at first, but before his death had become a full wife.[6]

8. Zaynab bint Jaḥsh (Asad b. Khuzaymah), married Muḥammad in 627/5 after her divorce from Zayd b. Ḥārithah, aged 38; her mother was a maternal aunt of Muḥammad's, and her father a client of the clan of 'Abd Shams of Quraysh.[7]

9. Māriyah the Copt, a slave-concubine presented to Muḥammad by the ruler of Egypt in 628/6 or earlier, who bore him a son called Ibrāhīm; she remained a concubine.[8]

10. Umm Ḥabībah (Ramlah) bint Abī Sufyān (Quraysh—'Abd Shams), married on Muḥammad's return from Khaybar in 628/7, aged about 35; she was the widow of 'Ubaydallāh b. Jaḥsh, with whom she had made the *hijrah* to Abyssinia.[9]

11. Ṣafīyah bint Ḥuyayy (Jewish—an-Naḍīr), captured at Khaybar in 628/7 and assigned to Muḥammad; aged 17; was perhaps

[1] IS, viii. 35–39; Ṭab. i. 1767–9; Caetani, i. 312.
[2] IS, viii. 39–56; Ṭab. i. 1769 f.; Caetani, i. 424.
[3] IS, viii. 56–60; Ṭab. i. 1771; Caetani, i. 540.
[4] IS, viii. 60–67; Ṭab. i. 1771; Caetani, i. 588 f.
[5] IS, viii. 82; Ṭab. i. 1775 f.; Caetani, i. 588 f.
[6] IS, viii. 83–85; Ṭab. i. 1772; Caetani, i. 601.
[7] IS, viii. 71–82; Ṭab. i. 1772 f.; Caetani, i. 610 f.
[8] IS, viii. 153–6; Ṭab. i. 1775; Caetani, i. 730.
[9] IS, viii. 68–71; Ṭab. i. 1772; Caetani, ii. 55.

a concubine at first, but apparently accepted Islam and was set free.[1]

12. Maymūnah bint al-Ḥārith ('Āmir b. Ṣa'ṣa'ah—Hilāl), married as Muḥammad returned from the 'pilgrimage of fulfilment' in 629/7, aged 27; sister of the wife of al-'Abbās, &c.[2]

13. Rayḥānah bint Zayd (Jewish—an-Naḍīr), captured with Banū Qurayẓah to which her husband belonged, in 627/5; became Muḥammad's concubine, and apparently retained that status; died before him in 632/10.[3]

These are the women who may be regarded as having been properly united to Muḥammad as wives or concubines. At his death three were already dead, and Māriyah was only a concubine. The remaining nine became the 'mothers of the believers'. About a score of other women are mentioned as having been at least thought of as wives for Muḥammad. There is much obscurity and dubiety about some of them; many tribes were doubtless eager to claim a matrimonial relationship with Muḥammad, and to make the most of vague reminiscences. Thus it is widely held that Muḥammad married a woman of Kilāb, but several completely different versions are given of her name. The one thing that seems certain about this supplementary list is that none of the women in it formed a lasting union with Muḥammad.[4]

1. Asmā' bint an-Nu'mān (Kindah—Jawn), said to have been married to Muḥammad in June 630 (iii/9) and according to some versions divorced before the marriage was consummated (but the story of the divorce is told of several other women); also said to have observed the veil and been counted as one of the 'mothers of the believers', but this is denied by some accounts, and she is said to have married a husband after leaving Muḥammad.[5]

2. Qutaylah bint Qays (Kindah), sister of al-Ash'ath b. Qays who revolted against Abū Bakr but later became an important Muslim leader; was on her way to marry Muḥammad when he died.[6]

3. Mulaykah bint Ka'b (Layth), said to have been divorced from

[1] IS, viii. 85–92; Ṭab. i. 1773 ; Caetani, ii. 34 ff., 49.

[2] IS, viii. 94–100; Ṭab. i. 1773; Caetani, ii. 66.

[3] IS, viii. 92–94; Ṭab. i. 1775; Caetani, i. 634, ii. 369.

[4] Cf. G. H. Stern, *Marriage in Early Islam*, 151–7; Caetani, ii. 478 f.; Wellhausen, 'Die Ehe bei den Arabern', 464 f.

[5] IS, viii. 102–5, 158. 13, 25; Ṭab. i. 1775. 3; IH, 1004 f.

[6] IS, viii. 105 f., 158. 16; Ṭab. i. 1776. 5; IH, 1004. 15 (?).

Muḥammad before consummation of the marriage, or to have married him in January 630 (ix/8) and then died; it is also denied that Muḥammad married any woman of Kinānah (of which Layth was a part).[1]

4. Bint Jundub b. Ḍamrah (Kinānah); her marriage to Muḥammad both asserted and denied.[2]

5. Fāṭimah bint aḍ-Ḍaḥḥāk (Kilāb), one of the names given for the 'woman of Kilāb' who is generally agreed to have been among Muḥammad's wives and to have been divorced; the date of the marriage is given as March 630 (xi/8).[3]

6. 'Amrah bint Yazīd (Kilāb), perhaps variant of above.[4]

7. 'Āliyah bint Ẓabyān (Kilāb), another variant.[5]

8. Sabā bint Sufyān (Kilāb), another variant.[6]

9. Nashāh bint Rifā'ah (Kilāb), another variant; but it is also said that her clan were confederates of the Jewish clan of Qurayẓah.[7]

10. Ghazīyah bint Jābir, Umm Sharīk (Kilāb or Kindah or Quraysh-'Āmir or Daws or Anṣār); there is a wide agreement that the fifth clause of the Qur'anic verse discussed above (about the believing woman who gives herself to the prophet) refers to a woman called Umm Sharīk, and she is sometimes identified with Ghazīyah; but there is another version according to which the proposal came from Muḥammad, and Ghazīyah was divorced before the marriage was consummated.[8]

11. Fāṭimah bint Shurayḥ; perhaps a corruption of another name since no details are given.[9]

12. Sanā or Sabā bint (Asmā' b.) aṣ-Ṣalt (Sulaym), died before her marriage to Muḥammad was consummated.[10]

13. ash-Shanbā' bint 'Amr (Ghifār, confederates of Qurayẓah, or Qurayẓah), divorced because she made a sceptical remark on the death of Muḥammad's son Ibrāhīm.[11]

14. Khawlah bint al-Hudhayl (Taghlib), niece of Diḥyah b. Khalīfah al-Kalbī, married to Muḥammad, but died on her way to him.[12]

[1] IS, viii. 106, 158. 8, 11.
[2] IS, viii. 106.
[3] IS, viii. 100. 24, 101. 6, 158. 9, 26.
[4] IS, viii. 100. 25, 102. 7; Ṭab. i. 1777.3; IH, 1004 f.
[5] IS, viii. 100. 26, 102. 10; Ṭab. i. 1776. 2.
[6] IS, viii. 101. 1, 102. 5.
[7] Ṭab. i. 1774. 3.
[8] IS, viii. 110–12; Ṭab. i. 1774. 15, 1776. 7; IH, 1004. 3.
[9] Ṭab. i. 1776. 7.
[10] IS, viii. 106 f.; Ṭab. i. 1774. 6.
[11] Ṭab. i. 1774. 10.
[12] IS, viii. 114 f.; Ṭab. i. 1776. 12.

15. Sharāf bint Khalīfah (Kalb), maternal aunt of Khawlah, took her place on her death.[1]

16. Khawlah bint Ḥakīm (Sulaym), daughter of a woman of the Meccan clan of 'Abd Shams and related to the clan of Hāshim, 'was one of those who gave themselves to the prophet, and he put her off (*arja'a-hā*) and she used to serve him', this being presumably after the death of her husband 'Uthmān b. Maẓ'ūn about the time of the battle of Uḥud (she had been long married to 'Uthmān since her son as-Sā'ib b. 'Uthmān fought at Badr).[2] (Perhaps, as she was the widow of an early Muslim, Muḥammad gave her shelter under his roof, but refused to marry her because she was too old or for some other reason.)

Finally there are seven women between whom and Muḥammad there was some talk of marriage without the plans ever being carried out. Two were women of the Anṣār who arranged the marriages themselves but were forced by their families to abandon them, perhaps through fear that Muḥammad would cease to be impartial.

1. Ḥabībah bint Sahl (Anṣār—Mālik b. an-Najjār).[3]
2. Laylā bint al-Khaṭīm (Anṣār—Ẓafar).[4]
3. Umm Hāni' bint Abī Ṭālib (Quraysh—Hāshim).[5]
4. Umm Ḥabīb bint al-'Abbās (Quraysh—Hāshim).[6]
5. Ḍubā'ah bint 'Āmir ('Āmir b. Ṣa'ṣa'ah).[7]
6. Ṣafīyah bint Bashshāmah (Tamīm—al-'Anbar).[8]
7. 'Ammārah (or Umāmah) bint Ḥamzah (Quraysh—Hāshim).[9]

[1] IS, viii. 115; Ṭab. i. 1776. 1.
[2] IS. viii. 113.
[3] IS, viii. 326 f.
[4] IS, viii. 107 f.; Ṭab. i. 1776. 14.
[5] IS, viii. 108 f.; Ṭab. i. 1777. 5.
[6] Ṭab. i. 1777. 15.
[7] IS, viii. 109 f.; Ṭab. i. 1777. 7
[8] IS, viii. 110; Ṭab. i. 1777. 13.
[9] IS, viii. 113 f.

INDEX

Names of authors occurring in the footnotes are included in the index only where the footnote contains bibliographical information. Names on the map on p. 152 are not indexed. 'B.' after a name is short for Banū, 'sons of', and indicates a tribe or clan. Where the name of a man's clan or tribe appears after his name, it is not usually indexed separately, but accompanies the man's name in the index. The article *al-*, *ad-*, &c., is disregarded in the alphabetical ordering.

al-Ḥārith (Khazraj), B., 89, 154, 156, 164, 167 f., 170 f., 180, 194, 222 f.
— b. 'Abd Manāt b. Kinānah, 57, 81–83.
— b. Abī Shāmir (or Shimr), prince of Ghassān, 41, 345 f.
— b. 'Āmir, 14, 56.
— b. 'Amr (Jumaḥ), 262.
— b. 'Awf, 94.
— b. Hishām (Makhzūm), 57 f., 62, 67, 74, 76.
— b. Ka'b, B., 82, 124, 127, 343, 359, 367.
— b. Nawfal, 238.
— b. Uhbān, 356.
— b. 'Umayr al-Azdī, 113.
Ḥārithah (Aws), B., 23 f., 153 f., 156 f., 159–61, 163 f., 169–71, 174, 210 f., 216, 227.
— b. Qaṭan, 363 f.
al-Ḥarrah, 341.
Hāshim, B., 95, 257, 260, 374, 380 f., 399.
Ḥassān b. Thābit, 18, 32, 42, 165, 186, 210, 271, 321, 345.
Ḥāṭib b. Abī Balta'ah, 112, 344 f.
— b. Qays, 156, 163.
— b. Umayyah (Ẓafar), 214.
— War of, 156, 163.
Ḥātim aṭ-Ṭā'ī, 89, 381.
Hawāzin, 53, 66, 70–75, 81 f., 87, 91, 95–105, 147, 149, 342, 364.
Hawdhah b. 'Alī (Ḥanīfah), 41, 132–6, 345, 347.
Ḥawwā', 386.
ḥazz, 357.
Hebrew, 192, 213, 240.
Hebron, 112.
Hell, 24, 125, 190, 207, 233, 258, 269 f., 297, 301.
Hellenism, 205, 334.
Heraclius, 113 f., 116, 239.
Ḥibrā, 112.
ḥijāb, 284.
Ḥijāz, 14, 76, 108, 219, 242, 301, 310, 316.
Hijrah, 33, 72, 83–85, 97, 102, 119, 135, 143, 146, 151, 155 f., 158, 160–2, 164–70, 173, 175, 177, 179, 181, 194–6, 198 f., 202, 217, 227, 234, 248–51, 264, 268, 273, 284, 289, 303, 307, 316 f., 329, 331 f., 339, 373, 378, 386–88.
hijrah, 1 f., 242, 357, 396; see also *hājara*, *muhājirūn*.
al-Hilāl, B., 81, 98, 100, 360.
ḥilf, 169, 172, 192, 245, 248.
ḥilm, 264.
Ḥims, 246.
Himyar(-ite), 82, 120, 125, 366, 380.
Hind bint 'Awf, 380.
— — Aws (Khaṭmah), 377.
— — al-Mughīrah, 387; *see also* Umm Salamah.
— — Qays (Salimah), 387.
— — Simāk (Balī), 158, 163, 376.
— — 'Utbah, 69, 384.
al-Ḥīrah, 132, 137, 140 f.
Hirschfeld, H., 192.
Hishām b. 'Amr, 74.
— b. al-'Āṣ (Sahm), 3, 342.
— b. al-Mughīrah, 376.
— b. Ṣubābah, 263.
Ḥismā, 108 f., 341.
Ḥiṣn b. Abī Qays, 377.
ḥizb Allāh, 109, 247, 357.
Hoenerbach, W., 95.
Holy Land, 324.
— Rood, 114, 116.
— Spirit, 320.
Horovitz, J., 1, 338.
House, 311.
al-Ḥubāb b. al-Mundhir (Salimah), 181, 215, 343.
Hubayrah b. Abī Wahb (Makhzūm), 65, 67, 76.
Ḥubayyib, 154, 163.
al-Ḥublā, B., 154, 156, 166–9, 171, 174–6, 182, 210.
al-Ḥudaybiyah, 40–42, 46, 51–53, 58 f., 62, 65, 67, 84, 87, 102, 109, 133, 144, 187, 189, 218, 230, 234 f., 243, 254, 307, 311, 327 f., 341, 345 f.
Ḥudaylah, B., 154, 165, 378.
al-Ḥuḍayr b. Simāk, 156–9, 161–3, 165, 174, 176.
Ḥudhayfah b. Badr, 91.
Hudhayl, B., 30, 64, 66, 81, 90, 101.
ḥukm, 143.
ḥulafā', 172.
al-Hūn b. Khuzaymah, B., 81, 88.
al-Hunayd, 108 f.
Ḥunayn, 53, 60, 70–73, 76, 87, 94–102, 117, 144, 147, 179, 236, 254–7, 259 f., 302, 307, 319, 342, 347, 350.
al-Ḥuraqah (Juhaynah), B., 355.
Hurgronje, C. Snouck, 204, 307, 390.
al-Ḥurr b. Qays, 94.
ḥurr, 356.
al-Ḥuṣayn b. Niyār, 139.
— b. Sallām (Qaynuqā'), 197.
al-Ḥuṭam b. Ḍubay'ah (Bakr b. Wā'il), 132, 141.
al-Ḥutāt b. Yazīd (Tamīm), 140, 249.
al-Ḥuwayrith b. Nuqaydh (Quraysh), 69.
Ḥuwayṭib b. 'Abd al-'Uzzā, 56, 67, 74, 76.
Ḥuyayy b. Akhṭab (an-Naḍīr), 38, 189, 212 f.

al-Mas'ūdī, 114.
Ma'ūnah, 31.
mawālī'l-yahūd, 193.
Māwiyah, 381.
mawlā, *mawālī*, 222, 239, 247, 294.
al-Maydānī, 383.
Mayfa'ah, 342.
Maymūnah bint al-Ḥārith ('Āmir b. Ṣa'ṣa'ah), 60, 69, 288, 380, 394, 397.
maysir, 233, 298 f.
Māzin b. an-Najjār (-i), B., 154, 156, 165.
Mecca(-n) (-ns), *passim*.
Medina(-n) (-ns), *passim*.
— Constitution of, *see* Constitution.
Merciful, 135, 221, 310, 356–8.
Messenger, 23, 27, 121, 244, 350.
— of God, 11, 50, 74, 109, 188, 221, 224 f., 235, 308, 312, 348, 354–63, 395.
Messiah, 316 f., 319 f.
Middle East, 146, 220.
Mihja' b. Ṣāliḥ, 344.
Miḥṣan, 165.
millat Ibrāhīm, 205.
al-Miqdād b. 'Amr, 3, 111.
Miqyas b. Ḍubābah al-Laythī, 68, 263.
Mirba' b. Qayẓi (Ḥārithah), 161.
Misma', 141.
mīthāq, 245.
Moles, 184.
Moses, 16, 103–5, 240, 358, 369.
Mosque of the Two Qiblahs, 202.
Mu'abbis, 157.
Mu'ādh b. 'Āmir b. Jāriyah (Ḍubay'ah), 376, 387.
— b. al-Ḥārith (b. 'Afrā'), 166, 378.
— b. Jabal (Salimah), 122, 237, 366.
— b. an-Nu'mān, 156, 158, 272, 387.
mu'adhdhin, 305.
mu'ākhāh, 248.
al-Mu'allā, B., 172, 271.
al-mu'allafah qulūbu-hum, 74, 348 f., 352 f.
Mu'attib b. Qushayr (Ḍubay'ah of 'Amr b. 'Awf), 214.
Mu'āwiyah, B., 154, 161–5, 192, 216, 249.
— b. Abī Sufyān, 73, 140.
— b. Kindah, B., 122, 366 f.
— b. Mālik, 162.
Mu'awwidh b. 'Afrā', 166, 378.
Muḍar, 356.
Mudarris, 157.
Mudlij, B., 3, 81 f., 84.
Mudrikah, B., 81.
al-Mughīrah b. Shu'bah, 102–4, 266, 359 f., 375.
al-Muhājir b. Abī Umayyah (Makhzūm), 122 f., 130, 366.
muhājirāt, 243.
Muhājirūn, *muhājirūn*, 1, 228, 242, 247, 357; *see also* Emigrants.
Muḥammad, *passim*; *see also* Messenger of God.
— 'Abd al-Fattāḥ Ibrāhīm, 10.
— b. 'Abdallāh, 47, 235.
— b. al-Ḥanafīyah, 374.
— b. Ibrāhīm b. al-Ḥārith, 351.
— b. Ka'b al-Quraẓī, 196, 377.
— b. Maslamah, 92, 160 f., 210–12, 214, 236, 340 f.
Muḥārib, B., 17, 43, 81, 90 f., 340 f.
al-Muḥarram, 8.
muḥdith, 223.
muḥṣanāt, 390.
muḥṣināt, *muḥṣinīn*, 389 f.
Mujāhid, 351.
Mukharribah, 375.
Mukhayrīq, 197, 257.
Mulawwiḥ, 52, 342.
Mulaykah bint Ka'b (Layth), 397.
— — Khārijah, 377.
mulk as-samā, 136.
Mullah (Kinānah), 356.
mulūk, 120, 346.
mu'minūn, 303.
Munabbih b. al-Ḥajjāj, 14, 56.
munāfiqūn, 180, 184, 197; *see also* Hypocrites.
al-Mundhir b. 'Amr, 180, 340.
— b. Ḥarām, 377.
(al-Mundhir b.) al-Ḥārith b. Abī Shimr (Ghassān), 113.
al-Mundhir b. Qadāmah, 209.
— b. Sāwā al-'Abdī, 131 f., 360 f.
Muqā'is, 139.
Muqawqis, 41, 112, 345 f.
Murād, B., 82, 119.
al-Muraysī', 35, 68, 86, 185, 341.
Murrah b. al-Aws, B., 154, 163, 177.
— (Ghaṭafān), B., 36, 52, 81, 87, 91, 94, 342.
Muṣ'ab b. 'Umayr, 198.
muṣaddiq, 253, 367.
musāfiḥāt, *musāfiḥīn*, 389 f.
muṣallā, 306, 308.
Musaylimah, 79, 124, 132–6, 139, 148.
Musayyir, 161.
Mushallal, 69.
mushrik, 223.
Muslim(-s), *passim*.
muslim, 205, 304.
Muslim Brotherhood, 301.
muslimūn, 358.
al-Muṣṭaliq (Khuzā'ah), B., 35, 81–84, 237, 287, 341, 367.
al-Mustawrid b. 'Amr, 360.

PRINTED IN
GREAT BRITAIN
AT THE
UNIVERSITY PRESS
OXFORD
BY
CHARLES BATEY
PRINTER
TO THE
UNIVERSITY